THE INVENTION OF THE COLONIAL AMERICAS

THE INVENTION OF THE
COLONIAL AMERICAS

DATA,
ARCHITECTURE,
AND THE ARCHIVE
OF THE INDIES
1781–1844

BYRON ELLSWORTH HAMANN

GETTY RESEARCH INSTITUTE

LOS ANGELES

For Christian, Amanda, and Angelina

CONTENTS

vii	Preface
xvi	Acknowledgments
xvii	Abbreviations
xviii	Note from the Author
1	**Introduction:** Archives, Architecture, and the Data of the New World
37	**Chapter 1:** The Archive of the Indies in 1818
73	**Chapter 2:** The Source Archives
125	**Chapter 3:** Archive as Apparatus
165	**Chapter 4:** Data Retrieval
227	**Chapter 5:** The Monsters of Reason
243	**Epilogue:** Archival Memory
251	Appendix A: The Finances of the Archive of the Indies: Account Books and Receipts, 1785–1832
252	Appendix B: From Archivists to Soldiers: The Employees of the Archive of the Indies, 1785–1844
256	Appendix C: Parasols, Shields, Butterfly: The Document Case Metopes of the Archive of the Indies, 1786–88
260	Illustration Credits
261	About the Author
262	Index

INVENCION. s. f. La accion de inventar. *Inventio.*

INVENCION. Se toma algunas veces por la misma cosa inventada. *Inventum.*

INVENCION. Lo mismo que HALLAZGO.

INVENCION. Se toma muchas veces por ficcion, engaño, ó mentira. *Figmentum.*

INVENCION. Artificio retórico, con que el orador dispone, con solícito estudio, las especies que le han de servir para algun discurso, y su exôrnacion. *Inventio.*

HACER INVENCIONES. f. Lo mismo que hacer gestos, ó visages, ú otras acciones parecidas á estas, ó caricias y expresiones fuera de propósito. *Gesticulari, nutibus intempestivis blandiri.*

—Diccionario de la lengua castellana compuesto por la Real Academia Española, reducido á un tomo para su mas fácil uso, 1780[1]

INVENTION. Feminine substantive. The act of inventing. Latin *Inventio.*

INVENTION. It sometimes means the invented thing. *Inventum.* INVENTION. The same as FINDING. INVENTION. It often means fiction, deception, or lie. *Figmentum.* INVENTION. Rhetorical artifice, by which the orator achieves, with careful application, those effects which serve him for a particular discourse, and its embellishment. *Inventio.* TO MAKE INVENTIONS. Phrase. The same as to make gestures, or faces, or other actions similar to these, or inappropriate cajoleries and expressions. *Gesticulari, nutibus intempestivis blandiri.*

PREFACE

In the opening pages of *The Invention of America* (1961), Mexican historian Edmundo O'Gorman asks the following question:

> Let us suppose that the caretaker of an archive comes across an ancient papyrus in a cellar. The next day he brings it to the attention of a professor of classical literature, who after careful study realizes that it is a hitherto unknown text by Aristotle. Who is the discoverer of this document, the caretaker who found it or the professor who identified it?[2]

O'Gorman's book takes place in the decades following 1492, and shows how Europeans came to realize that the lands across the Atlantic were not the edges of Asia, but rather an entirely new continent. For O'Gorman, *discovery* (as a literal uncovering) implies the revelation of things already imagined, already thought to exist. *Invention*, in contrast, is a jarring recognition of the previously unknown—a recognition that forces a radical reconsideration of existing ideas and worldviews.[3] The *invention* of America was not simply the identification of a new continent.[4] It was also a profound rethinking of the world itself, and its inhabitants. Medieval visions of a land-island surrounded by water were replaced by a "terraqueous globe" of oceans divided by continents.[5] Even the Adamic oneness of humanity was challenged.[6]

In O'Gorman's archival anecdote, the caretaker acts as Christopher Columbus, encountering something he was not really surprised to find (a papyrus in an archive, just as Columbus expected to find land by sailing west). In contrast, the professor is the more important character, because he (like geographers in Columbus's wake) realizes that the papyrus is a document both unexpected and—for the world of classical studies—profoundly transformative.

This book takes place three centuries after Columbus's voyages, but it also concerns the imagination of geography and the connections linking architectures of space to architectures of knowledge (fig. P.1). Where O'Gorman frames his parable in terms of archivists and scholars, the pages that follow add another participant: the archival architecture in which encounters of papyrus, archivist, and scholar occur.

vii

FIGURE P.1
Looking west down the southern gallery of the Archive of the Indies, before the shelf reformations of the late 1920s.
The curtained doorway leads to the corner room for Royal Patronage (Patronato Real) documents.
Archivo ABC, Reference Number 5708678.

FIGURE P.2
Aerial view of Seville looking southeast, October 1926.
The massive cathedral dominates the center of the photo, and just to the south (right) is the square Lonja building. To the southeast of both cathedral and Lonja are the patio-filled buildings of the royal palace and its sprawling wooded gardens.
Fototeca Municipal de Sevilla, Fondo Sánchez del Pando, Signatura sp4_pu-vi_sf_047.

FIGURE P.3
Entrance to the Archive of the Indies in the western facade of Seville's Lonja, May 2016.

Where O'Gorman's story is about how imaginations of the Old World (the earth-island of Europe, Africa, and Asia) were replaced by a new planetary vision (the New World redefines the world as a whole), my story is about how, in the late eighteenth century, the Americas were newly imagined as lands *separate,* and *separable from,* the Old World. The invention of the colonial Americas—"invention" in all of the senses defined by Spain's Royal Academy (Real Academia Española) in 1780 (the word *colonial* will not appear in the academy's dictionary until 1837)[7]—was central to this process of separation, a separation that still shapes how we imagine the past and its legacies in the present.

In February 1785, King Carlos III of Spain approved designs for the General Archive of the Indies (el Archivo General de Indias, AGI). The new archive was to be installed on the upper floor of a sixteenth-century building in Seville (figs. P.2, P.3) and would house all Spanish government documents related to the New World written before 1760—that is, before Carlos III came to power in mid-August 1759, and before his economically extractive Bourbon reforms began in Spanish America.[8] In part, the

PREFACE ix

creation of this archive was a defensive act of intellectual warfare. It was meant to combat recent polemics by British, French, and Dutch authors, who since the early 1760s had argued that the Americas and their inhabitants were intrinsically inferior: degenerate and degenerating.[9] These attacks also renewed the long tradition of Black Legend critiques of imperial Spain—at the very same time that Britain and France were launching what would become the second age of global imperialism. To counter these biased "philosophical histories," the Sevillian archive was designed to be a space where new, empirically grounded histories of the New World could be written.

In scholarship today, the creation of the Archive of the Indies is usually heralded as Spain's greatest contribution to Enlightenment practices of historiography and archival research.[10] But what is generally overlooked, or left unexamined, is that this new archive was created by dismembering *already existing archives* throughout Spain, archives in which documentary sources about the history of the Americas were *integrated* with documentary sources about the history of Europe. In other words, the Archive of the Indies created a repository in which it was easier to imagine the history of the Americas as a history independent from the history of Europe—and vice versa. Documentary sources on America's past were newly segregated, in a very material sense, from documentary sources on Europe's past. By stressing and materially institutionalizing America's separateness and difference, the Archive of the Indies paradoxically reinscribed the terms of the Enlightenment Dispute of the New World that it was meant to combat.[11]

That these ideas of "colonial" difference and separation rose to prominence during the second half of the eighteenth century is no accident. This was an era of revolutionary independence movements across the Atlantic world, and transatlantic-panhemispheric warfare profoundly shaped the Archive of the Indies.[12] The violence even determined when the archive could be created. The AGI as an idea was first approved by Carlos III in 1781. But Spain's involvement in the American War of the Thirteen Colonies made the project impossible "until peace is achieved"—that is, until the Treaty of Paris in 1783 (fig. P.4).[13]

This geopolitical context is one of many reasons why George Washington (fig. P.5) appears on this book's frontispiece, and why each chapter begins by quoting one of the Figaro operas.[14] Figaro's creator—Pierre-Augustin Caron de Beaumarchais—was a lifelong supporter of the American revolution that created the United States. A decade into his career as a dramatist, Beaumarchais was also supplying weapons to rebels in the Thirteen Colonies, weapons decisive in the 1777 Battle of Saratoga. In a 1785 letter published by the *Journal de Paris,* he referred to himself as "*Beaumarchais* l'Américain."[15] And six years later, for his third Figaro play, Beaumarchais placed a bust of George Washington in the study of Sevillian nobleman Count Almaviva—a detail the play's villain tries to exploit in the penultimate scene.[16]

This Washingtonian flourish is the most directly political reference in a trilogy that had always played with ancien régime hierarchies. Audiences first met Almaviva (and his ex-valet Figaro and love interest Rosina) in Seville itself (*The Barber of Seville,*

FIGURE P.4
Francisco de Goya y Lucientes (Spanish, 1746–1828).
The Tobacco Guards, 1780, oil on canvas, 262 × 137 cm. Featuring heavily armed men in Andalusian dress— one wearing a sash embroidered *Renta de Tabaco*—this was among the eleven tapestry cartoons completed by Francisco de Goya in late January 1780. These were the last tapestries Goya designed before the Royal Tapestry Factory (Real Fábrica de Tapices) was shut down for eight years due to the financial strains of Spain's involvement in the War of the Thirteen Colonies. Tobacco was a New World crop and royal monopoly, imported to Spain for most of the eighteenth century via the port of Cádiz.
Madrid, Museo Nacional del Prado, cat. no. P000788.

1775). Their story's second act (*The Marriage of Figaro,* 1784) is set in the Sevillian countryside, on the count's estate of Aguas-Frescas. Then, after serving as viceroy of Mexico, Almaviva was appointed Spanish ambassador to revolutionary Paris, where the trilogy's final adventure (*The Guilty Mother,* 1791) takes place.

Seville, the Thirteen Colonies, Mexico, Paris: the geopolitics of Beaumarchais's dramas resonate, as will be seen, with those of the Archive of the Indies. Also resonant are Beaumarchais's deeply archival plots. They are driven by paperwork. Song lyrics, love letters, household inventories, military commissions, political correspondence, and even receipts are dropped, pocketed, hidden, revealed. Documents propel these narratives forward, madcap-foolscap.

But the most important resonance is of timelines, archival and operatic. The first three operas based on Beaumarchais's plays are exactly contemporary with the creation of the Archive of the Indies: its planning, its implementation, and its initial indexing. Giovanni Paisiello's *The Barber of Seville* (1782) was published one year after the AGI concept received royal approval. Wolfgang Amadeus Mozart's *The Marriage of Figaro* (1786) opened the same year that shipments of documents were arriving at the new archive from repositories in Cádiz and Madrid. And by the time Gioachino Rossini's *The Barber of Seville* premiered (1816), archivist Diego Juárez was halfway through indexing the Royal Patronage (Patronato Real) section, a project that when finished (three years later) would complete the AGI's first collection of finding aids.[17]

Incidentally but not insignificantly, 1816 was also the year Napoleon Bonaparte (then in exile on the southern Atlantic island of Saint Helena) famously described *The Marriage of Figaro* as "the Revolution already put into action."[18]

FIGURE P.5
Joseph Perovani (U.S. American, 1765–1835).
Portrait of George Washington, 1796, oil on canvas, 220 × 145 cm.
This portrait (commemorating the "Treaty of Friendship, Limits and Navigation between Spain and the United States. Done at San Lorenzo el Real this 27th day of October 1795") was commissioned in 1796 by José de Jáudenes (Spanish ambassador in Philadelphia) as a gift for Spanish prime minister Manuel Godoy. Madrid, Museo de la Real Academia de Bellas Artes de San Fernando, inv. no. 0693.

NOTES

1 *Diccionario de la lengua castellana* (Madrid: Joaquín Ibarra, 1780), 560.

2 Edmundo O'Gorman, *The Invention of America: An Inquiry into the Historical Nature of the New World and the Meaning of Its History* (Bloomington: Indiana University Press, 1961), 15; originally published in Spanish as *La invención de América: El universalismo de la cultura de occidente* (Mexico: Fondo de Cultura Económica, 1958). For relations of archivists, historians, and archives today, see Alexandra Walsham, Kate Peters, and Liesbeth Corens, "Introduction," in *Archives and Information in the Early Modern World,* ed. Liesbeth Corens, Kate Peters, and Alexandra Walsham (Oxford: Oxford University Press, 2018), 1–26.

3 The use of *inventio* and its variants in titles of books about the Americas has a broader history. Two responses to O'Gorman appeared in the early 1990s. In 1992, Reyes Mate and Friedrich Niewöhner published *El precio de la "invención" de América* (Barcelona: Anthropos Editorial del Hombre, 1992), an edited volume based on talks at the III Encuentro Hispano-Alemán in the Monastery of Guadalupe, Spain. The main evocation of O'Gorman appears in the editors' opening comments: "De la lectura de los siguientes textos se desprende que América es el precipitado no sólo de diversas culturas sino, sobre todo, de distintas miradas: a veces reproducción de Europa, a veces invento de Europa y, al final, autodescubrimiento de Europa....El descubrimiento de lo otro no podía hacerse más que al precio de una transformación de sí mismo. Ese proceso lento y doloroso tuvo muchos vaivenes" (7–8). The following year, José Rabasa published *Inventing America: Spanish Historiography and the Formation of Eurocentrism* (Norman: University of Oklahoma Press, 1993). Although critical of how O'Gorman contrasts *invention* with *discovery* (Rabasa places his own use of *invention* in a genealogy of 1980s inventionology), and annoyed by the high modernist metaphysics with which O'Gorman concludes, Rabasa shares O'Gorman's insistence that America has no preexisting essence or identity but is instead a "discursive formation" that changes over time in the writings of European commentators. Rabasa also points out that O'Gorman's title finds a precedent, four centuries earlier, in Fernán

Pérez de Oliva's nine-chapter manuscript on the *Historia de la invención de las Indias* (History of the invention of the Indies). Written around 1528, the manuscript summarizes Christopher Columbus's travels to the Americas, with a final chapter on Taíno culture in the Caribbean; see Fernán Pérez de Oliva, *Historia de la invención de las Indias* (Madrid: Siglo XXI, 1991). For a more recent discussion of early modern "invention," see Bernhard Siegert, *Cultural Techniques: Grids, Filters, Doors, and Other Articulations of the Real,* trans. Geoffrey Winthrop-Young (New York: Fordham University Press, 2015), 135.

4 "America" in this book does not, of course, refer narrowly to the United States, but rather to the entire fourth continent, named (in a 1507 world map by Martin Waldseemüller) after Florentine navigator Amerigo Vespucci.

5 O'Gorman, *Invention,* 54.

6 On the Adamic crisis, see O'Gorman, *Invention,* 55–56, 86–87, 138; and, more recently, Martin W. Lewis and Kären E. Wigen, *The Myth of Continents: A Critique of Metageography* (Berkeley: University of California Press, 1997), 24–26. Their book's watery conclusions are amplified in "A Maritime Response to the Crisis in Area Studies," *Geographical Review* 89, no. 1 (1999): 161–68.

7 Real Academia Española, *Diccionario de la lengua castellana por la Academia Española,* 8th ed. (Madrid: Imprenta Nacional, 1837), 179.

8 Jacques Barbier, "The Culmination of the Bourbon Reforms, 1787–1792," *Hispanic American Historical Review* 57, no. 1 (1977): 51–68; John Fisher, "Critique of Jacques A. Barbier's 'The Culmination of the Bourbon Reforms, 1787–1792,'" *Hispanic American Historical Review* 58, no. 1 (1978): 83–86; Allan J. Kuethe, "More on 'The Culmination of the Bourbon Reforms': A Perspective from New Granada," *Hispanic American Historical Review* 58, no. 3 (1978): 477–80; Ilona Katzew, *Casta Painting: Images of Race in Eighteenth-Century Mexico* (New Haven: Yale University Press, 2004); Barbara E. Mundy, "The Images of Eighteenth-Century Urban Reform in Mexico City and the Plan of José Antonio Alzate," *Colonial Latin American Review* 21, no. 1 (2012): 45–75; and Gabriel B. Paquette,

Enlightenment, Governance, and Reform in Spain and Its Empire, 1759–1808 (New York: Palgrave Macmillan, 2008). For a parallel economic history of the North American Thirteen Colonies in the mid-eighteenth century, see James Deetz, *In Small Things Forgotten: The Archaeology of Early American Life* (Garden City, NY: Anchor, 1977), 36–40.

9 Classic discussions of these polemics are offered by Antonello Gerbi, *The Dispute of the New World: The History of a Polemic, 1750–1900,* trans. and ed. Jeremy Moyle (Pittsburgh, PA: University of Pittsburgh Press, 1973); and Jorge Cañizares-Esguerra, *How to Write the History of the New World: Historiographies, Epistemologies, and Identities in the Eighteenth-Century Atlantic World* (Stanford, CA: Stanford University Press, 2001). These polemics are explored further in my next chapter.

10 Pedro González García, ed., *Discovering the Americas: The Archive of the Indies* (New York: Vendome, 1997), 12; David F. Slade, "Imagining from Within: Archives, History, and Ibero-American Enlightenment Discourse," in *Lumières et histoire / Enlightenment and History,* ed. Tristan Coignard, Peggy Davis, and Alicia C. Montoya (Paris: Editions Honoré Champion, 2010), 200; and Nicolás Bas Martín, *El cosmógrafo e historiador Juan Bautista Muñoz (1745–1799)* (Valencia: Universitat de València, 2002), 147–50. For a lavishly illustrated overview of the trade exchange building and its history, see Antonio Campos Alcaide, "La Lonja de Sevilla: Arquigrafía de un edificio" (PhD diss., Universidad de Sevilla, 2017).

11 For further discussion of the Dispute of the New World, see this volume, introduction.

12 On transnational-Atlantic and hemispheric-American histories of the Age of Revolutions, see Eric Beerman, *España y la independencia de Estados Unidos* (Madrid: Fundación Mapfre América, 1992); François Xavier Guerra, "Identidad y soberanía: Una relación compleja," in *Revoluciones hispánicas: Independencias americanas y liberalismo español,* ed. François-Xavier Guerra (Madrid: Editorial Complutense, 1995), 207–39; François Xavier Guerra, "The Implosion of the Spanish American Empire: Emerging Statehood and Collective Identities," in *The Collective and the Public in Latin*

America: Cultural Identities and Political Order, ed. Luis Roniger and Tamar Herzog (Brighton: Sussex Academic Press, 2000), 71–94; Jaime E. Rodríguez O., *The Independence of Spanish America* (Cambridge: Cambridge Latin American Studies, 1998), and, in response, Rafe Blaufarb, "The Western Question: The Geopolitics of Latin American Independence," *American Historical Review* 112, no. 3 (2007): 742–63; David Armitage, *The Declaration of Independence: A Global History* (Cambridge, MA: Harvard University Press, 2007); Ralph Bauer, "Hemispheric Studies," *PMLA* 124, no. 1 (2009): 234–50; Ralph Bauer, "Thomas Jefferson, the Hispanic Enlightenment, and the Birth of Hemispheric American Studies," *Dieciocho* 4 (2009): 49–82; David Armitage and Sanjay Subrahmanyam, eds., *The Age of Revolutions in Global Context, c. 1760–1840* (New York: Palgrave Macmillan, 2010); and Daniela Bleichmar, *Visible Empire: Botanical Expeditions and Visual Culture in the Hispanic Enlightenment* (Chicago: University of Chicago Press, 2012). See also Jorge Cañizares-Esguerra, *Puritan Conquistadors: Iberianizing the Atlantic, 1550–1700* (Stanford, CA: Stanford University Press, 2006).

13 "tiene resuelto el Rey que todos los papeles de Indias se trasladen, hecha la paz, a la Casa Lonja de Sevilla" (AGI IG 1852, José de Gálvez, 19 and 22 November 1781). Spain's involvement in the War of the Thirteen Colonies had many other repercussions: for example, it led to the temporary closing of the Royal Tapestry Factory (Real Fábrica de Tapices), for which Francisco de Goya had provided designs since his arrival in Madrid in 1775. See Janis A. Tomlinson, *Francisco Goya: The Tapestry Cartoons and Early Career at the Court of Madrid* (Cambridge: Cambridge University Press, 1989), 108, 124; and Juliet Wilson-Bareau, *Goya in the Norton Simon Museum* (Pasadena, CA: Norton Simon Museum, 2016), 77.

14 And as one reviewer pointed out (indicating yet another facet of the United States-Spain connections that run through this project), the single thing most people in the U.S. know about Seville is that an opera about a barber takes place there, thanks to the 1950 "Rabbit of Seville" *Looney Tunes* cartoon. See Daniel Goldmark, *Tunes for 'Tunes: Music and the Hollywood Cartoon* (Berkeley: University of California Press, 2005), 107, 114, 119, 120, 126, 135, 156, 193; and Edmond Johnson, "Figaro! Figaro! Figaro? The Intersection of Opera and Animation in *Looney Tunes* and *Merrie Melodies*" (paper presented at the Music and the Moving Image Conference, University of California at Santa Barbara, 15 January 2006). On the problem

of music's marginalization in our imaginations of the past, see Byron Ellsworth Hamann, "A *Tesoro de la Lengua Castellana o Español* Version 2.0: Review of *Lexikon of the Hispanic Baroque*, ed. Evonne Levy and Kenneth Mills," *Journal of Art Historiography* 11 (2014), https://arthistoriography.files.wordpress.com/2014/11/hamann-review.pdf.

15 Robert Darnton, *George Washington's False Teeth: An Unconventional Guide to the Eighteenth Century* (New York: W. W. Norton & Company, 2003), 120, 182n1.

16 David Coward, "Introduction," in Pierre Beaumarchais, *The Figaro Trilogy*, ed. and trans. David Coward (Oxford: Oxford University Press, 2003), xviii; Hugh Thomas, *Beaumarchais in Seville: An Intermezzo* (New Haven, CT: Yale University Press, 2007); and Neil L. York, "Clandestine Aid and the American Revolutionary War Effort: A Re-Examination," *Military Affairs* 43, no. 1 (1979): 26–30. On the culture and architecture of opera in the Enlightenment Iberian world, see Robin L. Thomas, *Architecture and Statecraft: Charles of Bourbon's Naples 1734–1759* (University Park: Pennsylvania State University Press, 2013), 15–45. The 1795 "Treaty of Friendship" commemorated by the Washington portrait (see fig. P.5) specified that "the Southern boundary of the United States which divides their territory from the Spanish Colonies of East and West Florida, shall be designated by a line beginning on the River Mississippi at the Northernmost part of the thirty first degree of latitude North of the Equator, which from thence shall be drawn due East to the middle of the River Apalachicola or Catahouche, thence along the middle thereof to its junction with the Flint, thence straight to the head of St Mary's River, and thence down the middle thereof to the Atlantic Ocean" ("Treaty of Friendship, Limits, and Navigation Between Spain and The United States; October 27, 1795," *The Avalon Project: Documents in Law, History and Diplomacy,* http://avalon.law.yale.edu/18th_century/sp1795.asp). For more on the treaty, see Richard L. Kagan, *The Spanish Craze: America's Fascination with the Hispanic World, 1779–1939* (Lincoln: University of Nebraska Press, 2019), 27–28, 41. On eighteenth-century Florida, see Bruce Sterling and Lewis Shiner, "Mozart in Mirrorshades," *Omni* 7, no. 12 (1985): 70.

17 As a coda to this operatic history of Figaro adaptations, John Corigliano and William Hoffman's *The Ghosts of Versailles* (inspired by Beaumarchais's *The Guilty Mother*) premiered on 19 December 1991, mere days before the start of a 1992 Columbus Quincentenary that would explode taken-for-granteds about the connected

histories of Europe and the Americas. *The Ghosts of Versailles* provides this book's epilogue epigraph.

18 Count de Classes, *Memoirs of the Life, Exile, and Conversations of the Emperor Napoleon*, vol. 3 (London: Henry Colburn, 1836), 55; and Byron Ellsworth Hamann, "How to Chronologize with a Hammer, Or, The Myth of Homogeneous, Empty Time," *HAU: Journal of Ethnographic Theory* 6, no. 1 (2016): 69–101. As a final temporal note, research on this book began in March 2014. The manuscript was completed in September 2017. Earlier presentations were given as the keynote lecture for the graduate symposium The Margin Is the Centre, Department of Art History, Visual Art, and Theory, University of British Columbia (2016; special thanks to Weiyi Chang, Kristine Olson, and Ignacio Adriasola); the keynote lecture for the XXXI Colóquio do Comitê Brasileiro de História da Arte: Arte em Ação, Universidade Estadual de Campinas/UNICAMP (2016; special thanks to Claudia Mattos); and a lecture at the Center for Seventeenth- and Eighteenth-Century Studies, University of California, Los Angeles (2018; special thanks to Barbara Fuchs and Charlene Villaseñor Black). Last but certainly not least: my archival work in general is deeply indebted to the expertise of historian and finding-aid genius Linda Arnold.

ACKNOWLEDGMENTS

This project would have been impossible without the help of archivists and librarians. Many thanks to:

Archivo General de la Administración
Archivo General de Indias

Archivo General Militar
Archivo General de Simancas

Archivo Histórico de Cádiz
Archivo Histórico Nacional
Archivo Histórico Provincial de Cádiz
Archivo del Jardín Botánico
Archivo del Museo Naval

Archivo Municipal de Sevilla
Bancroft Library
Biblioteca del Palacio Real
Biblioteca del Servicio de Archivo,
   Hemeroteca y Publicaciones
Delegación del Gobierno de la Junta de
   Andalucía en Sevilla
Hispanic Society of America

New York Public Library
University of Virginia Library

Daniel Gozalbo Gimeno
Manuel Ravina Martín and
Pilar Lázaro de la Escosura
Diego Quiros Montero
Julia Teresa Rodríguez de Diego,
Isabel Aguirre Landa, and
José María Burrieza Mateos
Javier Fernández Reina
Iván Vivanco Izquierdo
Manuel María Cañas Moya
Esther García Guillén
Juan Carlos Martínez Alonso and
María del Pilar del Campo
Inmaculada Franco Idígoras
James A. Eason
Pablo Andrés Escapa

Rafael Cid-Rodríguez

Rebeca Rull Fernández
Patrick Lenaghan, Noemi Espinosa,
and John O'Neill
Meredith Mann
David Whitesell

ABBREVIATIONS

AGA	Archivo General de la Administración, Alcalá de Henares, Spain	
AGI	Archivo General de Indias, Seville, Spain	
	IG	Indiferente General
	MP	Mapas y Planos
AGM	Archivo General Militar, Segovia, Spain	
AGS	Archivo General de Simancas, Simancas, Spain	
	ARC	Archivo
	MPD	Mapas, Planos, y Dibujos
AHC	Archivo Histórico de Cádiz, Cádiz, Spain	
AHN	Archivo Histórico Nacional, Madrid, Spain	
	MPD	Mapas, Planos, y Dibujos
AHPC	Archivo Histórico Provincial de Cádiz, Cádiz, Spain	
AHPS	Archivo Histórico Provincial de Sevilla, Seville, Spain	
AJB	Archivo del Jardín Botánico, Madrid, Spain	
AMN	Archivo del Museo Naval, Madrid, Spain	
AMS	Archivo Municipal de Sevilla, Seville, Spain	
ARAH	Archivo de la Real Academia de la Historia, Madrid, Spain	
BNE	Biblioteca Nacional de España, Madrid, Spain	
	DIB	Dibujos
BPR	Biblioteca del Palacio Real, Madrid, Spain	
BSAHP	Biblioteca del Servicio de Archivo, Hemeroteca y Publicaciones, Seville, Spain	
DGJAS	Delegación del Gobierno de la Junta de Andalucía en Sevilla, Seville, Spain	
HSA	Hispanic Society of America, New York City, United States	
NYPL	New York Public Library, New York City, United States	
UVL	University of Virginia Library, Charlottesville, United States	

carp.	carpeta
doc.	documento
exp.	expediente
fol.	folio
leg.	legajo
lib.	libro
top.	topográfico

NOTE FROM THE AUTHOR

Unless otherwise indicated, all French, Italian, Portuguese, and Spanish translations are my own. When quoting from original texts, spelling variations have not been standardized (for example, Paw instead of Pauw, or labarynths instead of labyrinths). Similarly, the use (or not) of accents has not been modernized. Titles of bound manuscript catalogs are italicized.

SUSANNA

Piegato è il foglio…or come si sigilla?
(*piega la lettera.*)

The letter is folded…now how to seal it?
(*folds the letter.*)

COUNTESS

Ecco - - - prendi una spilla:
si cava una spilla e gliela dà.
Servirà di sigillo, attendi - - - scrivi
Sul riverso del foglio,
Rimandate il sigilo:

Here - - - take a pin:
she removes a pin and gives it to her.
It will serve for a seal, wait - - - write
on the back of the letter,
Return the pin:

SUSANNA

E' più bizzarro
Di quel della patente.

It's stranger
than the seal on the commission.

COUNTESS

Presto nascondi: io sento venir gente.

Quick hide it: I hear people coming.

(*Susanna si mette il biglietto nel seno.*)

(*Susanna tucks the letter in her bodice.*)

—Wolfgang Amadeus Mozart (music) and Lorenzo da Ponte (libretto), *The Marriage of Figaro*, 1786[1]

INTRODUCTION
ARCHIVES, ARCHITECTURE, AND THE DATA OF THE NEW WORLD

This is a book about information storage and retrieval, about the creation of an apparatus mediating relations between users and previously recorded data—an apparatus generative of new, synthetic knowledge. It is a book that begins in the late eighteenth century, in Enlightenment Spain. But despite describing events that took place more than two hundred years ago, this book's stories—about power in the database, storage as erasure, and politically charged histories of "colonial America"—resonate with our world today.[2] These present-day resonances are not accidental. They exist because of direct connections between the now and the then.

Let's start by asking a rather curious question. When did the Americas become colonial?

This question may seem ridiculous. Surely the Americas were colonial for around three hundred years, beginning in 1492 and ending with the Age of Revolutions in the long late eighteenth century. There is certainly lots of scholarship about the New World during this period that uses "becoming colonial" as a title, or in the text.[3] But history is a bit stranger. The idea that the Americas were colonial, a space of colonization, and that the period from 1492 to circa 1800 was an era of colonial history, did not emerge until the so-called colonial period was almost over—that is, in the second half of the eighteenth century. This is true in English, French, Spanish, and Portuguese sources.

Certainly, some parts of the early modern Americas were referred to as colonies. But that word, derived from ancient Latin, simply meant settlements, and it was very different in political charge from the categories of colonial, colonization, and colonialism that we take for granted now. Furthermore, as scholars of the Spanish Empire have long pointed out (from Ricardo Levene to Anthony Pagden to François-Xavier Guerra to Paula De Vos to Mark Burkholder), the Spanish word *colonia* was almost never used to describe Spanish America before the end of the eighteenth century.[4] (This is in contrast to sources in English, which did refer to New World settlements as colonies.)[5] When Spanish-language authors began to write about American *colonias* in the late eighteenth century, they were making a self-conscious, highly strategic move. This new categorization was used to justify new economic and political subordinations—or to denounce them.[6]

Before the late eighteenth century, then, the word *colonia* existed in Spanish, but it was rarely used. The adjective *colonial,* in contrast, did not exist *in any European language* before the 1700s. It first shows up in English in the late 1720s but does not become common until the middle of the century—at which point it also appears in French and migrates to Spanish and Portuguese. The same basic history holds for *colonization,* which appears around 1749. *Colonialism* and its cognates do not emerge until the nineteenth century.

Claims about "the colonial" and "coloniality" have always, therefore, been political, comparative claims. They posit that certain regions (the Americas, for example) are "colonial" spaces in which practices, policies, and mentalities are fundamentally different from those in noncolonial spaces (Europe, for example). Oddly, however, very little scholarly work on coloniality (and especially in the Iberian New World) is actually comparative.[7] It assumes that practices in, say, the Americas (especially those related to power and violence) must have been different—and uniformly so, across "colonial" American space—from practices in Europe.[8] But these assumptions are seldom verified by parallel research projects that join archival analysis of European history to archival analysis of American history.[9] The question should always be: Is a practice in the sixteenth- or seventeenth- or eighteenth-century Americas truly "colonial"?[10] That is, truly without parallel in Europe? Or is the practice merely symptomatic of a violent and hierarchical early modern world?

Relying on secondary sources about Europe's history really does not help here. Due to the paired legacies of nationalist historiography and archival variation (different kinds of documents were written in, and preserved from, sixteenth-century Granada versus sixteenth-century New Granada versus sixteenth-century Guadalajara), the (nationalist) histories of Europe have been written using questions and assumptions very different from those at play in the (nationalist) histories of the Americas. European and American nationalist-historiographic traditions are often difficult to compare when using secondary sources. Adequate comparisons often require new archival research.[11] And so the following pages ask how it became possible, in a precise, material sense, to *write* histories of the New World—and specifically histories of early modernity, when the Americas were linked to global empires administered from Europe—separate from histories of the Old World. Rather than starting with sweeping, transhistorical claims about coloniality or colonialism, this project follows the deflational, technique-focused strategies of anthropologist Bruno Latour and media archaeologist Bernhard Siegert.[12] That is, what were the material-archival conditions that enabled scholars to assume "colonial" American difference from the start, rather than establishing that difference through careful archival comparison of American and European sources?

THE STRANGE CAREER OF THE ARCHIVE

Since the late 1960s, debates about "the archive" have been of great interest across disciplines: philosophy, history, art history, anthropology, media archaeology. And yet, on sitting down to read these varied and very useful studies, it turns out that the archive they discuss is usually a *metaphoric* archive. This tendency can be traced back to Michel Foucault's *The Archaeology of Knowledge* (1969). There, "the archive" was not a place or even a collection of documents. It was a set of conditions for knowing, thinking, writing:

> **All these systems of statements (whether events or things)...I propose to call *archive*. By this term I do not mean the sum of all the texts that a culture has kept upon its person as documents attesting to its own past, or as evidence of a continuing identity, nor do I mean the institutions, which, in a given society, make it possible to record and preserve those discourses that one wishes to remember and keep in circulation....The archive is first the law of what can be said, the system that governs the appearances of statements as unique events.[13]**

Drawing on Foucault, evocations of "the archive" from the 1980s to the 2000s often referred to historical traces in general. The archive was "not a building, nor even a collection of texts, but the collective imagined junction of all that was known or knowable, a fantastic representation of an epistemological master pattern."[14] On the one hand, this archival expansion was extremely useful. Not all traces of the past are alphabetical documents inked on paper. Thinking about the archive in an expanded sense provides us with a richer set of sources for imagining past lives, as well as for thinking about what has not survived, or why certain histories are told instead of others. As anthropologist Michel-Rolph Trouillot writes in *Silencing the Past,* "history begins with bodies and artifacts: living brains, fossils, texts, buildings."[15]

But this expansion of "the archive" was perhaps excessive. In 2009, one historian complained that "the archive has become a preapproved allegory for any and all modes of contestation."[16] And, from 2012: "Such literature suggests that the archive concept has been a fashion victim and risks collapsing under the weight of metaphoric overextension. If everything is an archive, then what do we call the buildings that house the old files?"[17] In response, over the past decade plus, anthropologists, historians, art historians, and media archaeologists have refocused the sweeping metaphorics of "the archive" onto the materiality of *paperwork:* files, folders, indexes, forms. This new "archival turn" concerns above all the documents *stored* in archival repositories—how they were written, what they are written on, the norms and accidents their surfaces encode, how they smell and feel, how they influence action and understanding.[18]

But even with these new, document-focused approaches, the archive in a more basic, more literal sense—a dynamic assemblage of architecture, storage containers, documents, and people—has been little studied.[19] There are notable exceptions, of course. Pioneering examples are Peter Rück's work on the ducal archive in fifteenth-century Savoy (published 1971) and Luciana Duranti's meditation on the relations between archival architecture and authority from republican Rome to the French Revolution to her own electronic present (published 1996). Studies from the past few years include Randolph C. Head's illustrated explorations of early modern archives

ARCHIVES, ARCHITECTURE, AND THE DATA OF THE NEW WORLD 3

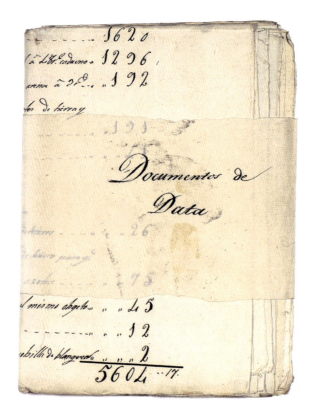

in Baden, Innsbruck, Lucerne, Würzburg, and Zurich; Markus Friedrich's innovative vision of archives in society ("first and foremost, we must emphasize the physicality of archives"); and Filippo de Vivo's tantalizing glimpses of archival spaces and furniture in early modern Italy.[20] Yet the overall neglect of archives in the narrow sense is striking, and surprising. The architecture of archival space is not a passive background for document storage and access. It is the active framework for a dynamic system in which storage and access shape what documents can *mean*.[21]

THE DATA OF THE ARCHIVE

Although a project on the concrete materiality of an eighteenth-century archive may seem nostalgically old-fashioned in our present-day world of disembodied data and instant access, it is no such thing. It reminds us of the (usually forgotten) architectures that enable our own archival situation. The wireless dematerializations of cloud computing are only possible because of massive server buildings sprawling across the globe. Covering thousands of acres of land from the United States to Canada to Scandinavia to China, and required to function 24/7 without interruption, their backup systems are infamously toxic generators of e-pollution.[22] In a nicely eighteenth-century turn, Vincent Mosco argues that these structures need to be seen as factories, reviving the "dark satanic mills" of the early Industrial Revolution.[23]

FIGURE I.1
Documentos de Data receipt packet, within AGI Indiferente General legajo 1858J, 1830. Seville, Archivo General de Indias.

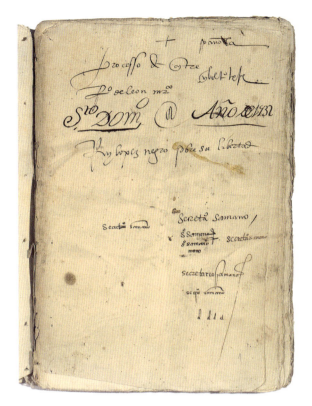

FIGURE I.2
Original sixteenth-century cover for lawsuit number 2, "Ruy López negro sobre su libertad," within AGI Justicia legajo 11.
Seville, Archivo General de Indias.

FIGURE I.3
Added cover sheet for lawsuit number 2 within AGI Justicia legajo 11, once sewn directly to the original sixteenth-century documents (see holes near left edge).
In contrast to the outer cover sheet shown in figure I.4, this sheet includes only the most basic place-date-names-topic information.
Seville, Archivo General de Indias.

In the wake of cloud computing, the "digital humanities" have been narrowly redefined as projects that analyze database metadata. The story of the Archive of the Indies provides a strange prehistory: the media archaeology of a paperwork warehouse at the dawn of the Electrical Age.[24] From its foundation, the Archive of the Indies was designed as a space where data could become information, a space generative of new historical knowledge. And when completed, it was a metadata-tagged *database*. That word, so popular today, would not be coined until 1955. But the idea of "data" already existed by the eighteenth century.[25] Three entries for **DATA** appear in the first dictionary of Spain's Royal Academy, published in 1732—and by 1791, the entry for **DATA** had four different senses.[26] Some documents stored within the AGI itself were explicitly labeled *documentos de data,* as with packets of payment receipts (fig. I.1).[27]

What would now be called metadata was central to the archive's functioning. Documents were tagged with keywords, and that information was gathered in the archive's handwritten *Índice* (Index) and *Inventario* (Inventory) books. This created a "system of coordination" (as described in 1790) still preserved today.[28] Older documents were embedded within a dual layer of metadata (fig. I.2). A new sheet of paper was sewn to the cover of the old document, tagged with brief summaries of names, dates, places, and topics (fig. I.3). The original document and its new cover were then placed inside a paper folder whose cover provided a more detailed content summary (figs. I.4, I.5).

ARCHIVES, ARCHITECTURE, AND THE DATA OF THE NEW WORLD   5

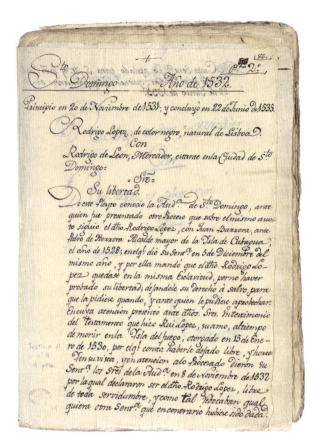
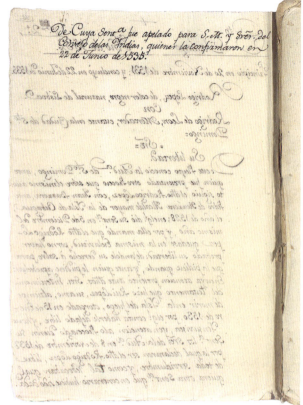

FIGURE I.4
Late eighteenth-century cover sheet (recto) for lawsuit number 2 within AGI Justicia legajo 11. The contents of the lawsuit are summarized in detail in the handwriting of Pedro Navarro, archival *oficial supernumerario* from April 1787 to October 1800. Seville, Archivo General de Indias.

FIGURE I.5
Late eighteenth-century cover sheet (verso) for lawsuit number 2 within AGI Justicia legajo 11. Seville, Archivo General de Indias.

Groups of these dually tagged documents were assembled into larger bundles, which were in turn given their own covers tagged with summaries of the subfolders they contained (figs. I.6, I.7). All of this metadata was then linked to cross-referenced finding aids, which allowed researchers to locate documents by either shelf mark location (in the *Inventario* books; fig. I.8) or content (in the *Índice* books; fig. I.9). The result (as described in 1791) was "order and clarity."[29]

Given this strikingly familiar system of tagging and indexing and cellular filing, all forming an assemblage designed to be *productive,* it is useful to think of the AGI in relation to present-day architectural and media theory. In his conclusions to *The Interface: IBM and the Transformation of Corporate Design,* John Harwood laments that architectural historians have too often limited themselves to the symbolism of how buildings look, versus the mechanics of how they function:

> **Emphasis on the aesthetic outcomes of the design program can all too easily be misunderstood as an emphasis on the beauty of its products, as a matter of imagism. I have argued throughout that the outward appearance of objects is only of secondary importance when considering how these objects (and indeed systems of objects,

6 INTRODUCTION

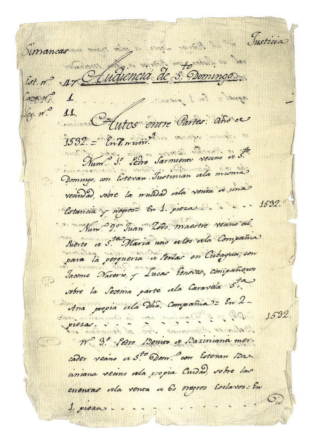 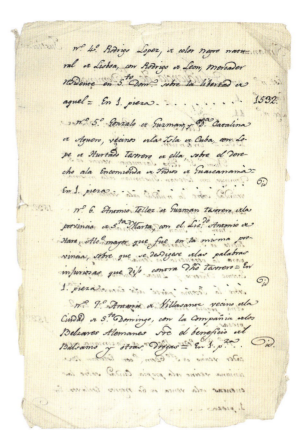

FIGURE I.6
Early nineteenth-century cover sheet (recto) for AGI Justicia legajo 11, containing civil lawsuits from 1532.
The legajo's source archive (Simancas) and AGI location (case 47, shelf 1, bundle 11) are indicated on the left; its component documents are summarized in the hand of Antonio Tariego y Somoza, archival commissioner from April 1799 to April 1809. Seville, Archivo General de Indias.

FIGURE I.7
Early nineteenth-century cover sheet (verso) for AGI Justicia legajo 11.
Seville, Archivo General de Indias.

processes, and concepts) came to be. Even considered as a surface, the interface is anything but superficial. As we have seen, the graphics, machine casings and I/O [input/output] devices, curtain and cellular walls, and exhibition techniques that related the human being to the computer and corporation alike all played a determining role in the way these machines interact. However, art and architectural history all too often remain mired in the institutional imperatives toward aestheticization, fixing machines as objects rather than as apparatuses, as images rather than as interfaces.[30]

Harwood explores recursive aesthetic-engineering systems, in which the design and functioning of IBM computers paralleled the office buildings where those computers were developed and used. Imagining architecture as a productive, functioning apparatus has a long history: consider Le Corbusier's 1923 claim that the house was a "machine for living in."[31] But the tradition of designing architecture as apparatus goes back—appropriately for my project—to at least the eighteenth century.

Perhaps the best-known Enlightenment architectural apparatus is Jeremy Bentham's Panopticon prison. It was dreamed up in the late 1780s, at the very same time that Seville's Renaissance trade exchange (the Lonja de Mercaderes) was being renovated

ARCHIVES, ARCHITECTURE, AND THE DATA OF THE NEW WORLD 7

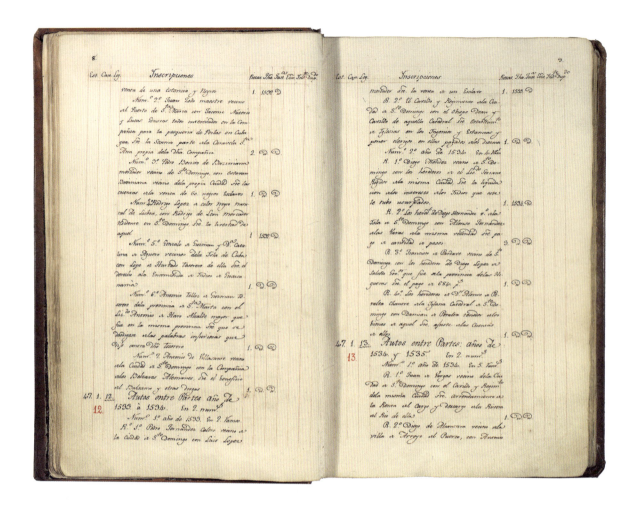

FIGURE I.8
Inventario **for the Justice (Justicia) section of the AGI, completed by Antonio Tariego y Somoza and Ysidoro Antillón in 1809.**
The volume is opened to show entries for case 47, shelf 1, bundles 11, 12, and 13, pages 8–9. On the left is the entry for the case file of Rodrigo López ("de color negro, natural de Lisboa"); see also figs. I.2–I.7. Seville, Archivo General de Indias.

into an archive. Described repeatedly by Michel Foucault as an "apparatus" or "mechanism" or "marvelous machine," the Panopticon was not simply an aesthetic construction: it was a device designed to enable specific effects.[32] Famously, the Panopticon's cells all faced a central observation tower, whose single guard could look directly at any one of the prisoners without ever being seen. This architecture of prisoner storage enabled (and inspired) experimental, information-generating practices:

> The Panopticon was also a laboratory; it could be used as a machine to carry out experiments to alter behaviour, to train or correct individuals. To experiment with medicines and their effects. To try out different punishments on prisoners, according to their crimes and character, and to seek the most effective ones. To teach different techniques simultaneously to the workers, to decide which is the best. To try out pedagogical experiments.[33]

More broadly, architectural historian Anthony Vidler sees the "instrumentalizing" of built space as a hallmark of Enlightenment design, including—but not limited

8 INTRODUCTION

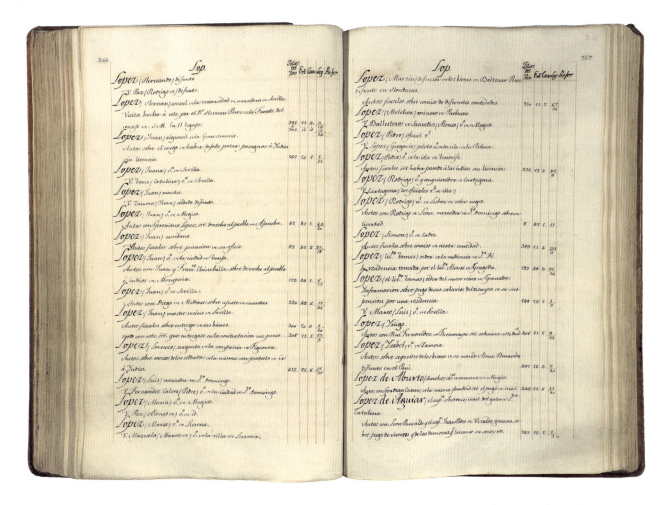

FIGURE I.9
Índice for the Justice (Justicia) section of the AGI, completed by Antonio Tariego y Somoza and Ysidoro Antillón in 1809.
On the right is the entry for Rodrigo López's case file; see also figs. I.2–I.8.
Seville, Archivo General de Indias.

to—the Foucauldian sites of prisons, hospitals, and factories: "The traditional sense of a building that embodied 'beauty' in its proportions and its three-dimensional geometries was gradually subordinated to the idea of a geometrical order that followed the dictates of social or environmental needs.... In this 'primitive functionalism,' the organization of the plan, the division of built space, was isolated as a tool of social control and reform."[34]

This all brings us back to Seville. In the very same years Bentham was dreaming up his Panopticon, and utopian architect Claude-Nicolas Ledoux his Maison de Plaisir, the still-searchable apparatus that is the Archive of the Indies was first assembled. Why?

THE DISPUTE OF THE NEW WORLD

Early in August 1784, Juan Bautista Muñoz and Francisco Miguel Maestre wrote a letter to José de Gálvez, Spain's minister of the Indies. Muñoz and Maestre were in Seville

ARCHIVES, ARCHITECTURE, AND THE DATA OF THE NEW WORLD   9

and had just prepared a renovation proposal for turning the city's sixteenth-century trade exchange into an archive. They saw their project as a polemic intervention into the Republic of Letters:

> Today the Indies are viewed in all of Europe with true enthusiasm. The wisest pens are dedicated to explaining their riches—acquiring a great deal of their own glory in the prestige of the subject matter. Which is really, truly dignified, and no one is more interested in it than the Spaniards, whose deeds in the New World scarcely allow comparison with those of other nations.[35]

Just over a year later, Muñoz still saw the new archive (then being assembled) as an intellectual intervention. But he was much harsher in tone:

> Once the New World was found by the Catholic Monarchs, Spain began to be envied for the glory of the discovery. The envy increased as our colonies and conquests grew, and not even the slow passage of nearly three hundred years has been enough to calm this vile emotion. Even in this century, when Philosophers always brag about not believing or asserting anything without close inspection, it is extremely common among foreigners to speak of our deeds in America without consulting reason, copying without judgment the worn-out pronouncements of shallow, biased men.[36]

To understand these polemic references—and their direct connection to the archive's origins—we must cross the Pyrenees and travel a quarter century back in time.

Paris, 1761. Georges-Louis Leclerc, the future Comte de Buffon, was a decade into publishing what would eventually become a thirty-six-volume *Histoire naturelle* (*Natural History*). As director of the king's garden (and its associated cabinet-museum), Buffon had access to a vast collection of biological specimens, living and preserved.[37] His *Histoire naturelle* is filled with their engraved images—skeletons, stuffed animals, organs preserved in fluid.

The first three volumes came out in 1749. Volume 1 opens with an essay about how to study natural history, followed by an overview of theories about the history of the earth. Volume 2 begins with a "Histoire générale des animaux" (General history of animals), followed by part 1 of a "Histoire naturelle de l'homme" (Natural history of man). Volume 3 starts with a description of the king's natural history cabinet, and then presents part 2 of the "Histoire naturelle de l'homme."[38]

The project continued in 1753 with the first of nine volumes on quadrupeds; these would appear at the rate of about one a year until 1764. In general, their contents are straightforward: a series of chapters, each dedicated to a specific animal. The table of contents in the final volume, for example, begins with chapters on "Le Zèbre" (The zebra), "L'Hippopotame" (The hippopotamus), and "L'Élan & le Renne" (The moose and the reindeer). But in 1761, with the publication of *Histoire naturelle* volume 9, this regular structure was, strangely, disrupted. Chapter 1 concerns the lion. Chapter 2 tigers. But then, in the midst of this menagerie, there appear three general chapters on "Animaux de l'ancien Continent" (Animals of the old continent), "Animaux du

10 INTRODUCTION

nouveau Monde" (Animals of the New World), and "Animaux communs aux deux Continens" (Animals common to the two continents).

Their titles seem demure, but their contents unleashed a debate that would rage for decades. The chapter on animals of the New World is à scathing denunciation.[39] It claims that the Americas were much colder than the Old World, and also wetter, more humid.[40] As a result, there were fewer animal species, all of them stunted. Animals brought to the Americas from Europe became smaller. Native Americans were weak, their talents imperfect, their ideas undeveloped. All of which suggests that the New World really was *new:* it had only recently emerged from the ocean (an idea based on Buffon's earlier, general theory of global geologic processes).[41] Furthermore, Buffon claims, historical sources for understanding the New World were deeply flawed. Spanish chroniclers, "to enhance the glory of their military victories, prodigiously exaggerated the number of their enemies." The stagnant and cold Americas could never support the large populations described in fifteenth- and sixteenth-century Spanish accounts.[42]

Exactly how Buffon came up with this theory—and why he decided to insert it (seemingly at random) amid the lions and tigers of volume 9—is unclear. Back in 1749, at the end of volume 3, he had written about Native Americans as part of a globe-surveying chapter on the "Variétés dans l'espèce humaine" (Varieties of the human species). But that account of the Americas, which began in the Arctic and ended in Patagonia, described a diversity of New World societies, even as it argued for a general unity in physical type (evidence against a latitude-based theory of human difference inherited from the ancient Greeks). Buffon went as far as to characterize the Aztecs and Inkas as *hommes civilisés* and the people of Panama as *de bonne taille.*[43] He did claim that the "torrid zone" of the New World was less hot (*moins chaud*) than the same zone in Europe; he also critiqued Spanish accounts of military conquests as exaggerated.[44] But the overall tone in 1749 was fairly neutral—radically different from Buffon's sweeping 1761 condemnations of America's geography, inhabitants, and historical sources.

Perhaps recent events can explain Buffon's harsh (and unexpected) change in tone. The Seven Years' War between France and Britain (1754–63), which involved battles on both new and old continents, was going badly. By 1760, the British had taken all French territories on the mainland of North America. Buffon certainly recognized the national loss of prestige resulting from these conquests, and the strain war placed on France's finances. Writing from Paris in mid-November 1759, he complained that "everything here is expensive, everything is sad." He had just sent his gold and silver dishes to the royal treasury so that they could be melted down to support the war effort.[45] Wartime austerity even limited Buffon's ability to acquire specimens for the king's cabinet-museum, such as Michel Adanson's Senegalese collections in 1759.[46]

A second factor shaping Buffon's 1761 spleen may be literary. While he was writing volume 9, he was reading Charles de Brosses's just-published, fetishism-inventing *Du culte des dieux fétisches* (On the cult of the fetish gods).[47] Its philosophizing may have inspired Buffon to do some philosophizing of his own. Indeed, Buffon felt that the arguments in *Du culte* had, out of caution, not been pushed far enough. As he explained to Brosses in a July 1760 letter:

> The substance of your ideas seems to me just and true; it only seemed to me that you were sometimes embarrassed to put them in their full light for the reasons that embarrass us all when we want to tell the truth. We can only praise you for this prudence, at the same time that we regret the excellent things it has caused you to suppress.[48]

But whatever the reasons for their creation, Buffon's harsh claims in *Histoire naturelle* volume 9 triggered a transatlantic "Dispute of the New World."[49]

The dispute's second installment came seven years later, when Dutch canon Cornelius de Pauw published his *Recherches philosophiques sur les Américains* (Philosophical researches on the Americans). Volume 1 appeared in 1768; volume 2 in 1769. The first chapter (130 pages) is a ruthless amplification of Buffon's ideas. For starters, America was an inferior continent. It was cold, fetid, and wet, just as Buffon had said. But where Buffon claimed this was because the New World was immature, Pauw claims the New World was old and degraded.[50] "It is, without a doubt, a terrible spectacle," he begins, "to see half of the globe so disgraced by nature, so that everything was either degenerate, or monstrous."[51] The continent's human and animal inhabitants were corrupted and weak—and the same fate awaited immigrants of any species.[52] America was even the birthplace of syphilis.[53] Like Buffon, Pauw argues that Spanish sources from the fifteenth and sixteenth centuries could not be trusted, as they were filled with exaggerations.[54] But Pauw's main contribution to the Dispute of the New World is his evocation of Black Legend critiques of the Spaniards themselves. Spaniards were not simply bad chroniclers, as Buffon had claimed. They were morally reprehensible. These accusations appear in early paragraphs of the introduction and continue throughout the first chapter. Spaniards are described as "lazy" and "fanatic"; they "massacred" and committed "savageries" against indigenous people.[55] The Spanish invasion was a world-historical cataclysm: "The conquest of the New World, so famous and so unjust, was the greatest misfortune that humanity has suffered."[56]

Yet Pauw's politics were complicated. On the one hand, he complained that philosophers "did not cease, by their seditious writings, to encourage Princes to invade the Southern Lands"—invasions that led to chain-reaction global conflagrations, like the Seven Years' War:

> And when Europe is at war, the whole universe is: all the points of the globe are successively shaken as by an electric force; the theater of massacres and carnage has been enlarged from Canton to Arkhangelsk, from Buenos Aires to Quebec. The trade of the Europeans having intimately bound the different parts of the world by the same chain, these are likewise drawn into the revolutions and vicissitudes of attack and defense, and not even Asia can remain neutral when merchants in America have quarrels over beaver skins or Campeche wood.[57]

On the other hand, Pauw was not opposed, in theory, to European expansion. He claimed over and over again that nature made Europeans superior to Native Americans.[58] The only problem was the violence Europeans used to assert their authority. The *Recherches philosophiques* thus set Pauw up as a competent philosopher able to advise on expansionist policy: "The Europeans, instead of employing open force and outrageous methods to destroy the American hordes, ought to have employed only the sweetness and superiority of their genius and talents in order to tame them."[59] Ethical empire, Pauw argued, was possible.

Three years later, the third key entry in the Dispute of the New World was published: Guillaume Raynal's *Histoire philosophique et politique, des établissements & du commerce des Européens dans les deux Indes* (*A Philosophical and Political History of the Settlements and Trade of the Europeans in the East and West Indies*).[60] Despite the work's title, which suggests a binary comparison of the East and West Indies, Raynal's project is global, connecting Europe, Africa, Asia, and the Americas. Although the *Histoire* went through multiple printings (several of which were famously expanded by Denis Diderot himself), the project's basic structure was established in the first edition. It consists of four parts. The first part (books 1–5) concerns European expansion to Africa and Asia. The second (books 6–9) focuses on expansion to Mexico and South America. The third (books 10–14) discusses the Caribbean and, because of the slave trade, West Africa. Finally, the fourth part (books 15–18) covers North America. A pan-European cast of imperial powers is involved: Portugal, France, Britain, and Spain (of course), but also Denmark, Russia, Prussia, Sweden, and the Netherlands.

Raynal's politics, like Pauw's, were complicated. Raynal denounced the violence that accompanied European expansions. The worst culprits, following Pauw, were the Spaniards. As the *Histoire*'s villains, Spaniards are constantly condemned.[61] Yet at the same time, Raynal (like Pauw) believed in the "civilizing" mission of Europe and in the importance of global trade—and thus many of his sections actually end with recommendations for more efficient European rule abroad![62] Raynal is famous today for prophesying the Haitian Revolution of 1791, as part of his discussion of Caribbean slavery: "Where is he, that great man, who Nature owes to her vexed, oppressed, tormented children? Where is he? He will appear, he will raise the sacred standard of liberty . . . [and] tyrants will become the prey of iron and flame."[63] This is not the only passage where the *Histoire* warns of coming rebellion: also imagined is a bloody uprising in British India.[64] But Raynal (who was very critical of the French Revolution, when it came) did not offer these prophecies hoping they would come true.[65] He offered them hoping European governments would implement preventative reforms. Raynal is quite clear about his advisory aspirations, his dreams of influencing expansionist policy: "There has never been a development so important for the human species in general, and for the peoples of Europe in particular, as the discovery of the New World, and the passage to the [East] Indies via the Cape of Good Hope. . . . Europe has founded Colonies everywhere: but does she know the principles on which to found them?"[66]

ARCHIVES, ARCHITECTURE, AND THE DATA OF THE NEW WORLD　13

Raynal doesn't get around to talking about degraded nature in the Americas until the very end of his project, at the start of book 17. There, he begins the story of British presence in North America with a condemnation of the New World as a whole. Buffon seems to be his direct source. America was cold, wet, stagnant: a land of swamps and vast rivers and eternal snows even in the tropics. The animals were less diverse, smaller, and weaker than those in Europe. Native Americans were "degraded and degenerated." The laziness of their men forced their women into servitude. Drawing on Buffon, Raynal blames a cataclysmic deluge, from which the continent has only recently emerged. America was still recovering, still drying.[67]

The fourth and final key contribution to the Dispute of the New World appeared five years after Raynal: William Robertson's *History of America* (1777). Robertson—a Scottish Enlightenment professor at the University of Edinburgh—had worked on this project for about a decade, following his earlier *History of the Reign of Charles V* (1769). The *History of America* consists of eight "books," divided between two volumes of more than five hundred pages each. The first volume chronicles a history of Old World navigation (from the ancient Egyptians to the Portuguese in Africa), the voyages of Columbus, and the invasion of the Caribbean to 1518; it also includes an overview of American climate, geography, and natural history. The second volume covers Hernán Cortés in Mexico, Francisco Pizarro in Peru, and indigenous societies in Mexico and South America; it also provides a political and religious overview of Spain's New World empire (from the mid-sixteenth century to the Bourbon reforms of Robertson's present day).[68]

Robertson criticizes the recent "attention of philosophers" to American themes: "too impatient to inquire, they hastened to decide; and began to erect systems, when they should have been searching for facts on which to establish their foundations."[69] Yet he still parrots the clichés of American inferiority established by Buffon a decade and a half earlier. In the first volume's book 4, we read that the American continent is cold, filled with "stagnating water" from which "putrid exhalations arise."[70] "The principle of life seems to have been less active and vigorous there, than in the ancient continent," and so there are fewer animal species, all stunted. The same "pernicious" degeneration awaits European animals brought to the Americas.[71] Indigenous people are of "feeble frame and languid desire." The men "treat their women with coldness and indifference."[72]

In terms of the Spaniards, Robertson is more nuanced than his predecessors. Although he twice repeats the claim that Spanish sources are unreliable, he nevertheless cites Spanish sources constantly.[73] At the conclusion of his work, he even includes a short overview, annotated-bibliography style, of the main Spanish chroniclers of the Americas (Hernán Cortés, Francisco López de Gómara, Bernal Díaz del Castillo, Antonio de Herrera), followed by a thirteen-page bibliography. Robertson also points out, in his introduction, that he had tried to consult documents in the Archive of Simancas (Archivo General de Simancas) but was denied access: "Spain, with an excess of caution, has uniformly thrown a veil over her transactions in America."[74] Although Robertson does not deny the violence of conquest, his introduction blames this on the faults of individual Spaniards, not on royal policy: "From what I have experienced in the course of my inquiries, I am satisfied, that upon a more minute scrutiny into their early operations in the New World, however reprehensible the actions of individuals may appear, the conduct of the nation will be placed in a more favourable light."[75] And so throughout the subsequent pages, Robertson highlights efforts by kings and missionaries to protect Native Americans and rein in the conquistadors.[76]

Buffon, Pauw, Raynal, Robertson: these four "philosophical historians" were connected to each other through citations.[77] Pauw and Raynal reference Buffon; Robertson references Buffon, Pauw, and Raynal. They were also connected, in condemnation, by their critics. In 1780 and 1781, exiled Jesuit Francisco Clavijero named (and refuted) all four authors throughout his *Storia antica del Messico* (Ancient history of Mexico). Although Juan Bautista Muñoz named no "Philosophers" in his Dispute-referencing letters of 1784 and 1785, his library inventory included the works of Buffon, Pauw, Raynal, and Robertson.[78] Around 1789, exiled Jesuit Juan de Velasco's *Historia del Reino de Quito* (History of the Kingdom of Quito) denounced "the chimerical systems of Pauw, Raynal, Marmontel, Buffon, and Robertson, who without leaving the Old World have wanted to perform the most lamentable dissection of the New."[79] And in 1792, the English translator of Jacques-Pierre Brissot's *Nouveau voyage dans les états-unis de l'Amérique septentrionale* (New voyage to the United States of Northern America) complained about New World myths in his preface: "You find them by regiments pressed into the service of De Paw, tortured into discipline and taught to move to the music of Raynal, and then mounted among the heavy armed cavalry of Robertson."[80]

In Spain, however, a defense was mounted to block Robertson's cavalry. A Spanish translation of *History of America* was approved, undertaken...and then denied publication. But although that project failed, it triggered the creation of the AGI.

THE ARCHIVE OF THE INDIES AND THE ATLANTIC REVOLUTIONS

Robertson's two-volume work was published in Dublin in late May 1777.[81] Copies reached Spain a few months later, and on 8 August a member of the Royal Academy of History (Real Academia de la Historia) proposed that *History of America* be translated into Spanish. As noted above, the project was approved. A first-round draft was ready by the end of the year.[82]

One of the original publication's limitations—about which Robertson lamented in his preface—was that *History of America* did not use Spanish archival sources. In contrast, the Spanish academicians hoped to annotate their translation with new primary-source references. They requested archival access from José de Gálvez (minister of the Indies), and he approved their petition on 1 January 1778.[83] Later that month, six members of the academy began to meet twice a week to work on adding references.[84] The full manuscript of their newly annotated translation was ready by the end of April. A copy was given to Gálvez so that it could be read by an external reviewer. The review was returned in late November. It was incredibly hostile. So hostile, in fact, that in late December King Carlos III suspended the translation's publication. He even took authority for writing official chronicles of the Americas away from the Royal Academy of History.[85]

The first references to the creation of "el Archivo general de Yndias" (the article *el* is significant) emerge against this fraught scholarly background. On 11 October 1778—just over a month before making public the scathing review of the Robertson translation—Gálvez ordered Fernando Martínez de Huete to Seville to "carefully investigate whether the Lonja building in Seville would be appropriate for installing the General Archive of the Indies."[86]

This was not, initially, why Martínez de Huete was being sent to Andalusia. Back in early February, the Council of the Indies (Consejo de Indias) proposed that he, along with Francisco Ortiz de Solorzano and Juan de Echevarría, travel to the Archive of Simancas to order and index the documents stored there from the council's offices in Madrid.[87] The three men were chosen for this initiative because they had previously (1770–77) organized and indexed the papers of the council's Office of Chamber Clerks (Escribanía de Cámara).[88] Exactly why the Simancas archival initiative was proposed on 5 February is unclear. But it may not be a coincidence that two weeks earlier, on 20 January, the Council of the Indies received a long petition for documents in its Madrid archives from academy member José Miguel de Flores, one of the six men tasked with adding annotations to Robertson's translated *History of America*.[89]

Whatever the cause, the council's plan in early February was an indexing-research project at Simancas. But by mid-June, the project had grown. Ortiz de Solorzano and Echevarría would still go to Simancas, but Martínez de Huete would visit Seville and survey the New World documents there.[90] Four months later, in the official commission letter of 11 October, Martínez de Huete's tasks were expanded even further. He was to visit both Seville and Cádiz. He was to prepare index-reports on the documents in House of Trade (Casa de la Contratación) archives of both cities, as well as on the holdings of Seville's Columbian Library (Biblioteca Colombina). And he was to evaluate Seville's sixteenth-century Lonja as a possible home for "el Archivo general de Yndias."

Why, between June and October, did creating *the* General Archive of the Indies emerge as a possibility?

As far as I know, by October 1778 Gálvez had still not received the hostile review of the Robertson translation. But the translation project had already raised many questions about Spanish and foreign access to New World documents. Furthermore, Gálvez had long been thinking about archival reforms. Five years earlier, in 1773, he had gone to Simancas to seek documents in support of canonizing Juan de Palafox y Mendoza.[91] Palafox (a mid-seventeenth-century bishop from Puebla, Mexico) had been a noted critic of the Jesuits; his example offered historical justification for the order's expulsion from Spain's empire in 1767 (an expulsion Gálvez enforced as inspector general of New Spain from 1765 to 1771).[92] But although Gálvez was able to locate Palafoxian documents during his Simancan visit in 1773, he was annoyed with the state of the archive, and so he wrote a report to the Marquis of Grimaldi (then secretary of state to Carlos III). As a result, a year later (in May 1774) royal architect

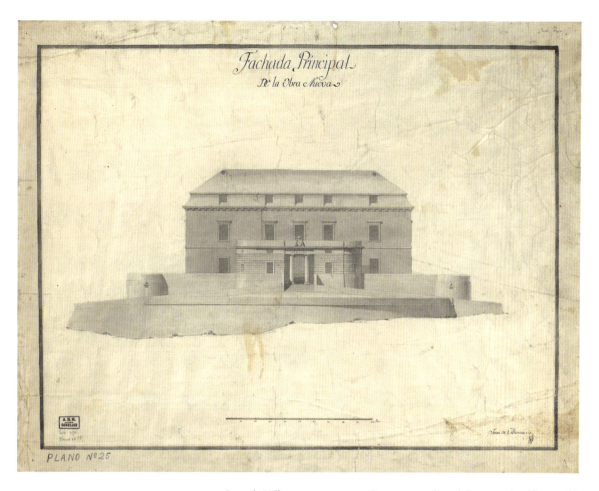

FIGURE I.10
Juan de Villanueva (Spanish, 1739–1811).
Fachada Principal de la Obra Nueva (Front facade of the new building), 1774, ink on paper, 48 × 61.5 cm. Madrid, Archivo Histórico Nacional, Consejos MPD 25.

Juan de Villanueva was sent to Simancas castle and drew up plans for an addition—an addition that was never built.[93] Villanueva proposed a minimalist, classicizing building (fig. I.10). Organized around a central patio, it would have expanded the castle's irregular footprint southwest. The basement would have kitchens, storage spaces, and barracks for soldiers (fig. I.11).[94] The lower floor would house documents (to the west) and offices (to the east; fig. I.12).[95] The upper floor and attic would be entirely devoted to document storage (fig. I.13).[96]

But that was simply a plan to *expand* Simancas, and to maintain its centuries-old mixture of Old and New World documents. Gálvez's proposal in October 1778, for creating a new—*the* new—"Archivo general de Yndias," was quite different. Instead of maintaining Simancas as a truly imperial archive, merging documents from Europe and the Americas, a new archival space would be created for a purified collection of America-only documents: some relocated from within Seville, and others brought from repositories in other cities. This would simultaneously free space in the Simancas castle so that its rooms could focus solely on the history of Europe.[97]

ARCHIVES, ARCHITECTURE, AND THE DATA OF THE NEW WORLD   17

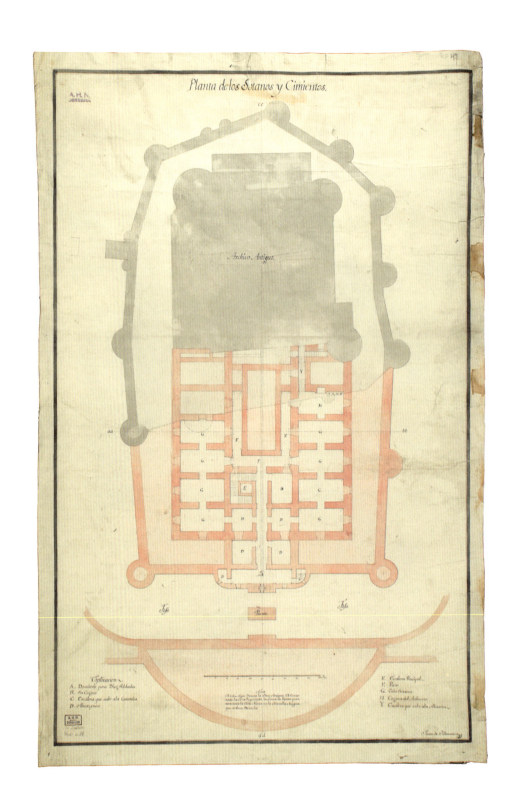

FIGURE I.11
Juan de Villanueva (Spanish, 1739–1811).
Planta de los Sotanos y Cimientos (Plan of the basements and foundations), 1774, ink on paper, 95 × 61 cm.
Plan for an expansion of the Archive of Simancas, basement level.
Key: **A** Dormitory for ten soldiers. **B** Their kitchen. **C** Staircase that goes up to the guard house. **D** Storage. **E** Main staircase. **F** Corridor. **G** Eight basements. **H** Kitchen of the archivist. **Y** Staircase that goes up to the living quarters.
Note: The color black denotes the old building. Red the proposed building. The line of dots that crosses the new building is the old wall that must be torn down.
Madrid, Archivo Histórico Nacional, Consejos MPD 54.

FIGURE I.12
Juan de Villanueva (Spanish, 1739–1811).
Planta del Quarto Vajo (Plan of the lower floor), 1774, ink on paper, 94 × 57 cm.
Plan for an expansion of the Archive of Simancas, lower level. The original castle is in black, the proposed expansion in red.
Key: **A** Plaza with two entrances, one to the town and the other to the countryside. **B** Bridge and guardhouse large enough for ten men and their leader. **D** Wall and outer bailey that surround the new and old buildings. **E** Main entrance and front room. **F** Staircase that connects to all upper floors. **G** Antechamber that leads to the office and living quarters of the secretary. **H** Room for the office. **Y** Living quarters of the secretary. **J** Rooms for papers. **K** Patio with colonnade that connects to the old archive. **L** Secret staircase for all floors.
Madrid, Archivo Histórico Nacional, Consejos MPD 323.

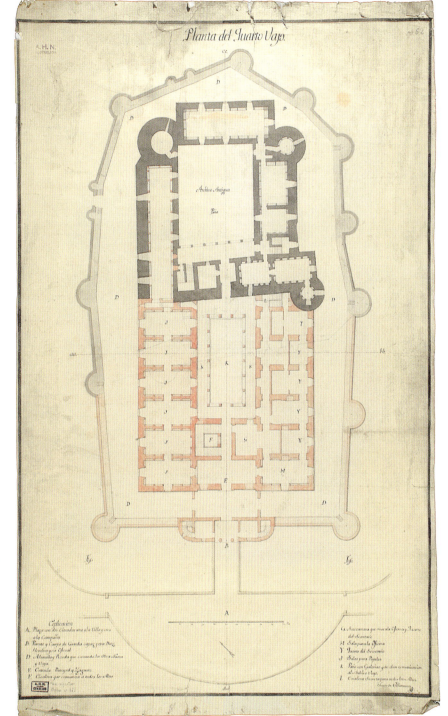

ARCHIVES, ARCHITECTURE, AND THE DATA OF THE NEW WORLD 19

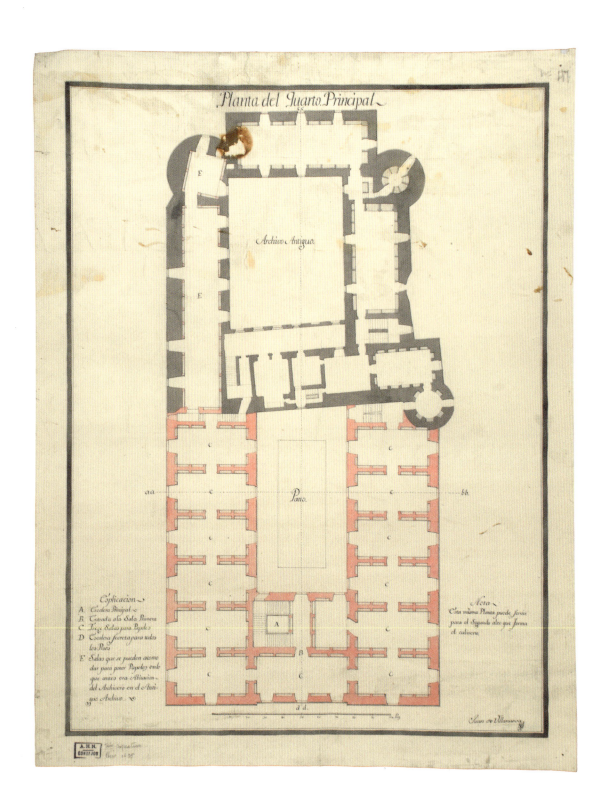

Nevertheless, Gálvez's October 1778 initiative did not go forward. Martínez de Huete, the man appointed to "carefully investigate whether the Lonja building in Seville would be appropriate for installing the General Archive of the Indies," never even made it to Seville. He worked in Cádiz for a year and a half, and then returned to Madrid.[98]

The next reference to dreams of an American archive is from two years later. Remember that after the Robertson translation fiasco of 1778, Carlos III took the privilege of writing histories of the Americas away from the Royal Academy. Six months later, on 8 June 1779, thirty-four-year-old royal cosmographer Juan Bautista Muñoz wrote to the king asking permission to begin research on his own history of the New World. The king approved the request ten days later, on 17 June.[99] As will be seen in chapter 1, Muñoz began researching right away, starting with the Council of the Indies archives in Madrid. He spent nearly two years there, before heading north to the Archive of Simancas in April 1781. On 18 August 1781, Muñoz wrote to Gálvez complaining about the archive's organization—and imagining an alternative: "For the rest, my inclination would be (when it should please God) to improve the state of things, and to join in an Archive meant *only for papers from the Indies,* both those here [in Simancas] as well as in Madrid, Cádiz, and Seville."[100] This letter reactivated Gálvez's archival dreams from the 1770s, and so he drafted a new proposal to the king on 7 November 1781.[101] Two weeks later, on 22 November, Gálvez wrote to Muñoz with news of the king's response:

> **His Majesty being informed, he resolved that the Council [of the Indies] favorably consider my proposal from '74 to expand the Castle of Simancas (owing to my report and as a result of the study I made of that archive in 1773); but since current urgencies do not allow such a costly work to be undertaken, the king has resolved that all the papers of the Indies should be transferred, once peace is achieved, to the Lonja building in Seville.**[102]

The "current urgencies" and future "peace" were those with Britain in the War of the Thirteen Colonies. Spain had been secretly supplying the rebels since 1776, and in July 1778 began open hostilities against Britain in the Caribbean. But the war soon proved costly, in part because of a British naval blockade. This stopped American cargoes from arriving in Spain—cargoes that amounted to as much as one quarter of Spain's ordinary revenues.[103]

War ended with the signing of the Treaty of Paris on 3 September 1783. Five months later, on 15 February 1784, Muñoz arrived in Seville to begin a new phase of research. A month into his stay, on 12 March 1784, he wrote a letter to Gálvez that has since been described as the Magna Carta of the Archive of the Indies[104]—"Magna Carta" not because this was the first time the idea of such an archive had been proposed but because this letter at last succeeded in making that archive a reality.[105] Peace had indeed been achieved, and so on 23 April Gálvez wrote back: Muñoz should examine the Lonja in Seville, as well as the House of Trade headquarters in Cádiz, and report as to which was more promising for the creation of a new archive. Muñoz received

FIGURE I.13
Juan de Villanueva (Spanish, 1739–1811).
Planta del Quarto Principal (Plan of the main floor), 1774, ink on paper, 62 × 48 cm.
Plan for an expansion of the Archive of Simancas, main level. The original castle is in black, the proposed expansion in red.
Key: **A** Main staircase. **B** Entrance to the first room. **C** Thirteen rooms for papers. **D** Secret staircase for all floors. **E** Rooms that could be used to store papers, in what was formerly the living area of the archivist in the old archive. Note: This same plan can serve for the upper floor, which creates the attic.
Madrid, Archivo Histórico Nacional, Consejos MPD 55.

this letter in early May, and on 24 May he toured Seville's Lonja with architects Félix Carazas and Lucas Cintora. Muñoz wrote a glowing description for Gálvez on 8 June. On 27 June, Gálvez responded, telling Muñoz that his initial report on the Lonja had been approved, and that the next step was a more formal renovation proposal. The proposal was ready on 4 August. It was sent to Gálvez, who again was pleased with what he read.[106]

The next task was removing the Lonja's current residents so that the walls dividing the upper floor into separate apartments could be ripped out. A royal eviction order was forwarded by Gálvez on 21 September: the Lonja's inhabitants (men and women connected to Seville's merchant guild, offices of which were on the ground floor) would be relocated to new lodgings.[107] There were complications, of course, but on 3 December, Muñoz reported that the apartments would be empty by the end of the month.[108] The holidays began, and 1785 arrived. On Thursday, 3 February—one day after Candlemas, the official end of the long Christmas season—Gálvez wrote to Muñoz with good news. His August 1784 renovation proposal had been approved by the king. The work of demolition and reconstruction could begin.[109]

Three years and nine months later, on 5 November 1788, the archive was ready.[110]

This book's exploration of the invention of colonial America continues in chapter 1, with a trip to Seville in 1818. Through the journal of young Bostonian George Ticknor, we will visit the Archive of the Indies in its first decades of existence, seeing how spaces were organized and furnished, and how documents were arranged and indexed.

Chapter 2 then moves back in time to the 1770s and 1780s, surveying the donor archives plundered to provide the initially empty Archive of the Indies with documents: first the Palace of the Councils (Palacio de los Consejos) in Madrid, then the Archive of Simancas, and finally the House of Trade's archive in Seville's royal palace and a rented house in Cádiz. As champion of a new American archive, royal cosmographer Juan Bautista Muñoz had harsh things to say about these other repositories when he visited them in the early 1780s. Muñoz's critiques are usually taken at face value. But they are not the only records of what those other archives were like before they were dismembered. Reconstructing their arrangements circa 1780 reveals a very different archival logic from the one that triumphed at the Archive of the Indies.

Chapter 3 looks in detail at the AGI's physical creation: how, starting in the spring of 1785, a sixteenth-century building was radically and controversially renovated to make it an archival space. The design of that space (its flooring, its spatial divisions, its document cases) went through major changes between 1785 and 1788, transformations that made the Renaissance trade exchange not just a place to store papers but also a dynamic apparatus generative of new knowledge. This potential was made possible through novel interactions of architecture, documents, and humans.

But since theory is one thing and practice quite another, chapter 4 tracks research projects undertaken in the Archive of the Indies from the 1790s to 1830. For most of these projects, the paper trails are very short. But for Washington Irving in the late 1820s and Martín Fernández de Navarrete in the mid-1790s, a more complete picture of archival practice can be reconstructed.

Finally, chapter 5 uses a famous print by Francisco de Goya (a close friend of Juan Agustín Ceán Bermúdez, the AGI's first archival commissioner) to explore questions of light, darkness, and the revolutionary linguistic history by which the words *colonial, colonization,* and *colonialism* came to inhabit our present-day vocabulary.

CODA: THE LONGITUDE OF INDEPENDENCE

> Since the Longitude Act of 1714, which offer'd Prizes up to twenty thousand Pounds for a reliable way to find the true Longitude at Sea, the Observatory had become a Target for Suggestions, Schemes, Rants, Sermons, full-length Books, all directed to Bradley's Attention, upon the Problem of the Longitude. Though some were cagy, hinting at Amazing Simplicity and Ingenious Devising, whilst giving no details, most of the letters were all-out philosophick confessions, showing either an unhealthy naïveté, or an inner certainty that the Scheme would never work anyway. For many, it was at least a chance to Rattle at length to a World that was ignoring them. Others were more passionate as to the worth of their Inventions, though employing Arts more of the Actor-Projector than of the Geometer. Occasionally Insanity roll'd a sly Eye-ball into the picture.
>
> —Thomas Pynchon, *Mason & Dixon,* 1997[111]

(Citing a work by Thomas Pynchon is a genre-feature in the world of media archaeology, so I'm delighted to be able to join the fun: *Mason & Dixon* takes place between Christmastide 1760 and Christmastide 1786.)[112]

In *The Tropics of Empire* (a fascinating book published by MIT in 2008), Nicolás Wey-Gómez asks why Christopher Columbus wrote about sailing *south,* and not simply west, in his Atlantic explorations. Wey-Gómez connects Columbus's counterintuitive (and often overlooked) directionality to enduring geographic theories inherited from the ancient Greeks. According to this antique theory of zones, the earth's climate could be divided into five regions encircling the planet. Surrounding the poles north and south were two arctic zones, frozen and all but uninhabitable. Next came the two temperate zones; Europe was located in the northern one. Finally, the fifth, torrid zone was a band surrounding the equator. It was supposedly a place of scorching heat, all but uninhabitable.

Zonal theory did not simply divide the world by climate. It also claimed that similar peoples with similar institutions would be found throughout each zone. Inhabitants of the same zone had the same capacity for rulership—or servitude. Thus, in the sixteenth century, the Indies in the Americas were understood to be comparable with the Indies in Asia not simply because of an accidental error in naming but because both regions were located in the torrid zone—and so in theory featured comparable inhabitants and ways of life.[113]

This zonal model of geography was closely connected to mapping technologies. Calculating global latitude—one's position to the north or south of the equator—was, by the sixteenth century, a well-established practice. One would measure the height of the sun or the polestar above the horizon, and then perform some basic calculations. These allowed for a measurement of latitude within one or two degrees.[114] In contrast, calculating global longitude—one's position east or west—was a completely different matter, above all if at sea on an unstable ship. A first wayfinding method involved fluctuations in the earth's magnetic field. Another used eclipses on the moons of Jupiter. But in theory, the easiest method involved having a good clock. On leaving a port, that clock would be set to local time. As one traveled (crossing what in the future would be mapped as time zones), one would calculate *local* time based on celestial phenomena. Local longitude was then revealed by a few more calculations based on the difference between local time and the time on the clock. In theory, all fairly straightforward. The problem was the clock. It had to stay accurate for months at a time—even 99.99% accuracy was not really good enough. Its mechanisms (metals, woods, grease) could not be disrupted by changes in temperature or humidity or the corrosive effects of salty air. And it had to be sturdy, resistant to the rocking of a ship.[115]

Since the sixteenth century, various governments had offered prizes for an accurate method of measuring longitude at sea. The Spanish king Felipe III promoted one such award in 1598.[116] But it was not until the 1750s that English clockmaker John Harrison developed timekeepers accurate enough for longitude calculation. He worked on several models, but after key breakthroughs with his H3 clock in the late 1750s, his H4 (ready for testing by 1761) finally succeeded as an oceanworthy timepiece (fig. I.14). Although Harrison would not be fully awarded the Longitude Prize until 1773 (after many political complications), his devices quickly became famous throughout Europe. They were targets of French industrial espionage as early as 1763.[117]

The years surrounding 1760, the years Harrison was perfecting a device that enabled longitude calculation, were also the years that the Seven Years' War began and ended, followed by the Stamp Act's imposition on the Thirteen Colonies—an important moment in our story, as chapter 5 will explain. These were also the years when, in English and French, *colonial* and *colonization* exploded into popular use. And these were the years when the Dispute of the New World began. Is there a connection linking emergent, eighteenth-century geopolitics of Atlantic coloniality to emergent, eighteenth-century techniques of calculating longitude?

Remember that latitude climatology united the globe. The New World as well as the Old were connected by zonal bands. Both had torrid tropics. In contrast, the verticality of longitude provided a new way to imagine a separation of Eastern and Western Hemispheres, and to justify models of American difference radically distinct from anything encountered in Afroeurasia. The tropical model of a hot zone encircling the

FIGURE I.14
Philippe Joseph Tassaert (Flemish, 1732–1803), after Thomas King (British, died before 1769).
Portrait of John Harrison, 1768, mezzotint, sheet trimmed to 41 × 31.5 cm.
Based on a 1767 painting by King, in the background is Harrison's third marine timekeeper (H3). Harrison's prizewinning fourth design (H4) is on the table.
London, Science Museum, inv. no. 1884-217.

earth was replaced by a continental model in which all of the Americas were uniquely *cold*. The zonal system was global, and could not be used to fragment and demonize the Americas as utterly unlike the other continents. Longitude calculations overthrew this older imaginary, and provided a new, technical means by which to precisely establish lines of difference separating the Old World from the New.

It is not incidental, then, that all four creators of the Dispute of the New World used America's continental chill to directly challenge the globe-encircling, latitude-based theory of zones. As usual, Buffon set up the basic model:

> The heat is in general much less in this part of the world, and the humidity much greater: if we compare the cold and the heat in all degrees of latitude, we shall find that in Quebec, which is the same [latitude] as that of Paris, the water of the rivers freezes every year to a thickness of several feet.... This difference of temperature under the same latitude in the temperate zone, though very great, is still perhaps less than

that of heat under the torrid zone: one burns in Senegal, and under the same line one enjoys a gentle temperature in Peru; it is the same in all the other latitudes that one would wish to compare.[118]

Seven years later, Pauw repeated these Paris-Quebec, Senegal-Peru models, and added a new comparison of his own: the Thames and Hudson Bay. All of these pairs reveal the same thing: they challenge theories of zonal unities through globe-spanning differences within "the same latitude."[119] A few years after Pauw, Raynal created his own comparisons of hot and cold places supposedly in the same zone: France and America (between the thirty-fifth and thirty-sixth latitudes) as well as North Africa and Louisiana.[120] And in 1777, Robertson repeated Buffon:

> If we proceed along the American continent into the torrid zone, we shall find the cold prevalent in the New World extending itself also to this region of the globe, and mitigating the excess of its fervour. While the negro on the coast of Africa is scorched with unremitting heat, the inhabitant of Peru breathes an air equally mild and temperate.[121]

Starting in the 1760s, zonal unities based on latitude were no longer valid. They were displaced by the absolute rupture of hemispheric difference.

> Treatises on "Parageography" arriv'd, with alternative Maps of the World superimpos'd upon the more familiar ones. Many,— as had the elder Cabot upon his deathbed,— claim'd to've been told the Secrets of the Longitude by God (or, as some preferr'd, Thatwhichever Created Earth and her Rate of Spin). Others told of Rapture by creatures not precisely Angels, nor yet Demons,— styl'd "Agents of Altitude." That they were taken aloft and shewn the Earth as it appear'd from the Distance of the Sun, and that the Navigator of the Vessel us'd a kind of Micrometer, whose Lines were clapp'd to the Diameter of the Earth, and that the measuring device read 8.75 seconds of Arc, "not in our numbers of course, not until accurately transnumerated, from theirs.—"[122]

NOTES

1 Lorenzo da Ponte, *Le nozze di Figaro, o sia la folle giornata* (Prague: Giuseppe Emanuele Diesbach, 1786), 73. See also https://www.youtube.com/watch?v=_OYtlGpApc0 (at 2:07:27): Concerto Köln, conductor René Jacobs, Paris, Le Théâtre des Champs-Elysées, 2001.

2 Jill Lepore, *The Whites of their Eyes: The Tea Party's Revolution and the Battle over American History* (Princeton, NJ: Princeton University Press, 2010); and Ray Hernández-Duran, *The Academy of San Carlos and Mexican Art History: Politics, History, and Art in Nineteenth-Century Mexico* (London: Routledge, 2017), 140–41.

3 Thomas B. F. Cummins, "The Madonna and the Horse: Becoming Colonial in New Spain and Peru," *Phoebus* 7 (1995): 52–83; Ann Laura Stoler, "Tense and Tender Ties: The Politics of Comparison in North American History and (Post) Colonial Studies," *Journal of American History* 88, no. 3 (2001): 830; Robert Blair St. George, *Possible Pasts: Becoming Colonial in Early America* (Ithaca, NY: Cornell University Press, 2000); Louise M. Burkhart, "Death and the Colonial Nahua," in *Nahuatl Theater: Death and Life in Colonial Nahua Mexico,* ed. Barry D. Sell, Louise M. Burkhart, and Gregory Spira (Norman: University of Oklahoma Press, 2004), 29; and Helena M. Wall, "'In These Meane Spaces': Becoming Colonial in the British Atlantic," *Journal of Colonialism and Colonial History* 15, no. 3 (2014).

4 Ricardo Levene, *Las Indias no eran colonias* (Madrid: Espasa-Calpe, 1951); Anthony Pagden, "Identity Formation in Spanish America," in *Colonial Identity in the Atlantic World, 1500–1800,* ed. Nicholas Canny and Anthony Pagden (Princeton, NJ: Princeton University Press, 1987), 64–65; François-Xavier Guerra, "The Implosion of the Spanish Empire: Emerging Statehood and Collective Identities," in *The Collective and the Public in Latin America: Cultural Identities and Political Order,* ed. Luis Roniger and Tamar Herzog (Brighton: Sussex Academic Press, 2000), 72–73; Paula De Vos, "From Herbs to Alchemy: The Introduction of Chemical Medicine to Mexican Pharmacies in the Seventeenth and Eighteenth Centuries,"

Journal of Spanish Cultural Studies 8, no. 2 (2007): 138; and Mark A. Burkholder, "Spain's America: From Kingdoms to Colonies," *Colonial Latin American Review* 25, no. 2 (2016): 125–53.

5 Burkholder, "Spain's America," 125, 127. But even the English example is complicated: D. B. Quinn's classic "Renaissance Influences in English Colonization: The Prothero Lecture," *Transactions of the Royal Historical Society* 26 (1976): 73–93, has several references to early modern authors *avoiding* use of the term *colony* in their writings.

6 Guerra, "The Implosion of the Spanish Empire," 72, 78, 89; and Burkholder, "Spain's America." On the postindependence and present-day political charge of these categories, see Jorge Klor de Alva, "Colonialism and Postcolonialism as (Latin) American Mirages," *Colonial Latin American Review* 1 (1992): 3–23; Jorge Klor de Alva, "The Postcolonization of the (Latin) American Experience: A Reconsideration of 'Colonialism,' 'Postcolonialism,' and 'Mestizaje,'" in *After Colonialism: Imperial Histories and Postcolonial Displacements,* ed. Gyan Prakash (Princeton, NJ: Princeton University Press, 1994), 241–75; and Cecilia Méndez Gastelumendi, "¿Una larga espera? Ironías de la cruzada postcolonialista en Hispanoamérica," *Histórica* 30, no. 2 (2006): 117–28; as well as the still-essential Frederick Cooper, *Colonialism in Question: Theory, Knowledge, History* (Berkeley: University of California Press, 2005), 3–55 (for example, the risks of a "dilute use of the concept of the colonial" are diagnosed on p. 26).

7 On the British Atlantic, see critiques by David Armitage, "Greater Britain: A Useful Category of Historical Analysis?," *American Historical Review* 104, no. 2 (1999): 427–45; and Michael Warner, "What's Colonial about Colonial America?," in *Possible Pasts: Becoming Colonial in Early America,* ed. Robert Blair St. George (Ithaca, NY: Cornell University Press, 2000), 49–70. On the Spanish Atlantic, see Tamar Herzog, *Defining Nations: Immigrants and Citizens in Early Modern Spain and Spanish America* (New Haven, CT: Yale University Press, 2003); Byron Ellsworth Hamann, *The Translations of Nebrija: Language, Culture, and*

Circulation in the Early Modern World (Amherst: University of Massachusetts Press, 2015); and Byron Ellsworth Hamann, *Bad Christians, New Spains: Muslims, Catholics, and Native Americans in a Mediterratlantic World* (New York: Routledge, 2020).

8 For case-study critiques of such one-sidedness, see Anthony Grafton, "The Rest vs. the West," *New York Review of Books* (10 April 1997): 57–64; Byron Ellsworth Hamann, "How to Chronologize with a Hammer, Or, The Myth of Homogeneous, Empty Time," *HAU: Journal of Ethnographic Theory* 6, no. 1 (2016): 269; and Byron Ellsworth Hamann, "*Las relaciones mediterratlánticas:* Comparative Antiquarianism and Everyday Archaeologies in Castile and Spanish America (1575–1586)," in *Antiquarianisms: Contact, Conflict, and Comparison,* ed. Benjamin Anderson and Felipe Rojas (Oxford: Oxbow, 2017), 49–71. See also Byron Ellsworth Hamann, "A *Tesoro de la Lengua Castellana o Español* Version 2.0: Review of *Lexikon of the Hispanic Baroque,* edited by Evonne Levy and Kenneth Mills," *Journal of Art Historiography* 11 (2014), https://arthistoriography.files.wordpress.com/2014/11/hamann-review.pdf.

9 This is not to say that comparative archival projects are never undertaken for the early modern Iberian empires. They certainly have been written, especially over the past decade plus. Significantly, these projects tend not to be centered on demonstrating the "colonial" status of the Americas by contrast to contemporary European society; other questions about transatlantic early modernity are at issue. Indeed, some of these studies dispense with the category of "colonial" altogether: Jorge Cañizares-Esguerra, *How to Write the History of the New World: Histories, Epistemologies, and Identities in the Eighteenth-Century Atlantic World* (Stanford, CA: Stanford University Press, 2001); Herzog, *Defining Nations;* Marcy Norton, *Sacred Gifts, Profane Pleasures: A History of Tobacco and Chocolate in the Atlantic World* (Ithaca, NY: Cornell University Press, 2008); Ana Díaz Serrano, "El modelo político de la monarquía hispánica desde una perspectiva comparada: Las repúblicas de Murcia y Tlaxcala durante el siglo XVI" (PhD diss., Universidad de Murcia, 2010); Hamann, *Translations of Nebrija;* and Hamann, *Bad Christians, New Spains.* An important exception is the must-read work of Aaron Hyman, which thinks through questions of the colonial in a comparative, Euro-American framework. See Barbara E. Mundy and Aaron M. Hyman, "Out of the Shadow of Vasari: Towards a New Model of the 'Artist' in Colonial Latin America," *Colonial Latin American Review* 24, no. 3 (2015): 283–317; Aaron M. Hyman, "Inventing Painting: Cristóbal de Villalpando, Juan Correa, and New Spain's Transatlantic Canon," *Art Bulletin* 99, no. 2 (2017): 102–35; and Aaron M. Hyman, *Rubens in Repeat: The Logic of the Copy in Colonial Latin America* (Los Angeles: Getty Research Institute, 2021).

10 See, for example, the (negative) answer to the question "What Is Colonial about This Picture?," in Kathryn Burns, *Into the Archive: Writing and Power in Colonial Peru* (Durham, NC: Duke University Press, 2010), 138–43.

11 Hamann, *Bad Christians, New Spains,* 4–5, 8n13; and Hamann, "*Tesoro.*"

12 Bruno Latour, "Drawing Things Together," in *Representation in Scientific Practice,* ed. Michael Lynch and Steve Woolgar (Cambridge, MA: MIT Press, 1990), 19–68 (his comments on bureaucracy and the bureau are particularly relevant here, 52–54); and Bernhard Siegert, *Cultural Techniques: Grids, Filters, Doors, and Other Articulations of the Real,* trans. Geoffrey Winthrop-Young (New York: Fordham University Press, 2015), 9. See also Miruna Achim, *From Idols to Antiquity: Forging the National Museum of Mexico* (Lincoln: University of Nebraska Press, 2017).

13 Michel Foucault, *The Archaeology of Knowledge* [1969], trans. A. M. Sheridan Smith (New York: Pantheon, 1972), 128.

14 Thomas Richards, *The Imperial Archive: Knowledge and the Fantasy of Empire* (London: Verso, 1993), 3. Consider a few classic writings from this period with *Archive* prominently featured in their titles. In Nicholas B. Dirks's "Colonial Histories and Native Informants: Biography of an Archive," in *Orientalism and the Postcolonial Predicament,* ed. Carol A. Breckenridge and Peter van der Veer (Philadelphia: University of Pennsylvania Press, 1993), 279–313, one has to search the endnotes carefully to figure out where the documentary collection he discusses is located. In contrast, Dirks's "Annals of the Archive: Ethnographic Notes on the

Sources of History," in *From the Margins: Historical Anthropology and Its Futures,* ed. Brian Keith Axel (Durham, NC: Duke University Press, 2002), 47–65, provides autobiographical reflections on the process of researching in archives, much like Arlette Farge's classic *The Allure of the Archives,* trans. Thomas Scott-Railton (New Haven, CT: Yale University Press, 2013). Ann Laura Stoler's *Along the Archival Grain: Epistemic Anxieties and Colonial Common Sense* (Princeton, NJ: Princeton University Press, 2009) is about the classifications used by governments to rule their subjects. John Bender and Michael Marrinan's *Regimes of Description: In the Archive of the Eighteenth Century* (Stanford, CA: Stanford University Press, 2005) is a compilation of academic essays about the eighteenth century. Last but not least, Kathryn Burns disarmingly begins her *Into the Archive* by admitting that, while it is really a book about notaries, a friend advised her to use (and provided her with) a more compelling, archive-referencing title (xi).

15 Michel-Rolph Trouillot, *Silencing the Past: Power and the Production of History* (Boston: Beacon, 1995), 29; see also Constantin Fasolt, *The Limits of History* (Chicago: University of Chicago Press, 2004), xiv; Jorge Cañizares-Esguerra, "Categories as Archives: From Silence to Social Justice," *disClosure: A Journal of Social Theory* 27 (2018): 15–20; and Aaron M. Hyman and Dana Leibsohn, "Washing the Archive," *Early American Literature* 55, no. 2 (2020): 419–44.

16 Anjali Arondekar, *For the Record: On Sexuality and the Colonial Archive in India* (Durham, NC: Duke University Press, 2009), 2.

17 David Zeitlyn, "Anthropology in and of the Archives: Possible Futures and Contingent Pasts; Archives as Anthropological Surrogates," *Annual Review of Anthropology* 41 (2012): 461–80. More recently, see Elizabeth Yale, "Focus: The History of Archives and the History of Science," *Isis* 107, no. 1 (2016): 76: "In May 2015 Rick Prelinger, meta-archivist and founder of the Prelinger Library and Prelinger Archives, wrote, via Twitter, that 'the "archive" is overtheorized; "archives" (where the labor of record keeping takes place) are undertheorized and underfunded.'"

18 On this latest "archival turn," see Filippo de Vivo and Maria Pia Donato, "Scholarly Practices in the Archives, 1500–1800," *Storia della storiografia* 68, no. 2 (2015): 15; Randolph C. Head, "Configuring European Archives: Spaces,

Materials, and Practices in the Differentiation of Repositories from the Late Middle Ages to 1700," *European History Quarterly* 46, no. 3 (2016): 514. Also note that a previous "archival turn" had been proclaimed in postcolonial studies, with "the archive" functioning at its broad metaphorical level as a system of governance and classification: Ann Laura Stoler, "Colonial Archives and the Arts of Governance: On the Content in the Form," *Archival Science* 2 (2002): 87–90; and Burns, *Into the Archive,* 146. For general comments, see Ann Blair and Jennifer Milligan, "Introduction: Towards a Cultural History of Archives," *Archival Science* 7 (2007): 289–96; Matthew Hull, "Documents and Bureaucracy," *Annual Review of Anthropology* 41 (2012): 251–67; and Zeitlyn, "Anthropology in and of the Archives." Case studies include Cornelia Vismann, *Files: Law and Media Technology,* trans. Geoffrey Winthrop-Young (Stanford, CA: Stanford University Press, 2008); Robin E. Kelsey, "Viewing the Archive: Timothy O'Sullivan's Photographs for the Wheeler Survey, 1871–74," *Art Bulletin* 85, no. 4 (2003): 702–23; Sven Spieker, *The Big Archive: Art from Bureaucracy* (Cambridge, MA: MIT Press, 2008); Ann Blair and Peter Stallybrass, "Mediating Information 1450–1800," in *This Is Enlightenment,* ed. Clifford Siskin and William Warner (Chicago: University of Chicago Press, 2010), 139–63; Ann Blair, *Too Much to Know: Managing Scholarly Information before the Modern Age* (New Haven, CT: Yale University Press, 2010); Siegert, *Cultural Techniques,* 82–96; Arndt Brendecke, *The Empirical Empire: Spanish Colonial Rule and the Politics of Knowledge,* trans. Jeremiah Riemer (Berlin: De Gruyter Oldenbourg, 2016); Filippo de Vivo, "Ordering the Archive in Early Modern Venice (1400–1650)," *Archival Science* 10 (2010): 231–48; John Tagg, "The Archiving Machine; Or, The Camera and the Filing Cabinet," *Grey Room* 47 (2012): 27–31; and Fabien Montcher, "Archives and Empire: Scholarly Archival Practices, Royal Historiographers and Historical Writing across the Iberian Empire (Late 16th and Early 17th Century)," *Storia della storiografia* 68, no. 2 (2015): 21–35. Allan Sekula's "The Body and the Archive," *October* 39 (1986): 3–64, although interested in "the archive" in a broad, Foucauldian sense, does engage with documentary cataloging and storage (of photographs, in this case). I would also file Aleida Assmann's *Cultural Memory and Western Civilization: Functions, Media, Archives* (Cambridge: Cambridge University Press, 2011) under the sign of document studies (as connected to individual and social memory), but see her brief chapter "Archives," 327–32. On the trope of the academic "turn," see Tom Boellstorff, "For Whom the Ontology Turns: Theorizing the Digital Real," *Current Anthropology* 57, no. 4 (2016): 387–407.

19 "We need an architectural history of archives": Peter Burke, "Commentary," *Archival Science* 7 (2007): 394; see also the proposals in Daniel Nemser, "Eviction and the Archive: Materials for an Archaeology of the Archivo General de Indias," *Journal of Spanish Cultural Studies* 16, no. 2 (2015): 124–27. My architectural focus is not meant to imply that, in the Western tradition, references to archives have always been references to buildings filled with documents. Early modern sources often link document storage to archive-chests (arks). But these chests were themselves always stored somewhere, even if they were mobile, and so the history of document storage (and of the meanings and power of those documents) is always a history both architectural and social. See Arndt Brendecke, "'*Arca, archivillo, archive*': The Keeping, Use and Status of Historical Documents about the Spanish *Conquista*," *Archival Science* 10 (2010): 267–83; Sundar Henry, "Archiving the Archive: Scribal and Material Culture in 17th-Century Zurich," in *Archives and Information in the Early Modern World*, ed. Liesbeth Corens, Kate Peters, and Alexandra Walsham (Oxford: Oxford University Press, 2018), 210–12; José Carlos de la Puente Luna, *Andean Cosmopolitans: Seeking Justice and Reward at the Spanish Royal Court* (Austin: University of Texas Press, 2018), 42–43; and Markus Friedrich, *The Birth of the Archive: A History of Knowledge*, trans. John Noël Dillon (Ann Arbor: University of Michigan Press, 2019), 80–82.

20 Peter Rück, "Die Ordnung der herzoglich savoyischen Archive unter Amadeus VIII (1398–1451)," *Archivalische Zeitschrift* 67 (1971): 11–101; Luciana Duranti, "Archives as a Place," *Archives and Manuscripts* 24, no. 2 (1996): 242–55; Head, "Configuring European Archives"; Head, *Making Archives*; Friedrich, *Birth of the Archive*, 5, see also 111–38; and Filippo de Vivo, "Archival Intelligence: Diplomatic Correspondence, Information Overload, and Information Management in Italy, 1450–1650," in *Archives and Information in the Early Modern World*, ed. Liesbeth Corens, Kate Peters, and Alexandra Walsham (Oxford: Oxford University Press, 2018), 53–86. Many thanks to Julie Park for telling me about Duranti's work, and to Constantin Fasolt for telling me about Head's work. I can also recommend two case studies on modern France: Vincent Duclert, "Un palais pour

les archives: Le projet Napoléon dans l'histoire," *Sociétés & Représentations* 19 (2005): 79–94; and Elsa Marguin-Hamon and France Saïe-Belaïsch, "Du modèle à la création: Les bâtiments d'archives en France depuis 1960," *Sociétés & Représentations* 19 (2005): 95–104. Painstaking reconstructions of the spatial layouts and storage systems of medieval and early modern libraries are provided by A. J. Piper, "The Libraries of the Monks of Durham," in *Medieval Scribes, Manuscripts and Libraries: Essays Presented to N. R. Ker*, ed. M. B. Parkes and Andrew G. Watson (London: Scolar, 1978), 213–49; Thomas Kimball Brooker, "Upright Works: The Emergence of the Vertical Library in the Sixteenth Century" (PhD diss., University of Chicago, 1996); and Angela Dressen, *The Library of the Badia Fiesolana: Intellectual History and Education under the Medici (1462–1494)* (Florence: SISMEL Edizioni del Galluzzo, 2013); see also this volume, chapter 3. More recent libraries are discussed in Anthony Vidler, "Books in Space: Tradition and Transparency in the Bibliothèque de France," *Representations* 42 (1993): 115–34; Patrick Joyce, "The Politics of the Liberal Archive," *History of the Human Sciences* 12, no. 2 (1999): 35–49 (on the British Library, and by extension the Library of Congress, in the mid-nineteenth century); Zeynep Çelik Alexander, "Stacks, Shelves, and the Law: Restructuring the Library of Congress," *Grey Room* 82 (2021): 6–29 (on the Library of Congress); and John M. Ganim, "The President's Address 2017," *Pacific Coast Philology* 52, no. 2 (2017): 149–65 (a broader survey of the symbolics and functionality of library designs from the nineteenth century to the present).

21 Other writers have considered general categories of archival space and document storage. These are all useful, but are distinct from the close-grained exploration of architecture, storage layouts, documents, and people that I pursue here. In philosophy, Jacques Derrida famously (if briefly) began *Archive Fever* by talking about the ancient Greek word for archive and the architectural space it referred to; Jacques Derrida, *Archive Fever: A Freudian Impression*, trans. Eric Prenowitz (Chicago: University of Chicago Press, 1996). That he initially presented these ideas in a conference at the Freud House in London is not incidental; Carolyn Steedman, "Something She Called a Fever: Michelet, Derrida, and Dust," *American Historical Review* 106, no. 4 (2001): 1159–80. In history, Arlette Farge's delightful *The Allure of the Archives* devotes several of its shorter prose-poem chapters to archival spaces of research access (the

reading room, the entrance, the index room)—but not, significantly, to archival spaces of *storage* (and see also Philippe Artières's engaging "Présentation; Espaces d'archives," *Sociétés & Représentations* 19 [2005]: 5–11, which uses Farge as its point of departure). In media archaeology, Cornelia Vismann's *Files* begins with the bureaucratic spaces imagined in Kafka's writings (13–29), and later includes a brief discussion of Roman archival spaces (57–59); Brendecke's "'*Arca, archivillo, archive*'" investigates the chest, the private archive, and the state archive as typical sites for document storage in the early modern Spanish empire (see also Brendecke, *Empirical Empire*). And Heather Wolfe and Peter Stallybrass (in a must-read essay) chronicle the different sub-building technologies of early modern document storage from strings to chests to desks to cabinets, methods they illustrate with period images showing how these were incorporated into rooms; Heather Wolfe and Peter Stallybrass, "The Material Culture of Record-Keeping in Early Modern England," in *Archives and Information in the Early Modern World*, ed. Liesbeth Corens, Kate Peters, and Alexandra Walsham (Oxford: Oxford University Press, 2018), 179–208. The issue of archival buildings appears at the very end of their essay: Wolfe and Stallybrass, "Material Culture," 206–7. Hussein Omar explores the politics of (in)accessibility in the Egyptian National Archives over the past century-plus: "The State of the Archive: Manipulating Memory in Modern Egypt and the Writing of Egyptological Histories," in *Histories of Egyptology: Interdisciplinary Measures*, ed. William Carruthers (New York: Routledge, 2003), 174–84. Laura Fernández-González considers Spain's Archive of Simancas in the sixteenth century: "The Architecture of the Treasure-Archive: The Archive at Simancas Fortress 1540–1569," in *Felix Austria: Lazos familiares, cultura política y mecenazgo artístico entre las cortes de los Habsburgo / Family Ties, Political Culture and Artistic Patronage between the Habsburg Courts*, ed. Bernardo J. García García and Vanessa de Cruz Medina (Madrid: Fundación Carlos de Amberes, 2016), 1–44. Other historians have studied networks of archive–archive relationships; see Markus Friedrich, "Archives as Networks: The Geography of Record-Keeping in the Society of Jesus (1540–1773)," *Archival Science* 10 (2010): 285–98 (on the global connections of Jesuit archives); and María M. Portuondo, "Finding 'Science' in the Archives of the Spanish Monarchy," *Isis* 107, no. 1 (2016): 95–105 (on the *matryoshka*-doll-like layering of archival repositories in Spain). Tamar

Herzog's *Mediación, archivos y ejercicio: Los escribanos de Quito (siglo XVII)* (Frankfurt: V. Klostermann, 1996) has important comments about the generation (and social life) of bureaucratic archival collections as personal property in early modern Quito (and, by extension, in the Spanish Empire overall); see also Fernando Bouza, *Corre manuscrito: Una historia cultural del Siglo de Oro* (Madrid: Marcial Pons, 2001), 242–70. And in anthropology, Liam Buckley considers the ruination of archival buildings and the ruination of the documents stored therein at the National Archives of The Gambia: Liam Buckley, "Objects of Love and Decay: Colonial Photographs in a Postcolonial Archive," *Cultural Anthropology* 20, no. 2 (2005): 249–70.

22 John Harwood, *The Interface: IBM and the Transformation of Corporate Design, 1945–1976* (Minneapolis: University of Minnesota Press, 2011), 66; and Vincent Mosco, *To the Cloud: Big Data in a Turbulent World* (Boulder: Paradigm, 2014), 32–39, 71–74, 123–37. For cloud infrastructures near you, see http://newcloudatlas.org.

23 Mosco, *To the Cloud,* 157. On the politicization of industrial smoke as early as 1804, see Jorge Otero-Pailos, "The Ambivalence of Smoke: Pollution and Modern Architectural Historiography," *Grey Room* 44 (2011): 100.

24 On the strategy of replacing breathless claims of radical technological newness with deeper genealogies, see Vincent Mosco, *The Digital Sublime: Myth, Power, and Cyberspace* (Cambridge, MA: MIT Press, 2004); Siegert, *Cultural Techniques;* Vismann, *Files;* and citations in Byron Ellsworth Hamann, "Object, Image, Cleverness: The *Lienzo de Tlaxcala,*" *Art History* 36, no. 3 (2013): 542, and Byron Ellsworth Hamann, "An Artificial Mind in Mexico City (Autumn 1559)," *Grey Room* 67 (2017): 42n89. On Francisco de Goya's attempts to cure his Seville-acquired deafness with electricity in the 1790s, see Gudrun Maurer, "Goya, sordo, y la 'máquina eléctrica,'" *Boletín del Museo del Prado* 30, no. 48 (2012): 94–98. On electrical spectacles in late eighteenth-century Spain, see Jesusa Vega, *Ciencia, arte e ilusión en la España ilustrada* (Madrid: CSIC, 2010), 101, 159. Finally, on archival metadata, see Randolph C. Head, *Making Archives,* 54, 59, 67, 103.

25 In his 1788 *Lectures on History and General Policy,* Joseph Priestley refers to the facts of history as "data"—and data is a key term throughout his

experimental and historical writings. See Daniel Rosenberg, "Data before the Fact," in *"Raw Data" Is an Oxymoron,* ed. Lisa Gitelman (Cambridge, MA: MIT Press, 2013), 15–40, for an excellent discussion of the emergence of Enlightenment data in English sources. For nondigital paper "databases," see Ellen Gruber Garvey, "facts and FACTS: Abolitionists' Database Innovations," in *"Raw Data" Is an Oxymoron,* ed. Lisa Gitelman (Cambridge, MA: MIT Press, 2013), 89–102; Markus Krajewski, *Paper Machines: About Cards & Catalogs, 1548–1929,* trans. Peter Krapp (Cambridge, MA: MIT Press, 2011); and Çelik Alexander, "Stacks, Shelves, and the Law." For the mid-twentieth-century emergence of the word *database,* see the *Oxford English Dictionary.* On the method of "strategic anachronisms," see William Warner, "Transmitting Liberty: The Boston Committee of Correspondence's Revolutionary Experiments in Enlightenment Mediation," in *This Is Enlightenment,* ed. Clifford Siskin and William Warner (Chicago: University of Chicago Press, 2010), 109–10; and Hamann, "An Artificial Mind," 9–10, 31–34. Note that the genealogy of *data* in Spanish sources goes back to at least the 1520s; a manuscript book of expenses paid by Seville's House of Trade (Casa de la Contratación) is headed by the word *Data,* underlined (AGI Contaduría 269).

26 Real Academia Española, *Diccionario de la lengua castellana,* vol. 3 (Madrid: Imprenta de la Real Academia Española, 1732), 28.

27 Various examples are found in AGI IG 1858J. Starting in 1793, annual financial records for the archive are titled "Cuenta con Cargo, y data del Arca de caudales del R[ea]l Archivo gener[al] de Yndias," but *data* is used as early as 1785 for archival financial records (AGI IG 1858H). On data versus information, see Alexander R. Galloway, *The Interface Effect* (Cambridge: Polity, 2012), 81–84; and Lisa Gitelman and Virginia Jackson, "Introduction," in *"Raw Data" Is an Oxymoron,* ed. Lisa Gitelman (Cambridge, MA: MIT Press, 2013), 8–9.

28 Guidelines for running the AGI were published in 1790: *Ordenanzas para el Archivo General de Indias* (Madrid: Imprenta de la Viuda de Ibarra, 1790). They remained in effect for nearly a century, and have been reprinted in Pedro Torres Lanzas and Germán Latorre, *Archivo General de Indias: Catálogo; Cuadro general de la documentación* (Seville: Tipografía Zarzuela, 1918), 23–40; and at the end of Francisco de Solano, Margarita Gómez

Gómez, and Manuel Romero Tallafigo, eds., *Ordenanzas del Archivo General de Indias* (Seville: Dirección General del Libro, Bibliotecas y Archivos, Consejería de Cultura, Junta de Andalucía, 1986). The "system of coordination" is described as follows: "Para complemento del nuevo sistema de coordinacion deberá ser incesante la diligencia de sacar en quartillas sueltas apuntamientos con notas remisivas de aquellos papeles que toquen ó ilustren diferentes puntos, y de colocar dichas quartillas en los correspondientes legajos; con el designio de facilitar el hallazgo de qualquier papel, y de conseguir prontamente en qualquier materia toda la luz que sea capaz de suministrar el Archivo" (*Ordenanzas* [1790], 26–27).

29 "Por el llama el comisionado los legajos que estan en los estantes, y despues de limpios y sacudidos por el Portero, entrega uno à cada oficial, quien le exâmina, le divide y subdivide, si es necesario, y abraza cada separacion con medio pliego de papel y en él explica sucintamente lo que contiene y su f[ec]ha. Le vuelve despues al comisionado, este le comprueba; ya hallandole arreglado numera las subdivisiones y las junta con otra cubierta de papel, que dice quantas son, de que tratan en g[ene]ral y sus años: numera estas divisiones, y en otra cubierta que las abraza todas, pone un resumen de lo que contienen y por caveza la misma inscripcion que está en el inventario, que es la propia que tiene la cartela pendiente por defuera del legajo; y al margen de este resumen se escribe el archivo de donde vino, el num[er]o del estante, el de la tabla ó caxon en que se ha de colocar, el que tiene el legajo segun la numeracion del inventario y el que le corresponde en la misma tabla. . . . Y ultimamente se cubre y ata el legajo como previene el capitulo 50 del Reglamento, poniendo en la cartela sobre su inscripcion los numeros del estante, caxon y legajo que le corresponde. No hay duda, Ex[celentísi]mo s[eñ]or que esta operacion parece prolixa (bien que cada dia se hace con mas facilidad, por que en los principios se camina despacio, y con la experiencia y conocimiento que se adquiere se simplifican las divisiones y subdivisiones) pero es precisa, es indispensable. Ella instruye à los oficiales de todo lo que contiene el Archivo, pues todo lo exâminan: ordena los legajos, que por lo regular lo no están: los clasifica, los divide, subdivide y algunas veces vuelve á subdividir para darles todo el orden y claridad posible" (AGI IG 1854A, Juan Agustín Ceán Bermúdez to the Marquis de Baxamar, Seville, 27 July 1791). These linked document tagging systems, three-part shelf marks, and index and inventory volumes were recommended in a number of eighteenth-century treatises on archival organization; see "Mémoire instructif pour l'arrengement des Archives," *Journal Oeconomique* (March 1751): 152, 168, 173; Pierre Camille Le Moine, *Diplomatique-Pratique, ou traité de l'arrangement des archives et trésors des chartes* (Metz: Joseph Antoine, 1765); Oliver Legipont, *Itinerario en que se contiene el modo de hacer con utilidad los viajes à cortes estrangeras* [1751], trans. Joaquín Marín (Valencia: Benito Monfort, 1759), 269, 299; and Eutimio Sastre Santos, *Una instrucción de Jovellanos para el arreglo del archivo del Monasterio Santiaguista de Sancti Spiritus, Salamanca, 1790* (Madrid: Hidalguía, 1995): 76, 79. On linked inventory and index books in early sixteenth-century Görz, see Head, *Making Archives,* 163–64.

30 Harwood, *Interface,* 224; and Kris Paulsen, *Here/There: Telepresence, Touch, and Art at the Interface* (Cambridge, MA: MIT Press, 2017). For Foucault's discussion of the apparatus as "a thoroughly heterogeneous set consisting of discourses, institutions, architectural forms," see Giorgio Agamben, *What Is an Apparatus? And Other Essays* (Stanford, CA: Stanford University Press, 2009), 2.

31 Le Corbusier, *Toward an Architecture* [1923], trans. John Goodman (Santa Monica, CA: Getty Research Institute, 2007), 151, 299; see also case studies cited in Rajiv C. Shah and Jay P. Kesan, "How Architecture Regulates," *Journal of Architectural and Planning Research* 24, no. 4 (2007): 350–59.

32 Michel Foucault, *Discipline and Punish: The Birth of the Prison,* trans. Alan Sheridan (New York: Vantage, 1977), 201, 204 ("apparatus"); 200, 202, 204, 205, 206, 207 ("mechanism"); 201, 202, 203, 207 ("machine"). However, although Foucault imagines how various panoptic structures could generate written documents (189–90), he (alas) never explores the spatiality of document storage—that is, the archive in a narrow sense. See also Agamben, *What Is an Apparatus?,* 1–24.

33 Foucault, *Discipline and Punish,* 203–4.

34 Anthony Vidler, *The Writing of the Walls: Architectural Theory in the Late Enlightenment* (Princeton, NJ: Princeton Architectural Press, 1987), 3; see also his chapters "Spaces of Production" ("each *métier* had its own space, at once an extension and completion of its machines and activities and a kind of machine on its own terms," 23–34) and

"The Design of Punishment" ("after the Revolution, any sublimity in the prison, whether panoptical or not, had to be found solely in the implacable silence of a mechanism wherein, as Baltard put it, 'the buildings functioned like a machine submitted to the action of a single motor,'" 73–82). Note that although Vidler is critical of some of Foucault's claims about panoptic visibility—and how these ideas have been simplified by later architectural historians (39)—he agrees with the general idea of architecture as apparatus. See Vidler, "Transparency and Utopia: Constructing the Void from Pascal to Foucault," in *Regimes of Description: In the Archive of the Eighteenth Century,* ed. John Bender and Michael Marrinan (Stanford, CA: Stanford University Press, 2005), 177–83.

35 See this volume, chapter 3, 158–59n21 (AGI IG 1853, Juan Bautista Muñoz and Francisco Miguel Maestre to José de Gálvez, Seville, 4 August 1784). Already in June 1779, in his proposal to Carlos III for writing a new New World history, Muñoz saw his work as an intervention that would "desagraviar a la nación de los injustos cargos de los estrangeros." Cited in Nicolás Bas Martín, *El cosmógrafo e historiador Juan Bautista Muñoz (1745–1799)* (Valencia: Universitat de València, 2002), 96 (see also 108 for comments in 1783); and Margarita Gómez Gómez, "El Archivo General de Indias: Génesis histórica de sus ordenanzas," in *Ordenanzas del Archivo General de Indias,* ed. Francisco de Solano, Margarita Gómez Gómez, and Manuel Romero Tallafigo (Seville: Dirección General del Libro, Bibliotecas y Archivos, Consejería de Cultura, Junta de Andalucía, 1986), 64.

36 "Desde que se halló el nuevo Mundo por los Reyes Catolicos, empezaron a envidiar á españa la gloria del descubrimiento. Crecio la embidia segun se ivan acrecentando nuestras colonias i conquistas; ni la dilatada serie de casi trecientos años ha bastado para aquietar aquella vil pasion. Aun en este siglo, quando tanto se precian de Filosofos, de no admitir ni proferir nada sin examen, es comunisimo entre los Estrangeros hablar de nuestros hechos en America sin consultar la razon, copiando sin dicernimiento las declamaciones antiguas de hombres ligeros i apasionados" (AHN Diversos-Colecciones 29 N17, "Razon de la obra cometida a D.[on] Juan B[autis]ta Muñoz," Juan Bautista Muñoz to José de Gálvez, Madrid). Another copy, dated 16 November 1785, can be found in AJB Div. XIII leg. 5 carp. 8 doc. 10. Thanks to AJB archivist Esther García Guillén for helping me track down these various copies.

37 Jacques Roger, *Buffon: A Life in Natural History,* ed. L. Pearce Williams, trans. Sarah Lucille Bonnefoi (Ithaca, NY: Cornell University Press, 1997), 44–61, 220–21, 273–74, 280, 353.

38 Roger, *Buffon,* 65–201.

39 Georges-Louis Leclerc, Comte de Buffon, *Histoire naturelle, générale et particulière, avec la description du Cabinet du Roi,* 20 vols. (Paris: L'Imprimerie Royale, 1749–88), 9:85–128.

40 The idea that the Americas were cold can also be found in various seventeenth-century texts; see Jorge Cañizares-Esguerra, "New World, New Stars: Patriotic Astrology and the Invention of Indian and Creole Bodies in Colonial Spanish America, 1600–1650," *American Historical Review* 104, no. 1 (1999): 33–68. The connection between these earlier ideas and Buffon's theories is unclear.

41 Roger, *Buffon,* 104–5.

42 Buffon, *Histoire naturelle,* 9:114.

43 Buffon, *Histoire naturelle,* 3:493, 499; on the critique of latitude theories, see 3:484, 493, 502.

44 Buffon, *Histoire naturelle,* 3:511, 512, 514.

45 Roger, *Buffon,* 207.

46 Anna Raitières, "Lettres à Buffon dans les 'Registres de l'Ancien Regime' (1739–1788)," *Histoire et nature* 17–18 (1981): 96. An annuity-exchange was arranged with Adanson the following year. This earlier experience of North American warfare may explain why Buffon was later opposed to France's involvement in the War of the Thirteen Colonies: Roger, *Buffon,* 421.

47 Georges-Louis Leclerc, Comte de Buffon, *Correspondence,* 2 vols., in *Oeuvres Complètes de Buffon,* ed. Jean-Louis de Lanessan, new ed. (Paris: Libraire Abel Pilon, 1884), 1:113 (Buffon to Charles de Brosses, 5 May 1760). On Brosses and the coinage of the term *fetishism,* see William Pietz, "The Problem of the Fetish, II. The Origin of the Fetish," *Res: Anthropology and Aesthetics* 13 (1987): 23–45.

48 Buffon, *Correspondence,* 1:113–14 (Buffon to Charles de Brosses, 14 July 1760).

49 Classic accounts of this Dispute of the New World include Henry Ward Church, "Corneille De Pauw, and the Controversy over His *Recherches Philosophiques Sur Les Américains,*" *PMLA* 51, no. 1 (1936): 178–206; Benjamin Keen, *The Aztec Image*

in Western Thought (New Brunswick, NJ: Rutgers University Press, 1973), 217–309; Antonello Gerbi, *The Dispute of the New World: The History of a Polemic, 1750–1900,* trans. and ed. Jeremy Moyle (Pittsburgh, PA: University of Pittsburgh Press, 1973), 217–309; and Cañizares-Esguerra, *How to Write the History of the New World.*

50 Cornelius de Pauw, *Recherches philosophiques sur les Américains; Ou mémoires intéressants pour servir à l'histoire de l'espèce humaine,* 2 vols. (Berlin: George Jacques Decker, 1768–69), 1:5–7, 11, 22–26, 44, 104–6.

51 Pauw, *Recherches philosophiques,* 1:i; see also 23 and 30 for his direct critiques of Buffon.

52 Pauw, *Recherches philosophiques,* 1:x, 4, 9, 12–13, 28, 34–35, 54.

53 Pauw, *Recherches philosophiques,* 1:19–22.

54 Pauw, *Recherches philosophiques,* 1:57, 68, 93.

55 Pauw, *Recherches philosophiques,* 1:ix, 26, 66, 73, 84, 88, 93.

56 Pauw, *Recherches philosophiques,* 1:ii.

57 Pauw, *Recherches philosophiques,* 1:90.

58 Susanne Zantop, "Dialectics and Colonialism: The Underside of the Enlightenment," in *Impure Reason: Dialectic of Enlightenment in Germany,* ed. David W. Wilson and Robert C. Holub (Detroit: Wayne State University Press, 1993), 306–7.

59 Pauw, *Recherches philosophiques,* 1:118. For a pro-expansion reading of Pauw, see Zantop, "Dialectics"; and cf. Ottmar Ette, "Archeologies of Globalization: European Reflections on Two Phases of Accelerated Globalization in Cornelius de Pauw, Georg Forster, Guillaume-Thomas Raynal and Alexander von Humboldt," *Culture & History Digital Journal* 1, no. 1 (2012): 1–17.

60 On discussions of this work in the Spanish press, see Bas Martín, *El cosmógrafo,* 67–68. Although printed in France in 1772, the work carried a 1770 Amsterdam imprint (common subterfuges for radical Enlightenment literature); see Anthony Pagden, *The Enlightenment and Why It Still Matters* (New York: Random House, 2013), 200–201; and Robert Darnton, *The Forbidden Best-Sellers of Pre-Revolutionary France* (New York: W. W. Norton, 1995).

61 William Randall Womack, "Eighteenth-Century Themes in the *Histoire Philosophique et*

Politique des Deux Indes of Guillaume Raynal" (PhD diss., University of Oklahoma, 1970), 17–18. For example, when chapter titles were added to the 1780 edition, two of them (book 6, chapter 7; and book 7, chapter 2) concerned the "cruelties" of the Spaniards—the only European power to receive this dubious honor.

62 Womack, "Eighteenth-Century Themes," 13, 16, 25, 30–39, 50; Trouillot, *Silencing the Past,* 81–82; and Pagden, *The Enlightenment,* 200–202, 262–63. See also Dallas D. Irvine, "The Abbé Raynal and British Humanitarianism," *Journal of Modern History* 3, no. 4 (1931): 564–77.

63 This particular quotation would not appear until the revised edition of 1780; the original 1770s version simply called on European monarchs to end the slave trade: Guillaume-Thomas Raynal, *Histoire philosophique et politique, des établissemens & du commerce des Européens dans les deux Indes,* 6 vols. (Amsterdam: 1770), 4:174; and Guillaume-Thomas Raynal, *Histoire philosophique et politique, des établissemens & du commerce des Européens dans les deux Indes,* rev. ed., 10 vols. (Geneva: Jean-Leonard Pellet, 1780), 3:204. Raynal's Haitian prophecy is mentioned in Irvine, "Abbé Raynal," 567; Womack, "Eighteenth-Century Themes," 45–46; and Darcy Grimaldo Grigsby, *Extremities: Painting Empire in Post-Revolutionary France* (New Haven, CT: Yale University Press, 2002), 19.

64 Raynal, *Histoire* (1770), 1:383–84; and Raynal, *Histoire* (1780), 1:397–98.

65 Womack, "Eighteenth-Century Themes," 4; and Grigsby, *Extremities,* 40.

66 Raynal, *Histoire* (1770), 1:1–2.

67 Raynal, *Histoire* (1770), 6:192–97.

68 William Robertson, *History of America,* 2 vols. (Dublin: Whitestone et al., 1777), 2:406–34. On the connection of Robertson's arguments to the renewal of European imperialism, see David F. Slade, "Enlightened Archi-Textures: Founding Colonial Archives in the Hispanic Eighteenth Century" (PhD diss., Emory University, 2005), 73–75.

69 Robertson, *History of America,* 1:286.

70 Robertson, *History of America,* 1:258–59.

71 Robertson, *History of America,* 1:259–61.

72 Robertson, *History of America,* 1:292–93, 319.

73 Robertson, *History of America,* 1:285, 379.

74 Robertson, *History of America,* 1:ix.

75 Robertson, *History of America,* 1:x.

76 Robertson, *History of America,* 1:215–18; 2:185, 228, 348–49, 351, 375.

77 On Enlightenment "philosophical history," see Cañizares-Esguerra, *How to Write the History of the New World,* 1–27; and Pagden, *The Enlightenment,* 179–283.

78 Nicolás Bas Martín, "Una aproximación a la biblioteca del ilustrado valenciano Juan Bautista Muñoz (1745–1799)," *Saitabi* 48 (1998): 130, 143, 142, 143.

79 Juan de Velasco, *Historia del Reino de Quito en la América Meridional,* 3 vols. (Quito: Imprenta de Gobierno, por Juan Campuzano, 1841–44), 1:iii, as well as 3:54 on "the deception and injustice of Pauw, Raynal, and Robertson." See also Gerbi, *Dispute of the New World,* 217; and Cañizares-Esguerra, *How to Write the History of the New World,* 204, 249–53. Jean Marmontel published *Les Incas* in 1777 (see Gerbi, *Dispute of the New World,* 50–51).

80 Jacques-Pierre Brissot de Warville, *New Travels in the United States of America, Performed in 1788,* trans. Joel Barlow (Dublin: W. Corbet, 1792), iv.

81 R. A. Humphries, "William Robertson and His History of America," in *Tradition and Revolt in Latin America and Other Essays* (New York: Columbia University Press, 1969), 18; Thomas Crawford, ed., *The Correspondence of James Boswell and William Johnson Temple, 1756–1795, Part 1* (Edinburgh: Edinburgh University Press, 1997), 420; and Stewart J. Brown, *William Robertson and the Expansion of Empire* (Cambridge: Cambridge University Press, 2008), 154.

82 On the Robertson affair, see María Teresa Nava Rodríguez, "Robertson, Juan Bautista Muñoz, y la Academia de la Historia," *Boletín de la Real Academia de la Historia* 187, no. 2 (1990): 435–56; Cañizares-Esguerra, *How to Write the History of the New World,* 160–85; and Richard L. Kagan, *Clio and the Crown: The Politics of History in Medieval and Early Modern Spain* (Baltimore: Johns Hopkins University Press, 2010), 283–87.

83 Cañizares-Esguerra, *How to Write the History of the New World,* 375n169. One peer reviewer of the book you are now reading pointed out that the team-archival-annotation of another author's work also took place elsewhere in Spanish Enlightenment scholarship; for an example from the history of architecture, see Daniel Crespo Delgado and Miriam Cera Brea, "Ceán y la arquitectura," in *Ceán Bermúdez: Historiador del arte y coleccionista ilustrado,* ed. Elena María Santiago Páez (Madrid: Biblioteca Nacional de España, 2016), 247, 249, 265.

84 Cañizares-Esguerra, *How to Write the History of the New World,* 177; but cf. Nava Rodríguez, "Robertson," 443n21.

85 Richard L. Kagan situates these conflicts over translation, and the subsequent (and controversial) appointment of Muñoz, in the context of factional rivalry between Gálvez (minister of the Indies) and Pedro Rodríguez de Campomanes (director of the Royal Academy of History); Kagan, *Clio and the Crown,* 281–88.

86 "examinanda menudamente si la Casa-Lonja que existe en Sevilla será al proposito para colocar el Archivo G[ene]ral de Yndias," (AGI IG 1852, letter of commission to Fernando Martínez de Huete, San Lorenzo, 11 October 1778); the earliest reference to this mandate I have found is in a 6 October note added to a letter to Miguel de San Martín Cueto: "Que vea si la Casa Lonja existente en ella serà à proposito para colocar en ella el Archivo general de Yndias" (AGI IG 1852, Aranjuez, 19 June 1778). See also Alberto Humanes Bustamante, "De la Real Casa Lonja de Sevilla al Archivo General de Indias," in *La América española en la época de Carlos III: Sevilla, diciembre 1985–marzo 1986* (Seville: Ministerio de Cultura, Instituto de Cooperación Iberoamericana and Archivo General de Indias, 1985), 74; and Gómez Gómez, "El Archivo," 66.

87 AGI IG 1852, "Cons[ej]o de Yndias 5 de Febrero de 1778. Por el fallecimiento de d[on] Antonio de Salazar…" Projects of archival indexing and documentation had been important in Spain throughout the eighteenth century. For a general overview, see Agustín Millares Carlo, "El siglo XVIII español y los intentos de formación de un corpus diplomático," *Revista de la Biblioteca, Archivo y Museo* 2 (1925): 515–30. Both Susan Boynton, *Silent Music: Medieval Song and the Construction of History in Eighteenth-Century Spain* (Oxford: Oxford University Press, 2011), and María Gloria Aparicio Valero, *Regalismo borbónico e historia crítica: Las comisiones de archivos; Su recopilación documental (1749–1756)* (Valencia: Institució

Alfons el Magnànim, 2013) discuss the massive, midcentury multisite Commission of Archives Project. In addition, Boynton, *Silent Music,* 166, examines Manuel Abad y Lasierra's survey of archival documents in Aragon. Also important is Juan Antonio Enríquez's November 1780 report on the archives and libraries throughout Spain that held manuscripts on the Americas, a list later used by Juan Bautista Muñoz (AGI IG 1565); Nicolás Bas Martín, *Juan Bautista Muñoz (1754–1799) y la fundación del Archivo General de Indias* (Valencia: Generalitat Valenciana, 2000), 32.

88 On this earlier project, see AGI IG 1852, "Cons[ej]o de Yndias 5 de Febrero 1778, Por fallecimiento de d[o]n Antonio de Salazar"; and AGI IG 1852, Francisco Ortiz de Solorzano, Simancas, 14 May 1785. In the 1770s, Escribanía de Cámara documents seem to have been stored in a house in front of the Church of Santa María de la Almudena (just across the street, to the north, from the Palace of the Councils): "la Ess[criba]nia de Camara de el Sup[re]mo Consejo de Indias, y los Papeles de ella de muchos años à esta parte se hallan en uno de los Quartos segundos de la Casa que frente de la Puerta de los Pies de la Iglesia Parroquial de Santa Maria de la Almudena de esta Corte, y llaman del Platero" (AHN Consejos leg. 1288, Vicente de Alfaro, Madrid, 13 September 1781).

89 AGI IG 1656, "Noticias que se solicitan de las dos secretarias del Real y Supremo Consejo y Camara de las Indias"; and Cañizares-Esguerra, *How to Write the History of the New World,* 375.

90 "el expresado d[o]n Fernando Mart[ín]ez de Huete destinado á la recoleccion de los papeles de Yndias que existen en Sevilla" (AGI IG 1852, letter to Miguel de San Martín Cueto, Aranjuez, 19 June 1778). In 1781, Muñoz would be very critical of the two years of work by Ortiz de Solorzano and Echevarría (who died 23 September 1780 and was replaced by Estevan de Larrañaga): "Ya que estavan aqui bastantes dias los dos oficiales que fueron embiados al principio, recibieron la Ynstruccion por Febrero de 1779. Parecio la empresa, como lo era en la realidad, mui superior a las fuerzas de los sugetos…no han tocado en lo substancial de la obra" (AGI IG 1852, Juan Bautista Muñoz to José de Gálvez, 18 August 1781; on Echevarría's death, see AGI IG 1852, Manuel de Ayala y Rosales to José de Gálvez, Simancas, 25 September 1780).

91 For references to Gálvez's 1773 visit, see AGI IG 1852, Francisco Ortiz de Solorzano and Estevan de

Larrañaga to José de Gálvez, Simancas, 14 August 1784; and AGI IG 1854A, "Expediente sobre el establecimiento i progresos del Archivo de Yndias de Sevilla" ("Nota" under the year 1784). Four notes on the Palafox documents, dated 1773, are tucked into a parchment-bound manuscript in AGI IG 1858C titled *Ymbentario De los Papeles de la Secretaria de Yndias de la Negociazion del Reyno de N[ue]va España.*

92 Francisco de Solano, "José de Gálvez: Fundador del Archivo de Indias," in *Ordenanzas del Archivo General de Indias,* ed. Francisco de Solano, Margarita Gómez Gómez, and Manuel Romero Tallafigo (Seville: Dirección General del Libro, Bibliotecas y Archivos, Consejería de Cultura, Junta de Andalucía, 1986), 27–28.

93 Margarita Gómez Gómez, "Carlos III y José de Gálvez: El proyecto ilustrado de un sistema de archivos," in *IV Encuentro, De la ilustración al romanticismo: Carlos III, dos siglos después,* ed. Mariano Peñalver, vol. 2 (Cádiz: Universidad de Cádiz, 1994), 39–49; and Daniela Calabró, "Referencias históricas sobre la villa de Simancas," *Castillos de España* 110–11 (1998): 59–74. See also the letter on the plans from José de Gálvez to Simancas archivist Manuel Ayala de Rosales, Madrid, 27 December 1774 (AGS ARC 7, 2, 219); thanks to Isabel Aguirre Landa for helping me track down this document.

94 The key for figure I.11 reads: "A Dormitorio para Diez Soldados. B Su Cozina. C Escalera que sube a la Guardia. D Almazenes. E Escalera Principal. F Paso. G Ocho Sotanos. H Cozina del Archivero. Y Escalera que sube ala Abitacion. Nota El color Negro Denota la Obra Antigua. El Encarnado la Obra Proyectada. La linea de Puntos que atraviesa la Obra Nueva es la Muralla Antigua que se deve Demoler." The corresponding caption contains the English translation.

95 The key for figure I.12 reads: "A Plaza con dos entradas una a la Villa y otra a la Campaña. B Puente y Cuerpo de Guardia capaz para Diez Hombres y su Oficial. D Muralla y Ronda que circunda la Obra Nueva y Vieja. E Entrada Principal y Zaguan. F Escalera que comunica a todas los Altos. G Antecamara que sirve a la Oficina y Quarto del Secretario. H Sala para la Oficina. Y Quarto del Secretario. J Salas para Papeles. K Patio con Galerias que dan comunicacion al Archivo Viejo. L Escalera secreta para todos los Altos." The corresponding caption contains the English translation.

96 The key for figure I.13 reads: "A Escalera Principal. B Entrada a la Sala Primera. C Treze Salas para Papeles. D Escalera secreta para todos los Pisos. E Salas que se pueden acomodar para poner Papeles en lo que antes era Abitacion del Archivero en el Antiguo Archivo. Nota Esta misma planta puede servir para el Segundo alto que Forma el cubirerto." The corresponding caption contains the English translation.

97 This dual separation was clearly described when the king approved the new Indies archive in 1781: "todos los papeles de Indias se trasladen, hecha la paz, a la Casa Lonja de Sevilla, para que en ella se coloquen con orden debido y entera separación de los respectivos a España, que podrán entonces caber en la fortaleza de Simancas" (AGI IG 1852, José de Gálvez, 19 and 22 November 1781); quoted in Pedro Torres Lanzas, "Archivo General de Indias de Sevilla," in *Guía histórica y descriptiva de los archivos, bibliotecas, y museos arqueológicos de España,* ed. Francisco Rodríguez Marín (Madrid: Tipografía de la "Revista de Archivos, Bibliotecas, y Museos," 1916), 377; and Gómez Gómez, "El Archivo," 67–68.

98 Martínez de Huete arrived in Cádiz on 4 December 1778 and sent various reports back to Gálvez over the next year and a half. He began to request permission to return to Madrid in January 1780. Permission was granted in late March, and by 2 May, Martínez de Huete was back in Madrid. His archival commission was officially ended 11 January 1781. See the various letters from Martínez de Huete to José de Gálvez scattered throughout AGI IG 1852.

99 ARAH, 9/6462, Juan Bautista Muñoz, "Oficio al rey pidiendole se le permita escribir la historia geografica de America y que al mismo tiempo se le franquen todos los archivos y bibliotecas con libros y papeles tocantes a este tema," 8 June 1779 (unpaginated). Carlos III approved the request on 17 June 1779.

100 AGI IG 1852, Juan Bautista Muñoz to José de Gálvez, Simancas, 18 August 1781 (italics mine). See this volume, chapter 2, 114n6.

101 "1781. Oficio del Secretario del Consejo de 7 de Noviembre 1781 sobre la conveniencia de ensanchar la fortaleza de Simancas, refiriéndose a un informe de su Archivero hecho con motivo de la dificultad de ordenar los Papeles de Yndias según la instrucción dada por dicho Tribunal a sus comisionados" (AGI IG 1854A, Juan Bautista Muñoz).

102 "Enterado S[u] M[ajestad], ha resuelto se prevenga al Consejo que mi determinacion del año 74 para ampliar el Castillo de Simancas fue tomada en consideracion a consecuencia de mi informe y de resulta del reconocimiento que hice de aquel Archivo en el de 1773; pero no permitiendo las urgencias actuales se ponga en ejecución aquella costosa obra, tiene resuelto el Rey que todos los papeles de Indias se trasladen, hecha la paz, a la Casa Lonja de Sevilla" (AGI IG 1852, José de Gálvez, 19 and 22 November 1781; quoted in Torres Lanzas, "Archivo," 377; and Gómez Gómez, "El Archivo," 67–68). In a letter to Gálvez dated 1 May 1784, Francisco Ortiz de Solorzano and Estevan de Larrañaga (writing from Simancas) describe the royal order: "la R[ea]l or[de]n de 22. de Noviembre de 1781 para la translacion de todos los papeles de Yndias existentes en este Archivo, á la casa Lonja de Sevilla para que en ella se coloquen con el orden devido, y entera separacion de los de españa, à cuyo unico fin se fuesen haciendo los Ynventarios" (AGI IG 1852).

103 Richard Herr, *The Eighteenth-Century Revolution in Spain* (Princeton, NJ: Princeton University Press, 1958), 140; and John Lynch, *Bourbon Spain: 1700–1808* (London: Basil Blackwell, 1989), 326.

104 Manuel Ballesteros Beretta, "D. Juan Bautista Muñoz: La Historia del Nuevo Mundo," *Revista de Indias* 10 (1942): 589.

105 Indeed, in the 1780s the men working to create the Archive of the Indies generally felt the foundational document was the king's decree of 22 November 1781 (AGI IG 1854A, Juan Bautista Muñoz, "La Real Resolucion, en cuya virtud se establecio el Archivo general de Yndias en Sevilla").

106 For this history of correspondence, see AMS Sección 11 Papeles del Conde de Águila tomo 4 no. 13, fols. 27r–45v.

107 AMS Sección 11 Papeles del Conde de Águila tomo 4 no. 13, fol. 45v; AGI IG 1853, José de Gálvez to Consulado de Mercaderes, San Ildefonso, 21 September 1784; Slade, "Enlightened Archi-Textures," 124–25; and Nemser, "Eviction and the Archive," 123, 134–35. Lonja residents were initially to displace the occupants of the old House of Trade in the northwest corner of the royal palace, but those occupants (not surprisingly) protested, and in November, money was acquired from the merchants' guild in Cádiz to help the former habitants of the Lonja find new lodgings. On the complaints, see AGI IG 1853; on the eventual

housing subvention, see AMS Sección 11 Papeles del Conde de Águila tomo 4 no. 13, fol. 52r, José de Gálvez to Juan Bautista Muñoz, San Lorenzo, 19 November 1784: "Respecto de que esta prevenido lo conveniente para que se desocupe la Casa Lonxa, y que la contratacion subsista sin novedad en los destinos que tiene esto el dia, por haverse àllanado él Consulado De Cadiz á dar ayudas de costa á sus Dependientes para que paguen sus hauitaciones fuera de la casa Lonxa."

108 AMS Sección 11 Papeles del Conde de Águila tomo 4 no. 13, fol. 53r.

109 AMS Sección 11 Papeles del Conde de Águila tomo 4 no. 13, fol. 58r–v. A sixteen-folio economic register on construction work at the Lonja by Manuel de Zuazo y Yañez (from 11 March to 13 September 1785) describes the tearing-down of the apartments in this way: "por quarenta y quatro dias que ubo de trabajo en el Derribo de las Avitaciones que havia en la lonxa, que se dio por un tanto y son desde la dia diez y nuebe de febrero hasta el diez y seis de Abril de este año ambos inclusives" (AGI IG 1858H, document "Num.º 1.º," entry for 30 April 1785).

110 AGI IG 1854A: "se hà concluido la obra material de este su Archivo."

111 Thomas Pynchon, *Mason & Dixon* (New York: Henry Holt and Company, 1997), 141.

112 Friedrich A. Kittler, "Rock Music: A Misuse of Military Equipment," in *The Truth of the Technological World: Essays on the Genealogy of Presence,* trans. Erik Butler (Stanford, CA: Stanford University Press, 2013), 155; Reinhold Martin, *The Organizational Complex: Architecture, Media, and Corporate Space* (Cambridge, MA: MIT Press, 2003), 230; John Harwood, "The Other End of the Trajectory: Danger Zones," *Grey Room* 54 (2014): 81, 84, 99; Assmann, *Cultural Memory,* 202–3; Siegert, *Cultural Techniques,* 48–52; Geoffrey Winthrop-Young, "'Well, What Socks Is Pynchon Wearing Today?' A Freiburg Scrapbook in Memory of Friedrich Kittler," *Cultural Politics* 8, no. 3 (2012): 361–73; and John Harwood, "On Wires," *Grey Room* 69 (2017): 113.

113 On the (zonal) distinctions of India versus Cathay in Columbus's writings, see Nicolás Wey-Gómez, *The Tropics of Empire: Why Columbus Sailed South to the Indies* (Cambridge, MA: MIT Press, 2008), 18, 46, 137, 335–88.

114 David S. Landes, "Finding the Point at Sea," in *The Quest for Longitude,* ed. William J. H. Andrewes (Cambridge, MA: Collection of Historical Scientific Instruments, Harvard University, 1996), 23–24.

115 William J. H. Andrewes, "Introduction," in *The Quest for Longitude,* ed. William J. H. Andrewes (Cambridge, MA: Collection of Historical Scientific Instruments, Harvard University, 1996), 2–3; and Andrew L. King, "'John Harrison, Clockmaker at Barrow; Near Barton upon Humber; Lincolnshire': The Wooden Clocks, 1713–1730," in *The Quest for Longitude,* ed. William J. H. Andrewes (Cambridge, MA: Collection of Historical Scientific Instruments, Harvard University, 1996), 167–87. Dava Sobel and William J. H. Andrewes's *The Illustrated Longitude* (New York: Walker and Company, 1996), also generated by Harvard's 1993 Longitude Symposium, has an excellent discussion of Harrison's painted versus printed portrait on 151–53.

116 Andrewes, "Introduction," 2.

117 Anthony G. Randall, "The Timekeeper That Won the Longitude Prize," in *The Quest for Longitude,* ed. William J. H. Andrewes (Cambridge, MA: Collection of Historical Scientific Instruments, Harvard University, 1996), 244–45, 250.

118 Buffon, *Histoire naturelle,* 9:107. For an earlier comparison of Senegal and America (limited in its implications to theories of skin color), see Buffon, *Histoire naturelle,* 3:484 and 3:502 (Darien-Africa-Ceylon).

119 Pauw, *Recherches philosophiques,* 1:11–12: "la même latitude."

120 Raynal, *Histoire* (1770), 6:109.

121 Robertson, *History of America,* 1:253.

122 Pynchon, *Mason & Dixon,* 141–42. For Harrison's "timepiece" and longitude calculation, see 155–56, 200–201, 283, 322, 437, 728–31; and also Neal Stephenson, *The System of the World: Volume III of The Baroque Cycle* (New York: William Morrow, 2004), 62, 72, 76, 343, 349, 384, 528.

COUNT
Hai messo ancor guidizio?.,

Are you behaving yourself?

FIGARO
Oh è come! ed ella
Come in Siviglia?..

And how! And you,
why in Seville?

COUNT
Or te Io spiego   Al Prado
V di un fior di bellezza, una fanciulla
Figlia d' un certo medico barbogio
Che quá da pochi dì s' è stabilito,
Io di questa invaghito
Lasciai patria, e parenti, e quà men venni.
E quì la notte e il giorno
Passo girando a que balconi intorno.

I'll explain   On the Prado
I beheld a flower of beauty, a maiden,
daughter of a certain doddering physician
who recently established himself here,
I became infatuated with her,
left home and family; and here I came.
And here night and day,
I walk back and forth in front of that balcony.

FIGARO
A que' balconi?.. un medico?.. o cospetto
Siete ben fortunato;
Su' i maccheroni il cascio v'è cascato.

That balcony? A physician?.. Here in front
You are very fortunate;
the cheese fell right on the macaroni.

COUNT
Come?..

Can you explain?..

FIGARO
Certo. Là dentro
Io son barbiere, perucchier, chirurgo,
Botanico, spezial, veterinario,
Il faccendier di casa.

Certainly. There within
I am barber, hairdresser, surgeon,
botanist, apothecary, veterinary,
the guy who runs the house.

COUNT
Oh che sorte!

Oh, what luck!

—Gioachino Rossini (music) and Cesare Sterbini (libretto), *The Barber of Seville*, 1816[1]

CHAPTER 1
THE ARCHIVE OF THE INDIES IN 1818

During the second week of October 1818, George Ticknor spent seven days in Seville. The young Bostonian had just finished two years of graduate study at Georg-August-Universität in Göttingen. He was enjoying a Grand Tour before returning to Massachusetts, where the Smith Professorship of French and Spanish awaited him at Harvard.[2]

One of the places Ticknor visited in Seville—and described in his journal—was the Archive of the Indies (fig. 1.1). The building had already become a tourist destination, and Ticknor's timing was lucky: the archive was especially busy.[3] Archival third official Diego Juárez was finishing a four-volume index to the archive's Royal Patronage (Patronato Real) section, a project he started in 1814.[4] Former archival commissioner Juan Agustín Ceán Bermúdez was also there, visiting from Madrid. He may have been consulting documents for his biography of the building's sixteenth-century architect, Juan de Herrera.[5] Using Ticknor's journal as a guide, we can follow in his footsteps, and imagine what the Archive of the Indies was like during the first decades of its existence.

At the very same time, across the ocean, the Spanish American wars of independence had been burning for a decade, and would soon be over. Ticknor was certainly aware of these events. The revolutions in "South America" were hot topics of conversation the previous year in France, when the Bostonian was hanging out with Alexander von Humboldt, William H. Prescott, and Sir Humphry Davy.[6] Ticknor's journal entry for 19 April 1817 reads: "The conversation turned much on South America, of which everyone has been talking in Paris since the publication of the Abbé de Pradt's book, in which he expresses the most sanguine expectation of its speedy emancipation."[7] A few months later, in early August 1817, Ticknor wrote: "Alluding to the troubles in South America, he [Marshal Davout] said almost impatiently, 'Je ne crois plus aux révolutions!'"[8]

In other words, as the initial indexing of the Archive of the Indies neared its completion, Spain's imperial presence in the Americas was, violently, coming to an end.

After describing Seville's cathedral, the adjacent Columbian Library, and the Casa de Pilatos palace, Ticknor brings the reader to the Archive of the Indies:

> Another establishment here that must be interesting to an American is the *Archivo de las Indias,* now preserved in the *lonja* or exchange. This is an admirable building of almost unexceptionable proportions and purity in its architecture, built by Herrera in the same simple, severe style with the Escorial, and, I presume, his last and, I think, his best work, since he died in 1597, and the *lonja* was not finished until 1598 [fig. 1.2]. In the days when Seville was the grand mart and exclusive deposit for everything that came from the Americas, this exchange was one of the most active, busy spots in Europe; but after the monopoly was transferred to Cadiz, it became empty and useless until the government determined to make it the grand deposit for all publick papers relating to the Americas, from their first discovery and the first discussions about their discovery to that time, and continuing it for the same purpose in the future. This excellent plan has been executed since the year 1785.[9]

FIGURE 1.1
Seville's cathedral and, to the south, the Archive of the Indies.
The gardens to the west of the Lonja are newly planted (only one palm tree!), dating the photograph to ca. 1932.
Fototeca Municipal de Sevilla, Fondo Sánchez del Pando, Signatura sp4_pu-vi_sf_049.

FIGURE 1.2
The Lonja's dedication stone, above the building's northern entrance, July 2017.
The inscription reads EL CATHOLICO Y MVY ALTO Y POD[E]RO / SSO DON PHELIPE SEGVNDO REI DE / LAS ESPAÑAS MANDO HAZER ESTA / LONJA, A COSTA DE LA VNIVERSIDAD / DE LOS MERCADERES, DE LA QVAL HI / ZO ADMINISTRADORES PERPETVOS / AL PRIOR Y CONSVLES DE LA DICHA / VNIBERSIDAD. COMENÇOSE A NEGO / ÇIAR EN ELLA EN .14. DIAS . DE . EL . MES / DE AGOSTO . DE . 1598 . AÑOS (The Catholic and most high and powerful don Felipe II, King of the Spains, commanded the building of this Lonja, to be paid for by the merchants' guild, from which he made as permanent administrators the prior and consuls of the said guild. Business began to be conducted therein on 14 August 1598).

Raised up on a stepped platform from the surrounding plaza, the Archive of the Indies is located just northwest of Seville's royal palace (Real Alcázar) and just south of the cathedral. Although originally designed with entrances on all four sides, by the early nineteenth century the principal doorway faced west (and is still the main entrance used today). Ticknor would have walked up the platform's steps and entered the building through this main door (fig. 1.3). Straight ahead, he would have seen the building's light-filled central patio (fig. 1.4). But his destination was just to the right: a monumental flight of stairs ascended to the upper floor (fig. 1.5). This grand staircase was one of the renovations to the Lonja made by architect Lucas Cintora in the 1780s, and, like much of Cintora's work, it was (and remained) controversial. Although its massive slabs of dark-pink jasper do echo the similarly colored brick on the building's exterior, their combination with black and white marble detailing creates a darker, baroque ambience.[10] Already in 1792, only a few years after the staircase renovation was completed, Antonio Ponz complained that it "is rich with marbles, but doesn't harmonize with the character of the older architecture."[11]

If nothing else, this color-saturated stairway creates a space of transition, even separation—a liminal zone through which the visitor must pass in order to reach the documentary treasures housed above. During the first decades of the archive's existence, the ground floor of the building was used for nonarchival offices, and the basement's cistern was a publicly accessible source of water.[12] Plans to control access to the archive with an iron gate were debated, and finally approved by the king, in the late 1780s.[13] But even without such a literal barrier, the stairway itself provides a symbolic separation through color and material. If archaeology accesses the past by moving downward, through excavation (Pompeii and Herculaneum had been discovered in Spanish Naples the previous century), at the Archive of the Indies one reached the past by going *up*.[14]

THE ARCHIVE OF THE INDIES IN 1818   39

FIGURE 1.3
The Lonja building seen from the northwest.
To the viewer's left, above the northern facade's central doorway, is a light-colored stone with the dedicatory inscription from 1598 (see fig. 1.2). Based on the state of the gardens, the photograph was taken in the 1930s.
Fototeca Municipal de Sevilla, Fondo Serrano, Signatura se16_e-c2_sf_008.

FIGURE 1.4
The central patio of the Lonja in the 1890s, before the upper and lower galleries were fully enclosed in the 1920s.
The central fountain features a statue of Christopher Columbus.
From Max Junghändel, *Die baukunst Spaniens* (Dresden: J. Bleyl, 1893–98), plate 138.
Los Angeles, Getty Research Institute, NA1301.J8 1888.

FIGURE 1.5
The main staircase of the Lonja, as redesigned in the late 1780s by architect Lucas Cintora, May 2016.

40 CHAPTER 1

FIGURE 1.6
The floating spiral staircase of the Lonja (constructed in 1609–11 by architect Miguel de Zumárraga), leading up to the roof, June 2017.

FIGURE 1.7
The roof of the Lonja, looking northeast across its central patio to the cathedral, June 2017.

42 CHAPTER 1

FIGURE 1.8
Looking west down the northern gallery of the Archive of the Indies, after the shelving reforms of the late 1920s.
The curtained doorway at the far end leads to what was originally the archive's front office.
Seville, Archivo General de Indias, fotos antiguas 007.

This grand stairway is oriented north–south, with one landing; after reaching the top, Ticknor would have seen the central patio to his right and soaring west-facing windows to his left. Straight ahead were two wooden doorways. The one on the right concealed a spiral staircase to the building's roof—a popular end-of-tour destination in decades to come, if not by 1818 (figs. 1.6, 1.7).[15] The door on the left led to the archive.[16] Beyond was a small "reception room or doorman's office." This, in turn, led to a square room in the building's northwest corner. A vaulted, coffered stone ceiling soared above a space filled with tables, chairs, and bookshelves of mahogany and walnut. This was the main office, where six archivists worked to inventory, index, and copy the documents under their care.[17] Perhaps it was here that Ticknor was introduced to the legendary Ceán Bermúdez, and to Diego Juárez as well. Perhaps all three men then continued through the office's eastern door and entered the archive itself.

It was (and still is) a monumental, U-shaped space, taking up the northern, eastern, and southern sides of the building. Each gallery is thirty feet high, twenty-six feet wide, and one hundred and fifty feet long (fig. 1.8). The floor is richly patterned in black, white, and dark-pink stone, highly polished; in 1844, Félix González de León wrote that "one could say that it serves as a continuous mirror where all objects are reflected, for the brilliance and polish of stones that seem to be glass."[18] The walls left and right are lined with tall cases of dark mahogany, rising to more than fifteen feet.

THE ARCHIVE OF THE INDIES IN 1818   43

FIGURE 1.9
Document cases 3, 4, 5, and 6 (built from 1787 to 1788 by Blas Molner y Zamora) on the western wall of the eastern gallery of the Archive of the Indies, November 2016.

FIGURES 1.10–1.15
Blas Molner y Zamora (Spanish, 1737–1812).
Row 1 (l–r): Case 3, metope carving of crossed arrows and round shield; case 3, metope carving of drum.
Row 2 (l–r): Case 4, metope carving of crossed quivers; case 4, metope carving of parasol (upright).
Row 3 (l–r): Case 4, metope carving of feather headdress (profile, facing left); case 4, metope carving of the "two worlds" motif.
1787–88.
Seville, Archivo General de Indias.

Most cases contained six shelves, piled with bundled documents, all wrapped in paper and carefully labeled:

> The building, the room, and the cases in which they are preserved, are the best I ever saw for such a purpose. Luckily a man capable of making use of them was employed. The learned, accurate, and indefatigable Cean Bermúdez came here in 1791, and spent sixteen years of his life at the rate of fourteen or fifteen hours a day, and is now here on a visit, in arranging these papers and forming the indices. Every paper has an envelope thrown round it, numbered, and containing an abstract of its contents, and is placed in the bundle to which it belongs. This, again, is marked with a label of wood that hangs out, and is then put up in the case where its date and matter fix it.[19]

This wrapping and labeling was in keeping with the archive's *Ordenanzas* (Ordinances), published in 1790.[20] Many of the descriptive cover sheets survive (see figs. I.2–I.7).[21] The wooden labels are more elusive. Cardboard labels from later in the nineteenth century can occasionally be found,[22] and their visual effect is revealed by old photographs, which show how the shelves looked before modifications in the late 1920s (see figs. P.1, 1.25, 1.31, 1.32).

Along the top of all the cases—which are separated from one another by grooved bands of Doric pilasters—runs a long decorative frieze (fig. 1.9). It is made up of panels carved with symbols of navigation, conquest, and the Americas (figs. 1.10–1.21). There are shields with crossed spears, bows and arrows, ships, drums, pairs of globes (the "two worlds" motif), and the Pillars of Hercules. There are feathered shields and headdresses and even parasols (perhaps to evoke the East Indies). There are armored

44 CHAPTER 1

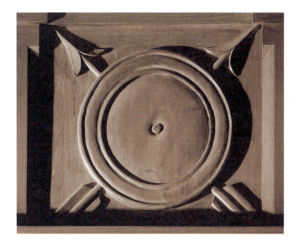

THE ARCHIVE OF THE INDIES IN 1818   45

FIGURES 1.16–1.21
Blas Molner y Zamora (Spanish, 1737–1812).
Row 1 (l–r): Case 71, metope carving of crossed arrows and irregular shield; case 71, metope carving of parasol (upright).
Row 2 (l–r): Case 73, metope carving of feather headdress (profile, facing left), with the square banner representing the number 20; case 75, metope carving of crossed arrows and round shield.
Row 3 (l–r): Case 77, metope carving of feather headdress (frontal); case 78, metope carving of torso (note exposed tripartite liver).
1787–88.
Seville, Archivo General de Indias.

FIGURE 1.22
Blas Molner y Zamora (Spanish, 1737–1812).
Case 73, metope carvings representing (left to right) a butterfly battle standard, a warrior bodysuit (as torso), and a feather headdress (marked with a rectangular banner for the number 20), 1787–88.
Seville, Archivo General de Indias.

cuirasses, some with feather skirts, and which sometimes seem to morph into butchered human torsos. All of these reference the feathered bodysuits of Aztec warriors, copied from a circa 1519 tribute document published in Francisco Antonio Lorenzana y Buitrón's *Historia de Nueva-España* (1770; History of New Spain). The best evidence for this iconographic connection appears in three panels over case 73 (fig. 1.22). One shows a butterfly battle standard, a detail that appears in a number of the *Historia*'s engravings. To the right is a feathered bodysuit, marked below the ribs with an upside-down fleur-de-lis: this is a liver glyph, which graces several of the *Historia*'s warrior costumes. Finally, there is a feather headdress marked with a rectangular banner: the Aztec symbol for the number 20. This specific headdress-plus-banner combination appears in plate 5 of the *Historia* (fig. 1.23).

Crowning this richly carved frieze is a sharp cornice that projects out into the room, creating horizontal bands left and right that unite the space of each gallery into a visual whole (fig. 1.24). This projecting cornice makes the monumental shelves feel a bit like giant waves, cresting above the visitor on both sides. In French, Arlette Farge points out, the same word is used for a collection of documents and the depths of the ocean: *le fond*. This also holds true in Spanish: *el fondo*.[23] But the visitor is prevented from drowning in this paper sea by a subtle feature of the cases, at first easy to overlook. Each is marked, high above, with a wooden cartouche, engraved with a number (see

THE ARCHIVE OF THE INDIES IN 1818 47

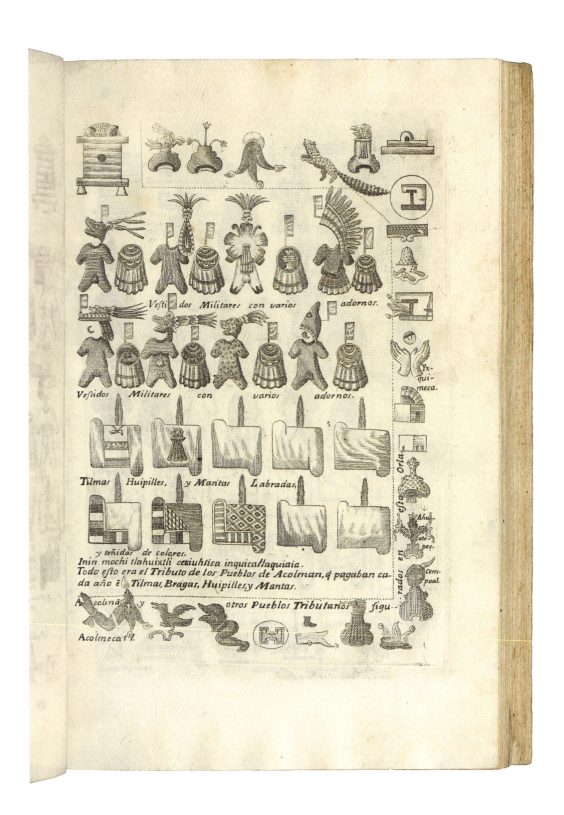

FIGURE 1.23
Plate 5 of Francisco Antonio Lorenzana y Buitrón's *Historia de Nueva-España* (Mexico: Imprenta del Superior Gobierno, 1770).

This is an engraving of fol. 3r (the tribute province of Acolman) from the *Matrícula de tributos*, an Aztec tribute document created ca. 1519. A large round butterfly decorates the third warrior bodysuit in the first row; the bodysuit to the right is topped with a massive feather headdress marked by a rectangular banner glyph (representing the number 20). These probably inspired the butterfly and headdress-plus-banner metopes above case 73 (see figs. 1.18 and 1.22). In the row of costumes below, a trilobed liver glyph decorates the second military bodysuit on the left, which probably inspired another metope carving above case 73 (see fig. 1.22). Los Angeles, Getty Research Institute, F1230.C82.

FIGURE 1.24
Looking south down the eastern gallery of the Archive of the Indies, November 2016.

fig. 1.22).[24] There are eighty-one in total. Their arrangement seems perplexing. The numbers in the northern, entry-arm of the archive do not begin 1, 2, 3, but rather 26, 27 (to the right), 28, 29 (to the left). I will return to this important detail in chapter 3.

The already underway numeration serves as a path, leading the tour forward. Numbers on the left keep rising, numbers on the right count backward. Halfway down the northern gallery, a doorway interrupts the right-hand wall. Above is squeezed one shelf for documents (case 20; see fig. 1.8); beyond, out the door, is the upper gallery that runs around the Lonja's central patio. By the time of Ticknor's visit, the open archways on three sides of this gallery had been enclosed, and were used to store documents that had yet to be officially shelved.[25]

The tour continues down the northern gallery. At case number 14, the shelving turns a corner, revealing the eastern gallery (see fig. 1.24). The numbers on the right keep dropping: 13, 12, 11, 10. Halfway down is a doorway facing west: it leads to the aforementioned patio storage space. Above this doorway is a single shelf, case 7.

THE ARCHIVE OF THE INDIES IN 1818 49

Continuing onward, the right-hand case numbers keep dropping: 6, 5, 4. At last, just before the eastern gallery turns into the southern, those case numbers reach 1—and around the corner the entire series ends, with case 81.

I will return to the contents of these eighty-one cases shortly, but first let us complete the tour with Ticknor, as preserved in his journal. He (and his guides) would have continued down the southern gallery to a door beckoning in the wall at the western end (fig. 1.25). It opened onto a square room with two additional floor-to-ceiling mahogany cases (fig. 1.26). This was the archive's Holy of Holies, a room—according to a remodeling plan from 1785—*para las cosas preciosas,* "for precious things." Some of these precious things were works of art.[26] They included a plaster statue of pilot Juan Sebastián Elcano (who completed Ferdinand Magellan's circumnavigation of the globe in 1522);[27] a supposedly original portrait of Christopher Columbus (donated by his descendant the Duke of Veragua);[28] and paintings of Hernán Cortés and King Fernando VII (the latter crowned by a cloth canopy).[29] Maps were eventually displayed here as well, but the real treasures in the room were its documents on paper and parchment.

Some, bearing famous signatures, were later framed under glass for the perusal of visitors.[30] But most of the room's archival preciosities were stored in its two glass-fronted mahogany cases. Unlike the main galleries of the archive, which contained the day-to-day traces of government bureaucracy, this corner room housed documents directly connected to royal privilege and patronage: Patronato Real. Transferred from a similarly sequestered room in the Archive of Simancas (discussed further in the next chapter), these were the documents being indexed by royal permission (granted in 1814) when Ticknor happened to stop by:[31]

> The indices which have been making since 1791, and are still going on, amount already to fourteen folio volumes, referring to all the papers relating to the government, economy, administration of justice, etc., of the colonies. Two, however, are extremely interesting. The first contains a notice of all the papers in the archives that have more an European than an American character and yet relate to America, such as papal bulls, kings' edicts, petitions of the early navigators, beginning in 1480 and coming down to 1697, with the materials ready to finish it to the present day, and only waiting to be copied. The second contains a notice of the papers more American than European, and, of course, comprises everything relating to the voyages of the navigators, the discoveries, the natives, the history of the country since, etc., and begins in 1486, and is already finished to 1703. These indices, like all the others, are excellent in their kind, and leave little to desire, for, besides that they are chronological, they are divided into epochs, classed by matters, and contain a notice and abstract of every paper, however small, which they record. In fact, I consider the entire establishment as the most perfect of the kind, and whoever wishes hereafter to write an account of America has here all the early documents that belong to the Spanish government arranged to his hand.[32]

The two thematic divisions that Ticknor mentions refer to the two-part division of documents in the corner room's cases. All of case 1, and the first shelf of case 2,

FIGURE 1.25
Looking west down the southern gallery of the Archive of the Indies, before the shelving reforms of the late 1920s.
Based on a comparable photo published by Pedro Torres Lanzas, a more precise date may be ca. 1916. The curtained doorway at the far end of the gallery leads to the corner room where Royal Patronage documents are stored.
Seville, Archivo General de Indias, fotos antiguas 008.

FIGURE 1.26
The room of Royal Patronage in the southwest corner of the Lonja's upper floor, 1930s.
Beyond the door curtains, the (postrenovation) shelves of the archive's southern gallery are visible.
Fototeca Municipal de Sevilla, Fondo Serrano, Signatura se16_e-c2_sf_009.

contained papers with more a "European than an American character," including (as Ticknor notes) papal bulls, briefs, and petitions and lawsuits relating to conqueror-explorers such as Columbus and Cortés. These documents were covered by the first of the Royal Patronage *Inventario* and *Índice* finding aids. The remaining shelves in case 2 contained "papers more American than European," including letters from the New World, accounts of rebellions in New Spain in 1624 and 1692, and documents related to the seventeenth-century anti-Jesuit bishop Juan de Palafox y Mendoza. (Note that Ticknor seems to have scrambled his dates: the case 1 and 2 documents covered in the first *Inventario* and *Índice* volumes actually date from 1486 to 1703, as outlined by the summary sheet on the third folio of this section's *Inventario;* the case 2 documents covered in the second *Inventario* and *Índice* volumes date from 1480 to 1697, as outlined by the summary sheet on the second folio of this section's *Inventario.*)

Ticknor is correct when he says that fourteen folio volumes of finding aids already existed when he visited in 1818—and when the Royal Patronage indexing was finally completed a year later, their number would rise to seventeen.[33] He is also correct when he says (as quoted earlier) that Ceán Bermúdez began the archival indexing project in 1791. Yet despite being created over a span of three decades, all of these finding aids share the same organizing system. Each document is identified with a three-part number. The first number refers to the case: 1 to 81, plus two additional cases (1 and 2) in the Royal Patronage room. The second number refers to the shelf within the case: usually 1 to 6, although, as mentioned earlier, some over-door cases have only one shelf. The third number refers to the document's ordinal position on the shelf—although if the document is part of a longer series, then there are actually two numbers, the first indicating the document's ordinal position within a thematic series, and the second indicating its ordinal position on the shelf. For example, 47–1–12 points to a document in case 47, shelf 1, bundle 12 on the shelf (see fig. 1.8). Similarly, 5–5–4/20 points to a document in case 5, shelf 5, bundle 20 on the shelf (and item 4 in a longer thematic series).

All of these finding-aid volumes, filled with three-part shelf marks, still survive. Guided by their contents, we can reconstruct—case by case, shelf by shelf, document by document—how the archive's contents were originally ordered (fig. 1.27). And so now we will temporarily exit the room of Royal Patronage and walk back to the eastern gallery. This was where the archive's installation began.[34]

CONTADURÍA, CASES 1–11: THE ACCOUNTING DEPARTMENT OF THE COUNCIL OF THE INDIES (MADRID)

The first documents to be shelved—and the first to be indexed—were from the Contaduría, or Accounting department, of the Council of the Indies. These documents left the council's offices in Madrid on 3 November 1786 and reached Seville (in 98 chests) on 24 November.[35] The AGI's superintendent director, Antonio de Lara y Zúñiga, later commented that these papers arrived "well organized, and ready to be installed in their respective cases without any difficulty."[36] They were not, however,

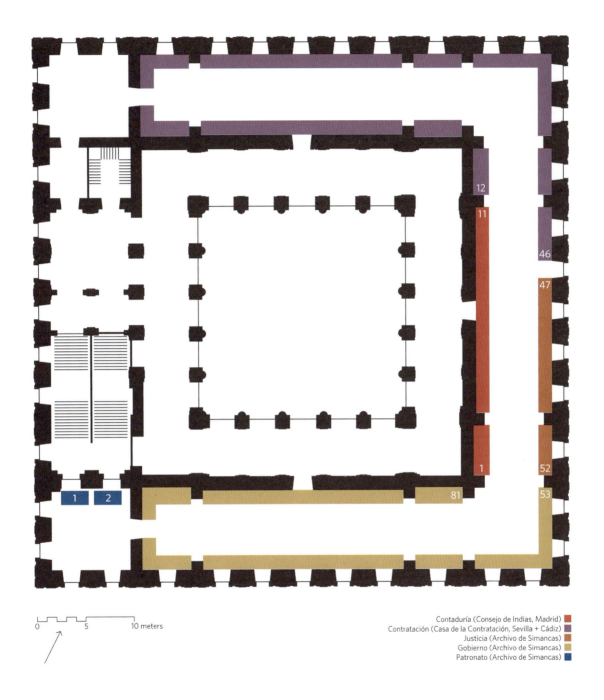

FIGURE 1.27
Spatial arrangement of documents on the upper floor of the Archive of the Indies, ca. 1820.
North is at the top of the plan.

THE ARCHIVE OF THE INDIES IN 1818 53

FIGURE 1.28
Tomás López (Spanish, 1730–1802).
Mapa General de España (Map of all Spain), 1795, engraving, 48.5 × 58.5 cm.
Darker dots have been added to indicate the locations of the four main donor archives for the Archive of the Indies. From top to bottom, they are: Simancas, Madrid, Seville, and, on the Atlantic coast, Cádiz. Madrid, Biblioteca Nacional de España, MR/2/057.

the first documents transferred to the newly founded archive from elsewhere in Spain. A year earlier, on 14 October 1785, twenty-four wagons arrived in Seville, bearing 254 chests of documents from the Archive of Simancas, far to the north (fig. 1.28).[37] Some of those papers were eventually filed under Royal Patronage, others in the Justice (Justicia) section of the archive's eastern gallery, and others in the Government (Gobierno) section of the archive's southern gallery. But in contrast to the Accounting documents from Madrid, most of the Simancas documents came "without order, nor inventory"—and so their installation was delayed as archivists tried to organize and catalog them.[38] And even before the Simancas shipment arrived, archivists seem to have been transferring documents from Seville's House of Trade archive, located in the royal palace just around the corner.[39]

The Accounting documents filled cases 1–11, taking up most of the space on the eastern gallery's west-facing inner wall (fig. 1.29; see fig. 1.27). Their contents were indexed in two volumes by the man described by George Ticknor as "the learned, accurate, and indefatigable Ceán Bermúdez." As Ticknor explains, this archivist came to Seville in 1791 and would eventually live there for "sixteen years of his life." He is an important figure in the early history of the archive, but he did not choose to work in Seville.

Juan Agustín Ceán Bermúdez was appointed archival commissioner on 31 December 1790. Over the course of the next four decades, he would become Spain's leading scholar of architecture, art history, and archaeology. But in 1790, despite having studied painting with Anton Rafael Mengs and being friends with artist Francisco de Goya, the future archivist was above all a political functionary, closely linked to statesman Gaspar Melchor de Jovellanos (a childhood friend from Gijón, in northern Spain). Indeed, it was because of Jovellanos that Ceán Bermúdez was sent to Seville—not for his historical expertise, but because he was in exile.

The French Revolution began in July 1789. Its unfolding events were viewed with increasing concern from the other side of the Pyrenees. Starting that fall, the Count of Floridablanca, King Carlos IV's first secretary of state, attempted to prevent the revolution's spread. News from France was suppressed. In November, all foreign and Spanish nonresidents were ordered to leave Madrid. Men thought sympathetic to Enlightenment reforms were also targeted, and over the course of 1790, members of Jovellanos's circle were exiled: first Francisco de Cabarrús in June (sent to prison in A Coruña), then Jovellanos himself in August (sent to report on coal mines in Asturias), and finally Ceán Bermúdez in December.[40]

By mid-February 1791, Ceán Bermúdez arrived in Seville with his family and took rooms on Calle de las Cruces (near the Puerta de la Carne gate, on the southeastern edge of the city). Within a month he began the Herculean task of cataloging the archive's contents, which brings us back to the eleven cases of Accounting documents.[41] He indexed their contents in two volumes: the first, the *Inventario,* listed documents as they were ordered in the wall cases; the second, the *Índice,* was organized by names, themes, provinces, and towns. Ceán Bermúdez completed this project in less than a year: he began on 10 March 1791 and finished on 17 January 1792.

What were these papers about? The Accounting department of the Council of the Indies kept records on the sources of royal income (monopoly profits, tax and tribute revenues) as well as outpayments to maintain the empire and its infrastructure. Thus case 1, shelf 1, bundle 21 concerned the costs of printing and distributing copies of the four-volume *Recopilación de las Leyes de las Indias* (Compilation of the laws of the Indies) from 1706 to 1757 (the first edition had been published in 1681, a second in 1756). Moving to the right, case 2, shelf 1, bundle 233/29 detailed the costs of furnishing the council's own offices and chapel from 1579 to 1733. Case 4, shelf 5, bundle 127/28 included accounts related to the royal monopoly on playing cards from 1687 to 1692. Case 6, shelf 1, bundle 15/8 itemized the costs of providing the Church in Guatemala with wine and oil from 1690 to 1734. The single shelf of case 7 (above the doorway to the archive's central patio) included a document on the payment of warehouse guards in Havana from 1 March 1728 to 8 August 1757. Military expenditures for the

Nº 3º

Numero de Estantes, Caxones y Legajos en que estan colocados los papeles del Ynventario de la Contaduria grãl de Yndias.

Estantes.	Caxones.	Legajos.	Suma de los legajos de cada Estante.
I	1	50	204
	2	29	
	3	22	
	4	29	
	5	28	
	6	46	
II	1	39	206
	2	24	
	3	46	
	4	35	
	5	22	
	6	40	
III	1	56	229
	2	56	
	3	27	
	4	33	
	5	27	
	6	30	
IV	1	27	181
	2	28	
	3	30	
	4	32	
	5	28	
	6	36	
V	1	24	153
	2	18	
	3	22	
	4	25	
	5	30	
	6	34	
VI	1	45	191
	2	20	
	3	26	
	4	30	
	5	34	
	6	36	
VII	Es una sobre puerta, 1	por lo que tiene un solo caxon 25	25
VIII	1	37	175
	2	31	
	3	22	
	4	34	
	5	28	
	6	23	
IX	1	45	209
	2	19	
	3	37	
	4	36	
	5	22	
	6	43	
X	1	47	197
	2	36	
	3	28	
	4	34	
	5	27	
	6	25	
XI	1	33	186
	2	26	
	3	28	
	4	26	
	5	22	
	6	45	
			1.956.

"pacification" of Manila by General Legazpi in 1576 were in case 8, shelf 1, bundle 7/14, part of a longer series of documents about the Philippines. Income accounts from the Royal Fifth of pearls harvested on the island of Margarita from mid-June 1602 to the end of January 1611 were in case 10, shelf 3, bundle 3/12. The lower half of case 10 (starting on shelf 3, and taking up all of shelves 4, 5, and 6) was filled with two centuries of paperwork (1532–1733) for Lima's royal revenues (Real Hacienda)—a series continued from 1734 to 1760 in the first shelf of case 11. That was the last case of the Accounting section. Its final document, in shelf 6, tallied the costs of royal expeditions to find the source of the Orinoco River from 1754 to 1769.

CONTRATACIÓN, CASES 12–46: PAPERWORK FROM THE HOUSE OF TRADE (SEVILLE AND CÁDIZ)

A new section began in cases 12 and 13, continued around the corner to fill all of the northern gallery (cases 14–40), and finally overflowed into cases 41–46 on the building's eastern wall (see fig. 1.27). These were documents from the Casa de la Contratación, the House of Trade for the New World.

This section of the archive had a complicated history. The House of Trade was founded in 1503, and occupied offices attached to Seville's royal palace.[42] Seville was an inland port, connected to the ocean (some fifty miles to the southwest) by the Guadalquivir River. This was a good strategy for defense—early modern Europe had a number of other inland ports, including Hamburg, Antwerp, and Nantes—but became more and more impractical as ships grew larger and the river filled with silt.[43] In 1718, the center for Spain's commerce with the Americas was transferred to Cádiz, a coastal city on a peninsula jutting directly into the Atlantic (see fig. 1.28). The House of Trade established new offices there, and half of its archive was relocated as well—but the other half remained in Seville, and managed to survive at least one eighteenth-century fire.[44] George Ticknor makes a brief reference to this complicated peregrination of papers: "of those relating to America copies had generally been sent to Seville, though these had been injured and partly destroyed by a fire, and finally in Cadiz, where an American law-court sat, there were others."[45]

When the Archive of the Indies was founded in the 1780s, the Cádiz documents returned to Seville in two convoys. The first twenty-four chests arrived on 8 and 9 January 1786; thirty more chests followed in the early days of August.[46] In other words, the House of Trade documents from Cádiz arrived between the shipments from Simancas (in October 1785) and Madrid (in November 1786). These papers were then (re)integrated with the House of Trade documents that had remained in Seville. The still-in-Seville half of the archive was apparently transferred to the Lonja building right after the initial staff of the archive was appointed on 29 August 1785; these were probably the first documents to take up residence in the yet-to-be-renovated building.[47]

House of Trade was the second section of the archive to be indexed, but the process took much longer than for Accounting. While this was in part because many more documents were involved, other factors were also at play. Nine finding-aid volumes

FIGURE 1.29
Schematic representation of the eleven cases of documents in Accounting (Contaduría), drafted by Juan Agustín Ceán Bermúdez in 1791–92.
Seville, Archivo General de Indias, Indiferente General 1854B.

would eventually be created. Following the model established by Accounting, the first four inventories were organized case by case, listing each document in order. The remaining five indexes were thematic: the first four indexed persons, and the fifth covered themes and places. Once again, Ceán Bermúdez was in charge. If one assumes that he began to work on House of Trade right after finishing the inventories for Accounting, then the first *Inventario* volume (for cases 12–15) took just over a year: it was completed on 6 March 1793. As it happens, this was about a month after Francisco de Goya came south from Madrid to visit Ceán Bermúdez. It was a fateful trip: in Seville the artist came down with an illness that left him deaf for the rest of his life. (By late February, Goya had recovered enough to go to Cádiz, where he convalesced in the home of Sebastián Pérez Martínez, a merchant and art collector.)[48]

The second *Inventario* volume of House of Trade documents (for cases 16–17) was also a year-plus in the making, completed 17 September 1794. But on finishing this second volume, Ceán Bermúdez became caught up in research for a project of his own: a *Diccionario histórico de los mas ilustres profesores de las bellas artes en España* (Historical dictionary of the most illustrious practitioners of fine arts in Spain), published in 1800.[49] As a result, the third House of Trade *Inventario* (cases 18–29, plus the first two shelves of case 30) took two and a half years—it was not completed until 18 March 1797. That December, Ceán Bermúdez's exile was lifted: he was appointed to a post in the Secretariat of Grace and Justice for the Indies (Secretaría de Gracia y Justicia de Indias). He returned to Madrid, leaving the work of the fourth House of Trade *Inventario* (cases 30–46, plus the completion of the five topical indexes as well) to other archival commissioners appointed to replace him. The first was José Acevedo Villaroel, followed by Antonio Tariego y Somoza (who signed his name to the fourth *Inventario* volume when it was finished on 12 August 1801).

House of Trade officials oversaw all aspects of commerce with the New World. For journeys leaving from Spain to the Americas, they issued travel licenses, trained pilots, created maps, purchased export goods (including the quicksilver so central for New World mining), and oversaw the maintenance of ships (from rigging to hold to hull). For journeys arriving in Spain from the Americas, they collected import taxes, claimed the precious metals and jewels owed to the Crown, and reviewed and stored the detailed shipping registers required of any vessel traveling to or from the New World. They also dealt with the estates of men and women who had died abroad. To enforce its powers, the House of Trade ran a courtroom as well. It was authorized to judge cases involving violations of trade law, as well as conflicts between merchants and sailors.

These various capacities were all reflected in the documents housed in the northern part of the archive. Pilot examinations, for example, were stored in case 12, shelf 2, bundles 1/9 to 7/15. "Autos sobre bienes de difuntos"—paperwork related to the property of European men and women who died in the Indies—began in case 13, filling shelves 2–6, and then continued to fill all six shelves of case 14, the first two shelves of case 15, and scattered shelves thereafter (including case 17, shelves 2–5). Case 16 was completely filled with criminal and civil lawsuits tried before the House of Trade, a series that continued in the first shelf of case 17. For example, the first bundle on the first shelf of case 16 contained a 1545 lawsuit between Pedro de Velasco and Pedro Sánchez over the value of a parcel of hardtack; on the same shelf, another bundle contained a 1595 lawsuit between Captain Francisco Díaz Pimienta and the owners of some chests of cochineal that the captain had transported across the Atlantic. It had been a rough crossing, and Díaz Pimienta wanted partial reimbursement for the *avería* trade tax (used to pay for fleet defenses) that he paid on hides which had been lost in a (successful) effort to save the cochineal.

Registries of ships sailing *to* the Americas began in case 18, taking up part of shelf 1 and all of shelves 2–6. These registries continued to fill all six shelves of case 19, the single above-door shelf of case 20 (this was the door that led out to the patio gallery), all six shelves of case 21, and almost all six shelves of case 22. The final twenty-three bundles of case 22, shelf 6, however (bundles 1/15 to 23/37), began a new series: registries of ships returning *from* the Americas. These accounts were packed into the cases surrounding the door leading to the archive's front office: all six shelves of cases 23–28, as well as the first five shelves of case 29. For example, case 25, shelf 5 contained the registries for *Nuestra Señora de Atocha,* a vessel that capsized during a hurricane in 1622 (and was rediscovered in the 1970s). Twenty-three bundles of slave-trade registries filled the first shelf in case 30, and part of the second.

The accounts of specific paymasters (*pagadores*) for American shipping (overseeing costs of the Armada, or artillery) began in case 32, shelf 5, bundle 1, and continued to case 34, shelf 6, bundle 41/14. Accounts by collectors of the *avería* trade tax took up the lower half of case 36 (shelves 4–6) and all of case 37. Documents related to the House of Trade's treasurer—account books filled with imports of gold, silver, copper, and brazilwood—filled almost all of cases 38 and 39.[50] Royal decrees (*cédulas*) relating to the House of Trade were stored in the first set of shelves on the building's east-facing wall: case 41, shelf 4, bundle 1/11 to shelf 6, bundle 11/34. Documents related to the granting of licenses for travel to the New World—perhaps the most famous series in the archive—began in case 42, shelf 2, bundle 1/5 and ended in case 45, shelf 2, bundle 1/12. The remaining shelves of case 45, and all six shelves of case 46, closed the House of Trade section with a miscellany of themes (ranging from additional "Autos sobre bienes de difuntos," to documents on the slave trade, to more pilot exams).

JUSTICIA, CASES 47–52: LEGAL PROCEEDINGS FROM THE COUNCIL OF THE INDIES (MADRID, VIA SIMANCAS)

The third section to be installed and indexed was Justice (Justicia). This series began where the House of Trade documents ended, and it filled six cases (numbers 47–52) along the archive's eastern outer wall. As with the Accounting documents installed in cases 1–11, the documents in Justice had been generated by the Council of the Indies. But whereas the Accounting documents had been shipped directly from the council's offices in Madrid, the documents that made up the Justice section had previously been sent from Madrid for storage in the Archive of Simancas.

As mentioned above, 254 chests of Simancas documents arrived in Seville on 14 October 1785. Superintendent director Antonio de Lara y Zúñiga later complained that these documents arrived "without order, nor inventory."[51] But this was only partly true. A few years earlier, in 1781, royal cosmographer Juan Bautista Muñoz visited Simancas to research what would become his *Historia del Nuevo-Mundo* (History of the New World). He found that the main gallery for documents from the Council of the Indies was "divided more or less in two sections: to one side, those related to Justice, that is, lawsuits, residencies, inspections, and reports; to the other side, all the rest, which under the general name of 'Government' presented a confused miscellany."[52] Confused, and copious: it would take decades for the Government files to be organized and shelved at the AGI, filling its southern gallery and overflowing into its enclosed patio. But the documents related to Justice presented less of a problem. There were far fewer of them, and Muñoz suggests they were already organized at Simancas—meaning they were easier to separate and shelve once they reached Seville.

These papers were documented in a two-volume finding aid: the *Inventario* listed each document case by case; the *Índice* was organized by subject. The first 479 pages of the *Inventario* were written by archival commissioner Antonio de Tariego y Somoza (who had finished the fourth volume of the House of Trade inventories back in 1801); the remaining entries were completed by his successor, commissioner Ysidoro Antillón, on 20 June 1809—one year into the Napoleonic invasion of Spain and two months after thirty-one crates of AGI documents were shipped from Seville southwest to Cádiz for safety.[53]

Where the documents in the Accounting section of the Archive of the Indies preserved the actions of the Council of the Indies directly related to economic questions, the documents in Justice centered on the council's capacities as a court of law. Justice documents can be divided into two sections. The first involved cases initially tried in the Americas, or in the courtroom of the House of Trade (in Seville or Cádiz), but then appealed and sent on for a final hearing by the Council of the Indies in Madrid. Such cases included lawsuits (*autos entre partes*), financial reviews (*autos fiscales*), and documents generated by inspections of government officials working in the Americas (*visitas, residencias,* or *comisiones*). These documents ran from shelf 1 of case 47 to shelf 5 of case 51. The second section focused on litigation presented directly before the Council of the Indies. It was therefore much smaller, running from case 51, shelf 5 to case 52, shelf 6. Three legal genres were represented in this section: lawsuits (*autos entre partes*), financial reviews (*autos fiscales*), and complaints and reports (*informaciones y probanzas*). Both sections of Justice were arranged by royal high court jurisdictions (*audiencias*), from Santo Domingo to Guatemala to Quito to Chile.[54]

For example, case 47, shelf 1, bundle 5 contained a lawsuit between doña María de Toledo and the city government of Santo Domingo over parcels of land that her deceased husband, don Diego Colón (son of Christopher Columbus) had left to the city. Case 48, shelf 1, bundle 20/2 preserved the massive amounts of paperwork generated by Francisco Tello de Sandoval's four-year review of government officials in New

Spain (from Viceroy Antonio de Mendoza on down) between 1544 and 1548.[55] One shelf to the right, a very different set of documents was stored: case 49, shelf 6, bundle 5/35 contained a lawsuit between Francisco de las Casas (*encomendero* of Yanhuitlán in New Spain) and Pedro de Alvarado (governor of Guatemala) over the 450-peso value of a mule that the former had sold to the latter in October 1526.

Moving to litigation presented directly before the council, case 51, shelf 1, bundle 5/1 included a petition by imprisoned pilot Francisco Hernández over the fines he was being asked to pay for the loss of his ship. Later on the same shelf, bundle 1/22 contained a report (*información*) "made by the royal high court of New Galicia about certain Turkish or Moorish ships that arrived on the coast." A number of proceedings related to the civil wars of Peru were filed in case 52, shelf 3, bundle 17/8—such as 1561 appeals by the heirs of Toribio Galíndez de la Riva against the confiscation of his property "as complicit in the rebellion of Peru," or by the abbess and nuns of the Convent of Santa Marina in Zafra over rights to the property of Juan Rodríguez Barragán, "condemned to death in Peru."

PATRONATO: ROYAL PATRONAGE AND PATRIMONY (SIMANCAS)

Together, the documents of Accounting, House of Trade, and Justice filled the northern and eastern arms of the archive, with fifty-two cases in all. This left the thirty-odd cases of the southern gallery (from 53 to 81). However, the next indexing project after the Justice volumes were finished in June 1809 did not begin until late 1814, and it involved the documents of Royal Patronage—documents stored not in the archive's main galleries but in their own private chamber (see figs. 1.26, 1.27).

That no indexing was completed between June 1809 and December 1814 is not surprising. This was the era of the Napoleonic Wars and Joseph Bonaparte's rule as king of Spain—Joseph himself entered Seville as conqueror on 1 February 1810. This history also explains why, once King Fernando VII returned to power in March 1814, the next indexing project at the Archive of the Indies would center on papers detailing the privileges of the Spanish monarchy and its rights to rule in the New World.

Royal Patronage was the most famous part of the archive, as George Ticknor's breathless description makes clear:

> Some of them [the documents] are extremely curious. I sought in vain, however, for a scrap of Columbus's handwriting. Probably it does not exist, unless it be in an unsigned codicil to his will in the *escribano*'s office at Valladolid, a copy of which is preserved here; but there are original letters of Cortes to Charles V, letters of Magallanes, a collection of the MSS. of Las Casas, of Sebastian Cabot, etc., letters of Pizarro signed with his mark, because he could not write, MSS. of Diego Columbus, heir and successor of the discoverer, and, in short, something of nearly every name that occurs in the early history of South America. Among other things, too, is the most important of all the documents we yet know for the life of Cervantes, who on his return from captivity asked for an office in South America, and presented eight papers whose originals, duly

authenticated, are here (estante II, cajon 5, legajo 1), setting forth his services in the army and at the battle of Lepanto, and his sufferings in Algiers, in short containing in minute detail the most important, the most interesting, and the most obscure part of his life. He was fortunately refused, or we should never have had *Don Quixote;* and these precious documents have slept here ever since until Cean's diligence discovered and sent them to Navarrete, who will soon print them with his new edition of *Don Quixote* and his new life of Cervantes.[56]

The four-volume finding aid to the archive's Royal Patronage section, underway during Ticknor's visit, was completed by archivist Diego Juárez in late November 1819. It consists of two inventories organized by shelf mark, one index of names, and another index of themes.

On the shelves, this precious collection began with seven bundles of papal bulls and briefs legitimating Spanish rights in the Americas; all of these were stored in case 1, shelf 1. These were followed, on the same shelf, by documents related to Columbus and his two sons Diego and Fernando (including an account of Diego's death, about which Ticknor writes elsewhere in his journal). The first shelf of the first case ended with papers relating to Magellan and the Moluccas (from which Ceán Bermúdez had taken notes for an unpublished history),[57] a series that continued on shelf 2 (bundles 1/1 to 2/16). The remaining shelves in the first case were taken up with documents related to the deeds of conquistadors and early settlers in the Caribbean, Philippines, New Spain, and South America. For example, documents related to Francisco Pizarro and his descendants in Peru could be found in at least two bundles on shelf 4. In contrast, case 2 was mostly filled with documents about governance and its failures. Accounts of the 1692 maize riots in Mexico City and Tlaxcala, for example, were on shelf 4, document 1. The final shelves of case 2 contained documents related to famous individuals (the descendants of Moctezuma and potential saints on shelf 4, Miguel de Cervantes on shelf 5), naval power (the attacks of Francis Drake and other pirates later on shelf 5), and royal decrees (shelf 6).

Before leaving this space and returning to the southern gallery, we should briefly consider the symbolic location of these documents within the building as a whole. Royal Patronage was located in the square room in the southwest corner of the Lonja; it was therefore the structural opposite of the square room in the northwest corner, where the archive's front offices were located. If those offices were relatively public spaces for work, Royal Patronage, in contrast, was the least accessible (and therefore most protected) section of the archive. Similar spatial symbolisms were at work in the Archive of Simancas, as we will see in the next chapter.

GOBIERNO, CASES 53–81: PAPERWORK FROM THE COUNCIL OF THE INDIES (MADRID, VIA SIMANCAS)

Royalist and revolutionary pressures were not the only reasons that the room of Royal Patronage, and not the southern gallery, was the fourth section of the archive to be indexed. Documentary chaos was an important factor as well. Remember that the shipment of Accounting papers from Madrid's Council of the Indies totaled 98 chests, filling 11 archival cases. The shipment from the House of Trade in Cádiz totaled 54 chests that, augmented by the House of Trade documents that had stayed in Seville, filled 35 archival cases. In contrast, the shipment of documents from Simancas filled a massive 254 chests. Only a small percentage of their contents were used to fill the 6 cases of Justice (and to augment the 2 cases of Royal Patronage, as will be seen in chapter 4). The remaining documents from Simancas—dealing with all of Spain's ultramarine territories, from the Caribbean to Chile to the Philippines, and involving a vast range of document types (letters from viceroys, governors, and archbishops; royal decrees; economic documents on mining, minting, tobacco, and fortifications)—were apparently (as mentioned above) badly organized, and quite possibly exceeded the storage space available on the shelves in the southern gallery.

This core of Government documents was slowly expanded with additional collections over the next decades: in 1788, a shipment of 60 crates of documents from the Secretariat of Peru (in Madrid);[58] in 1790, 232 crates from the Secretariat of New Spain (also in Madrid);[59] in 1822, 23 crates from the Maritime Court (in Cádiz),[60] and in 1828, yet more crates from the Secretariats of New Spain and Peru.[61] Although additional shelves were added to the enclosed upper gallery of the Lonja's patio in 1830,[62] it was not until the 1860s that archivist Aniceto de la Higuera finally organized and indexed the vast bulk of Simancan documentation—a process that required creating new shelving in new areas of the Lonja.[63] For several decades, then, the organization of the southern gallery of the archive remained incomplete.

However, archivists before Higuera had worked to tame this "confused forest" of papers, and traces of their efforts can be found in the AGI's documentation.[64] Starting in January 1802, Ceán Bermúdez (exiled again in Seville from June 1801 to May 1808, after Jovellanos fell from favor a second time) directed work sorting and organizing the *papeles de gobierno,* working through various *audiencias* (Chile, the Philippines, Guadalajara). This project was continued by new head archivist Manuel de Valbuena until autumn 1809.[65] Our best evidence that the southern gallery was actually used around the time of George Ticknor's visit for a provisional organization of Government documents is a one-sheet list outlining how "the papers from the eleven *Audiencias* of America that came from the Archive of Simancas are placed in the shelves" (fig. 1.30). Although undated, the list is in the handwriting of Ventura Collar y Castro (AGI employee from 1785, promoted to head archivist in March 1819), and is written on paper with a distinctive ROMEU watermark—an unusual brand, but one being used for other documents dated late 1818 to 1819.[66] Perhaps this paper indicates a shelving or indexing initiative by Ventura Collar around the time of his promotion.

According to its outline, case 53 seems to have been left empty, separating the Government documents from the last of the Justice documents in case 52. Documents from Mexico were stored in cases 54 and 55, followed by those from Charcas in case 57, Quito in case 58, and Guadalajara in case 59. Miscellaneous papers were stored in the

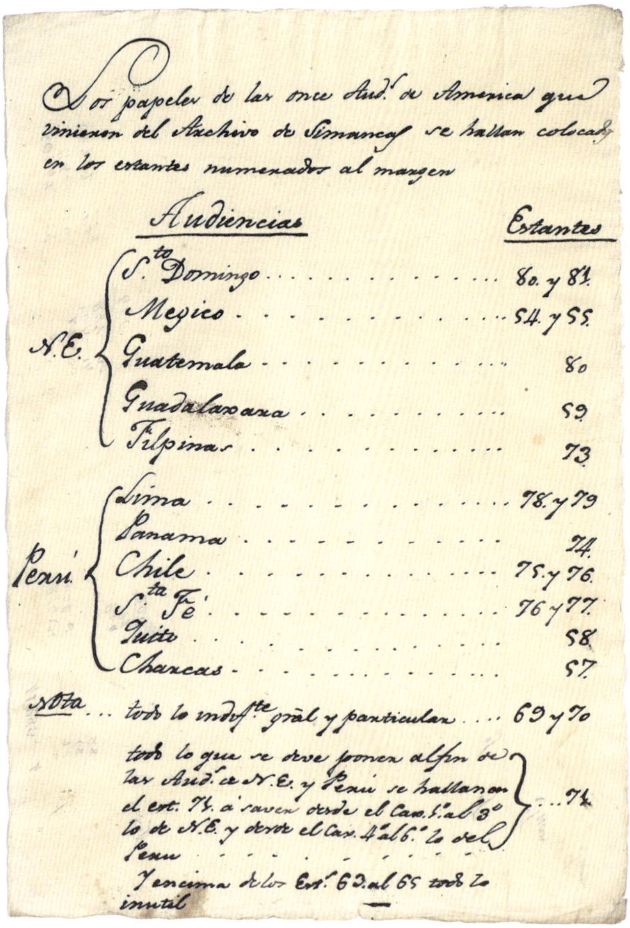

Los papeles de las once Aud.s de America que vinieron del Archivo de Simancas se hallan colocad[os] en los estantes numerados al margen

Audiencias		Estantes
N.E.	S.to Domingo	80. y 81.
	Megico	54. y 55.
	Guatemala	80
	Guadalaxara	59
	Filipinas	73
Perú	Lima	78. y 79
	Panama	74
	Chile	75. y 76.
	S.ta Fe	76 y 77
	Quito	58
	Charcas	57

Nota … todo lo indif.te gral y particular … 69 y 70

todo lo que se deve poner al fin de las Aud.s de N.E. y Perú se hallan en el est. 74. a saver desde el Cax. 1.o al 3.o lo de N.E. y desde el Cax. 4.o al 6.o lo del Perú … 74

Y encima de los Est.s 63 al 65 todo lo inutil

FIGURE 1.30

Plan for shelving documents in the cases of the southern gallery by Ventura Collar y Castro, 1819 (?).

Seville, Archivo General de Indias, Indiferente General 1855.

upper shelves of cases 63, 64, and 65. The cases surrounding the doorway to Royal Patronage's corner room seem not to have been used. Turning to the southern gallery's northern wall, *todo lo indif[eren]te g[e]n[er]al y particular* (a mixed miscellany of files) was housed in cases 69 and 70, more miscellaneous documents in case 71, documents from the Philippines in case 73, Panama in case 74, Chile in cases 75 and 76, Santa Fe in cases 76 and 77, Lima in cases 78 and 79, Guatemala in case 80, and, finally, Santo Domingo in cases 80 and 81. Although dozens of tourists wrote accounts of their visits to the Lonja from 1792 through the 1850s, none mentioned noticeably empty shelving or documents stacked on the floor of the main gallery. This suggests that the southern gallery's shelves were filled with documents, at least for storage if not yet fully sorted. Other unsorted documents, as mentioned above, were housed in the rooms created by closing off the patio's upper galleries in 1800 and 1801.[67]

In contrast, by 1874 the archive's main galleries were filled with stacked piles of documents: Argentine researcher Vicente Quesada described "colossal heaps" on the floor.[68] During the previous two decades, the AGI had received a number of additional archival collections. Between 1856 and 1864, documents arrived from the Ministry of Grace and Justice (Ministerio de Gracia y Justicia), the Ministry of Finance (Ministerio de Hacienda), and the General Overseas Office of the Ministry of War (Dirección General de Ultramar en el Ministerio de la Guerra). In 1871, documents arrived from the Ministry of State (Ministerio de Estado). Yet more materials from the General Overseas Office arrived in 1887 (papers relating to Cuba, Puerto Rico, Louisiana, Florida, and the Philippines) and 1888 to 1889 (Cuba), followed by a section of "Indies Archive" documents from the Provincial Library of Cádiz (Biblioteca Provincial de Cádiz) in 1903.[69] Photos taken by Carnegie Institution researcher Roscoe R. Hill (who worked at the AGI from January 1911 to April 1913) reveal documents on pallets in the eastern gallery (figs. 1.31, 1.32), as well as bundled "Papers from Cuba" (Papeles de Cuba) on the ground floor (fig. 1.33). These storage issues were partially addressed in 1913—the fourth centenary of Vasco Núñez de Balboa's arrival at the Pacific—when the ground-floor gallery was enclosed and equipped with metal shelves.[70]

By the end of the twentieth century, it was estimated that the archive housed more than 43,000 *legajos* (document bundles), amounting to some 90,000,000 pages, or nine kilometers of shelving.[71]

This is the archive as it existed when its first four sets of finding aids—for Accounting, House of Trade, Justice, and Royal Patronage documents—were completed by 1819. The next two chapters move back in time to the 1780s, first to explore the donor archives dismembered to provide the Archive of the Indies with papers, and then to study the processes, and poetics, of the building's radical and controversial renovation.

FIGURE 1.31
Roscoe R. Hill (U.S. American, 1880–1960).
Documents stored on pallets in the eastern gallery in front of cases 12 and 13 (note the paper wrappers enclosing each shelved document bundle), Archive of the Indies, 1911–13.
Berkeley, University of California at Berkeley, Bancroft Library, Roscoe R. Hill Photograph Collection, BANC PIC 1962.024 Box 1.

THE ARCHIVE OF THE INDIES IN 1818   65

FIGURE 1.32
Roscoe R. Hill (U.S. American, 1880–1960).
Documents stored on pallets in the eastern gallery, Archive of the Indies, 1911–13.
Berkeley, University of California at Berkeley, Bancroft Library, Roscoe R. Hill Photograph Collection, BANC PIC 1962.024 Box 1.

FIGURE 1.33
Roscoe R. Hill (U.S. American, 1880–1960).
The "Papers from Cuba," Archive of the Indies, 1911–13.
Berkeley, University of California at Berkeley, Bancroft Library, Roscoe R. Hill Photograph Collection, BANC PIC 1962.024 Box 1.

NOTES

1 Cesare Sterbini Romano, *Almaviva, o sia l'inutile precuazione* (Rome: Crispino Puccinelli, 1816), 11–12. See also https://www.youtube.com /watch?v=enEVvo2f6bo (at 25:39): Teatro alla Scala, conductor Riccardo Chailly, Milan, Teatro alla Scala, 1999.

2 George Ticknor, *Life, Letters, and Journals of George Ticknor,* 2 vols. (Boston: Houghton Mifflin, 1909); George Ticknor, *George Ticknor's Travels in Spain,* ed. G. T. Northrup (Toronto: University Library, University of Toronto, 1913); and Richard L. Kagan, *The Spanish Craze: America's Fascination with the Hispanic World, 1779–1939* (Lincoln: University of Nebraska Press, 2019), 178–79. Ticknor was the future biographer of William Hickling Prescott, his friend and a pioneering U.S. historian of Spain and Mexico: George Ticknor, *Life of William Hickling Prescott* (Boston: Ticknor and Fields, 1864).

3 "El edificio es grandioso: sea pues todo correspondiente, por manera que si un viajero curioso viene a Sevilla, no admire solamente los restos de su opulencia antigua, sino tambien halle un monumento que acredite nuestro espritiu i gusto en el presente siglo" (AGI IG 1853, Juan Bautista Muñoz and Francisco Miguel Maestre to Joséde Gálvez, 4 August 1784).

4 A document in AGI IG 1858G (a draft of the "Yndice Alfabetico de Juarez" in a cardboard-covered folder labeled "Yndice perteneciente al Tomo 2°") says that Royal Patronage indexing work was "Concluido en 24 de Noviembre de 1819." Juárez had been working in the AGI since the 1780s (see this volume, appendix B), and before that (from 1781) he was a scribe assistant working for Muñoz in Spain and Portugal. See his petition for a post as a scribe in AGI IG 1854A (Diego Juárez, Madrid, 15 December 1789), although he would not be hired as a scribe until June 1796 (see AGI IG 1857A; appointment is added as a note to a letter on scribal replacements for Joséf Águilera, deceased, Seville, 23 March 1796). Juárez recounts his employment history in AGI IG 1857B (Diego Juárez, Seville, 21 September 1814).

5 Ceán Bermúdez had been asked to write an encomium about Herrera in February 1812 by the Royal Academy of History. He apparently prepared

this in a few days, but continued to work on the essay over the next decade: Real Academia de la Historia, *Memorias de la Real Academia de la Historia,* vol. 5 (Madrid: Imprenta de Sancha, 1817), lvii; and José Clisson Aldama, *Juan Agustín Ceán-Bermúdez escritor y crítico de Bellas Artes* (Oviedo: Instituto de Estudios Asturianos, 1982), 291–93. This was one of the projects he was researching in the fall of 1818 when Ticknor met him in Seville. Letters to the main archivist of Simancas (Tomás González) on 8 August, 7 November, and 19 December 1818 (written from Madrid) all refer to his then-current efforts to locate documents on Herrera's early years. Note that I have been unable to find independent confirmation of Ticknor's claim that Ceán Bermúdez was in Seville in early October 1818; however, his monthly letters to González from August 1818 to January 1819 are suggestive. The first, from Madrid, is dated 8 August, but the next two, also from Madrid, are dated 17 October and 7 November. Perhaps the gap in letters from early August to mid-October indirectly reflects a trip to Seville: Manuel Serrano Sanz, "Cartas de D. Martín Fernández de Navarrete, D. Agustin Ceán Bermúdez y D. Diego Clemecín, á D. Tomás González, archivero de Simancas," *Revue Hispanique* 6 (1899): 107–18. The biography of Herrera was finally published in 1870, and on several pages it cites documents in the Archive of the Indies: Juan Agustín Ceán Bermúdez, *Ocios de don Juan Agustín Ceán Bermúdez sobre Bellas Artes (hasta ahora inéditos)* (Madrid: Imprenta de Berenguillo, 1870), 5, 56, 90. In addition, one Herreran document from the Archive of the Indies (on instruments he designed for calculating longitude) had been included in Eugenio Llaguno y Amirola and Juan Agustín Ceán Bermúdez, *Noticias de los arquitectos y arquitectura de España desde su restauración,* vol. 2 (Madrid: La Imprenta Real, 1829), 363–64; see also Clisson Aldama, *Juan Agustín Ceán-Bermúdez,* 93–94, 229–32.

6 On Davy's circle of friends, and his key role in Romantic science during the late eighteenth and early nineteenth centuries, see Richard Holmes, *The Age of Wonder* (New York: Pantheon, 2008). Thanks to Christian Kleinbub and Amanda Gluibizzi for this recommendation.

7 Ticknor, *Life, Letters, and Journals,* 128–29. Dominique de Pradt's two-volume *Des colonies et de la révolution actuelle de l'Amérique* (Paris: F. Bechet and A. Égron, 1817) had just been published.

8 Ticknor, *Life, Letters, and Journals,* 147.

9 Ticknor, *George Ticknor's Travels,* 47. For an excellent history of the Lonja's construction in the late sixteenth and early seventeenth centuries, see Alfredo J. Morales, "El Archivo de Indias," *Apuntes del Real Alcázar de Sevilla* 14 (2013): 50–71, 287–95.

10 The color scheme, and Lucas Cintora's original plans for a gilded iron gate, may have been inspired by the monumental baroque stairway (begun in 1617 and completed in 1654) leading down to the royal burial chamber of the Escorial monastery-palace. See AGI IG 1854A (Lucas Cintora, Seville, 18 October 1787: "ponerle rejas De yerro sencillas y proporcionad[a]s ala magnificiencia De la escalera"); Francisco de los Santos, *Descripción del Real Monasterio de San Lorenzo de El Escorial* (Madrid: Juan García Infançon, 1698), 146 (on construction history); and Andrés Ximénez, *Descripción del Real Monasterio de San Lorenzo de El Escorial* (Madrid: Antonio Marín, 1764), engraving between pages 380 and 381 (iron entry gate). The Archive of the Indies, like the Escorial, was a royal institution, and of course the pantheon of the Escorial was a kind of archive for royal corpses embodying the past history of Spain. Alfonso Pleguezuelo Hernández argues that despite Cintora's interventions, the overall structure of the staircase dates to its original construction in 1614–32: Alfonso Pleguezuelo Hernández, "La Lonja de Mercaderes de Sevilla: De los proyectos a la ejecución," *Archivo Español de Arte* 249 (1990): 35–37; and María Antonio Colomar Albajar, ed., *La Casa Lonja de Sevilla: Una casa de ricos tesoros* (Madrid: Ministerio de Cultura, 2005), 192–97.

11 "La nueva escalera es rica de mármoles; pero no dice con el caracter de la obra Antigua": Antonio Ponz, *Viage de España, en que se da noticia de las cosas mas apreciables, y dignas de saberse, que hay en ella,* vol. 17, *Trata de Andalucia* (Madrid: La Viuda de Joaquín Ibarra, 1792), 215. Ponz's criticisms are part of a broader neoclassical discourse against baroque design, in which AGI employee Ceán

Bermúdez was also an important critic: Juan Agustín Ceán Bermúdez, "El churriguerismo" [1816], *Boletín de la Biblioteca Menéndez y Pelayo* 3, no. 6 (1921): 285–300; Yves Bottineau, "La 'fortune' de l'architecture baroque espagnole," *Revue de l'Art* 11 (1971): 87–96; Juan Miguel Serrera, "Los ideales neoclásicos y la destrucción del barroco: Ceán Bermúdez y Jerónimo Balbás," *Archivo Hispalense* 223 (1990): 135–59; Daniel Crespo Delgado, "La arquitectura del Museo del Prado vista por sus contemporáneos (1789–1815)," *Madrid: Revista de Arte, Geografía e Historia* 8 (2006): 333; and Francisco Ollero Lobato, "Ceán Bermúdez, Itálica, y las artes en Sevilla," *Academia: Boletín de la Real Academia de Bellas Artes de San Fernando* 106–7 (2008): 49–64.

12 In the center of the patio was "una fuente espaciosa De marmoles con abundancia De agua De los Caños De Carmona (cuyo nacimiento es un Arcala De los panaderos) y sus derramas se recojen en un grande y ermoso Arjibe desde donde se distribuye a el Comun" (AGI IG 1853, Felix Carasa and Lucas Cintora, Seville, 24 May 1784); "su Atrio està vn Lugar publico p[ar]a aguas menores; vn Escotillon q[u]e vaja al Algibe....Y debiendo acompañar à la suntuosidad de esta fabrica todas las precauciones correspondientes â su conservacion, aseo, y seguridad, estimada muy oportuno para su logro q[u]e la referida entrada del Poniente fuese privativa del Archivo; en cuio caso cerrandose la Puerta q[u]e continua à la Galeria vaja con llaves p[o]r dentro, y fuera, de modo q[u]e solo pueda servir alguna vez extraordinaria; abriendose la vajada del Algibe en otro lugar que le tiene, y suprimiendo como inutil el paraje destinado p[ar]a aguas menores" (AGI IG 1854A, Antonio de Lara y Zúñiga to Antonio Porlier, Seville, 26 January 1788).

13 "De la subida, y miran á el patio: los cuales pueden cerrarse y seguir los adornos referidos, o ponerle rejas De yerro sencillas y proporcionad[a]s ala magnificiencia De la escalera y De todo el edificio: sin embargo le parece à este Architecto que puestas las rejas en los referidos arcos quedara la escalera con mas ermosura, diafanidad, luz, y una ermosa vista para el patio" (AGI IG 1854, Lucas Cintora, Seville, 18 October 1787); see also the many back-and-forth letters on this issue in AGI IG 1854A, including correspondence from Antonio Porlier (Aranjuez, 27 June 1788) and Juan Manuel de Villanueva (15 July 1788). The account books from 1789 include expenses "por el importe de la Puerta de hierro, que se puso en el Zaguan" in August, and "Al Maestro Pintor, por dar de verde à la rexa del Zaguan" in October (AGI IG 1858H;

the *zaguán* was the corridor connecting the building's western door to its central patio, according to a plan from 2 May 1789: AGI IG MPD 47 086). This may be the gate mentioned a half century later by Félix González de León, who in 1844 described "la parte baja que dá al patio cerrada con fuerte reja"; Félix González de León, *Noticia artística, histórica y curiosa de todos los edificios públicos, sagrados, y profanos, de esta muy noble, muy leal, muy heróica e invicta ciudad de Sevilla,* vol. 1 (Seville: José Hidalgo y Compañía, 1844), 88.

14 For an excellent discussion of Enlightenment archaeology in the Spanish Empire, see Irina Podgorny, "The Reliability of the Ruins," *Journal of Spanish Cultural Studies* 8, no. 2 (2007): 213–33; for the connections linking Herculaneum, Pompeii, and Spanish America, see Joanne Pillsbury and Lisa Trever, "The King, the Bishop, and the Creation of an American Antiquity," *Ñawpa Pacha* 29 (2008): 191–219.

15 José Herrera Dávila, *Guía de forasteros de la ciudad de Sevilla* (Seville: Diario de Comercio, 1832), 31; and González de León, *Noticia artística,* 89: "A la subida de la escalera principal, y junto á la entrada del archivo, se vé la escalera segunda que dá subida á las azotes en que remata el edificio."

16 Nicolás de la Cruz, *Viage de España, Francia, é Italia,* vol. 14 (Cádiz: Imprenta de D. Manuel Bosch, 1813), 230, describing a visit in 1801: "El quarto frente ocupa el lado de la escalera y oficinas."

17 The archive's original *Ordenanzas* established six ranks within the archive: the head archivist (*archivero*), four numbered archivists (*oficiales*), an assistant (*mozo*) and a doorman (*portero*); *Ordenanzas para el Archivo General de Indias* (Madrid: Imprenta de la Viuda de Ibarra, 1790), 2–3. However, for the first decade-plus of the archive's existence, an additional three archivists (*supernumerarios*) as well as a scribe (*escribano*) were hired to help with the organizing, shelving, and initial indexing of incoming documents (see this volume, appendix B; and AGI IG 1854A, Juan Bautista Muñoz, "Razón del origen, progreso, i actual estado del Archivo general de Indias," 3 August 1787: "En cuanto a los individuos de la Oficina, en el principio se nombraron un Archivero y cuatro Oficiales con las graduaciones de 1°. 2°. 3°. y 4°. Pero habiéndose tratado a fines del pasado 86 sobre la necesidad de más gente para el arreglo y disposición general, determinó S[u] M[ajestad] que por ahora se pusiesen además cuatro sujetos hábiles con honores y sueldo de Oficiales mayores, y dos Escribientes, y efectivamente

se han nombrado tres de los primeros, y uno de los segundos." Furniture for the AGI—four tables and twelve chairs—was originally provided on loan by Gregorio de Fuentes, shortly after his appointment as interim treasurer (*thesorero interino*) in March 1786 (AGI IG 1854A, Antonio de Lara y Zúñiga, Seville, 26 May 1787; AGI IG 1854A, Gregorio de Fuentes, Seville, 26 May 1787). Purpose-built furnishings—ten mahogany desks with drawers and twelve walnut chairs—were completed in September and October 1787 (AGI IG 1854A, Antonio de Lara y Zúñiga, Seville, 18 October 1787). Lara hoped to add another four tables and fourteen chairs (AGI IG 1854A, Antonio de Lara y Zúñiga, Seville, 24 November 1787), but based on later inventories it is unclear if he was successful. At least two such inventories exist, one dated 12 September 1798 (and subsequently reviewed and annotated on 1 September 1801), and the other dated 9 March 1809. Both "Ymbentarios" are in AGI IG 1856.

18 "El pavimento de losas grandes de marmol encarnadas y blancas, puede decirse que sirve de espejo continuado donde reflejan todos los objetos, por la brillantez y pulimento de las piedras que paracen de cristal" (González de León, *Noticia artística,* 89).

19 Ticknor, *George Ticknor's Travels,* 47–48.

20 *Ordenanzas,* 39–40.

21 In addition to the examples from AGI Justicia 11, illustrated in this volume's introduction, other well-preserved sets can be found in AGI Justicia 264 and AGI Contaduría 233.

22 Surviving examples (about the size of a 3 × 5 index card) can be found in AGI Santo Domingo 1 (label for 53-1-1); AGI IG 1858A (147-5-10); AGI IG 1858E (14-5-7); AGI IG 1858D (147-5-75/147-5-10); AGI IG 1858H (147-5-13); and AGI IG 1858I (147-5-16). A related example (made of multiple layers of folded paper with horizontal cuts at top and bottom for threading a ribbon tie) is included in AGI IG 1852. Although it has no shelf mark information, the label reads "Secretaria de Nueva España / Expediente / Sobre envio de los papeles de su Archivo desde / 1700 a 1759 al General de Sevilla / Año de 1785 á 1793." One of the papers folded up to make this label is a printed sheet dated "Madrid á 8 de Setiembre de 1820."

23 Arlette Farge, *The Allure of the Archives,* trans. Thomas Scott-Railton (New Haven, CT: Yale University Press, 2013), 4; see also Markus Friedrich, *The Birth of the Archive: A History of Knowledge,* trans. John Noël Dillon (Ann Arbor: University of

Michigan Press, 2019), 71. For Spanish-language oceanic-archival metaphors, see José Antonio Benito, "Perú en el Archivo General de Simancas (A.G.S.)," *BIRA* 21 (1994): 289 (*el océano de sus legajos*); María Teresa Triguero Rodríguez, "América y el Archivo de Simancas," *Studia Historica: Historia Moderna* 7 (1989): 798 (*bucear*); and Julio F. Guillén y Tato, "Prólogo," in *Índice de la colección de documentos de Fernández de Navarrete que posee el Museo Naval*, ed. V. Vicente Vela (Madrid: Instituto Histórico de Marina, 1946), xv (*bucear por el Archivo*).

24 On cartouche shelf labels, see also Eric Garberson, *Eighteenth-Century Monastic Libraries in Southern Germany and Austria: Architecture and Decorations* (Baden-Baden: Verlag Valentin Koerner, 1998), 84–86.

25 The enclosure of the archways took place from 1800 to 1801, and was carried out first by architect Lucas Cintora and then, on his death, by his son Manuel. An itemized day-by-day list of expenditures for this work from January 1801 is preserved in the AGI's Archivo del Archivo: Manuel Zintora, "Cuenta diaria de lo gastado en acavar de cerrar los Arcos de la galeria del Archivo g[ene]ral de Yndias," 2 January 1801. A copy of the first folio of this letter was reproduced in a panel for the exhibition *La Casa Lonja de Sevilla: Historia de las intervenciones en el renacentista "Cubo Herreriano,"* installed on the AGI's ground-floor gallery since 2016. See also AGI IG 1856 (a letter on royal approval of the gallery enclosure, from Joséf Antonio Caballero to Pedro Reales y Colarte, Aranjuez, 27 February 1800).

26 These works were often mentioned by later tourists, including Isidore Taylor, *Voyage Pittoresque en Espagne, en Portugal et sur la cote d'Afrique de Tanger a Tétouan* (Paris: Librairie de Gide Fils, 1826), 173; Alexander Slidell Mackenzie, *A Year in Spain, by a Young American* (Boston: Hillard, Gray, Little, and Wilkins, 1829), 287; Captain C. Rochfort Scott, *Excursions in the Mountains of Ronda and Granada, with Characteristic Sketches of the Inhabitants of the South of Spain*, vol. 2 (London: Henry Colburn, 1838), 107; and George Dennis, *A Summer in Andalucia*, vol. 1 (London: Richard Bentley, 1839), 204. Both Baron Charles Dembowski, in *Deux ans en Espagne et en Portugal pendant la Guerre Civile, 1838–1840* (Paris: Librairie de Charles Gosselin, 1841), 166, and González de León (*Noticia artística*, 89) make clear these works were all still housed together in the room for Royal Patronage; Richard Ford, in *A Hand-Book for Travellers in Spain, and Readers at Home*, vol. 1 (London: John Murray, 1845), 251, only mentions

Columbus. By 1847, the paintings had been rearranged: the Columbus portrait had moved to the front office and the Cortés portrait stayed in the Royal Patronage room. See Severn Teackle Wallis, *Glimpses of Spain, Or, Notes of an Unfinished Tour in 1847* (New York: Harper & Brothers, 1849), 223; and Antoine de Latour, *Études sur l'Espagne: Séville et l'Andalousie* (Paris: Michel Lévy Frères, 1855), 110–11.

27 This seems to have been acquired in the spring of 1808 (AGI IG 1856, list of expenses dated 28 February 1809; AGI IG 1856, receipt number 11 signed by Manuel Agustín Sánchez, 20 May 1808).

28 The painting was donated in December 1814 (AGI IG 1857A, Ventura Collar y Castro, Seville, 24 December 1814). Unfortunately, it was not in good shape and so had to be restored ("por la compostura que he hecho en un retrato original de cuerpo entero de d[o]n cristoval colon, descubridor del nuevo mundo, poniendole un bastidor, forrandole con lienzo, y quitandole algunas imperfecciones"; AGI IG 1857B, accounts for 1816, receipt number 29 signed by Joaquín de Cabral y Bejarano, 20 July 1816).

29 Both were painted by Joaquín Cortés, *Pintor de Cámara* and director general of Seville's Escuela de las Tres Nobles Artes; Luis Quesada, *Los Cortés: Una dinastía de pintores en Sevilla y Francia entre los siglos XVIII y XIX* (Seville: Guadalquivir Ediciones, 2001), 21–32. The portrait of Cortés was based on a painting (supposedly by Titian) owned by Seville resident Francisco Saavedra; Joaquín Cortés was paid for the copy in August 1813 (AGI IG 1857A, book of accounts for 1813, receipt signed by Joaquín Cortés, 19 August 1813). The portrait of Fernando VII was commissioned in June 1816, in anticipation of a visit to Seville by the queen and infanta in September: "Por el retrato de n[uest]ro soberano el S[eñ]or d[o]n Fernando 7°, que por no haberle en la oficina, se compró para quando pasase por esta Ciudad la Reina n[uest]ra S[eño]ra, y S[eño]ra Ynfanta, y se halla colocado en el dosel de la Sala del R[ea]l Patronato" (AGI IG 1857B, book of accounts for 1816, receipt number 27 signed by Joaquín Cortés, 22 June 1816). See also Quesada, *Los Cortés*, 27.

30 The earliest references to this that I have found are from visits made in the 1830s: Scott, *Excursions*, 107 ("the keeper of the archives requesting me, at the same time, not to press too hard upon the valuable MS., and assuring us, that most persons were obliged to be satisfied with looking at the precious document bearing the signature of the adventurous Columbus, in its glass case"); and

Dembowski, *Deux ans*, 166 ("Quatre cartes au glaises complètent les décors de cette pièce"). These documents, or perhaps the entire Royal Patronage room, seem to have been off-limits to visitors in 1840: both Elizabeth M. Grosvenor, in *Narrative of a Yacht Voyage in the Mediterranean during the Years 1840–41*, vol. 1 (London: John Murray, 1842), 48, and Théophile Gautier, in *Voyage en Espagne* (Paris: Charpentier, 1845), 363, complain that no documents were on display when they visited in the fall of that year. See also Louisa Tenison, *Castile and Andalucia* (London: Richard Bentley, 1853), 176: "There are some curious documents relating to Cervantes, and his application to the government for some situation in America, which was refused him. They set forth all the sufferings of his life, his wars and captivity in Algiers; but a deaf ear was turned to his petition, and he remained in Spain, to write Don Quixote, and immortalize his name. Many of these interesting manuscripts used formerly to be shown to strangers, but the glass-cases which enclose them will not open anymore, thanks to the exploits of one of our own country-women, who managed one day to abstract a page from this valuable collection as a gentle souvenir of Cervantes." On the innovation of glass framing, see Jesusa Vega, *Ciencia, arte e ilusión en la España ilustrada* (Madrid: CSIC, 2010), 253–54.

31 On the transfer of these Royal Patronage documents to Seville from the Royal Patronage section of the Archive of Simancas, see Ángel de la Plaza Bores, *Archivo General de Simancas: Guía del investigador*, 4th ed. (Madrid: Ministerio de Cultura, 1992), 94; and AGI IG 1854A, Antonio de Lara y Zúñiga to Antonio Porlier, Seville, 18 October 1787: "Yo cuidarè de los correspondientes à Patronato, q[u]e pienso colocar solas en la vltima pieza. . . . La sala (n[umer]o 7.°) està sin Estantes, tendrà solo dos para los Papeles de Patronato en los Huecos."

32 Ticknor, *George Ticknor's Travels*, 48.

33 Finding-aid totals in 1818 were: two volumes for Accounting, nine volumes for House of Trade, two volumes for Justice, and the first (of four) volumes for Royal Patronage.

34 Installation of cases for the galleries was completed in May 1788 ("En el mes vltimo se acabaron, y pusieron los Estantes de la tercera crujia de este Archivo, con que se completaron los acordados por V[uestra] E[xcelencia]: solo restan los dos pequeños que han de servir p[ar]a los Papeles de Patronato"; AGI IG 1854A, Antonio de Lara y Zúñiga to Antonio Porlier, Seville, 18 June 1788); see also AGI IG 1845B, receipt 11, signed by Blas

Molner y Zamora and Antonio de Lara y Zúñiga, Seville, 26 May 1788. By 20 June, many of the documents had been put into place: "Concluida ya la estanteria de ese Archivo, i colocados en ella gran parte de sus papeles" (AGI IG 1854A, letter from Antonio de Lara y Zúñiga to Antonio Porlier, Seville, 20 June 1788).

35 AGI IG 1853 (José de Gálvez?, San Ildefonso, 7 November 1786); "el Jueves ultimo llegaron los papeles" (AGI IG 1853, Antonio de Lara y Zúñiga, Seville, 25 November 1786 [Friday]); AGI IG 1854A, Juan Bautista Muñoz, "Expediente sobre el establecimiento i progresos del Archivo General de Indias," fol. 21r, 31 July 1787; "se llevaron de Cadiz cincuenta Cajones, de la Contaduria g[ene]ral. 98 y de Simancas 254" (AGI IG 1854A, Antonio de Lara y Zúñiga to Antonio Porlier, Seville, 27 October 1787).

36 "los q[u]e embio la contaduria del Consejo en 98 Cajones estan bien coordinados, y en disposicion de trasladarse à sus respectivos Estantes sin travajo alguno" (AGI IG 1854A, Antonio de Lara y Zúñiga to Antonio Porlier, Seville, 18 October 1787); see also Margarita Gómez Gómez, "El Archivo General de Indias: Génesis histórica de sus ordenanzas," in *Ordenanzas del Archivo General de Indias,* ed. Francisco de Solano, Margarita Gómez Gómez, and Manuel Romero Tallafigo (Seville: Dirección General del Libro, Bibliotecas y Archivos, Consejería de Cultura, Junta de Andalucía, 1986), 72.

37 AGI IG 1852, Antonio de Lara y Zúñiga, 14 October 1785; AGI IG 1852, Francisco Ortiz de Solorzano and Hipólito de la Vega (they headed the two wagon trains), 19 October 1785; and AGI IG 1854A, Juan Bautista Muñoz, "Expediente sobre el establecimiento i progresos del Archivo General de Indias," fols. 17v–20r, 31 July 1787—note that folio 19r numbers the chests at 253, not 254, as do two unsigned letters (presumably written by José de Gálvez) sent from San Ildefonso (AGI IG 1852, unsigned letter, 23 September 1785; and AGI IG 1852, unsigned letter 4 October 1785). Previous scholarship has numbered the chests at 253, 254, and 257.

38 "los q[u]e vinieron del Archivo de Simancas en 254 cajones sin orden, ni Ynventario" (AGI IG 1854A, Antonio de Lara y Zúñiga to Antonio Porlier, Seville, 18 October 1787).

39 AGI IG 1853, Antonio de Lara y Zúñiga, 11 February 1786; and AGI IG 1854A, Juan Bautista Muñoz, "Expediente sobre el establecimiento i progresos del Archivo General de Indias," fols. 20v–21r, 31 July 1787.

40 Richard Herr, *The Eighteenth-Century Revolution in Spain* (Princeton, NJ: Princeton University Press, 1958), 261; John Lynch, *Bourbon Spain: 1700–1808* (London: Basil Blackwell, 2016), 377; Clisson Aldama, *Juan Agustín Ceán-Bermúdez,* 62–64; Mauricio Domínguez y Domínguez-Adame, "Juan Agustín Ceán-Bermúdez (1749–1829) y Sevilla," in *Juan Agustín Ceán-Bermúdez (1749–1829): Algo más que una calle,* ed. Concha Álvarez Moro (Seville: Publicaciones del Centro Asturiano en Sevilla, 2001), 30–33; Magdalena Canellas Anoz, "Juan Agustín Ceán-Bermúdez en el Archivo General de Indias," in *Juan Agustín Ceán-Bermúdez, asturiano en Sevilla: 250 aniversario de su nacimiento (1749–1829)* (Seville: Publicaciones del Centro Asturiano en Sevilla, 1999), 41–55; and Javier González Santos, "Cronología: Los trabajos y los días: Ceán en el tiempo," in *Ceán Bermúdez: Historiador del arte y coleccionista ilustrado,* ed. Elena María Santiago Páez (Madrid: Biblioteca Nacional de España, 2016), 6.

41 Ceán Bermúdez's appointment letter and other related documents can be found in AGI IG 1854A.

42 For details, see this volume, chapter 2.

43 Sergio Rodríguez Lorenzo, *La carrera de Indias (la ruta, los hombres, las mercancías)* (Santa María de Cayón, Spain: Esles de Cayón, 2012), 19.

44 In 1784, Muñoz claimed that "los Papeles conducidos en vezes de Sevilla" to the Cádiz House of Trade "apenas componen la mitad del Archivo" (AGI IG 1853, Juan Bautista Muñoz to José de Gálvez, Seville, 8 June 1784). On the fire, see AGI Contratación 4879A ("Causa sobre el fuego ocasionado en la R[ea]l Cassa de la contrattas[io]n Desta ciu[da]d el dia 31 de Jullio de 1753"), as well as this volume, chapter 2.

45 Ticknor, *George Ticknor's Travels,* 47.

46 AGI IG 1853, Antonio de Lara y Zúñiga, 11 February 1786; AGI IG 1854A, Juan Bautista Muñoz, "Expediente sobre el establecimiento i progresos del Archivo General de Indias," fols. 20v–21r, 31 July 1787; cf. José Torre Revello, *El Archivo General de Indias de Sevilla: Historia y clasificación de sus fondos* (Buenos Aires: Talleres S. A. Casa Jacobo Peuser, 1929), 37, 62. Note that Lara would later write that a total of fifty chests (and not fifty-four) arrived from Cádiz: "los Papeles q[u]e han venido de Cadiz en cinquenta cajones" (AGI IG 1854A, Antonio de Lara y Zúñiga, Seville, 18 October 1787); see also AGI IG 1854, Antonio de Lara y Zúñiga, Seville, 27 October 1787. More chests of documents were shipped to the AGI from Cádiz in 1798: the House of Trade there had been

dissolved in 1790. AGI IG 1858H, payment "por el flete de 39. cajones de papeles, que conduxo de la casa de Contratas[io]n de Cadiz," book of accounts for July 1798; and AGI IG 1858H, payment "por el flete de 17 caxones de papeles, que condujo de la contratas[io]n de Cadiz," book of accounts for August 1798.

47 "Zuazo, y Collar estan limpiando, y coordinando p[o]r clases, y años los papeles q[u]e existen en este Archivo, y Casa de aquel. . . . Entretanto q[u]e V[uestra] E[xcelencia] no dispone otra cosa, se colocaràn estos, y demas papeles q[u]e lleguen de esa tierra, en vna pieza vaja de la casa Lonja, vnica q[u]e resta, y franquès el consulado para la construccion de Estantes, y Ventanas; y harè q[u]e los oficiales travajen en sus corredores del mejor modo, y con la menor incomodidad, q[u]e se pueda" (AGI IG 1853, Antonio de Lara y Zúñiga to José de Gálvez, Seville, 17 September 1785). "Digo: que en 29 de Agosto de 785 se dignò S[u] M[ajestad] poner à mi cuidado su direccion . . . desde entonces encarguè à los quatro Oficiales la separacion por clases, y años de los papeles q[u]e custodiaba en su casa el Primero, y traslado à esta Lonja; en que entendieron hasta el Mes de Mayo proximo [1786]" (AGI IG 1854A, Antonio de Lara y Zúñiga to Antonio Porlier, Seville, 18 October 1787). A 6 August 1785 letter from Gregorio de Fuentes to Gálvez suggests that document transfers had not yet begun: "por estar proxima la estacion oportuna para la remision de papeles, los que desde luego puede V[uestra] E[xcelencia] mandar conducir, por tener en esta Casa Lonja sitio al proposito resguardado y decente, donde esten custodiados, el que me facilitan el Prior y Consules de este Consulado" (AGI IG 1852).

48 Gudrun Maurer, "Una leyenda persistente: El viaje de Goya a Andalucía en 1793," *Boletín del Museo del Prado* 28, no. 46 (2010): 76.

49 David García López, "Más parece hecha por una sociedad de lavoriosos yndividuos, que por uno solo: El método de trabajo de Ceán Bermúdez," in *Ceán Bermúdez: Historiador del arte y coleccionista ilustrado,* ed. Elena María Santiago Páez (Madrid: Biblioteca Nacional de España, 2016), 92.

50 Rafael Donoso Anes, "La documentación contable en la Tesorería de la Casa de la Contratación de las Indias de Sevilla (1530–1717)," *Compatabilités* 3 (2012): 1–22.

51 "los q[u]e vinieron del Archivo de Simancas en 254 cajones sin orden, ni Ynventario" (AGI

IG 1854A, Antonio de Lara y Zúñiga to Antonio Porlier, Seville, 18 October 1787).

52 AGI IG 1854A, Juan Bautista Muñoz, "Razón del origen, progreso i estado actual del Archivo General de Indias," August 1787. For the full quotation, see this volume, chapter 2, 118n63.

53 For details, see this volume, chapter 4. Although the *Índice* does not have any authorship or date information, the handwriting is that of Ysidoro Antillón. (Note that Antillón took over the writing of the *Inventario* volume on page 479, not 499 as claimed by that volume's colophon. A key distinction can be seen in the tails of each man's lowercase letter *g:* Tariego's are a smooth looping curve, whereas Antillón's look like a letter *s.*)

54 Torre Revello, *El Archivo General de Indias,* 76–78.

55 Ethelia Ruiz Medrano, *Reshaping New Spain: Government and Private Interests in the Colonial Bureaucracy, 1531–1550* (Boulder: University Press of Colorado, 2006).

56 Ticknor, *George Ticknor's Travels,* 48–49.

57 See BNE MS 5622.

58 AGI IG 1854A, Antonio de Lara y Zúñiga to Antonio Porlier, Seville, 13 February 1788.

59 AGI IG 1852, shipping contract signed by Visente Muñoz and others, Madrid, 3 October 1790.

60 *Juzgado de Arribadas:* AGI IG 1858J, letter 15 March 1822; and AGI IG 1858J, letter 30 December 1827.

61 Torre Revello, *El Archivo General de Indias,* 38; see also this comment on the archive in 1830: "la multitud de remesas de papeles que se han hecho à aquel Archivo del Juzgado de Arribadas de Cadiz, Ministerio de Hacienda, S[ecreta]rias del Perù y Nueva España y ultimam[en]te por la Cont[adu]ria gen[er]al de Yndias en cerca de 350 cajones" (AGI IG 1858J, José de la Higuera y Lara, Seville, 29 October 1830).

62 AGI IG 1858J, documents in subfolder "Sobre la Obra de la Estanteria." These upper galleries were enclosed for document storage in 1800–1801; see n25 above.

63 From (at least) the early 1850s, visitors noted the use of two different colors of paper to wrap document bundles. In 1853, Louisa Tenison (*Castile and Andalucia,* 176) published this account:

"The Lonja, as it now stands, is an emblem of the actual condition of Spain; its halls deserted, not a sign of life about it. It has a very fine patio, paved with marble. A polished marble staircase leads to a superb gallery, running round three sides of the building, full of the records of Spain's past greatness. Here are ranged on shelves, the archives of the New World from the time of its discovery. But the gallery is deserted, the blue and brown paper parcels, ticketed and numbered, look cold and voiceless, and no one seems to think of studying their records." When Vicente G. Quesada visited the archive two decades later, in the 1870s, he noted that white and blue papers were used to wrap document bundles. His account suggests that blue paper was used for the documents newly ordered and shelved in the southern gallery by archivist Aniceto de la Higuera (hired in 1844 on the retirement of his uncle, José de la Higuera y Lara: AHN Ultramar 2430 exp. 2): "Cada legajo está envuelto en papel, blanco lo que se refiere á la Contaduria de Indias, y azul los de las Audiencias y sus subdivisiones: cada paquete tiene un tejuelo grande cuadrilongo en el qual está escrito el año, la materia y el órden de colocacion, exactamente igual á la referencia de los inventarios. En la parte superior tiene un carton del tamaño del legajo, y este está liado con una cinta de algodon" (Vicente G. Quesada, "Sevilla: El Archivo General de Indias," *Revista del Río de la Plata* 9 [1874]: 683). On Aniceto, see María Antonia Colomar Albajar and Pilar Lázaro de la Escosura, "Los 'Papeles de Gobierno' del Archivo General de Indias," in *Archivo General de Indias: El valor del documento y la escritura en el Gobierno de América,* ed. Reyes Rojas García (Madrid: Ministerio de Educación, Cultura y Deporte, 2016), 213–20. In her poem on the AGI from the mid-1920s, Irene A. Wright describes "blue-wrapped bundles, pack on pack," in "The Archives of the Indies at Seville," *Hispanic American Historical Review* 6, no. 1 (1926): 3. On the shelving reforms of the late 1920s, see this volume, chapter 4, 224n171.

64 "una selva confusa": AGI IG 1857B, Diego Suárez to Miguel de Lardizaba, Seville, 1 April 1815.

65 See monthly work summaries scattered throughout AGI IG 1856, and also the discussion in the final section of this volume's chapter 4. On Jovellanos and Ceán Bermúdez in 1801, see Canellas Anoz, "Juan Agustín Ceán-Bermúdez," 55–57; Domínguez y Domínguez-Adame, "Juan Agustín Ceán-Bermúdez," 33–36; and González Santos, "Cronología," 28–30.

66 The earliest document on ROMEU-watermarked paper that I have found is a letter in AGI IG 1857B from Diego Juárez to Juan Estevan Lozano de Torres, 11 November 1818. The paper is also used in a series of payment receipts from late 1818 and early 1819 included in AGI IG 1857B (no. 4, payment to Diego Juárez, 31 December 1818; no. 6, payment to Luis Pérez, 31 December 1818; no. 8, payment to Manuel Águilar Sánchez, 24 December 1818; no. 9, payment to Antonio Lorenzo, 31 December 1818; no. 1, payment to Ventura Collar, 1 April 1819; no. 14, payment to Manuel Águilar Sánchez, 31 March 1819; and no. 18, payment to Francisco García Suárez y Castañeda, 24 April 1819). Other examples of this paper are included in two cardboard-cover ribbon-tied document folders in AGI IG 1858G, labeled "Yndice perteneciente al tomo 1.°" and "Yndice perteneciente al Tomo 2.°."

67 On the patio storage rooms and their 1830 shelving, see AGI IG 1858J, documents in subfolder "Sobre la Obra de la Estanteria." Touristic accounts of these rooms are made in an 1809 letter by William Jacob (*Travels in the South of Spain in Letters Written A.D. 1809 and 1810* [London: J. Johnson and Co., 1811], 79): "the apartments consist of three rooms in front, each one hundred and eighty feet long, and four others, lighted from the patio, of smaller dimensions"; and in an 1844 guidebook by González de León (*Noticia artística,* 89): "Otros ángulos mas hacia el interior, hay tambien con papeles, pero en estantes de otras maderas mas comunes, para lo cual cerraron los arcos que daban al patio dejando un balcon en cada uno que no hace buen efecto con lo magnifico de la obra."

68 Quesada, "Sevilla," 669: "hay multitud de legajos que forman en el piso colosales pilas, porque ya no hay local para ponerlos."

69 Pedro Torres Lanzas, "Archivo General de Indias de Sevilla," in *Guía histórica y descriptiva de los archivos, bibliotecas, y museos arqueológicos de España,* ed. Francisco Rodríguez Marín (Madrid: Tipografía de la "Revista de Archivos, Bibliotecas, y Museos," 1916), 386–87; and Torre Revello, *El Archivo General de Indias,* 38, 435.

70 Torres Lanzas, "Archivo," 384–85, 429–36; and Pedro González García, "Introduction," in *Discovering the Americas: The Archive of the Indies,* ed. Pedro González García (New York: Vendome, 1997), 23.

71 Ministerio de Cultura (Dirección General de Bellas Artes y Archivos), Fundación Ramón Areces, and IBM España, *Proyecto de informatización del Archivo General de Indias* (Torrejón de Ardoz, Madrid: Julio Soto Impresor, 1990), 14, 22.

FIGARO

Scorsi gia molti Paesi	I have passed through many lands
In Madrid io debuttai	I made my debut in Madrid
Feci un Opera, e cascai	I wrote an opera, and failed
E col mio bagaglio addosso	and with a pack on my back
Me ne corsi a più non posso	I ran as fast as I could
In Castiglia, e nella Mancia—	to Castile, and to La Mancha—
Nell'Asturie in Catalogna—	to Asturias to Catalonia—
Poi passai l'Andaluzia—	then I went to Andalusia—
E girai l'Estremadura—	and toured Extremadura—
Come ancor si era Morena—	and also the Sierra Morena—
Ed alfin nella Gallicia;	and finally Galicia;
In un luogo ben accolto.	In one place well received.
E in un altro in lacci avvolto.	And in another hog-tied.
Ma pero di buon umore.	But always in good spirits.
D'ogni evento superior.	Always coming out on top.
Col sol rasojo senza contanti,	With only a razor and no money,
Facendo barbe tirai avanti,	I made my living as a barber,
Or qui in Siviglia fò permanenza	and now I live here in Seville
Pronto a servire vostar Eccellenza,	ready to serve Your Excellency,
Se pur io merito sì grande onor.	if I should merit such a great honor.

COUNT

La tua filosofia è assai giojosa,	Your philosophy is most jolly,

— Giovanni Paisiello (music) and Giuseppe Petrosellini (libretto), *The Barber of Seville*, 1782[1]

CHAPTER 2

THE SOURCE ARCHIVES

In 1779, King Carlos III of Spain commissioned his royal cosmographer, Juan Bautista Muñoz, to write a new history of the Americas. The project was to be Spain's intervention in the Dispute of the New World, a series of anti-Spanish polemics that, over the previous two decades, had developed in a succession of books in French and English. Its most recent installation—William Robertson's *History of America* (1777)—was initially well received in Spain, and Robertson was even elected to Spain's Royal Academy of History. But although a Spanish translation was started, a reviewer took issue with the book's claims, and late in 1778 the translation's publication was blocked.[2]

Muñoz received permission to write his own history six months later, and he began researching right away.[3] He started with a yearlong study of documents in the archives of the Council of the Indies in Madrid. In May 1781, he received royal permission to continue his research elsewhere in Spain.[4] Over the next four years, Muñoz would travel throughout the peninsula, from León to Biscay to Andalusia to Portugal. Thanks to the help of up to six scribal assistants, more than 150 notebooks were filled with copied documents potentially useful for a new history of Spanish America.[5] As Muñoz researched, another idea emerged: centralizing all government documents about the New World in a single archive.[6] Others had imagined such a project before, but Muñoz would make it a reality.

This chapter explores the four main donor archives to the Archive of the Indies, archives Muñoz visited during his first six years of research (see fig. 1.28). They are the office archives of the Council of the Indies in Madrid; the Archive of Simancas (just outside Valladolid); and the divided archive of Spain's House of Trade (which by the 1780s was split between original offices in Seville and new offices in Cádiz). Muñoz had harsh things to say about most of these repositories, and his critiques have been repeatedly cited in studies about the creation of the Archive of the Indies.[7]

But Muñoz was hardly a neutral observer. Before a new Archive of the Indies could be born in Seville, Muñoz had to justify the dismemberment of already existing repositories. It was from their fragments that the new archive would be stocked. Fortunately, the royal cosmographer is not our only source of information for what these other archival spaces were like in the eighteenth century, before their contents were dispersed. Using the descriptions and diagrams of other witnesses, we can reconstruct those older archival spaces in detail—and thus realize that Muñoz's critiques are not as straightforward and reliable as previously assumed.

This chapter follows in Muñoz's footsteps. We begin at the Council of the Indies in Madrid, where Muñoz researched from July 1779 to the summer of 1780. We then travel with him north, to the Archive of Simancas, where Muñoz was based for more than two and a half years: late April 1781 to mid-November 1783.[8] Finally, we go south to Andalusia. Muñoz left Madrid for Seville in late January 1784, and en route he stopped in various archives and libraries, including those of Valdepeñas, Córdoba, and Écija. He arrived in Seville in mid-February 1784, and used the city as a research base for more than nine months. He began by visiting a number of Seville's libraries and manuscript collections, including the archive of the original House of Trade. A month into his stay, on 12 March, Muñoz wrote a letter to the minister of the Indies, José de Gálvez, proposing the creation of a centralized archive for American documents. Gálvez supported the proposal (as noted in the introduction, he had thought about such a project before), and early in June, Muñoz sent a glowing report on the archival potential of Seville's sixteenth-century Lonja. After spending the summer and fall in and around Seville (in late July he traveled to Granada and Málaga), at the end of November the royal cosmographer continued southwest to Cádiz. He was there for over a month, and among other repositories visited the House of Trade's new offices and archive.

Muñoz was back in Seville by 6 February 1785. A few days later, he learned that his plans for implementing a new Archive of the Indies had been officially approved by the king. This was less than a year after he had first written to Gálvez with the idea. What happened next is a story for chapter 3.

MADRID: THE PALACE OF THE COUNCILS

When Muñoz began his research in July 1779, the offices of the Council of the Indies were housed on the western edge of Madrid, in a retrofitted seventeenth-century palace (fig. 2.1). The building was called the Palacio de los Consejos—the Palace of the Councils, plural—because crammed within its walls were the offices of a half dozen royal institutions. The Council of the Indies was joined by the Council of Castile (Consejo de Castilla), the Council of the Chamber of Castile (Consejo de la Cámara de Castilla), the Council of Military Orders (Consejo de las Órdenes Militares), the accounting section of the Council of the Crusade (Consejo de la Cruzada), and, above all, the many departments of the Council of Finance (Consejo de Hacienda).[9]

Although Latin Americanists may be tempted to treat the Council of the Indies in isolation, doing so would be deceptive.[10] The royal councils were conceived as the component parts of a single governing body. "The councils must be studied as an institutional complex, and not as isolated units," writes legal historian Francisco Tomás y Valiente. "Contemporaries studied all the councils as forming part of an indivisible whole."[11] Or, in the words of a seventeenth-century adviser to King Felipe IV: "In them [the Councils] is represented Your Majesty, and you are their Head, and of Your Majesty and these Ministers is constituted one body."[12]

74 CHAPTER 2

FIGURE 2.1
Palace of the Councils, Madrid, July 2017.
Today the Palace of the Councils is divided between the Council of State and the Captaincy General of the Army.

Given this corporate model, the same men sometimes held posts in more than one council at a time,[13] and promotions transferred officeholders from one council to another—such as from the Council of Finance to the Council of the Indies, or from the Council of the Indies to the Council of Castile.[14] During the reorganizations of 1718, for example (about which more below), the Council of the Indies' secretary for New Spain was named secretary of the Council of Military Orders. This reappointment triggered a chain reaction of reappointments throughout the councils as a whole. The newly vacant secretary for New Spain post was filled by the secretary of the Council of the Chamber of Castile, whose post was filled by the secretary for Peru in the Council of the Indies, whose post was filled in turn by the secretary of the Council of Finance.[15] The cohabitation of several royal councils within the Palace of the Councils was therefore not simply a matter of expediency or available real estate. It was the architectural manifestation of a conceptual and functional unity. Indeed, although symbolically appropriate, this cohabitation was not necessarily practical, or comfortable—as we will soon see.

The consular system first developed in the late fifteenth and early sixteenth centuries. Each council averaged around a dozen members, although these numbers could increase or decrease over time. The councils served as advisory bodies to the king. Day-to-day obligations included answering correspondence, discussing policy, making official appointments (from judges to archbishops), and in some cases serving as a final court of appeal for legal disputes. Councils met separately, several times a week.

THE SOURCE ARCHIVES   75

FIGURE 2.2
Louis Meunier (French, ca. 1630–ca. 1680).
Veue de la Court du Palais de Madrid / Vista del primer patio del Palacio de Madrid (View of the first patio of the Palace of Madrid), 1665–68, engraving, 13.3 × 24.3 cm.
Despite inaccuracies of relative scale, architectural details, and printed orientation (this looking-south view should be mirror-reversed so that the triangular clock tower is on the viewer's right), the engraving gives a sense of the palace's Courtyard of the Queen as a dynamic social space.
Madrid, Museo de Historia de Madrid, inv. no. 00001.861.

As a whole, the councils can be divided into two main groups: general and territorial.[16] At the height of the consular system in the early seventeenth century, there were thirteen.[17] General councils were those of the Inquisition (created in 1487), Military Orders (1495), Crusade (1509?), State (1521), War (1522), and Finance (1523). Territorial councils were those of Castile (1480), Aragon (1494), the Chamber of Castile (1518, an offshoot of the Council of Castile), the Indies (1524), Italy (1556), Portugal (1582), and Flanders (1588).[18] When the royal court was more or less permanently established in Madrid in 1561, the offices of most of these councils were set up within the royal palace itself, and specifically in rooms surrounding the Courtyard of the Queen in the eastern half of the building (fig. 2.2). Hidden corridors and screened windows within the palace allowed the king to monitor council meetings unobserved, or to make sudden, unexpected appearances.[19] Two seventeenth-century authors, Gil González Dávila (in 1623) and Antoine de Brunel (in 1665) make clear the way in which the royal palace mingled residences and offices in a manifestation of kingly power:

> In the Western part of Madrid, in what was originally the Royal Castle [Alcaçar Real], the Palace of our illustrious Monarchs is located, which represents—by what one can see from the outside—the greatness and authority of its Ruler, adorned with towers, capitals, doors, windows, balconies, and lookouts. The inside of the Palace is made up

of patios, corridors, galleries, halls, Chapel, Oratories, chambers, privies, parks, gardens, and orchards; from there one can see valleys, rivers, forests, and trees, lingering on the peaks of the Guadarrama and Buytrago Mountains, and that which borders on the Royal Convent of the Escorial. In the principal patios the Councils of Castile, Aragon, State, War, Italy, and Portugal have their offices; and in another to the side the Councils of the Indies, Military Orders, Finance, and Accounting.[20]

In the second patio of the Palace are held, in various Rooms, different Councils: that of the State is held beneath the apartment of the King, where the general good of all of his Realms is dealt with; that of War also meets there, where the means of carrying it out successfully is planned, according to that which has been resolved in that of State; next door is the Council of Castile, which they call *Royal,* and which is of great importance, and it has sixteen Councilors, and one President, many matters from other Councils pass through their hands, and above all those of the Indies, because of the great interests that the people of both Castiles have there. There is one [a Council] for Aragon, Italy has its own, and Flanders also, that of the Indies is held in another place, as well as that of Finances, which they call *de la Hacienda;* another, *de las ordenes,* which deals with the affairs of the Orders of Knighthood, and judges the proofs of Nobility of those who seek it, which meets in the same place as the two previous ones. Of all of these, there is not one which is not within the precinct of the Palace. That of the Inquisition has its Tribunal in the house of the President of the Holy Office. That of the Crusade, which deals with dispensations for eating meat on Saturday, and of similar revenues, which the King controls by authority of the Popes, meets in the house of its President.[21]

That was in Habsburg times. But after the Bourbons emerged triumphant at the end of the War of the Spanish Succession (1701–14), a decision was made (in 1717) to move most council offices to their own building, just to the south. Originally built for the Duke of Uceda from 1613 to 1618, this palace was still owned by the Uceda family, and so was rented from them by the Crown. Like the royal palace itself, the building was rectangular in plan and organized around two internal patios.[22] This physical removal of council offices from the king's residence was, it should be noted, a political displacement. The Bourbons introduced a personalized government of secretariats (focused on individual ministers rather than advisory collectives) that appropriated many of the powers formerly exercised by the councils.[23] Banishing council offices from the royal residence symbolized their reduced importance in Bourbon governmentality.

Their relocation was complicated, but it could have been more so. By the early eighteenth century, the number of councils had decreased. Of the thirteen councils that existed at the beginning of the seventeenth century, only nine remained by the time of the move. The councils of Portugal, Flanders, Aragon, and Italy had all been disbanded (in 1668, 1702, 1707, and 1717).[24] Of the nine councils that were left, only six were relocated. As Antoine de Brunel points out in the quotation above, the Council

THE SOURCE ARCHIVES 77

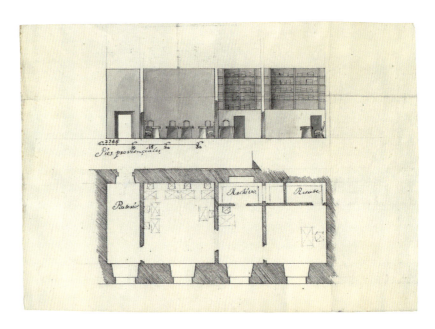

FIGURE 2.3
Joséph Pérez.
Plans for remodeling the rooms of the "Secretaría del Consejo de Estado y Guerra en el palacio del duque de Uceda" (Secretariat of the Council of State and War in the palace of the Duke of Uceda), 1742, ink on paper, 27 × 37.7 cm.
Madrid, Archivo Histórico Nacional, Estado MPD 1121.

of the Inquisition and the Council of the Crusade already had their own buildings. The Inquisition's headquarters were a few blocks to the northeast of the palace, and the Crusade's a few blocks due east—on a street still called Calle de la Cruzada.[25] The Council of State—presided over by the king himself, and closely connected to him—would continue to meet within the royal palace.[26]

So, early in 1717, the councils of Military Orders, War, Finance, Castile, the Chamber of Castile, and the Indies moved to their new quarters. But even this roster was not fixed. Late in 1748, the Council of the Crusade sold its long-established home and relocated most of its offices to a building some distance away (on Calle de Atocha, next to the Convent of La Magdalena). Its accounting department (Contaduría), however, was moved into the Palace of the Councils, where it joined the accounting departments of other councils.[27] In 1774, the Council of War offices (fig. 2.3) were removed to their own building a few blocks to the southeast.[28] Thus, when Juan Bautista Muñoz began his research in 1779, he entered a building that housed, in full or in part, six royal councils: Military Orders, Crusade, Finance, Castile, the Chamber of Castile, and the Indies.

The Palace of the Councils was a complicated space. It had originally been built as a private residence, so figuring out how to fit six councils within its three aboveground floors was a challenge. The first two floors had soaring twenty-one-foot-high ceilings, which meant that in many areas loftlike mezzanines (*entresuelos,* literally "between-floors") could be built to increase available space. Even so, as plans for the move developed, it became apparent that there was no room in the new building for each council's full archives. Therefore, a massive transfer of documents to the Archive of Simancas began in 1718. (This transfer of offices and archives turned out to be lucky:

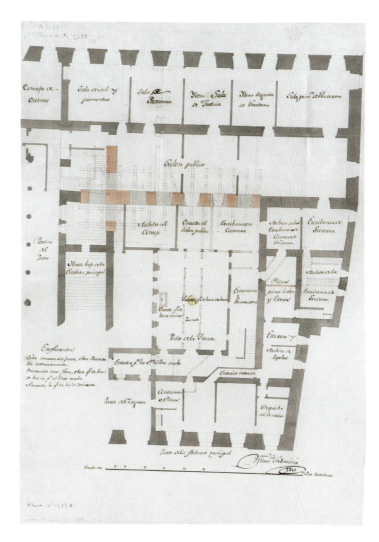

FIGURE 2.4
Francisco Sabatini (Italian, 1721–97).
Plan of the western half of the Palace of the Councils, 1781, ink on paper, 74 × 53 cm.
Red ink indicates target areas for repairs, and dotted lines show a proposed scaffold-support system.
Madrid, Archivo Histórico Nacional, Consejos MPD 1239.

the royal palace burned to the ground in a devastating fire on Christmas Day 1734.) As will be seen below, these transferred documents had not yet been integrated into Simancas's main collections when Muñoz visited in 1781.[29]

The Palace of the Councils still stands, divided between the (new) Council of State (created in 1812) and the Captaincy General of the Army (Capitanía General del Ejercito). The building was damaged in the fascist bombing of Madrid during the Spanish Civil War, and it required extensive reconstruction in the 1940s. Even so, its structural shell survived intact, something that quickly becomes apparent when plans of the building postrestoration are superimposed over plans of the building from the early 1780s (plans drafted when interior walls began to crack under the weight of attic-stored documents; figs. 2.4, 2.5, 2.6).[30] These visual records are complemented by alphabetic records attesting how the palace's floors were divided among its resident councils. One account, dated 11 March 1786, even includes room-by-room measurements.[31] Together, these sources allow us to reconstruct what the Palace of the

THE SOURCE ARCHIVES 79

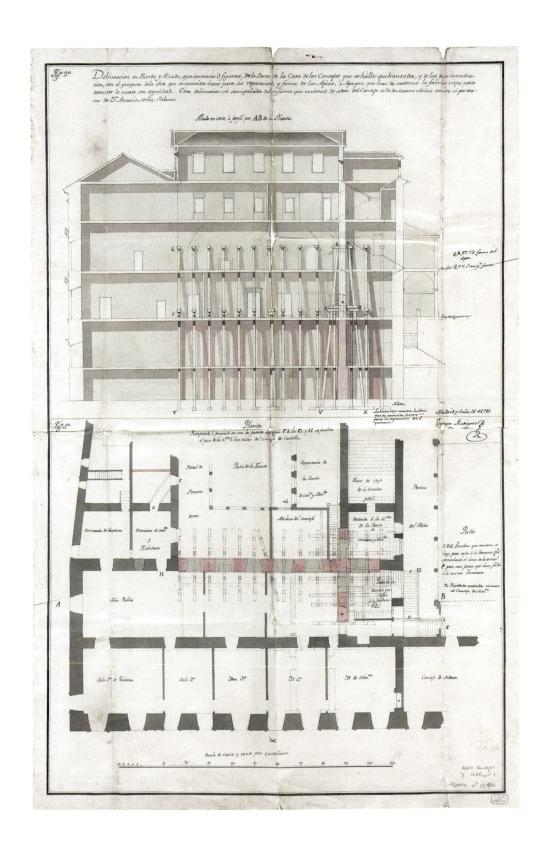

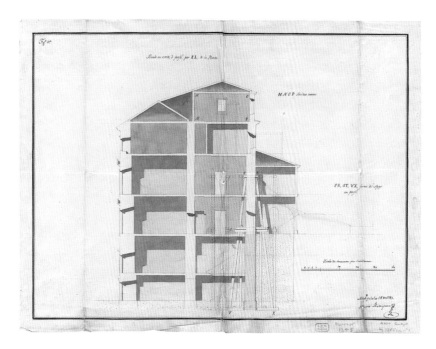

FIGURE 2.5
Ventura Rodríguez (Spanish, 1717–85).
Delineacion en Planta y Alzado, que contiene 3 figuras, de la parte de la Casa de los Consejos que se halla quebrantada, y de las de su inmediacion, con el proyecto de la obra que se necesita hacer para su reparacion, y forma de los Apeos, o Apoyos, que han de sostener la fabrica vieja para executar la nueva con seguridad. Esta delineacion va acompañada del informe que en virtud de orden del Consejo de 30 de Marzo ultimo remito oi por mano de D[o]n Antonio M[a]r[ti]n[e]z Salazar, Fig[ur]a 2ª (Plan and section drawings, in three figures, of the part of the House of the Councils that is damaged, as well as the surrounding areas, with plans for the work needed for repairs, and the structure of the scaffolding, or supports, which have to hold up the old structure in order to carry out the new work safely. This representation is accompanied by a report that, obeying an order by the Council this past 30 March, I turn in today via don Antonio Martínez de Salazar, Figure 2.), 17 July 1781, ink on paper, 98 × 64.4 cm.
Section (viewed looking north) and plan (north at top) of the southwest corner of the Palace of the Councils. As in figure 2.4, red ink indicates target areas for repairs; also indicated are the beams for a proposed scaffold-support system.
Madrid, Archivo Histórico Nacional, Consejos MPD 1244.

FIGURE 2.6
Ventura Rodríguez (Spanish, 1717–85).
Fig[ur]a 3ª (Figure 3), 17 July 1781, ink on paper, 48.5 × 64.6 cm.
Section of the southwest corner of the Palace of the Councils, viewed looking west. As in figures 2.4 and 2.5, red ink indicates target areas for repairs, which are surrounded by the beams for a proposed scaffold-support system.
Madrid, Archivo Histórico Nacional, Consejos MPD 1245.

Councils was like when Muñoz visited in the 1780s (fig. 2.7). Especially important is what these sources reveal about the spatial relations of Council of the Indies offices to those of its neighbors.[32]

The palace is constructed at the top of a southward-sloping hill. This topographic situation means that the main (northern) facade has two stories plus an attic level (see figs. 2.1, 2.7), while the southern facade has a basement, three stories, and an attic (fig. 2.8; see fig 2.6). Two massive granite-framed doorways ornament the front facade. The main entrance to the palace is through the door on the right. Inside was a once-grand entrance hall large enough for a carriage to enter, drop off its occupants, and then continue out through the second massive doorway farther down the facade. By the 1780s, however, this impressive space had been divided into a series of rooms for the building's guards (fig. 2.9).[33] In contrast to the western main-entry door, the eastern door seems to have been sealed off.

Security cleared, visitors continued on to a square room at the base of a monumental flight of stairs up to the first floor. Doors opened to the left and right. A left-hand door led out to the building's largest patio, which had a shaded colonnade running around all four sides. To the north and east of this open space were the main offices of the Council of the Indies. To the south was the Council of Military Orders.[34] By continuing down the western colonnade (that is, heading south), visitors would find (on the right) another stairway, going up and down in square-spiral fashion. Descending, visitors could access the two lower floors, used for the treasury and storage. Ascending, they could access the first and second floors as well as a new attic archive. But before exploring these other levels, let us return to the square entry room, at the base of the monumental staircase, in order to explore the western half of the ground floor.

THE SOURCE ARCHIVES   81

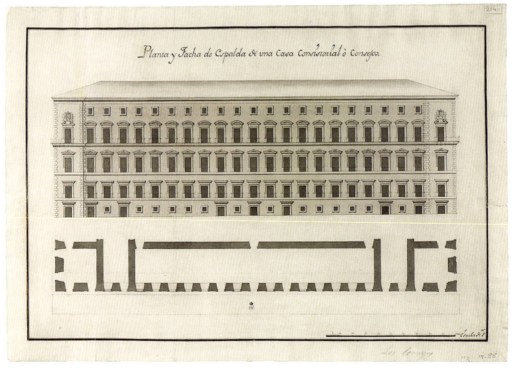

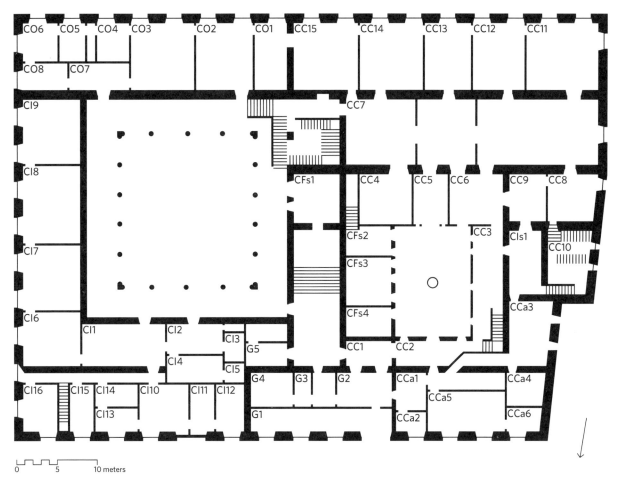

FIGURE 2.7
Fachada principal de la Casa de los Reales Consejos (Front facade of the Palace of the Royal Councils), 1770s, pencil and ink on paper, 23.1 × 35.2 cm. Madrid, Biblioteca Nacional de España, DIB/14/45/3.

FIGURE 2.8
Planta y Fachada de Espalda de una Casa Consistorial ò Consejos (Plan and facade of the back of a consistory or councils building), 1780s (?), ink on paper, 48.2 × 69.3 cm. Madrid, Biblioteca Nacional de España, DIB/15/86/3.

FIGURE 2.9
Reconstruction of room layouts on the ground floor (Calle Mayor level) of the Palace of the Councils in 1786, based on the room-by-room measurements and descriptions of Joséph de la Ballena.
North (and the Calle Mayor) is at the bottom. Most doorway locations are approximate. **G (Guard rooms):** **1** entry, **2** hall, **3** alcove, **4** kitchen, **5** dormitory. **CCa (Council of Castile, Accounting for Chamber Fines and Justice Expenses of the Kingdom):** **1** doorman's room, **2** storage room for charcoal, **3** archive, **4** treasurer's office, **5** officials' workroom, **6** head accountant's office. **CC (Council of Castile): 1** entry, **2** procurator's workroom, **3** procurators' workroom, **4** archive and procurators' workroom, **5** entrance to Public Hall, **6** chamber clerks' office, **7** Public Hall, **8** government chamber clerks' office, **9** archive of government chamber clerks, **10** archive of government clerks, **11** First Hall of Government, **12** Second Hall of Government, **13** Hall of Justice, **14** Hall *de Provincia,* Hall *de Milquinientas.* **CIs (Council of the Indies, secretary of Peru):** **1** storage room for charcoal and mats. **CFs (Council of Finance, secretary of the Committee on Commerce and Money): 1** entry and doorman's room, **2** office, **3** office, **4** office. **CO (Council of Military Orders): 1** chamber scribe's office, **2** Hall of Justice, **3** Hall of Government, **4** attorney's office, **5** archive, **6** treasury, **7** public entry, **8** doorman's room. **CI (Council of the Indies): 1** public entry, **2** pages' and doorman's room, **3** doorman's room, **4** clerks' and scribes' room, **5** small room, **6** chapel, **7** Hall of Justice, **8** First Hall of Government, **9** Second Hall of Government, **10** first accounting room, **11** second accounting room, **12** third accounting room, **13** head official's office, **14** archive, **15** archive, **16** lord accountant's office.

THE SOURCE ARCHIVES   83

By choosing the door to the right of the main staircase, visitors arrived at the entrance room for the offices of the Council of Castile, which filled most of this side of the building's ground floor. Beyond this entrance was a long room filled with tables for procurators (*procuradores,* or "legal paper-pushers," in Kathryn Burns's memorable gloss).[35] There, to the right (that is, to the north) was a door leading to the offices of Accounting for Chamber Fines and Justice Expenses of the Kingdom (Contaduría de Penas de Cámara y Gastos de Justicia del Reyno), a division of the Council of Castile that filled the northwestern corner of the ground floor.[36] To the left, three doors opened onto the patio at the heart of this half of the building. Rectangular instead of square, its center contained the circular basin from which the space got its name: the Patio of the Fountain. Along the patio's western (right-hand) side was a long room filled with more desks for procurators; along its eastern side were offices for the Secretariat of the Committee on Commerce and Money (Secretaría de la Junta de Comercio y Moneda), a section of the Council of Finance. To the south was a small colonnaded space that led to the public hall (*salón público*) of the Council of Castile.

In theory—like the palace's carriageway entrance—this public hall was an impressive, monumental space: 110 feet long, 26 feet wide, with five doorways in its southern wall leading to the Council of Castile's formal chambers: the First Hall of Government, the Second Hall of Government, the Hall of Justice (Sala Primera de Gobierno, Sala Segunda de Gobierno, Sala de Justicia), and two rooms for appeals courts (the Sala de Provincia and Sala de Milquinientos). But by the 1780s, the vast public hall had been subdivided into smaller rooms. A window at the western end of this once-grand space looked out onto Madrid's surrounding countryside. To its left, a door led into the previously mentioned First Hall of Government; to its right, another door led into the scribal offices, archives, and storage spaces that filled the cluster of ground-floor rooms at the center of the building's angled west facade. These rooms belonged to several different councils, as will be seen shortly.

To summarize, most of the palace's ground floor was occupied by the main offices of three councils: the Council of the Indies around the northeast corner, the Council of Military Orders along the eastern half of the southern facade, and the Council of Castile around the Patio of the Fountain in the building's western half. But the ground floor did not provide enough space, so additional offices for these councils were distributed throughout the rest of the building.

The Council of Military Orders had offices on all three aboveground floors. Or, actually, on three *and a half* aboveground floors. The five rooms of Encomienda Accounting (Contaduría de Encomiendas) were packed into a raised mezzanine above its offices in the palace's southwest corner. Offices for the Secretariat of Military Orders (Secretaría de Órdenes Militares) were on the first floor, probably in a suite of rooms centered on the palace's northern facade. Offices for General Accounting of Military Orders (Contaduría General de Órdenes Militares) were on the second floor, and they also seem to have been centered on the northern facade.

Similarly, the Council of the Indies had offices on both the ground and first floors. But while its ground-floor offices were in the building's northeastern corner, its first-floor offices—for the Secretariat of New Spain and the Secretariat of Peru—ran around the building's northwestern corner.[37] In other words, as we just saw for the Secretariat of Military Orders, office distributions within the Palace of the Councils were not vertically consistent. Different parts of different councils occupied different sections of different floors.

Space was at such a premium that sometimes a room belonging to one council was lodged in the midst of rooms belonging to another. This was the case with the storage room ("for placing matting, charcoal, and other furnishings") belonging to the Secretariat of Peru.[38] It was located directly below the secretariat's main first-floor offices in the palace's northwest corner, surrounded by ground-floor archives and workrooms belonging to the Council of Castile. This storage room is even labeled on the plan drawn up by Francisco Sabatini around 1781: *Pieza para Carbon y Esteras* (see figs. 2.4, 2.9-CIs1).

One effect of these irregular distributions—and of the need to cram as many offices as possible into the available space—is that personnel from different councils were constantly interacting with each other. This was to be expected, given that the councils as a whole were imagined as part of a single body, and given that the same men could hold posts on more than one council at a time. But this mixing, and the cheek-to-jowl spatial layout, could also cause problems—of secrecy, for one. Several of the councils ran courtrooms, or otherwise dealt with sensitive information. Controlling this information was difficult in the packed and intermingled bureaucratic offices. A 1785 letter about building new, larger headquarters for the royal councils complained that

> the procurators are scattered throughout the front rooms of all the councils, so that in order to call them to that of Castile, for example, it is often necessary to go look for where they have their tables among all the others; and these, due to the smallness of the space, are found so close one to the other that one hears and sees what others are working on nearby, even without wanting to notice, which many times causes unfortunate consequences for the interested parties, because the subalterns of the Councils, the lawyers, and the other subalterns are mixed with the multitude of people who come together in the front rooms.[39]

Cramped quarters could cause material problems as well. One of the archive rooms for the Council of Castile's Government Chamber Secretariat (Secretaría de Cámara de Gobierno del Consejo de Castilla) was on the ground floor of the palace. Located at the center of the building's angled west-facing facade (to the viewer's right in Francisco Sabatini's floor plan), this *Archivo de la Escribania de Govierno* contained several staircases (see figs. 2.4, 2.9-CC10). These descended to more storage space in the excavated basement, as well as to a mezzanine (*entresuelo*) raised above that basement space. In turn, another mezzanine space was built *above* this ground-floor archive. That room was also an archive: it housed documents for the Secretariat of Peru, and was connected to that secretariat's first-floor offices by another staircase.[40] In other words, there were six interpenetrating spaces in this part of the palace: the Secretariat of Peru offices on the first floor, below which was a mezzanine archive, below which was the archive of the Government Chamber Secretariat on the ground floor, below which was another mezzanine, below which was the basement. Paper is heavy, so the weight of the Secretariat of Peru's mezzanine archive caused problems for the ceiling and walls below. Architect Joséph de la Ballena was brought in to look at the matter in mid-September 1785. He recommended that the mezzanine archive's papers be removed, at least temporarily, so that construction work could be carried out below to reinforce supporting walls in the basement.[41]

Together, these anecdotes (on information control and architectural infrastructure) provide vivid images of the delicate, interconnected ecosystem that was the Palace of the Councils. And so when Juan Bautista Muñoz began to work in this environment in July 1779, where did he go? He certainly spent time in the Secretariat of Peru's mezzanine archive, but this was only one of five archival spaces in that suite of offices. The spacious (thirty-by-twenty-three foot) office of the secretary's head official (*oficial mayor*) contained two small closets for papers, and above this office was built yet another mezzanine archive (measuring seven by thirteen feet). A room next to the office of the lord secretary (*señor secretario*) contained a stairway down to another mezzanine archive, this one housing seventy-five shelves for papers.[42]

An additional stop for Muñoz would have been right next door: just to the north of the Secretariat of Peru were the offices of the Secretariat of New Spain. These contained three archival spaces: one in a corridor-like room measuring twenty-four by six feet, and two more in subfloor mezzanine spaces measuring twenty-six by fourteen feet and thirty-eight by twenty-four feet.[43]

A third destination would have been the archival rooms in the ground-floor offices of the Council of the Indies, which, as just seen, were located on the other, eastern side of the building. To reach them from the (first-floor) Secretariats of Peru and New Spain, Muñoz had a couple of options. From the Secretariat of Peru offices, he could have taken the staircase down to the ground floor (passing the storage room that said secretariat had for matting and charcoal), continued through the Council of Castile offices surrounding the Patio of the Fountain, and then on past the main staircase and into the eastern patio. Alternatively, he could have exited the secretary of New Spain's offices and passed through the offices of the Secretariat of the Chamber and Royal Patronage of Castile (Secretaría de la Cámara y Real Patronato de Castilla, part of the Council of the Chamber of Castile).[44] These offices surrounded, and looked down onto, the Patio of the Fountain: Muñoz would have had to traverse quite a few of them before reaching, at the southeast corner of the patio, the upper landing of the palace's grand stairway. This would bring him down to the ground floor and into the eastern patio.

There, at the far end of the northern colonnade, a door opened on the left. This brought Muñoz into the front entrance room (*pieza de entrada*) for the ground-floor offices of the Council of the Indies. It was sparsely furnished, with four old pine benches, four pine ladders, a door screen, and some maps of the New World.[45] In the eastern wall of this room was another doorway, which led to a series of spacious formal rooms, far better decorated. They followed one after the other north to south along the eastern wall of the palace: the chapel, the Hall of Justice, the First Hall of Government, the Second Hall of Government. All of their east-facing windows were screened with Persian blinds, and all were hung with paintings (a Virgin of Guadalupe, a Santo Toribio of Lima, an Adoration of the Magi). The three halls were well stocked with books, which Muñoz probably consulted: each had at least one copy of the *Recopilación de las Leyes de las Indias* (Compilation of the laws of the Indies) and *Política Indiana* (Governance of the Indies).[46] But to reach the Council of the Indies' archives, he would need to leave the front entry room by another door, in its northern wall. This opened onto a long corridor connecting a series of accounting offices: the first, second, and third rooms (with tables, chairs, and pewter writing sets for bureaucrats), the office of the head official, the office of the lord accountant (*señor contador*), and two smallish archival rooms, each eleven by twenty-two feet. Near them, a flight of stairs led up: they provided access to the largest collection of New World documents in the Palace of the Councils. A mezzanine above the actuarial rooms contained four archival spaces: the first twenty-four by twenty-two feet, the next twelve by twenty-two feet, the third fourteen by twenty-two feet, and the last twenty-five by twenty-two feet. We can imagine documents of interest to Muñoz being brought down for him (and his scribal assistants) to consult and copy in one of the three accounting offices.

All together, the Council of the Indies packed fourteen archival rooms into the floors and mezzanines of the Palace of the Councils. Muñoz and his scribal assistants spent a year consulting the papers therein, and making copies.

What does this reconstruction suggest about the hierarchies and geographies of knowledge within the Palace of the Councils? First, it reveals that the building contained no Europe versus Americas binary. The Council of the Indies and the Council of Castile both had their main offices on the ground floor, along with the Council of Military Orders, and all three councils had additional office spaces extending into floors above and below. The Council of the Indies was not relegated to a marginal space within the building (such as the basement or the uppermost floor). Indeed, given the limitations of space within the palace, it is probably a mistake to argue for any hierarchy based on location. The uppermost floor housed most of the offices and archives of the Council of Finance—hardly an unimportant government body. Close to the Secretariats of New Spain and Peru on the first floor were, as we have seen, offices of the Council of the Chamber of Castile, as well as the Accounting department of the Council of the Crusade. Getting from one suite of offices to another within the same umbrella council meant moving through the spaces, and interacting with the bureaucrats, of those other organizations. There was no Atlantic in the Palace of the Councils.

Muñoz met with a similar situation—a retrofitted building, space at a premium, and a merging (as opposed to segregation) of New and Old World spaces—the following year, when he traveled north to Simancas.

FIGURE 2.10
The Archive of Simancas, viewed from the southwest, July 2019.
The corner tower to the viewer's right housed the Chamber of Works and Forests. Its brick addition rises up out of the earlier stone crenellations.

SIMANCAS: THE ARCHIVE OF SIMANCAS

The castle that now houses the Archive of Simancas was originally built in the fifteenth century. Its current appearance is due to extensive sixteenth-century renovations that transformed the fortress into a place for housing documents (fig. 2.10).

The idea of using the castle as an archive dates to the summer and early fall of 1540. In a letter from 26 June, royal secretary Francisco de los Cobos mentioned plans to establish the Simancas archive later that summer; on 16 September, Emperor Carlos V issued a royal decree for documents to be sent there.[47] At first, only part of the castle was to be used as an archive: the top of the northeast tower, where, in 1543, an extra level—in brick—was added for document storage. This material contrast is still visible today (fig. 2.11).[48] A number of royal orders commanding the sending of documents were issued in 1543 and 1544: on 19 February 1543 for an archive in the castle of La Mota in Medina del Campo; on 11 February 1544 for Privileges of Nobility from the Monastery of San Benito in Valladolid; and on 30 June 1544 for documents on the Americas in possession of the Council of the Indies' Secretary Juan

88 CHAPTER 2

FIGURE 2.11
The Archive of Simancas, looking northeast from within the castle's walls, July 2019.
At center is the tower with a brick addition for the Chamber of Works and Forests.

de Sámano, as well as those in Seville's House of Trade. In terms of personnel, the first archival officials for Simancas were named on 5 May 1545.[49] And although papers were not always transferred when requested, one thing is clear: from the very beginning, the Archive of Simancas was to house documents from throughout Carlos V's empire, not simply his possessions in Iberia.

The next major transformation of Simancas took place thirty years later, during the reign of Felipe II. Starting in 1575, construction work began to turn the entire castle into an archival space. In part, expansion was needed because documents had continued to arrive in Simancas, so many that one tower was not enough to hold them. But in addition, the very conception of Simancas had changed. Carlos V saw the archive as dedicated, above all, to documents establishing his personal authority. In contrast, his son Felipe II had a much broader vision. Simancas would be the depository for *all* documents generated by the royal bureaucracy, not simply those related to the prestige and privileges of the king.[50] Indeed, Felipe II even imagined that other, private archives might be incorporated into Simancas: at one point he described the building as an archive "for my said kingdoms and vassals" (*a los dichos mis reinos y vasallos*).[51]

This changing documentary vision is reflected in the castle's spatial layout. The archive had its origins at the top of the northeast tower: the brick-walled chamber built by Carlos V. Felipe II was not indifferent to the importance of documents supporting his royal authority, and so in the 1570s renovations, directly beneath his father's archive, he added his own two-story archive for documents of Royal Patronage: *Patronazgo Real*. But in addition, surrounding this anchoring tower were new rooms created on the castle's northern and eastern sides to house less-exalted papers.[52] In turn, the castle's western side (at least on the two lower floors) was converted into

THE SOURCE ARCHIVES 89

offices as well as the residence of the live-in archivist. Finally, the archive's southern side, where the main entrance is located, was divided between offices and document storage.[53]

The renovations took more than a decade, and in 1578, architect Juan de Herrera (hard at work building Felipe's Escorial monastery-palace far to the south) was brought in to revise the plans. New documents continued to arrive during construction.[54] In 1588—although the renovation work was not yet finished—a thirty-point list (*Instrucción*) of guidelines for running the archive was written, a list that, three centuries later, would inspire a similar set of *Ordenanzas* for the Archive of the Indies.[55] Around this time, a cutaway diagram of the renovated archive was drafted. It perfectly represents the two-part conception of the archive's holdings (fig. 2.12). To the left, in its own tower, are the documents of Royal Patronage (*patronadgo*). But most of the building's floors are taken up with more mundane documentation: "of the Indies" (*de Indias*) on the topmost floor, and below it, "accounting of finances and accounts" (*contadurias de hazienda y cuentas*).

Over the next three centuries, documents continued to arrive at Simancas.[56] One of the most important additions took place starting in 1718. As seen in the previous

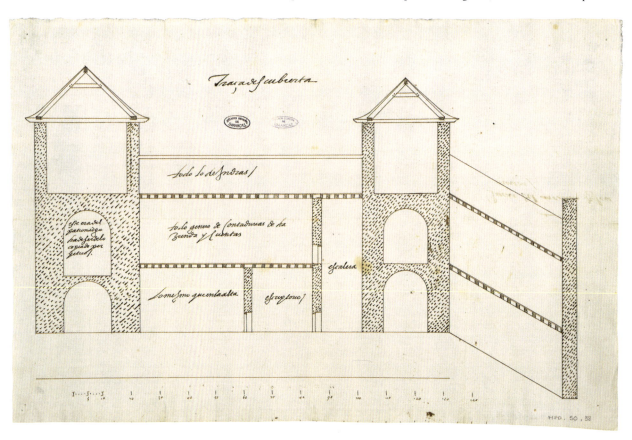

90 CHAPTER 2

section, in 1717 King Felipe V decided to move the offices of his royal councils out of the royal palace and into the Palace of the Councils nearby.[57] But since space was at a premium in those new lodgings, a great deal of documentation from the councils was sent on to Simancas. This transfer was not simply a functionalist question of floor space; it was also a way for the new Bourbon regime to distance itself, in a literal and material way, from the historical weight of Habsburg governmental precedent. The dating of these transferred documents is also significant: they were from before 1700—that is, prior to the War of the Spanish Succession and Bourbon ascendancy.[58]

On their arrival at Simancas, these new shipments—perhaps because of their sheer scale—were not integrated into the already existing archival spaces, but simply put together in a room of their own. And so when Juan Bautista Muñoz visited sixty years later, these papers were easily distinguished: "it seems that no more work had been done than shelving, where possible, the documents that were sent from the court on various occasions since the time of Felipe II until 1718. Only those of the ultimate shipment were in a separate room, well ordered."[59]

This brings us to Muñoz's famous and much-cited complaints about the Archive of Simancas. Some four months into his stay, on 18 August 1781, Muñoz wrote this damning description to José de Gálvez:

> It is incredible the confusion that rules in a large part of the documents, especially in the large room called Government.... The interest with which I look at some very important documents, and the sadness to see the majority of them badly placed in this large room of the Indies, which although it has the name and appearances of a Hall is nothing more than a garret exposed to the elements of all the seasons, encouraging polecats and other pests.[60]

Muñoz researched at Simancas for two years, until late March 1783.[61] That fall, on 28 November 1783, he wrote this unflattering recollection from Madrid:

> I examined the archive of Simancas, and almost immediately was met with a bountiful harvest [of documents], but so entangled and disorganized that, honestly, it seemed impossible to avoid darkness and confusion in the notes and extracts, without first undertaking a detailed study of that great pile of papers, separating the useful ones, and organizing them by dates and subjects.[62]

Time did not mellow his opinions. He penned these recollections on 3 August 1787:

> I went to Simancas in April of 1781, and I found the papers of the Indies badly stored, most of them in a large room in the attic. Most notable was the confusion and disorder with which most of them were placed. It seemed that nothing more had been done than store wherever possible the documents that had been sent from the Royal Court on various occasions since the time of Felipe II up until 1718. Only those from the last shipment were in a separate room, neatly ordered. The rest were divided more or less in two sections: to one side, those related to Justice, that is, lawsuits, residencies,

FIGURE 2.12
Traça descubierta (section drawing) of spaces within the Archive of Simancas, 1589, ink on paper, 33 × 50.5 cm.
Simancas, Archivo General de Simancas, MPD L-38.

FIGURE 2.13
Ventura Rodríguez (Spanish, 1717–85).
Elevation drawing of the castle viewed from the south, 1762, pencil and ink on paper, 46.5 × 66.2 cm. From *Descripción Geométrica del Real Archivo de Simancas* (Scaled drawings of the Royal Archive of Simancas), no. 1.
Madrid, Biblioteca Nacional de España, DIB/14/6/6.

inspections, and reports; to the other side, all the rest, which under the general name of "Government" presented a confused miscellany.[63]

On the surface, this all sounds very bad. Fortunately, Muñoz is not our only source of information on the Archive of Simancas in the eighteenth century. Extended descriptions were penned by four other visitors, in 1726, 1749, 1751, and 1791. Visual documentation also survives: a set of amazing sections and floor plans drafted by Ventura Rodríguez in 1762 (figs. 2.13–2.15, 2.17–2.20), as well as plans for a never-built expansion by Juan de Villanueva in 1774 (see figs. I.10–I.13). Finally, the Archive of Simancas houses alphabetic documentation on the history of its own physical upkeep.[64] Together, these sources allow us to reevaluate Muñoz's accusations. They also enable us to tour the eighteenth-century building. Our main guides will be Francisco Nangle's report from 1749 and Ventura Rodríguez's drawings from 1762, which are in close and overlapping agreement. These will be supplemented with Santiago Agustín Riol's report from 1726 and José Marcos's account from 1751. Once we have toured the castle, we will be in a better position to judge Muñoz's critiques of it.

92 CHAPTER 2

FIGURE 2.14
Ventura Rodríguez (Spanish, 1717–85).
Plan of the ground floor, 1762, pencil and ink on paper, 46.5 × 66.2 cm.
From *Descripción Geométrica del Real Archivo de Simancas* (Scaled drawings of the Royal Archive of Simancas), no. 2.
Key: **1** Bridge over the moat, which provides the main entrance to the archive. **2** Door and front room of the said entrance. **3** Door to the patio. **4** General Court Registry. **5** Business of Naples, Milan, and Sicily, etc. **6** The same. **7** Room for Inspections from the Kingdom of Naples, Sicily, and the State of Milan. **8** General Court Registry. **9** The same. **10** Tower of books of contracts and general Chamber books. **11** Main staircase to the most important rooms. **12** Staircase for the living quarters of the archivist. **13** Rooms for the said living quarters on this lower floor. **14** Bridge of the Fountain of the King, which provides a secondary entrance to the archive. **15** Outer bailey.
Madrid, Biblioteca Nacional de España, DIB/14/6/7.

In the past as in the present, the archive is reached by crossing a bridge over the building's deep moat (see fig. 2.14-1), and then turning left (west) to the colonnaded main entrance (see fig. 2.14-2).[65] There, visitors pass into a tower room (on the right), through impressive wooden doors, and finally into a squarish room that opens onto a colonnade at the southern end of the castle's central patio (see fig. 2.14-3). The main archival spaces of the building are to the north and east (that is, directly in front of the visitor, and to the right). The residence of the archivist took up the first two levels on the west side of the castle (that is, to the visitor's left).

Following in the steps of Francisco Nangle, who visited the castle in late summer of 1749, we turn right in the patio's colonnade, and enter the wide doorway that opens onto the castle's main staircase (see fig. 2.14-11). But we do not ascend right away. To our left and right are doorways, and we choose the one on the right. This brings us to a suite of three rooms in the castle's southeast corner (all paved in "fine brick," wrote Santiago Agustín Riol in 1726).[66] The first (see fig. 2.14-4), its walls lined with brick and plaster shelving, houses "various books of the General Court Register, and some bundles of papers from the Secretariat of State."[67] A door in the east wall leads

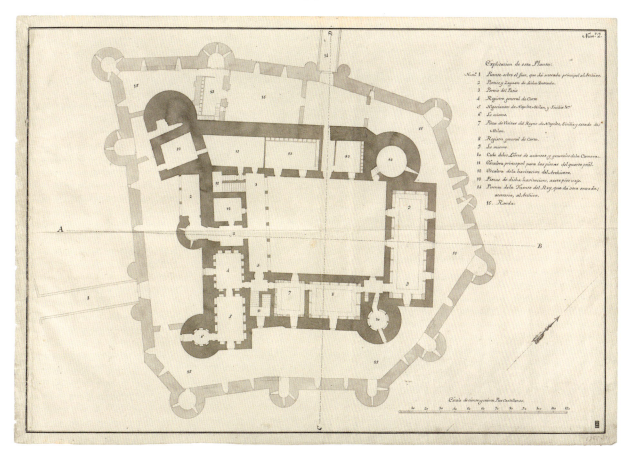

THE SOURCE ARCHIVES 93

to the next room (see fig. 2.14-5), which houses more papers from the Secretariat of State, as well as papers from the provincial Secretariats of Flanders, Portugal, and Italy (specifically, "Naples, Milan, and Sicily").[68] According to José Marcos, who visited in 1751, this was also the place where the shipments of documents sent from Madrid in 1718 were stored.[69] There is a window in the eastern wall; a door to the right leads to a final room, a circular space in the base of a tower (see fig. 2.14-6). It contains more Secretariat of State documents.

Nangle then retraces his steps back to the main staircase (see fig. 2.14-11) and takes the door to the left. Beyond is a square room with windows east and west (see fig. 2.14-7). More state papers are here: both Riol and Rodríguez specify them as *visitas* for Naples, Milan, and Sicily.[70] The next room is rectangular, lined with shelves closed by wood-framed metal grille doors (see fig. 2.14-8). More General Court Registry documents are here, as well as (at least in 1749) paperwork from the Royal Council of Castile.[71] Next—we have been moving south to north through this suite of rooms—is a small antechamber. Just beyond a narrow flight of ascending stairs is the door to a round tower room (see fig. 2.14-10). Books from the Chamber of Castile are stored there: "libros de asientos, y generales de la Camara." In 1749, these included documents about Navarre as well as about the conquest of Granada.[72]

Returning to the antechamber, we continue north through a door that leads to one of the largest and most impressive rooms in the archive: "truly royal and magnificent for its beauty, spaciousness, and light."[73] Its ceiling is two stories high (see fig. 2.14-9). Its walls are lined with wooden cases, and a wooden walkway provides access to documents in the upper level. More General Court Registry documents are here, and in 1726 Riol was unstinting in his praise: "separated and arranged by month.... These books or registers of the seal are not only the most complete that exist in the Archive but also the most precious mineral from which one can extract (as I have extracted) most precious information."[74]

Rejoining Nangle, we go back to the antechamber and ascend its narrow flight of stairs. These lead to the most famous chamber within the archive (see fig. 2.15-7).[75] An inscription painted black-on-white above the entrance declares its holdings: *Patronazgo Real.*[76] On entering, we find ourselves inside a two-story cylinder of dark wooden doors, the upper level reached by a walkway, and above everything an elaborately carved wooden ceiling. The geography of its contents is the geography of the Spanish Empire. There are documents on Crown authority over religious institutions (*Patronazgo*) for the Indies, Granada, and Iberia as a whole. There are treaties (*capitulaziones*) with Italy, with Muslims and knights in Castile, with Aragon, Navarre, Portugal, England, France, the House of Austria.

Leaving the tower, we continue to explore this new level of the archive. To the right (that is, to the north) a door opens onto the walkway that runs around the second level of the General Court Registry room (see fig. 2.15-6; see also fig. 2.14-9). To the left, we enter a long rectangular room almost as large (see fig. 2.15-5). On the western wall, two windows open out onto the building's central patio. They are mirrored

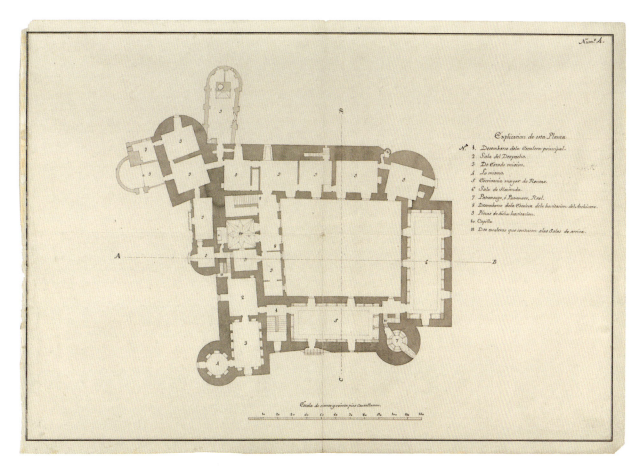

FIGURE 2.15
Ventura Rodríguez (Spanish, 1717–85).
Plan of first floor, 1762, pencil and ink on paper, 46.5 × 66.2 cm.
From *Descripción Geométrica del Real Archivo de Simancas* (Scaled drawings of the Royal Archive of Simancas), no. 4.
Key: **1** Landing of main staircase. **2** Office. **3** State correspondence. **4** The same. **5** Main accounting of rents. **6** Room for Accounting. **7** Royal Patronage. **8** Landing for the staircase of the living quarters of the archivist. **9** Rooms of the said living quarters. **10** Chapel. **11** Two staircases that lead to the upper rooms.
Madrid, Biblioteca Nacional de España, DIB/14/6/9.

by two openings on the eastern wall: one is a window, and the other leads out to a small iron-enclosed balcony. The room itself is lined with shelves, which store economic documents described as "General Accounts" (*Contadurías Generales*), according to Nangle in 1749; and "Main Accounting of Rents" (*Escrivania mayor de Rentas*), according to Rodríguez in 1762.[77]

A door in the southern wall leads out to the upper landing of the archive's main staircase; straight ahead, another door leads to a suite of three offices that echo the layout of the rooms below. All have soaring two-story ceilings. The first (see fig. 2.15-2) houses the winter offices, located above ground for additional warmth during the coldest months of the year. This is where the main archivist works, and a long table enables approved visitors to consult and copy documents.[78] Shelves on the wall house the archive's dozens of finding aids.

Dominating the eastern wall is an elaborate doorway topped by the coat of arms of Felipe II and a carved inscription: PATRONAZGO REAL (fig. 2.16). Given that, as just seen, the main collection of documents related to royal patronage was always kept in the castle's northeast tower, this ornate entrance has been perplexing.[79] In the

THE SOURCE ARCHIVES 95

FIGURE 2.16
Entrance to Royal Patronage (Patronazgo Real), Archive of Simancas, ca. 1930.
Archivo ABC, Reference Number 4482994.

FIGURE 2.17
Ventura Rodríguez (Spanish, 1717–85).
Plan of second floor, 1762, pencil and ink on paper, 46.5 × 66.2 cm.
From *Descripción Geométrica del Real Archivo de Simancas* (Scaled drawings of the Royal Archive of Simancas), no. 6.
Key: **1** Landings of the two stairways that provide access to this floor. **2** Room for the Council of War. **3** Room for the Council of War, of the Secretariat for Sea and Land. **4** The same. **5** General accounts departments. **6** Tower of Aragon. **7** Walkways for rooms 5 and 6 on the main floor. **8** The same for the tower of Royal Patronage. **9** Space above the main staircase. **10** Spaces above rooms 2, 3, and 4 of the main floor. **11** Accounts office. **12** Space above the chapel. **13** Rooms for the living quarters of the archivist.
Madrid, Biblioteca Nacional de España, DIB/14/6/11.

eighteenth century, the room beyond held state papers (see fig. 2.15-3).[80] It is impressively appointed. The floor is paved in black and white jasper, the ceiling is vaulted, and the walls are lined with open shelving, which allows the well-archived documents to literally *shine:* "they do not have doors, and this makes it [the room] brighter, because of the uniformity or placement of the documents, each one with a very white paper wrapping, and their labels all of the same size, which is delectable to the eye. To the east is a very large window that fills it [the room] with light."[81] Beyond, in the castle's southeast tower, are more state archives (see fig. 2.15-4).

Back in the winter office, a small doorway in the northwest corner opens onto a narrow flight of stairs. Going down, they lead to the building's chapel (see fig. 2.15-10) and to the upper level of the extensive suite of rooms where the archivist lived (see fig. 2.15-9; see also fig. 2.14-13 for his rooms on the ground floor). But we, following Nangle, instead take the stairs up to the next level (see fig. 2.17). To the left, in a squarish room in one of the castle's towers, is the archive's pay office (*pagaduría;* see fig. 2.17-11).[82] To the right and down a few steps is a room housing papers from the Secretariat of War (Secretaría de Guerra), mixed—at least in 1749—with documents pertaining

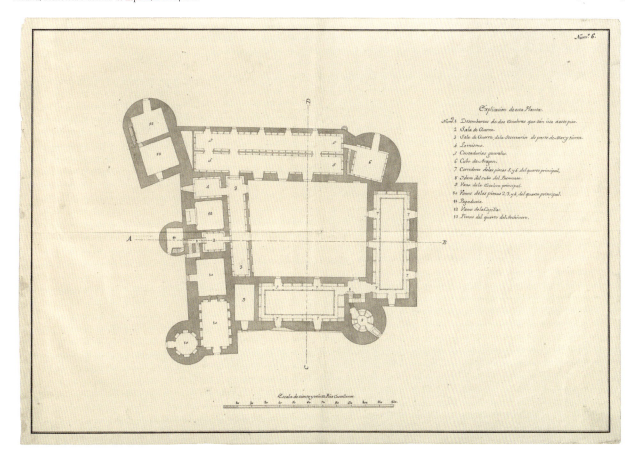

THE SOURCE ARCHIVES 97

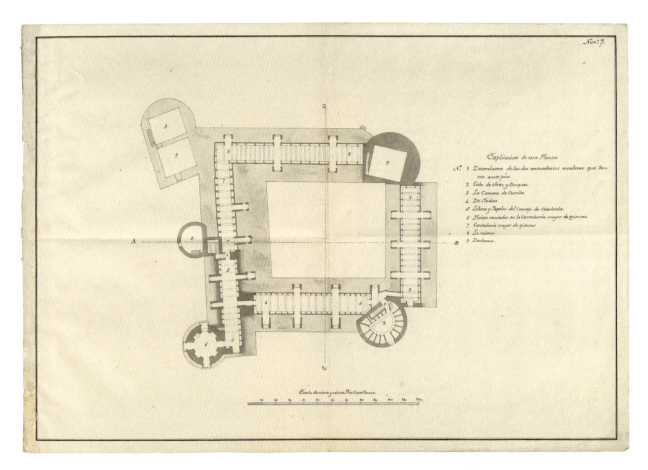

FIGURE 2.18
Ventura Rodríguez (Spanish, 1717–85).
Plan of attic, 1762, pencil and ink on paper, 46.5 × 66.2 cm.
From *Descripción Geométrica del Real Archivo de Simancas* (Scaled drawings of the Royal Archive of Simancas), no. 7.
Key: **1** Landings for the two stairways that provide access to this floor. **2** Tower of Works and Forests. **3** The Chamber of Castile. **4** Of the Indies. **5** Books and papers of the Council of Finance. **6** Lawsuits presented in the Main Finance Office. **7** Main Accounting Office. **8** The same. **9** Spaces above rooms on the lower floors.
Madrid, Biblioteca Nacional de España, DIB/14/6/12.

to don Juan de Austria (Felipe II's illegitimate brother) and the Committee of Works and Forests (Junta de Obras y Bosques) (see fig. 2.17-2).[83] A door in the northern wall leads to a long, narrow gallery overlooking the patio (see fig. 2.17-3). More Secretariat of War documents are here: specifically, from the Secretariat of Sea and Land (Secretaría de Mar y Tierra), although in 1749 Nangle reported that the room also housed documents from the Secretariats of the Indies.[84]

In the room's western far end, a door in the southern wall leads to yet more Secretariat of War storage (see fig. 2.17-4). A door in the western wall opens onto a massive gallery, larger than any we have yet encountered. Its walls are lined with shelves, and another row of shelving (according to Rodríguez's drawing) divides the room in two (see fig. 2.17-5). The shelves store documents on general accounting (*contadurías generales*).[85] Continuing north down the length of the room leads to a square two-story chamber in the castle's northwest tower, containing documents for the Kingdom of Aragon (see fig. 2.17-6). There is no exit from here, so we must retrace our steps back to the small staircase that led to the pay office (see figs. 2.17-1, 2.17-11). Continuing up, the stairs bring us to the attic level of the castle.

Located within the castle's slanted roof, the rooms here are in general quite narrow but extremely long. The first spans the castle's southern side, split into eastern and western halves at the top of the stairs just climbed (see fig. 2.18-1).[86] The room to the east (reinforced with metal bars still visible today) houses documents from the Council of Finance (see fig. 2.18-5).[87] A tower room at its far end contains fiscal lawsuits: from the Council of Finance, according to Nangle; and from the Main Accounting Office (Contaduría Mayor de Cuentas), according to Rodríguez (see fig. 2.18-6).[88] The eastern end of this long gallery holds more documents from the Main Accounting Office (see fig. 2.18-7), which continues down the gallery of the castle's western roof (see fig. 2.18-8). This has no exit, so we must return to the gallery of the metal bars and follow a narrow corridor in its northern wall, which leads us to a long room running the length of the archive's eastern roof. Here are the papers of both the Council and Secretariat of the Indies (see fig. 2.18-4). At the far northern end is the oldest archival space within the castle: the brick-walled, wood-shelf-lined Chamber of Works and Forests (Cubo de Obras y Bosques) created by Carlos V in the early 1540s (see fig. 2.18-2; see also fig. 2.11).[89] And beyond that, running the length of the castle's northern side, is storage for the Council of the Chamber of Castile (see fig. 2.18-3).[90]

FIGURE 2.19
Ventura Rodríguez (Spanish, 1717–85).
Section drawing of the castle across line C–D of the plans, looking northeast, 1762, pencil and ink on paper, 46.5 × 66.2 cm.
From *Descripción Geométrica del Real Archivo de Simancas* (Scaled drawings of the Royal Archive of Simancas), no. 3.
Madrid, Biblioteca Nacional de España, DIB/14/6/8.

FIGURE 2.20
Ventura Rodríguez (Spanish, 1717–85).
Section drawing of the castle across line A–B of the plans, looking northwest, 1762, pencil and ink on paper, 46.5 × 66.2 cm.
From *Descripción Geométrica del Real Archivo de Simancas* (Scaled drawings of the Royal Archive of Simancas), no. 5.
Madrid, Biblioteca Nacional de España, DIB/14/6/10.

Our tour concludes here (see figs. 2.19, 2.20). It isn't easy to get out—this was one reason Carlos V chose to establish his original archive on this level, for security—and so we must walk back down the gallery of the Indies, turn right into the gallery of the Council of Finance, descend two flights of narrow stairs to the winter office, and, finally, descend the much wider staircase that returns us to the castle's patio on the ground floor.

The first thing our tour reveals—assembled as it was from accounts in 1726, 1749, 1751, and 1762—is that spaces within the archive had fairly stable identities over the course of the eighteenth century (and in some cases back to the sixteenth, as the 1589 diagram shows). This is not surprising: paper is heavy, bulky, and hard to move, and there was a limited amount of space in the castle. (Expansion plans were drawn up in 1774, as mentioned earlier, but they were never built.) Such organizational stability allows us to move forward in time, from 1762 to 1781, to reconsider the influential vision of Simancas that Muñoz left for posterity.

What do we make of his complaint that the documents of the Indies were badly stored in an "attic" or "garret"—a space exposed to the elements? Well, it certainly is true that one of the attic rooms in the castle was dedicated to documents *de Yndias*. This had been true since the sixteenth century, as the 1589 diagram shows (see fig. 2.12). However, these were not the only documents stored in the castle's uppermost story. The room beyond Indies storage was dedicated to documents from the Council of the Chamber of Castile (that is, documents about central Spain), and between these Indian and Iberian rooms was the brick-walled Chamber of Works and Forests—the very first archival room built into the castle when Carlos V decided to gather archives there in the 1540s. In other words, documents about the Indies were indeed stored in the attic, but they were not alone: documents about Europe were in the attic as well. The attic was not a marginal space within the Simancas archive. On the contrary, it was the highest—and therefore most secure—level within the castle.[91] It was the level where the archive first began.

Ventura Rodríguez's drawings from 1762 reveal that the attic's roof was pierced with a number of windows for light (see figs. 2.19, 2.20). Apparently these were leaking when Muñoz visited in 1781, exposing documents to the elements. Was this not a clear sign of neglect? Again, things are not so simple. Windows are always a point of weakness in a building. This is as true in 2022 as it was in 1781. Windows need constant upkeep, if not replacement, every few years. In the eighteenth century, the windows at Simancas were replaced about every decade. When Francisco Nangle visited the castle in the summer of 1749, he wrote up a list of necessary repairs, including the windows—repairs carried out that fall by Ambrosio Marnara.[92] When Rodríguez drew his carefully labeled plans of the castle in 1762, he also made a list of repairs needed on the roof, doors, and windows, and these renovations were made over the next two years. Not quite a decade later, in 1770, the castle's windows again needed replacing, and Isidoro Álvarez was brought in to do the work, along with carpenter Agustín Redondo. And so when Muñoz visited Simancas a decade later, in 1781, the windows (not surprisingly) yet again needed repair, repairs carried out in 1782.[93] Another decade later, in May 1791, money for the general upkeep of roof, doors, and windows was provided to archivist Manuel de la Cruz. When Gaspar Melchor de Jovellanos visited the archive that fall, on 1 October, he praised the "good repairs" (*buenas reparaciones*) recently carried out.[94]

Thus what Muñoz presents as scandalous architectural neglect is instead simply the timing of his visit relative to an established schedule of repairs every decade or so. That said, it certainly would have been better to inspect and repair the archive's roof every year—archivist Manuel de Ayala y Rosales suggested this in 1784—and so in 1792, just after Jovellanos's visit, funds were (finally) provided to the archive for annual maintenance.[95] Note that two years before, an annual roof inspection for the Archive of the Indies was mandated in its 1790 *Ordenanzas*. The AGI's account books make clear that this decree was enforced. Every year, an architect was paid to inspect the roof.[96]

Muñoz's complaints about disorder and disrepair also distract from a more basic structural feature of the Archive of Simancas. Since the archive's foundation, documents about the history of the Americas had been housed in the same building as documents about the history of Europe: there was a room for documents from the Indies, another for documents from Castile, another for Aragon, but also rooms for Naples, Sicily, and Milan. In some cases, documents about European history and American history were stored in the same rooms. Occasionally, this may reflect a temporary solution; for example, in 1749, Francisco Nangle wrote that documents from the Secretariats of the Indies were stored in the same room as documents for the Council of War's Secretariat of Sea and Land, but only the Secretariat of Sea and Land was listed by Rodríguez in 1762 (see fig. 2.17-3). However, in other cases, the structural mixing of European and American documents in the same room, in the same documentary category, was intentional, even fundamental. The most important example of this was the room for Royal Patronage. Like the room it inspired in the Archive of the Indies, this room was filled with documents related to royal privileges. In Simancas, these were documents about privileges both in Europe *and* the Americas, stored together. But when the Archive of the Indies was created, the contents of this tower room were dismembered. American documents were sifted out and sent to Seville, and the Simancan tower was left to focus on documents about Europe alone.

Indeed, as already seen at the Palace of the Councils, the very governance of Spain's empire did not always respect sharp divisions between the Old World and the New. This intermixing also contributed to documentary "confusions" at Simancas. From 1590 to 1610, Juan de Ibarra was secretary for both the Council of the Indies and the Committee of Works and Forests—a committee that oversaw the maintenance of royal properties, from palaces to woodlands.[97] Official paperwork was removed from Ibarra's house upon his death, and eventually made its way to the brick-walled tower built by Carlos V. A mixing of texts about woodlands in Castile and territories in the New World would not have bothered Carlos V, had he been alive, and the overlapping of these subjects was part of Juan de Ibarra's daily experience for twenty years. But such a combination was intolerable for Enlightenment archivists, who in the spring of 1785 worked to purify Simancas's brick-walled tower of its New World contents and send them on to the new archive in Seville.[98]

SEVILLE: THE HOUSE OF TRADE

Starting in mid-February 1784, Muñoz spent fourteen months in Andalusia. First in Seville and later in Cádiz, he visited the divided archives of the Casa de la Contratación: the New World House of Trade.

As discussed in the previous chapter, the House of Trade was founded in Seville in 1503 and occupied an ever-expanding suite of offices in the northwest corner of the royal palace.[99] Official trade with and travel to the New World was regulated by the Crown, so House of Trade officials oversaw all aspects of these transatlantic connections: sending and receiving royally monopolized merchandise (including the Royal Fifth of precious metals and jewels owed to the king), compiling and drafting maps, running a courtroom to judge trade disputes, and safeguarding documents (such as shipping registers, the testaments of men and women who died in the Americas, or the paperwork generated by the House of Trade's own courtroom). In 1718, the new Bourbon government transferred Spain's center for New World shipping—and the House of Trade as well—to Cádiz. Nevertheless, the House of Trade offices in Seville were not entirely abandoned. A skeleton crew remained, including an archivist who oversaw the documentary collections not sent to the coast.[100]

In contrast to his account of the Archive of Simancas (and to his account of the House of Trade offices in Cádiz, as will be seen in the next section), Muñoz says very little about the architectural surroundings that housed what was left of Seville's House of Trade archive. Perhaps he wished to avoid any risk of lèse majesté: he was a royally appointed cosmographer working on a royally approved history of the New World, and his critical accounts of the then-current state of Spain's archives were meant to reach King Carlos III. Critiquing the physical fabric of archival offices located in one of the king's palaces was probably not prudent.[101] Muñoz also seems to have wanted to stay in the good graces of archivist Manuel de Zuazo y Yañez. This man's help would be needed to transfer the Seville House of Trade documents to the new Archive of the Indies a block away, and also—more importantly—to reintegrate those documents with their companions from Cádiz. Indeed, Zuazo had been calling for this reunion for several decades (although he assumed documents would return to the Sevillian palace).[102] Thus, instead of interrogating the architecture, Muñoz's account of the House of Trade in Seville (written on 8 June 1784, four months after his arrival) focuses on the state of the documents themselves, and the hardships they had undergone before the tenure of the then-current archivist:

> More attention is merited to that which is said, with great accuracy, about the sorry state of many papers, and one could add the absence of others: if only it were possible to repair these damages, or prevent them in the future with an exemplary punishment. But there is no suspect against whom one could establish a lawsuit. I found that in various books the blank pages had been besmirched with doodles and other games of the pen, which are clearly from the previous century: and one can believe anything possible from someone who would treat public papers this way. Many of them were no doubt burned in the repeated fires that took place in the House during that era, and of which today remain vestiges in various singed books. I leave aside wormholes, mildew, and other injuries of time, especially from the aforementioned period of ignorance and neglect.
>
> In the present century, with its new light and Letters, such public papers have been viewed with more interest and love. And I know for certain that those of the House and Court of Trade have received notable benefit with the creation of the office of the Archivist, which according to all evidence has been praisefully exercised by the Zuazos, father [Joséph de Zuazo y Castillo] and son [Manuel de Zuazo y Yañez].[103] This one [Manuel], who has served for forty-four years, seems to me a man of honor, and goodly zeal, and of much intelligence and application. It is true that there are a number of Papers among those under his care that are bundled without order or

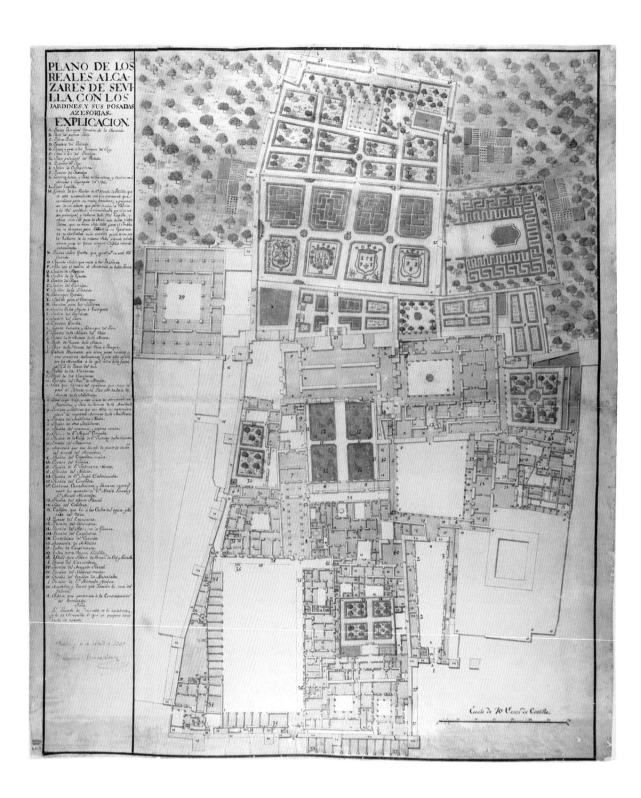

division by topics; in my judgment they were found this way before the creation of his post. More importantly, in a great part of these I see evidences of his diligence in the labels, where he has noted with prolixity the subject matter of the documents. Coordinated with these labels is the inventory that he created; which, if it does have various imperfections (as a work made by a man by himself, without the means nor ability to revolutionize the papers and give them a new order and organization) is nevertheless very worthy of praise and reward.

I praise anyone who applies his body to work, and does what he can according to his abilities, talents, and training. But when one is dealing with a new establishment, I desire the greatest completion and perfection. The idea of the General Archive of the Indies is of the utmost nobility, and well executed it will enhance in a grand manner the honor of the present Reign, and of the Ministry of Your Excellency [José de Gálvez, minister of the Indies].[104]

Exactly where, architecturally speaking, were these besmirched and burned and partially organized documents stored when Muñoz came to inspect them in the summer of 1784? We can begin with two images created in the second half of the eighteenth century. First is the beautiful—if frustrating—architectural plan of Seville's royal palace drafted by Sebastian van der Borcht and dated 10 April 1759 (fig. 2.21). The vast majority of ground-floor rooms are carefully drawn and labeled. Yet when we turn to the northwest corner of the complex, where the House of Trade was located, we are presented with a void. The outer walls are indicated, and the central patio and its gallery, but none of the internal rooms are mapped. The second image was created a decade and a half later. Francisco Manuel Coelho's 1771 city plan of Seville presents the House of Trade building with a two-story western facade (figs. 2.22, 2.23).[105] Together, these images provide a point of departure, and with the help of three centuries of alphabetic accounts we can sketch out the internal divisions of the House of Trade, and see how they changed over time.

Sixteenth-century documents describe two floors of rooms arranged around a central patio: there was a warehouse, chapel, jail, stables, and ever-expanding offices and residences for House of Trade employees, beginning with the accountant (*contador*), treasurer (*tesorero*), and commissioner (*factor*). House of Trade ordinances from 1531 called for the creation of a locked archive within the building's warehouse.[106] In later decades, it seems that document storage was divided among the organization's different offices. In 1603, for example, a series of shelves was installed in the offices of the *avería* tax accountants (*contaduría de averías*); apparently their registry books had become so numerous that many were stacked on the floor.[107]

In the following year, 1604, a devastating fire swept through the House of Trade, and the costly repairs took several years. Plans for a new jail, in a separate building, were drawn up in 1608. When the work was completed in 1613, the rooms of the old jail were turned into a hall for the (institutionally distinct) merchants' guild (Consulado de Mercaderes).[108] Another fire struck the House of Trade in May 1691; the

FIGURE 2.21
Sebastian van der Borcht (Dutch, 1725–?).
Plano de los Reales Alcázares de Sevilla con sus jardines y sus posadas azesorias (Plan of the Royal Palace of Seville with its gardens and its various rooms), 10 April 1759, ink and watercolor on paper, 88.2 × 74.5 cm. North is at the bottom. The House of Trade offices (their rooms unfortunately not delineated) were located around the patio to the viewer's lower right. Madrid, Archivo General del Palacio Real, Planos, Mapas y Dibujos, PLA 5956.

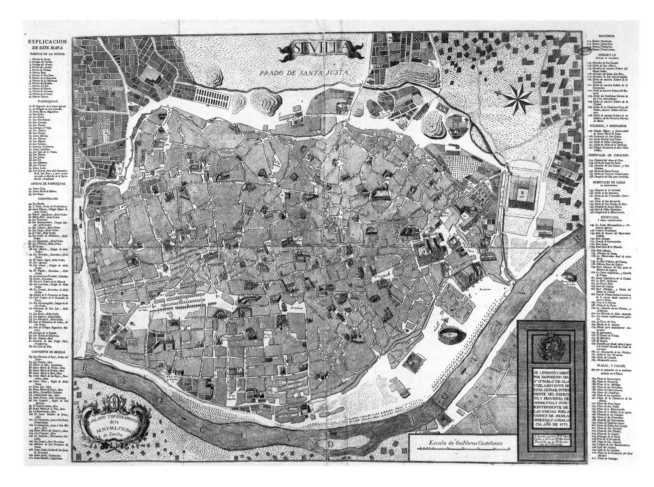

FIGURE 2.22
Francisco Manuel Coelho, cartographer; and José Braulio Amat y Garay (Spanish, 1747–?), engraver.
Plano Topográphico de la M.[uy] N.[oble] Y M.[uy] L.[eal] Ciudad de Sevilla (Topographic map of the very noble and very loyal city of Seville), 1771, etching, 93.5 × 137 cm.
North is to the left. The House of Trade is in the southern part of the city, along with the cathedral, the Lonja, and the royal palace.
Madrid, Real Academia de la Historia, Departamento de Cartografía y Artes Gráficas, C-Atlas E, II, 17.

FIGURE 2.23
Detail of fig. 2.22.
The House of Trade is at 151, the Lonja (the future Archive of the Indies) is at 152, and the cathedral is at 147, in the lower left corner.

repairs took two years.[109] A quarter century later, in 1718, the majority of the House of Trade's offices were transferred to Cádiz.

At this point, the rooms in Seville's left-behind building were in general given over to residences (much like the upper floor of the nearby Lonja). Or, to be more precise, the many apartments already in the House of Trade building continued to be occupied. In 1722, for example, doña Ursula Ulloquí (the widow of a former employee) petitioned for, and received, permission to continue living in her husband's rooms. She is only the first of a half dozen widow-residents documented in the building over the course of the eighteenth century. Male bureaucrats lived there as well. In 1784, occupants included widow María Antonia Montero, House of Trade scribe José Antonio de Andrade, House of Trade judge Rodrigo Marqués de la Plata, and, of course, House of Trade archivist Manuel de Zuazo y Yañez.[110]

Yet the building's history as a site of mercantile offices and warehouses was not entirely forgotten. In 1748, the Royal Company of Commerce and Manufactures of San Fernando (Real Compañía de Comercio y Fábricas de San Fernando, founded in

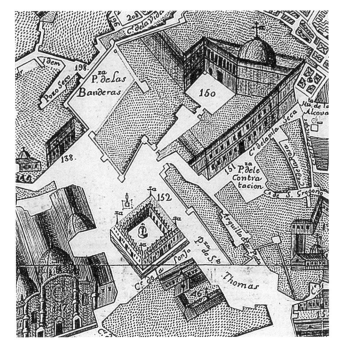

1747 to conduct trade with the Indies) was granted prime office and living spaces within the emptied-out House of Trade, including a warehouse room along the front facade. The company would eventually take over about half of the building.[111] Several of the ground-floor spaces, however, were already occupied: they held "the Archives of papers ancient and modern from the Tribunal of Trade." But when the Royal Company moved in, those documents were transferred to rooms on the upper floor by archivist Zuazo, "so that in the future there should be no confusion or disorder." Two large document cases, "extremely difficult to move," remained on the ground floor—but in return, the Royal Company agreed to pay for new shelving on the upper floors.[112] That was in June 1749. Three months later, the Royal Company still had not fulfilled its obligation, and the result was chaos (at least according to a letter of complaint by Zuazo): "document bundles piled on top of one another, and the others untied."[113]

The next reference to these now upper-floor archives is from four years later. On 3 May 1753, another fire struck the building. It raged through the upper galleries and the rooms along the northeastern and northwestern sides of the patio. An investigation conducted afterward revealed that the fire had threatened the living quarters of archivist Zuazo as well as the relocated archives; all of these rooms were situated around the patio's western corner, on the upper floor.[114] Fortunately, quick work by the archivist and a team of workers called in from the adjacent palace (they cut a fire barrier into the fabric of the building) saved the documents from destruction.[115]

Zuazo and the archive were still resident in these rooms twenty years later. In 1771 and 1773, two reports were drafted about House of Trade installations in Seville, and they provide a final glimpse of the archive before Muñoz came to visit a decade later.

The first report, prepared by Zuazo himself in late July 1771, includes a compilation of documents relating to the spaces of the House of Trade offices since 1718, when most operations were moved to Cádiz. It is filled with fascinating anecdotes: one describes an improvised basement tavern for card-playing (and selling contraband aguardiente and tobacco); another recounts how the building's main patio became a parking lot for carriages; others detail the various repairs and reforms carried out in different apartments. In its final pages, several references to the archival rooms appear. The transfer of papers from the ground floor to the upper floor in 1749 had caused problems. Commentaries from 1756, 1768, and 1771 all complain that the upper-floor rooms were "terribly hot" in the summer, and had a leaking roof that both damaged the archive's documents and enabled easy snacking access for rodents:

THE SOURCE ARCHIVES 107

> Because in the rooms in which they are today reduced, [the papers] reach almost to the ceiling, these animals (which thrive in the attics) without any barrier walk upon the papers, as can be proven by the cords they are tied with, which appear gnawed, and I fear they will begin on the said papers, which would cause harm and prejudice to the king and other interested parties.[116]

The rooms were also very small, so in the summer of 1756, Zuazo was granted another upper-floor room for archival storage: a room directly above the main entrance, which also featured a balcony looking out onto a plaza—a place still called the Plaza de la Contratación today.[117]

Not quite two years after Zuazo compiled this report, in January 1773, he was visited by Judge of the Indies don Rodrigo Marqués de la Plata, who wrote up a short description of the archival rooms. There were five rooms in total. The first (eight and a half by seven *varas*—a *vara* is eighty-four centimeters, or just under a yard) was filled with three-*vara*-high document cases. The next room (three and a quarter by four *varas*) had two document cases, two *varas* high and two and a half *varas* wide. The third and fourth rooms (four by eight and a quarter *varas,* eight by eight and three-quarters *varas*) were both lined with the three-*vara*-high document cases also found in the first room. The final room (thirteen by three and a half *varas*) was probably along the front facade balcony; only one wall had document cases, which (as in the second room) were two *varas* tall. In total, the five rooms contained 5,546 *resmas* worth of documents—nearly three million pages.[118]

CÁDIZ: THE HOUSE OF TRADE

The centuries-long stability of the House of Trade in Seville contrasts with the institution's peripatetic history in Cádiz. In May 1717, King Felipe V ordered that the House of Trade's offices be transferred from Seville to Cádiz. This was, you will remember, just a few months after he ordered the relocation of the royal councils from Madrid's royal palace to the new Palace of the Councils.[119]

The actual move to Cádiz took place less than a year later. In March 1718, a new headquarters (a house belonging to the Count of Alcúdia) was rented on the Plaza of San Agustín. This was in the eastern part of the peninsular city, and the House of Trade would stay there for more than five decades (fig. 2.24). But by 1765—at least according to complaints by House of Trade officials—that building needed extensive renovations and repairs, work the widowed Countess of Alcúdia was unwilling to pay for. And so in late September 1772, the House of Trade moved its offices to a new location several blocks away.[120] Two adjacent buildings were rented from the Marquis of Torresoto. Together, they occupied the northern end of a trapezoidal city block bounded by Calle de San Francisco (on the east), Calle del Rosario (on the west), and Calle del Baluarte (now Beato Diego de Cádiz, on the north). In late eighteenth-century census records, the eastern building's address was San Francisco 41 (now 5); its western companion was at Rosario 109 (now 6).[121] The building on Calle

108 CHAPTER 2

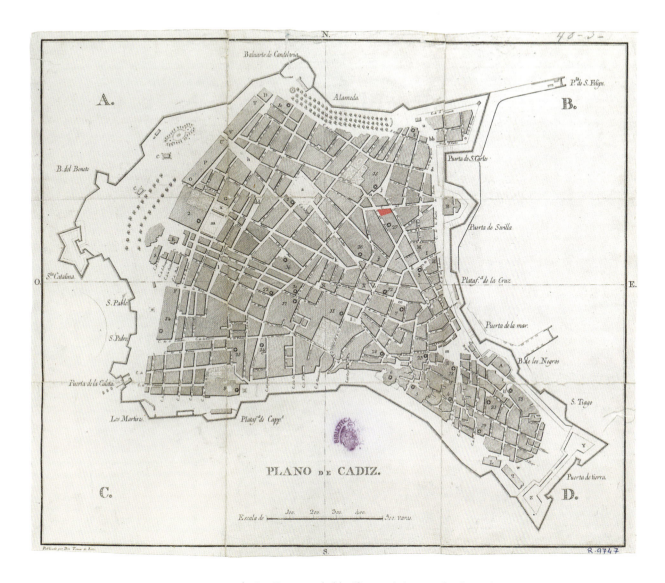

FIGURE 2.24
Tomás de Sisto (Spanish, 1778–1826).
Plano de Cádiz (Map of Cádiz), 1811, engraving, 28 × 33 cm.
Starting in 1772, the House of Trade offices (and café) were located in the buildings highlighted in red (added by author). The Plaza of San Agustín, where the House of Trade offices were first located, is labeled with a *b* three streets to the southeast.
Madrid, Biblioteca Nacional de España, MV/12.

de San Francisco held offices and the president's residence; the building on Calle del Rosario held a café.[122] A *French* café, at least according to a city census from 1773: the owner, forty-six-year-old Gillermo Cansect, was from "Tolasa, in France"; the waiters were *Gascon* Francisco Fernandez (aged thirty-eight) and *Limosins* Pedro Maticu (aged twenty-one) and Jacobo Bernin (aged twenty).[123] A massive wooden model of the city completed in 1779, as well as a street plan published in 1811, together give some sense of what these buildings looked like and how they fit into a broader urban fabric. Each had its own central patio and shared parts of a third (figs. 2.25, 2.26).[124]

The House of Trade offices were still in these buildings when Muñoz came to inspect their archives in the spring of 1784.[125] He was not pleased:

THE SOURCE ARCHIVES   109

Then I went to Cádiz, where the House of Trade occupies a rented house, rather middling. In it lives the President; the necessary offices are there without any extra room; and all that they have been able to spare for the papers brought from Seville (which make up half of the Archive) are three uncomfortable and ridiculous rooms, two in the highest and one in the lowest floors of this house. And even if the majority of the house should be made into an Archive, the building has none of the qualities needed for that purpose.[126]

Muñoz's first complaint, then, is that the House of Trade was in a rented house of scornworthy size (*una casa alquilada, mui mediana*). But the House of Trade had always occupied rented buildings in Cádiz, and in any case this was not at all unusual for government offices.[127] As seen above, the Palace of the Councils in Madrid was also a building rented from its noble owner, the Duke of Uceda.

Plans for a purpose-built House of Trade building in Cádiz were drafted several times over the second half of the eighteenth century, but none of these were ever

FIGURE 2.25
Alfonso Jiménez and Francisco Gamberini, project leaders.
Model of Cádiz, 1777–79, ácana, beech, cedar, ebony, guaiacum, mahogany, palo santo, pearwood, pine, sandalwood, ivory, bone, silver, silk, paper, and feathers, 12.52 × 6.92 m.
Starting in 1772, the offices of the House of Trade were just southeast of the Monastery of San Francisco, which can be located by its rectangular garden toward the northern/left-hand side of the photograph.
Cádiz, Museo de la Ciudad.

FIGURE 2.26
Alfonso Jiménez and Francisco Gamberini, project leaders.
Model of Cádiz (detail), 1777–79, ácana, beech, cedar, ebony, guaiacum, mahogany, palo santo, pearwood, pine, sandalwood, ivory, bone, silver, silk, paper, and feathers.
The buildings occupied by the House of Trade were just below the skewed pentagonal block near the center of the photograph; at the top of the photograph is the Monastery of San Francisco.
Cádiz, Museo de la Ciudad.

constructed—and here, too, we find a parallel to Madrid's Palace of the Councils.[128] In the mid-1780s, the Crown considered buying the Madrid palace outright from the Duke of Uceda. But as more and more structural problems appeared, royal architect Francisco Sabatini proposed the construction of a new, purpose-designed building. Unfortunately, plans were never drafted, and in 1804, the Crown finally bought the Palace of the Councils from the Duke of Frías and Uceda.[129]

What about Muñoz's complaint that, in these rented offices, archival documents were stored in "three uncomfortable and meager rooms, two in the highest and one in the lowest floors of this house"? Just as with his comments about the "attic" location of New World documents in the Archive of Simancas, these seemingly straightforward criticisms conceal a more complex situation.

Starting in the late seventeenth century, Cádiz developed a distinctive style of architecture—a uniquely vertical style, which is not at all surprising given that the city was built on a peninsula, with a limited amount of land.[130] Buildings, especially those connected to the Indies trade, typically had four stories, plus a basement with a cistern to gather and store rainwater (fresh water being another premium on this rocky promontory surrounded by salty ocean). The lower two floors of these structures were given over to business and had relatively low ceilings. The ground floor was used as warehouse space for storing goods. The floor above (often called the *entresuelo*) was occupied by offices. The next floor up, in contrast, was residential, with high ceilings. It is presumably on this second floor that the House of Trade president, mentioned in Muñoz's description, would have lived.[131] Finally, the uppermost floor returned to low ceilings and provided living space for servants, additional household storage, and access to the building's roof (which offered not only spectacular views but also space for drying laundry). English traveler Henry Swinburne visited Cádiz a few years before Muñoz, in the mid-1770s, and wrote the following description of the city's characteristic architecture:

> The houses are lofty, with each a vestibule, which being left open till night, serve passengers to retire to: this custom, which prevails throughout Spain, renders these places exceedingly offensive. In the middle of the house is a court like a deep well, under which is generally a cistern, the breeding-place of gnats and mosquitos; the ground-floors are ware-houses, the first stories compting-house or kitchen, and the principal apartment up two pair of stairs. The roofs are flat, covered with an impenetrable cement, and few are without a *mirador* or turret for the purpose of commanding a view of the sea. Round the parapet-wall at top are placed rows of square pillars, meant either for ornament, according to some traditional mode of decoration, or to fix awnings to, that such as sit there for the benefit of the sea-breeze may be sheltered from the rays of the sun; but the most common use made of them, is to fasten ropes for drying linen upon.[132]

In other words, it is probably true that the Cádiz House of Trade did not group all of its archival documents together in a single room on a single floor, but instead divided them "two in the highest and one in the lowest floors of this house." However, the division of archives into multiple rooms across multiple floors of a building was, as we have seen several times, a common practice in late eighteenth-century Spain. The Archive of Simancas was arranged this way, as were the various office archives—often crammed into makeshift mezzanines—in Madrid's Palace of the Councils.

Furthermore, the storage of House of Trade documents in rooms on the ground floor and uppermost floor wasn't really a cause for complaint. According to architectural customs in Cádiz, such distributed locations were totally appropriate: these were spaces traditionally used for storage.

With these four tours, I have argued that the archives of the Palace of the Councils, the Archive of Simancas, and the two halves of the House of Trade in Seville and Cádiz were not simply chaotic and disorganized, as Juan Bautista Muñoz would have us believe. They had their own systems of order, their own logical relations to the buildings in which they were housed. And they often merged paperwork from the Old and New Worlds. But these systems and logics were different from the ones that Muñoz thought desirable. The archives in Madrid, Simancas, Seville, and Cádiz were organized according to ancien régime traditions.[133] In their place, Muñoz wanted an archive that, quite literally, manifested Enlightenment. This brings us to the next chapter.

NOTES

1 Giuseppe Petrosellini, *Il barbiere di Siviglia: Dramma Giocoso per Musica in quattro Atti* (Prague: Giuseppe Emanuele Diesbach, 1784), 14–16. See also https://www.youtube.com/watch?v=GzlrkidYS58 (at 9:01): The Greek National Opera, conductor Chrissantos Alisafis, Athens, Theater Hall of the Michael Cacoyannis Foundation, 2010. On Paisiello, see Robin L. Thomas, *Architecture and Statecraft: Charles of Bourbon's Naples 1734–1759* (University Park: Pennsylvania State University Press, 2013), 16.

2 Jorge Cañizares-Esguerra, *How to Write the History of the New World: Histories, Epistemologies, and Identities in the Eighteenth-Century Atlantic World* (Stanford, CA: Stanford University Press, 2001), 171–82.

3 ARAH 9/6462; and Manuel Ballesteros Beretta, "Don Juan Bautista Muñoz, dos facetas científicas," *Revista de Indias* 3 (1941): 11.

4 Ballesteros Beretta, "Don Juan Bautista Muñoz," 14.

5 "Siempre he llevado conmigo dos escrivientes habiles en el conocimiento de caracteres antiguos, que no han cesado ni cesan de trabajar; i a las veces han sido menester hasta seis" (AHN Diversos-Colecciones 29 N17 3r, "Razon de la obra cometida a D.[on] Juan B[autis]ta Muñoz," 16 November 1785). Such peripatetic archival research trips had a long history in Spain; see Richard L. Kagan, *Clio and the Crown: The Politics of History in Medieval and Early Modern Spain* (Baltimore: Johns Hopkins University Press, 2010), 111, 281.

6 "Por lo demas mi parecer seria, que quando quiera Dios mejorar el semblante de las cosas, i se junten en un Archivo destinado solo para los papeles de Yndias, asi los de aqui, como los de Madrid, Cadiz i Sevilla: entonces se destinen sugetos capaces para ordenarlos, i disponer un buen Ynventario conforme a las sabias intenciones del Gobierno" (AGI IG 1852, Juan Bautista Muñoz to José de Gálvez, 18 August 1781).

7 Complaining about archival chaos was already a well-established trope; see Randolph C. Head, *Making Archives in Early Modern Europe: Proof, Information, and Record-Keeping 1400–1700* (Cambridge: Cambridge University Press, 2019), 153.

8 Muñoz lived in Valladolid and commuted daily to Simancas; during this period he also made shorter research trips to Palencia, Salamanca, Tolosa, and Bayona. Nicolás Bas Martín, *El cosmógrafo e historiador Juan Bautista Muñoz (1745–1799)* (Valencia: Universitat de València, 2002), 104–6.

9 These offices, as discussed below, were moved to the Palace of the Councils during a reorganization of the Council of the Crusade in 1748; the council itself was disbanded in 1750 and replaced by the Directorate and General Accounting of the Three Graces of Crusade, Church Revenue Tithe, and Estate Tithe (Dirección y Contaduría General de las Tres Gracias de Cruzada, Subsidio, y Excusado)—which was in turn renamed as the Commissary General of the Crusade (Comisaría General de Cruzada) in 1754.

10 The classic study of the Council of the Indies is Ernesto Schäfer, *El Consejo Real y Supremo de las Indias*, 2 vols. (Seville: M. Carmona, 1935–47); more recently, see Arndt Brendecke, *The Empirical Empire: Spanish Colonial Rule and the Politics of Knowledge*, trans. Jeremiah Riemer (Berlin: De Gruyter Oldenbourg, 2016).

11 "En cuanto a los Consejos entiendo que deben ser contemplados como un complejo institucional y no como unidades aisladas…los contemporáneos, quienes, como veremos estudiaban todos los Consejos como formando parte de un todo indivisible": Francisco Tomás y Valiente, "El gobierno de la monarquía y la administración de los reinos en la España del siglo XVII," in *La España de Felipe IV: El gobierno de la monarquía, la crisis de 1640, y el fracaso de la hegemonía europea* (Madrid: Espasa-Calpe, 1982), 84, 88.

12 "Consejos de la Corte…En ellos está representado V[uestra] M[ajestad], y es su cabeza, y de V[uestra] M[ajestad] y de estos Ministros se constituye un cuerpo": "Instruccion que se dio al Señor Felipe Quarto sobre materias del gobierno de estos reynos y sus agregados," *Semanario Erudito* 11 (1788): 195.

13 In 1635, for example, the 176 consular offices were staffed by 144 men. One José González served on four different councils: Quintín Aldea, "Los

miembros de todos los consejos de España en la década de 1630 a 1640," *Anuario de Historia del Derecho Español* 50 (1980): 204–5. See also Feliciano Barrios, *Los Reales Consejos: El gobierno central de la Monarquia en los escritores sobre Madrid del siglo XVII* (Madrid: Universidad Complutense, 1988), 70, 96, 99, 110–11, 163, 166–67, 184, 224, 232; and Tomás y Valiente, "El gobierno de la monarquía," 126, 132, 136, 141, 143, 144, 146, 147.

14 Concepción García-Gallo, "La información administrativa en el Consejo de Indias: Las 'Noticias' de Díez de la Calle," in *III Congreso del Instituto Internacional de Historia del Derecho Indiano* (Madrid: Instituto Nacional de Estudios Jurídicos, 1973), 372; Mark A. Burkholder, "The Council of the Indies in the Late Eighteenth Century: A New Perspective," *Hispanic American Historical Review* 56, no. 3 (1976): 408–9; and Pere Molas Ribalta, "'Aragón' en el Consejo de Castilla," *Cuadernos Dieciochistas* 2 (2001): 13–35.

15 José Antonio Escudero López, "La reconstrucción de la administración central en el siglo XVIII," in *Historia de España: La época de los primeros Borbones*, vol. 1, *La nueva monarquía y su posición en Europa (1700–1759)* (Madrid: Espasa-Calpe, 1985), 119.

16 Agustín Bermúdez Aznar, "Las instituciones: El rey y los reinos," in *Historia general de España y América*, vol. 8, *La crisis de la hegemonía española, siglo XVI*, ed. José Andrés-Gallego (Madrid: Rialp, 1986), 349–51; and Tomás y Valiente, "El gobierno de la monarquía," 84.

17 Despite its name, the Council of Navarre, based in Pamplona, is usually excluded from the main tally of state councils. See Tomás y Valiente, "El gobierno de la monarquía," 166n5.

18 Exact foundation dates for some of the councils are debated, in part because royal decrees of (re)organization may be transforming previously existing advisory bodies. In general, see Jaime Vicens Vives, "Estructura administrativa estatal en los siglos XVI y XVII," in *Coyuntura económica y reformismo burgués, y otros estudios de la historia de España* (Barcelona: Ediciones Ariel, 1968), 120–24; and Tomás y Valiente, "El gobierno de la monarquía," 130–46. Barrios, *Los Reales Consejos*, dedicates separate chapters to each council, with very useful footnotes on dating debates. Carlos Javier de Carlos Morales, ed., *Los consejos y los consejeros de Carlos V* (Madrid: Sociedad Estatal para la Conmemoración de los Centenarios de Felipe II y Carlos V, 2000), provides an overview of the system of councils during the reign of Carlos V. For the Council of the Inquisition (Consejo de la Inquisición), see José Antonio Escudero López, "Los orígenes del Consejo de la Suprema Inquisición," *Anuario de historia del derecho español* 53 (1983): 238–89. For the Council of the Crusade (Consejo de Cruzada), see José Goñi Gaztambide, "El archivo de la Cruzada," *Hispania Sacra* 2 (1949): 199; and José Martínez Millán and Carlos Javier de Carlos Morales, "Los orígenes del Consejo de Cruzada (siglo XVI)," *Hispania: Revista Española de Historia* 51, no. 179 (1991): 901–32. For the Council of State (Consejo de Estado), see Feliciano Barrios, *El Consejo de Estado de la monarquía española, 1521–1812* (Madrid: Consejo de Estado, 1984). For the Council of War (Consejo de Guerra), see Francisco Andújar Castillo, *Consejo y Consejeros de Guerra en el siglo XVIII* (Granada: Universidad de Granada, 1996); and Juan Carlos Domínguez Nafría, *El Real y Supremo Consejo de Guerra (siglos XVI–XVIII)* (Madrid: Centro de Estudios Políticos y Constitucionales, 2001), 53–62. For the Council of Finance (Consejo de Hacienda), see Carlos Javier de Carlos Morales, "El Consejo de Hacienda de Castilla en el reinado de Carlos V (1523–1556)," *Anuario de Historia del Derecho Español* 59 (1989): 49–160; and Juan F. Gelabert, "Sobre la fundación del Consejo de Hacienda," in *Política y hacienda en el antiguo régimen,* ed. José Ignacio Fortea Pérez and Carmen María Cremades Griñán, vol. 1 (Murcia: Universidad de Murcia, 1993), 83–95. For the Council of Castile (Consejo de Castilla), see José María Puyol Montereo, "El consejo real de Castilla en el reinado de Fernando VII" (PhD diss., Universidad Complutense de Madrid, 1991). For the Council of Aragon (Consejo de Aragón), see Pilar Arregui Zamorano, "Ordenanzas del Consejo de Aragón," *Anuario de Historia del Derecho Español 55* (1985): 705–33; Jon Arrieta Alberdi, *El Consejo Supremo de la Corona de Aragón (1494–1707)* (Zaragoza: Institución "Fernando el Católico", 1994); Miguel Ángel González de San Segundo, "Notas sobre miembros del Consejo de Aragón en la administración indiana (1621–1707)," in *XI Congreso del Instituto Internacional de Historia del Derecho Indiano: Buenos Aires, 4 al 9 de septiembre de 1995: Actas y estudios,* vol. 3 (Buenos Aires: Instituto de Investigaciones de Historia del Derecho, 1997), 38;

and Molas Ribalta, "'Aragón.'" For the Council of the Chamber of Castile (Consejo de Cámara de Castilla), see José Antonio Escudero López, "El Consejo de Cámara de Castilla y la reforma de 1588," *Anuario de Historia del Derecho Español* 67 (1997): 927–28. For the Council of the Indies (Consejo de Indias), see Schäfer, *El Consejo Real;* García-Gallo, "La información administrativa," 361–63; and Brendecke, *Empirical Empire,* 93–100. For the Council of Italy (Consejo de Italia), see Arregui Zamorano, "Notas," 710; Manuel Rivero Rodríguez, "El consejo de Aragón y la fundación del Consejo de Italia," *Pedralbes: Revista d'Història Moderna* 9 (1989): 57–90; Manuel Rivero Rodríguez, "El Consejo de Italia y el gobierno de los dominios italianos de la monarquía hispana durante el reinado de Felipe II (1556–1598)" (PhD diss., Universidad Autónoma de Madrid, 1991); and Manuel Rivero Rodríguez, "El Consejo de Italia: La gobernación de los dominios hispánicos (1556–1717)," *Historia 16,* no. 197 (1992): 55–58.

19 Barrios, *Los Reales Consejos,* 46–49; José Miguel Morán Turina, "El palacio como laberinto y las transformaciones de Felipe V en el Alcázar de Madrid," *Anales del Instituto de Estudios Madrileños* 18 (1981): 251–63; Fernando Checa Cremades, "Monarchic Liturgies and the 'Hidden King': The Function and Meaning of Spanish Royal Portraiture in the Sixteenth and Seventeenth Centuries," in *Iconography, Propaganda, and Legitimation,* ed. Allan Ellenius (Oxford: Clarendon, 1998), 89–104; and Brendecke, *Empirical Empire,* 72–73, 100. The many institutions housed within Spain's royal (and viceroyal) palaces connected to theories of the king as an embodiment of justice; see Michael J. Schreffler, *The Art of Allegiance: Visual Culture and Imperial Power in Baroque New Spain* (University Park: Pennsylvania State University Press, 2007), 9–35.

20 Gil González Dávila, *Teatro de las Grandezas de la Villa de Madrid Corte de los Reyes Catolicos de España* (Madrid: Tomas Junti, 1623), 309.

21 Antoine de Brunel, *Voyage d'Espagne* (Paris: Charles de Sercy, 1665), 54.

22 For the text of the two royal decrees implementing the move, see Barrios, *El Consejo de Estado,* 748–52. The first decree specifically prohibits bureaucrats from taking documents out of the new building (and to their private homes). This home-storage practice was quite common among early modern bureaucrats: see José Luis Rodríguez de Diego, *Instrucción para el gobierno del Archivo de Simancas (Año 1588)* (Madrid: Ministerio de

Cultura, 1988), 28–29; Tamar Herzog, *Mediación, archivos y ejercicio: Los escribanos de Quito (siglo XVII)* (Frankfurt: V. Klostermann, 1996), 21–25; and Tamar Herzog, *Upholding Justice: Society, State, and the Penal System in Quito (1650–1750)* (Ann Arbor: University of Michigan Press, 2004), 49–50. Nevertheless, Santiago Agustín Riol complained about the practice (and the documentary losses it caused) in his 1726 report to King Felipe V on "el estado que hoy tiene los papeles de sus Archivos": "Informe que hizo a su magestad el 16 de junio 1726," *Semanario Erudito, Tomo Tercero,* ed. Antonio Valladares de Sotomayor (Madrid: Don Blas Roman, 1787), 122–24, 127–30, 219. On the council building and its history, see Virginia Tovar Martín, "El palacio del Duque de Uceda en Madrid: Edificio capital del siglo XVII," *Reales Sitios* 17, no. 64 (1980): 37–44; Inocencio Cardiñanos Bardecí, "Ventura Rodríguez, Sabatini, y la Casa de los Consejos," *Villa de Madrid* 27, no. 101 (1989): 33–44; José María Puyol, "El palacio de Uceda, sede de los Reales Consejos de la Monarquía," *Torre de los Lujanes* 46 (2002): 189–211 ("muchas veces nos ayuda a entender mejor una institución política o administrativa si penetramos en el marco físico en el que desarrolló sus funciones y en el que trabajaron sus empleados," 191); José María Puyol, "El palacio de Uceda: Sede de los Reales Consejos de la Monarquía, Capítulo II: La adquisición del Palacio por el Estado (1717–1804)," *Torre de los Lujanes* 47 (2002): 131–63; Daniel Crespo Delgado, "La arquitectura del Museo del Prado vista por sus contemporáneos (1789–1815)," *Madrid: Revista de Arte, Geografía e Historia* 8 (2006): 333–34; and Cristóbal Marín Tovar and Emilio Borque Lafuente, *El Palacio de Uceda: La Capitanía General de Madrid* (Madrid: Ministerio de Defensa, 2017).

23 Pedro González García, "Introduction," in *Discovering the Americas: The Archive of the Indies,* ed. Pedro González García (New York: Vendome, 1997), 20–21; Purificación Medina Encina, "The Secretariats of State and the Indies," in *Discovering the Americas: The Archive of the Indies,* ed. Pedro González García (New York: Vendome, 1997), 209–46; Magdalena Canellas Anoz, "El Archivo General de Indias: La recreación de un espacio para la cultura," in *La Casa Lonja de Sevilla: Una casa de ricos tesoros,* ed. María Antonio Colomar Albajar (Madrid: Ministerio de Cultura, 2005), 20; and José Antonio Escudero López, "Reformas del Consejo de Indias a la entrada del siglo XVIII," in *La América hispana en los albores de la emancipación: Actas del IX Congreso de Academias Iberoamericanas de la Historia,* ed. Rafael del Pino y

Moreno, Gonzalo Anes, and Álvarez de Castrillón (Madrid: Marcial Pons, 2005), 675–84.

24 Ángel de la Plaza Bores, *Archivo General de Simancas: Guía del investigador,* 4th ed. (Madrid: Ministerio de Cultura, 1992), 128–29.

25 Isabel Mendoza García, "Propiedades urbanas de la Inquisición en la villa de Madrid (siglo XVIII)," in *Política, religión e inquisición en la España moderna: Homenaje a Joaquín Pérez Villanueva,* ed. Pablo Fernández Albaladejo, Virgilio Pinto Crespo, and José Martínez Millán (Madrid: Universidad Autónoma de Madrid, 1996), 483–96; José Fernández Llamazares, *Historia de la Bula de la Santa Cruzada* (Madrid: Eusebio Aguado, 1859), 347–48; and Riol, "Informe que hizo a su magestad," 177.

26 Barrios, *El Consejo de Estado,* 297–300.

27 Fernández Llamazares, *Historia de la Bula,* 348.

28 Domínguez Nafría, *El Real y Supremo Consejo de Guerra,* 563–64.

29 A similar documentary displacement would take place more than a century later. When Queen Isabel II took the throne in 1834 (ushering in a new era of constitutional monarchy), thousands of documents were again transferred to Simancas. Over half of the archive's current holdings arrived between 1826 and 1852; see José Luis Rodríguez de Diego, "La apertura de Simancas a la investigación histórica en el año 1844," in *Archivi e storia nell'Europa del XIX secolo: Alle radici dell'identità culturale europea,* ed. Irene Cotta and Rosalia Manno Tolu, vol. 2 (Rome: Direzione generale per gli archivi, 2006), 608.

30 The post–Civil War reconstruction of the building is described in Roberto Martín Artajo, "El 'Palacio de los Consejos,'" *Reconstrucción: Dirección General de Regiones Devastadas y Reparaciones* 50 (1945): 33–36; and Alberto Camuñas, "La reconstrucción del Palacio del Consejo de Estado," *Reconstrucción: Dirección General de Regiones Devastadas y Reparaciones* 50 (1945): 37–56. See also AGA caja 2376; caja 2372 top. 76/04-12 exp. 2; caja 20056 top. 76/13-17; caja 20057 top. 76/13-17; caja 20058 top. 76/13-17; as well as an envelope of photographs in the AGA's Dirección General de Regiones Devastadas photographic archive: (04)082.000 caja F/04218 sobre 1. Thanks to Daniel Gozalbo Gimeno, Jefe de la Sección de Información, for his help in locating these materials. Note that only the sections of the building pertaining to the Council of State (the

northwest corner of the ground floor, and the first and second floors) are reported; the sections pertaining to the Captaincy General are kept secret—but see *Plano parcial de Madrid* (Madrid: Instituto Geográfico y Estadístico, 1874), Hoja N.° 10. Four (partial) eighteenth-century architectural plans of the building exist. Three (AHN Consejos MPD 1239, 1244, and 1245; see this volume, figs. 2.4, 2.5, 2.6) were drafted as part of the project to repair and strengthen the southern wall of the Patio of the Fountain in 1781: due to a new attic archive, and the fact that the building had "false foundations," this and adjacent supporting walls were cracking (see also Cardiñanos Bardecí, "Ventura Rodríguez"). Four decades earlier, in 1742, architect Joséph Pérez was hired to reform two rooms pertaining to the "Secretaría del Consejo de Estado y Guerra"; three letters on the project are in AHN Estado 3496, and a room plan and elevation is now in AHN Estado MPD 1121 (see this volume, fig. 2.3; see also Domínguez Nafría, *El Real y Supremo Consejo de Guerra,* 563).

31 AHN Consejos leg. 1288 caja 2 exp. 1, fols. 65r–81v (Joséph de la Ballena, "Relación individual," 11 March 1786). Additional, if fragmentary, details on the distribution of offices within the Palacio de Consejos can be found throughout cajas 1 and 2 of AHN Consejos leg. 1288. Inventories of the ground-floor offices of the Council of the Indies are found in AGI IG 845; see note 34 below for more details.

32 Reconstructing the layouts of early modern buildings from alphanumeric documents faces several challenges. Descriptions may be incomplete or composite—see Lena Cowen Orlin, "Fictions of the Early Modern English Probate Inventory," in *The Culture of Capital: Property, Cities, and Knowledge in Early Modern England,* ed. Henry S. Turner (New York: Routledge, 2002), 41–83; and Thomas, *Architecture and Statecraft,* 28. The numbers themselves may be estimated, or even symbolic— Schreffler, *Art of Allegiance,* 39–42—and thus less objective and empirical than they first appear. For the Palace of the Councils, only partial plans of only the first floor survive from the eighteenth century (see note 30 above), and although Ballena's room-by-room alphabetic account from 1786 is incredibly rich, he does not always indicate on which floor a suite of offices is located. Also, with the exception of the two lowest floors (the *planta de lo mas bajo* and *planta del entresuelo*), Ballena's descriptions do not move through the palace one floor at a time: he follows his list of ground-floor offices for the Council of Military Orders with a

list of its offices in the mezzanine above, then on the first floor, and then on the second floor. He then returns to the ground floor to describe the Council of Indies, then to the first floor to describe offices of the Secretariat of Peru and Secretariat of New Spain, and then up to the second floor for the main offices and archives of the Council of Finance, and so on up and down through the building's various levels.

33 On the carriageway, see Martín Artajo, "El 'Palacio de los Consejos,'" 36.

34 A number of archival references locate the main Council of the Indies offices around the eastern patio of the Palace of the Councils, and in particular along its eastern wall: "en la pared del oriente acia donde tiene su residencia el Cons[ej]o de Yndias" (AHN Consejos leg. 1288 caja 1 exp. 9, unsigned letter 25 February 1785); "La Pared de la fachada entrando a mano derecha, q[u]e mira a Oriente, en el Patio immediato al Consejo de Yndias" (AHN Consejos leg. 1288 caja 2 exp. 15, "Relación" from Joséph de la Ballena and Manuel de Vera, 26 March 1788); and "à la circumbalacion del Patio que està â las entradas De los Consejos de Yndias, y Ordenes" (AHN Consejos leg. 1288 caja 2 exp. 13, fol. 68r, "Relacion individual" of Joséph de la Ballena, 11 March 1786). Although this half of the palace is, unfortunately, not included in Francisco Sabatini's floor plan (see fig. 2.4), Sabatini does indicate that the offices of the Council of Military Orders begin along the midpoint of the southern facade. Ballena's room-by-room description from March 1786 reveals that those offices would have perfectly filled the available space along the rest of the southern facade. This left, on the ground floor, the spaces on the eastern and northern sides of the building's eastern patio. Both the Ballena description and inventories from 1776 and 1779 (AGI IG 845) suggest that the council's formal rooms (Sala Primera de Gobierno, Sala Segunda de Gobierno, Sala de Justicia, and Sala del Oratorio) were arranged one after another in series (although these different sources list the rooms in different orders). Their location along the palace's eastern wall is confirmed by two points of evidence. First, measurementwise, there was enough space on this side to contain all four rooms (following Ballena's estimates). Second, this wall of the palace had enough windows. The 1779 inventory lists two pairs of Persian blinds (*persianas*) in the three *salas* and one pair in the chapel, thus requiring seven windows total, which were available along the eastern but not the northern facade. Since the office of the lord accountant

(Despacho del Señor Contador) was the only room in the council's accounting offices to have a set of Persian blinds in the inventories of 1776 and 1779, this suggests it had one east-facing window, hence its location in my reconstruction at the northeast corner of the building.

35 Kathryn Burns, *Into the Archive: Writing and Power in Colonial Peru* (Durham, NC: Duke University Press, 2010), 3.

36 The connection of these offices to the Council of Castile is indicated in a document, probably from 1789, listing the various rooms that would be necessary if a new building were to be constructed to house the various councils. Also on this list pertaining to the Council of Castile are *La de mil y quinientas, La Ess[criba]nia de Gobierno de Castilla,* the *Escribano de Camara de Gobierno,* and the *Escribania de Gobierno de Aragon* (the latter recently incorporated into the Council of Castile; see Puyol Montero, *El consejo,* 333; AHN Consejos leg. 1288 caja 2 exp. 13, fols. 134r–135r).

37 I lack direct proof that the Secretariat of New Spain's offices were on the first floor. I locate the offices there in part because they are listed directly after the (securely located) rooms of the Secretariat of Peru in Ballena's 1786 account (AHN Consejos leg. 1288 caja 2 exp. 1, fols. 74v–76r) and also because the floor space needed for its rooms fits well within the adjacent northwest corner (a distribution limited by the structural walls of the building). Furthermore, from Ballena's account and other documents in AHN Consejos leg. 1288 (see note 34 above), secure information exists on the names of the four offices up on the second floor—and together, when mapped out, their footprints neatly consume all available floor space there.

38 Ballena's 1786 survey describes the room as follows: "de esta misma Secretaria del Perú, en el Piso bajo y entrando inmediato à las Mesas De Procuradores una Pieza para meter esteras, Carbon y otras muebles De veinte y cinco por diez y nuebe" (AHN Consejos leg. 1288 caja 2 exp. 13, fol. 75r–75v).

39 "Los Procuradores estan dispersos en las ante salas de todos los consejos, de forma q[u]e para llamarlos en el de Castilla, por exemplo, es preciso muchas veces, irlos á buscar por los demas donde tienen sus Mesas; estas por la estrechez del lugar se hallan tan cercanas unas à otras, que se oye, y ve lo que en ellas trabajan por los immediatos, aunque no quieran poner atencion en ello, lo que muchas

veces trae malas consecuencias à los intereses de las partes; de forma, que los subalternos de los Consejos, los Abogados, y demas subalternos estàn mezclados con la multitud de gentes, que concurre à las antes salas" (AHN Consejos 1288 caja 2 exp. 1, fol. 9r–9v, Juan Francisco de Lastiri, 21 May 1785).

40 Ballena's 1786 survey describes the room as follows: "Archibo en un entresuelo que cae sobre el que tiene la Secretaria de Camara de Gobierno Del Consejo de Castilla" (AHN Consejos leg. 1288 caja 2 exp. 13, fol. 74v).

41 "Muy Señor mio: En el Deposito, ô Archibo de Papeles que tiene V[uestra] m[ajestad] en su Despacho de la Secretaria de Cam[a]ra de gouierno se halla el Pavimento del Piso del q[uar]to baxo, el entresuelito que tiene, su escalerita q[u]e baja al sotano, dos tabiques de sus dibisiones, y parte de su techo q[u]e coge un pedazo del Archibo de la Secretaria del Perú proxmio â arruinarse, y debiendo hacer el corresp[onden]te apeo, y reparos precisos p[a]ra su seguridad, teniendo p[a]ra estto q[ue] sacar â fuera la tierra con q[ue] pensaron macizar el sotanillo, creyendo serbiria de algun util p[a]ra contener la ruina, y p[a]ra aligerar el peso, y q[u]e se pueda trabajar con alguna libertad, hasta dejarlo todo enteram[en]te asegurado, es Yndispensable se despojen los Papeles, q[ue] hay en aquella parte, y tambien los pertenecientes, y q[u]e cargan sobre el techo, y suelo del nominado Archibo dela mencionada secretaria del Peru, lo q[u]e he de merecer â V[uestra] m[ajesta]d se sirba hacer pres[en]tte à los S[eño]res del consejo, paraq[u]e inteligenciados de todo lo referido, se sirban dar las ordenes Correspondienttes, â fin de que se despoje q[uan]to antes sea possible" (AHN Consejos 1288 caja 1 exp. 11, letter from Jośeph de la Ballena, 18 September 1785).

42 "otra Pieza de catorce por once: con una escalera para un entresuelo, y en ella algunos 75 estantes de Papeles...otra en que està el Oficial mayor De treinta por veinte y tres: inclusive en ella dos Piececitas en que hay varios Papeles: Sobre la Pieza del señor Secretario un Archibito de diez y siete por trece" (AHN Consejos leg. 1288 caja 2 exp. 13, fols. 74v–75r).

43 "tras De d[ic]has Piezas otra que sirbe De Archibo De veinte y quatro por seis: otro Archibo que baja à un entresuelito De veinte y seis por catorce: Otra De treinta y ocho por veinte y quatro" (AHN Consejos leg. 1288 caja 2 exp. 13, fol. 75v).

44 The Council of the Chamber of Castile had three component secretariats: Royal Patronage,

Grace, and Justice (Patronato Real, Gracia, and Justicia) (Barrios, *Los Reales Consejos,* 184–93). The Secretariat of the Chamber of Grace and Justice and the State of Castile (Secretaría de la Cámara de Gracia y Justica y Estado de Castilla) was also housed in the Palace of the Councils, on the second floor. This is made clear in a letter from Ventura Rodríguez on 23 November 1779 about repairs needed to the palace's roof and walls, and how this would impact other second-floor offices of the Secretariat of Aragon and the Council of Finance (AHN Consejos leg. 1288 caja 1 exp. 1, fols. 17r–20r). See also Escudero López, "El Consejo de Cámara de Castilla," 934.

45 See the "Pieza de entrada al Cons[ej]o" section of the 1779 inventory (AGI IG 845). For published work on the furnishings and books in these offices, see Antonio Muro Orejón and Fernando Muro Romero, "Los libros impresos y manuscritos del Consejo de Indias," *Anuario de Estudios Americanos* 33 (1976): 713–854 (an article that, despite its title, does not only deal with books); and Margarita Gómez Gómez and Isabel González Ferrín, "El archivo secreto del Consejo de Indias y sus fondos bibliográficos," *Historia Instituciones Documentos* 19 (1992): 187–214.

46 See the 1776 and 1779 inventories (AGI IG 845), as well as Muro Orejón and Muro Romero, "Los libros impresos."

47 Plaza Bores, *Archivo General de Simancas,* 26.

48 Laura Fernández-González, "The Architecture of the Treasure-Archive: The Archive at Simancas Fortress 1540–1569," in *Felix Austria: Lazos familiares, cultura política y mecenazgo artístico entre las cortes de los Habsburgo / Family Ties, Political Culture and Artistic Patronage between the Habsburg Courts,* ed. Bernardo J. García García and Vanessa de Cruz Medina (Madrid: Fundación Carlos de Amberes, 2016), 1–4.

49 Pedro Torres Lanzas and Germán Latorre, *Archivo General de Indias: Catálogo; Cuadro general de la documentación* (Seville: Tipografía Zarzuela, 1918), 9; and Plaza Bores, *Archivo General de Simancas,* 27–28.

50 Rodríguez de Diego, *Instrucción,* 43; and José Luis Rodríguez de Diego, "La formación del archivo de Simancas en el siglo XVI: Función y orden interno," in *El libro antiguo español IV: Coleccionismo y bibliotecas (siglos XV–XVIII),* ed. María Luisa López-Vidriero and Pedro M. Cátedra (Salamanca: Ediciones Universidad de Salamanca, 1998), 525–30.

THE SOURCE ARCHIVES 117

51 Rodríguez de Diego, *Instrucción,* 64; and José Luis Rodríguez de Diego and Julia T. Rodríguez de Diego, "Un archivo no sólo para el rey: Significado social del proyecto simanquino en el siglo XVI," in *Felipe II (1527–1598): Europa y la monarquía católica,* ed. José Martínez Millán, vol. 4 (Madrid: Parteluz, 1998), 465.

52 Rodríguez de Diego, *Instrucción,* 66–68; and Rodríguez de Diego and Rodríguez de Diego, "Un archivo no sólo para el rey," 465.

53 Riol, "Informe que hizo a su magestad," 204.

54 Plaza Bores, *Archivo General de Simancas,* 36.

55 Rodríguez de Diego, *Instrucción.*

56 José Torre Revello, *El Archivo General de Indias de Sevilla: Historia y clasificación de sus fondos* (Buenos Aires: Talleres S. A. Casa Jacobo Peuser, 1929), 31.

57 Plaza Bores, *Archivo General de Simancas,* 58; and Riol, "Informe que hizo a su magestad," 86.

58 Thanks to AGS Subdirector José María Burrieza Mateos for confirming the 1700-and-earlier dates of these shipments. See the archive's "Listado de Instrumentos de Descripción 'Antiguos'" (IDD/AGS/VAR/INV-02); Plaza Bores, *Archivo General de Simancas,* 58, 180; and note 67 below.

59 See note 62 below. On earlier shipments of documents from Madrid to Simancas (specifically, papers from the Council of the Indies), see Torre Revello, *El Archivo General de Indias,* 31.

60 "Es increible la confusion que reina en una grandisima parte de legajos, especialmente en los de la sala grande que llaman de governo....La aficion con que miro unos documentos tan importantes, i el dolor de ver los mas de ellos mal colocados en esta pieza grande de Yndias, que aunque tiene nombre i apariencias de sala no es sino un desvan expuesto a las inclemencias de todas estaciones, i ocasionado a Garduñas i otras sabandijas" (AGI IG 1852, Juan Bautista Muñoz to José de Gálvez, 18 August 1781). Complaints about polecats in Simancas also appear in a 1 May 1784 letter from Francisco Ortiz de Solorzano and Estevan de Larrañaga to Gálvez: "Garduñas (especie de Raposos ô Gatos monteses de que esta plagado el archivo y hacen un sumo destrozo en los Papeles)" (AGI IG 1852).

61 Ballesteros Beretta, "Don Juan Bautista Muñoz," 24.

62 "Recurri al de Simancas, i no bien me havia internado en su reconocimiento, quando se me presentó una mies copiosisima, pero tan embrollada i desordenada, que parecia moralmente imposible evitar la obscuridad i confusion en los apuntamientos i extractos, a menos de preceder un prolijo escrutinio de aquella gran mole de Papeles, separar los utiles, i ordenarlos por tiempos i materias" (AHN Diversos-Colecciones 29 N16, Juan Bautista Muñoz, "Idea de la Historia general de America, i del estado de ella," fols. 3v–4r, Madrid, 28 November 1783).

63 "Pasé a Simancas por abril de 81 i hallé los papeles de Indias mal custodiados, todos los más en una sala grande aguardillada. Aun más notable era la confusion i el desorden con que estaban puestos por la mayor parte. Al parecer no se había hecho más operación que ir colocando a la ventura los legajos que se enviaron de la Corte en diversas veces desde el tiempo de Felipe II hasta 1718. Solamente los de la última remesa estaban en pieza separada regularmente ordenados. Los restantes estaban divididos casí por mitad, a un lado los llamados de justicia, esto es, pleitos, residencias, visitas e informaciones: a otro lado todos los demás, que bajo el nombre general de gobierno comporúan una confusa miscelanea" (AGI IG 1854A, Juan Bautista Muñoz, "Razón del origen, progreso i estado actual del AGI," fols. 1v–2r, 3 August 1787).

64 The 1726 account is by Santiago Agustín Riol, published in 1787 ("Informe que hizo a su magestad"). The 1749 account is in a report by Francisco Nangle (AGS Secretaría de Guerra leg. 3295). The 1751 account is in a 22 December letter from José Marcos (AHN Estado leg. 3554). The 1791 account is in the diary of Gaspar Melchor de Jovellanos, published in 1953 (Gaspar Melchor de Jovellanos, *Diarios, Tomo I* (Oviedo: Instituto de Estudios Asturianos, 1953). The 1762 drawings are by Ventura Rodríguez, apparently created as part of an inspection of the building after the Lisbon earthquake in 1755 (Plaza Bores, *Archivo General de Simancas,* 63–64; BNE DIB 14/6/6-14/6/12). The 1774 expansion plans are in AHN Consejos MPD 25, 54, 323, 55; see also Daniela Calabró, "Referencias históricas sobre la villa de Simancas," *Castillos de España* 110–11 (1998): 68–69.

65 The key for figure 2.14 reads: "1 Puente sobre el foso, que dá entrada principal al Archivo. 2 Portico, y Zaguan de dicha entrada. 3 Portico del Patio. 4 Registro general de Corte. 5 Negociacion de Napoles, Milan, y Sicilia &a. 6 Lo mismo. 7 Pieza de Visitas del Reyno de Napoles, Sicilia y estado de Milan. 8 Registro general de Corte. 9 Lo mismo. 10 Cubo de los Libros de asientos, y generales de la Camara. 11 Escalera principal para las piezas del quarto pr[incip]al. 12 Escalera de la havitacion del Archivero. 13 Piezas de dicha havitacion, a este piso vajo. 14 Puente de la Fuente del Rey, que dá otra entrada, accesoria, al Archivo. 15 Ronda." The corresponding caption contains the English translation.

66 Riol, "Informe que hizo a su magestad," 204.

67 AGS Secretaría de Guerra leg. 3295; and Plaza Bores, *Archivo General de Simancas,* 167–71.

68 AGS Secretaría de Guerra leg. 3295; and Plaza Bores, *Archivo General de Simancas,* 103–25, 127–35.

69 "La 2.ª pieza que es quadrada como la antecedente, tiene todos los Andenes llenos de papeles, y aun hai al rededor en el suelo varias Papeleras con papeles, como se traxeron en el año 1718....La quarta y ultima Remision de Pap[ele]s fue en el año de 1718. que D[o]n Marcelo Muñoz y Lariz traxo Pap[ele]s de las mas de las oficinas de Madrid. Los de Estado son de todas las Negociaciones extrangeras, y empiezan en unas desde el año 1610. en otras desde el de 1620. en otras despues, y acaban en el año de 1699. Estan en la pieza segunda de las bajas de la Torre. Estos Pap[ele]s vinieron con un Inventario tan por mayor, como el de la remision antecedente. V[uestra] E[xcelencia] puede informarse del mal estado de este Inventario; pues en esse Archivo hai copia puntual del que aqui quedo, y escrito de una misma mano. Tampoco de esta remision se ha hecho nuevo Inventario" (AHN Estado 3554 caja 1, José Marcos to José Carvajal, Simancas, 22 December 1751).

70 Plaza Bores, *Archivo General de Simancas,* 130–32.

71 AGS Secretaría de Guerra leg. 3295; and Plaza Bores, *Archivo General de Simancas,* 141–43.

72 AGS Secretaría de Guerra leg. 3295; and Plaza Bores, *Archivo General de Simancas,* 145–51.

73 Riol, "Informe que hizo a su magestad," 205.

74 Riol, "Informe que hizo a su magestad," 205.

75 The key for figure 2.15 reads: "1 Desembarco dela escalera principal. 2 Sala del Despacho. 3 De Estado misivo. 4 Lo mismo. 5 Escrivanía mayor de Rentas. 6 Sala de Hacienda. 7 Patronazgo, ó Patronato, Real. 8 Desembarco dela Escalera de la havitacion del Archivero. 9 Piezas de dicha havitacion. 10 Capilla. 11 Dos escaleras que conduzen a las Salas de arriva." The corresponding caption contains the English translation.

76 Plaza Bores, *Archivo General de Simancas,* 93–102.

77 Plaza Bores, *Archivo General de Simancas,* 235–44, 245–48.

78 "En esta pieza trabaja el oficial mayor; y en ella misma en otra mesa larga trabajamos mi Compañero, y yo, y aqui se trahen todos los Papeles que son menester para unos y para otros" (AHN Estado 3554 caja 1, José Marcos to José Carvajal, Simancas, 22 December 1751).

79 Plaza Bores, *Archivo General de Simancas,* 94.

80 Plaza Bores, *Archivo General de Simancas,* 41–43.

81 Riol, "Informe que hizo a su magestad," 207.

82 The key to figure 2.17 reads: "1 Desembarcos de dos escaleras que dan uso a este piso. 2 Sala de Guerra. 3 Sala de Guerra, de la Secretaria de parte de Mar, y tierra. 4 Lo mismo. 5 Contadurías generales. 6 Cubo de Aragon. 7 Corredores de las piezas 5, y 6 del quarto principal. 8 Ydem del cubo del Patronato. 9 Vano de la escalera principal. 10 Vanos de las piezas 2, 3, y 4, del quarto principal. 11 Pagaduria. 12 Vano de la capilla. 13 Piezas del quarto del Archivero." The corresponding caption contains the English translation.

83 Plaza Bores, *Archivo General de Simancas,* 183–207, 58, 173–77.

84 Plaza Bores, *Archivo General de Simancas,* 179–82.

85 Plaza Bores, *Archivo General de Simancas,* 257–65.

86 The key for figure 2.18 reads: "1 Desembarcos de las dos antecedentes escaleras que dan uso a este piso. 2 Cubo de obras y Bosques. 3 La Camara de Castilla. 4 De Yndias. 5 Libros, y Papeles del Consejo de Hacienda. 6 Pleitos causados en la Contaduría mayor de Qüentas. 7 Contaduría mayor de qüentas. 8 Lo mismo. 9 Desbanes." The corresponding caption contains the English translation.

87 Plaza Bores, *Archivo General de Simancas,* 221–28.

88 Plaza Bores, *Archivo General de Simancas,* 221–28, 267–74.

89 Plaza Bores, *Archivo General de Simancas,* 173–77.

90 Plaza Bores, *Archivo General de Simancas,* 145–51.

91 Fernández-González, "The Architecture of the Treasure-Archive," 5–6; and Arndt Brendecke, "'*Arca, archivillo, archivo*': The Keeping, Use and Status of Historical Documents about the Spanish *Conquista*," *Archival Science* 10 (2010): 269. The castle's upper floors were also less prone to humidity than those lower down: Plaza Bores, *Archivo General de Simancas,* 62, 87.

92 AGS Secretaría de Guerra leg. 3295.

93 Plaza Bores, *Archivo General de Simancas,* 63–65. On the 1770 repairs specifically, see AGI IG 1852, Manuel de Ayala y Rosales to José de Gálvez, Simancas, 14 May 1784, quoted in note 95 below.

94 Jovellanos, *Diarios,* 1:222; and Plaza Bores, *Archivo General de Simancas,* 68.

95 "En lo demas de hallarse inutilizados Algunos â causa de las Goteras i Garduñas, procede de no repararse todos los años (como debia) los texados de este Real Archivo, aviendo faltado de larguisimo tiempo â esta parte sus anuales consignaciones, para obras, y estar con tal comunicacion abiertas las socarrenes de él que no alcanzan las Garduñeras puestas en las salas altas i baxas ni otros adbitrios para descastar semejantes Animalejos. Para lo primero tengo hechas tres Representaciones al ex[celentísim]o s[eñ]or conde de Floridablanca y la ultima con f[ec]ha de 10 de este mes exponiendo à S[u] E[xcelencia] la urgente necesidad De reparos indispensables en este Real edificio por no averse executado desde el año de 1770" (AGI IG 1852, Manuel de Ayala y Rosales to José de Gálvez, Simancas, 14 May 1784). See also Plaza Bores, *Archivo General de Simancas,* 68.

96 *Ordenanzas para el Archivo General de Indias* (Madrid: Imprenta de la Viuda de Ibarra, 1790), 47–48: "Con especialidad deberán precaverse las goteras: á cuyo fin se dispondrá todos los años por otoño, que el Arquitecto visite y reconozca las azoteas."

97 Plaza Bores, *Archivo General de Simancas,* 173–77.

98 "Como sin embargo del exacto reconoci-m[ien]to q[u]e se ha hecho en ese Archivo de los papeles tocantes a Indias, se echan menos alg[uno]s que es presumible se hallen confundidos con los de otras clases…han de registrarse en los

papeles tocantes ala Junta de obras y bosques los causados desde el año de 1590 hasta el de 1610: pues consta q[u]e p[o]r muerte de Juan de Ibarra secret[ari]o q[u]e fue del Cons[ej]o de Indias, y al mimso tiempo de d[ic]ha Junta se recogieron de su casa entre los corresp[ondien]tes a obras y bosques muchos papeles del Cons[ej]o de Indias, y aunq[ue] p[o]r este se reclamaron muchas veces, no hay noticia de que se huviesen vuelto. Lo prevengo a V[uestra] m[ajestad] de or[de]n de S[u] M[ajestad] a fin de q[ue] por su p[ar]te contribuya a la mas pronta execucion de tan importante diligencia franqueando a los comisionados los auxilios necesarios" (AGI IG 1852, José de Gálvez to Manuel de Ayala y Rosales, Aranjuez, 31 March 1785). This was not an isolated case: see also (in AGI IG 1852) the "Lista de los unicos Documentos relativos a Indias, que se han encontrado en el reconocimiento actuado en el rexistro General del sello desde el año de 1511 hasta 1524," as well as the complaints about archival mixing in an earlier 1 May 1784 letter from Francisco Ortiz de Solorzano and Estevan de Larrañaga to José de Gálvez: "hàn resultado y entresacado muchissimos Papeles correspondientes à la Camara de Castilla, Conss[ej]o de Hacienda, Junta de Obras y Bosques, y otros varios que estavan mezclados con los de Yndias." See also comments by Gálvez in Margarita Gómez Gómez, "Documentos y archivos para el gobierno de las Indias: El valor de la escritura en la gestión de los negocios," in *Archivo General de Indias: El valor del documento y la escritura en el Gobierno de América,* ed. Reyes Rojas García (Madrid: Ministerio de Educación, Cultura y Deporte, 2016), 88. That the purge of American documents was never complete is nicely illustrated in a recent exhibition and catalog: *Las Yndias: El recuerdo permanente del Archivo de Simancas* (Archivo General de Simancas, 15 October 2019 to 15 April 2020), http://www.culturaydeporte.gob.es/cultura/areas/archivos/mc/archivos/ags/destacados/2019/indias.html.

99 On the offices of the House of Trade in Seville, see Gildas Bernard, "La Casa de la Contratación de Sevilla, luego de Cádiz, en el siglo XVIII," *Anuario de Estudios Americanos* 12 (1955): 253–54; Juana Gil-Bermejo García, "La Casa de Contratación de Sevilla (algunos aspectos de su historia)," *Anuario de Estudios Americanos* 30 (1973): 679–761; Juana Gil-Bermejo García, "Traslado de la Casa de la Contratación de Sevilla a Cádiz," in *La burguesía mercantil gaditana (1650–1868): Ponencias presentadas en el XXXI Congreso Luso-Español para el Progreso de las Ciencias, celebrado en Cádiz* (Cádiz: Instituto de Estudios Gaditanos, 1976), 139–44; Luis Navarro García, "La Casa de la Contratación

THE SOURCE ARCHIVES 119

en Cádiz," in *La burguesía mercantil gaditana (1650–1868): Ponencias presentadas en el XXXI Congreso Luso-Español para el Progreso de las Ciencias, celebrado en Cádiz* (Cádiz: Instituto de Estudios Gaditanos, 1976), 45; José Muñoz Pérez, "Repercusiones en la subdelegación sevillana de la supresión de la Casa de la Contratación de Cádiz (1790)," *Anuario de Estudios Americanos* 38 (1981): 362–407; Carmen Galbis Díez, "The Casa de la Contratación," in *Discovering the Americas: The Archive of the Indies*, ed. Pedro González García (New York: Vendome, 1997), 91–128; and Ramón María Serrera Contreras, "La Casa de la Contratación en Sevilla (1503–1717)," in *España y América, un océano de negocios: Quinto centenario de la Casa de la Contratación, 1503–2003*, ed. Guiomar de Carlos Boutet (Seville: Sociedad Estatal Quinto Centenario, 2003), 47–64.

100 On House of Trade *subdelegados* still in Seville, see AHPC caja 10796–16 ("Informe sobre el estado de la Casa de Contratación en Sevilla," 27 July 1771); see also Muñoz Pérez, "Repercusiones en la subdelegación sevillana," 375–81.

101 Muñoz Pérez ("Repercusiones en la subdelegación sevillana," 368–72) details the status of the House of Trade as pertaining to the royal palace.

102 Torre Revello, *El Archivo General de Indias*, 61–62; see also the many letters and petitions of Zuazo y Yañez in AGI IG 1853. Zuazo was appointed archivist of the House of Trade in Seville on 13 February 1751; see his three-folio "Relacion de Meritos y Servicios" (submitted, without success, in hopes of a promotion to Cádiz) dated 20 October 1772 (AGI IG 2030).

103 For brief biographies, see AHPC caja 10796–16, "Informe sobre el estado de la Casa de Contratación en Sevilla," fol. 1r, 27 July 1771.

104 "Mas atención merecería lo que se dice con mucha verdad acerca del mal estado de muchos papeles, i puede añadirse de la falta de otros; si fuese posible resarcir estos daños, o precaberlos para en adelante con un escarmiento. Pero no existe sugeto contra quien pueda formarse sospecha alguna. Hallo en varios libros, afeados los blancos con rasguños i otros juegos de pluma, que manifiestamente son del siglo pasado: i es de creer qualquier cosa de quien asi trataba los Papeles públicos. Muchos de ellos se quemaron sin duda en los repetidos incendios que en aquella era hubo en la Casa, i de que hoy quedan vestigios en varios libros chamuscados. Dejo aparte la polilla, la

humedad, i otras injurias del tiempo, en particular del indicado tiempo de ignorancia i descuido.

"En el presente siglo, con la nueva luz e las Letras, se han mirado los Papeles públicos con más interes i amor. Y tengo por cierto que los de la Casa Audiencia de Contratación han recibido notable beneficio con la creación del empleo de Archivero, que según todas las apariencias han egercido loablemente los Zuazos Padre e Hijo. Este, que lo sirve hace 44 años, me parece un hombre de honor, de buen zelo, i de bastante inteligencia i aplicación. Es cierto que hay número de Papeles entre los de su cargo enlegajados sin orden ni distinción de materias, según en mi juicio se hallaban antes de la creación de su empleo. Más aun en gran parte de estos veo muestras de su diligencia en las cartelas, donde ha notado con proligidad los asuntos de los documentos. Correspondiente a esas cartelas es el inventario que formó; el qual, si bien tiene varias imperfecciones, como hecho por un hombre solo sin medios ni facultad para trastornar los papeles i darles nueva orden i colocación, es sin embargo muy digno de alabanza y de premio.

"Yo alabo a qualquiera que aplica el hombre al trabajo, i hace lo que puede según sus proporciones, sus talentos, i su instrucción. Pero quando se trata de un nuevo establecimiento, deseo lo mas acabado i perfecto. La idea del Archivo general de Indias es nobilísima, i bien egecutada acrecentará en gran manera el honor del presente Reinado, i del Ministerio de V[uestra] E[xcelencia]" (AGI IG 1853, Juan Bautista Muñoz to José de Gálvez, Seville, 8 June 1784). Note that "papeles públicos" meant, in the eighteenth century, primary manuscript sources (as opposed to printed books: Cañizares-Esguerra, *How to Write the History of the New World*, 8). See also Eric Garberson, "Libraries, Memory, and the Space of Knowledge," *Journal of the History of Collections* 18, no. 2 (2006): 115, on the "early modern sense of public, serving the common good, regardless of ownership."

105 On the map, see Muñoz Pérez, "Repercusiones en la subdelegación sevillana," 366–67.

106 Leopoldo Zumalacárregui, "Las Ordenanzas de 1531 para la Casa de la Contratación de las Indias," *Revista de Indias* 30 (1947): 754.

107 Gil-Bermejo García, "La Casa de Contratación," 715.

108 Gil-Bermejo García, "La Casa de Contratación," 736; and Muñoz Pérez, "Repercusiones en la subdelegación sevillana," 398–99.

109 Ernst Schäfer, "Curiosos pormenores del incendio de la Casa de la Contratación de Sevilla en 1691," *Investigación y Progreso* 9, no. 12 (1934): 357–61; and Francisco Morales Padrón, *Memorias de Sevilla (1600–1678)* (Córdoba: Publicaciones del Monte de Piedad y Caja de Ahorros de Córdoba, 1981), 147–49.

110 Rodrigo Marqués de la Plata to José de Gálvez, Seville, 27 October 1784. On the longer history of inhabitants, see Gil-Bermejo García, "La Casa de Contratación," 733; Muñoz Pérez, "Repercusiones en la subdelegación sevillana," 381–89, 402–4; and the especially colorful account in AHPC caja 10796–16 ("Informe sobre el estado de la Casa de Contratación en Sevilla," 27 July 1771), which among other things reveals that some of the occupants of the building in 1784 were already living there in 1771. See also, for scribe Francisco de Andrade's residency in 1770–71, AGI IG 2030, folder "Años de 1770 á 71 Expediente en que manda conservar…"

111 Gil-Bermejo García, "La Casa de Contratación," 734; and Muñoz Pérez, "Repercusiones en la subdelegación sevillana," 392–93.

112 "Sevilla Junio 6 de 1749 = Mediante a que por Real orden de S[u] M[ajestad] me esta mandado, establesca la R[ea]l Compañia de S[a]n Fernando en esta R[ea]l Casa de contratacion en la parte que le sea util para sus oficinas y quarto de direccion, y haviendoseme manifestado, serle a d[ic]ha R[ea]l Compañia ocupar los sitios, donde actualmente estan los Archivos de papeles antiguos y modernos del Tribunal de la Contratacion, de lo que habiendo dado quenta al Ill[ustrísi]mo S[eñ]or d[o]n Francisco de Varays i Valdes mi Presidente en d[ic]ho Tribunal, ha venido S[u] Ill[ustrísi]mo en que d[ic]hos papeles se muden de d[ic]hos sitios vajos a otros altos de esta misma R[ea]l casa, donde esten con comodidad; d[o]n Manuel Zuaso Yañez archivista practicara la remocion de d[ic]hos papeles a los d[ic]hos quartos altos, que le estan señalados, en el mejor modo posible, para que no haya en adelante confusion ni estaravio, cuyo costo tiene facilitado la parte de d[ic]ha R[ea]l Compañia, y executado, entregue las llaves de d[ic]hos quartos vajos, que paran en su poder, al portero de esta R[ea]l Casa, para que las tenga a disposicion de d[ic]ha R[ea]l Compañia con mis ordenes, y respecto que los dos armarios de papeles son dificultosos de Remover, y que la R[ea]l Compania esta conforme, en que se mantengan dentro de d[ic]hos quartos, y por ellos poner estantes a su costa en d[ic]hos quartos altos, donde se coloquen los paples que estos ocupaban, lo tendra entendido d[ic]ho Archivista para su cumplimiento" (AGI IG 1853, Manuel de Zuazo y Yañez, Seville, 12 September 1749). On the Royal Company more generally, see Muñoz Pérez, "Repercusiones en la subdelegación sevillana," 384, 389–97; Carlos Alberto González Sánchez, "En torno al establecimiento de la Real Compañía de Comercio y Fábricas San Fernando de Sevilla," in *La burguesía de negocios en la Andalucía de la Ilustración,* ed. Antonio García-Baquero, vol. 2 (Cádiz: Diputación de Cádiz, 1991), 63–72; and Carlos Alberto González Sánchez, "La organización del tráfico comercial con las Indias en la Real Compañía de San Fernando de Sevilla," in *Andalucía, América y el mar: Actas de las IX Jornadas de Andalucía y América (Universidad de Santa María de la Rábida, octubre 1989),* ed. Bibiano Torres Ramírez (Seville: Diputación de Huelva, 1991), 241–53.

113 "Bien consta a V[uestra] S[enoría] como que lo esta viendo a lo menos dos veces cada dia la infeliz situacion, en que se hallan los papeles de este Archivo de Contratacion mudados de los quartos vajos a los altos, en fuerza de decreto de V[uestra] S[enoría], pues ha tres meses, que existen amontonados los legajos unos sobre otros, y los mas desatados, todo por esperar la disposicion, que ha de dar la Compañía de S[a]n Fernando, que ha motivado este atropellamiento, pues habiendo ofrecido; que por los armarios que tienen las piezas, que se le han apropriado, habian de costear estantes, no lo han complido" (AGI IG 1853, Manuel de Zuazo y Yañez, Seville, 12 September 1749).

114 "las techumbres de los quarttos, altos que corren desde la auitacion de la archivista que esta en el angulo de poniente hasta parte de la auitacion de Su S[eño]ria, que estta en el angulo ópuesto, comprehendiendo las galerias y q[uar]tos del angulo Ynttermedio" (AGI Contratación 4879A, testimony of Jacobo Josséph Sánches Samaniego, 1 August 1753, in "Causa sobre el fuego ocasionado en la R[ea]l Cassa de la contrattas[io]n Desta ciu[da]d el dia 31 de Jullio de 1753"). This western-corner location is confirmed by a letter written by Zuazo after torrential rains in Seville in early January 1785. The storms came from the south and thus threatened the documents in south-facing archival rooms. Zuazo worked with two hired men to remove at-risk documents from their shelves, and he also hired carpenters to fix roof leaks. Zuazo's 7 January 1784 letter to José de Gálvez requested reimbursements for the expenses these preventative measures required (AGI IG 2032).

115 Or at least according to Zuazo: "Dijo que el dia de ayer a las tres de la tarde, vio humo, Ynmediato de su q[uar]to p[ara] la cossina, y que con el aire se inclinaua, assia el quarto de la auitacion del s[eño]r oydor D[on] Jacobo Samaniego, p[or] lo qual empesso a llamar gente y auiendo acudido los m[aest]ros del Alcazar, Y aruaniles y otros, empesaron a hacer el Cortte mas de dos varas fuera de la cossina del quarto de este testigo, hauiendo quedado esta sin leccion, y solo otro citio ynediato que seruia de Caruonera, fue donde se hisso el corte quedando lo demas del quarto entero, sin que aprenteo fixose p[ar]a donde empesso el fuego, y d[ic]ho s[eñ]or dio prouidencia p[ar]a la seg[uridad] de los papeles que esta, a cargo de este t[estig]o con las que se logro el sacar todos los papeles i ponerlos en partte segura que es lo q[ue] saue puede decir la verdad socargo de su juram[en]to firmo y que es de edad de treinta a[ño]s. Manuel de Zuazo" (AGI Contratación 4879A, testimony of Manuel de Zuazo y Yañez, 1 August 1753, in "Causa sobre el fuego ocasionado en la R[ea]l Cassa de la contrattas[io]n Desta ciu[da]d el dia 31 de Jullio de 1753").

116 "p[o]r q[ue] como en las Piezas a que hoy estan Reducidos, llegan hasta la techumbre, estos Animales que se crihan en los desbanes, sin tener detencion andan sobre los Papeles como se Comprueba con los hilos con que estan atados que se veen Rohidos y temo empiezen con los citados Papeles, en que causarian el Daño y Perjuicio al Rey y Otros Ynteresados" (AHPC caja 10796-16, fol. 17r; see also fol. 9r–9v on summer heat in 1771, and fols. 14v–15r on ceiling repairs in 1761).

117 AHPC caja 10796-16, fol. 18r.

118 "d[ic]hos Papeles, y Libros, y por estas unidas, cotejo de las resmas que producen, segun d[ic]ho s[eño]r Presidente se sirve ordenarlo, resultò que habrà <u>cinco mil quinientas quarenta y seis de d[ic]has resmas</u>" (AHPC caja 10796-18, fol. 1v). A *resma* is 500 sheets of paper: Delia Pezzat Arzave, *Guía para la interpretación de vocablos en documentos novohispanos, siglos XVI–XVIII* (Mexico City: Adabi and Fundación Alfredo Harp Helú, 2009), 198.

119 For the House of Trade's history in Cádiz, see Bernard, "La Casa de la Contratación"; Victor Fernández Cano, "Disputa por la sede de la Casa de la Contratación en 1725," *Anuario de Estudios Americanos* 26 (1969): 357–83; Pablo Antón Solé, "El Oratorio de la Audiencia y Casa de Contratación de Cádiz y la distribución de sus enseres entre las parroquías pobres de la Diócesis

(1784–1791)," *Anuario de Estudios Americanos* 29 (1972): 625–35; Gil-Bermejo García, "Traslado"; Navarro García, "La Casa de la Contratación"; José Muñoz Pérez, "Cádiz y los años finales de su Casa de Contratación," *Cádiz Iberoamérica* 4 (1986): 14–17; José Muñoz Pérez, "Manuel González Guiral, último Presidente de la Casa de Contratación de Cádiz," *Gades* 20 (1992): 65–128; Carlos Simón Alonso Diez, "El traslado de la Casa de la Contratación a Cádiz 1717," *Revista da Faculdade de Letras: História* 13 (1996): 353–64; and Antonio García-Baquero González, "La etapa de residencia en Cádiz hasta su extinción (1717–1793)," in *España y América, un océano de negocios: Quinto centenario de la Casa de la Contratación, 1503–2003,* ed. Guiomar de Carlos Boutet (Seville: Sociedad Estatal Quinto Centenario, 2003), 65–80.

120 For overviews of the House of Trade's locations in Cádiz, see Navarro García, "La Casa de la Contratación," 42–45; and Alonso Diez, "El traslado," 361. The House's post-1772 locations are described in an appraisal and writ in AGI Indiferente General 2031A. Appraisal (*aprecio*) dated 24 January 1774: "casa propria del s[eño]r Marques de Torre soto, que ocupan los Tribunales de Contratacion, y consulado, con sus agregados, como son dos Acesorias con sus entresuelos que se hallan en el frente de la Portada principal, y tambien la Casa continuga que sirue de Cafee con algunos entresuelos, que haze esquina a la calle del Rosario." Writ (*auto*) dated 25 January 1774: "pasamos a la Calle que nombran de s[a]n Francisco a ver, reconoser, medir y Apreciar las Acesorias que se hallan a el frente de la Casa que oy ocupa la R[ea]l Contratacion, es la primera la de la derecha hasia la yglesia del Rosario, la que vista y reconocida damos de valor. . . . Sigue la Acesoria que esta a la izquierda hasia s[a]n Francisco, la que vista y reconosida damos de valor a lo que pertenece a su Albañileria y terreno. . . . Y assimismo pasamos a la Calle del Rosario a ver, reconoser, medir y apreciar la casa que ocupa el Cafe, la que vista . . . dos Acesorias continguas, y Casa del Cafe (que son independientes) . . . las dos Acesorias, Cafee, y entresuelos que con separacion tiene arrendadas el referido Marques. . . . Por lo que haze ala primera Acesoria que esta a la derecha hasia la Yglesia Auxiliar del Rosario. . . . La segunda Acesoria que haze esquina ala Calle de s[a]n Francisco. . . . Y la parte de Cassa que ocupa la oficina del Cafee."

121 In the city census (*padrón*) from 1773 (AHC lib. 1006), San Francisco 44 (residence of the "Marques del Real Tesoro, Presidente de Contratacion," and his staff of servants) is listed on page 168; Rosario 109 (and its French occupants) is listed on 193. Both locations are described as belonging to the "Marques de Torre Soto" in *Cuaderno V: Barrio del Rosario* of the 1797–99 census (AHC lib. 1014, pp. 2 and 3).

122 Cádiz had a thriving café culture in the late eighteenth century; see Charles de Bourbon, "Voyage du Compte d'Artois a Gibraltar, 1782," *Revue retrospective, ou, Bibliothèque Historique,* 3rd ser., 2 (1838): 74; Luis Miguel Enciso Recio, "Actividades de los franceses en Cádiz," *Hispania* 19, no. 75 (1959): 269–86; Manuel Ravina Martín, "El mundo del libro en el Cádiz de la Ilustración," *Cuadernos de Ilustración y Romanticismo* 9 (2001): 92–93; Alberto González Troyano, "Tabernas, tertulias y cafés en la imagen literaria de Andalucía," in *Redes y espacios de opinión pública de la Ilustración al Romanticismo: Cádiz, América y Europa ante la Modernidad: 1750–1850,* ed. Marieta Cantos Casenave (Cádiz: Servicio de Publicaciones de la Universidad de Cádiz, 2006), 379–82; Virtudes Narváez Alba, "El café gaditano en la época de las Cortes," in *Redes y espacios de opinión pública de la Ilustración al Romanticismo: Cádiz, América y Europa ante la Modernidad: 1750–1850,* ed. Marieta Cantos Casenave (Cádiz: Servicio de Publicaciones de la Universidad de Cádiz, 2006), 207–17; Antonio Bonet Correa, *Los cafés históricos* (Madrid: Ediciones Cátedra, 2014), 18–20; and Javier Osuna García, "Los cafés de Cádiz: De la discusión liberal al café cantante," *Los fardos de Pericón (1512)* (blog), 31 January 2014, http://losfardos.blogspot .com/2014/01/los-cafes-de-cadiz-de-la-discusion .html. On café culture in Enlightenment Spain more generally, see María del Carmen Cayetano Martín, Cristina Gállego Rubio, and Pilar Flores Guerrero, "El café y los cafés en Madrid (1699–1835): Una perspectiva municipal," *Anales del Instituto de Estudios Madrileños* 36 (1996): 237–48; Javier Fernández Sebastián, "Los primeros cafés en España (1758–1809)," in *La imagen de Francia en España durante la segunda mitad del siglo XVIII / L'image de la France en Espagne pendant la seconde moité du XVIIIe siècle,* ed. J. R. Ayes (Alicante and Paris: Instituto de Cultura Juan Gil-Albert, Diputación Provincial de Alicante / Presses de la Sorbonne Nouvelle, 1996), 63–84; María de los Ángeles Pérez Samper, "Espacios y prácticas de sociabilidad en el siglo XVIII: Tertulias, refrescos y cafés de Barcelona," *Cuadernos de Historia Moderna* 26 (2001): 39–51; and Jesusa Vega, *Ciencia, arte e ilusión en la España ilustrada* (Madrid: CSIC, 2010), 91–92.

123 AHC lib. 1006, 193.

124 On the model, see Luis Francisco Martínez Montiel, "La maqueta de Cádiz, algunos apuntes sobre la construcción y su autor," *Laboratorio de Arte* 12 (1999): 279–91; Fernando Marías, "From Madrid to Cádiz: The Last Baroque Cathedral for the New Economic Capital of Spain," in *Circa 1700: Architecture in Europe and the Americas,* ed. Henry A. Millon (Washington, DC: National Gallery of Art, 2005), 139–59. Thanks to Jesús Escobar for suggesting Marías's essay.

125 Muñoz's spring 1784 visit to Cádiz is poorly documented (Bas Martín, *El cosmógrafo,* 120; Manuel Ballesteros Beretta, "Juan Bautista Muñoz: La creación del Archivo de Indias," *Revista de Indias* 4 [1941]: 67–73); he returned late in 1784, when he also visited the Naval Archive (Archivo de Marina), located in "three large rooms" of a naval installation on the Isla de León, across a bay to the southeast of the Cádiz peninsula. See this volume, chapter 4 and fig. 4.9; William Dalrymple, *Travels through Spain and Portugal in 1774* (London: J. Almon, 1777), 168; and Antonio Ponz, *Viage de España, en que se da noticia de las cosas mas apreciables, y dignas de saberse, que hay en ella,* vol. 17, *Trata de Andalucia* (Madrid: La Viuda de Joaquin Ibarra, 1792), 292–316. Those documents, which Muñoz thought originated in Seville's House of Trade, had been stored until 1771 in Cádiz's Monastery of San Francisco (close to the House of Trade headquarters, and now home to the Museo de Cádiz). Muñoz copied an inventory of those documents during his stay, and that inventory is preserved in one of the Muñoz Collection volumes in Madrid's Royal Academy of History: ARAH 9/4855, fols. 240r–253v; Ballesteros Beretta, "Juan Bautista Muñoz," 80. I attempted to correlate documents mentioned in this copied inventory with documents in PARES (Portal de Archivos Españoles, Spain's online index of national historic archives) but was unsuccessful, so I do not know whether any of the documents stored in the Naval Archive in 1784 were ever transferred to the Archive of the Indies. A more systematic study of this index may produce better results. Muñoz famously described the documents stored on the Isla de León as in danger of turning into an "archive of garbage": "No puedo disimular el dolor con que vi aquel cumulo de Papeles en tres grandes salas, asi llamadas por mal nombre, porque en realidad son desvanes. La intemperie i las goteras bastan para dar fin de los papeles. Pero no es esto lo peor. No hai quien mire con amor i cuidado aquel deposito: asi ni hai orden, ni inventario, ni

se llega a un legajo e muchos años. Muchos de los antiguos estan ya totalmente perdidos: aun de los modernos está apoderada la polilla. Si no se pone breve remedio, antes de mucho sera un Archivo de uasura" (AGI IG 1853, Juan Bautista Muñoz to José de Gálvez, 17 December 1784).

126 "Luego pasé a Cádiz, donde la Audiencia de Contratación está en una casa alquilada mui mediana. En ella vive el Presidente, estan las oficinas necesarias sin ninguna holgura; i no han podido destinarse para los Papeles conducidos en vezes de Sevilla, que apenas componen la mitad del Archivo, sino tres piezas incomodas i ridículas, dos en lo mas alto, i una en lo mas bajo de esta Casa. Aun cuando lo mejor de ella quisiere destinarse para Archivo, ninguna circunstancia tiene el edificio de las que se requieren para ese fin" (AGI IG 1853, Juan Bautista Muñoz to José de Gálvez, Seville, 8 June 1784).

127 In the late 1700s, Juan Ignacio González del Castillo wrote two sainetes (short plays)—*La casa nueva* and *La casa de vecindad*—that satirized the monopoly on housing and rentals of the nobility and clergy in Cádiz; Juan Ignacio González del Castillo, *El café de Cádiz,* ed. Alberto Romero Ferrer (Seville: Junta de Andalucía, Consejería de Cultura, 2011), 51–52.

128 José Antonio Calderón Quijano reproduces (in black and white) a number of these unbuilt projects: *Cartografía militar y marítima de Cádiz,* vol. 2 (Sevilla: Escuela de Estudios Hispanoamericanos, 1978), figs. 293, 315, 317, 318, 320, 326, 336. A color image of facade elevations for Antonio Hurtado's 1778 proposal is reproduced in Teodoro Falcón Márquez, *La bahía de Cádiz en tiempos de Carlos III* (Cádiz: Consejería de Obras Públicas y Transportes de la Junta de Andalucía, 1988), 24; see also Navarro García, "La Casa de la Contratación," 44. A new customs (aduana) building was constructed in Cádiz from 1765 to 1773; on this, and on connected (if failed) plans for a new House of Trade, see Muñoz Pérez, "Cádiz," 16.

129 Cardiñanos Bardecí, "Ventura Rodríguez," 39–43; and África Martínez Medina, "Proyecto para una nueva Casa de Consejos," in *Francisco Sabatini, 1721–1797: La arquitectura como metáfora del poder,* ed. Delfín Rodríguez Ruiz (Madrid: Electa, 1993), 428–31.

130 Juan Alonso de la Sierra Fernández, *Las torres-miradores de Cádiz* (Cádiz: Ediciones de la Caja de Ahorros, 1984), 36–52; and Juan Miguel Suárez-Cantón Huertas, "La casa gaditana: Análisis

de un proceso de evolución y creación tipológica"
(PhD diss., Universidad de Sevilla, 1996).

131 Francisco Manjón was the House of Trade
president from 11 June 1776 until early 1784,
when illness forced him to step down; he was
replaced by interim presidents don Bartolomé
de Ortega (9 March 1784 to 28 November 1786)
and don Ramón Rivera (28 November 1786 to 25
September 1787). However, Manjón continued to
live in the House of Trade, so new lodgings were
set up for the interim presidents in the House
of Trade's lawcourt (*audiencia*) building. When
Francisco Manjón died in 1787, Carlos III granted
Manjón's widow permission to continue living in
their rooms in the House of Trade. However, the
incoming president Manuel González Guiral was
not pleased with this situation, and so arranged
for the widow to be transferred to another house
(the rent of which was paid for: Muñoz Pérez,
"Manuel González Guiral," 104–5). For a list of
House of Trade presidents, see Bernard, "La Casa
de la Contratación," 276–78; for the 1 August 1777
joint testament of President Francisco Manjón and
his wife, doña Maria Teresa Micón, see Manuel
Ravina Martín, *23 testamentos del Cádiz de la
Ilustración* (Sevilla: Junta de Andalucía, Consejería
de Cultura, 2008), 107–12.

132 Henry Swinburne, *Travels through Spain, in
the Years 1775 and 1776* (London: Elmsly, 1779),
216–17.

133 Brendecke, *Empirical Empire,* discusses early
modern understandings of archival access and storage, understandings quite distinct from our own;
see also Kagan, *Clio and the Crown,* 163.

Antonio con cappello in mano,
e il Conte

Antonio with a hat in his hand,
and the Count

ANTONIO

Io vi dico Signor, che Cherubino
E ancora nel castello
E vedete per prova il suo cappello.

I am telling you, my lord, that Cherubino
is still in the castle
and you can see that his hat proves it.

COUNT

Ma come, se a quest'ora
Esser giunto a Siviglia egli dovria.

But how, if by this time
he should have arrived in Seville.

ANTONIO

Scusate, oggi Siviglia è casa mia.
Là vestissi da donna, y là lasciati
Ha gli altri abiti suoi:

Forgive me; today Seville is my house.
There he dressed as a woman, and there left
his other clothes:

COUNT

Perfidi!

Rogues!

—Wolfgang Amadeus Mozart (music) and Lorenzo da Ponte (libretto), *The Marriage of Figaro,* 1786[1]

CHAPTER 3

ARCHIVE AS APPARATUS

Between the fall of 1785 and the fall of 1786, thousands of documents moved into the Archive of the Indies. Perhaps as early as September 1785, papers were transferred from Seville's House of Trade archive, just around the corner. On 14 October 1785, 254 document crates arrived from the Archive of Simancas. On 8 and 9 January 1786, 24 crates arrived from the House of Trade in Cádiz; another 30 arrived on 5 August. On 25 November, 98 crates arrived from the Council of the Indies in Madrid.[2]

But when these mountains of paperwork were delivered, they entered storage limbo. Renovation plans for the archive's future home—the Lonja, or trade exchange building, designed by architect Juan de Herrera in the early 1570s—had only been approved in February 1785, a mere eight months before the first shipment of documents arrived from Simancas. The transformation of the Lonja took several years to complete, and the plans were dramatically (and controversially) changed as work progressed. Even the shelving went through three design phases, over a period of two years.[3] It was not until February 1788—more than two years after the first shipping crates arrived in Seville—that superintendent general Antonio de Lara y Zúñiga began to install documents on the shelves, starting with the well-organized Accounting papers from Madrid.[4] But even then, not all of the document cases were finished. The archive's southern gallery would not be outfitted in mahogany and cedar until June 1788, and the two cases in the Royal Patronage room were not ready until late December.[5]

Yet although additional furniture would continue to be built in 1789, major work on the archive was completed on 5 November 1788. On that day, Lara wrote to Antonio Porlier (minister of Grace and Justice of the Indies), telling him to inform King Carlos III that "the material work on this, his Archive of the Indies, has been finished."[6]

This chapter chronicles the four-year transformation of Seville's Lonja into an archive: from the renovation of its interior spaces to the construction of its shelving to the installation of its documents (table 3.1). Like many architectural projects, the Archive of the Indies was not the work of a single designer. It was a collaborative effort, and its team of personnel changed over time.[7] From June 1784 to April 1785, the key player was Juan Bautista Muñoz. He developed an initial renovation strategy with project director Francisco Miguel Maestre,[8] project commissioner Gregorio de Fuentes,[9] and architects

125

	GALLERIES	CASES	STAIRCASE	DOCUMENTS
1785				
April		30 April: Model completed of case design #1 (AGI IG 1858H)		
May				
June				
July				
August				
September	17 September: Three galleries proposed (AGI IG 1853)	17 September: Case design #2 proposed (AGI IG 1853)		
October				
November				
December				
1786				
January				
February				
March	15 March: Five arches completed (AGI IG 1853)			
April				
May				
June		17 June: Case design #3 proposed (AGI IG 1854A)		
July			20 July: Cintora maps existing stairs (AGI IG 1853)	
August			4 August: Cintora design #1 rejected (AGI IG 1853)	
September			13 September: Cintora design #2 proposed (AGI IG 1853)	
October				
November		8 November: Cases under construction (AGI IG 1854A)		
December				

TABLE 3.1

Comparative chronology of renovation projects at the Archive of the Indies, April 1785 to December 1788.

	GALLERIES	CASES	STAIRCASE	DOCUMENTS
1787				
January				
February		28 February: First case installed (AGI IG 1854A)		
March				
April				
May		3 May: Blas Molner y Zamora signs contract for all cases (AGI IG 1854B)		
June				
July				
August				
September				
October	18 October: Ten arches completed (AGI IG 1854A)		18 October: Cintora design #3 proposed (AGI IG 1854A)	
November				
December				
1788				
January				
February		13 February: Gallery 2 case installation (AGI IG 1854A)		13 February: Documents being installed (AGI IG 1854A)
March				
April				
May		28 May: Cases installed in gallery 3 (AGI IG 1854A)		
June			18 June: Stair revetments completed (AGI IG 1854A)	20 June: Most documents installed (AGI IG 1854A)
July				
August			23 August: Final polishing of stairs (AGI IG 1854B)	
September				
October				
November				
December		24 December: Patronato cases completed (AGI IG 1858H)		

ARCHIVE AS APPARATUS 127

Félix Carazas and Lucas Cintora. Late in the spring of 1785, Muñoz left to do research in Portugal; from then on he would oversee the archive's transformation from afar.

A second phase of the project began on 29 August 1785, when Sevillian inquisitor Antonio de Lara y Zúñiga was appointed the archive's superintendent director.[10] Over the next three-plus years, Lara worked with Cintora, now project architect, to physically transform the Lonja. When the renovations were completed in November 1788, Lara began initial attempts at cataloging.

Lara's commission was terminated on 1 February 1791. He was replaced by a new archival commissioner, Juan Agustín Ceán Bermúdez, who arrived from Madrid to continue the work of document labeling and finding-aid preparation.[11] Ceán Bermúdez's initial period of employment lasted until December 1797, when he was summoned back to Madrid. As we saw in chapter 1, it was during Ceán Bermúdez's tenure in Seville that the archive's first *Inventario* and *Índice* books were written.

But although the archive's final organization involved ideas and input from a half dozen historians, archivists, and architects, there is a consistency to the overall vision of the project as it developed over time. Design changes that on the surface seem radically disruptive turn out, on closer inspection, to serve a shared understanding of how an archival apparatus should function.

CHOOSING THE LONJA

Royal cosmographer Juan Bautista Muñoz arrived in Seville in mid-February 1784. He was five years into his research project for a new history of the New World. A month after his arrival, on 12 March, he wrote a letter to José de Gálvez (minister of the Indies) proposing the creation of a centralized archive for American documents.[12] Gálvez had already been thinking about this possibility for over a decade, and so on 23 April he wrote back: Muñoz should move forward with the idea and look in both Seville and Cádiz for an appropriate building. Muñoz received this letter in early May, and on 24 May he toured Seville's Lonja with Félix Carazas and Lucas Cintora.[13] All three men were enthusiastic about what they saw.

The Lonja was designed around 1572 by Juan de Herrera, who by then had been working on the construction of Felipe II's Escorial monastery-palace (near Madrid) since 1563 (fig. 3.1).[14] Construction on the Lonja—intended to provide offices and warehouses for Seville's merchants—began in the 1580s. The northern rooms of the ground floor were finished in August 1598, an event commemorated by the dedicatory inscription above the north facade's central door (see fig. 1.2). The rest of the building's ground floor was mostly completed the next year, after which construction started on the upper level. The project was suspended in 1601 due to financial problems, and although construction began again in 1609, the building was not finished until 1646.[15] By 1660—in the aftermath of Seville's devastating plague of 1649, which killed half the city—the Lonja may have been all but abandoned by merchants. From 1660 to 1674, a short-lived painting academy was set up in one of its rooms by Bartolomé Esteban Murillo.[16]

A century later, the upper floor had been divided into apartments. Here is how Muñoz described the building in a letter to Gálvez on 8 June 1784, shortly after his initial tour with Carazas and Cintora:

> The Lonja building, a freestanding structure, has no rival in solidity, and appears made to order for the purpose [of creating an archive]. It contains not an atom of wood, apart from the doors and windows: its ceilings are stone vaults, impressively worked. Which means that it is free of fires. This is also true of flooding, which in Seville is very important to consider. The terrain on which it is built is higher than the level of the waters of the Guadalquivir River during its highest flooding, and to this elevation one must add the stepped foundation, by which one ascends to a walkway that runs all along the building, adorning it and fortifying it, and placing its ground floor much higher than that of the nearby Cathedral, where there is no memory of floodwaters ever reaching, not by a long shot.
>
> In terms of disposition and convenience for the proposed use, on the upper floor alone, which is the main one of the two that make up the building, there seems to be enough space (and even room to spare for the papers that will have to be integrated in the future). Each one of the four equal facades is two hundred feet long: [each side is] occupied by five rooms, one in the middle magnificently long, two square ones in the corners, and between these and the middle room another two (somewhat smaller than the corner rooms). Only the western side is different, because it has the staircase in the center, which provides entry to the gallery that runs around the patio, which also gives access to all the rooms (which connect one to the other). This [western] side could be left empty, for it might be useful to install offices totally separated from the documents. The other three [sides] could be decorated with a body of raised

FIGURE 3.1
Postcard of the Escorial palace-monastery, viewed from the northwest.
Weltkunstkarte Nr. 32 / El Escorial bei Madrid, 1563–1584 (The Escorial near Madrid, 1563–1584), ca. 1941. Printed by Bärenreiter-Verlag Kassel, photograph by Kunstgeschichtliches Seminar Marburg.
The library is located in the rectangular substructure on the upper level of the colonnaded facade of the building's main entrance (toward the viewer's right).

ARCHIVE AS APPARATUS 129

shelves, perhaps halfway up the walls, which will surely be enough for [documents from] the offices of the Court. And this body [of shelves] should be worked with a certain elegant simplicity, considering that perhaps in the future, above it, one might add another body divided from the first with some walkways running around each of the rooms. And perhaps it would be best to dress one of them [the rooms] with these two [levels] of shelving divided by walkways (according to the design chosen), which would serve as a model for the others later on.

Today the interior of the Lonja building is made unattractive and disfigured with many partitions and false walls, by which it has been divided into many apartments, some of medium size, others tiny, occupied by the Accountant, Secretary, Scribe, and Doorman of the [Merchants'] Guild, and other ancient Dependencies thereof, or widows of the same. For the purposes of the General Archive, one only has to return the building to its original form, tearing down these superpositions of poor construction. If the present inhabitants of the Lonja, or some of them, wish to continue their privilege of free lodgings, one could either provide them with an annual equivalent in money, or relocate them to other buildings owned by the Department of the Indies. For example: the old House of Trade, occupied today by the Trading Company of San Fernando, the archive of [the House of] Trade and apartment of its archivist, the subdelegate judge of the same organization, and a few others; or a house divided off from the same building with a new door to the north, where the scribe of the Navy lives for free; or finally the so-called Jail of Trade, at present unused, which occupies a great deal of space in front of the said house.[17]

Gálvez shared these observations with Carlos III, and later that month—on 27 June 1784—the king issued a royal order: Muñoz, with the help of Seville resident Francisco Miguel Maestre (Knight Commander of the Order of San Juan), was to draw up a proposal outlining the work needed to transform the Lonja into an Archive of the Indies.[18] Later that summer—on 4 August—Muñoz and Maestre wrote to Gálvez, detailing their ideas for the building.

Their letter is worth quoting at length, because it reveals how the archive was initially imagined, and it sets a precedent for later transformations. Muñoz and Maestre begin by describing the demolition work needed to reveal the building's original structure:

Excellent Sir:

In fulfillment of the Royal Order of His Majesty that Your Excellency was pleased to communicate to us with the date of 27 June, we carefully revisited the Lonja building, with the assistance of architects don Lucas Cintora and don Félix Carazas, who also did the first inspection. After having discussed and deliberated (with all necessary prudence), we agree that the first step is to remove the partitions, false walls, and other bad impositions with which (in order to create apartments) such a sumptuous structure has been disfigured. And these have marred it not only by disfiguring its original layout and openness but also with a variety of floorings corresponding to the new divisions, with repair-patches, with the smoke of the kitchens, etcetera. All must be returned to its original simplicity and beauty, scraping away plaster and soot, giving to all the rooms a wash the color of natural stone, and paving them with uniformity. The flooring will be sufficient if of common brick, if well selected, polished, and trimmed for close-fit paving. To these works should be added the closing of the doors of the corner rooms (which are to one side), and opening them [new doors] in the middle; and constructing a sturdy platform (which should project a little more than a half a yard from the wall, and should be up to a third [a yard] in height), which will serve as a base for shelving and will protect the papers in the lowest shelf (at the very least) from the damages caused to things directly on the floor. For greater strength and durability, this base should have on its exterior a stone veneer three or four inches thick; this should be enough so that when looking at it only stone can be seen. As regards to quality, our opinion is that it should be at least a jasper from Morón [de la Frontera, near Seville], something from this country that can be gotten for a moderate price. In keeping with this idea, guidelines for the masonry work have been made by the aforementioned architects, whose document is attached (number 1).[19]

After some clarifying comments about the attached document,[20] Muñoz and Maestre then move from the building's rooms to the cases that will house its archival treasures.

In regards to the shelving, we have thought with some passion. Today the Indies are viewed in all of Europe with true enthusiasm. The wisest pens are dedicated to explaining their riches—acquiring a great deal of their own glory in the prestige of the subject matter. Which is really, truly dignified, and no one is more interested in it than the Spaniards, whose deeds in the New World scarcely allow comparison with those of other nations. Your Excellency is deeply convinced of these truths, and in accordance with them advances the true glories of the fatherland. The papers, faithful depositories of these [glories], are now going to be brought together in this General Archive, which will be a treasure of great value. All good patriots, all men of taste and knowledge (both natives and foreigners) view this undertaking with great interest: and it will be appropriate to satisfy, even in the very materiality of the work, the desires of the good and the expectations of the many. The building is magnificent: everything else should be as well, so that if a curious traveler comes to Seville, he will not only admire the remains of its ancient opulence but also find a monument that is a credit to our spirit and taste in the present century.

Such are our desires, and we believe they will be fully achieved if, on top of the aforementioned platform base (the visible part sheathed in marble), there should be raised a body [of shelving] in the Doric order, which is presented in the attached design (number 2) [fig. 3.2]. Its height is determined by the bottom of the [ceiling] vaults, whose distance from the floor is five and two-thirds yards, and since the base has to remain visible so as not to diminish the beauty of the rooms, the cases should rise not much higher than five yards. The base plus ornamentation total over one yard,

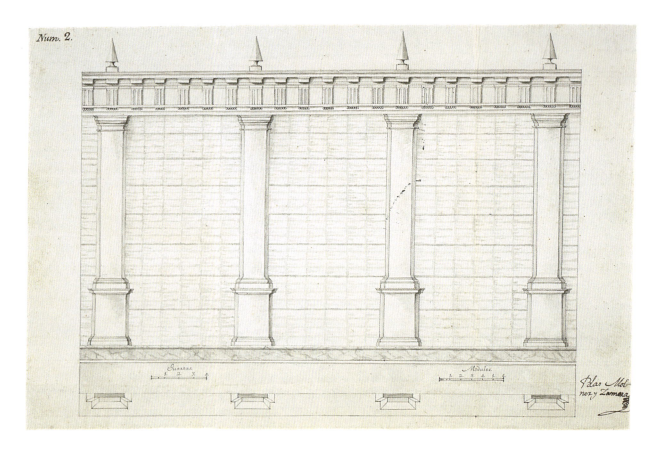

FIGURE 3.2
Blas Molner y Zamora (Spanish, 1737–1812).
First document case design for the Archive of the Indies, 4 August 1784, ink on paper, 24.3 × 37.5 cm. Seville, Archivo General de Indias, MP Europa y Africa 34.

and so there will remain four [yards] totally useable [for holding documents], which can be divided into seven or eight shelves, which filled with papers made elegant with attractive labels will give shape to the design, and against this the pilasters and their bases will stand out. The spacing of the intercolumns, or interpilasters, will be a bit greater than appears in the drawing, because if the location requires it they should be narrowed, so that in the hollows (as the useless parts of a structure) the height should be double, or a bit more than double, than the width.

With the woods for a work like this one it is necessary to be attentive to beauty as well as durability, especially in this land dominated by excessive humidity and heat. Both qualities are found in mahogany and cedar, to which should be added the ease of acquiring the necessary quantity from Havana, possibly with greater speed than one could gather any other woods from the peninsula (other than the common kinds, which in no way should be used in works such as these). It seems to us that all the exterior body should be of mahogany, that is to say pilasters with pedestals, and ornament; the ladders, the shelves, and the boards that the shelves have to have in back, all of cedar. The fronts of the tables, and most especially the body of the architecture, must be perfectly worked and polished. From this plan will emerge a work so durable, so simple, so beautiful and noble, that not even Envy will be able to criticize it.[21]

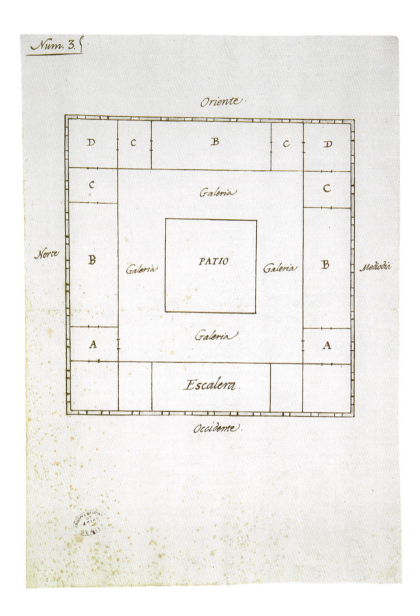

FIGURE 3.3
Juan Bautista Muñoz (Spanish, 1745–99) and Francisco Miguel Maestre (?–1784).
Plan for the upper floor of the Lonja, 4 August 1784, ink on paper, 30 × 21 cm.
The doors in all rooms are aligned. Despite what is said in the accompanying letter, exactly which doorways were to be left open and which were to receive actual doors is not indicated.
Seville, Archivo General de Indias, MP Europa y Africa 32.

This discussion leads directly to portable furniture, and to the building's doors:

The tables and benches for the rooms of the Archive must be of the same woods; that is, cedar for the benches and legs of the tables, and mahogany for their flat surfaces. And so that all goes together, it is necessary that the doors by which the rooms are connected should also be covered in mahogany, and all those which provide entry to the Archive. Service doors, however, can be dispensed with: they are not needed, and their open frames will probably look better to the viewer. According to this plan, six doors will be sufficient, as can be seen by looking at the plan (number 3) [fig. 3.3], which represents the Lonja building.[22]

ARCHIVE AS APPARATUS 133

The final paragraphs of this August proposal then cover a number of themes: the placement of offices on the western, staircase side of the building; estimates of costs and materials; and the need for an eviction order to remove the building's occupants before remodeling can begin. Muñoz and Maestre conclude by returning to documents and shelving. First, they recommend that papers be installed according to the order in which they were stored in their source archives—an innovative approach in the eighteenth century, and described by archivists today as the "principle of provenance." Second, they explain that the document cases will *not* be closed with doors or wire screens: good archival practices will protect documents from theft better than any physical barrier.

This 4 August 1784 proposal was approved by José de Gálvez two weeks later. A royal order for evicting the Lonja's residents was secured in late September, and the building was vacated by the end of the year.[23] Official, royal approval for the 4 August designs was granted on 3 February 1785, and renovations began on 11 March.[24] The first steps involved tearing out walls not original to the sixteenth-century building, and cleaning soot from the ceilings. On 27 April, as he prepared to leave Seville for Lisbon, Muñoz wrote another letter to Gálvez. He described how the work was progressing and what was left to be done (based on the proposal from the previous summer).[25] His April instructions included a plan of the upper floor showing where doors needed to be added and where they needed to be closed up—a point to which I will return (see fig. 3.4).

By early June, Muñoz was copying documents in Portugal's Torre do Tombo archive. He returned to Spain in November, and by mid-December was just northwest of Madrid, researching at the Escorial's library. Although a letter from the second half of March 1787 reveals Muñoz went to Seville at least once to check in on the project, this seems to be unusual: he was mostly living and working in Madrid or its courtly environs.[26] But he continued to oversee the construction works in Seville from afar: not as a paper architect, with additional drawings, but as an alphabetic one, with words.[27]

VISIONS OF ORDER

These initial imaginations of the archive, proposed in August 1784 and repeated in April 1785, are fascinating and perplexing. On one level, they lay out basic imperatives for design and construction over the next four years. At the same time, the archive they imagine is quite different from the archive that was completed in 1788. Most significantly, the series of small rooms described and illustrated in 1784 and 1785 (lined with shelving, their doorways aligned) were, by 1788, ripped open and expanded into a continuous space of three connected galleries.

But before seeing what the archive became, let us consider how it was originally conceived. Notably, although much of what Muñoz and Maestre proposed seems to focus on surface effects, those surface effects had deeper functions. Recalling John Harwood's ideas from the introduction, we can say that aesthetics supported an apparatus. Architectural imagism served archival interface.[28]

134 CHAPTER 3

Central to Muñoz's initial vision for the archive was the aesthetic of simplicity (*simplicidad*). Later additions to the building needed to be purged: "All must be returned to its original simplicity and beauty, scraping away plaster and soot."[29] The shelving, too, "should be worked with a certain elegant simplicity."[30] In sum, "from this plan will emerge a work so durable, so simple, so beautiful and noble, that not even Envy will be able to criticize it.... In what we propose are joined together, in our view, good taste in the arts with a noble and majestic simplicity."[31]

But the creation of simplicity—especially in a building like the Lonja, with a long history of occupation and interventions—required a lot of effort. Again and again, Muñoz outlined specific strategies for creating simplicity, often through visual and material unity—another key category (*igualdad, uniformidad*). Some of these strategies involved color. Once they had been cleaned, the soot-stained vaults of the Lonja's ceiling should be painted with a wash (*baño*) "of stone-color, in such a way that the color becomes the same in all the vaults."[32] This visual unification was also recommended for the staircase, landing, entry hall, and gallery: to all "will be given a light wash of stone-color, something brighter than what now exists, so that everything becomes equal."[33]

In the case of the archive's extensive new woodwork, a desired unity of color was, paradoxically, compromised by unity of materials. Wood, unlike paint, is a natural product; its hue and grain are what they are. But even here Muñoz made recommendations, which underscore just how obsessed he was with unity and simplicity:

> **Much care will be taken in the selection of the wood, especially the mahogany, achieving the greatest evenness possible in the color of all the parts of each room, and even more so in the parts that are the same. For example, the pilasters, the pedestals, the triglyphs, the mouldings, etcetera, should be as similar among themselves in color and grain as can be achieved. If some small variation can be detected, it should be within the different parts. Thus it will not be inconvenient if the color of the triglyph should be lighter or darker than that of the metope; the metopes should always be uniform amongst themselves, and also the triglyphs. To improve selection, it will be useful to begin by sawing the greater part of the wood, to divide in keeping with the relevant measurements.[34]**

Material unity was also an issue underfoot. The division of the Lonja into apartments had not only produced a chaos of interior walls but also generated a "variety of floorings corresponding to the new divisions." This visual chaos needed to be repaved "with uniformity."[35] "All of the rooms of the upper floor will be paved in perfect evenness [*igualdad*] with slabs of stone from Málaga, achieving maximum excellence and beauty, both in their selection and juxtaposition side by side, as in their union among each other and with the base for the shelves."[36]

A further manifestation of this desire for unification was just above floor level: a raised stone platform was to run along the edges of each room. Its direct purpose was to elevate the mahogany document cases, but it would work in visual ways as well: "The base for the shelving, which now is cut off in the alcoves of the windows, should

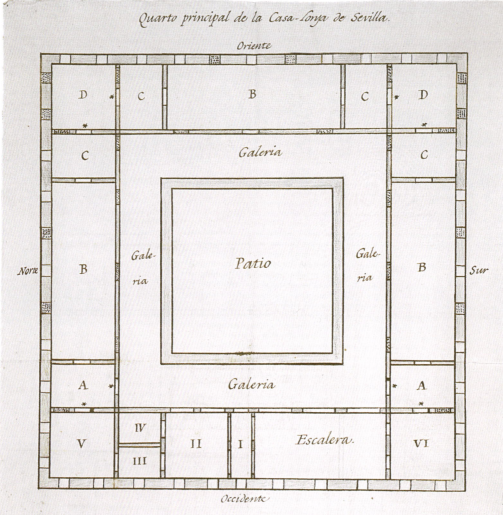

Quarto principal de la Casa-Lonja de Sevilla.

I. Desembarcadero de la escalera, con una ventana a la calle, i arcos a tres frentes.
II. Glorieta, o sea Vestibulo, con arcos a dos frentes, puertas i ventanas a otros dos.
III. Pieza de recibimiento.
IV. Subida a las azoteas.

Todas las puertas i ventanas notadas con puntos quedan cerradas i sin uso, pero en lo exterior como corresponde a la uniformidad i hermosura del edificio. Donde va esta señal ✱ se indican puertas que se abren de nuevo.

be continued within them as well, so that it runs through all the rooms where there is shelving, without any other interruption than that which is necessary for the doors, at whose sides it will stop with very little distance between them and the angle of the opening."[37]

As below, so too above: Muñoz imagined that a cornice running along the top of his mahogany cases would provide another band of visual unification: "The entablature will run continuously, without any interruption along the four walls of all of the halls, creating a crown that as a whole will serve as a foundation for the vaults and will produce a better visual effect than the real foundation, which will be hidden."[38]

Finally, the continuous floor- and ceiling-lines uniting each room were to be combined with a visual unification of rooms to each other. Although Herrera's sixteenth-century design probably aligned the doors in all rooms, by the eighteenth century, door placements had become irregular. Doors in the building's four corner rooms were off-center, close to the building's outer walls. In contrast, the doors in the main halls on the north, east, and south sides of the building were (still) centered. Muñoz wanted to change this. *All* doorways were to be centered in their walls (and thus aligned to one another), creating a visual corridor uniting each side of the archive. In his accompanying drawing of the Lonja's upper floor (fig. 3.4), existing doors (and windows) to be sealed up are shaded with stippled dots.[39] Doors (and windows) to be left open appear as empty rectangles. Closed-up doors to be reopened are marked by an asterisk. Muñoz's letters explain further: "To these works should be added the closing of the doors of the corner rooms, which are to one side, and opening [new doors] in the middle."[40] "The four corner rooms have their doors at the sides. With attention to the visual effect and impressiveness, they will be closed, and openings will be made in the middle [of each wall], creating arches of brick, which is the material of the wall where they have to be opened."[41] Such visual alignments were a popular feature of baroque and neoclassical architecture, and even have their own technical name: rooms enfilade.[42] Indeed, when Juan de Villanueva drew up plans for expanding the Archive of Simancas in 1774, the new building's rooms were organized enfilade—in contrast to the jumbled and off-center spaces in the original castle (see figs. I.11–I.13).

These aesthetics of simplicity and unity were not without precedent in Iberian archives—something Muñoz knew quite well. For example, they shaped several of the spaces at Simancas. In his room-by-room description from 1726, Santiago Agustín Riol was attentive to occasional visual unities in floors and walls. Just inside the entryway were "three very spacious rooms, with worked-wood ceilings and floors of fine brick." The main staircase had "risers and walls of white stone, wide, with two landings or resting places, and much light."[43] But perhaps the most impressively unified room in Simancas was the one beyond a stone doorway labeled *Patronazgo Real* (see fig. 2.16). "One discovers a very large hall, almost square, all of marvelous architecture, because the floor is of black and white jasper, and the ceiling a beautiful vault, and all around are equally sized and spacious cupboards for the papers: they do not have doors, and this makes it brighter, because of the uniformity or placement of the

---

FIGURE 3.4
Juan Bautista Muñoz (Spanish, 1745–99).
Quarto principal de la Casa-Lonja de Sevilla (Upper floor of the Lonja building in Seville), 27 April 1785, ink on paper, 36.1 × 26 cm.
Key: **I** Landing of the staircase, with a window overlooking the street, and arches on three sides. **II** Entry hall, or vestibule, with arches on two sides and doors and windows on the other two. **III** Reception room. **IV** Access up to the roof. All of the doors and windows shaded with dots will remain sealed and unused, although their appearance on the exterior facade will be determined by the uniformity and beauty of the building. This symbol * indicates doors that will be opened up again.
Seville, Archivo General de Indias, MP Europa y Africa 33.

documents, each one with a very white paper wrapping, and their labels all of the same size, which is delectable to the eye. To the east is a very large window that fills it [the room] with light."[44]

But these were *unusual* spaces of visual harmony, scattered throughout Simancas castle. In Seville, Muñoz wanted unity and simplicity to characterize the archive as a whole. In this, his design dreams were in dialogue with two broader cultural currents in late eighteenth-century Spain. The first relates to theories of economy and masculinity; the second to a renewed interest in Renaissance classicism and the buildings of Juan de Herrera. Muñoz's surface aesthetics had profound implications.

MASCULINE ECONOMY

As Rebecca Haidt reveals, one of the models for masculinity in Enlightenment Spain emphasized economy, restraint, and, above all, *simplicity.* The *hombre de bien* (gentleman, man of honor) contrasted with the *petimetre,* a frivolous, wasteful dandy.[45] In the early 1780s, for example, Luis María Cañuelo y Heredia (editor of *El Censor,* one of Madrid's periodicals) wrote that "my manner of dress will be supremely simple [*sencillo*] not because of modesty, but rather because of appropriateness. Flashiness and ostentation in dress are an extremely uncomfortable thing."[46] Uncomfortable—and economically unsound. Earlier in the century, Diego de Torres Villarroel had chastised men who "waste money on dressing-tables, and Castor oil (because they suffer from hysteria), powders, ribbons, beauty marks, and bracelets, and all the dissimulating cosmetics of a lady." A few years later, Juan Antonio Gómez Arias offered this advice to his male readers: "friend, don't go hungry just to be handsome."[47] The financial consequences of maintaining a fashionable facade were even dramatized in two satires about hairdressing from 1767 and 1787: the "Carta de un peluquero" (Letter from a hairdresser) and "Noticia de los peinados del peluquero francés" (Report on the hairstyles of the French hairdresser).[48] Just as the walls of the Lonja needed to be purified of their smoky grime, the *hombre de bien* should not be "marred" or "disfigured" by wasteful cosmetics or other fashionable accessories. These would detract from an "original simplicity."

Eighteenth-century Spaniards even imagined masculine-architectural analogies, undergirded by an aesthetic of simplicity. Consider this mid-1780s letter published in Madrid's *El Censor:*

> Sir: I am a man of good stature; thick of beard; beefy; in complexion rather dark, and my whole body is covered with fur. I do not fear the sun or water, and I do no more in caring for my hair than make sure that it is clean and does not inconvenience me; the tailor and the shoemaker leave me fully satisfied when my clothes and shoes are comfortable and easy to walk in. And with all of this I am as pleased with my manly body as the most plucked Adonis can be with his womanly one.... It is undeniable that the beauty of a body does not consist in any other thing than in the proportion and appropriateness found by the one who contemplates it, in the parts of which it is

made, for the purpose for which the whole has been made. Thus a facade is beautiful when the parts of which it is composed appear, to the sight of he who considers it, the most appropriate for the stability of the building, and indicate an interior layout most appropriate for the uses to which it is destined.[49]

Form should follow function; exterior clarity should align with interior order; excess and artificiality should be avoided. This was true of architecture and of men.

Additional parallels to this Enlightenment emphasis on "an ideal body moderate and restrained" can be found in how Muñoz discussed the costs of transforming the Lonja into an archive.[50] Muñoz did not see the simplicity and unity he imagined for the archive as frivolous superficiality or a falsely restrained facade. Unity and simplicity were to be achieved through fiscal economy. The appearance of the archive would not be a shallow product of paint and veneer: it would actually manifest, in built form, sound economic principles.

Such economic prudence was commanded by the king himself. As Gálvez wrote in his letter asking for a renovation proposal from Muñoz and Maestre:

> The king has understood with great satisfaction that which you have punctually and wisely related in your letter dated 8 of the present month [June 1784] concerning the current status and promising potential offered by the structure of the Casa Lonja of that city [Seville] for a General Archive of the papers of the Indies, as well as the works necessary to carry out such an important design. And so that this not be delayed, His Majesty has resolved that the same two men who made the inspection [architects Carazas and Cintora] should take your report and, in the part that deals with the necessary tasks for the construction of the archive, estimate as closely as possible how great the costs will be (based on what is proposed in the report), working with a prudent economy, yet never abandoning attention to the greatest proportion, convenience, and ornament that are possible.[51]

Just over a month later, this royal command was quoted at the conclusion of Muñoz and Maestre's proposal of 4 August 1784:

> We hope to proceed according to the wise comment by Your Majesty on the regulation of these works. Your Majesty commanded that they should be done "with a prudent economy, yet never abandoning attention to the greatest proportion, convenience, and ornament that are possible." Your Excellency has precise ideas about what prudent economy is—a virtue that would stop being so, if in dealing with a public work, it were not united with magnificence.[52]

So how was this prudent economy, united with magnificence, to be achieved? And what does it reveal about the depths of archival imagism?

To start, consider the woodwork. Muñoz argued that his extensive uses of American cedar and, above all, mahogany (an incredibly fashionable wood throughout the Euroamerican world in the late eighteenth century) should not be understood as wasteful luxury, or as material references that merely "symbolized" the New World.[53] First, these woods were not simply luxurious. They were also practical. They resisted heat, humidity, and insects, all important factors in a city like Seville.[54] Second, although these woods did come from the Americas (and so were on one level symbolically appropriate for an archive of the Indies), the fact that Spain's empire—and the king's royal prerogatives—extended across the Atlantic meant that large quantities of these precious woods could be acquired quickly and at a reasonable price:

> The cost of the woods has not been calculated, which doubtless would be greater if they had to be purchased from retailers; but gotten in Havana, and transported by account of Your Majesty in your royal mailboats and other ships, they will be acquired with such ease that even others from the peninsula will not be cheaper (disregarding the ordinary ones, which are not acceptable), and none of those could compare with cedar and mahogany, neither in durability nor in beauty.[55]

Discussion of the archive's unified floor treatment provides another example in which beauty and spatial symbolics were built on sound economic foundations. In their proposal of 4 August 1784, Muñoz and Maestre suggested that the base for the shelving be capped in "a jasper from Morón, something from this country that can be acquired at a moderate price." They also considered uniting the floor with "pavers from Genoa"—that is, stones imported from northwestern Italy—"lasting forever and at a tolerable cost."[56] Four days later, in a letter to Gálvez, Muñoz returned to the economics of flooring. "It would be without a doubt better," he wrote, to pave the archive with Spanish stone (*piedra del Reino*). Unfortunately, however, "this would greatly increase the cost."[57]

Yet the economics (and symbolics) of paving continued to bother Muñoz. More than a month later, a new flooring plan was announced, one that combined economy, material symbolism, and patriotism: "for the flooring I judge it preferable that pavers from Málaga should be used, which will be better than those from Genoa, and will perhaps come out more moderately priced."[58] When the procurement of stone began in April 1785, local Andalusian sources were indeed used: red jasper from Cerro de San Antón and white marble from Sierra de Mijas (fig. 3.5).[59]

The aesthetics of Enlightenment masculinity also resonated with late eighteenth-century architectural trends. Baroque and rococo ornamentation were rejected, replaced by a new vogue for classical severity. This was a pan-European movement, accompanied by a search for local, "national" representatives of an earlier Renaissance neoclassicism. In Spain, this led to a revival of interest in the late sixteenth-century buildings of Juan de Herrera—a body of work that included Seville's Lonja.[60]

HERRERAN CLASSICISM

Herrera's aesthetics—and especially his designs for the Escorial monastery-palace—were a constant point of reference in the transformation of the Lonja. This applies to the very vocabulary with which the Lonja reforms were imagined. Herrera's sixteenth-

century designs were repeatedly described in the late eighteenth century as having "unity" (*unidad*), "uniformity" (*uniformidad*), "proportion" (*proporción*), and "economy" (*economía*). They possessed a "noble simplicity" (*noble sencillez*), in keeping with "the great models of antiquity" (*los grandes modelos de la antiguedad*).[61] These traits—uniformity, economy, noble simplicity—are the same categories Muñoz used to describe his own project, as seen above.

These conceptual parallels are not accidental. Muñoz was familiar with the Escorial even before he conducted research there in December 1785. He owned a copy of José de Sigüenza's 1605 *Tercera parte de la historia de la orden de San Geronimo* (Third part of the history of the Order of San Gerónimo), which despite its title was a detailed description of the Escorial. Its prose may have shaped the language Muñoz then used to write about the Archive of the Indies.[62] Furthermore, Sigüenza's account of the Escorial's library helps explain some of the design transformations in the AGI's shelving, as well as Muñoz's concern with beautiful materials that *performed* in specific ways.

As mentioned above, Seville's document cases went through three design phases, starting in August 1784. An initial plan was one of only three illustrations accompanying Muñoz and Maestre's original archival proposal, which gives a sense of just how important they thought the document cases were (see figs. 3.2, 3.3). At the bottom of the drawing is a low platform of jasper, on which stand rectangular wooden supports for Doric pilasters, which in turn support a carved metope crowned with decorative spikes. Subsequent discussions of this design, however, complained that the pilasters took up too much space—valuable space that could be used for documents. And so the

FIGURE 3.5
Shipping receipt for bricks, white flagstones, and red flagstones transported from Málaga to Seville, 29 October 1787.
Seville, Archivo General de Indias, Indiferente General 1854B.

shelves were redesigned again, and again. Yet the initial rejection should not have been unexpected. Such an ornately architectural style for shelving was quite old-fashioned by the 1780s.

Starting in the late sixteenth century, shelving designs sought to maximize space on the walls, and so tended to provide only the most skeletal frameworks: consider Rome's Angelica and Palazzo Corsini libraries (1604, 1747) and Milan's Ambrosiana (1609).[63] The first shelving design for the Archive of the Indies had little in common with such minimalist forms. But it did look a great deal like shelving in the Escorial's library (figs. 3.6, 3.7). There, raised up on a low jasper platform, a series of rectangular wooden bases support Doric columns, which in turn support a carved metope crowned with wooden spheres.[64] Sigüenza's published account of the Escorial did not include engravings of the library's shelves, but it described them. These descriptions had a direct influence on the plans for document cases at the Archive of the Indies.

First, like the proposed designs for the Archive of the Indies, the shelves at the Escorial were made of several kinds of wood, wood with symbolic origins. The domestic joined the ultramarine. As Sigüenza writes in his 1605 description:

> The material and wood of which these shelves are made is all precious, the most ordinary being walnut, the rest brought from the Indies: mahogany of two kinds, which

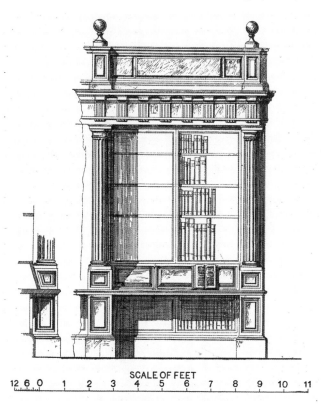

FIGURE 3.6
The library of the Escorial, late sixteenth century.
From Max Junghändel, *Die baukunst Spaniens* (Dresden: J. Bleyl, 1893–98), plate 259.
Compare the bookshelves with the document case design in figure 3.2.
Los Angeles, Getty Research Institute, NA1301.J8 1888.

FIGURE 3.7
Elevation of a bookcase, and section of a desk in the library of the Escorial.
From John Willis Clark, *The Care of Books: An Essay on the Development of Libraries and Their Fittings, from the Earliest Times to the End of the Eighteenth Century* (Cambridge: Cambridge University Press, 1901), 268.

ARCHIVE AS APPARATUS 143

FIGURE 3.8
Second document case design for the Archive of the Indies, 17 September 1785, ink on paper, 46.7 × 33.5 cm.
Seville, Archivo General de Indias, MP Europa y Africa 37.

they call male and female, the color of brazilwood a little less fiery. Ácana of dark chestnut color but somewhat more noble and fiery, such as of dark blood. Ebony, cedar, orange, mastic, from all of these, joined and interwoven, the surface of the whole is composed, a structure of the Doric order most handsome.⁶⁵

Similarly, Andrés Ximénez's 1764 *Descripción del Real Monasterio de San Lorenzo de El Escorial* mentions twice that the library's shelving combined woods "de España, y de las Indias."⁶⁶

But as beautiful as those varied woods were, time revealed that they had not been the best choice. The climate of the Guadarrama Mountains had been hard on the Escorial's carpentry. Sigüenza's account continues:

And although the material was quite extraordinary and beautiful, it didn't work very well, because it is very subject to changes in the weather, opening and closing and thus becoming deformed. It is very important to have experience with materials, and with the lands in which they are to be used.⁶⁷

These lines would have provided Muñoz with a cautionary tale about site-appropriate materials; they probably explain why he was so attentive to the possible effects of Seville's climate on the shelves in his new archive, and why he proposed the resilient two-wood system of mahogany and cedar.

In addition, by the eighteenth century, the Escorial's shelves were closed with gilded wire-mesh doors. This was a design feature initially rejected by Muñoz for Seville (see fig. 3.2), revived a year later in new design proposals by Antonio de Lara y Zúñiga (fig. 3.8), and ultimately rejected by the final design plans of 1786 (fig. 3.9).⁶⁸ But the very fact that Muñoz (and Lara) considered such doors as a possibility suggests another point of dialogue with the design of the Escorial's library, if only as a point of contrast.⁶⁹

The Escorial-Seville shelving comparison was made explicit in a progress report on the Archive of the Indies written by Muñoz in mid-March 1787, two years after approval for Muñoz and Maestre's initial proposal had been given. Muñoz's report even evokes Vitruvius, who is also referenced in Sigüenza's *Tercera parte:*⁷⁰

The shelving of the Library of the Escorial is built with the same taste and [Doric] order of architecture, although it has its faults, and is quite distant from the simplicity, majesty, and perfection of our own. I listened a few days ago to three Englishmen who had visited the finished section [in Seville], and they spoke of it with admiration and enthusiasm. In truth, it transports the spirit to the ancient times of Roman grandeur, and can even be considered worthy of Vitruvius himself: its grandiose halls with vaulted ceilings of worked stone and marble flooring, decorated to the height of the

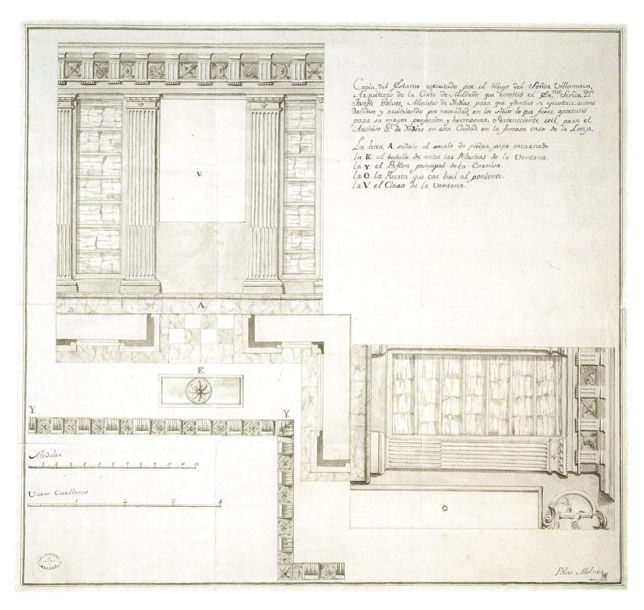

FIGURE 3.9
Juan de Villanueva (Spanish, 1739–1811), designer; and Blas Molner y Zamora (Spanish, 1737–1812), draftsman.
Third document case design for the Archive of the Indies, 17 June 1786 (design), 14 March 1787 (drawing after design), ink on paper, 47 × 51.4 cm.
Key: Copy of the shelving based on the drawing of Lord Villanueva, architect of the Court of Madrid: which was sent by the most excellent Lord don José de Gálvez, Minister of the Indies, so that it should be exactly constructed (modifying and adjusting as needed) in whatever places should be convenient for its greatest perfection, and beauty. These will belong to the General Archive of the Indies in this city; in the famous Lonja building. The letter A. indicates the base of red jasper stone. The E. the soffit panel between the pilasters and the window. The Y. the main soffit of the cornice. The O. the door located to the west. The V. the opening for the window.
Seville, Archivo General de Indias, MP Europa y Africa 54.

vault-bases with a body of Doric architecture six yards tall, on a base of jasper, with tables, windows, and other things of equal taste and nobility.[71]

But when this progress report was written, the appearance of the upper floor of the Lonja had been radically, and controversially, transformed. The archive-in-preparation was not how Muñoz and Maestre first imagined it in 1784. Yet although the revised design departed from the initial proposals, it kept with their spirit, pushing the original vision to a radical new level. Muñoz approved. The changes amplified the archive's simplicity and visual uniformity. They also evoked the layout of the Escorial's library. These were arguably changes following the tradition of Juan de Herrera himself. But for this new design to be implemented—to make Herrera's Lonja even more Herreran—a shocking intervention was perpetrated on the building's upper floor.

A PRESERVATION DEBATE IN EIGHTEENTH-CENTURY SEVILLE

Many of the construction details in Muñoz's progress report from July 1787 match his and Maestre's initial proposals from almost exactly three years before. There is an emphasis on returning the building to its original beauty and on unifying its flooring. An interest in the visual unifications possible through the combination of room layout and shelving was also maintained. But the 4 August 1784 proposals had focused on removing the added partitions of apartment dwellers and realigning the doors of Herrera's individual rooms to create an enfilade (all visually complemented with a continuous stone base for shelving below, and the shelving's own cornice above). By July 1787, a far more radical visual-spatial program had been implemented:

> I will now speak of the status in which are found the things of the said Archive. The building is a beautiful square of two hundred feet on each side, with two floors and stone vaults, built at the end of the sixteenth century by the celebrated Juan de Herrera. Its upper level, destined for the documents, had on each side five rooms, square ones in the corners, then two smaller ones, and in the middle a hall almost twenty-five yards wide and a width (common to all) of nine and a half [yards]. Only the west side was different, because of the staircase. This side has remained in its original form. *The other three have been joined into one great hall composed of three galleries by removing their dividing walls and replacing them with stone arches to support the ceilings.* Finding these marred and blackened for many reasons, they have been returned to their original beauty. The flooring was of a thousand styles, and all was unified with pavings of Málaga [stone] in two colors, which were brought to Seville by water in recent months, and already the paving is well advanced. The shelving corresponds to the majesty of the building: a body in the Doric order, with pilasters for columns, five and a half yards high, not counting the base which is a third of a yard, and is of Málaga jasper. Its entablature runs continuously, without any interruption, forming a crown that serves as a base for the vaults, and makes a better visual effect than the true base, which is covered up, because of how the cymatium and cornice meet. The said shelving is of perfectly polished mahogany on the outside, and on the inside is of cedar. Tables, benches, doors,

and windows are being made of the same woods. A good part of all this is built and installed, and the work continues with zeal. The shelving, which is the main work, is contracted by royal decree with don Blas Molner, director of the Academy of Noble Arts of Seville (in sculpture), who has agreed to finish within two years, which will end in May 1789. He is in charge of all stages, from sawing to polishing; and His Majesty provides him with wood and money in part-payment. At the same time work is being done to renovate and improve the staircase, which was constructed with less taste than the rest of the building, no doubt by a designer much inferior to the esteemed Herrera. I am confident that within two years the work will be fully completed, and Your Majesty will have an ornament of taste and value superior to all others of its kind known anywhere in Europe.[72]

This one sentence—"The other three have been joined into one great hall composed of three galleries by removing their dividing walls and replacing them with stone arches to support the ceilings"—is easy to overlook. But it points to a firestorm of controversy that raged in Seville for more than a year.

On 29 August 1785, Antonio de Lara y Zúñiga was appointed the archive's new superintendent director. He would spend the next three-plus years overseeing renovations. On inspecting the state of the Lonja in early September, he was immediately annoyed to find that nothing but demolition work had been accomplished since mid-April. Yet this lack of progress was also an advantage. It allowed Lara, and project architect Lucas Cintora, to modify the original designs. The result was an architecture that, once filled with documents, would galvanize new research.

Lara and Cintora must have clicked immediately. Or perhaps Cintora took advantage of Lara's arrival to implement an architectural knowledge-machine he had already dreamed up. Whatever the reason, the fate of the archive was changed less than three weeks after Lara's appointment. Here is how Lara, in his first report after visiting the Lonja, described the archive's revised design to José de Gálvez:

My dear lord: following that which I offered to Your Excellency in my previous [letter], I have reviewed the work on the Lonja building, which is destined for the General Archive of the Indies, and finding it not yet started, and in a state that allowed the projected [plans] to be improved, aligning myself to the intentions and desires of Your Excellence, I have resolved—with the ideas and approval of the Master Architect, and other intelligent men—to remove the walls that divide its rooms, substituting them with arches of stone, to form a single [space] that joins the northern, western, and southern sides, as is shown in the plan that I include [fig. 3.10], leaving only the [room] numbered 9, with its door numbered 8, for the storing of certain papers, or things most precious [the future room of Royal Patronage]. I have the satisfaction to assure Your Excellency that this idea has been generally applauded, and, accompanied by other small innovations (as indicated by the same plan and its explanation), forms a work and archival hall without equal in Europe, at least as far as I know.[73]

ARCHIVE AS APPARATUS 147

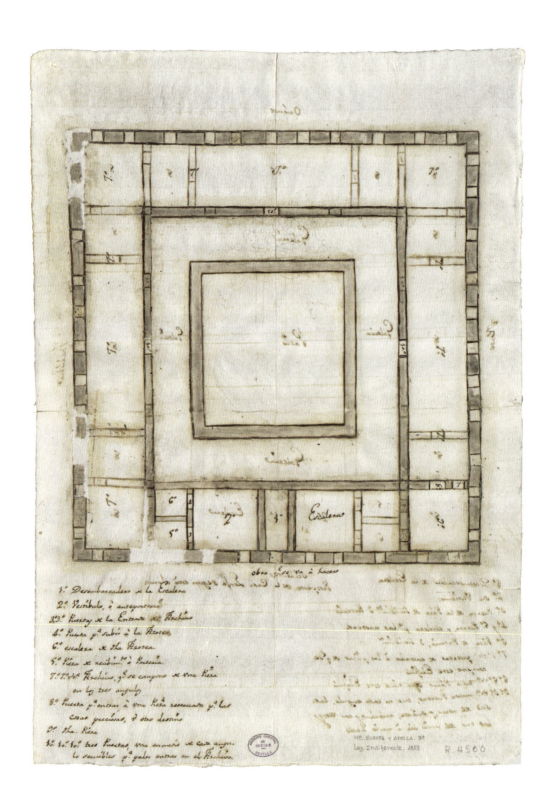

148 CHAPTER 3

The plan Lara mentions is very suggestive, especially when compared with earlier drawings of the same upper floor (see figs. 3.3, 3.4). Most of the building's walls are drawn with dark black lines, their spaces filled in with a gray wash. In contrast, the dividing walls to be torn down are drawn very lightly, and are not filled in. The effect is almost ghostly: these walls will soon disappear.

Fewer than nine months later, master architect Lucas Cintora described his own version of these events. Back in September, Lara had convened his first meeting with project employees, and was thinking about the designs inherited from Muñoz:

> That which don Juan Bautista Muñoz had planned seemed very appropriate to his Lordship [Lara]; but on entering and exiting the many halls and rooms that divide the three sides of the building with disproportionate massive walls fifty inches thick, he admitted that he was displeased with having to divide the archive into thirteen smaller archives separated one from the other, just because this was the number of rooms that occupied the three sides of the building destined for the said project. "Sir," I said, "what you describe isn't really that necessary. Would Your Lordship like to create an archive that perhaps has no equal in Europe? Would Your Lordship like to be free of these walls, which will obscure the shelving, and which now darken the building and diminish its magnificence with the many divisions they impose on it? Well, all of this is remedied by totally removing these walls and putting in their place arches of stone (matching the building), so that these [arches] support that which is now supported by those [walls], and Your Lordship will achieve with this all that you desire: three galleries sixty-two yards long, and in which, with a single glance, can be seen all of the document cases each one contains. This idea is not simple, nor is its execution among the easiest, but it is the most appropriate for the goal."[74]

The plan was implemented. By mid-March, half of the ten supporting arches were finished. Three of the now-unnecessary walls had been ripped out.[75] Then the scandal began. The rediscovery of Juan de Herrera as a Spanish architectural genius, and the recent emergence of preservationist aesthetics, meant that many people in Seville were horrified by what was being done inside the Lonja. By the end of the month, even people in Cádiz were talking, which led architect Miguel Olivares to write to Cintora asking for his side of the story.[76] In response, Cintora published a 110-page screed attacking his attackers and defending the renovations (fig. 3.11). It was published in early June. Its title took no prisoners:

JUST REFUTATION OF THE IGNORANT
AND OF MALIGN FOES.
A CRITICAL-DEFENSIVE LETTER
IN WHICH IS VINDICATED
THE WORK THAT IS BEING DONE
IN THE LONJA
OF SEVILLE.

FIGURE 3.10

Antonio de Lara y Zúñiga (Spanish, 1736–1802) and Lucas Cintora (Spanish, 1732–1800).
Plan for the upper floor of the Lonja, 17 September 1785, ink on paper, 44 × 31.4 cm.
Dividing-wall lines in the three galleries have been drawn very lightly; these walls are to be demolished and replaced by arches.
Key: **1** Landings of the staircase. **2** Vestibule, or antechamber. **3** Entry doors to the archive. **4** Door for going to the roof. **6** Staircase to the said roof. **5** Reception room or doorman's office. **7** Archive, which comprises a single space on the three sides [of the building]. **8** Door leading to a reserved room for precious things, or another purpose. **9** The said room. **10** Three doors, one in the middle of each side [of the patio gallery] enabling access to the archive.
Seville, Archivo General de Indias, MP Europa y Africa 31.

FIGURE 3.11
Lucas Cintora (Spanish, 1732–1800).
Title page of *Justa repulsa de ignorantes, y de émulos malignos* (Seville: Vázquez, Hidalgo, y Compañía, 1786).
Storrs, University of Connecticut, Dodd Research Library, A735.

This was not a prudent move on Cintora's part. In early October, Gálvez wrote to Lara: the screed had been published without permission and contained various errors. Cintora should be reprimanded and all copies of the book destroyed.[77] (Fortunately, at least two escaped: one is now in the Archive of the Indies' own library, and the other in the Dodd Research Library of the University of Connecticut at Storrs.)

But the controversial renovations continued. All ten arches were in place by mid-October 1787. The installation of document cases was also well underway (having started in February) and would be completed in late May 1788. On 20 June 1788, Lara reported that most of the archive's documents were in place.

"Three galleries sixty-two yards long, and in which, with a single glance, can be seen all of the document cases each one contains." This was not easy to achieve, either socially or architecturally—indeed, Cintora spent many pages of his screed explaining arch design. But as with so many aspects of the archive, this visual effect was meant to do more than simply impress visitors. It was to perform specific functions in the production of archival knowledge.

DATA VISUALIZATION

When wall-system shelf design emerged in the late sixteenth century, it was not merely a method for maximizing storage space. It was also a method for structuring information, making libraries easier to use. Visually speaking, the wall system created a unified, floor-to-ceiling expanse of books, preferably covering all four walls of a single large room. The way that books were shelved, and how they related to one another, was carefully planned. Book placement was to reflect the structure of the universe. Shelving subsections were organized by topic, and all joined together to form a coherent, continuous whole. As a result, according to theories driving wall-system display, visitors could take in the entire intellectual contents of a library with a single glance. And in that glance, visitors could simultaneously see what information the library contained as well as understand how that information related to the organization of the cosmos.

In 1661, Herman Conring argued against dividing libraries into many small rooms; far preferable was housing all books in a single space, a design that "causes more to be seen at once" and "presents everything as if to a single look of the eyes.... Truly it is greatly delightful, as it were, to learn in just one moment an almost infinite number of things, just as in fact often happens in other instances when much is suddenly given to be understood."[78] Not quite a century later, Oliver Legipont described wall-system organization as "a kind of architectural figure and an unbroken circle, in such a manner that progress may be made in appropriate and pleasing order from the introductory to the elevated, or on the other hand from the more sublime and universal to the specific...all is most suitably displayed to the eyes of the viewer, and thus is to hand for the learned, so that those who desire to teach or profess the disciplines can here contemplate and survey these same [disciplines] as if concentrated in a glass."[79] The wall system was not simply an aesthetic move: it was to produce a fusion between books, the universe, and the researcher's mind, facilitating library usage by actively enabling the production of new knowledge.[80] Starting in the eighteenth century, treatises on organizing archives were making the same visual claims for the arrangement of documents. Like Lucas Cintora's screed, they stressed the importance of taking in an archive's holdings "with a single glance" (*de un solo golpe de vista*).[81]

As it happens, the organization of Juan de Herrera's Escorial library was an early manifestation of wall-system theory. Although its shelves (as we have seen) were architectonic and not minimalist, their contents were grouped by subject matter, an arrangement symbolically reinforced by frescoes on the ceiling.[82] Given the deep impact of the Escorial's library on plans for the Archive of the Indies, it should be no surprise to find these spatial-intellectual ideas at play in Seville. Cintora, a fan of Herrera, mentions the Escorial three times in his 1786 *Justa repulsa* (Just refutation), so we can assume the monastery-palace's sixteenth-century library shaped his radical ideas for an eighteenth-century archive.[83]

Wall-system theory also explains many features of document arrangement at the Archive of the Indies. As mentioned during our tour with George Ticknor in chapter 1, the numbering system of document cases in the archive's three galleries seems odd. It begins not where visitors entered the archive (by the front offices in the northwest corner) but instead at the southern end of the inner wall of the eastern gallery (see fig. 1.27). Case 1 was there, case 7 above the door to the patio, and case 13 at the inner wall's northern extreme. Understood in terms of user access, it seems strange to begin numeration halfway through the archive. Understood in terms of of wall-system visuality, however, this starting point makes perfect spatial-symbolic sense. When looking at this wall of cases, the visitor is looking to the west—that is, toward the Americas, and, closer to home, to the Guadalquivir River, which was Seville's connection to the Atlantic. In libraries, wall-system theory created microcosms. At the Archive of the Indies, cases 1–13 aligned their viewer with planetary geography.

Furthermore, documents in Seville were arranged on the archive's walls to create the visual-conceptual unities central to wall systems. Look again at the thematic placements mapped in figure 1.27. All the documents of Accounting could be seen at once, stored on shelves 1–11 of that west-facing wall of the eastern gallery. House of Trade documents, starting in the eastern gallery, taking up all of the northern gallery, and finally overflowing into the eastern gallery again, were not really visible all at once, but would have surrounded the viewer who walked along them. The Justice documents, on shelves 47–52, could easily be seen in a single glance. The Government documents took up all four walls of the southern gallery: not visible all at once, but creating the immersive four-walls experience beloved of wall-system theorists. Finally, the two cases of precious Royal Patronage documents in the southwest corner room could also be viewed in a single glance. Remember that the sorting of the AGI's documents began with their scattered arrivals in the fall of 1785, years before document installation began in early 1788. This would have given archivists plenty of time to calculate how much space each documentary section would need, and thus where each section should be displayed to maximize single-glance visibility.

Wall-system theory also explains why so much emphasis was placed on uniformity and regularity in the archive's floors, walls, and ceilings. Visual unity in the architectural shell would create a consistent backdrop for the enhanced viewing of bundled documents. As Walter Benjamin argued in the 1930s, and as more recently demonstrated by Reinhold Martin and John Harwood, architectonic envelopes do a great deal of work, and are perhaps even more effective the farther they recede into the background.[84] At the AGI, archival architecture was to function like the frame for a painting or the bezel for a jewel: it was to amplify the visual impact of what it contained.

This emphasis on visual encounters with documents was a relatively new idea in archival design. As seen in the last chapter, the donor archives in Madrid, Simancas, Seville, and Cádiz all distributed their holdings in a number of separate rooms. At Simancas, which provides our best information on how documents were kept, we find a wide variety of storage systems: a few on open shelves, but the majority on shelves obscured behind doors or within velvet-lined locked chests. For the most part, Simancas guarded its documents as hidden treasures. As Riol put it in 1726, "these books or registers of the seal are not only the most complete that exist in the archive but also the most precious mineral, from which one can extract (as I have extracted) most precious information."[85]

In contrast to the buried riches of a mine, the Archive of the Indies presented its documents as visible components of a light-filled system of knowledge: all neatly arranged, all clearly labeled, all unified.

THE GRID

We might be tempted to think the AGI's wall-system arrangement of documents helped preserve memories of their different origins in different archives, from Simancas to Madrid to Seville to Cádiz. But I'm not sure this was the case. Yes, documents were grouped according to their archives of origin—yet exceptions were made and, as will be seen in the next chapter, sometimes sets of documents from one section were relocated to another. In addition, the ways documents were displayed, and the ways they were named, worked to erase their diverse origins. Only one of the sections, House of Trade, preserved the name of its donor archive—an archive previously split, you will remember, between Seville and Cádiz. All of the other shelving sections were named for their *subject matter,* not their institution of origin: Accounting, Justice, Government, and Royal Patronage. Furthermore, as George Ticknor described in 1818, the treatment of documents was also meant to create visual unity and erase divergent histories. Each bundle was wrapped in paper and given a new label. This prevented the visual chaos that stacked, unwrapped bundles of papers would produce; it also united all documents with a single style of filing, regardless of their origins. Document display worked to simultaneously clarify and conceal.

To better understand how a system designed for knowledge-producing visibility was also a system of information-obscuring invisibility, consider Bernhard Siegert's discussion of the grid.[86] For Siegert, the grid is a fascinating and powerful device because it can register both presence and absence, both data and address. Data can be removed from a grid for consultation and then returned to the same place—or, when a grid is applied to, say, unknown territory, it produces a system for ordering the unexpected. Document cases, of course, create a system of data and addresses: the case-unit is subdivided into shelf-units, which in turn contain bundled document packets (their various layers, as shown in the introduction, redundantly tagged with different levels of metadata; see figs. I.3–I.7).[87] Note that before the late 1920s, document bundles in Seville were not stored vertically but were stacked horizontally one on top of the other within a shelving alcove—a stacking that would have enhanced the grid-like appearance of the AGI's walls (see figs. P.1, 1.25, 1.31; cf. fig. 1.8).

What happens when we analyze these grid-arranged documents at another level of magnification (below the wall system's sweeping visual-thematic unities), using as our guides the case-by-case, shelf-by-shelf, document-by-document inventories created between 1791 and 1819? As mentioned in chapter 1, all documents were given a three-part address within archival space, referring to case, shelf, and bundle.[88] The eighty-one gallery cases, divided (usually) into six shelves, united the archive into a conceptual grid of eighty-one "columns," all containing (except for the three single-shelf overdoors) six "rows" each. An appendix of two more six-row columns was provided by the two document cases in the Royal Patronage room. Within this grid of columns and rows, the third level of document-addresses was often binomial, consisting of two parts. The lower number indicated the document's ordinal position on the shelf. The upper number indicated the document's ordinal position within a thematic subsection (a subsection that could run across any number of shelves).

Take, for example, the section of documents referred to on the Justice *Inventario* pages shown in figure I.8. Most of page 8 (on the left) continues the list of documents in case 47, shelf 1, bundle 11 that began on the previous page; at the very bottom begins a list of the documents in case 47, shelf 1, bundle 12: "Autos entre partes año de 1533 à 1534" (lawsuits between individuals, 1533–34). This list continues on the first two-thirds of page 9; the final third of the page then covers the documents in case 47, shelf 1, bundle 13: "Autos entre partes años de 1534 y 1535."

Figure 3.12 maps the contents of all six shelves in case 47 (as detailed on pages 1–90 of the Justice *Inventario*). For the documents in each shelf, the bottom row of numbers is progressive, starting with 1, and indicates how many document bundles total there were per shelf. The upper row of numbers indicates thematic series within the shelving system overall; these may begin on one shelf and end on another. The Justice section of the archive begins at case 47, and so that case's first shelf starts with the first thematic series in that section: the royal high court of Santo Domingo, and specifically "Autos entre partes" (lawsuits between individuals). Shelf 1 contains twenty-seven document bundles of such cases; the 1532 lawsuit documents illustrated in figures I.2–I.7 were located in bundle 11 (or, to give the full shelving location, 47.1.11). The twenty-eighth bundle on the shelf began a new series of Santo Domingo documents, "Autos fiscales" (financial lawsuits), which contained fourteen bundles of documents (47.1.1/28 through 14/41). Shelf 1 ended by beginning a new thematic series, "Residencias" (Reviews of government officials). This series contained sixty document bundles, five of which were on shelf 1 (47.1.1/42 through 5/46), thirty-eight of which were on shelf 2 (47.2.6/1 through 43/38), and seventeen of which were on shelf 3 (47.3.44/1 through 60/17). Near the end of shelf 3 were four bundles of "Visitas" (Inspections; 47.3.1/18 through 4/21), followed by one bundle of "Comisiones" (Commissions; 47.3.1/22). This bundle was the last within the Santo Domingo section; the final five bundles on shelf 3 moved to the royal high court of Mexico, with a series of

CASE 47

Shelf 1

Audiencia de Santo Domingo

Autos entre partes   Autos fiscales   Residencias
     1 2 3 4 5 6 7 8 9 10 11 12 13 14   1 2 3 4 5
1 2 3 4 5 6 7 8 9 10 11 12 13 14 15 16 17 18 19 20 21 22 23 24 25 26 27 28 29 30 31 32 33 34 35 36 37 38 39 40 41 42 43 44 45 46

Shelf 2

Audiencia de Santo Domingo

Residencias...
6 7 8 9 10 11 12 13 14 15 16 17 18 19 20 21 22 23 24 25 26 27 28 29 30 31 32 33 34 35 36 37 38 39 40 41 42 43
1 2 3 4 5 6 7 8 9 10 11 12 13 14 15 16 17 18 19 20 21 22 23 24 25 26 27 28 29 30 31 32 33 34 35 36 37 38

Shelf 3

Audiencia de Santo Domingo   Audiencia de México

Residencias...   Visitas   C   Autos entre partes
44 45 46 47 48 49 50 51 52 53 54 55 56 57 58 59 60   1   2   3   4   1   1   2   3   4   5
1   2   3   4   5   6   7   8   9   10   11   12   13   14   15   16   17   18   19   20   21   22   **23   24   25   26   27**

Shelf 4

Audiencia de México

Autos entre partes...
6 7 8 9 10 11 12 13 14 15 16 17 18 19 20 21 22 23 24 25 26 27 28 29 30 31 32 33 34 35 36 37 38 39 40 41 42 43 44
1 2 3 4 5 6 7 8 9 10 11 12 13 14 15 16 17 18 19 20 21 22 23 24 25 26 27 28 29 30 31 32 33 34 35 36 37 38 39

Shelf 5

Audiencia de México

Autos entre partes...   Autos fiscales
45 46 47 48 49 50 51 52 53 54 55 56 57 58 59 60 61 62 63 64 65 66 67 68 69 70 71 72 73 74 75 76 77 78   1   2   3   4   5
1   2   3   4   5   6   7   8   9   10   11   12   13   14   15   16   17   18   19   20   21   22   23   24   25   26   27   28   29   30   31   32 33 34 35 36 37 38 39

Shelf 6

Audiencia de México

Autos fiscales...   Residencias
6 7 8 9 10 11 12 13 14 15 16 17 18 19 20 21 22 23 24 25 26 27 28 29 30 31 32 33 34 35   1   2   3   4   5   6   7   8   9   10 11 12 13 14 15 16
1 2 3 4 5 6 7 8 9 10 11 12 13 14 15 16 17 18 19 20 21 22 23 24 25 26 27 28 29 30 31 32 33 34 35 36 37 38 39 40 41 42 43 44 45 46

FIGURE 3.12
A mapping of case 47's documentary contents,
showing the grid of the archive.

"Autos entre partes" (47.3.1/23 through 5/27). This series continued to fill all of shelf 4 (47.4.6/1 through 44/39) and most of shelf 5 (47.5.45/1 through 78/34). The last five bundles on shelf 5 began a new series of Mexican legal documents, "Autos fiscales" (47.5.1/35 through 5/39), a series that continued on shelf 6 (47.6.6/1 through 35/30). Shelf 6 concluded with seventeen "Residencias" bundles for Mexico (47.6.1/31 through 16/46), a series that continued on the first shelf of case 48.

Users consulting the archive's inventories were therefore not only given the address for finding a particular document on a specific shelf but were also, simultaneously, given information linking that document to a broader thematic sequence, to other documents that might be relevant for understanding the target document. Thus, within an abstract grid of positional numbers addressing archival space, the inventories of the archive also register another, more concrete level of meaning.

But if the grid makes presence and absence and series visible, it also only makes those presences and absences and series visible within the terms of its own organization. Once things—from documents to territory—are put in a grid, the grid works to deny, to erase, any coherence or absences found in older organizational structures. Once data is put in a grid, its histories prior to incorporation in that totalizing order are easily ignored.[89] Presences and absences can only be registered within a grid's framework, not beyond its limits or before its implementation.

The grid asserts a power to produce order. But the real power of the grid is to produce the *illusion* that the objects placed under its control had never been ordered before being captured in the grid's own totalizing net.[90] This is a problem Siegert points to in his example of the United States territorial survey, created by the Land Ordinance Act of, yes, our magic year 1785. That grid could produce squares of land for sale that fell in swamps or bodies of water, or even within "Indian Territory"—and so subject to a sovereignty previous to, and challenging of, the land divisions and ownership possibilities pronounced by the grid.

A similar erasure was produced on the shelves of the Archive of the Indies. The unified shelving and packaging worked to efface prior histories and replace them with a new eighty-plus-by-six storage grid: a new system of spatial addresses from which data could be removed, consulted, and returned in the process of producing new knowledge.[91]

How this grid of documents was actually used is explored in the next chapter.

NOTES

1 Lorenzo da Ponte, *Le nozze di Figaro, o sia la folle giornata* (Prague: Giuseppe Emanuele Diesbach, 1786), 71. See also https://www.youtube.com/watch?v=_OYtlGpApco (at 2:03:27): Concerto Köln, conductor René Jacobs, Paris, Le Théâtre des Champs-Elysées, 2001.

2 For the details of these shipment chronologies, see this volume, chapter 2.

3 María Antonio Colomar Albajar, *La Casa Lonja de Sevilla: Una casa de ricos tesoros* (Madrid: Ministerio de Cultura, 2005), 180–81, 185–89; see also this volume, table 3.1. On shelving design more generally, see Thomas Kimball Brooker, "Upright Works: The Emergence of the Vertical Library in the Sixteenth Century," 5 vols. (PhD diss., University of Chicago, 1996); Joseph Connors and E. Angela Dressen, "Biblioteche: L'architettura e l'ordinamento del sapere," in *Il Rinascimento Italiano e l'Europa*, vol. 6, *Luoghi, spazi, architetture,* ed. Donatella Calabi and Elena Svalduz (Treviso: Fondazione Cassamarca, 2009), 199–228; and Eric Garberson, *Eighteenth-Century Monastic Libraries in Southern Germany and Austria: Architecture and Decorations* (Baden-Baden: Verlag Valentin Koerner, 1998), 68–70, 83–87.

4 The first shelves (eight *varas* in length) were in place by 28 February 1787. Since they are described as built around windows, I assume they were on the northern wall of the northern gallery, just outside the archive's main office in the northwest corner: "El dia vltimo de febrero se concluió, y puso el primer estante de este Archivo.... El Estante concluido tiene ocho varas de largo con el hueco de vna ventana q[u]e hai en el" (AGI IG 1854A, Antonio de Lara y Zúñiga to José de Gálvez, Seville, 14 March 1787). By 18 October 1787, Lara wrote that the ninety-eight chests of Accounting documents were "ready to be moved to their respective cases." He also noted that the following week, all of the archive's papers would be moved to the building's upper floor, although this seems to refer to a seasonal changing of offices (from the cooler ground floor in the summer to the warmer upper floor in the winter) and not necessarily to the installation of documents per se: "los q[u]e embio la contaduria del Consejo en 98 Cajones estan bien coordinados, y en disposicion de trasladarse à sus respectivos Estantes sin travajo alguno.... Està cortado con tablas vn buen pedazo

de la obra nueva p[ar]a q[u]e sirua de Archivo en este Ynvierno; y poder obrar con menos embarazo; la semana proxima hazè subir à el todos los papeles, q[u]e acomodarè del mejor modo possible" (AGI IG 1854A, Antonio de Lara y Zúñiga to José de Gálvez, Seville). In any event, the cases of the eastern gallery would not be completed until 13 February 1788; on that day Lara wrote that at least some of the archive's documents had been installed in their cases: "el escultor encargado de los estantes concluya los de la segunda crugia, i suspenda el trabajo de los de la tercera hasta nuevo aviso. Pero juzga indispensable exponer, que segun el lugar que ocupan los Papeles colocados en una parte de la Estanteria, recela que en dos crugias no havra capacidad aun para los que tiene" (AGI IG 1854A, Antonio de Lara y Zúñiga to José de Gálvez, Seville). On 28 May 1788, Blas Molner y Zamora was paid for completing the archive's gallery cases (AGI IG 1854A, Blas Molner y Zamora to Antonio de Lara y Zúñiga, Seville), and on 18 June 1788, Lara wrote that documents were being installed: "Los Papeles se van acomodando en los Estantes" (AGI IG 1854A, Antonio de Lara y Zúñiga to José de Gálvez, Seville).

5 "Sabado 20 Las ocho Metopas p[ar]a estos Estantes de Patronato q[u]e hizo D[o]n Blas Molner, y menciona su recibo.... Miercoles 24 Los gastos cauzados en la Carpinteria... que han motivado los dos Estantes de Patronato, en vidrios, y herraje" (AGI IG 1858H, parchment-bound book of accounts March 1785–February 1789, entries for December 1788).

6 "Puede V[uestra] E[xcelencia] si lo tiene à bien, manifestar à S[u] M[ajestad] se hà concluido la obra material de este su Archivo de Yndias" (AGI IG 1854A, Antonio de Lara y Zúñiga to José de Gálvez, Seville, 5 November 1788). In terms of furniture, the account books for October 1789 report the following payment: "Dia 8 el Maestro Carpintero que se ocupó en componerse las mesas y disponer su subida al Archivo alto" (AGI IG 1858H, "Libro en que se sientan las Cuentas mensuales desde el mes de Marzo de 1789," parchment-bound book of accounts 1789–1810).

7 John Harwood's discussion of Eliot Noyes, design teams, and IBM provided me with a starting point for thinking about collaborative 1780s design work at the AGI; John Harwood, *The*

Interface: IBM and the Transformation of Corporate Design, 1945–1976 (Minneapolis: University of Minnesota Press, 2011). For an early modern parallel, see the (often conflictive) collaborative design of the Escorial: George Kubler, *Building the Escorial* (Princeton, NJ: Princeton University Press, 1982).

8 Maestre is described as "el govierno De la obra" in a 24 June 1784 letter (AMS Sección 11 Papeles del Conde de Águila tomo 4 no. 13, fol. 35v, José de Gálvez to Juan Bautista Muñoz, Aranjuez). He died on 9 November 1784 (AMS Sección 11 Papeles del Conde de Águila tomo 4 no. 13, fol. 51r, Seville, November 1784). This 1784 letter is probably referred to in AGI IG 1854A, "Expediente sobre el establecimiento i progresos del Archivo de Yndias de Sevilla," fol. 2v, Juan Bautista Muñoz, 31 July 1787.

9 Gregorio de Fuentes was named project commissioner on 2 February 1785: AMS Sección 11 Papeles del Conde de Águila tomo 4 no. 13, fols. 59r–59v, José de Gálvez to Gregorio de Fuentes, El Pardo, 2 February 1785 (appointment letter); AMS Sección 11 Papeles del Conde de Águila tomo 4 no. 13, fol. 58r, José de Gálvez to Juan Bautista Muñoz, El Pardo, 3 February 1785; and AGI IG 1854A, "Expediente sobre el establecimiento i progresos del Archivo de Yndias de Sevilla," fol. 3v, Juan Bautista Muñoz, 31 July 1787.

10 AGI IG 1854A, José de Gálvez?, San Ildefonso, 29 August 1785.

11 Dismissal of Lara: AGI IG 1854A, Antonio Porlier to Antonio de Lara y Zúñiga, Madrid, 1 February 1791; see also response in AGI IG 1854A, Antonio de Lara y Zúñiga to Antonio Porlier, Seville, 9 February 1791.

12 Reference to a "Carta de D. Juan Bautista Muñoz de 12 de Marzo instando por la egecución del Archivo general" (AGI IG 1854A, "Expediente sobre el establecimiento i progresos del Archivo de Yndias de Sevilla," Juan Bautista Muñoz, 31 July 1787).

13 "Con fecha de 23 de Abril se sirvió V[uestra] E[xcelencia] comunicarme Real Orden, con inserción de una representación del Archivero de la Casa de Contratación de Sevilla, i de los informes acerca de ella dados por el Presidente i Contador

Arnuero, D[o]n Fernando de Huete, i el Marqués del Surco; para que instruido de ellos reconozca la Casa Lonja de esta ciudad, con asistencia de Facultativos que informen de la capacidad i disposición de ella para formar un Archivo general de Indias resguardado de las injurias del tiempo" (AGI IG 1853, Juan Bautista Muñoz to José de Gálvez, Seville, 8 June 1784; see also AGI IG 1853, Félix Carazas and Lucas Cintora, Seville, 24 May 1784).

14 Carmen Méndez Zubiría, "La casa de Lonja y su transformación en Archivo de Indias," in *Primeras jornadas de Andalucía y América,* vol. 2 (Huelva, Spain: Instituto de Estudios Onubenses, 1981), 305–15; Alberto Humanes Bustamante, "De la Real Casa Lonja de Sevilla al Archivo General de Indias," in *La América española en la época de Carlos III: Sevilla, diciembre 1985–marzo 1986* (Seville: Ministerio de Cultura, Instituto de Cooperación Iberoamericana and Archivo General de Indias, 1985), 59–81; Alfonso Pleguezuelo Hernández, "La Lonja de Mercaderes de Sevilla: De los proyectos a la ejecución," *Archivo Español de Arte* 249 (1990): 15–41; and Catherine Wilkinson-Zerner, *Juan de Herrera: Architect to Philip II of Spain* (New Haven, CT: Yale University Press, 1993), 9, 39–41, 58, 81–83.

15 On the Lonja's seventeenth-century builders, see Juan Antonio Arenillas, *Del clasicismo al barroco: Arquitectura sevillana del siglo XVII* (Seville: Diputación de Sevilla, 2005), 221, 230–33, 242, 246.

16 On the possible abandonment, see Humanes Bustamante, "De la Real Casa Lonja de Sevilla," 73. On the academy, see Antonio de la Banda y Vargas, "Los estatutos de la Academia de Murillo," *Anales de la Universidad Hispalense* 42 (1961): 107–20; Antonio de la Banda y Vargas, "La Academia de Murillo," *Boletín de Bellas Artes* 11 (1983): 37–48; Humanes Bustamante, "De la Real Casa Lonja de Sevilla," 73; Peter Cherry, "Murillo's Drawing Academy," in *Bartolomé Esteban Murillo (1617–1682): Paintings from American Collections,* ed. Suzanne Stratton-Pruitt, exh. cat. (New York: Henry N. Abrams, 2002), 47–61; and Ramón Corzo Sánchez, *La Academia del Arte de la Pintura de Sevilla: 1660–1674* (Seville: Instituto de Academias de Andalucía, 2009).

17 "La Casa Lonja, edificio aislado, que en firmeza no tiene superior, i parece hecho de proposito para el intento. No hai en él un atomo de madera fuera de las puertas i ventanas: sus techumbres son bovedas de piedra grandemente labradas. Por manera que está libre de incendios. Lo está igualmente de inundaciones: cosa en Sevilla de mucha consideración. Ya el terreno sobre que se levanta la fábrica es de suyo más elevado que el nivel de las aguas del Guadaquivir en sus mayores crecidas: pues a esta altura deben añadirse las gradas, por las quales se sube a un andito que circunda el quadro, le adorna, le fortalece, i pone su primer piso harto superior al de la contigua Catedral, adonde no hai memoria que hayan llegado jamas las aguas ni con mucho.

"Quanto a disposición i comodidad para el fin propuesto, en solo el piso superior, que es el principal de los dos de que consta el edificio, hai quanta puede aparecerse, aun dejando lugar para los Papeles que se hayan de agregar en lo sucesivo. Tiene cada uno de los quatro frentes uniformes doscientos pies con poca diferencia: ocupan lo largo cinco salas, una en medio magnifica prolongada, dos quadradas en los angulos, i entre estas i la de en medio otras dos algo menores que los angulares. Solo el frente occidental varia, por tener en el centro la escalera, que da entrada a la galería que circunda el patio, i por esta a todas las salas que se comunican mutuamente. Este frente podria quedar desocupado, por si conviniere poner algunas oficinas con total separación de los Papeles. Los otros tres podrían vestirse de un cuerpo de estantes elevados como hasta la mitad del altura, los quales bastarán sin duda para las oficinas de la Corte. I este cuerpo debería labrarse con cierta simplicada elegante, antediendo a que en lo venidero pueda sobre el colocarse otro cuerpo dividido del primero con unos andenes a derredor de cada una de las salas. Y quizá sería lo mejor, vestir una de ellas con sus dos estantes divididos por los andenes según el plan que se adoptase, la qual sirviese de modelo para las otras en lo sucesivo.

"Hoi está envilecido i afeado lo interior de la Casa Lonja con muchos tabiques i doblados, por las quales se ha dividido en diversas habitaciones, unas medianas, unas chicas, ocupadas de Contador, Secretario, Escribano, i Portero del Consulado, i algunos antiguos Dependientes de el, o viudas de los mismos. Para el uso de Archivo general no hai que hacer otra cosa sino restablecer el edificio en su primer estado, derribando esos sobrepuestos de mala obra. Si a los presentes habitantes de la Lonja, o a algunos de ellos, se quiere continuar el beneficio de habitación de gracia, o bien puede consignarseles un equivalente anual en dinero, o recompensarles en otros edificios propios del departamento de Indias. Tal es la Casa de Contratación vieja, ocupada hoy dia por la Compañía de S.[an] Fernando; el Archivo de Contratación, i habitación de su Archivero; el Oidor subdelegado del mismo Tribunal, i algunos otros: tal, una Casa desmembrada del mismo edificio con nueva puerta hacia el Norte, donde habita de gracia el Escribano de Marina: tal finalmente la llamada Carcel de Contratación, al presente sin uso, que ocupa bastante extensión en frente de dicha casa" (AGI IG 1853, Juan Bautista Muñoz to José de Gálvez, Seville, 8 June 1784).

18 "Miguel Maestre cavallero comendador De la Orden de s[a]n Juan recidente en esa ciudad" (AMS Sección 11 Papeles del Conde de Águila tomo 4 no. 13, fol. 36r, José de Gálvez to Juan Bautista Muñoz, Aranjuez, 27 June 1784).

19 "Exc[elentísi]mo Señor: En cumplimiento de la R[ea]l Orden de S[u] M[ajestad] que V[uestra] E[xcelencia] se sirvio comunicarnos con fecha de 27. de Junio, reconocimos prolijamente la Casa-Lonja con asistenica de los Arquitectos D.[on] Lucas Zintora, i D.[on] Felix Carasas, los mismos que hicieron el primer reconocimiento. Despues de haver conferido i meditado con la madurez devida, convenimos en que lo primero era quitar los tabiques, doblados, i otros malos sobrepuestos, con que para disponer habitaciones se havia envilecido tan suntuosa fabrica. Y no solamente la havian afeado con desfigurar su primera distribucion i diafanidad, sino tambien con variedad de pavimentos acomodados a las nuevas divisiones, con los salvegados, con el humo de las cocinas &c. Todo deve restablecerse en su primitiva simplicidad i hermosura, raspando lo blanqueado i denegrido, dando a todas las salas un baño del color nativo de la piedra, i solandolas con uniformidad. El pavimento bastará que sea de ladrillos comunes, si bien escogidos, raspados, i cortados para su buena union. A estas obras se añade, cerrar las puertas de las salas angulares que estan a un lado, i abrirlas en el medio; i levantar un zòcalo macizado de material, que sobresalga poco mas de media vara de la pared, i tenga hasta una tercia de altura, el qual servira de pie a los estantes, i los preservarà, nada menos que a los papeles del nicho inferior, de las injurias a que estan ocasionadas las cosas imediatas al suelo. Para mayor firmeza i duracion devera ese zòcalo llevar por el frente una chapa de piedra del grueso de tres o quatro pulgadas, esto es quanto baste para q[u]e a la vista solamente se presente piedra. En la calidad de esta, nuestro juicio es que sea quando menos un jaspe de Mozon, genero del pais que se logra a precio moderado. Conforme a esta idea se han hecho las regulaciones de la obra de arbañileria por los Arquitectos nombrados, cuyo papel va adjunto (num. 1)" (AGI IG 1853, Juan Bautista Muñoz and Francisco Miguel Maestre to José de Gálvez, Seville, 4 August 1784).

20 Cintora and Caraza's report, dated 24 June 1784, is in AGI IG 1853.

21 "Acerca de los estantes hemos pensado con algun espiritu. Hoi dia se miran las Yndias en toda Europa con cierto entusiasmo. Las mas sabias plumas se dedican a ilustrar sus cosas, librando gran parte de su gloria en la dignidad del obgeto. Es dignisimo en realidad, i nadie mas interesado en él que los Españoles, con cuyos hechos en aquel Nuevo mundo apenas merecen entrar en comparacion los de las otras Naciones. V[uestra] E[xcelencia] está intimamente persuadido de estas verdades, i conforme a ellas promueve las verdaderas glorias de la patria. De ellas son fieles depositarios los papeles que ahora van a juntarse en este Archivo general, que sea un tesoro de sumo aprecio. Todos los buenos patricios, todos los hombres de gusto i de saber, asi naturales como estrangeros, mirarán esta empresa con particular atencion: i sera justo satisfacer, aun en lo material de la obra, a los deseos de los buenos, i a la expectacion general.

"El edificio es grandioso: sea pues todo correspondiente, por manera que si un viajero curioso viene a Sevilla, no admire solamente los restos de su opulencia antigua, sino tambien halle un monumento que acredite nuestro espritiu i gusto en el presente siglo.

"Tales son nuestras deseos, i creemos se lograrán cumplidamente, si sobre el indicado zòcalo, de jaspe en la parte visible, se levanta un cuerpo de Arquitectura Dorica, qual presenta el adjunto plano (num. 2). Su elevacion está determinada por la imposta de las bovedas, cuya distancia del piso es de cinco varas i dos tercias: i haviendo de quedar visible la imposta para no quitar a las salas su hermosura, devera subir el estante poco mas de cinco varas. Mas de una se llevan zócalo i ornamento: asi que vendran a quedar quatro entermente utiles, las quales podran dividirse en siete u ocho nichos, que ocupados de papeles bien elegajados con targetas graciosas formaràn el plano, i sobre este resaltaràn las pilastras con sus pedestales. Las distancias de los intercolunios, o sean entrepilastras, sera quando mas la que figura el dibujo; porque si el lugar pide otra cosa, deveran mas bien estrecharse, de forma que en los huecos, considerados como vanos de un edificio, sea la altura el duplo, o algo mas que el duplo de la anchura.

"En las maderas de una obra como esta es necesario atender a la hermosura, i aun mas a la duracion, principalmente en este pais donde reinan con exceso humedades i calores. Ambas qualidades se hallan en la Caoba i el Cedro macho; a que se añade la facilidad de acopiar la cantidad que se quiera trayendola de la Havana, quiza con mas brevedad que se Juntarian qualesquiera otras maderas de la peninsula, fuera de las comunes que por ningun caso deven emplearse en semejantes obras. Somos de parecer, que sea de Caoba todo el cuerpo, esto es pilastras con pedestales, i ornamento: las escalerillas, las tablas, i el forro que los

estantes han de llevar por la espalda, i la armazon del ornamento, todo de cedro. Los frentes de las tablas, i con mucha especialidad el cuerpo de Arquitectura, deveran labrarse i bruñirse perfectamente. Por esta idea saldra una obra tan durable, tan simple, tan hermosa i noble, que ni aun la embidia tendra que censurar" (AGI IG 1853, Juan Bautista Muñoz and Francisco Miguel Maestre to José de Gálvez, Seville, 4 August 1784).

22 "De las mismas maderas deven ser las mesas i los bancos de las salas del Archivo; esto es, de cedro los bancos i los pies de las mesas; los tableros de estas de caoba. Y para que todo corresponda, es menester que tambien vayan chapeteadas de Caoba las puertas por donde se comunican las Salas, i todas las que den entrada al Archivo. Aunque pueden escusarse las puertas de comunicacion: no hai necesidad de ellas, i por ventura pareceran mejor a la vista sus huecos despejados. En este caso bastarian seis puertas, segun se entendera dando una ojeada al plano (num. 3) que representa la Casa-Lonja" (AGI IG 1853, Juan Bautista Muñoz and Francisco Miguel Maestre to José de Gálvez, Seville, 4 August 1784).

23 AMS Sección II Papeles del Conde de Águila tomo 4 no. 13, fols. 38r–45v, 53r; AGI IG 1853, José de Gálvez to Consulado de Mercaderes, San Ildefonso, 21 September 1784.

24 "el dia II de Marzo, en q[u]e se principiò" (AGI IG 1858H, parchment-bound book of accounts March 1785–February 1789).

25 "Instruccion para las obras q[ue] han de hacerse en La Lonja de Sevilla para Archivo g[ene]-ral de Indias" (AGI IG 1853, JBM, 27 April 1785; incomplete copy in AMS Sección II Papeles del Conde de Águila tomo 4 no. 13, fols. 68r–73r).

26 AGI IG 1854A; the opening of the letter is dated "Sevilla 14. de Marzo 1787"; the conclusion is dated "31 de Marzo 1787." Among other things, the letter discusses debates over how the archive's document cases should be designed—and the very next letter in the file, also dated 14 March 1787, is from Lara, asserting his own views about the cases.

27 The most famous examples of this are Muñoz's summary-history of the archive project from 1781–87, "Expediente sobre el establecimiento i progresos del Archivo de Yndias de Sevilla" (dated 31 July 1787); and, a few days later, his 3 August 1787 "Razón del origen, progreso, i actual estado del Archivo general de Indias." Both can be found in AGI IG 1854A. For transcriptions, see David F. Slade, "Enlightened Archi-textures: Founding Colonial Archives in the Hispanic Eighteenth

Century" (PhD diss., Emory University, 2005), 321–27, 328–33; and (for the "Razón" only) see Margarita Gómez Gómez, "El Archivo General de Indias: Génesis histórica de sus ordenanzas," in *Ordenanzas del Archivo General de Indias,* ed. Francisco de Solano, Margarita Gómez Gómez, and Manuel Romero Tallafigo (Seville: Dirección General del Libro, Bibliotecas y Archivos, Consejería de Cultura, Junta de Andalucía, 1986), 91–96. Note that the "Expediente" is followed by shorter, materials-focused histories not included in Slade: "Expediente sobre Maderas para las obras del Archivo"; "Expediente sobre marmoles de malaga para la soleria i el zocalo de los estantes del Archivo"; "Exp[edien]te sobre la translacion de los Papeles de Yndias de Simancas al Archivo de Sevilla"; "Expediente de la translacion de Papeles de la Contratacion de Cadiz al Archivo de Sevilla"; and "Expediente de la translacion de Papeles de la Contaduria General al Archivo de Sevilla." A year later, on 1 November 1788, Muñoz wrote to Antonio Porlier with his suggestions for the official *Ordenanzas* of the new archive (AGI IG 1854A; copy in Gómez Gómez, "El Archivo General de Indias," 105–8). Finally, letters by Muñoz in AGI IG 1854B make clear that he regularly reviewed the monthly financial accounts of the work being carried out on the Lonja (see, for example, letters from 26 August 1787 and 20 June 1788).

28 Harwood, *Interface,* 224.

29 AGI IG 1853, Juan Bautista Muñoz and Francisco Miguel Maestre to José de Gálvez, Seville, 4 August 1784; for quote in Spanish, see note 19 above.

30 AGI IG 1853, Juan Bautista Muñoz to José de Gálvez, Seville, 8 June 1784; for quote in Spanish, see note 17 above.

31 "En lo que proponemos se junta, en nuestro juicio, una i otra con el buen gusto en las Artes, i con una simplicidad noble i magestuosa" (AGI IG 1853, Juan Bautista Muñoz and Francisco Miguel Maestre to José de Gálvez, Seville, 4 August 1784).

32 "Las bovedas dengridas del humo se acabaran de limpiar por el metodo que se ha empezado.... Se dará el baño de color de piedra, de tal manera que quede el color igual en todas las bovedas" (AGI IG 1853, Juan Bautista Muñoz to José de Gálvez, Seville, 27 April 1785).

33 "A la escalera, desembarcadero, glorieta i galeria se dara un baño ligero de color de piedra, algo mas claro que el que aora tiene; por manera que todo quede igual" (AGI IG 1853, Juan Bautista Muñoz to José de Gálvez, Seville, 27 April 1785).

34 "Se tendra mucho cuidado en la eleccion de las Maderas, especialmente en la caoba, procurando la maior igualdad posible en el color de todas las partes de cada sala, i mas aun en las partes semejantes. Por egemplo las pilastras, los pedestales, los triglifos, los modillones &c, sean tan semejantes entre si en color y vetas quanto puedan serlo. Si alguna pequeña variedad se observa, sea en partes diferentes, Asi no sera inconveniente que sea algo mas o menos claro el color del triglifo que el de la metopa, siempre en todas las metopas sean uniformes entre si, i tambien los triglifos. Para hacer mejor la eleccion, convendra ante todas cosas asserrar la maior parte de la madera, dividirla segun las medidas convenintes" (AGI IG 1853, Juan Bautista Muñoz to José de Gálvez, Seville, 27 April 1785). For later, comparable problems with architectural terracotta, see Jorge Otero-Pailos, "The Ambivalence of Smoke: Pollution and Modern Architectural Historiography," *Grey Room* 44 (2011): 104–6.

35 AGI IG 1853, Juan Bautista Muñoz and Francisco Miguel Maestre to José de Gálvez, Seville, 4 August 1784; for quote in Spanish, see note 19 above.

36 "Todas las salas del piso alto se solaran con perfecta igualdad de losetas de piedra de Malaga, procurando todo primor i hermosurea, asi en la eleccion i contraposisicon de las imediatas, como en la union de ellas entre si i con el zocalo" (AGI IG 1853, Juan Bautista Muñoz to José de Gálvez, Seville, 27 April 1785).

37 "El zocalo de los estantes que aora esta cortado en los vanos de las ventanas se completara tambien en ellos, por manera que siga por todas las salas donde haya estantes, sin otra interrupcion que la necesaria en las puertas, a cuyos lados rematara con mui pequeña distancia entre ellos i el angulo del vano" (AGI IG 1853, Juan Bautista Muñoz to José de Gálvez, Seville, 27 April 1785).

38 "El entablamento correra seguido sin ninguna interupcion por las quatro caras de todas las Salas, haciendo una coronacion que juntamente servira de imposta a las bovedas, i hara mejor vista que la imposta veradera, la qual que dara encubierta" (AGI IG 1853, Juan Bautista Muñoz to José de Gálvez, Seville, 27 April 1785).

39 The key for figure 3.4 reads: "I Desenbarcadero de la escalera, con una ventana a la calle, i arcos a tres frentes. II Glorieta, o sea Vestibulo, con arcos a dos frentes, puertas i ventanas a otros dos. III Pieza de recibimiento. IV Subida a las azoteas. Todas las puertas i ventanas notadas con puntos quedan cerradas i sin uso, pero en lo exterior como corresponde a la uniformidad i hermosura del

edificio. Donde va esta señal * se indican puertas que se abren de nuevo." The corresponding caption contains the English translation.

40 AGI IG 1853, Juan Bautista Muñoz and Francisco Miguel Maestre to José de Gálvez, Seville, 4 August 1784; for quote in Spanish, see note 19 above.

41 "Las quatro Salas angulares tienen las puertas a los lados. Con atencion a al vista i grandiosidad se cerrara, i se abriran en medio haciendo arcos de ladrillo, que es la materia de la pared donde han de abrirse" (AGI IG 1853, Juan Bautista Muñoz to José de Gálvez, Seville, 27 April 1785).

42 Thomas Ford Reese, *The Architecture of Ventura Rodríguez*, vol. 1 (New York: Garland, 1976), 101.

43 Santiago Agustín Riol, "Informe que hizo a su magestad el 16 de junio 1726," *Semanario Erudito, Tomo Tercero*, ed. Antonio Valladares de Sotomayor (Madrid: Don Blas Roman, 1787), 207, 205, 204, 206.

44 Riol, "Informe que hizo a su magestad," 206.

45 On the *hombre de bien* and the *petimetre*, see Rebecca Haidt, *Embodying Enlightenment: Knowing the Body in Eighteenth-Century Spanish Literature and Culture* (New York: St. Martin's, 1998). On the *hombre de bien* alone, see Kelly Donahue-Wallace, *Jerónimo Antonio Gil and the Idea of the Spanish Enlightenment* (Albuquerque: University of New Mexico Press, 2017).

46 "Mi modo de vestir seria sumamente sencillo no por modestia, sino por conveniencia. El brillo, la ostentacion en el vestir es una cosa sumamente incomoda" (Luis María Cañuelo y Heredia, "Discurso XXXIX," *El Censor* 2 [1781]: 616; cited in Haidt, *Embodying Enlightenment*, 118).

47 "Estos gastan tocador, y azeyte de sucino, porque padecen males de madre, polvos, lazos, lunares, y brazaletes, y todos los dissimulados afeytes de vna Dama" (Diego de Torres Villarroel, "Vision y visita dezima: Los pitimetres, y lindos," in *Visiones y visitas de Torres con D. Francisco de Quevedo, por la Corte* [Madrid: Antonio Marin, 1727], 31); "pues, amigo, tu no andes guapo por no comer" (Juan Antonio Gómez Arias, *Recetas morales, politicas, y precisas para vivir en la Corte con conveniencia todo genero de personas* [Madrid: Luis Gutiérrez, 1734], 59; see also Haidt, *Embodying Enlightenment*, 118, 122).

48 For the "Carta" (which includes costs charged for its outrageous invented styles), see José Clavijo y Fajardo, "Pensamiento LVII," *El Pensador* 5 (Madrid: Joachín Ibarra, 1767): 75–90. The "Noticias" is a tonadilla in manuscript at Madrid's

Biblioteca Municipal (Haidt, *Embodying Enlightenment*, 248). Both works are discussed in Haidt, *Embodying Enlightenment*, 132; see also Jesusa Vega, *Ciencia, arte e ilusión en la España ilustrada* (Madrid: CSIC, 2010), 44, and, on the ideally restrained dress of scientists, 45–48.

49 "Señor: soy un hombre de buena estatura; cerrado de barba; membrudo; de un color un tanto atezado, y tengo cubierto de vello el cuerpo todo. No temo al sol ni al agua: cuido de mi cabello lo preciso no más para que ande limpio, y para que no me incomode: el sastre y el zapatero me tienen plenamente satisfecho, quando la ropa y el calzado me viene comoda y vagarosa. Y con todo eso estoy tan enamorado de mi figura de hombre, como el Adonis mas acepillado puede estarlo de la suya de muger.... Es innegable que la hermosura de un cuerpo no consiste en otra cosa, que en la proporcion y aptitud que halla el alma que le contempla, en las partes que le componen, para el fin para que el todo ha sido hecho. En tanto es hermosa una fachada, en quanto las partes de que consta aparecen á la vista de quien la considera las mas aptas para la firmeza del edificio, y la representan en lo interior una disposicion la mas conveniente a los usos á que se destina" (Luis María Cañuelo y Heredia [as "Andrés Morphalazon"], "Discurso LXXII," *El Censor* 3 [1784?]: 73–74, 78; see also Haidt, *Embodying Enlightenment*, 123, 137–38).

50 Haidt, *Embodying Enlightenment*, 107.

51 "El Rey se ha enterado con mucha Satisfaccion de quanto V[uestra] M[ajestad] a informado con puntualidad y conocimiento en Su carta de 8 del presente mes asi en orden al estado actual y bellas disposiciones que presta el Edificio de la Casa Lonja de esa Ciudad, para Archivo general de los Papeles de Yndias como a las obras que necesitan hazerse para poner en execucion tan importante designio. Y a fin de que esta no se retarde, ha resuelto S[u] M[ajestad] que los mimsos dos Peritos que han hecho el reconocimiento con presencia del Ynforme de V[uestra] M[ajestad] en la parte que toca á las obras necesarias a la construccion de Archivo en la forma que ally se propone regulen con toda es pesificacion los costos a que ascenderán, haciendose con una prudente economia, sin que por esto dexe de atenderse al mejor proporcion comodidades y ornato que sean posibles" (AMS Sección II Papeles del Conde de Águila tomo 4 no. 13, fol. 35v, José de Gálvez to Juan Bautista Muñoz, Aranjuez, 27 June 1784).

52 "Por otra parte creemos andar conformes con la sabia expresion de S[u] M[ajestad] sobre la regulacion de estas obras. Manda S[u] M[ajestad] que se hagan 'con una prudente economia, sin que por esto dege de atenderse a la mejor proporcion, comodidades i ornato que sean posibles.' V[uestra] E[xcelencia] tiene exactas nociones de lo que es prudente economia; virtud que dejaria de serlo, si tratandose de una obra publica no anduviese unida con la magnificencia" (AGI IG 1853, Juan Bautista Muñoz and Francisco Miguel Maestre to José de Gálvez, Seville, 4 August 1784).

53 David F. Slade, "Imagining from Within: Archives, History, and Ibero-American Enlightenment Discourse," in *Lumières et histoire / Enlightenment and History,* ed. Tristan Coignard, Peggy Davis, and Alicia C. Montoya (Paris: Editions Honoré Champion, 2010), 197, argues that the use of mahogany was a riposte to the Dispute of the New World. On eighteenth-century mahogany more broadly, see Madeleine Dobie, "Orientalism, Colonialism, and Furniture in Eighteenth-Century France," in *Furnishing the Eighteenth Century: What Furniture Can Tell Us about the European and American Past,* ed. Dena Goodman and Kathryn Norberg (New York: Routledge, 2007), 13–36; Chaela Pastore, "Mahogany as Status Symbol: Race and Luxury in Saint Domingue at the End of the Eighteenth Century," in *Furnishing the Eighteenth Century: What Furniture Can Tell Us about the European and American Past,* ed. Dena Goodman and Kathryn Norberg (New York: Routledge, 2007), 37–48; Ana Amigo Requejo, "Nota de las maderas finas que podrán hacerse conducir de La Habana, para muebles y otros adornos del Real Palacio Nuevo," in *Barroco Iberoamericano: Identidades culturales de un imperio,* vol. 2, ed. Carme López Calderón, María de los Ángeles Fernández Valle, and María Inmaculada Rodríguez Moya (Santiago de Compostela: Editorial Andavira, 2013), 367–80; and Matthew C. Hunter, "Joshua Reynolds' 'Nice Chymistry': Action and Accident in the 1770s," *Art Bulletin* 97, no. 1 (2015): 71, 76n154. See also E. H. Gombrich, *The Sense of Order: A Study in the Psychology of Decorative Art* (Ithaca, NY: Cornell University Press, 1984), 32, 65–67; Leora Auslander, "Beyond Words," *American Historical Review* 110, no. 4 (2005): 1030; and Glenn Adamson, "The Labor of Division: Cabinetmaking and the Production of Knowledge," in *Ways of Making and Knowing: The Material Culture of Empirical Knowledge,* ed. Pamela H. Smith, Amy R. W. Meyers, and Harold J. Cook (Ann Arbor: University of Michigan Press, 2014), 247.

54 The resistant properties of mahogany were later questioned, and verified, by Antonio de Lara y Zúñiga in August and September 1786, after Juan de Villanueva had proposed (in November 1785) that the archive's shelving be made of plaster instead: AGI IG 1853, Juan de Villanueva to José de

Gálvez, 23 November 1785; AGI IG 1853, Antonio de Lara y Zúñiga to José de Gálvez, Seville, 28 June 1786; AGI IG 1853, Antonio de Lara y Zúñiga to José de Gálvez, Seville, 29 August 1786 ("Para resolver sí los estantes de ese Archivo han de hacerse de Yesteria, o de maderas preciosas"); and AGI IG 1853, Antonio de Lara y Zúñiga to José de Gálvez, Seville, 6 September 1786 ("La caoba no se apolilla en esta tierra, segun me informan los Ynteligentes").

55 "No se ha calculado el importe de las maderas, que sin duda seria crecido si huviesen de comprarse a regatones: pero tomadas en la Havana, i traidas por cuenta de S[u] M[ajestad] en sus reales Paquebotes i otros buques, se lograrán con tanta comodiad, que acaso no costarian menos otras de la peninsula fuera de las ordinarias que no son admisibles, i ninguna de ellas puede compararse con el Cedro i la Caoba, ni en la duracion, ni en la hermosura" (AGI IG 1853, Juan Bautista Muñoz and Francisco Miguel Maestre to José de Gálvez, Seville, 4 August 1784).

56 "En la calidad de esta, nuestro juicio es que sea quando menos un jaspe de Mozon, genero del pais que se logra a precio moderado....En la partida 3.ª nos lastima ver tanto gasto en una mala soleria, cuyos reparos serian un censo contiuo: fuera mejor hacer el pavimento de losetas de Genova, obra eterna i de costa tolerable" (AGI IG 1853, Juan Bautista Muñoz and Francisco Miguel Maestre to José de Gálvez, Seville, 4 August 1784).

57 AMS Sección 11 Papeles del Conde de Águila tomo 4 no. 13, fol. 44v, Juan Bautista Muñoz to José de Gálvez, Seville, 8 August 1784; see also copy in AGI IG 1853.

58 "Para el pavimento tengo p[o]r mas conv[enien]te que se empleen lozetas de Malaga que seran mejores que las de Genova, y saldran tal vez a precios mas equitativos" (AMS Sección 11 Papeles del Conde de Águila tomo 4 no. 13, fol. 45v, Francisco Miguel Maestre and Juan Bautista Muñoz to José de Gálvez, Seville, 21 September 1784; see also copy in AGI IG 1853).

59 AGI IG 1852, Joséph de Ortega to José de Gálvez, Málaga, 27 April 1787; see also, later in the same bundle, the folder labeled "1785–87 Arch[iv]o g[ene]ral Exp[edien]te sobre Marmoles i Jaspes de malaga para las obras del Archivo de Sev[ill]a." On Andalusian fine stone quarries, see José Luis Romero Torres, "El escultor Fernando Ortiz, Osuna y las canteras barrocas," *Cuadernos de los Amigos de los Museos de Osuna* 11 (2009): 73–79.

60 Reese, *The Architecture of Ventura Rodríguez,* 1:143–77; Kubler, *Building the Escorial,* 102; Delfín

Rodríguez Ruiz, "En El Escorial 'murió la Arquitectura,'" in *El Monasterio del Escorial y la arquitectura,* ed. Francico Javier Campos y Fernández de Sevilla (San Lorenzo del Escorial: Estudios Superiores del Escorial, 2002), 313–32; Daniel Crespo Delgado, "De *conformidades y cariño:* El Escorial y Juan de Herrera en el *Viage de España* (1772–1794) de Antonio Ponz," in *El Monasterio del Escorial y la arquitectura,* ed. Francisco Javier Campos y Fernández de Sevilla (San Lorenzo del Escorial: Estudios Superiores del Escorial, 2002), 571–93; Fernando Marías, "Cuando El Escorial era francés: Problemas de interpretación y apropriación de la arquitectura española," *Anuario del Departamento de Historia y Teoría del Arte (UAM)* 27 (2005): 21–32; Daniel Crespo Delgado, "La arquitectura del Museo del Prado vista por sus contemporáneos (1789–1815)," *Madrid: Revista de Arte, Geografía e Historia* 8 (2006): 333, 339; Vega, *Ciencia, arte e ilusión,* 401–6 (on Spain); Andrew McClellan, *Inventing the Louvre: Art, Politics, and the Origins of the Modern Museum in Eighteenth-Century Paris* (Cambridge: Cambridge University Press, 1994), 188–89; and Paul B. Niell and Stacie G. Widdifield, *Buen Gusto and Classicism in the Visual Cultures of Latin America, 1780–1910* (Albuquerque: University of New Mexico Press, 2013). On late eighteenth-century "historic preservation" in Spain, see Humanes Bustamante, "De la Real Casa Lonja de Sevilla," 59; in France, see Richard Wittmann, *Architecture, Print Culture, and the Public Sphere in Eighteenth-Century France* (New York: Routledge, 2007), 67–69. For Muñoz and an eighteenth-century revival of Renaissance textual humanism, see Jorge Cañizares-Esguerra, *How to Write the History of the New World: Histories, Epistemologies, and Identities in the Eighteenth-Century Atlantic World* (Stanford, CA: Stanford University Press, 2001), 191–93.

61 Andrés Ximénez, *Descripción del Real Monasterio de San Lorenzo de El Escorial* (Madrid: Antonio Marin, 1764), 45, 48, 59, 70, 139, 145, 159, 184, 188 (*uniformidad*); 6 (*organizado*); 6, 10 (*proporción*). See also "Juan de Herrera," in *Retratos de los españoles ilustres, con un epítome de sus vidas* (Madrid: Imprenta Real, 1791), n.p. (*los grandes modelos de la antigüedad, unidad, simetría, gusto noble y sencillo en los adornos, economía, proporcion, noble sencillez*).

62 Nicolás Bas Martín, "Una aproximación a la biblioteca del ilustrado valenciano Juan Bautista Muñoz (1745–1799)," *Saitabi* 48 (1998): 145.

63 Heather Hyde Minor, *The Culture of Architecture in Enlightenment Rome* (University Park: Pennsylvania State University Press, 2010), 216–40; and Connors and Dressen, "Biblioteche," 226.

See also Garberson, *Eighteenth-Century Monastic Libraries,* 37–38; and Eric Garberson, "Libraries, Memory, and the Space of Knowledge," *Journal of the History of Collections* 18, no. 2 (2006): 105–36. Vertical shelving for side-by-side book storage did not emerge until the first half of the sixteenth century, a history brilliantly reconstructed in Brooker, "Upright Works."

64 María Paz Aguiló Alonso, *Orden y decoro: Felipe II y el amueblemiento de El Escorial* (Madrid: Sociedad Estatal para la Conmemoración de los Centenarios de Felipe II y Carlos V, 2001), 59–71.

65 José de Sigüenza, *Tercera parte de la historia de la orden de San Geronimo* (Madrid: Imprenta Real, 1605), 753–54.

66 Ximénez, *Descripción del Real Monasterio,* 187, 405.

67 Sigüenza, *Tercera parte,* 754.

68 The key for figure 3.9 reads: "Copia, del estante egecutado por el dibujo del Señor Villanueva, Arquitecto de la Corte de Madrid: que remitió el ex[celentísi]mo Señor D[o]n Josefh Galves, Ministro de Yndias, para que ydentico se ejecutace, acomodandose y arvitriando por nececidad, en los sitios lo que fuere oportuno para su mayor perfeccion, y hermosura. Perteneciente esté, para el Archivo G[enera]l de Yndias en esta Ciudad; en la famosa casa de la Lonja. La letra, A. señala el zocalo de piedra jaspe encarnado. la E. el techillo de entre las Pilastras de la ventana. la Y. el Pañon principal de la Cornisa. la O. la Puerta que cae haci al poniente. la V. el Claro de la ventana." The corresponding caption contains the English translation.

69 "Los Estantes se cierran tambien con doradas redecillas de Alambre" (Ximénez, *Descripción del Real Monasterio,* 187).

70 Sigüenza, *Tercera parte,* 753.

71 "La estanteria de la Biblioteca del Escorial está construida con el mismo gusto i orden de Arquitectura, aunque tiene sus defectos, i dista mucho de la simplicidad, magestad i perfeccion de la nuestra. Oí en dias pasados a tres Yngleses que han visto la parte concluida, i hablavan de ella con admiracion i entusiasmo. A la verdad se transporta el espiritu a los tiempos antinguas de la grandeza Romana, al considerar aquel edificio digno del mismo Vitruvio, i sus grandiosas salas con bovedas de canteria i solado de marmol, vestidas hasta el altura de la imposta de un cuerpo de Arquitectura dorica de seis varas sobre un zocalo de jaspe, con mesas, ventanas, i demas cosas de igual gusto i

nobleza" (AGI IG 1854A, Juan Bautista Muñoz, Seville, 14 and 31 March 1787).

72 "Dije ahora del estado en que se hallan las cosas de aquel Archivo. El edificio es un hermoso cuadro de a doscientos pies por frente, de dos cuerpos de arquitectura, con bovedas de piedra, labrado a fines del siglo XVI por el celebre Juan de Herrera. Su piso alto, destinado para los Papeles, tenía en cada lado cinco salas, dos cuadradas en los ángulos, junto a estas otras dos poco menores, y en medio un salón de casi 25 varas de largo sobre el ancho común de nueve y media. Solo difería la frente occidente por razón de la escalera. Este ha quedado en su antigua disposición. *Los otros tres se han reducido a un gran salón compuesto de tres crugias, quitando las paredes divisiorias, y substituiendo en su lugar arcos de piedra para sostener los techos.* Hallábanse estos afeados y denegridos por muchas causas, y se han restablecidos en su primitiva hermosura. El pavimento era de mil formas, y se mandó hacer todo uniforme de losetas de Málaga de dos colores: las cuales se condugeron a Sevilla por agua en meses pasados, y ya va muy adelantada la solería. Los estantes son correspondientes a la majestad del edificio: un cuerpo de Arquitectura Dórica, pilastras por colunas, alto 5 1/2 varas, sin el zócalo que tiene una tercia, i es de jaspe de Málaga. Su entablamento corre continuado sin interrupción alguna, formando una coronación que sirve de imposta a las bóvedas, y hace mejor vista que la imposta verdadera, la cual queda encubierta, porque enrasa con el cimacio de ella el del entablamiento. Dicha estantería es de caoba perfectamente pulida en todo lo visible, en lo interior de cedro macho. De las mismas maderas se hacen mesas, bancos, puertas, y ventanas. De todo está construida y puesta en su lugar una buena parte, y se continua trabajando con ardor. La estanteria, que es la obra principal, se hace por contrata celebrada de orden de S[u] M[ajestad] con D. Blas Molner Director de la Academia de Nobles Artes de Sevilla en la clase de escultura, quien se ha obligado a darla concluida en dos años que fenecerán en mayo de 89. De su cuenta son todas las labores desde el aserrado hasta el pulimento; y de la de S[u] [Majestad] proveerle de maderas, y de dinero a buena cuenta. Al mismo tiempo se trabaja en renovar y mejorar la escalera, que se construyó con menos gusto que el resto del edificio, sin duda por artífice muy inferior al insigne Herrera. Confio que dentro de dos años quedará la obra concluida en todas sus partes, y tendrá S[u] M[ajestad] una alhaja de un gusto y precio superior a cuantas se conocen de este género en toda la Europa" (AGI IG 1854A, Juan Bautista Muñoz, "Expediente sobre el establecimiento i progresos del Archivo

de Yndias de Sevilla," Madrid, 31 July 1787; italics added).

73 "Muy señor mio: consiguiente à lo q[ue] ofreci a V[uestra] E[xcelencia] en mi anterior, hè reconocido la obra de la casa Lonja, que se destina p[ar]a archivo G[enera]l de Yndias, y hallandola sin principiarse, y en estado de mejorar la proiectada, arreglandome à las intenciones, y deseos de V[uestra] E[xcelencia] hè acordado con dictamen, y aprobacion del Maestro Arquitecto, y otros Ynteligentes, quitar las paredes que dividen sus piezas, y sostituiendolas arcos de piedra, formar vna q[u]e coja los tres angulos de norte, oriente, mediodia, segun manifiesta el Plan q[u]e [h]e incluido; dejando solo la del numero 90 con su puerta numero 8° para resguardo de algunas papeles, ò cosas mas preciosas: tengo la satisfaccion de asegurar a V[uestra] E[xcelencia] q[u]e esta idea hà sido generalm[en]te aplaudida, y acompañada de las demas particularidades pequeñas, q[u]e indica el mismo plan, y su explicacion, compone vna obra, y salon de Archivo sin igual en la Europa; al menos q[u]e yo sepa" (AGI IG 1853, Antonio de Lara y Zúñiga to José de Gálvez, Seville, 17 September 1785). The key for figure 3.10 reads: "1 Desembocaderos de la Escalera. 2 Vestibulo, ò anteportería. 3 Puertas de la Entrada del Archivo. 4 Puerta p[ar]a subir à la Azotea. 6 escalera de d[ic]ha Azotea. 5 Pieza de recibim[ien]to ò Portería. 7 Archivo, q[u]e se compone de vna Pieza en los tres angulos. 8 Puerta p[ar]a entrar, à vna Pieza reseruata p[ar]a las cosas preciosas, v otro destino. 9 D[ic]ha Pieza. 10 tres Puertas, vna en medio de cada angulo servibles p[ar]a poder entrar en el Archivo." The corresponding caption contains the English translation.

74 Lucas Cintora, *Justa repulsa de ignorantes, y de emulos malignos* (Seville: Vázquez, Hidalgo, y Compañía, 1786), 32–33; see copy at https://archives.lib.uconn.edu/islandora/object/20002%3A860074007.

75 AGI IG 1853, Antonio de Lara y Zúñiga to José de Gálvez, Seville, 15 March 1786.

76 Cintora, *Justa repulsa de ignorantes,* 11–13. On architectural screeds in the early modern Iberian world, see Rodríguez Ruiz, "En El Escorial," 324–25; and Fernando Marías, "From Madrid to Cádiz: The Last Baroque Cathedral for the New Economic Capital of Spain," in *Circa 1700: Architecture in Europe and the Americas,* ed. Henry A. Millon (Washington, DC: National Gallery of Art, 2005), 145. On print culture and architectural debates in Enlightenment France, see Wittmann, *Architecture, Print Culture, and the Public Sphere;*

for Madrid, see Crespo Delgado, "La arquitectura del Museo del Prado."

77 AGI IG 1853, José de Gálvez to Antonio de Lara y Zúñiga, San Ildefonso, 3 October 1786. Lara responded a week and a half later, saying he had rounded up the copies, and Cintora wrote a letter of apology: AGI IG 1853, Antonio de Lara y Zúñiga to José de Gálvez, Seville, 14 October 1786; and AGI IG 1853, Lucas Cintora to José de Gálvez, Seville, 14 October 1786.

78 Garberson, "Libraries," 127. Already in 1588, Michel de Montaigne arranged the shelves of his own library so as to be visible in a single glance: "m'offrant en se courbant, d'une veuë, tous mes livres" (Brooker, "Upright Works," 3:720).

79 Garberson, *Eighteenth-Century Monastic Libraries,* 49–50.

80 "'The Library!' Leibniz answered, surging past the younger man and hurling himself against an immense door. There was a bit of preliminary cracking and tinkling as ice shattered and fell from its hinges. Then it yawned open to afford Fatio a view across several hundred yards of flat snow-covered ground to a dark uneven mountainous structure that was a-building there. 'No fair making comparisons with the one Wren's building at Trinity College,' Leibniz said cheerfully. '*His* will be an ornament—not that there is anything wrong with that—*mine* will be a tool, an engine of knowledge'" (Neal Stephenson, *The Confusion: Volume II of The Baroque Cycle* [New York: William Morrow, 2004], 295; more generally, see 292–309). Garberson (*Eighteenth-Century Monastic Libraries;* "Libraries") is optimistic about the functionality of this system, while Jeffrey Garrett ("Redefining Order in the German Library, 1775–1825," *Eighteenth-Century Studies* 33 [1999]: 103–23) is more skeptical, especially when library collections became, in the nineteenth century, too large to hold in one room, or to navigate without good catalogs. (I will return to Garrett's ideas in the epilogue.) The same optically illuminating theory also applied to the arrangement of eighteenth-century natural history collections: McClellan, *Inventing the Louvre,* 80.

81 Indeed, the authors of organizational treatises often dealt simultaneously with libraries and archives: Christoval Rodríguez, "Forma i modo de componer, i coordinar qualesquier archivos publicos generales, y particulares [ca. 1730]," *Iragi* 5 (1992–93): 235, 260; Oliver Legipont, *Itinerario en que se contiene el modo de hacer con utilidad los viajes à cortes estrangeras* [1751], trans. Joaquín Marín (Valencia: Benito Monfort, 1759), 155–293

(libraries), 294–304 (archives); and M. Mariée, *Traité des archives* (Paris: L'auteur and Cailleau, 1779), 104. On archival visuality, see Rodríguez, "Forma i modo," 260; Pierre Camille Le Moine, *Diplomatique-Pratique, ou traité de l'arrangement des archives et trésors des chartes* (Metz, France: Joseph Antoine, 1765), 18, 20 (*premier coup d'oeil*); and Manuel José de Ayala, "Discurso sobre el arreglo de los Archivos" (ca. 1767–97), BPR II/2851, fol. 184r (*su vista ès mas agradable, y su hallazgo mas pronto al primer golpe de vista*).

82 Brooker, "Upright Works," 1:13, 3:761–72; Garberson, *Eighteenth-Century Monastic Libraries,* 37–38; and María M. Portuondo, "The Study of Nature, Philosophy, and the Royal Library of San Lorenzo of the Escorial," *Renaissance Quarterly* 63 (2010): 1106–50. Note that John Shearman, in a splendid essay on the changing relations of decoration and function in the papal apartments of the Vatican, suggests that a ca. 1525 portrait of Melchiorre Baldassini in the collections of the Doria Pamphilj family shows (more than a half century before the Escorial) a bookcase with wall-system display: "The Vatican Stanze: Functions and Decoration," *Proceedings of the British Academy* 57 (1973): 41n98; see also Andrea G. de. Marchi, *Collezione Doria Pamphilj: Catalogo generale dei dipinti* (Cinisello Balsamo: Silvana, 2016), 402–3. However, I was able to see the Baldassini portrait in February 2020 (in the Phaeton Room of the Palazzo del Principe in Genoa), and the bookcase in the background, like the shelving units in the foreground, in fact displays books according to much more traditional methods: cover outward (first, second, third, and fifth shelves from the top in the background; middle shelf in the foreground), stacked on their sides (bottom shelf in the background; top shelf in the foreground), and opened to face the viewer (fourth shelf from the top in the background; middle shelf in the foreground).

83 Cintora, *Justa repulsa de ignorantes,* 46, 85.

84 Walter Benjamin, "The Work of Art in the Age of Its Technological Reproducibility," trans. Edmund Jephcott and Harry Zohn, in *The Work of Art in the Age of Its Technological Reproducibility and Other Writings on Media,* ed. Michael W. Jennings, Brigid Doherty, and Thomas Y. Levin (Cambridge, MA: Belknap, 2008), 40; Reinhold Martin, *The Organizational Complex: Architecture, Media, and Corporate Space* (Cambridge, MA: MIT Press, 2003); and Harwood, *Interface.*

85 Riol, "Informe que hizo a su magestad," 205.

86 Bernhard Siegert, *Cultural Techniques: Grids, Filters, Doors, and Other Articulations of the Real,*

trans. Geoffrey Winthrop-Young (New York: Fordham University Press, 2015), 97–120.

87 See also Garberson, *Eighteenth-Century Monastic Libraries,* 47–48.

88 The Escorial referenced its books using a similar three-part organizational code of case, shelf, and position on the shelf (Brooker, "Upright Works," 3:770).

89 For example, consider recent attempts to evaluate "database quality" in the digital humanities, which turn out to be hermetically sealed analyses of databases *as databases* and leave undiscussed how well the data represents a world *beyond* the storage server: Maximilian Shich, "Revealing Matrices," in *Beautiful Visualization: Looking at Data through the Eyes of Experts,* ed. Julie Steele and Noah Iliinsky (Sebastopol, CA: O'Reilly, 2010), 227–54; and Maximilian Shich et al., "A Network Framework of Cultural History," *Science* 345, no. 6196 (2014), supplementary materials (https://www.science .org/lookup/doi/10.1126/science.1240064). This is a classic example of data fetishism (*fetishism,* as seen in this volume's introduction, being a term coined in 1757), wherein the contents of databases are not recognized to be limited, human-generated reconstructions of the world, but are instead taken to be the world itself. See Vincent Mosco, *To the Cloud: Big Data in a Turbulent World* (Boulder: Paradigm, 2014), 175–206; as well as Luciana Duranti, "Archives as a Place," *Archives and Manuscripts* 24, no. 2 (1996): 252. On this big-data "shift to forms of representation whose reference is reflexive rather than indexical," see Orit Halpern, *Beautiful Data: A History of Vision and Reason since 1945* (Durham, NC: Duke University Press, 2014), 40. On the database as "not so much a representation of the world as a reconstruction of it," see Zeynep Çelik Alexander, "Stacks, Shelves, and the Law: Restructuring the Library of Congress," *Grey Room* 82 (2021): 24.

90 See also the discussion of "enframing" in Timothy Mitchell, *Colonising Egypt* (Cambridge: Cambridge University Press, 1988), 78–87.

91 Note that the first sheet of metadata inside each document bundle listed the archive of origin (see this volume, fig. I.6)—but to see this tag, the user had to take a bundle down from the shelf, untie its cords, and unwrap its protective sheath of paper.

BARTOLO
Curiosa voi non siete
Di leggere la carta, che v'há dato

It's strange you don't want
to read the letter, that he gave you

ROSINA
Che carta, non v'intendo?

What letter, I don't understand?

BARTOLO
Quella che lá metteste—
accenna la scarsella

The one you put there—
Pointing to her pocket

ROSINA
Ah si, per distrazione.

Oh yes, absent-mindedly.

BARTOLO
Deh fatela veder.

Let me see it.

ROSINA
Quest'è il biglietto
Che jeri ricevi da mio cugino,

It's the letter
that yesterday I received from my cousin,

BARTOLO
E veder nol potrei?

And may I not see it?

ROSINA
Nò Signorino
Guardate indegnità?

No your lordship
Can't you see that's rude?

— Giovanni Paisiello (music) and Giuseppe Petrosellini (libretto), *The Barber of Seville,* 1782[1]

CHAPTER 4
DATA RETRIEVAL

Reconstructing how this Andalusian apparatus was used during the first decades of its existence is challenging. In contrast to the Archive of Simancas, the Archive of the Indies lacks sustained records of the searches (*buscas*) petitioned throughout its history. At Simancas, this archive-within-an-archive spans nearly five centuries, enabling studies of changing patterns in document use over time (by the royal court, by church and state institutions, and by private individuals).[2] Yet although not systematically preserved in Seville, scattered evidence for early archival consultations does survive, and this allows us not only to see what kinds of requests were made, and by who, but also—for one exceptional research project—to reconstruct how a team of investigators worked through the archive's holdings to gather data.

FROM LOANS TO TOURISM: THE *ORDENANZAS*

For the first century-plus of its existence, the use of Seville's documents was regulated by *Ordenanzas para el Archivo General de Indias* (Ordinances for the General Archive of the Indies), published in 1790.[3] Of particular interest are items 56–63, which begin with loans and end with tourism. They are worth quoting in full—and note that since the just-created archive was understood to be restricted-access royal patrimony, these regulations are written in the voice of the king.[4]

56

No paper may ever be removed from the archive for any reason except by my express order, communicated by my Secretary of State and of the Office of Grace and Justice of the Indies: and in such a case, there will be put in the place of the loaned document a copy (if it be short), or if not, an extract and note indicating its destination, the date, and reason for the loan. Another note will be kept at hand by the Archivist, in order to reclaim the document, if after a significant space of time it has not been returned.[5]

57

Accounts, extracts, and copies of the documents can and shall only be sent when requested by any of the offices of my Secretaries of State and of the Universal Cabinet, the Supreme Council and Chamber of the Indies, and the Tribunal of Trade of Cádiz.[6]

58

If certain interested parties, either institutions or private persons, should need certain documents to support their rights, ennoble their families, or another honest end, on petitioning by writing the Archivist with an explanation of the reasons, these will be searched for and a basic report on their existence will be given, so that they [interested parties] are able to solicit through the Ministry of Grace and Justice of the Indies my Royal Permission to obtain the accounts or copies that they should need, verified against the originals and authorized by the signature of the Archivist.[7]

59

Otherwise, to no one will be given a copy or account of any document, nor even to insinuate its existence. Nor will it be granted to any person to handle the inventories and indexes, nor to be present during their consultation, and much less during the search and retrieval of documents of any kind.[8]

60

When by virtue of my order, as has been explained, there should be given to parties extracts or copies of certain papers, there will be charged for the search, copying, verification, and signing twenty-four reales of *vellón,* if the copy is not longer than an ordinary sheet of paper; but if it should be longer, for each extra sheet that should be needed there will be paid three reales: understanding well that each sheet should contain at least twenty-two lines of regular and clear writing, without more than two blank inches distributed between the two lateral margins. Of the sums that these regulations generate, the Archivist will receive a third, and the remainder will be divided among the archival Officials in equal parts.[9]

61

No other benefits can be requested or received from the parties, and in order to prevent abuses, I command that at the foot of the copies the Archivist should note in his own hand the quantity that has been charged by reason of these regulations.[10]

62

If at some point for reasons of my Royal service or of the Public Good it should be useful to command that documents from the Archive should be made available to certain subjects, care will be taken that they should be limited to the objectives of their commission, and that they not bring with them copyists nor assistants. However, they will be permitted to have one or more scribes in the entry room, or in another room where no documents are stored, to copy those that they should need with previous permission from the Archivist.[11]

63

All decent persons who should wish to see the Archive will be granted entrance during work hours, pending the agreement of the Supervisor and his permission; he will assign one of the employees to guide them and accompany them up to the exit, without allowing them to touch the documents.[12]

To see these eight commands in use, this chapter begins with the boxes of AGI documents filed under Indiferente General, numbers 1852–1858J. Their contents concern the archive's own history, and include scattered petitions for documentary copies and archival access.

DATA RETRIEVAL (1): GOVERNANCE

As item 57 of the *Ordenanzas* would predict, some of the research projects conducted in the Archive of the Indies were related to government requests from the "offices of my Secretaries of State and of the Universal Cabinet, the Supreme Council and Chamber of the Indies, and the Tribunal of Trade of Cádiz." Four will be considered here.

Example 1: In mid-December 1807, third archivist Diego Juárez reported on a request made by the finance minister (*fiscal*) of the Council of the Indies. Back in the late 1790s, the Duke of Alva petitioned the council for an annual payment of 8,000 ducats from Peru, a privilege supposedly granted to his ancestor in 1614. The finance minister asked archivists in Seville to seek out supporting documentation.[13] Initially, documents were found that seemed to back the duke's claims.[14] Nevertheless, Juárez continued to research, "with the aim of having complete knowledge of the papers in this Archive (as well as for the affection he has for them), as well as for having previously handled them in the company of don Juan Bautista Muñoz." Juárez eventually produced a nine-folio booklet of document summaries and quotations related to the issue. These included royal grants of income (from case 46, shelf 4, bundle 1/30), the 1578 ship's register for *Nuestra Señora de Belén* (from case 25, shelf 2, bundle 363/21), and even testimonies about Sir Francis Drake's piratical 1579 capture of *Nuestra Señora de la Concepción* (documentation in Royal Patronage case 2, shelf 5, bundle 2/21).[15] Juárez concluded his report with three arguments *against* the Duke of Alva's claims. Significantly, none of his cited sources were directly locatable using the archive's then-existing finding aids; tracking these varied references down would have required an indirect, exploratory research process, based on the embodied knowledge of Juárez and his fellow employees.

Example 2: Juárez mentioned the Alva project again in September 1814, as part of a letter that also described how he helped a royally commissioned engineer look for documents about the "province of Texas."[16] This refers to the late October 1805 arrival of don Joséf de Gabriel at the AGI. Gabriel's mission was to consult "the papers, maps, and topographic documents that might be connected to the debate over the western limits of Louisiana." In other words, this was a research project related to the Louisiana Purchase.

DATA RETRIEVAL   167

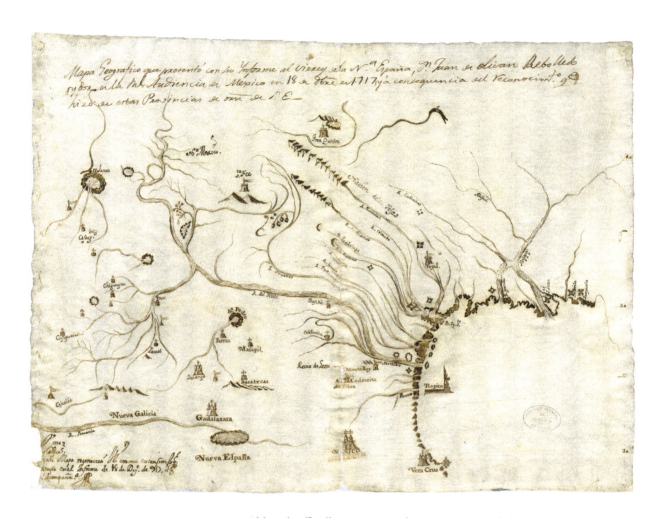

FIGURE 4.1
Juan de Oliván Rebolledo (1676–1738).
Mapa Geográfico que presentó con su Ynforme al virrey de la N[uev]a España (Geographical map presented with a report to the viceroy of New Spain), 1717, ink on paper, 31 × 42.5 cm.
Seville, Archivo General de Indias, MP-Mexico 110.

Although officially a transaction between France and the United States, the lands in question had been formally transferred to France from Spain on 30 November 1803, only a few weeks before the United States took possession on 20 December. A boundary dispute then ensued between Spain and the U.S., which was the reason for Gabriel's arrival at the AGI in 1805. As explained by Juan Agustín Ceán Bermúdez in his monthly work report from 30 October, "On the 29th of this month the Sergeant Major of Engineers don Joséf de Gabriel (with a captain from the same body) began research in this archive for the commission on the Limits of Louisiana and the province of Texas."[17] The two engineers were in Seville until the end of March, and they copied at least one relevant map in late February 1806. It was located in what is now the Mexico section of the archive, which (as part of the Government papers brought from Simancas) would not be officially indexed and shelved until the mid-nineteenth century. However, since at least 1802, Ceán Bermúdez and his corps of archivists had been working through the mountain of uncataloged documents from Simancas, and

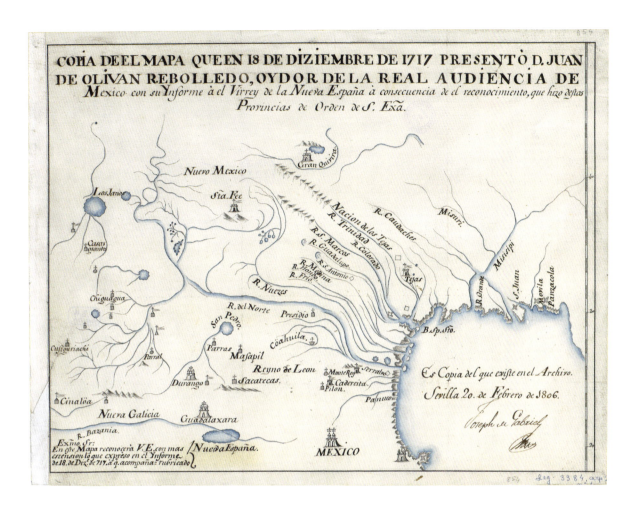

FIGURE 4.2
Joséf de Gabriel (Spanish, 1769–1811).
Copia de el mapa que en 18 de diziembre de 1717 presentò D. Juan de Oliván Rebolledo, oydor de la Real Audiencia de México con su ynforme à el virrey de la Nueva España (Copy of the map that, on 18 December 1717, was presented with its report by don Juan de Oliván Rebolledo, judge of the Royal High Court of Mexico, to the viceroy of New Spain), 1806, ink on paper, 34.5 × 44.5 cm.
Madrid, Archivo Histórico Nacional, Estado MPD 854.

their preliminary sorting may have helped to locate the map.[18] The browned-ink original, created in 1717, shows the Gulf of Mexico's coastline from Veracruz to Pensacola, as well as rivers and lakes and settlements, including Guadalajara and Santa Fe (fig. 4.1). The 1806 copy is carefully drafted and much easier to read, using blue ink to highlight the different bodies of water (fig. 4.2).[19] In any case, the border dispute between Spain and the United States would go on for another decade plus, and was not resolved until the Adams-Onís Treaty of 1819. By then, Joseph de Gabriel had been dead for eight years. He was killed in the Battle of Santa Engracia, just outside of Badajoz, on 19 February 1811.[20]

Example 3: Another request involved the physical loan of documents from the Archive of the Indies to a specific government office, a lending policy established in item 56 of the *Ordenanzas*. In late October 1821—two months after Spain recognized the independence of New Spain—the Council of State needed to consult a 1736 royal decree issued to the archbishop of the Philippines. The decree dealt with the king's authority to

DATA RETRIEVAL 169

make ecclesiastical appointments, a deep legacy of royal patronage powers established in the fifteenth century. The century-old Philippines ruling was of interest because such appointments had been discussed in a June 1821 recommendation by the Council of State to the king—a recommendation that triggered an angry response from the papal ambassador in Madrid. The subsequent back-and-forth debate lasted over a year.[21]

In this heated context, the request for documentary research was forwarded to Vicente Cano Manuel (of the Office of Grace and Justice of the Indies), and on 14 November 1821, he wrote to don Ramón López Pelegrín, secretary of the Office of Overseas Governance (Despacho de la Gobernación de Ultramar).[22] Approval for the search and loan of documents was granted on 20 November, and sent on to AGI head archivist Ventura Collar.

In Seville, things moved quickly. A week and a half later, on 1 December, Collar wrote to López Pelegrín to say that he was sending not only the decree from 1736 but also a number of other related documents (some earlier and some later) he felt were relevant to the case. An itemized list was included as well; the 1736 decree, Collar pointed out, was the document marked "Number 7." Collar also mentioned that he looked forward to getting those loaned documents back: "hoping that Your Excellency should be able to return all of them to me, once they have served the need for which they were requested from me, in order to return them to their respective files, in accordance with that which is outlined in Chapter 56 of the Royal Ordinances that govern this office."[23] The documents reached López Pelegrín in Madrid by 7 December (he then wrote a letter of thanks to Cano Manuel) and were on their way back to Seville just under a month later, on 4 January 1822.

Example 4: The most cosmopolitan government request for documents I have found is from 1830. It involves a complicated social network. On 1 May, Luis López Ballesteros (secretary of the Office of Finance) filed a petition on behalf of Manuel González Salmón (secretary of state) on behalf of Juan Miguel Páez de la Cadena (the Spanish ambassador to Russia).[24] Páez had recently met Alexander von Humboldt in Saint Petersburg: Humboldt stayed there mid-November to mid-December 1829 after a six-month natural history expedition in Siberia.[25] On talking with Páez, the Prussian savant (who had of course long been a scholar of the Iberian New World) expressed his interest in a copy of official Spanish mining regulations. Páez agreed to look into the matter and (apparently in a letter from 21 February) passed the request on to González Salmón, who then forwarded the request to López Ballesteros (on 4 April), who in turn presented the petition to the secretary of the Office of Grace and Justice of the Indies (on 1 May) so that it could be considered by the king.[26] Royal approval was granted in the Palace of Aranjuez (Palacio Real de Aranjuez) on 31 May, and a request for "all that there should be concerning the ancient legislation about mines" was forwarded to the Archive of the Indies.

The archivists got to work. Within a month (according to a letter from 7 July 1830), they compiled an "index of the ordinances, instructions, and replies relating to said section existing in said Archive, which encompasses seventeen items from the year

1576 to 1743, of printed and manuscript documents." Their letter went on to mention that many other documents relating to this theme could be provided, depending on Humboldt's specific interests.[27]

What happened next is unclear. Humboldt may have never even received the list of documents. One possibility is that the list sent from Seville to González Salmón in Madrid was then forwarded to Páez in Saint Petersburg, who would have then sent the documents on to Berlin. Alternatively, the list could have been forwarded directly to the Spanish ambassador in Berlin, Luis Fernández de Córdoba. This would have been a less auspicious route. Fernández de Córdoba saw Humboldt as an antimonarchical revolutionary, and in early May 1830 he wrote an angry letter to González Salmón opposing any Humboldt project in Spain.[28] In fact, Humboldt *was* very critical of Spanish politics at that moment (the final years of Ferdinand VII) and had no interest in returning to Iberia, as a June 1830 letter to Count Ferdinand von Galow reveals.[29]

DATA RETRIEVAL (2): FAMILY HISTORY

A second category of document requests relates to situations raised by *Ordenanzas* item 58: when "interested parties, either institutions or private persons, should need certain documents to support their rights, ennoble their families, or another honest end." Many of these requests were for certified copies of documents known (or suspected) by petitioners to be in the Archive of the Indies. Such requests were usually quite specific in terms of names and dates, which would have made locating documents much easier for archivists. We can often reconstruct their research process today.

Example 1: In the spring of 1802, Rafael García Serrano, a citizen (*vecino*) of Seville, wrote a letter to newly appointed head archivist Andrés María Bustos y Martínez. García Serrano was acting on behalf of Joséf Antonio Pérez de Laserna, citizen of Romeral (in La Mancha), who was trying to track down the last will and testament of his brother-in-law, don Francisco Antonio Díaz y Herrero (who had died at sea in 1784, en route from New Spain to Cádiz).[30] As per item 58 of the *Ordenanzas,* the will was then "searched for," so as to provide "a basic report" on its existence within the archive.

The wills of people who died in the Indies pertained to the House of Trade section of the archive, whose indexing (at the time of this request) had just been completed the year before, in 1801. Wills dating up to 1753 were stored in cases 13, 14, 15, and 17. Wills dating up to 1790, however, were stored in case 46. Archivist Bustos would therefore have gone to the fourth *Índice* for the House of Trade section (an index that covered shelves 30–46) and looked under D for "Díaz y Herrero." On page 116, he would have found this entry:

> **Díaz y Herrero, D. Francisco Antonio / natu**
> **ral de la Mancha y difunto abordo con testamento.**
> **Autos sobre bienes**   532 46 2 120/8

The concluding string of numbers begins with the page number for the same item in the corresponding shelf-by-shelf *Inventario* volume, followed by the location of Díaz y Herrero's will and testament within the archive: case 46, shelf 2, bundle 120/8.[31]

Papers located, Bustos then added this note to the bottom of García Serrano's original petition letter:

> **The document mentioned by this memorial exists in this General Archive under my care, about which I will provide information pending a royal order from the Ministry of Grace and Justice of the Indies. Seville, 29 May 1802.**[32]

Thus the next step was for Pérez de Laserna to receive royal permission for a copy.[33] He made his request via a representative in Madrid, Ramon Martínez Quadrado. On 24 July 1802 (that is, about two months after Bustos confirmed the existence of the will in the AGI), the petition was drafted on official bureaucratic paper for presentation to the minister of Grace and Justice of the Indies. As was common in these cases, the submitted petition was then redrafted by a court notary (apparently on 28 July), who made some slight adjustments to style and detail.[34] The notary specified that an "exact certified copy" of the will was needed, and even added a final note quoting item 58 of the archive's *Ordenanzas:* "In Article 58 of the Rules of the said Archive it is commanded that if certain interested parties, either institutions or private persons, should need certain documents...."[35] The petition was successful and took just over a week to be approved. A permission letter was written to Bustos on 2 August 1802, and when that letter reached Seville, an official copy of the requested testament would have been made for Pérez de Laserna.

Example 2: One month later (on 4 September 1802), another petition process began. Sevillian merchant Miguel Esteban de Val wrote to the minister of Grace and Justice of the Indies requesting a certified copy of the license issued to Ramón Méndez in 1768 for travel to the New World.[36] Val's request was received in Barcelona on 19 September (the king and his court arrived there on 11 September), and it was approved on 30 September.[37] A copy of the permission was then sent to AGI archivist Andrés María Bustos y Martínez.

According to Val's September petition, he had already visited the archive to verify that a copy of Méndez's travel license was indeed there. Travel licenses for the Indies were housed in the House of Trade section, from case 42, shelf 2, bundle 1/5 to case 45, shelf 2, bundle 1/12. They were organized chronologically by year, and by consulting this section's *Inventario,* archivists would have found that documents for 1768 were stored in case 44, shelf 6, bundle 294/31. That bundle contained hundreds of licenses, organized chronologically by month and day. Although the creation of a full index for "Pasajeros a Indias" (Passengers to the Indies) documents was one of the first projects started in the archive (by February 1786), it was never completed. The 1802 search for Méndez within the 1768 bundle had to be done document by document.[38] His petition dates to late October, making it one of the last documents in the set. But it was there (and still is).[39]

172 CHAPTER 4

As is often the case with these travel applications, Méndez's twenty-five-page file is filled with biographical information—some aspect of which is probably why Miguel Esteban de Val needed a copy. Méndez was traveling as the servant (*criado*) of Andrés Montaner y Virgil, who along with Manuel Moreno had been appointed to establish a Chair in Practical Anatomy at the Royal Hospital of Indians (Hospital Real de Indios) in Mexico City.[40] Documents provided in support of Méndez's travels included proof of his baptism in Madrid (24 October 1750, in the parish church of San Ginés), as well as a four-part statement by Méndez's father (followed by supporting testimony from four witnesses) about the family's background as "Old Christians, free from every bad race [*raza*] of Moors, Jews, heretics, or those newly converted to our Holy Catholic Faith, or punished or penitenced at any time by the Tribunal of the Holy Office [of the Inquisition], or having worked in dishonorable or manual occupations [*oficios viles, ni Mecanicos*], or descended from those families who are prohibited by the laws of these kingdoms from traveling to the Indies."[41]

Example 3: Just under six years later, in January 1808, another genre of House of Trade document was requested by Pedro Fernández Barrera.[42] Writing on behalf of his brother (a merchant in Veracruz, New Spain), Fernández Barrera wanted a certified proof of payment of import taxes for five large bags of cochineal, which had been shipped to Cádiz from Veracruz aboard the warship *San Joachín* in 1778. Significantly, Fernández Barrera also knew that the ship's *maestre* (official responsible for loading cargo) was Manuel de Laraviedra. This was a key detail, as will be seen shortly. Fernández Barrera initially went to the tribunal of the merchants' guild in Cádiz, but there he was told that such documents had been transferred to Seville and that a royal order was needed to get copies. And so in Madrid on 14 January, Fernández Barrera wrote his letter of petition. It was reviewed two days later and approved on 29 January. This approval was sent on to Seville, and on 17 February archivist Andrés María de Bustos y Martínez wrote to Joséf Antonio Cavallero (secretary of state and of the Office of Grace and Justice) reporting his compliance with the request.

The archival research process can be reconstructed as follows. Shipping records of vessels to and from the Americas were, as with the previous two examples, stored in the House of Trade section. Specifically, registries of ships arriving in Spain from the New World were kept in cases 22 to 30. They were organized by year. To track down this request, an archivist could have begun by looking up the last name of the ship's *maestre* in the *Índice* for this section of the House of Trade documents. It contains one entry for

Laraviedra (D. Manuel Ubaldo de) m[aest]re del navio
San Joaquin.
  Rexistro de lo que traxo de Veracruz en 1779 362 27 6 804/5

As seen earlier, the string of numbers after Laraviedra's entry begins with the page number for the same item in the corresponding shelf-by-shelf *Inventario* volume, followed by the location of the document within the archive: case 27, shelf 6, bundle 804/5 (that is, in the building's northwest corner).[43]

On locating and opening this bundle, archivists first would have seen a metadata sheet on the bundle's overall contents:

Registers of arrivals for the years 1779 to 1784, of the single ships that came from Veracruz, divided into three numbers.

> **Number 1, Year 1779, don Manuel Ubaldo de Laraviedra, *maestre* of the ship *San Joaquín;***
>
> **Number 2, Year 1783, don Francisco Yglesias, accountant and *maestre* of the frigate *Santa Lucía;***
>
> **Number 3, Year 1784, don Francisco Yglesias, accountant and *maestre* of the frigate *Santa Lucía.***

Inside, most of this bundle concerns the *San Joaquín* (the *Santa Lucía* documents are two slim booklets of bound papers). At the end of the bound *San Joaquín* registry book is an ABC index of names. "Gaspar Ant.º Leal" is listed under *G,* followed by the numbers 41 and 120–121. These refer to page numbers earlier in the registry. On 41r is item 151 / Ch. 354, for a shipment of 5,747 pesos to Gaspar Leal. On 120v–121r is item 202 / 678: "the said *maestre* registers than he has received from don Remigio Fernández, five large bags of fine cochineal...to be delivered in Cádiz to don Gaspar Antonio Leal."

If further documentation were needed, archivists could then have turned to the unbound printed shipping receipts that take up most of this bundle's contents. Three receipts relate to shipments sent by Remigio Fernández: 5,747 silver pesos for delivery to Gaspar Antonio Leal, 634 silver pesos for delivery to the Count of Reparaz, and, on receipt N.º 678, "cinco Zurrones de Grana fina" for delivery to Gaspar Antonio Leal (figs. 4.3, 4.4). The upper half of this last printed receipt records the basic details of the shipment; the lower half, and much of the reverse side, is filled with handwritten notes on import taxes (most of which were waived, as per a 12 October 1778 decree).

Example 4: Two decades later, on 21 January 1829, another registry-related request was filed by Seville resident don José González y Moro.[44] Back in 1781, his father (don Luis González) had sent José and his brother (Manuel) 4,997 pesos from Havana, divided among the warships *Guerrero, Arrogante,* and *Gallardo.* José went directly to the Archive of the Indies for official documentation but (as he writes in his petition) was told by archivists that they could not provide anything without official authorization ("los Directores del mencionado archivo...manifestaron al Exponente, no poder facilitar alguna [certificación], sin orden"). And so he filed his request.

Three weeks later, on 11 February, official approval was granted in the Palace of El Pardo, and a confirmation letter was sent on to the AGI. In contrast to the search for shipping records of the *San Joaquín,* González y Moro did not provide the name of any *maestre,* so archivists would have started with volume 3 of the *Inventario* of the House of Trade section, which lists the contents of cases 18–30 shelf by shelf. Registries

FIGURE 4.3
Shipping receipt for "five bags of fine cochineal" (recto), 1779.
Seville, Archivo General de Indias, Contratación 2589.

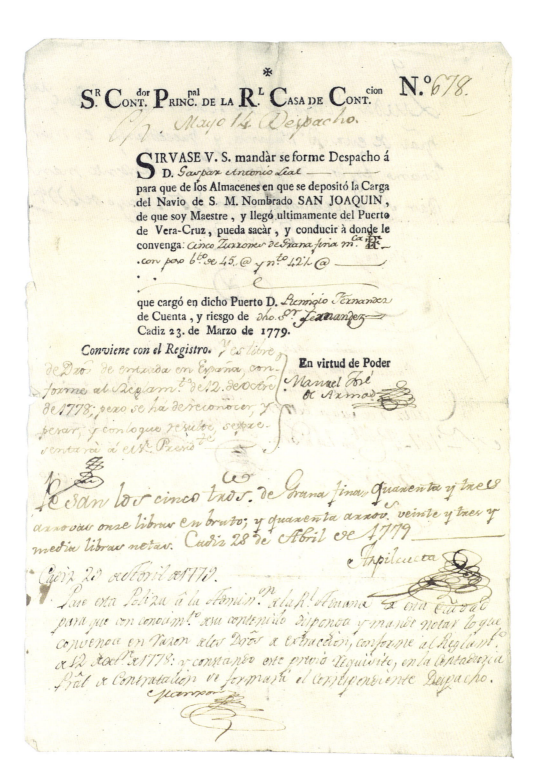

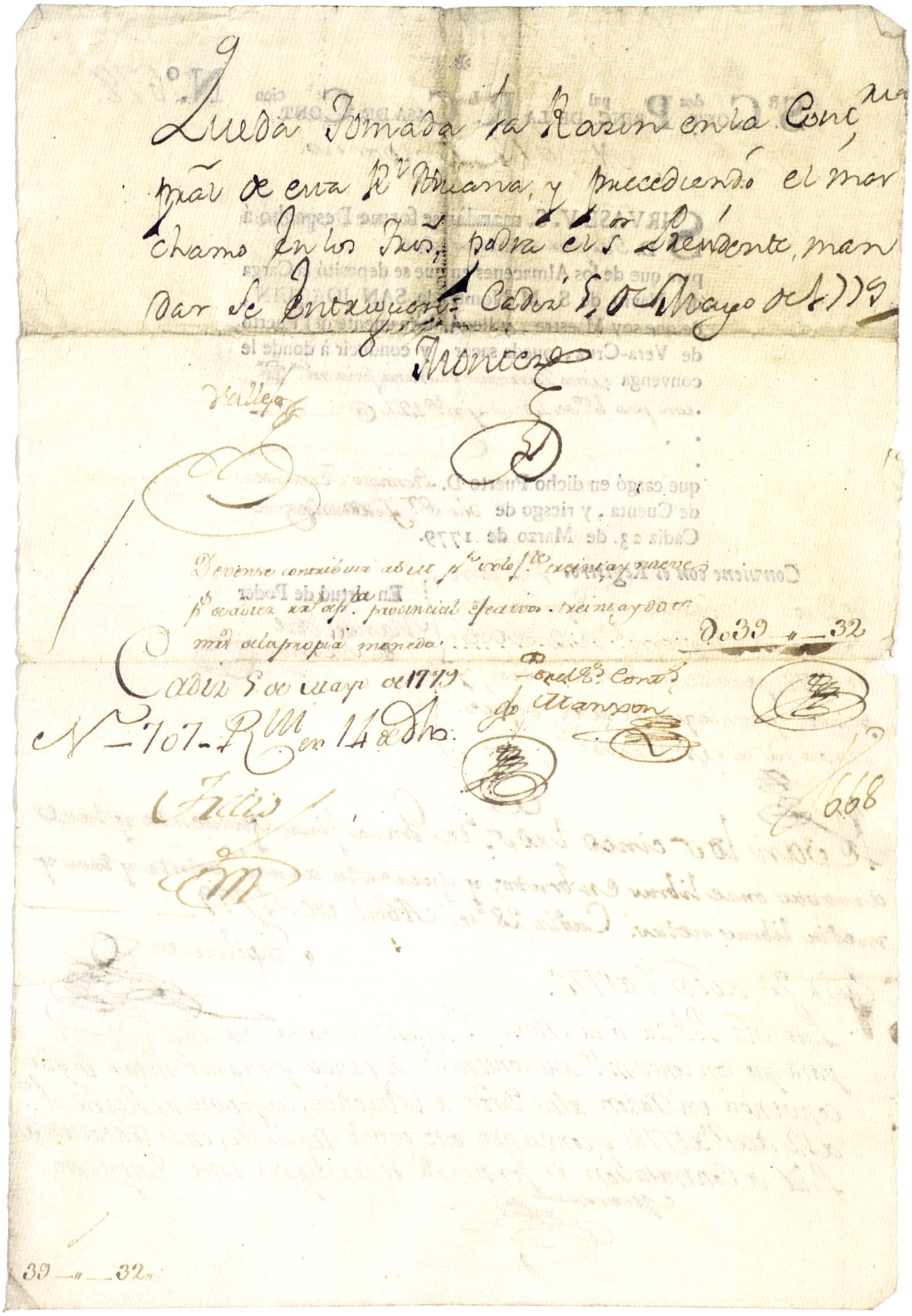

Queda Tomada la Razon en la Conta
ria de esta Rl Aduana, y precediendo el mar
chamo en los Rs para el S Presidente, man
dar se entreguen. Cadiz, 9 de Mayo de 1779

Monteros

Vallejo

Cadiz 9 de mayo de 1779

Nº 707 — R.M en 14 de Dho

Fras

of incoming ships begin on page 211 (at case 22, shelf 6). Arrivals entries are divided into two main groups: first the ships that traveled in official convoys, and then the ships that traveled alone. Within both sections, entries are organized chronologically by port of departure, with the year of each item written in a column on the right (making it easier for archivists to search for particular years).

Arrivals in convoy from New Spain in 1781 appear on pages 245 and 246 (the ships would leave Veracruz, then stop in Havana before crossing the Atlantic). Their documents were stored in case 25, shelf 1, bundles 317/1, 318/2, 319/3, and 320/4.[45]

The first bundle contained the bound ship's register for the *Arrogante.* Although Luis González is not listed in that registry book's own index (which is organized alphabetically by first name), under *J* is found "Josef y Man.¹ Gonz.ˡᵉᶻ," followed by two registry numbers: 920 and 923. These numbers would have allowed the archivists to find not only the entries for the money sent within the registry volume itself (divided into two lots, one with 1,333 pesos and the other with 332 pesos) but also the original (unbound) shipping receipts included in this bundle. The next bundle, 318/2, contained a similar cluster of documents: the bound ship's register for the *Gallardo,* as well as unbound shipping receipts. José and Manuel's money was once again divided into two lots (of 1,333 and 332 pesos; registry numbers 812 and 814). Finally, the bound ship's register for the *Guerrero* was in bundle 319/3; the money for José and Manuel was again divided into two lots (of 1,334 pesos and 333 pesos, 6 reales; registry numbers 1053 and 1055). The printed shipping receipts for the *Guerrero* were included in the next bundle, 320/4. Altogether, adding the amounts listed in these various bundles (1,333 + 332 + 1,333 + 332 + 1,334 + 333 pesos, 6 reales) produces a total of 4,997 pesos, 6 reales. This matches the sum mentioned by José in his 1829 petition.

The four examples above all involved searches for very specific items. But archivists also received general requests for any documents on such-and-such family. Their responses to this kind of petition varied.

Example 5: On 14 January 1817, Brigadier don Miguel Alcega wrote a letter asking for official copies of all those documents "that might relate to the family."[46] He had heard that the archive held "various notices and documents of some Admirals and Generals who carried the name Alzega whose services were very useful to the Crown in the discovery and conquest of the Americas." Royal authorization was granted a week later, on 21 January, and a permission letter went on to Seville. But because this request was rather vague—entries for the last name "Alcega" appear throughout the then-completed *Índice* books for Accounting, Justice, and House of Trade—and because Alcega was living in Seville at the time, on 5 February, archivist Ventura Collar wrote back to Madrid, basically saying that he would need more information: "I will fulfill this sovereign resolution after the aforementioned Brigadier should present himself to indicate the documents that he needs."[47]

Example 6: In contrast, three years later (on 17 May 1820), the king authorized Diego Colón (a descendant of Christopher Columbus and an official in the Secretariat of the Office of State) to "make certified copies of some documents present in

FIGURE 4.4
Shipping receipt for "five bags of fine cochineal" (verso), 1779.
Seville, Archivo General de Indias, Contratación 2589.

DATA RETRIEVAL 177

the Archive of the Indies," which Diego and his father (José Colón) needed "for the better preservation of the rights of their house." Father and son were especially interested in documents from "the section that don Diego Juárez (official of the said archive) has extracted, analyzed, and inventoried."[48] This inventoried section was, of course, Royal Patronage—a five-year project that had just been completed in late November 1819. Within Royal Patronage, documents related to the Colón family were concentrated in seven bundles on the first shelf of the first case (numbers 1/8 to 7/14). It was a documentary trove easy to find, and so (unlike the thwarted 1817 request by Brigadier Alcega) on 21 May, the archivist Collar wrote that he would provide don Diego Colón with copies "right away."[49]

Less than a decade later, Washington Irving received royal permission to consult the same section of documents, as part of his research on Christopher Columbus. This brings us to a third kind of research undertaken at the Archive of the Indies: projects for the writing of history.

DATA RETRIEVAL (3): SCHOLARSHIP

As seen in previous chapters, the creation of the Archive of the Indies had its origins in Juan Bautista Muñoz's commission to write a new, archivally grounded history of Spanish America. Ironically, Muñoz never seems to have used the archival space he brought into being, and the first volume of his *Historia del Nuevo-Mundo* was based on previously published sources. Nevertheless, other researchers quickly took advantage of the new repository to seek out documentation for their own projects.

The most extensive of these projects, headed by naval officer Martín Fernández de Navarrete, began in 1793. But that was a complicated undertaking, involving a half dozen scribes generating thousands of copies, so I will leave it to the end of this chapter and begin instead with smaller-scale requests.

Example 1: In the fall of 1807, Vicente Bérriz (lieutenant colonel of artillery) made a request to "study the papers of the archive, and copy those documents and notices related to weapons, which could be useful for the history of artillery."[50] His request was initially rejected by the archive, even though he carried an official permission to consult provincial archives ("los Archivos de las Provincias") for the project. Bérriz then requested a royal order to consult the Archive of the Indies specifically, which was granted in the Escorial on 17 October 1807.[51] As far as I can tell, Bérriz never wrote this history; perhaps his project was interrupted, and then abandoned, due to the seven years of Napoleonic violence that had just broken out on the peninsula.[52]

Example 2: A year after peace was restored, another research petition was sent to Miguel de Lardizabál, secretary of state and of the Universal Office of the Indies:

Most Excellent Sir:

Finding myself residing in Seville by order of His Majesty with the commission of the Company for Navigation of the Guadalquivir, and needing to acquire various interesting notices not only concerning the ancient state of the river and trade of that city in the first epoch of the discovery of America, and preparation for the most celebrated expeditions but also relating to the diverse mineral productions of overseas, and the history and advancements of their benefit, influence, and alteration that has been produced in the commercial relations of Europe, Asia, etcetera, etcetera, for a certain study on which I am working, I beg that your Excellency be served by attaining for me license from His Majesty to be able to examine and transcribe, according to the established regulations, the papers touching on these themes that exist in the General Archive of the Indies of Seville, by which I will receive particular favor. May God protect Your Excellency many years. Madrid, 1 June 1815.

Most excellent Sir,
Gregorio González Azaola[53]

In contrast to the artillery project of Lieutenant Colonel Bérriz, here we can say much more. The petitioner, Gregorio González Azaola, was a classic man of the Enlightenment. This research project would have united his varied interests in history, technology, mineralogy, and commerce—or, to use a period phrase, in "nature and art." González Azaola's writings on art include a report on the Roman antiquities he excavated near Burgos (1806);[54] an article on the prints of Goya's *Caprichos* (1811);[55] and a translation of Alexander Pope's 1734 *Essay on Man* (1821).[56] Writings on nature include several translations: an 1801 chemistry book by the Comte de Fourcroy;[57] an 1806 article on grape sugar by Joseph Louis Proust;[58] and Thomas Tredgold's physics-heavy 1825 *A Practical Treatise on Rail-Roads and Carriages*.[59] Original works include a proposal (with Alexandro Briarly) for the navigation of the Guadalquivir River (1815);[60] a polemic monograph about Spanish industrialization (1829);[61] and a prizewinning article on "the taste of wood that wines in casks usually have, and the methods to correct this" (1832).[62] González Azaola even designed a new cannon (in 1809, as a member of the Royal Artillery) and, in 1816, drafted plans for the Guadalquivir's Fernandino Canal as part of his work with the Company for Navigation of the Guadalquivir (Compañía de Navegación del Guadalquivir).

As far as I can tell, González Azaola never published the history he proposed to research at the Archive of the Indies. He may have been too busy to even look at documents, because the first years of the Company for Navigation—which, as his petition makes clear, was why González Azaola was in Seville—were hectic. Established by royal decrees of September and December 1814 (only a few months after King Fernando VII returned to power after the fall of Napoleon), the company was created to spearhead a series of development projects in and alongside the Guadalquivir River, with the goal of rejuvenating the economy of southwestern Andalusia.[63]

But in addition to those applied, then-present-day goals, historical research was envisioned as part of González Azaola's company duties from the very beginning. When González Azaola was first summoned for the project, on 6 September 1814, the king ordered (perhaps prematurely) "that he should bring with him all the plans, documents, and papers that he should be able to gather relating to the river."[64] The

DATA RETRIEVAL 179

FIGURE 4.5
Antonio Tis-Sandier (Spanish, 1804–?) and Manuel Spínola de Quintana (Spanish, 1770–1833).
Plano del Barco de Vapor llamado el Fernandino (á[lias]) el Betis (Plan of the steamboat called the Fernandino, aka the Betis), 1819 (original) and 1948 (reproduction), lithograph on paper, 42.5 × 57.5 cm.

company's published manifesto, coauthored by González Azaola and Briarly and dated 24 January 1815, begins with two pages of historical background (from the Romans to Felipe II to Enlightenment intellectuals) as context for the specific proposals that occupy most of the manifesto. Many of those ideas were never carried out, but two projects were successful and had long-lasting effects—and connect us to two other would-be researchers at the Archive of the Indies.

The first project was a canal in one of the oxbow-bends of the Guadalquivir, twenty kilometers south-southwest of Seville. The new waterway shortened the journey to Sanlúcar and the Atlantic by three leagues and transformed the river's flow: floods that in the past could last for five days now drained in less than ten hours. Excavations began on 1 June 1815, and González Azaola was closely involved with the design (along with mathematician Félix Albao and engineer José Agustín de Larramendi); he signed watercolor plans for the project on 19 June. Four and a half months later, on 6 November, the channel was complete.[65]

The company followed its new canal with another lasting innovation: regular steamboat service between Cádiz and Seville.[66] On 16 June 1816, the *Real Fernandino* (nicknamed the *Betis*) made its first journey (fig. 4.5).[67] It would continue to ply the Guadalquivir for decades. This was the vessel that brought Washington Irving to Seville in April 1828, when Irving was hoping to conduct research at the Archive of the Indies for a second edition of his just-published *History of the Life and Voyages of Christopher Columbus.*

I will turn to Irving shortly, but first want to end this section by considering another petition for archival research dating (like that of Gregorio González Azaola) to June 1815. As it happens, the petition was filed by a man who later became friends with the American author.

Example 3:

Most Excellent Sir:

Don Juan Wetherell, of the English nation, and resident in the City of Seville, appears before Your Excellency and says that, having heard that in the General Archive of the Indies of this City there exist various Manuscripts of don Miguel Cervantes Saavedra, and this petitioner desiring to understand their content, and if possible to make a copy of them for their study, supplicates Your Excellency, if it should be agreeable to you, that you would be pleased to give your Order to the Head of the aforementioned Archive so that he should be given access to the cited manuscripts. For which he hopes to be deserving of the generosity of Your Excellency, whose life may God preserve for many years. Seville, 17 June 1815.[68]

John Wetherell was the son of the English industrialist Nathan Wetherell, who had established a successful leatherworks in Seville in 1784. The Wetherells would be important figures in Sevillian society for the following half century. For example, at the same time that his son was thinking about Cervantes, Nathan was one of the chief investors in, and an early codirector of, the Company for Navigation of the Guadalquivir.[69] Indeed, the engine that powered the *Betis* steamboat was acquired in England by the Wetherells.[70] Perhaps it was purchased by John himself, who was closely involved in the family business and often made trips abroad to report on new technology.

John Wetherell also took part in Spain's humanistic circles, and in Seville he even created a collection of Roman and Mexican antiquities mentioned in tourist guides (and eventually purchased by the British Museum).[71] He was also a lifelong fan of *Don Quixote*. In November 1828, during Washington Irving's visit to Seville, Wetherell introduced the American writer to Ramón Feliu, then preparing a *Quixote* dictionary.[72] In his later years, Wetherell became friends with Nicolás Díaz de Benjumea, who published controversial esoteric-symbolic interpretations of the novel in the 1860s and 1870s.[73]

Wetherell's 1815 interest in the AGI's Cervantes documents (which deal with the future novelist's unsuccessful petition for a post in the Indies) was well informed. The documents had been located by archival commissioner Juan Agustín Ceán

Bermúdez on 12 January 1808; he promptly sent a copy on to the Royal Academy of History in Madrid. But this archival find would not be published for more than a decade.[74] In the weeks following Ceán Bermúdez's discovery, Spain's alliance with Napoleonic France began to collapse. Carlos IV abdicated the Spanish throne on 19 March, as did his son and successor Fernando VII on 6 May—four days after a failed anti-Napoleonic uprising in Madrid. One month later, on 6 June, Napoleon placed his brother Joseph on the Spanish throne. Six years of violence followed. Andalusia would not be invaded by Napoleonic forces until January 1810, but the year before, in early April 1809, thirty-one chests of documents from the Archive of the Indies were sent south to Cádiz for safety. The Cervantes documents were in chest 5.[75] On arrival, the chests were stored in Cádiz's customs house (*aduana*). This archival evacuation proved to be a smart move: although Joseph Bonaparte entered Seville on 1 February 1810, Cádiz was never conquered.

The Wetherells themselves fled to Cádiz in 1810, and the Archive of the Indies seems to have been closed in 1810 and 1811.[76] The French left Seville in August 1812, but it was not until June 1814 that archivist Diego Juárez traveled down to Cádiz to bring the exiled document chests back to the AGI.[77] Exactly when during these turbulent times John Wetherell learned of the Cervantine discoveries of 1808 is unclear. By 1815, the Peninsular War had been over for a year, and it was perhaps Wetherell's earliest opportunity to seek out the documents.

Unfortunately, as with the petitions of Lieutenant Colonel Vicente Bérriz and Lieutenant Colonel Gregorio González Azaola, I have not been able to determine if Wetherell ever consulted the documents he petitioned to see. In any case, they were published four years later by Martín Fernández de Navarrete, in the second half of his *Vida de Miguel de Cervantes Saavedra* (1819; *Life and Writings of Miguel de Cervantes Saavedra*).[78]

Wetherell and Navarrete bring us to another historian who sought permission to consult documents in the Archive of the Indies: Washington Irving.

TALES OF THE ARCHIVO

Our story begins with three items of AGI paperwork, all from 1828.[79] The first has an initial paragraph dated 21 May, followed by an addendum on 14 July. The second, a short note, is dated 7 June. The third, a short letter, is dated 3 August. Together, they track the process by which Washington Irving received permission to consult AGI documents related to Christopher Columbus: from a formal request to the Council of the Indies (May); to receipt of the request for consideration in San Sebastián, where King Fernando VII and his court were spending the summer (June–July); to sending official approval (August). Irving received the good news in Seville on 15 August (a Friday) and on the following Monday was reading documents at the archive.

As we have already seen, this three-part bureaucratic saga (petition, presentation-deliberation, decision) has been preserved for a dozen other archival requests from the first decades of the nineteenth century. What makes Irving's example particularly

182 CHAPTER 4

interesting is that—thanks to his voluminous diaries, letters, and best-selling publications—we can reconstruct not only the previous research that led him to the Archive of the Indies but also what he did when he gained access, and the effect archival consultations had on his writings. Furthermore, Irving's Sevillian story closely intertwined with that of scholar and naval officer Martín Fernández de Navarrete, who will provide the final research project in this chapter.

To understand why a U.S. citizen wanted to look at AGI documents in the spring of 1828, we have to go back in time some two and a half years.

Bordeaux, the second week of January, 1826. Irving and his younger brother Peter had been living there since mid-November.[80] Elsewhere in the same French city, artist Francisco de Goya and author Leandro Fernández de Moratín were living in exile, having fled the conservative Spain of Fernando VII (fig. 4.6). Irving even visited

FIGURE 4.6
Francisco de Goya y Lucientes (Spanish, 1746–1828).
Portrait of Leandro Fernández de Moratín, 1824, oil on canvas, 60 × 49.5 cm.
Bilbao, Museo de Bellas Artes, inv. no. 69/III.

DATA RETRIEVAL   183

Moratín on 30 January 1826, and later recommended his work to friends.[81] At this point, the American writer had been traveling in England, France, and the German states for more than a decade. But the new year of 1826 found him in a moment of financial and creative crisis.[82] It was a turning point in Irving's career. Six years later, he was an honorary member of Spain's Royal Academy of History, held an honorary doctorate in civil law from Oxford, and was the author of four best-selling books about Spain: *A History of the Life and Voyages of Christopher Columbus* (1828), *Chronicle of the Conquest of Granada* (1829), *Voyages and Discoveries of the Companions of Columbus* (1831), and (perhaps most famously) *The Alhambra: A Series of Tales and Sketches of the Moors and Spaniards* (1832).[83]

The catalyst for Irving's transformation into a world-famous Hispanist was a letter he received in Bordeaux on 9 January 1826. He tells the story at the beginning of his 1828 history of Columbus:

> Being at Bordeaux, in the winter of 1825–6, I received a letter from Mr. Alexander Everett, Minister Plenipotentiary of the United States at Madrid, informing me of a work then in the press, edited by Don Martin Fernandez de Navarrete, Secretary of the Royal Academy of History, &c, &c, containing a collection of documents relative to the voyages of Columbus, among which were many of a highly important nature, recently discovered. Mr. Everett, at the same time, expressed an opinion that a version of the work into English, by one of our own country, would be peculiarly desirable. I concurred with him in the opinion; and, having for some time intended a visit to Madrid, I shortly afterwards set off for that capital, with an idea of undertaking, while there, the translation of the work.[84]

Irving wrote back to Alexander Everett the next day, on 10 January. Two days later, he wrote again. The previous summer in Paris, Everett had offered to officially attach Irving to the American embassy in Madrid. On 12 January, Irving was finally ready to accept.[85] Irving's interest in an Iberian project was not entirely random: he had read *The Civil Wars of Granada* and *Don Quixote* when young, and he began studying Spanish in December 1824, while still in Paris.[86]

On 30 January, a passport from Everett arrived in Bordeaux; on 10 February, "at 6 oclock," Irving and his brother left for Madrid.[87] The journey took five days. The Americans arrived at ten in the morning on Wednesday, 15 February. They arranged temporary lodgings (which were apparently hard to find) at the Fonda del Ángel, just south of the Puerta del Sol plaza (fig. 4.7). They called on Everett in the afternoon, but the ambassador was out.[88] Everett's lodgings, and thus the American embassy as well, were located on Carrera de San Gerónimo, just east of Sol. Irving returned the following afternoon (after getting "our passports arranged" in the morning), and this time Everett was in. The two men then went to meet another American expat: Obadiah Rich, the embassy archivist and a bibliophile whose extensive library of Spanish books and manuscripts would be invaluable to Irving's writing in the months to come.[89] Rich lived in a house several blocks northeast of Puerta del Sol, on Calle de

184 CHAPTER 4

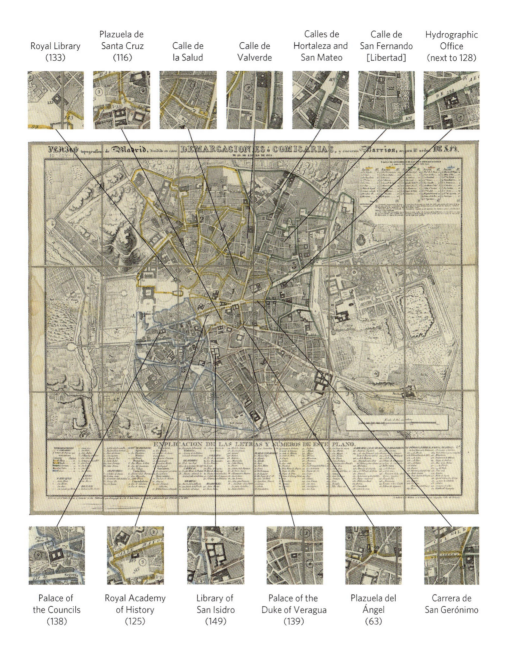

FIGURE 4.7
Washington Irving's Madrid, 1826–28.
Based on Pedro Lezcano y Carmona, draftsman; and Juan López de Vargas (Spanish, 1765–1825) and Pedro Martín de López, cartographers, *Plano topográfico de Madrid, dividido en cinco demarcaciones ó comisarias, y cincuenta Barrios* (Topographic plan of Madrid, divided into five parts or precincts, and fifty neighborhoods), 1835, engraving, 66.5 × 54.3 cm.

San Fernando, and that very Friday (17 February), Irving rented an apartment in the same building.[90] He moved in on Saturday:

> We are buried in the very depths of a great rambling Spanish house; our windows look upon a small garden, three parts of which are surrounded by the house. Our windows open to the floor; with iron grates to them—through one of which, we have a wicket

DATA RETRIEVAL 185

> by which we can enter the garden. We have the stillness of a cloister, with now & then the bell of a neighbouring convent to help the illusion. Our Consul Mr. Rich is a great collector & vendor of rare books, and I am surrounded by a curious library, entirely at my command.[91]

Irving used this library to get working on his Columbus project right away. On Sunday and Monday, he began to translate Bartolomé de las Casas's copy of Columbus's journal (a manuscript of which was in Rich's library). That Tuesday (21 February) Irving visited Martín Fernández de Navarrete, the "Secretary of the Royal Academy of History" whose Columbus research had lured Irving to Madrid.[92] The two men probably met in the Hydrographic Office (Depósito Hidrográfico) on Calle de Alcalá, where Navarrete worked, although the Royal Academy of History (in the old bakery building on the Plaza Mayor) is another possibility.[93] Navarrete showed Irving the first two volumes of his just-published *Colección de los viajes y descubrimientos que hicieron por mar los españoles* (Collection of voyages and discoveries which the Spaniards made by sea), advertised for sale less than a week before.[94] Although Irving praised Navarrete's work in a letter he wrote a few days later, he was apparently daunted, and depressed, at seeing the thousand-plus pages of documents. The two volumes were far more monumental than what Everett had led him to expect back in January. And so for the next month, Irving did no writing.[95]

By 15 March, Irving owned his own copy of the two-volume set, but even then his journals reveal continuing writer's block: "Much depressed....Weary & out of order."[96] Nevertheless, he began Spanish lessons again with a tutor on 18 March. The following week—Holy Week—he remained "listless," "dispirited," "uncommonly comfortless & depressed."[97] But on Holy Saturday, 25 March, Irving began to write. Over the next two and a half months, he completed a rough draft of his Columbus chronicle. Most of his research at this stage focused on the volumes of Navarrete and the wealth of materials in Obadiah Rich's library. Three weeks after he started writing, however, Irving began to explore other resources in Madrid: on 17 April, he "read in the library of the Jesuits" on Calle de Toledo (a few blocks south of the Plaza Mayor).[98] But that seems to have been an exception. More representative is his journal entry for Friday, 19 May: "Write at Columb. at home all day."[99]

After 12 June, Irving's daily references to writing on Columbus disappear for about a month. He began to prepare for a stage of manuscript revisions by rereading Navarrete's two volumes and making notes: "Reading Navarette all the morng....Read in Navarette—make notes &c....Make notes from various works for Columb."[100] On 3 July he visited the Royal Library (Biblioteca Real; just northeast of Madrid's royal palace, across the Plaza de Oriente) as a tourist; he would later return there as a researcher.[101] On 11 July, daily references to writing "at Columbus" return, thus beginning a second phase of the project. He worked more or less daily on Columbus from 3 July to 31 August, at which point his attention shifted for two and a half months to "Granad."—that is, what would become his 1829 *Chronicle of the Conquest of Granada.*

186 CHAPTER 4

Presumably, Irving continued to center his July–August research on the resources in Rich's library, although he did run into Navarrete at social gatherings on 6 August and 11 November.[102]

On 16 November, Irving moved into a new house. Located several blocks north of Calle de San Fernando, it was near the Santa Bárbara gate at the northern edge of the city, where Calle de Hortaleza and Calle San Mateo join. The Everetts had moved there in July, and Obadiah Rich seems to have relocated as well.[103] Irving later described exquisitely picturesque views from his new lodgings, including a Mercedarian monastery across the street and, several blocks beyond, the upper story of a Salesian nunnery:[104]

> About six weeks since Mr Richs family changed their residence and my brother & myself removed with them. They occupy the first floor of the house, we have rooms on the second. The house is one of those great habitations peculiar to Spain. Great entrances and staircases about which you might drive a French Diligence. Labarynths of rooms one within another, half of them unfurnished, of no use and never intended to be of any; for these Spaniards are mighty pompous in their dwellings and think it a mark of dignity to have a vast deal of waste room around them. Our house is in the highest part of Madrid, close by one of the Gates and commands a view over a great part of the city and the adjacent country. Directly opposite is a convent of fat friars into whose gardens & grounds our windows have a full prospect. If mortifying the flesh be necessary to salvation not one of these sleek fathers will ever get to heaven. Every day I see mules heavily laden with the good things of this world entering their gates, and the only flower to be seen in their garden is the Cauliflower.
>
> Beyond the domains of this holy brotherhood I have a view of all the upper part of an immense convent, one of the noblest in architecture in Madrid. It is a convent of nuns of noble families, and young ladies of distinction are educated there. Of course it is full of the most beautiful beings on the face of the earth. It is so far off that I cannot distinguish forms or features which is a great advantage, for if ever I descry any one peeping through the grated windows I set her down for the most beautiful and interesting young lady that ever was, weeping and wringing her hands, and pining away until no bigger round the wrist than a tissue paper, because she is shut up by her cruel parents—you can't think how pleasant it is.[105]

The day after he moved, 17 November, Irving returned to almost daily writing on Columbus, which would continue until early January. His journals include references to what would become the final main chapter of the published work (on "the character of 'Columbus,'" 26 November) as well as to some of the work's thirty-five appendices (17 and 22 December, 7 and 8 January).[106] Just after he began writing those appendices, on 19 December, Irving tried to visit both don Antonio de Uguina (on Calle de la Salud, just north of the Puerta del Sol plaza) and Navarrete. Uguina (personal treasurer to the Infante don Francisco de Paula) had been good friends with

Juan Bautista Muñoz, and he had inherited a collection of Muñoz's papers (including copies of New World–related documents), which is probably why Irving wanted to meet.[107] But neither Uguina nor Navarrete was home. With the holiday season beginning, Irving put these two social-research calls on hold for a month.

1827 began. Irving wrote on and off for the first week and a half, and starting on 11 January, he began a week "at Library taking notes" from various Columbian sources: Giovanni Battista Ramusio, Pascal-François-Joseph Gossellin, Alexander von Humboldt. This may have been at the Jesuit library Irving had visited the previous April, or perhaps at the Royal Library, which he had toured the previous July.[108] Then, on the morning of Thursday, 18 January—almost one month after his attempt in December—Irving called again on Navarrete, "through the hydrographical establishment."[109] Navarrete was in. This meeting seems to have unnerved Irving (much as their first meeting had done the previous April); nonetheless, it marks the beginning of a new, third phase of research and writing. Irving began to seek out manuscript sources held by private individuals in Madrid.

Although Irving was "Incapable of workg" on Friday, he called on Navarrete that Sunday at his home at 26 Calle de Valverde (a few blocks north of Puerta del Sol)—but, once again, Navarrete was away.[110] The next few days saw Irving at work late into the night (and, on 26 January, until dawn). He made another unsuccessful house call at Navarrete's on 26 January. Finally, on the 27th, after having gotten up at 3 a.m., Irving caught Navarrete at home. Irving was then loaned some manuscripts: "Call at Mr Navarettes. get MSS."[111] These may have been partial copies of documents about the lawsuits of Christopher Columbus's heirs that Navarrete received from the Archive of the Indies the previous summer, and which Irving refers to in one of the appendices for his 1828 history of Columbus:

> **The depositions of these witnesses are still extant in the archives of the Indies at Seville, amongst the papers belonging to the Admiral Don Luis Colon, and forming part of the proceedings relating to the preservation of his privileges, from 1515 to 1564. The author of the present work has two several copies of those interrogatories lying before him; one made by the late historian Muñoz and the other made in 1826, and signed by Don Jose de la Higuera y Lara, keeper of the general archives of the Indies in Seville.[112]**

Indeed, records of Navarrete's petitions for these documents, and of the copies sent by archivist José de la Higuera y Lara (on 23 August 1826) are on file, like many of this chapter's examples, in the Indiferente General section of the Archive of the Indies.[113]

More full days of writing followed, and then another visit to Navarrete on 30 January.[114] On 8 February, Irving went with a banker friend to call on an abbot "who promises to speak to Duke of Veragua to get me the examination of archives." (The dukes of Veragua were descendants of Columbus; their important private archive was acquired by the Archive of the Indies in 1926.)[115] On 22 February, Irving returned to the Hydrographic Office, there meeting not only Navarrete but also (at last) Antonio de Uguina. As Irving later wrote in the preface to *A History of the Life and Voyages,*

I must acknowledge, also, the liberality of the Duke of Veraguas, the descendant and representative of Columbus, who submitted the archives of his family to my inspection, and took a personal interest in exhibiting the treasures they contained. Nor, lastly, must I omit my deep obligations to my excellent friend Don Antonio de Ugina, treasurer of the Prince Francisco, a gentleman of talents and erudition, and particularly versed in the history of his country and its dependencies. To his unwearied investigations, and silent and unavowed contributions, the world is indebted for much of the accurate information, recently imparted, on points of early colonial history. In the possession of this gentleman are most of the papers of his deceased friend, the late historian Muños, who was cut off in the midst of his valuable labours. These, and various other documents, have been imparted to me by Don Antonio with a kindness and urbanity which greatly increased, yet lightened the obligation.[116]

A month and a half of almost daily (if often difficult) writing followed, partially leavened by Henry Wadsworth Longfellow's arrival in Madrid on 7 March.[117] In a letter back home to his father in Maine, the young poet wrote:

The society of Americans here is very limited here. Mr Everett and family—Mr. Smith his secretary—Mr. Rich, the consul—Washington Irving and his brother,—Lieut.[enant] Slidell of the Navy—and myself compose the whole. Mrs Everett is a very pleasant lady—and we pass very pleasant ev[en]ings at her house. She has not all the "pomp and circumstance" which Ambassadors' wives sometimes put on—and receives one in a friendly—not an official way. Mr. Rich's family circle is also a very agreeable one—and Washington Irving—who resides in the same house,—always makes one there in the evening. This is altogether delightful—for he is one of those men who put you at ease with them in a moment. He makes no ceremony whatever with one—and of course is a very fine man in society—all mirth and good humor.[118]

On Thursday, 10 May, Irving visited both Antonio de Uguina and, finally, the Duke of Veragua, "who shewd MS letters of the King of Portugal—King & Queen of Spain to Columbus."[119] Another six weeks of writing followed, and then a return to research at the royal and Jesuit libraries (on 20, 26, and 30 June and on 3 July).[120] Irving called on Antonio de Uguina again on 14 and 16 July, perhaps to see more of the Muñoz documents. On his second visit, Irving made "notes about Columbus," and was back to a library on 17 July.[121] The next day, Count Beaurepaire (sometime Spanish ambassador in Paris, like Beaumarchais's fictive Count Almaviva in *The Guilty Mother*) loaned Irving "Ms of Navarrete."[122] The day after that, Thursday, 19 July, Irving called on Navarrete himself to borrow a book about Amerigo Vespucci.[123] A week later, on Thursday, 26 July, Irving called on both Navarrete and Uguina, apparently for more manuscripts ("got Memoranda for Columb.")[124]

Irving was nearing the end of his year-plus marathon of writing. On 30 July, four days after visiting Navarrete and Uguina, Irving was "Preparing Parcels of Ms. to send by Mr Newman"—the British legation courier who would deliver the first half of the

DATA RETRIEVAL   189

Columbus manuscript to London publisher John Murray. Newman's actual departure was not until 9 August ("Mr Newman the British Courier departs this day and takes part of my MS. to Lond.[on] and Paris"). On 19 August, Irving was packing the second part of his manuscript "for London to go by Mr. Dedel the Dutch Minister who goes tomorrow."[125] Irving wanted to simultaneously publish in New York, so on 20 August he was "at American copy of Columb."[126]

The main body of the manuscript was completed; now Irving turned to the appendices (or "illustrations") started the previous December. In these, he would deal with controversial or tangential materials not included in the main narrative: "Amerigo Vespucci," "Martin Alonzo Pinzon," "Of the Atlantis of Plato." Irving worked on these "illustrations," as well as his preface, on and off for the next two months. He returned to the royal and Jesuit libraries several times, and on 21 and 26 September he again visited Antonio de Uguina.[127] Finally, on Thursday, 18 October, he prepared "parcels of the illustrations of Columb. to go by Mr. Rich tomorrow"—Obadiah Rich was leaving for a book-buying trip to London.

That October Thursday was an important moment: Irving's work on the Columbus manuscript was at last completed. On Friday, as Rich headed for London, Irving himself went on a weekend trip to the Escorial. Over the next few months, he researched other projects, moving back and forth from the Islamic world to Mexico: El Cid, Muhammad, Abderrahman, Moctezuma, and "Sahagun's Conquest of México." On 9 November, he changed his lodgings again, for "No 9 Plazuela St Cruz," just east of the Plaza Mayor.[128] On 6 December, Irving wrote a testy letter to John Murray, at last sending the Columbus preface (finished late August) and asking why the publisher had not contacted him.[129] Irving kept writing on Mahomet, Moors, and Moctezuma.[130] He would soon complete his second year of life in Madrid and was preparing for a change: a trip south to Andalusia with his brother.

On 8 February 1828, nearly two years after the project began, *A History of the Life and Voyages of Christopher Columbus* was published in London.[131] It received excellent reviews, one of which Irving received by mail in Madrid on 19 February.[132] Irving's self-reinvention from comic essayist to Romantic historian had worked. A week later, on 27 February (a Wednesday), Irving saw Navarrete at a dinner party. And two days later, at noon, Irving left Madrid for Andalusia. There he began a new period of research in libraries and archives, in part to revise his Columbus book for a second edition.

Irving's first destination was Córdoba, where he spent three days. (Due to health problems, his brother Peter stayed behind in Madrid.) Irving then went to Granada, where he stayed a week and a half. He continued down the Mediterranean coast to Málaga, then inland through Ronda, then on to coastal Gibraltar and Cádiz. On 14 April, a month and a half after leaving Madrid, Irving sailed out of Cádiz on the steamboat *Betis,* traveling along the coast and up the Guadalquivir to Seville. The *Betis* docked at half past five that afternoon. Irving would stay in Seville for over a year—and this brings me back, at last, to the Archive of the Indies.

For his first two weeks in Seville, Irving lodged at the Fonda de la Reyna on Calle Jimios, just northwest of the cathedral.[133] He began to explore the city's bibliographic and archival sources almost immediately. On Friday, 18 April (two days after Goya died in Bordeaux), Irving visited the cathedral's Columbian Library; the following Monday he went to the Archive of the Indies.

The Columbian Library had at its core a collection of books that once belonged to Columbus's son Fernando. Access was not a problem; Irving would spend many days there in the months to come. Among other things, he would come across Columbus's annotated copy of Pierre d'Ailly's *Imago Mundi* (Image of the world), as well as the navigator's manuscript *Libro de las profecías* (*Book of Prophecies*)—volumes that, a century and a half later, would be important for thinking about Columbus's apocalyptic motivations.[134]

Access to the Archive of the Indies, in contrast, was another matter. When Irving met archivist Higuera y Lara on Monday, 21 April, he presented a letter of introduction (perhaps the one Everett provided for Irving from the secretary of state on 24 February).[135] But Higuera y Lara informed Irving—in a response that should be familiar by this point in the chapter—that royal permission was needed before documents could be consulted. And so on 23 April (the same day Irving's portrait was painted by Scottish artist David Wilkie) (fig. 4.8), Irving included this request in a long letter to Everett:

> I have visited the archives of the Indias and presented a letter of introduction to the chief, Sen— Higuera y Lara. He tells me, however, that it is necessary to have an express order from the King before I can inspect the archives or make any extracts or copies. I wish very much to examine some documents prior to publishing the Second edition of my work. Can you, without inconvenience, in your intercourse at court, proporcionar me an order of the kind?[136]

Everett seems to have responded, for in a 7 May letter, Irving wrote:

> As to visiting the archives here, if it is a matter of such difficulty on the part of the government, I would not wish you to press it. I had supposed a simple application would have been sufficient. There are some documents concerning Columbus of which Mr. Navarrete has obtained copies, which he intends to publish in his third volume, and of which I have never been able to obtain a full sight at Madrid. I should have wished to get a sight of these, as I fear the third volume of Mr. Navarrete will be as long in making its appearance as the Jewish Messiah. It is not, however, a matter of much moment.[137]

Despite this pessimistic response by Irving, Everett began the process of requesting permission on 9 May, writing to secretary of state Manuel González Salmón.[138] In turn, on 21 May, González Salmón forwarded a (Spanish) copy of this request to the Council of the Indies, a notice of which forms the first piece of Irvingiana paperwork in the AGI.

Meanwhile, Irving kept busy in Seville. He had received copies of the London printing of *History of the Life and Voyages of Christopher Columbus* on 7 May, and got to work the next day making corrections for a second edition. Copies of the New York

DATA RETRIEVAL 191

FIGURE 4.8
David Wilkie (Scottish, 1785–1841).
Washington Irving, Seville, April 23.ᵈ, 1828, 1828, watercolor on paper, 36.8 × 26.6 cm. London, The John Murray Collection.

printing arrived soon after, on 21 May—the same day González Salmón sent Irving's access request to the council.[139] Over the next two months (during which González Salmón's letter reached the council on 7 June, and was reviewed and approved on 14 July), Irving alternated revisions on the Columbus history with work on *Chronicle of the Conquest of Granada*. Irving was now renting an apartment at "Mrs. Stalkers," located in the northwest corner of Seville's royal palace—in other words, in rooms that had once been House of Trade offices and archives. But when the Sevillian summer became too intense, Irving escaped to a cottage just outside of the city, owned by his friends the Wetherells (introduced above).[140]

On 5 August 1828—two days after the royal order granting Irving archival access was issued at the Palace of Aranjuez in San Ildefonso de la Granja—Irving sent John Murray his corrections to *History of the Life and Voyages* (corrections that, alas, would never be printed in London).[141] At the beginning of the following week, Irving went on a small coastal field trip and visited the descendants of Martín Alonzo Pinzón, pilot of *La Pinta* in 1492. In Palos, the American was granted access to Pinzón family papers (from which he made copies); at La Rábida, he had an intensely Romantic experience on the beach: "I cannot express to you what were my feelings on treading the shore which had once been animated by the bustle of departure, and whose sands had been printed by the last footstep of Columbus....I felt my heart swelling with emotions and my eyes filling with tears."[142]

Irving returned to Seville on 15 August, a Friday. Collecting his mail the next day, he received the 4 August letter from Everett "announcing the Kings permission for me to inspect the Archives of the Indias."[143] That Monday, Irving was at last able to consult documents: "Visit Archives of the Indias—Inspect papers of Christopher Columbus."[144] He returned to the archive the following day, at least for the morning.

But that seems to have been it. On Saturday, Irving took the *Betis* steamboat to Cádiz, where he would stay for more than two months. He spent his first week there revising the *History of the Life and Voyages* appendix that had to do with Martín Pinzón, inspired by his recent visit to Pinzón's heirs, and on 8 September sent copies of the revisions both to Murray in London and to his brother Ebenezer in New York.[145] Irving continued work on *Chronicle of the Conquest of Granada* and *Voyages and Discoveries of the Companions of Columbus* (both of which had been started in Madrid); in addition, to combat a recent piracy, he prepared an abridged version of the Columbus history, which was published the following year.[146] He returned to Seville on 3 November, and a week and a half later saw one of his favorite operas: *The Barber of Seville* (in situ, as it were). According to his journals, Irving had seen nearly twenty performances of the work since 1822 (in Prague, Paris, Bordeaux, and Madrid).

1829 began. Early in the new year, Irving returned to the Archive of the Indies one last time. On Monday, 5 January, he asked to see papers related to Vasco Nuñez de Balboa for *Voyages and Discoveries*. Unfortunately, and unsurprisingly, this request required new paperwork: "cannot examine the papers of Balboa without express order."[147] Or, as Irving put it in a letter to Everett on 14 February 1829,

> I have been disappointed in my hopes of being able to make researches in the archives of the Indias. I find the permission was confined to the papers relating to Columbus, and the keeper of the archives, though extremely civil and friendly, is rigorous in obeying the very letter of his instructions. I found it impossible, therefore, to obtain

an inspection of other papers relative to the early discoveries, and have not thought it worth while to make further application.[148]

In total, Washington Irving may have spent no more than a day and a half doing research at the Archive of the Indies. That said, he had a focused target (the lawsuit of Diego Columbus), which was easy to locate in the archive's index books for Royal Patronage: case 1, shelf 1, bundle 3/10, "Papers concerning don Diego and don Fernando Colón, sons of don Cristóbal." It was a document Irving had already seen several partial copies of in Madrid, in the houses of Navarrete and Uguina, so he was familiar with its contents. But did Irving's encounter with the original sixteenth-century documents impact his later works?

Yes and no. A first challenge—perhaps shock—Irving would have faced was the handwriting. The lawsuit documents are written in a labyrinthine early sixteenth-century script, filled with scribal abbreviations and difficult to read without a lot of practice—practice Irving probably didn't have. As we have seen, most of Irving's contact with archival documents in Madrid was through late eighteenth- and early nineteenth-century copies owned by Navarrete and Uguina. Obadiah Rich's manuscript of the Las Casas copy of Columbus's logbook, which today is in the New York Public Library, was also made in the late eighteenth century.[149] Perhaps Irving's only contact with centuries-old Spanish handwriting had been the documents he was shown in the personal archive of the Duke of Veragua on 10 May 1827. That said (applying my own experience, at least), if Irving had made his own copies of the copied Columbus documents in Madrid, these would have certainly helped him decipher—or navigate—the handwriting of the original papers in Seville.

In any case—perhaps because of the bureaucratic hurdles involved—Irving signposted his 1828 archival efforts in two subsequent publications. In the preface to *Voyages and Discoveries of the Companions of Columbus* (1831), Irving acknowledges

> how much he has been indebted to the third volume of the invaluable Historical collection [published in 1829] of Don Martin Fernandez de Navarrete, wherein he has exhibited his usual industry, accuracy and critical acumen.... He has had some assistance also from the documents of the law case between Don Diego Columbus and the Crown, which exists in the archives of the Indies; and for an inspection of which he is much indebted to the permission of the Spanish Government and the kind attentions of Don Joséf de La Higuera Lara, the keeper of the archives.[150]

The Diego Columbus law case is cited by Irving in footnotes on pages 20 and 28, but he never quotes from it directly. As Irving points out in his preface, the court documents had been published two years before by Navarrete, who himself credits his published version to manuscript copies made in the 1780s by Juan Bautista Muñoz and in the 1820s by José de la Higuera y Lara.[151]

Those were the same manuscript copies consulted by Irving in Madrid during his final year writing the Columbus manuscript in 1827. This brings up a second, and

194 CHAPTER 4

more complex, case study of how Irving's brief consultation at the AGI shaped his later publications: the 1831 "New Edition Revised and Corrected by the Author" of *History of the Life and Voyages of Christopher Columbus.*

In the first edition of 1828, Irving had already made various references to documents from "the archives of the Indies."[152] He had not yet been there, of course; he acknowledged that his secondhand sources were Navarrete's two 1826 volumes on Columbus, as well as copied manuscripts loaned by Navarrete and Uguina in Madrid. Yet despite the existence of these scattered pre-Sevillian citations in 1828, there is one section of the 1831 printing (and *only* one, as far as I can tell) that was extensively revised because of Irving's Andalusian research: appendix XI, on Martín Alonzo Pinzón. The 1828 version is around 673 words; the 1831 version is twice as long. The 1828 version is Englishonly; the 1831 version includes two Spanish-language quotes of witness testimonies from the Diego Columbus lawsuits in the AGI. Finally, the 1831 version highlights Irving's archival research in mid-August 1828. In the final paragraph, he writes:

> The extravagant testimony before mentioned appears never to have had any weight with the fiscal; and the accurate historian Muños, who extracted all these points of evidence from the papers of the lawsuit, has not deemed them worthy of mention in his work. As these matters, however, remain on record in the archives of the Indias, and in the archives of the Pinzon family, in both of which I have had a full opportunity of inspecting them, I have thought it adviseable to make these few observations on the subject; lest, in the rage for research, they might hereafter be drawn forth as a new discovery, on the strength of which to impugn the merits of Columbus.[153]

Remember that on 11 August 1828 (a Monday), Irving left Seville for a short trip to the coast, where he was warmly received by the descendants of the Pinzón family and allowed to consult their private papers. He returned to Seville that Friday, and on Saturday collected Everett's letter announcing permission to consult the Archive of the Indies. Irving visited the archive on Monday and Tuesday, and the following Saturday headed down to Cádiz. He spent his first week there revising the Pinzón appendix, and on 8 September sent copies of the revisions to London and New York. One manuscript draft of these revisions still survives, at the University of Virginia, bound into Irving's hand-corrected copy of the 1828 London printing.[154] The draft is a fascinating document: a working version, with lines crossed out and words revised. It was probably copied again for shipment to Irving's brother in New York (assuming this surviving version was sent to London), who then passed it along to the publishers to turn the clean copy into a printed page.

This revised Pinzón appendix is perhaps a disappointing coda to the saga of Irving's efforts to access the AGI: it took a lot of effort to consult documents there, but in the end they had little impact on Irving's Iberian histories. Yet such is often the fate of archival research.

DATA RETRIEVAL 195

FIGURE 4.9
Vicente Ignacio Imperial Digueri (Spanish, 1745–1821).
Plano de la bahia i ciudad de Cádiz (Plan of the bay and city of Cádiz), 1786, ink and watercolor on paper, 97 × 62 cm.
The city of Cádiz is depicted in red on the peninsula at the lower center of the map; the grid-planned Naval Academy of San Carlos appears in yellow on the mainland to the southeast (viewer's upper right). Madrid, Museo Naval, Sección de Cartografía E-LII-30.

FIGURE 4.10
Detail of figure 4.9.
The Isla de León, with existing buildings in red and the planned Naval Academy of San Carlos in yellow and gray. Image rotated so that north is at the top.

TOWARD A LIBRARY OF NAVAL SCIENCE

Four decades before Irving's visit to Seville, Martín Fernández de Navarrete was directing his own project of investigation at the Archive of the Indies.[155] But in contrast to the paper trails of Irving, Azaola, or even Wetherell, Navarrete's research is barely registered by the Indiferente General documents explored in this chapter. The one reference I have found is so slight, and so indirect, that it is easily overlooked. In the AGI's financial accounts for 1793, an entry in May lists the purchase of "a half dozen chairs for the scribes of Navarrete."[156]

Yet although this particular reference is extremely brief, thousands of pages documenting the two-plus years Navarrete and his scribes worked in Seville survive today in the archive of Madrid's Naval Museum (Museo Naval). These papers, dated from 23 April 1793 to 30 June 1795, provide a month-by-month glimpse of the first research project ever conducted in the AGI. They also reveal how organizational systems from the Archive of Simancas continued to structure the documents newly relocated to Seville.

In the fall of 1789, ambitious plans were made for a new Library of Naval Science (Biblioteca de Ciencia Naval) on the Isla de León. Located just southeast of Cádiz, this institution would form part of an under-construction academy dedicated to the Enlightenment renovation of Spain's navy (figs. 4.9, 4.10).[157] In order to stock the

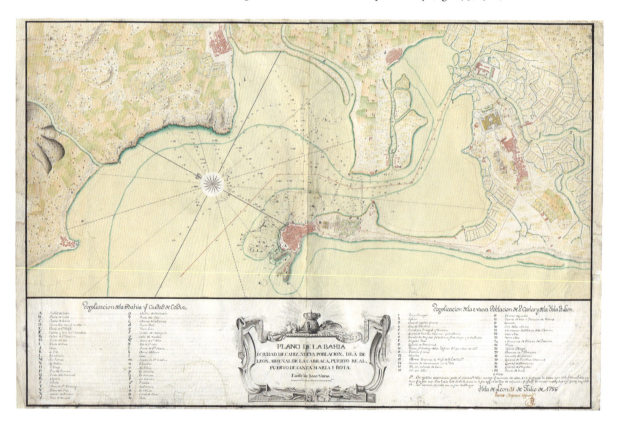

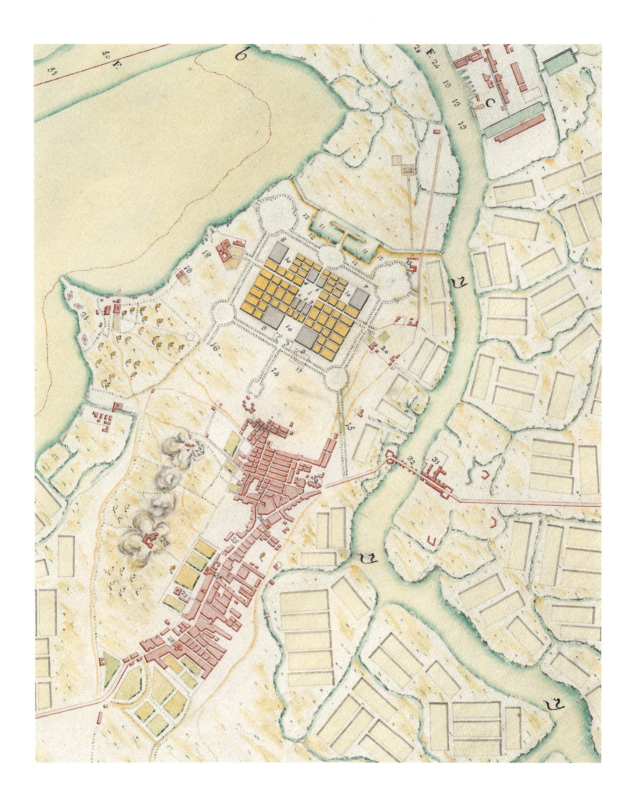

proposed library, three naval officers (including the twenty-four-year-old Navarrete) were commissioned by King Carlos III to seek out documents of maritime history in Spain's archives and libraries. Relevant materials were to be copied and the copies sent on to Cádiz so that, once a library building had been constructed, it could be stocked with a trove of unpublished primary sources.[158] In many ways, this project echoes that of Juan Bautista Muñoz, who (with his own team of scribes) undertook a similar copying tour of Spain's archives and libraries a decade earlier. But whereas Muñoz's document copies were, in theory, being gathered as sources for writing a new history of the Americas, the naval project commissioned in 1789 was open-ended. Copying documents was a goal in and of itself, not a first step toward the writing of an authoritative history. At the same time, and more broadly, the anthology aesthetic of both projects connects to the early modern genre of travel narrative compilations, in which previously published sources were gathered and reedited in massive multivolume editions.[159] The work of Muñoz and Navarrete (and their scribes) was a kind of bespoke analog to those printed collections.

Like Muñoz before him, Navarrete began his research in Madrid. He worked at the Royal Library and at the Jesuit library of San Isidro (both visited decades later by Irving), as well as in the private archives of the Marquis of Santa Cruz, the Marquis of Villafranca, and the Duke of Medinasidonia.[160] Navarrete spent the autumn of 1791 and 1792 at the Escorial, and in February 1793 headed south to Seville.[161] His team of six scribes followed in April—once they had finished their copying tasks in Madrid—and chairs were purchased for them in May. In June of the same year, Navarrete was summoned for duty in Spain's war against revolutionary France. But his team of scribes, led by Joséph de Basterrechea (who had assisted Navarrete since 1790), continued to search for and copy documents. Work went on for another two years, until a royal order in mid-June 1795 suspended the commission. A month later, the commission was dissolved.[162]

That October, Navarrete sent his copied documents to the Naval Academy (Academia de Guardias Marinas) on the Isla de León. The planned Library of Naval Science had never been built, and so in 1798, Navarrete's collection was sent to the archive of the Secretariat of the Naval Office (Secretaría del Despacho de Marina) in Madrid.[163] In 1812, the collection traveled south again to Cádiz. As with the thirty-one chests of documents sent there from the Archive of the Indies in 1809, this relocation was a protective measure against Napoleon's armies.

When the war ended in 1814, Navarrete's collection went back to Madrid, where it took up residence in the library-archive (*depósito*) of the Hydrographic Office.[164] In many ways, this new home was the kind of institution for which Navarrete's collection was created. Founded in the late eighteenth century, the Hydrographic Office had as its goal the Enlightenment renovation of Spanish nautical sciences. The office supported research, published new marine charts, and developed an impressive research collection, which by 1808 had as many as 7,000 volumes.[165] Located on Calle de Alcalá, just northeast of Puerta del Sol, the Hydrographic Office was where

Washington Irving visited Navarrete and first met Antonio de Uguina in January and February 1827 (see fig. 4.7). As noted earlier, Irving came to Madrid because Navarrete was publishing the results of his earlier archival work, starting with documents about Columbus. Eventually comprising five volumes, Navarrete's *Colección de los viajes y descubrimientos que hicieron por mar los españoles* (1825–37) was intended to display "the glory of the Spanish Nation." Ironically, of course, by the late 1820s Spain's overseas empire had all but disappeared.

Navarrete's copied manuscripts remained in the Hydrographic Deposit for over a century. In 1929, they traveled south to Seville, to be included in the displays of the Naval Pavilion at the Exposición Ibero-Americana (fig. 4.11).[166] In 1932, these and other documents from the Hydrographic Office were transferred to Madrid's Naval Museum, where they remain. A detailed index (by Vicente Vela, with an introduction by Captain Julio F. Guillén y Tato) was published in 1946, and a facsimile of the collection was printed in 1971. Today, the thirty-two volumes of the Navarrete collection

FIGURE 4.11
*Sevilla—Pabellón Marina de Guerra—"ALESDI,"
1929.*
The Naval Pavilion at the Exposición Ibero-Americana, viewed from the northwest.

DATA RETRIEVAL 199

contain 2,521 documents. Of these, nearly one thousand were copied in the Archive of the Indies from 1793 to 1795.

Using these manuscripts to reconstruct how Navarrete and his team conducted their research presents a number of challenges.[167] First, the surviving collection is incomplete. Some parts were lost in the century-plus between the commission's termination in 1795 and the binding of volumes for the Exposición Ibero-Americana in 1929. For example, page 241 of the first volume of Navarrete's 1825 *Colección* cites a document copied from the Archive of the Indies and double-checked by Navarrete on 30 May 1793. But that copied document (a 1494 memo from the Catholic monarchs to Columbus) is no longer part of the Navarrete collection.

Second, although each document copy was dated (as with the lost example just cited), those dates are not as straightforward as they first appear. The dates do not indicate when a document was first copied by one of Navarrete's scribes. Rather, the dates indicate when the copied document was *double-checked and corrected* against the original source by Navarrete or first assistant Joséph de Basterrechea. Depending on the workload, this double-checking could have taken place weeks or even months after the document was first copied. These document dates, in other words, only provide a general timeline for how Navarrete's team worked through the archive's contents, not a precise day-by-day register.

Third, with the occasional exception of Basterrechea, scribes did not sign their work. As a result, the authorship of particular copies is not immediately clear. This presents an initial challenge for analyzing how the work of copying was divided among the members of the team. Nevertheless, each scribe had distinctive handwriting; in addition, their names and when each was hired is also known. By a process of coordination and elimination, I propose the following correlation of names to handwriting.[168] The full team working in Seville included:

1 Joséph de Basterrechea, appointed 20 September 1790 (see fig. 4.13)
2 Félix Hernández Garriga, appointed 23 May 1791 (figs. 4.12, 4.13)
3 Miguel Sarmiento, appointed mid-January 1792 (figs. 4.14, 4.15)
4 Cipriano Suárez, appointed mid-January 1792 (figs. 4.16, 4.17)
5 Juaquín Finao, appointed 13 November 1792 (figs. 4.18, 4.19)
6 Joséph Miguel Martínez Abad, appointed 13 November 1792 (auxiliary scribe)

The team's general process of research and copying can be reconstructed as follows. The project leader (first Navarrete, then Basterrechea after June 1793) searched the archive's manuscripts for documents to copy. This could be very time consuming. In a letter to Navarrete dated 29 January 1795, Basterrechea lamented that "it sometimes happens that after spending many days reviewing from fifty to a hundred files I will not find anything."[169]

On locating a relevant document, the project leader would (usually) take out a sheet of paper and write a short document summary at the top. This first page, and the original document in question, would then be assigned to one of the other scribes, who would

200 CHAPTER 4

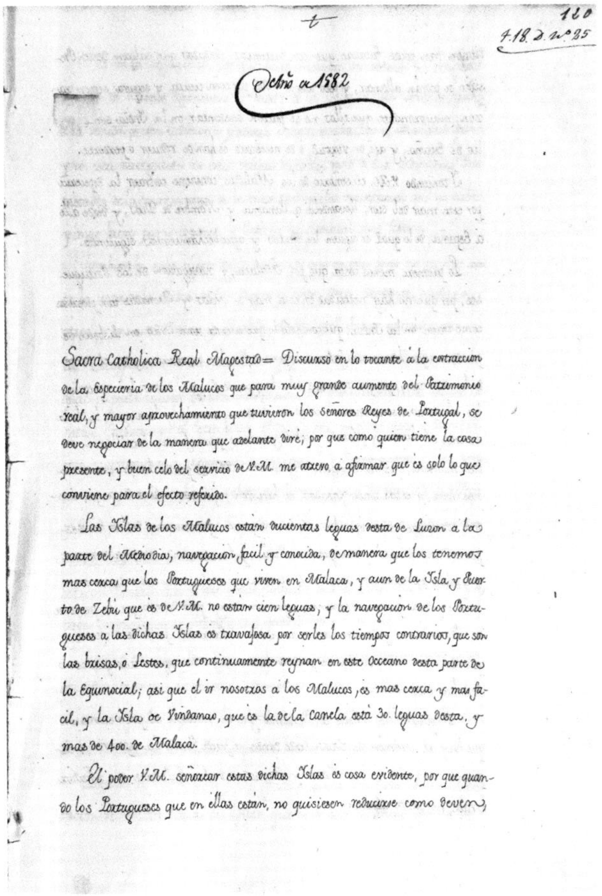

120

t. 18. D. nº 25

Año de 1582

Sacra Catholica Real Magestad = Discurso en lo tocante à la extraccion de la Especieria de los Malucos que para muy grande aumento del Patrimonio real, y mayor aprovechamiento que tuvieron los señores Reyes de Portugal, se deve negociar de la manera que adelante dire; por que como quien tiene la cosa presente, y buen celo del servicio de V. M. me atrevo a afirmar que es solo lo que conviene para el efecto referido.

Las Islas de los Malucos estan ducientas leguas desta de Luzon a la parte del Medio dia, navegacion facil y conocida, de manera que los tenemos mas cerca que los Portugueses que viven en Malaca, y aun de la Isla y Puerto de Zebu que es de V. M. no estan cien leguas, y la navegacion de los Portugueses a las dichas Islas es trabajosa por serles los tiempos contrarios, que son las brisas, ò Lestes, que continuamente reynan en este Occeano desta parte de la Equinocial; asi que el ir nosotros a los Malucos, es mas cerca y mas facil, y la Isla de Mindanao, que es la de la Canela està 30. leguas desta, y mas de 400. de Malaca.

El poder V. M. señorear estas dichas Islas es cosa evidente, por que quando los Portugueses que en ellas estan, no quisiesen reducirse como deven,

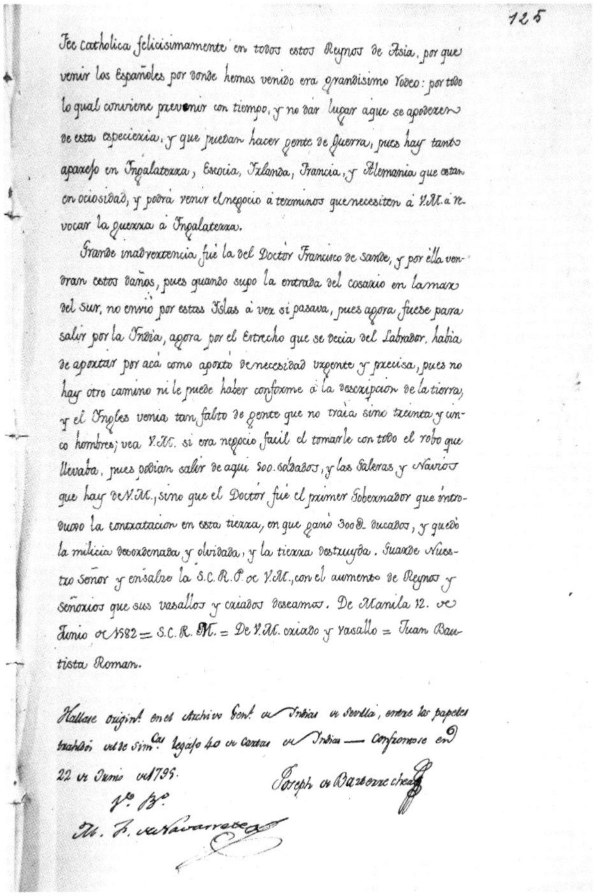

125

Fee catholica felicisimamente en todos estos Reynos de Asia, por que venir los Españoles por donde hemos venido era grandisimo rodeo: por todo lo qual conviene prevenir con tiempo, y no dar lugar a que se apoderen de esta especieria, y que puedan hacer gente de guerra, pues hay tanto aparejo en Ingalaterra, Escocia, Irlanda, Francia, y Alemania que estan en ociosidad, y podrà venir el negocio à terminos que necesiten à V. M. a revocar la guerra à Ingalaterra.

Grande inadvertencia fuè la del Doctor Francisco de Sande, y por èlla vendran estos daños, pues quando supo la entrada del cosario en la mar del sur, no envio por estas Islas à ver si pasava, pues agora fuese para salir por la India, agora por el Estrecho que se decia del Labrador, habia de aportar por acà como aporto de necesidad urgente y precisa, pues no hay otro camino ni le puede haber conforme à la descripcion de la tierra, y el Ingles venia tan falto de gente que no traìa sino treinta y cinco hombres; vea V. M. si era negocio facil el tomarle con todo el robo que llevaba, pues podian salir de aqui 500. soldados, y las Galeras y Navios que hay de V. M., sino que el Doctor fuè el primer Gobernador que introduxo la contratacion en esta tierra, en que ganò 300 D. ducados, y quedò la milicia desordenada y olvidada, y la tierra destruyda. Guarde Nuestro Señor y ensalze la S. C. R. P. de V. M., con el aumento de Reynos y señorios que sus vasallos y criados deseamos. De Manila 12. de Junio de 1582 = S. C. R. M. = De V. M. criado y vasallo = Juan Bautista Roman.

Hallase origin.l en el Archivo Gen.l de Indias de Sevilla, entre los papeles trahidos de Sim.cas legajo 40 de Cartas de Indias — Conforme se en 22 de Junio de 1795.

Joseph de Basterrechea

V.º B.º

M. F. de Navarrete

FIGURE 4.12
"Discurso en lo tocante a la extracción de la especería de los Malucos. Año 1582" (Comments about the exportation of spices from the Moluccas. 1582).
First page of an Archive of the Indies document copied by scribe 2 (Félix Hernández Garriga), verified and signed by Joséph de Basterrechea on 22 June 1795, and signed by Martín Fernández de Navarrete.
Madrid, Archivo del Museo Naval, Ms. 27 Colección Navarrete tomo 18 documento 25, fol. 120r.

FIGURE 4.13
"Discurso en lo tocante a la extracción de la especería de los Malucos. Año 1582" (Comments about the exportation of spices from the Moluccas. 1582).
Last page of an Archive of the Indies document copied by scribe 2 (Félix Hernández Garriga), verified and signed by Joséph de Basterrechea on 22 June 1795, and signed by Martín Fernández de Navarrete.
Madrid, Archivo del Museo Naval, Ms. 27 Colección Navarrete tomo 18 documento 25, fol. 125r.

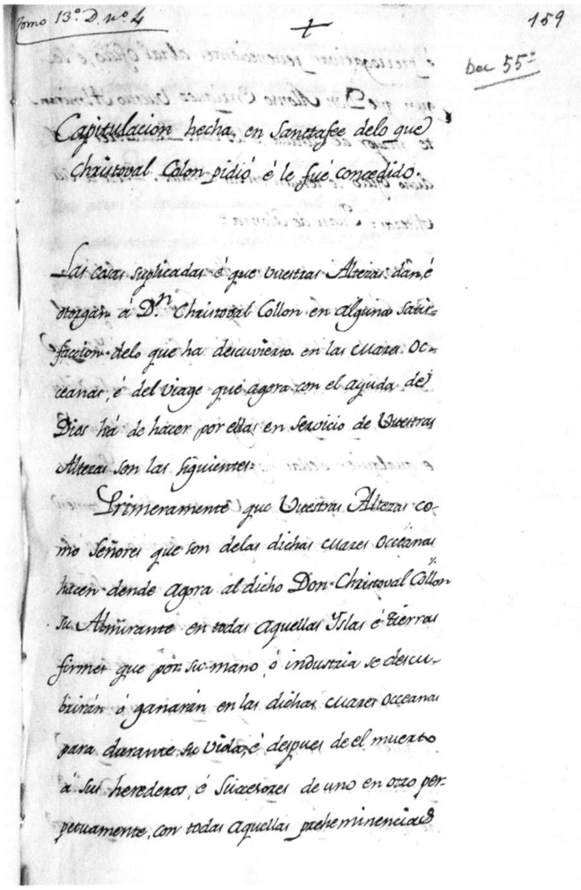

FIGURE 4.14

"Capitulación hecha en Santa Fe de lo que Cristóbal Colon pidió y le fue concedido. Año 1492" (Agreement reached in Santa Fe concerning that which Christopher Columbus requested and was granted. 1492).

First page of an Archive of the Indies document copied by scribe 3 (Miguel Sarmiento?) and verified and signed by Martín Fernández de Navarrete on 23 April 1793. Madrid, Archivo del Museo Naval, Ms. 22 Colección Navarrete tomo 13 documento 55, fol. 159r.

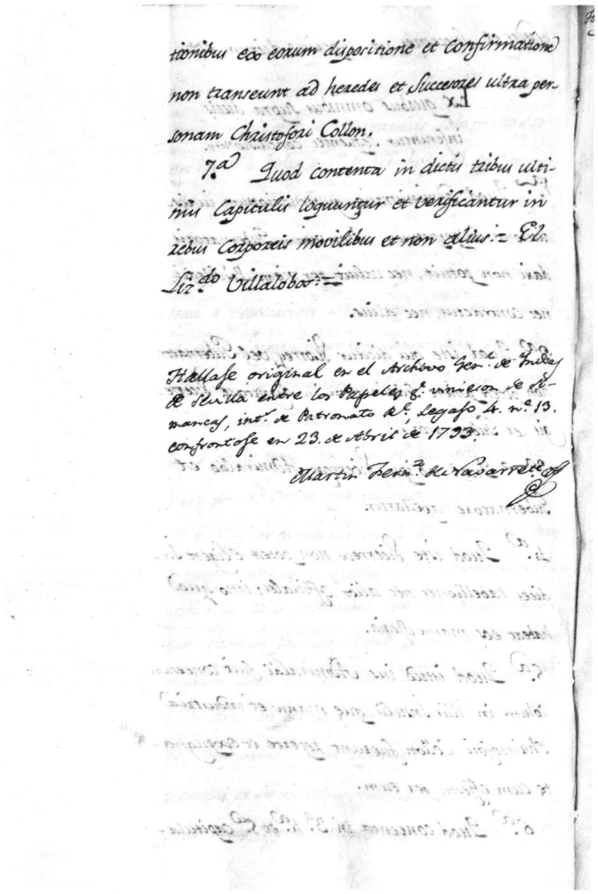

FIGURE 4.15

"Capitulación hecha en Santa Fe de lo que Cristóbal Colon pidió y le fue concedido. Año 1492" (Agreement reached in Santa Fe concerning that which Christopher Columbus requested and was granted. 1492).

Last page of an Archive of the Indies document copied by scribe 3 (Miguel Sarmiento?) and verified and signed by Martín Fernández de Navarrete on 23 April 1793. Madrid, Archivo del Museo Naval, Ms. 22 Colección Navarrete tomo 13 documento 55, fol. 180v.

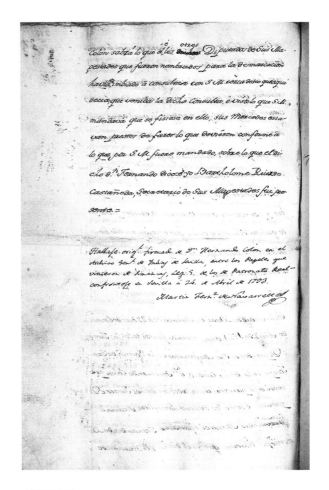

FIGURE 4.16
"Memorial que escribió Don Hernando Colón a los licenciados Acuña, Manuel, y Barrientos en Badajoz, pidiéndoles su parecer sobre la demarcación de la línea de la partición del Mar Océano y pertenencia del Maluco. Año 1524" (Memorandum written by don Hernando Colón to the licenciates Acuña, Manuel, and Barrientos in Badajoz, requesting their thoughts on the demarcation of the oceanic line of partition and its relevance to the Moluccas. 1524).
First page of an Archive of the Indies document summarized by Joséph de Basterrechea, copied by scribe 4 (Cipriano Suárez?), and verified and signed by Martín Fernández de Navarrete on 24 April 1793.
Madrid, Archivo del Museo Naval, Ms. 25 Colección Navarrete tomo 16 documento 41, fol. 395r.

FIGURE 4.17
"Memorial que escribió Don Hernando Colón a los licenciados Acuña, Manuel, y Barrientos en Badajoz, pidiéndoles su parecer sobre la demarcación de la línea de la partición del Mar Océano y pertenencia del Maluco. Año 1524" (Memorandum written by don Hernando Colón to the licenciates Acuña, Manuel, and Barrientos in Badajoz, requesting their thoughts on the demarcation of the oceanic line of partition and its relevance to the Moluccas. 1524).
Last page of an Archive of the Indies document summarized by Joséph de Basterrechea, copied by scribe 4 (Cipriano Suárez?), and verified and signed by Martín Fernández de Navarrete on 24 April 1793.
Madrid, Archivo del Museo Naval, Ms. 25 Colección Navarrete tomo 16 documento 41, fol. 396v.

DATA RETRIEVAL 203

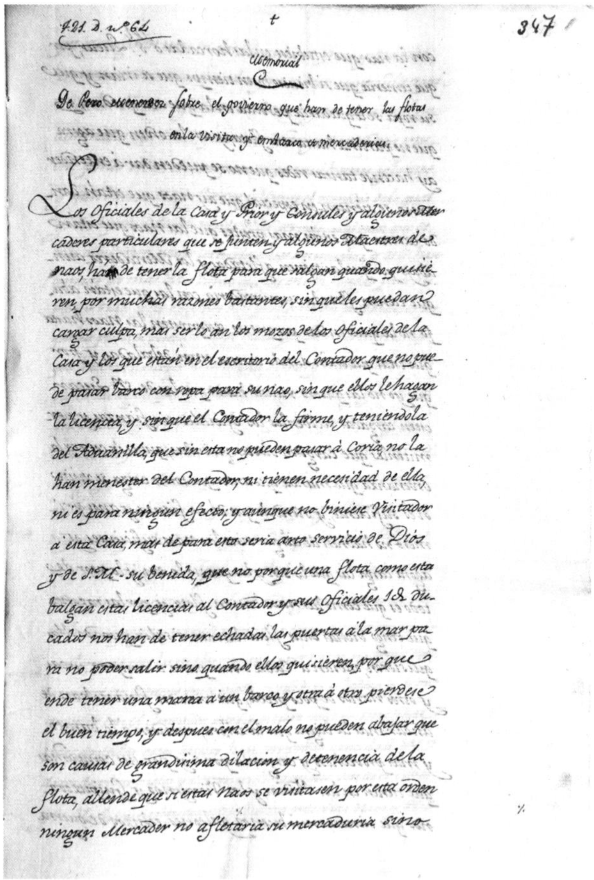

FIGURE 4.18

"Memorial De Pedro Menéndez sobre el gobierno que han de tener las flotas en la visita y embarco de mercaderías. Año 1561" (Memorandum by Pedro Menéndez about how the fleets should be managed during the inspection and the unloading of merchandise. 1561).

First page of an Archive of the Indies document summarized by Joséph de Basterrechea, copied by scribe 5 (Juaquín Finao?), and verified and signed by Martín Fernández de Navarrete on 23 May 1793.

Madrid, Archivo del Museo Naval, Ms. 30 Colección Navarrete tomo 21 documento 64, fol. 347r.

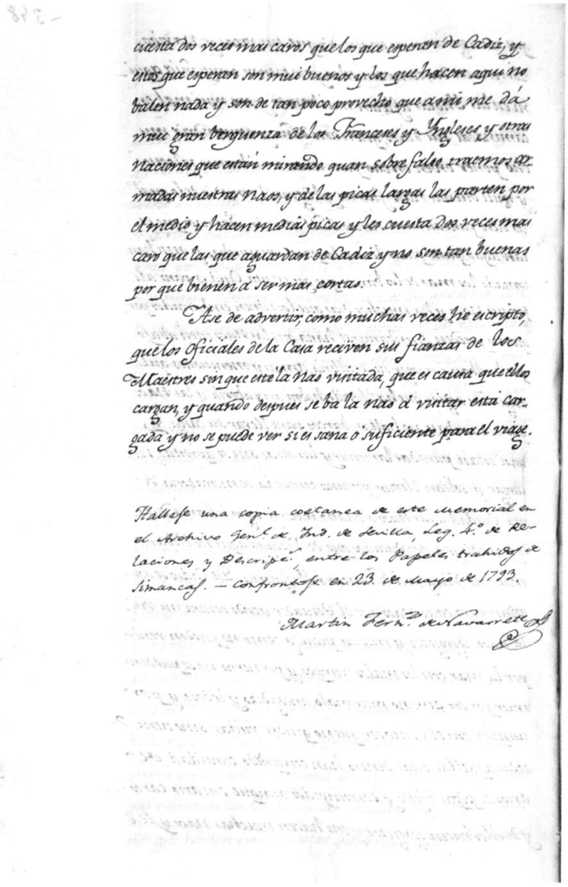

FIGURE 4.19

"Memorial De Pedro Menéndez sobre el gobierno que han de tener las flotas en la visita y embarco de mercaderías. Año 1561" (Memorandum by Pedro Menéndez about how the fleets should be managed during the inspection and the unloading of merchandise. 1561).

Last page of an Archive of the Indies document summarized by Joséph de Basterrechea, copied by scribe 5 (Juaquín Finao?), and verified and signed by Martín Fernández de Navarrete on 23 May 1793.

Madrid, Archivo del Museo Naval, Ms. 30 Colección Navarrete tomo 21 documento 64, fol. 348v.

copy out the full document. When completed, both the copy and the original text were given back to the project leader, who would then (with the help of one other team member) proofread the copy against the original, making corrections and additions as necessary.[170] Among other things, this system explains why so few full documents were copied by Basterrechea: most of his time was spent searching for documents (chart 4.1).

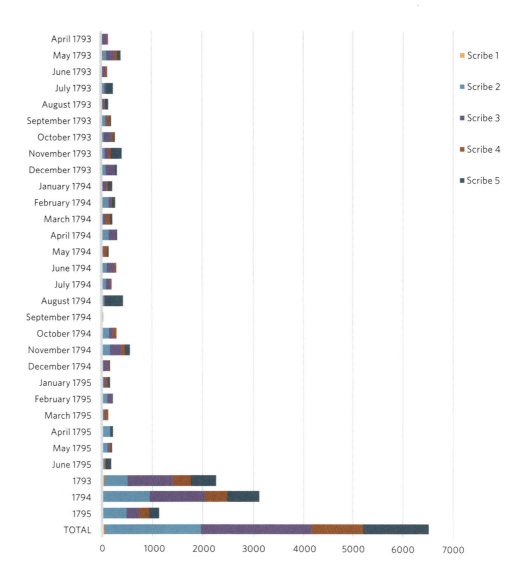

CHART 4.1
Scribal output at the Archive of the Indies, April 1793 to June 1795.
This chart shows the number of folios that each of Martín Fernández de Navarrete's scribes copied month by month and year by year.

This system may also explain why no full document copies are in the hand of the sixth scribe, Joséph Miguel Martínez Abad. He probably served as correction assistant.

For example, figures 4.16 and 4.17 show the first and last pages of a four-page document verified on 24 April 1793. At the top of the first page is a descriptive summary written by Basterrechea (with his distinctively tight hand and flourishes on end-of-line letters). Below begins a copy of the full document, probably by Cipriano Suárez (somewhat sloppy, with horizontal bars on the tail of the letter *p*). The first line of the copy contains a crossed-out correction, above which the word *capitulo* is written in Navarrete's hand. The first line of the last page also contains corrections, and after the main document ends, there is a note (in Navarrete's hand) indicating in what section of the archive the original document was located, the date of the document's verification, and Navarrete's signature.

That every document copy contains a reference to where its original source was located should, in theory, make it easy to track the team's progress through the holdings of the Archive of the Indies. But, as with document dating, things are not so simple. None of the copied documents are identified with the three-part case-shelf-document bundle system used from the 1790s to order and locate documents in the AGI. The April 1793 example above cites its source as "Leg.[ajo] 5. de los de Patronato Real." Another copy from April 1793 (figs. 4.14, 4.15) is from "Patronato R[ea]l, Legajo 4, n.° 13." By 1793, there was already a room set aside for Royal Patronage documents in the Lonja building, so presumably these two originals were stored there. But exactly where were they located in the room's two mahogany and cedar cases, each with six shelves? And what do we make of references to other document sources that seem to have no connection to the other main sections of the AGI (Accounting, House of Trade, Justice) that existed in the 1790s? The copy in figures 4.12 and 4.13, signed by Basterrechea and Navarrete in June 1795, is from "legajo 40 de Cartas de Yndias." The copy in figures 4.18 and 4.19 (verified 23 May 1793) is from "Leg.[ajo] 4° de Relaciones, y Descrip[cione]s."

Understanding these 1790s categories, and their location in the late eighteenth-century AGI, requires working backward from the present. In theory, there should be a clear ordinal correlation between the numbering of documents cataloged in the AGI today and the documents listed by Navarrete's scribes—for example, among the documents they label as legajos 1–8 of Patronato Real, or among legajos 1–11 of what they call "Relaciones y Descripciones." By searching keywords in PARES (Portal de Archivos Españoles, the online catalog for Spain's national archives), it is often possible to locate where documents copied by Navarrete and his team are located now. Thus the current location for the document copied in figures 4.16 and 4.17 described in 1793 as "Leg.[ajo] 5. de los de Patronato Real," is Patronato 48 (the two-part section-plus-number document identification system was introduced in the late 1920s).[171] Conveniently, document entries in PARES include the older, three-part identification system (case-shelf-bundle), which makes it easy to back-translate present-day catalog numbers. In this example, today's Patronato 48 corresponds to Patronato case 1, shelf 2, bundle 1/15. Two other documents from "Leg.[ajo] 5. de los de Patronato Real" were also copied in late April 1793 (Navarrete collection items 1594, 1600), and their current location, too, is Patronato 48 (or, formerly, case 1, shelf 2, bundle 1/15).

By extension, one would expect that documents copied in the 1790s from "Leg.[ajo] 6 de Patronato Real" would have been on an adjacent shelf in case 1—or, in the current system, a number shortly after Patronato 48. Unfortunately, this is not so. At least four of the "Leg.[ajo] 6 de Patronato Real" documents copied by scribe 3 in late April 1793 are now in Patronato 267—what was once case 2, shelf 5, bundle 1/22 (Navarrete collection items 233, 234, 237, and 1147). In other words, at least some documents from Navarrete's legajo 5 "de Patronato Real" were stored near the top of case 1, and some of the documents from Navarrete's legajo 6 "de Patronato Real" were stored near the bottom of case 2.

Further document correlations in PARES produce yet more complexity. Consider again case 2's shelf 5, item 22, which came from "Leg.[ajo] 6 de Patronato Real." Earlier on the same shelf, document bundles 13 and 14 were items from legajo 1 and legajo 3 of what Navarrete's scribes listed as "Relaciones y Descripciones."[172] Does this mean all of their "Relaciones y Descripciones" legajo 1 items will be found in case 2? No. In late April or early May 1793, scribe 2 copied a document from legajo 1 of "Relaciones y Descripciones" that is now in Patronato 18. This corresponds to case 1 (shelf 1, bundle 1/18).

Additional correlation work with the Navarrete copies produces similarly scattered results. On the one hand, despite their varied 1790s descriptions ("Patronato Real," "Relaciones y Descripciones," "Cartas de Indias," "Buen Gobierno"...), almost all of the documents copied by Navarrete's team are now in the Royal Patronage section of the AGI.[173] Yet at the same time, there is no clear correspondence between the ordering of the section-number systems referenced by Navarrete's scribes and the ordering of those documents in the AGI today—or, for that matter, in the AGI of 1814–19, which is when Diego Juárez created the first catalogs for Royal Patronage documents.

Fortunately, explanations are provided by a 150-page document (titled *Colecciones de Simancas*) in AGI Indiferente General 1858C.[174] The parchment-bound manuscript was created in the Archive of Simancas around 1784 by Fermín del Río y de la Vega, a scribe who since the spring of 1782 (and probably since the fall of 1780) had been helping Francisco Ortiz de Solorzano and Estevan de Larrañaga carry out their royal commission to order and catalog Council of the Indies documents in Simancas.[175] As explained in my introduction, this work was done so that, once the War of the Thirteen Colonies ended, those documents would be ready for transfer to a new Archive of the Indies.

The *Colecciones de Simancas* manuscript consists of four sections, each of which seems to be based on older, separate catalogs for American papers in the Simancas archive. The first section lists "Patronato Real" documents (pp. 1–38). The second section describes "Papeles de la Secretaría de Gouernacion del Consejo de Yndias à los dos Reynos de Nueva españa, y èl Peru" (pp. 39–82). The third describes "Papeles tocantes á la Secretaría de Nueva-españa" sent to Simancas in 1658 (pp. 83–112).[176] And the fourth describes "Papeles de la Secretaría del Perú," also sent to Simancas in 1658 (pp. 113–150). In sum:

1 Royal Patronage, 1492–1565
2 Secretariat of Governance of the Council of the Indies for the two kingdoms of New Spain and Peru, 1492–1604
3 Secretariat of New Spain, 1570–1648
4 Secretariat of Peru, 1550–1650

Within each of these four sections, the manuscript summarizes component legajos by theme and number. Table 4.1 compares the categories of this manuscript with the

CATEGORIES IN THE *COLECCIONES DE SIMANCAS* CATALOG (AGI INDIFERENTE GENERAL 1858C)	TOTAL NUMBER OF LEGAJOS ACCORDING TO THE *COLECCIONES DE SIMANCAS* CATALOG	CORRESPONDING NUMBER OF LEGAJOS FROM WHICH COPIES WERE MADE FOR THE NAVARRETE PROJECT (FOLLOWED BY SPECIFIC LEGAJO NUMBERS)
PATRONATO REAL		
Patronato Real [p. 1]	8 legajos	7 legajos copied (numbers 1, 3–8)
SECRETARÍA DE GOUERNACION DEL CONSEJO DE YNDIAS		
Consultas y Cartas del Consejo 1519–1566 [p. 39]	3 legajos	
Cartas de Sevilla, Cadiz, y otros Puertos 1520–1599 [p. 39]	27 legajos	2 legajos copied (numbers 1, 3)
Libros de Cartas enquadernadas de Sevilla, Cadiz, y otros Puertos 1551–1567 [p. 41]	2 legajos	2 legajos copied (numbers 1, 2)
Cartas de las Yndias escritas á S[u] M[ajestad] y àl Consexo 1513–1599 [p. 42]	64 legajos	49 legajos copied (numbers 1–10, 12–51)
Libros de Cartas enquadernadas de las Yndias 1533–1575 [p. 45]	3 legajos	
Memoriales y Peticiones del Consexo, 1526–1599 [p. 49]	49 legajos	
Memoriales, y Peticiones cuyos Decretos no tienen f[ec]ha [p. 49]	3 legajos	
Expedientes de Gobierno, encomendados à señores del Consexo [p. 52]	147 legajos	
Expedientes encomendados a s[eño]res del Consejo que han salido sobrantes [p. 57]	18 legajos	
Expedientes titulados de Govierno y Gracia [p. 58]	59 legajos	
Mas expedientes de Govierno y Gracia que salieron sobrantes [p. 63]	4 legajos	
Ynformaciones de Oficio, y Parte [pp. 63–67]	42 legajos	
Mas Ynformaciones de oficios y Partes en tres Legajos 1527–1576 [p. 67]	3 legajos	
Papeles tocantes al Buen Gouierno de las Yndias [p. 67]	25 legajos	19 legajos copied (numbers 1–9, 11–17, 19, 21, 22)
Papeles tocantes á Descripciones, Poblaciones (Muñoz collection) [p. 68]	11 legajos	11 legajos copied (numbers 1–11)
Registros y Relaciones del Oro y Plata 1526–1603 [p. 69]	9 legajos	
Legajos Particulares [pp. 70–72]	28 legajos	1 legajo copied (number 1)
Libros de Registro dèl Consejo 1528–1569 [p. 72]	23 legajos	1 legajo copied (number 1)
Libros de Registros de Peticiones 1572–1595 [p. 74]	4 legajos	
Libros Diferentes 1492–1597 [p. 75]	4 legajos	
Papeles Diversos 1508–1599 [p. 80]	17 legajos	12 legajos copied (numbers 1–4, 10–17)
SECRETARÍA DE NUEVA-ESPAÑA		
Cartas de Sevilla, Cadiz, y otros Puertos 1600–1648 [p. 83]	16 legajos	
Cartas del Distrito de la Audiencia de Mexico 1570–1648 [p. 84]	31 legajos	
Cartas de Vera-Cruz 1583–1640 [p. 86]	3 legajos	
Cartas de Yucatan 1592–1643 [p. 86]	2 legajos	
Cartas de Goathemala 1594–1644 [p. 86]	7 legajos	
Cartas de Guadalaxara 1590–1648 [p. 87]	4 legajos	

TABLE 4.1
Comparison of document categories in the *Colecciones de Simancas* manuscript catalog (from AGI IG 1858C) and document categories copied by Martín Fernández de Navarrete's scribes.
The first column indicates the section and subsection categories listed in the AGI's *Colecciones de Simancas* manuscript catalog. (In Seville, these documents were all stored in the Royal Patronage room.) The second column indicates the total number of legajos for each section or subsection. The third column indicates the total number of legajos from which Navarrete's scribes made copies, followed (in parentheses) by the specific identifying numbers of the legajos copied.

208 CHAPTER 4

CATEGORIES IN THE *COLECCIONES DE SIMANCAS* CATALOG (AGI INDIFERENTE GENERAL 1858C)	TOTAL NUMBER OF LEGAJOS ACCORDING TO THE *COLECCIONES DE SIMANCAS* CATALOG	CORRESPONDING NUMBER OF LEGAJOS FROM WHICH COPIES WERE MADE FOR THE NAVARRETE PROJECT (FOLLOWED BY SPECIFIC LEGAJO NUMBERS)
Cartas de Manila 1580–1643 [p. 87]	10 legajos	2 legajos copied (numbers 2, 7)
Cartas de Santo Domingo 1586–1644 [p. 88]	10 legajos	
Cartas de Havana y Cuba 1584–1648 [p. 89]	7 legajos	
Cartas de Puerto-Rico y la Florida 1594–1644 [p. 89]	5 legajos	
Cartas de Caracas, Cumana y la Margarita 1596–1644 [p. 89]	7 legajos	
Libros de Cartas enquadernadas de las Audiencias 1636–1640 [p. 90]	1 legajo	
Expedientes, Memoriales y encomiendas de Govierno 1597–1643 [p. 92]	60 legajos	
Expedientes, Memoriales, y encomiendas de Camara 1600–1643 [p. 94]	53 legajos	
Expedientes de Gracia [p. 97]	114 legajos	
Ynformaciones de Oficio y Parte [p. 101]	28 legajos	
Legajos Particulares [pp. 103–111]	80 legajos	4 legajos copied (numbers 1–4)
Papeles Diversos [pp. 111–112]	6 legajos	4 legajos copied (numbers 1, 3, 4, 6)
Papeles Diversos sin fecha [p. 112]	1 legajo	
SECRETARÍA DEL PERU		
Cartas de Sevilla, Cadiz, y otros Puertos 1600–1644 [p. 113]	42 legajos	
Cartas de los Virreyes del Peru 1599–1644 [p. 115]	13 legajos	
Cartas Audiencia de Lima 1583–1643 [p. 116]	30 legajos	
Cartas de las Charcas 1593–1642 [p. 118]	15 legajos	
Cartas de Tucuman, Buenos Ayres, y Rio de la Plata 1587–1640 [p. 119]	6 legajos	
Cartas de Chile 1600–1640 [p. 119]	7 legajos	
Cartas de Santa Feé 1590–1654 [p. 120]	22 legajos	
Cartas de Cartagena 1592–1642 [p. 121]	11 legajos	
Cartas de Santa Marta y Rio de la Hacha 1596–1639 [p. 122]	4 legajos	
Cartas de Quito 1594–1642 [p. 122]	8 legajos	
Cartas de Popayan 1597–1639 [p. 123]	2 legajos	
Cartas de Panama 1594–1641 [p. 123]	10 legajos	
Peticiones y Memoriales del Consejo y de la Camara 1600–1640 [p. 124]	72 legajos	
Peticiones y Memoriales sin fecha [p. 127]	11 legajos	
Expedientes, y encomiendas de Govierno sin fecha [p. 128]	37 legajos	
Expedientes de Govierno encomendados á Relatores del Consexo [p. 130]	39 legajos	
Confirmaciones de encomiendas de Yndias 1610–1640 [p. 133]	7 legajos	
Expedientes y encomiendas de Gracia [p. 133]	60 legajos	
Ynformaciones de Oficio y Parte [p. 136]	22 legajos	
Legajos Particulares [pp. 138–149]	79 legajos	1 legajo copied (number 1)
Papeles diversos 1590–1645 [p. 149]	4 legajos	3 legajos copied (numbers 1–3)
Papeles diversos sin fecha [p. 150]	2 legajos	2 legajos copied (numbers 1, 2)

FIGURE 4.20
Chest from Simancas now in the Archive of the Indies.
Second half of the sixteenth century, wood, gilded metal, and parchment, 33 × 65.5 × 41 cm. Seville, Archivo General de Indias, inv. no. 38.

categories of documents copied by Navarrete's four scribes. As can be seen, there is a strong correlation between the two. Not all of the documents listed in the manuscript were copied by Navarrete's scribes, but the section and subsection names, and numbers of legajos, match perfectly. For example, the manuscript lists eight legajos within "Patronato Real"; the "Patronato Real" documents copied by Navarrete's team in the 1790s have numbers ranging from 1 to 8. The manuscript lists eleven legajos of "Papeles tocantes á Descripciones" within "Secretaría de Gouernacion del Consejo de Yndias"; the equivalent "Relaciones y Descripciones" documents copied by Navarrete's team have numbers ranging from 1 to 11. And so on.

Presumably, these four sections of Simancas documents were shipped together to the Archive of the Indies in the fall of 1785. Exactly how they were divided up for travel is unclear: reports on the transport of documents from Simancas to Seville only list the weight of shipping crates, not their contents. The manuscript header for the "Patronato Real" documents specifies that, in Simancas, these eight legajos were "stored in a chest of walnut, with the Royal arms, the reinforcements and closure gilded."[177] The chest is mentioned again in AGI office inventories from September 1798 and March 1809, and it is still part of the AGI collections today (fig. 4.20).[178] The eight legajos of "Patronato Real" documents surely traveled together. The same was probably also true for the other three sections of documents listed in the *Colecciones de Simancas* manuscript: they would have been shipped as a group (even if divided among a series of crates), and on arrival in Seville were unloaded (and shelved?) in the Royal Patronage room. The contents of this corner chamber, as noted in chapter 1, were not indexed until after the restoration of Fernando VII in 1814.

210 CHAPTER 4

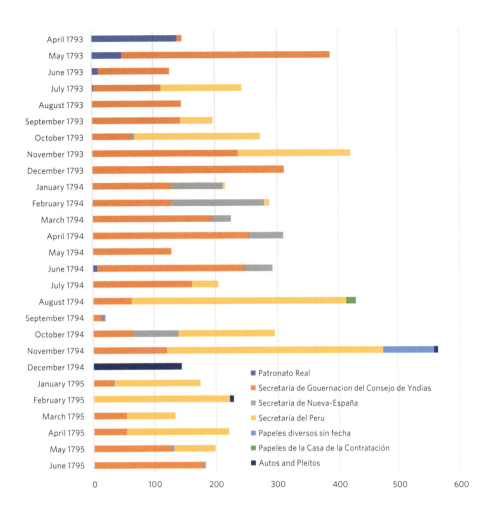

CHART 4.2
Archival processing at the Archive of the Indies, April 1793 to June 1795.
This chart tracks how many folios Martín Fernández de Navarrete's scribes copied month by month and from which document collections those folios originated.

But by then, the documents classified as Royal Patronage were no longer what they had been in the 1780s. Starting in 1804, archival first commissioner Juan Agustín Ceán Bermúdez began to augment the corner room's holdings with additional documents ("most curious and interesting") that he encountered when sorting and indexing files in other sections of the archive.[179] What this means is that the categories used by Navarrete's team in the 1790s (categories inherited from the Archive of Simancas) preserve for us the initial organization of the Royal Patronage collection *before* Ceán Bermúdez's intervention-expansion. They provide an otherwise undocumented snapshot of the AGI's early structure.

By plotting month by month the types of documents copied by Navarrete's team, a rough outline can be constructed of how scribes worked through these four collections of papers from Simancas (chart 4.2). Their work can be divided into five basic periods. The first lasted from late April to June 1793. The team began with "Patronato Real" documents (202 folios copied) and increasingly shifted emphasis to the eleven legajos

DATA RETRIEVAL 211

of "Relaciones y Descripciones" (456 folios). These—the manuscript catalog tells us in its second section—were a subcollection made by Juan Bautista Muñoz during his stay in Simancas from 1781 to 1783.[180] Like the eight legajos of "Patronato Real" documents, this Muñoz collection was also stored in a separate chest in Simancas (in the fall of 1785, at least).[181] If that same chest was used for shipment to Seville, it would have presented Navarrete's team with an already curated selection of interesting materials.[182] These first three months of work also included a short, exploratory copying of three folios each from "Buen Gobierno" and "Cartas Enquadernadas de Seville, Cadiz y Otros Puertos" (both, like "Relaciones y Descripciones," pertaining to the catalog's "Secretaría de Gouernacion del Consejo de Yndias").

The second period spanned July to December 1793. Copying continued in "Relaciones y Descripciones" (monthly work in this subsection would go on until July 1794), and work began in earnest on three additional subsections: "Legajos Particulares" from Peru (starting in July), "Buen Gobierno" (starting in September), and "Legajos Particulares" from New Spain and Peru (starting in November). "Legajos Particulares" from Peru pertained to the fourth section of documents described in the manuscript index ("Secretaría del Peru"); "Buen Gobierno" and the other "Legajos Particulares" documents pertained to the catalog's second section ("Secretaría de Gouernacion del Consejo de Yndias").

The third period of copying spanned January to November 1794. Research continued in "Legajos Particulares" from New Spain and Peru, as well as in "Legajos Particulares" from Peru. New copying began in the "Legajos Particulares" for New Spain (pertaining to the third section of the manuscript catalog, "Secretaría de Nueva-España"), as well as in "Consultas y Cartas del Consejo a Su Majestad," "Papeles de la Antigua Governacion de Nueva España y Peru," and "Cartas de Indias" (all pertaining to the second, "Secretaría de Gouernacion del Consejo de Yndias," section of the catalog). At the end of August, however, scribe 2 (probably Félix Hernández Garriga) was assigned a new, exploratory role: he left the collections stored in Royal Patronage's corner chamber and copied sixteen folios of Accounting documents "brought from the House of Trade." Specifically, he focused on a bundle of royal decrees (1541–56) in case 41, shelf 4, bundle 2/12.[183] Located on the eastern wall of the archive, just turning the northeast corner, this was the second book of decrees in a set of eighty. Spanning the years 1494 to 1782, the series took up most of shelves 4, 5, and 6. Remember that in 1794, this section of the archive was not yet indexed. Although Ceán Bermúdez completed the first two inventories for the Accounting section in 1793 and 1794 (for shelves 12–15 and 16–17), the *Inventario* for cases 18–30 was not completed until 1797, followed in 1801 by the *Inventario* for cases 30–46. Yet even without indexing, this chronologically ordered subsection of royal decrees would have been easy to navigate, which perhaps is why it was the target for exploratory copying. However, in the end this was an aborted exploration. After August, no more documents were copy-corrected from the Accounting section of the archive.[184]

By contrast, the fourth period of copying, from the last days of November through the end of December 1794, marked a radical change in strategy. Navarrete's team left the Royal Patronage room to explore the Justice section of the archive—specifically, documents on the lowest shelves of case 52 (the last case of Justice documents). As compared to the August adventure in Accounting, which only involved scribe 2, this foray involved all five of the active scribes. Scribe 1 (Basterrechea) looked for documents, wrote introduction-summaries, and assigned the work of copying to scribe 2 (Félix Hernández Garriga), scribe 3 (Miguel Sarmiento?), scribe 4 (Cipriano Suárez?), and scribe 5 (Juaquín Finao?). Only 145 folios of copies survive from this period, making December 1794 appear to be one of the commission's least productive months.

In January, Navarrete's team returned to the Royal Patronage room for what would be the final six months of the commission. Most of this period continued previous work in the "Legajos Particulares" from Peru (579 folios copied). January included a brief revisit of "Legajos Particulares" from New Spain and Peru (32 folios). A multi-month return to "Cartas de Indias" began in March (220 folios). Another multimonth return to "Cartas Enquadernadas de Sevilla, Cadiz y Otros Puertos" (a section first explored in May 1793) began in April (188 folios).

To summarize: using the four main sections of the *Colecciones de Simancas* manuscript catalog as a guide, we can see that the team began with "Patronato Real" documents (section 1), then expanded to documents from both "Secretaría de Gouernación del Consejo de Yndias" (section 2) and "Secretaría del Peru" (section 4). Papers from "Secretaría de Nueva-España" (section 3) were a focus of work during the halfway point of the project, from January to October 1794, which also featured, in August, a brief foray by scribe 2 into Accounting. After a month-plus exploration of Justice documents from late November to late December 1794, the team returned to "Secretaría de Gouernación del Consejo de Yndias" (section 2) and "Secretaría del Peru" (section 4). In other words, the project was always working simultaneously on multiple collections of documents at once, most of which were stored in Royal Patronage's corner room.

This multipronged strategy also holds true at the level of individual scribal practice. Only occasionally do the documents of a particular scribe pertain to just one thematic section over the course of several months (at least as reflected by when copied documents were double-checked and dated). From January to March 1794, for example, scribe 2 concentrated on "Papeles sobre el descubrimiento, conquista, y población de California" (in section 3, "Secretaría de Nueva-España"). From April to June 1794, he focused on "Papeles tocantes á las Islas de Maluco y Filipinas" (in section 2, "Secretaría de Gouernación del Consejo de Yndias"). From June to August 1793, scribe 3 and scribe 4 focused on "Relaciones y Descripciones" documents (in section 1, "Patronato Real"). But those periods of extended work on only a single section are unusual. The generally distributed nature of copying makes sense, given what we know about how the copying team worked. Individual scribes did not sit down with a single section of the archive to hunt for documents. Instead, the project leader searched for appropriate materials and then assigned their copying to individual scribes. Since different documents had different lengths, and since different scribes worked at different speeds, a certain irregularity would have been the rule for individual scribal practice.

DATA RETRIEVAL 213

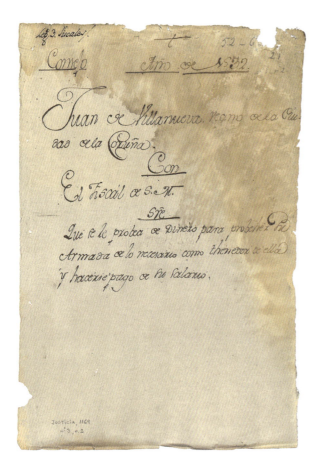
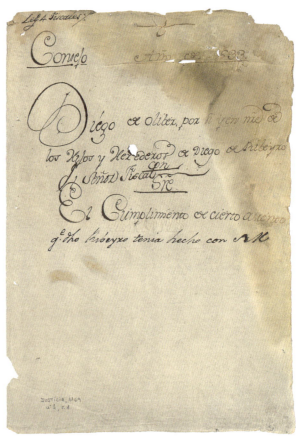

FIGURE 4.21
Cover sheet from "Legajos de Fiscales" 3, now filed in the Justice (Justicia) section of the AGI.
The "Leg. 3 Fiscales" label appears in the upper left corner.
Seville, Archivo General de Indias, Justicia 1169 N3 R2.

FIGURE 4.22
Cover sheet from "Legajos de Fiscales" 4, now filed in the Justice (Justicia) section of the AGI.
The "Leg. 4 Fiscales" label appears in the upper left corner.
Seville, Archivo General de Indias, Justicia 1169 N4 R1.

What can be said about the rates of individual scribal production (see chart 4.1)? Although both Navarrete and Basterrechea praised the work of some scribes (Hernández Garriga, Juaquín Finao) and criticized others (Miguel Sarmiento, Cipriano Suárez), these evaluations are not reflected in the output of each scribe as reflected in the surviving documents. Miguel Sarmiento was the most productive scribe over the twenty-seven-month period (copying an average of eighty-two folios per month), followed by Hernández Garriga (seventy folios per month). But these overall averages are deceptive, because month-by-month productivity varies widely. Sarmiento, for example, averaged ninety-seven monthly folios during 1793 and ninety in 1794, but only forty-three in 1795. In contrast, Hernández Garriga's monthly averages for those three years are fifty-two, seventy-nine, and seventy-nine. Month-by-month production for the team as a whole is also extremely irregular. Work hours were supposedly reduced during the hot summer months of June, July, and August, but this is not reflected by a drop in productivity in the surviving documents.[185] The least productive month was September 1794, with only twenty documents being verified. All of which recalls one

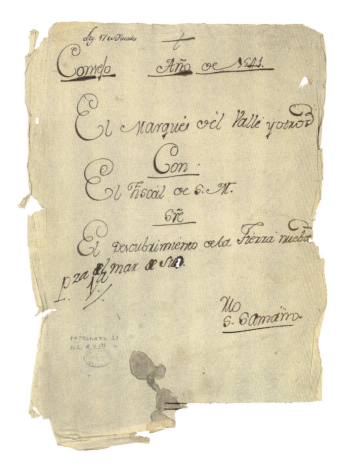

FIGURE 4.23
Cover sheet from "Legajos de Fiscales" 17, now filed in the Royal Patronage (Patronato Real) section of the AGI.
The "Leg. 17 de Fiscales" label appears in the upper left corner.
Seville, Archivo General de Indias, Patronato 21 N2 R4.

of the key limitations of the Navarrete collection: a number of the document copies seem to have been lost, making any fine-grained analyses deceptive.

Perhaps the most important feature of the Navarrete collection is that it provides a vision of how the archive was ordered in the first decade of its existence, when documentary arrangements were still in flux. I have already shown how Navarrete's copies attest to the reorganization of papers brought from Simancas within the shelves of Royal Patronage. In addition, these copies also reveal how some Simancan files, originally shelved in Justice, were later appropriated to enhance the Royal Patronage holdings.

Remember that from late November to late December 1794, Navarrete's team of scribes left the Royal Patronage room and focused instead on lawsuits in the Justice section's case 52. Many of these copied documents are still in Justice: legajo 27 of "Autos del Consejo" is now Justicia 1147 (Navarrete collection item 588); legajo 35 of "Autos del Consejo" is now Justicia 1164 (Navarrete collection item 1823). Legajos 3 and 4 of "Pleitos de Fiscales" are now both in Justicia 1169 (Navarrete collection items 1658, 1659). But other documents copied by Navarrete's team from these

DATA RETRIEVAL 215

sections—documents dealing with famous explorers and conquistadores—were relocated (probably by Ceán Bermúdez) to Royal Patronage. Thus, legajo 17 of "Autos del Consejo," on Nuño de Guzmán in Nueva Galicia, is now in Patronato 21 (Navarrete collection item 2209). Legajo 44 of "Autos del Consejo," a lawsuit involving Gonzalo Pizarro in Peru, is now in Patronato 19 (Navarrete collection item 1150). Although currently distributed between totally different sections of the archive, the cover sheets of these documents (labeled "Leg.° __ de Fiscales") reveal that they once formed part of a single series (figs. 4.21, 4.22, 4.23). As mentioned above, Ceán Bermúdez was involved in relocating documents from other sections of the archive to Royal Patronage from 1804 to 1808. The indexing of the Justice section did not take place until 1809, so those finding aids do not provide us with a guide to what Navarrete's team found on the shelves fifteen years earlier.

Fortunately—as with the previous exploration of subsections within the Royal Patronage holdings themselves—another "heirloom catalog" project enables triangulation of Navarrete's copies, documentary arrangements in the mid-1790s, and documentary arrangements after 1808. AGI Indiferente General 1858F contains two catalogs to Justice documents signed by Manuel de Zuazo y Yañez. As seen in chapter 2, Zuazo y Yañez was archivist in Seville's House of Trade until the fall of 1785, when he was hired to help with that archive's incorporation into the Archive of the Indies. He worked at the AGI for fifteen years, until his death in April 1800. (This was a plague year, but the outbreak of yellow fever in Seville did not begin until late July.)[186] In other words, the Zuazo y Yañez catalogs of Justice documents were created before 1800—and thus before Ceán Bermúdez began to extract documents from that section. The first catalog (*Ymbentario de Autos seguidos con el Fiscal del Consejo*) concerns financial reviews (*pleytos fiscales*); it describes fifty-six legajos of documents spanning the years 1524 to 1557. The second catalog (*Ymbentario y extracto de Autos entre partes*) concerns lawsuits (*autos entre partes*); it describes seventy legajos, currently spanning the years 1538 to 1582. (The catalog's first pages are missing.) Within the entry for each legajo, Zuazo y Yañez provided a short summary of the component court cases. These names and themes allow us to connect the catalogs' entries to Navarrete's copies as well as to the current location of documents within the AGI.

One point of potential confusion is that although Navarrete's team used four descriptive categories to refer to Justice documents ("Autos de fiscales," "Autos del Consejo," "Pleitos del Consejo," "Pleitos de fiscales"), the application of these categories is not divided neatly between Zuazo y Yañez's two catalogs. Documents listed in the *Autos seguidos con el Fiscal* catalog are described by Navarrete's team as "Autos del Consejo," "Pleitos del Consejo," and "Pleitos de fiscales." In turn, "Autos del Consejo" and "Pleitos del Consejo" are *also* used to describe documents that appear in the *Autos entre partes* catalog. (Only one document is described as coming from "Autos de fiscales," and probably connects to Zuazo y Yañez's second catalog.) However, despite these overlapping categories, what is consistent between the two catalogs and

Navarrete's copies are the legajo numbers (as well as the people named in each legajo), which match perfectly. The team copied from legajos numbered 4, 17, and 18 in the *Autos seguidos con el Fiscal* catalog, and from legajos numbered 27, 35, 44, 45 in the *Autos entre partes* catalog (and probably from legajos 2 and 5 as well). Although many of these papers are still in case 52 of the Justice section (Navarrete collection items 588, 1658, 1659, 1821, 1823, 1827), those relating to famous explorers (Christopher Columbus, Tristán de Luna, Gonzalo Pizarro, Nuño de Guzmán) have since been transferred to Royal Patronage. For example, at least two documents on Nuño de Guzmán (from 1533 and 1540), listed under legajo 17 of Zuazo y Yañez's *Autos seguidos con el Fiscal* catalog and identified as "legajo núm.[ero] 17" copies by Navarrete's scribes in 1794, are now in Patronato 21 (once case 1, shelf 1, bundle 2/21; Navarrete collection items 2206 and 2229). But their cover sheet retains its "Leg. 17 de Fiscales" label (see fig. 4.23).

In her recent discussion of Navarrete's project, María M. Portuondo argues that "tracing what Fernández de Navarrete found and where he found it may help reconstruct the inventories of his source archives, which in some instances—as I can attest—no longer hold the documents Fernández de Navarrete copied, these having been lost, stolen, or misplaced over the two hundred years that separate his project from ours."[187] The copied documents of Navarrete's project also reveal less dramatic changes: not the disappearance of documents, but their relocation within the same archival space.

NOTES

1 Giuseppe Petrosellini, *Il barbiere di Siviglia: Dramma Giocoso per Musica in quattro Atti* (Prague: Giuseppe Emanuele Diesbach, 1784), 60. See also https://www.youtube.com/watch?v=m3GgmX7cVzE (at 1:04:14): Freiburger Barockorchester, conductor René Jacobs, Vienna, Theater an der Wien, 2015. On Paisiello, see Robin L. Thomas, *Architecture and Statecraft: Charles of Bourbon's Naples 1734–1759* (University Park: Pennsylvania State University Press, 2013), 16.

2 José Luis Rodríguez de Diego and Julia T. Rodríguez de Diego, "Un archivo no sólo para el rey: Significado social del proyecto simanquino en el siglo XVI," in *Felipe II (1527–1598): Europa y la monarquía católica,* ed. José Martínez Millán, vol. 4, *Literatura, cultura, y arte,* ed. Virgilio Pinto Crespo (Madrid: Parteluz, 1998), 463–75; José Luis Rodríguez de Diego, "La apertura de Simancas a la investigación histórica en el año 1844," in *Archivi e storia nell'Europa del XIX secolo: Alle radici dell'identità culturale europea,* ed. Irene Cotta and Rosalia Manno Tolu, vol. 2 (Rome: Direzione generale per gli archivi, 2006), 601–26; Pedro Carasa Soto and Julia Teresa Rodríguez de Diego, "Una base de datos sobre historiografía española e hispanista: La investigación en el Archivo General de Simancas entre 1844 y 1990," in *Congreso internacional sobre sistemas de información histórica* (Álava, Spain: Juntas Generales de Álava, 1997), 415–27; and José Luis Rodríguez de Diego, "Archivos del poder, archivos de la administración, archivos de la historia (s. XVI–XVII)," in *Historia de los archivos y de la archivistica en España* (Valladolid: Secretariado de Publicaciones e Intercambio Científico, Universidad de Valladolid, 1998), 29–42.

3 On 20 April 1844, a royal decree by Queen Isabel II opened most Spanish state archives for historical research. See Antonio de Casas y Moral, *Recopilación legislativa de España desde 1810 a 1859,* vol. 3 (Granada: Imprenta de D. Manuel Garrido, 1859), 105–6. Nevertheless, the *Ordenanzas* continued to be in force and were affirmed as guidelines in 1862. New archival norms were established in 1894 under the Ministry of Development (Ministerio de Fomento) and in 1901 under the Ministry of Public Education (Ministerio de Instrucción Pública); see Palmira Vélez, *La historiografía americanista en España, 1755–1936* (Madrid: Iberoamericana, 2007), 98–100, 102.

4 These regulations on document access and circulation were based on the precedents established in 1588 for the Archive of Simancas: José Luis Rodríguez de Diego, *Instrucción para el gobierno del Archivo de Simancas (Año 1588)* (Madrid: Ministerio de Cultura, 1988), 110–11 and 113–14 (see items 16–21 and 27–30). On royal patrimony, *arcana imperii,* and archival control, see Rodríguez de Diego, "Archivos," 31–34; Richard L. Kagan, "Arcana imperii: Mapas, ciencia y poder en la corte de Felipe IV," in *El atlas del rey planeta: La "Descripción de España y de las cosas y puertos de sus reinos" de Pedro Texeira (1634),* ed. Felipe Pereda and Fernando Marías (Hondarribia, Spain: Editorial Nerea, 2002), 49–70; Richard L. Kagan, *Clio and the Crown: The Politics of History in Medieval and Early Modern Spain* (Baltimore: Johns Hopkins University Press, 2010), 163, 297; Richard L. Kagan, "The Secrets of Simancas," in *Hacer historia desde Simancas: Homenaje a José Luis Rodríguez de Diego,* ed. Alberto Marcos Martín (Valladolid: Junta de Castilla y León, 2011), 439; and Markus Friedrich, *The Birth of the Archive: A History of Knowledge,* trans. John Noël Dillon (Ann Arbor: University of Michigan Press, 2019), 72, 173, 176–80.

5 *Ordenanzas para el Archivo General de Indias* (Madrid: Imprenta de la Viuda de Ibarra, 1790), 42–43.

6 *Ordenanzas,* 43.

7 *Ordenanzas,* 43–44.

8 *Ordenanzas,* 44.

9 *Ordenanzas,* 44–45.

10 *Ordenanzas,* 45–46.

11 *Ordenanzas,* 46.

12 *Ordenanzas,* 46–47.

13 "Que con motivo de haverse solicitado en el Consejo de Yndias por el Duque de Alva se le diese satisfac[io]n de los caidos de la gracia de 8d. ducados anuales que en el año de 1614 se le señalaron en pueblos de Yndios vacos del Perú, el fiscal de d[ic]ho consejo expidio á este Archivo en años anteriores á el de 1800 various ordenes, encargando se buscase el Exped[ien]te que dio motivo á la

concesion de d[ic]hos 8d. ducados" (AGI IG 1856, Diego Juárez, Seville, 12 December 1807).

14 "Despues de muchas tareas, se pudieron hallar algunos docum[en]tos favorables á la Casa de Alva, los que se remitieron á dicho fiscal" (AGI IG 1856, Diego Juárez, Seville, 12 December 1807).

15 Although Juárez does not cite the Royal Patronage shelf marks in his text (in contrast to the documents from cases 25 and 46), his sources can be tracked down thanks to the summarized details he provides. The document described as "El Maestre del barco á quien acaecio el robo de los 360d. pesos, por su declaracion tomada en Panamá, por el oidor de aquella Aud[ienci]a el d[octo]r Alonso criado de cartilla" is currently Patronato 266 R10.

16 "Con semejantes conocim[ien]tos, ha ausiliado en este Archivo á un Comisionado que se presentó de orden del Rey, en busca de docum[en]tos s[ob]re limites en la provincia de Tejas" (AGI IG 1857B, Diego Juárez, Seville, 21 September 1814).

17 "El dia 29 de este mes comenzó á evacuar en este archivo la comision de Limites de la Luisiana y de la provincia de Texas el sargento mayor de ingenieros D. Josef de Gabriel con un capitan del mismo cuerpo" (AGI IG 1856, Juan Agustín Ceán-Bermúdez, "Acompaño à V[uestra] E[xcelencia] el plan de lo que se ha trabajado este mes en el archivo general de Yndias . . . Sevilla 31 de octubre de 1805"). Ceán Bermúdez's work reports for the next few months specify that the *Oficial 3º* (that is, Diego Juárez) was helping the engineers with their research.

18 Monthly progress reports, outlining what sections of documents each of the archivists had been working on, were filed by Ceán Bermúdez from (at least) 3 February 1802 through 31 March 1808 (scattered in several clusters throughout AGI IG 1856); see also Magdalena Canellas Anoz, "Juan Agustín Ceán-Bermúdez en el Archivo General de Indias," in *Juan Agustín Ceán-Bermúdez, asturiano en Sevilla: 250 aniversario de su nacimiento (1749–1829)* (Seville: Publicaciones del Centro Asturiano en Sevilla, 1999), 56–57.

19 Copy now in AHN Estado MPD 854; original AGI MP México 10 (from AGI México 633, fols. 816–52).

218 CHAPTER 4

20 "There were three great fortresses which guarded the border into Spain: Almeida, Badajoz and Ciudad Rodriguez. In the early months of 1811 all three were held by the French. While Wellington advanced upon the Almeida he despatched General Beresford with the Portuguese Army to besiege the fortress of Badajoz further south" (Susanna Clarke, *Jonathan Strange & Mr. Norrell* [New York: Bloomsbury, 2004], 306n3). On the visit of "Josef Gabriel" to the AGI, see the 26 October 1805 letter of head archivist Andres María de Bustos y Martínez to don Antonio Cavallero (AGI IG 1856; pink ribbon–bound folder of documents titled "Sevilla Año de 1806..."). On the border debate between Spain and the United States, see Philip Coolidge Brooks, *Diplomacy and the Borderlands: The Adams-Onís Treaty of 1819* (Berkeley: University of California Press, 1939). On Gabriel, see Nicolás Díaz y Pérez, "De-Gabriel y Estenoz (D. José)," in *Diccionario histórico, biográfico, crítico, y bibliográfico de autores, artistas, y extremeños ilustres*, vol. 1 (Madrid: Pérez y Boix, 1884), 193–95; and Álvaro Meléndez, "Brigadier José de Gabriel Estenoz," *Extremadura militar: Recuperación de la memoria militar extremeña y española*, 15 February 2011, http://alvaromelendez .blogspot.com/2011/02/brigadier-jose-de-gabriel -estenoz.html.

21 For copies of the original arguments (and the continued relevance of these issues two decades later), see Pedro González de Vallejo, *Discurso canónico-legal sobre los nombramientos de gobernadores hechos por los cabildos en los presentados por S. M. para obispos de sus iglesias* (Madrid: José María Repullés, 1839), 1–74. On the history of the Spanish Crown's ecclesiastical authority, see Byron Ellsworth Hamann, *Bad Christians, New Spains: Muslims, Catholics, and Native Americans in a Mediterratlantic World* (New York: Routledge, 2020), 95–98.

22 Correspondence on this search for documents is gathered in an (unlabeled) folder in AGI IG 1857B. For López Pelegrín, see *Guía política y militar* (Madrid: 1822), 38.

23 "En cumplimiento de la R[ea]l orden que V[uestra] E[xcelencia] se sirve comunicarme con f[ec]ha 20 del Nov[iembr]e proximo pasado, remito la adjunta nota con los documentos que manifiesta, en donde no tan solo acompaña el espediente, señalado con el numero 7° de que dimanò la R[ea]l cedula de 2. de Agosto de 1736, si tambien otros de f[ec]has anteriores y posteriores, que se han buscado y que me parece tienen referencia con el asunto de que trata el mismo espediente; esperando que V[uestra] E[xcelencia] disponga se me devuelva todo, luego que se haya evacuado el punto para que se mi piden, á fin de colocarlos en sus respectivos legajos, conforme à lo prevendio en el capitulo 56 de las R[eale]s ordenanzas que rigen en esta oficina" (AGI IG 1875B, Ventura Collar to Ramón López Pelegrín, Seville, 1 December 1821).

24 Cluster of documents in AGI IG 1858J. For González Salmón, see *Calendario manual y guía de forasteros en Madrid* (Madrid: Imprenta Real, 1830), 76; and Germán Bleiberg, "Sobre un viaje frustrado de Humboldt a España," *Estudios geográficos* 76 (1959): 373–89.

25 Friedrich Naumann, "Alexander von Humboldt in Russia: The 1829 Expedition," in *Four Centuries of Geological Travel: The Search for Knowledge on Foot, Bicycle, Sledge and Camel,* ed. P. N. Wyse Jackson (London: Geological Society, 2007), 161–75.

26 On 4 April, González Salmón also wrote back to Páez, indicating his intent to collect documentary information (Bleiberg, "Sobre un viaje frustrado," 377). For other examples of long-distance archival-copy requests, see Friedrich, *Birth of the Archive,* 190–91.

27 AGI IG 1858J.

28 Bleiberg, "Sobre un viaje frustrado," 379; see also Sandra Rebok, *Una doble mirada: Alexander von Humboldt y España en el siglo XIX* (Madrid: CSIC, 2009), 261–65.

29 Christian Suckow, "Humboldts spanische Option 1830—Eine Nachlese," *HiN Internationale Zeitschrift für Humboldt-Studien* 16 (2008): 37–40.

30 AGI IG 1856, folder labeled "A instancia de d[o]n J[ose]ph Antonio Perez..."

31 Currently AGI Contratación 5694.

32 "El documento que se expresa en este memorial existe en este Archivo G[ene]ral de mi cargo del que daré testimonio impetrando órden de S[u] M[ajestad] para ello por el Ministerio de Gracia y Justicia de Yndias: Sevilla" (AGI IG 1856, Andrés María Bustos y Martínez, Seville, 29 May 1802).

33 Royal permission was needed because the contents of state archives were considered royal property; see Rodríguez de Diego, "Archivos," 31–34; Kagan, "Arcana imperii," 63–68; Kagan, *Clio and the Crown,* 163, 297; Kagan, "Secrets of Simancas," 439; and Friedrich, *Birth of the Archive,* 72, 173, 176–80.

34 Other early nineteenth-century petitions in AGI IG 1856 also include two versions of the petition letter: one written by the petitioner on official sealed paper, and another, rewritten version (in a notably looping hand) with a second date a few days later (which I take to be the date of recopying), followed by a scrawled note of approval, followed by the date on which the approval was granted.

35 The same scribe quoted *Ordenanza* item 58 in his copy, sixteen years later, of a court case–related document request by the Marquis of Piedrasblancas: AGI IG 1857B, "Madrid 29 de Enero. El Marq[ué]s de Piedrasblancas, consejero de Ordenes."

36 AGI IG 1856, folder "A instancia de d[o]n Miguel Estevan del Val..."

37 María de los Ángeles Pérez Samper, *Barcelona, Corte: La visita de Carlos IV en 1802* (Barcelona: Edicions Universitat Barcelona, 1973).

38 On the indexing project, see AGI IG 1853, Antonio de Lara y Zúñiga to José de Gálvez, 1 February 1786, which includes a sample of his indexing of the "Pasajeros a Indias" documents from 1590. A year and a half later, the indexing of this section of the archive was being pursued in earnest, and 1,000 extracts had been written; AGI IG 1854A, Antonio de Lara y Zúñiga to Antonio Porlier, 18 October 1787. Partial indices of the "Pasajeros a Indias" documents survive for 1534–63 (AGI IG 1858C), 1590 (AGI IG 1853), 1640–57 (AGI IG 1858C), and 1661–91 (AGI IG 1858C). See also Manuel Romero Tallafigo, "La fundación del Archivo General de Indias: Fasto en la historia archivística europea," *Archivo Hispalense* 207–8 (1985): 14.

39 Currently AGI Contratación 5511B.

40 On Manuel Antonio Moreno, see Miruna Achim, "Making Lizards into Drugs: The Debates on the Medical Uses of Reptiles in Late Eighteenth-Century Mexico," *Journal of Spanish Cultural Studies* 8, no. 2 (2007): 169–91.

41 "Christianos viejos, limpios de toda mala raza de Moros, Judios, hereges, ni de los nuevamente convertido a nuestra santa fee Catholica, ni castigados ni penetenciados en tiempo alguno por el Tribunal del Santo oficio, ni han obtenido oficios viles, ni Mecanicos, ni descienden de las familias, a quienes por Leyes de estos Reynos está provehido el pase a los de Yndias" (AGI Contratación 5511B N2 R67).

42 AGI IG 1856, folder "Sevilla Año de 1808."

DATA RETRIEVAL 219

43 Currently AGI Contratación 2589.

44 AGI IG 1858J, folder "Accediendo el Rey N.[uestro] S.[eñor] à la instancia de d[o]n Jose Gonzalez Moro…"

45 Currently AGI Contratación 2102A–2105B.

46 AGI IG 1857B, folder "Madrid 21. de Enero de 1817…"

47 "Luego que se presente el citado Brigadier à designar los documentos que necesita" (AGI IG 1857B, Ventura Collar to Juan Estevan Lozano Torres, Seville, 5 February 1817).

48 "Accediendo el Rey á la solicitud de D[o]n Diego Colon, oficial de la Secretaria del Despacho de Estado, se ha servuido concederle licencia para sacar conforme á reglam[en]to copias sertificadas de algunos documentos existentes en el archivo general de Indias, en especial de entre los de la coleccion que ha estractado, analizado inventariado D[o]n Diego Juarez, oficial del referido archivo, respecto á que tanto él como su padre el S[eño]r D[o]n José Colon dicen necesitan estos docum[en]tos para la mejor conseruacion de los derechos de su casa" (AGI IG 1857B, Gobernación de Ultramar to Archivero General de Indias, Madrid, 17 May 1820).

49 "Conforme à lo que V[uestra] E[xcelencia] se sirve mandarme con su oficio de 17 del actual, de or[de]n de S[u] M[ajestad] estoy pronto en facilitar al S[eño]r d[o]n Diego Colon, oficial de la secretaria del despacho de Estado, las copias certificadas de los documentos existentes en esta oficial, de la coleccion analizada è inventariada por d[o]n Diego Juarez" (AGI IG 1857B, Ventura Collar to Antonio Porcel, Seville, 21 May 1820). The documents are currently AGI Patronato 8–14.

50 "reconocer los papeles de el Archivo, y extractar los documentos y noticias concernientes al ramo, que pueden ser utiles a la historia de la Artilleria" (AGI IG 1856, folder "22 de Oct[ub]re de 1807 Al Archivero del G[ene]ral de Ynd[ia]s en Sevilla").

51 AGI IG 1856, folder "22 de Oct[ub]re de 1807 Al Archivero del G[ene]ral de Ynd[ia]s en Sevilla."

52 Bérriz survived the war and was alive as late as 1832 (AGM, Hoja de Servicios Vicente Bérriz, 1a/b–2130). Thanks to archive director Diego Quiros Montero for helping me locate this personnel file.

53 "Ex[celentísi]mo Señor Hallandome residiendo en Sevilla de orden de S[u] M[ajestad] con la comision de la Compañia de Navegacion del Guadalq[uivi]r y necesitando adquirir varias noticias interesantes no solo acerca del antiguo estado del rio y contratacion de aquella ciudad en la epoca primera del descubrimiento de America y apresto de las mas celebres expediciones, sino tambien algunas otras relativas à diversas producciones minerales de ultramar historia y adelantamientos de su beneficio, influencia y alteracion que ha producido en las relaciones comerciales de Europa y Asia &c &c para cierta obra en que estoi trabajando, he de merecer à V[uestra] E[xcelencia] se sirva alcanzarme licencia de S[u] M[ajestad] para poder examinar y compulsar, bajo las precauciones de estilo, los papeles tocante à estas materias que existen en el Archibo general de Yndias de Sevilla, en que recibire especial favor. Dios gu[ard]e à V[uestra] E[xcelencia] m[ucho]s a[ño]s" (AGI IG 1857A, Gregorio González Azaola to Miguel de Lardizábal, Madrid, 1 June 1815).

54 Rosario Cebrián Fernández, *Comisión de Antigüedades de la Real Academia de la Historia: Antigüedades e inscripciones, 1748–1845; Catálogo e índices* (Madrid: Real Academia de la Historia, 2002), 136–40; and AHN Estado 2921 exp. 6.

55 Gregorio González Azaola, "Satiras de Goya," *Seminario Patrótico* 51 (27 March 1811): 25.

56 Alexander Pope, *Ensayo sobre el hombre,* trans. Gregorio González Azaola (Madrid: Imprenta Nacional, 1821).

57 Antoine-François Fourcroy, *Sistema de los conocimientos químicos y de sus aplicaciones á los fenómenos de la Naturaleza y del Arte,* trans. Pedro María de Olive and Gregorio González Azaola (Madrid: Imprenta Real, 1803–9).

58 Joseph Louis Proust, *Ensayo sobre el azúcar de uva,* trans. Gregorio González Azaola (Madrid: Imprenta Real, 1806).

59 Thomas Tredgold, *Caminos de hierro: Tratado practico,* trans. Gregorio González Azaola (Madrid: Oficina de D. Federico Moreno, 1831).

60 Alexandro Briarly and Gregorio González Azaola, *Navegación del Guadalquivir: Prospecto del plan y Compañía de Navegación del Guadalquivir* (Seville: Imprenta de D. Manuel de Aragón y Compañía, 1815).

61 Gregorio González Azaola, *Hornaguera y hierro* (Paris: La imprenta de David, 1829).

62 Gregorio González Azaola, "Memoria premiada sobre el gusto llamado vulgarmente de Madera que suelen contraer los vinos en las botas, y medios de corregirlo," in *Juntas públicas de la Real Sociedad Económica de Valencia celebradas el día 8 de diciembre de los años 1827, 1828, y 1829* (Valencia: Oficina de D. Benito Monfort, 1832), 20–45.

63 Alexandro Briarly, *Observaciones sobre la posibilidad y necesidad de mejorar la navegación del Río Guadalquivir* (Seville: Hidalgo, 1814); Briarly and González Azaola, *Navegación del Guadalquivir;* Ignacio García Pereda, "Los trabajos agronómicos de la Compañía del Guadalquivir en la primera mitad del siglo XIX," *Quaderns d'història de l'enginyera* 14 (2014): 155–79; Leandro Moral Ituarte, "Un intento frustrado de acondicionamiento del Guadalquivir: La actuación de la Real Compañía de Navegación en la primera mitad del siglo XIX; Nuevas aportaciones y replanteamiento geo-histórico de un tema polémico," *Mélanges de la Casa de Velázquez* 25 (1989): 327–53; Amalia Zapata Tinajero, "El río en el siglo XVIII y la Compañía de Navegación del Guadalquivir," in *El río, el bajo Guadalquivir* (Seville: Equipo 28, 1985), 64–67; and Teresa Sánchez Lázaro, "Cuatro proyectos de canales de navegación," in *El río Guadalquivir,* ed. Javier Rubiales Torrejón (Seville: Consejería de Obras Públicas y Transportes, 2008), 289–96.

64 Briarly and González Azaola, *Navegación del Guadalquivir,* 3.

65 Eduardo Camacho Rueda, "La ría y puerto de Sevilla (siglos XVIII y XX)," in *El río Guadalquivir,* ed. Javier Rubiales Torrejón (Seville: Consejería de Obras Públicas y Transportes, 2008), 244; Ezequiel Gómez Murga, "La captación del artesano inglés Nathan Wetherell," in *II Jornadas Andaluzas de Patrimonio Industrial y de la Obra Pública* (Cádiz: Fundación Patrimonio Industrial de Andalucía, 2012), 10; and García Pereda, "Los trabajos agronómicos," 162–64.

66 Gómez Murga, "La captación," 10; and Eduardo Camacho Rueda, "Barcos en la ría y puerto de Sevilla (siglos XIX y XX)," in *El río Guadalquivir,* ed. Javier Rubiales Torrejón (Seville: Consejería de Obras Públicas y Transportes, 2008), 266.

67 Gómez Murga, "La captación," 10–11.

68 "D[o]n Juan Wetherell de nacion Inglesa, y vecino de la Ciudad de Sevilla, ante V[uestra] E[xcelencia] parece y dice que teniendo noticia que en el Archivo General de Indias de esta Ciudad existen varios Manuscritos de D.[on] Miguel Cervantes Saavedra, y deseando el que expone enterarse de su contenido, y si preciso fuere sacar Copia de ellos para su ilustracion—Supp[li]ca a V[uestra] E[xcelencia] si biene a bien se sirva dar su Orden al Encargado del expresado Archivo a fin de que le facilite los Manuscritos citados. Lo que espera

220 CHAPTER 4

merecer de la bondad de V[uestra] E[xcelencia] cuya vida g[uar]de D[io]s m[ucho]s a[ño]s" (AGI IG 1857A, John Wetherell to Ministro Universal de Indias, Seville, 17 June 1815).

69 Gómez Murga, "La captación," 10–11; and García Pereda, "Los trabajos agronómicos," 158–59.

70 Ezequiel Gómez Murga, Jesús Barbero Rodríguez, and Charlotte Luisa Dinger, "Nathan Wetherell (1747–1831), un inglés por tierras de Dos Hermanas," *Dos Hermanas: Feria y Fiestas* 63 (2006): 78n11; and Gómez Murga, "La captación," 10.

71 Juan Wetherell, *Catálogo de una colección de antigüedades mejicanas con varios ídolos, adornos, y otros artefactos de los indios, que existe en poder de Juan Wetherell* (Seville: 1842); Felix González de León, *Noticia artística, histórica y curiosa de todos los edificios públicos, sagrados, y profanos, de esta muy noble, muy leal, muy heróica e invicta ciudad de Sevilla,* vol. 1 (Seville: José Hidalgo y Compañía, 1844), 167–69; and Richard Ford, *A Hand-Book for Travellers in Spain, and Readers at Home,* vol. 1 (London: John Murray, 1844), 247.

72 Washington Irving, *Journals and Notebooks,* vol. 4, *1826–1829,* ed. Wayne R. Kime and Andrew B. Myers (Boston: Twayne, 1984), 238.

73 Gómez Murga, "La captación," 9; and Doctor Thebussem, "Cuarta epístola droapiana (1865)," in *Segunda Ración de Artículos* (Madrid: [Sucesores de Rivadeneyra], 1894), 81–82.

74 On 4 June, secretary of the Royal Academy of History Joaquín Juan de Flores wrote a thank-you note to Ceán Bermúdez for documentary copies sent up to Madrid; see BNE MS 21456–5; Carlos Seco Serrano, "Vida y obra de Martín Fernández de Navarrete," in *Obras de D. Martin Fernández de Navarrete* (Madrid: Ediciones Atlas, 1954), xxxvii; and Martín Fernández de Navarrete, *Vida de Miguel de Cervantes Saavedra* (Madrid: La Real Academia Española, 1819), 231.

75 AGI IG 1857A, folder "Lista de los treinta y un caxones de papeles traidos a esta plaza de Cadiz del Archivo General de Yndias establecido en Sevilla." This documentary evacuation was prudent: in Napoleonic Rome, for example, some 3,239 chests of papers from the Vatican Archives were sent to Paris; many documents were thus lost or destroyed. Leonard E. Boyle, *A Survey of the Vatican Archives and of Its Medieval Holdings,* rev. ed. (Toronto: Pontifical Institute of Mediaeval Studies, 2001), 11.

76 Gómez Murga, "La captación," 5. For 1810, I have only been able to find a list of employee payments in the month of January; I could find

nothing for 1811. In 1812, investigations were conducted about the removal of the chests and the behavior of archival employees during the invasion (AGI IG 1857A, folder "Años de 1812 y 1813 Exped[ien]te relativo à la Suspension, y separacion del Archivero, oficiales, y depend[ien]tes del Archivo G[ene]ral de Yndias en Sevilla"). Regular employee payments began again in 1813 (AGI IG 1857A).

77 AGI IG 1857A, "Cuenta de los sueldos y gastos del real archivo general de Yndias en Sevilla perteneciente al año de 1814," receipt no. 28 (20 June 1814).

78 Navarrete, *Vida de Miguel de Cervantes Saavedra,* 311–49.

79 AGI IG 1858J.

80 Washington Irving, *Journals and Notebooks,* vol. 3, *1819–1827,* ed. Walter A. Reichart (Madison: University of Wisconsin Press, 1970), 542.

81 Irving, *Journals,* 3:563; and Washington Irving, *Letters,* vol. 2, *1823–1838,* ed. Ralph M. Aderman, Herbert L. Kleinfeld, and Jenifer S. Banks (Boston: Twayne, 1979), 186. On Goya and Moratín, see Edith F. Helman, "The Younger Moratín and Goya: On Duendes and Brujas," *Hispanic Review* 27, no. 1 (1959): 103–22; Jeannine Baticle, "La pintura de Goya en París y Burdeos, 1824–1828," in *Goya y Moratin: En Burdeos, 1824–1828,* exh. cat. (Bilbao: Museo de Bellas Artes de Bilbao, 1998), 37–54; and María Teresa Rodríguez Torres, "Francisco de Goya: Retratos de amigos; Zapater y Moratín," *Buletina = Boletín = Bulletin del Museo de Bellas Artes de Bilbao,* no. 2 (2006): 145–79. On Goya in Bordeaux, see Jonathan Brown and Susan Grace Galassi, *Goya's Last Works* (New Haven, CT: Yale University Press, 2006); as well as Carlos Saura's 1999 film *Goya en Burdeos.*

82 John Harmon McElroy, "Introduction," in Washington Irving, *The Life and Voyages of Christopher Columbus,* ed. John Harmon McElroy (Boston: Twayne, 1981), xviii–xxi. The following discussion of Irving's writing process draws heavily from McElroy.

83 On Irving's honorary LL.D. from Oxford, see Pierre M. Irving, *Life and Letters of Washington Irving,* vol. 2 (New York: G. P. Putnam, 1862), 430–32. On Irving and Romanticism, see Richard L. Kagan, *The Spanish Craze: America's Fascination with the Hispanic World, 1779–1939* (Lincoln: University of Nebraska Press, 2019), 137–40.

84 Washington Irving, *A History of the Life and Voyages of Christopher Columbus,* 4 vols. (London: John Murray, 1828), 1:iii.

85 Irving, *Letters,* 2:165–66.

86 Irving, *Journals,* 3:435; Washington Irving, *Letters,* vol. 1, *1802–1823,* ed. Ralph M. Aderman, Herbert L. Kleinfeld, and Jenifer S. Banks (Boston: Twayne, 1978), 232 (*Granada*), 365 (*Don Quixote*); and Stanley T. Williams, *The Spanish Background of American Literature,* vol. 2 (New Haven, CT: Yale University Press, 1955), 9–10. Irving probably read Thomas Rodd's 1803 *The Civil Wars of Granada,* which was a translation of Ginéz Pérez de Hita's two-part *Historia de los vandos de los zegries y abencerrages cavalleros moros de Granada, de las civiles guerras que huvo en ella, y batallas particulares que huvo en la vega entre moros y christianos, hasta que el rey don Fernando quinto la ganô,* first published in Zaragoza in 1595.

87 Irving, *Journals,* 3:563; and Irving, *Journals,* 4:5.

88 Irving, *Journals,* 4:9; and Kagan, *Spanish Craze,* 55.

89 In 1830, Rich was granted permission, extraordinarily, to visit the Archive of Simancas in search of books about the Americas published since 1700. The first volume of his *Bibliotheca Americana Nova* catalog was published in 1835 (see Kagan, "Secrets of Simancas," 439).

90 When Irving changed lodgings on 16 November 1826, he mentioned that he was moving from a "house in Calle S[a]n Fernando." Thanks to Meredith Mann of the Brooke Russell Astor Reading Room for Rare Books and Manuscripts, NYPL, for helping me double-check this reference in "Washington Irving Journal 21," Washington Irving papers, Manuscripts and Archives Division, NYPL. Although the printed Madrid maps of 1785 and 1835 do not feature a Calle de San Fernando, an 1831 Madrid guidebook reveals this was the new (monarchical) name for the street once called Libertad; Ramón de Mesonero Romanos, *Manual de Madrid: Descripción de la corte y de la villa* (Madrid: D. M. de Burgos, 1831), 166. An 1828 industrial exhibition guidebook confirms the use of the newer name as well as its location (via a cross street): "DOLLFUS (D. Enrique), calle de San Fernando, número 9, esquina á la de S. Marcos." Luis López Ballesteros, *Memoria de la Junta de Calificacion de los productos de la industria española remitidos á la Esposicion pública de 1827* (Madrid: D. L. Amarita, 1828), 111.

91 Irving, *Letters,* 2:178.

92 Irving, *Journals,* 4:13.

93 On the bakery's origins and fascinating history to 1830, see Jesús Escobar, *The Plaza Mayor and*

DATA RETRIEVAL 221

the *Shaping of Baroque Madrid* (Cambridge: Cambridge University Press, 2004), 9–11, 115–42, 241–58; see also Kelly Donahue-Wallace, *Jerónimo Antonio Gil and the Idea of the Spanish Enlightenment* (Albuquerque: University of New Mexico Press, 2017), 37, 49, 54.

94 An announcement had been published in the *Gaceta de Madrid* on 16 February, one day after Irving arrived: Eric Beerman, "Washington Irving en Madrid (1826–28): Cristóbal Colón," *Revista Complutense de Historia de América* 18 (1992): 199.

95 McElroy, "Introduction," xxxv–xxxvii.

96 Irving, *Letters,* 2:187; and Irving, *Journals,* 4:21.

97 Irving, *Journals,* 4:20–24.

98 Irving, *Journals,* 4:28; this was the library of the Reales Estudios de San Isidro. For its history and connection to an earlier Academia de Matemáticas, see Elena Ausejo, *Las matemáticas en el siglo XVII* (Madrid: Ediciones Akal, 1992), 40–43; and Amparo García Cuadrado, "Aproximación a la organización bibliotecaria española en el siglo XVIII," *Investigación bibliotecológica* 23 (1997): 114–15.

99 Irving, *Journals,* 4:33.

100 Irving, *Journals,* 4:37–38.

101 Irving, *Journals,* 4:39.

102 Irving, *Journals,* 4:44, 57.

103 Irving, *Journals,* 4:58; and Beerman, "Washington Irving en Madrid," 197, 200.

104 Irving, *Letters,* 2:214–15.

105 Washington Irving, *Washington Irving and the Storrows: Letters from England and the Continent, 1821–1828,* ed. Stanley Thomas Williams (Cambridge, MA: Harvard University Press, 1933), 102–3. Irving would later reprise—and autocritique—his convent fantasy of a tragically cloistered nun in *The Alhambra: A Series of Tales and Sketches of the Moors and Spaniards,* vol. 1 (Philadelphia: Carey and Lea, 1832), 112–17. This later nun-narrative even references Count Almaviva wooing Rosina in *The Barber of Seville.*

106 Irving, *Journals,* 4:63–65.

107 Nicolás Bas Martín, *El cosmógrafo e historiador Juan Bautista Muñoz (1745–1799)* (Valencia: Universitat de València, 2002), 190. Obadiah Rich chronicles the travels of this copy collection from Muñoz to Uguina and eventually to himself in *Catalogue of a Collection of Manuscripts Principally in Spanish Relating to America* (London: William Bowden, 1848). The collection was subsequently acquired by the NYPL: Edwin Blake Brownrigg, *Colonial Latin American Manuscripts and Transcripts in the Obadiah Rich Collection: An Inventory and Index* (New York: New York Public Library, 1978), vii–xviii. Note that when Muñoz died in July 1799, he willed his papers to King Carlos IV. They entered the Royal Library that August and were transferred to Madrid's Royal Academy of History in 1817: Real Academia de la Historia, *Catálogo de la colección de don Juan Bautista Muñoz,* vol. 1 (Madrid: Real Academia de la Historia, 1954), xlix–lii. On Uguina's Madrid address, see, in 1815, Joaquín Lorenzo Villanueva, *Apuntes sobre el arresto de los vocales de Cortes, Egecutado en Mayo de 1814* (Madrid: Diego García y Campoy y Compañía, 1820), 282 ("en la calle de la salud, núm. 2, en casa de don Antonio Ugina tesorero de los serenísimos señores infantes"); and, in 1827, Manuel José Quintana, *Epistolario inédito del poeta d. Manuel José Quintana,* ed. Eloy Díaz-Jiménez Molleda (Madrid: Librería General Victoriano Suárez, 1933), 100, 169, 174, 179.

108 Irving, *Journals,* 4:28, see also 65, 92, 101; and Irving, *Letters,* 2:266. On the Royal Library, see *Calendario manual y guía de forasteros en Madrid* (Madrid: Imprenta Real, 1827), 117–18; and García Cuadrado, "Aproximación," 103–9.

109 Irving, *Journals,* 4:67.

110 Irving, *Journals,* 4:67. The *Calendario manual y guía de forasteros en Madrid* lists Navarrete as living in the "calle de Valverde" from 1821 to 1834; his "expediente personal" in the Archivo General de la Marina records his death on 8 October 1844 taking place "en la calle Valverde no 26 cuarto 2°." See Dolores Higueras Rodríguez, "La colección Fernández de Navarrete del Museo Naval," in *Martín Fernández de Navarrete: El marino historiador (1765–1844); Ciclo de conferencias, noviembre 1994* (Madrid: Instituto de Historia y Cultura Naval, 1995), 58n30. Thanks to María del Pilar del Campo of the AMN for helping me track down this address.

111 Irving, *Journals,* 4:68.

112 Irving, *History of the Life and Voyages,* 4:178.

113 AGI IG 1858J, as part of 1826 folder of document copies that, starting 10 June 1826, Higuera y Lara was sending on to Navarrete: "Sevilla 23 de Agosto de 1826 Remite para el exp[resa]do Navarrete varias declarac[ione]s de Alonso de Ojeda y otros Pilotos sobre descub[rimien]tos de d[o]n Crist[óba]l Colon de los papeles de d[o]n Luis Colon desde 1515 à 1564 - pasados hoy 3 de Sep[tiemb]re de 1826." Also relevant is this later entry: "Sevilla à 7 de Nov[iemb]re de 1827 - Remite certifcac[ió]n de papeles pertenecientes al Almirante d[o]n Luis colon sobre conserbacion de sus privilegios año de 1515 à 1564 legajo n.° 2 de aquel Archivo compuesto de 24 piezas de autos. Pasados à Navarrete en Nov[iemb]re 15/827."

114 Irving, *Journals,* 4:68.

115 Vélez, *La historiografía americanista,* 106. Another collection of Columbus-related papers had been acquired by the Archive of the Indies in December 1813 (AGI IG 1857A, "Cuenta de los sueldos y gastos del archivo general de Ultramar en Sevilla correspondiente al Año de 1813"). See also Duque de Veragua, "El archivo de la casa ducal de Veragua," *Hidalguía* 6, no. 28 (1958): 413–24—an essay whose *posguerra* context the author makes quite clear.

116 Irving, *History of the Life and Voyages,* 1:viii–ix.

117 Irving, *Journals,* 4:73.

118 Henry Wadsworth Longfellow, *The Letters of Henry Wadsworth Longfellow,* vol. 1, *1814–1836,* ed. Andrew Hilen (Cambridge, MA: Belknap, 1966), 222.

119 Irving, *Journals,* 4:84. In the 1820s, the palace (and archive) of the dukes of Veragua was located at Calle del Olmos 28 (now 4; both numbers can be seen today on the building's *Asegurada de incendios* fire insurance facade tiles). Sometime after 1834, the family residence moved to Fuencarral 50 (now 46), a more fashionable part of the city. (That building's former owner was Raimundo Ettenhard y Salinas, whose will designated his cousin, doña Guillerma Remigia Ramírez de Baquedano, as heir. She, in turn, was the widow of the twelfth Duke of Veragua, who died in 1821.) In 1861, the family moved into a newly constructed palace at Calle San Mateo 7, a building still known as the Palacio del Duque de Veragua. See Joseph Señan y Velázquez, *Guía ó estado general de la real hacienda de España* (Madrid: Imprenta de Vega y Compañía, 1817), 4; Veragua, "El archivo de la casa ducal de Veragua," 413–14; Marqués de Saltillo, "Identificación de un retrato de Velázquez," *Archivo Español de Arte* 26, no. 101 (1953): 9; Anunciada Colón de Carvajal Gorosábel, "Pedro Colón de Larreátegui Ramírez de Baquedano," in Real Academia de la Historia, *Diccionario Biográfico electrónico,* http://dbe.rah .es/biografias/20416/pedro-colon-de-larreategui -ramirez-de-baquedano; and Cristina del Prado Higuera, "Espacios urbanos: La nobleza en Madrid

(1845–1900)," in *Del siglo XIX al XXI: Tendencias y debates; XIV Congreso de la Asociación de Historia Contemporánea,* ed. Rafael Fernández Sirvent and Rosa Ana Gutiérrez Lloret (Alicante: Biblioteca Virtual Miguel de Cervantes, 2019), 582, 588.

120 Irving, *Journals,* 4:90–92.

121 Irving, *Journals,* 4:94.

122 *Calendario manual* (1827), 76; and Irving, *Journals,* 4:94.

123 Irving, *Journals,* 4:95.

124 Irving, *Journals,* 4:96.

125 Irving, *Journals,* 4:98–99.

126 Irving, *Journals,* 4:99.

127 Irving, *Journals,* 4:99, 100, 102, 103, 104.

128 Irving, *Journals,* 4:112.

129 Irving, *Letters,* 2:257.

130 Irving, *Letters,* 2:253, 255, 256.

131 Irving, *Letters,* 2:269.

132 Irving, *Journals,* 4:13.

133 Irving, *Journals,* 4:189; and José de la Peña Cámara, "Washington Irving en Sevilla, 1828–1829," *Minervae Baeticae: Boletín de la Real Academia Sevillana de Buenas Letras* 15 (1987): 127.

134 Irving, *Letters,* 2:208; and Pauline Moffitt Watts, "On the Spiritual Origins of Christopher Columbus' 'Enterprise of the Indies,'" *American Historical Review* 90, no. 1 (1985): 73–102.

135 Irving, *Journals,* 4:131, 192.

136 Irving, *Letters,* 2:307. On Irving's friendship with artist David Wilkie, see Kagan, *Spanish Craze,* 140.

137 Irving, *Letters,* 2:309. In fact, Navarrete himself never seemed to have owned a complete transcript of these trial documents. When he published a version of them in the third volume of his *Colección de los viages y descubrimientos que hicieron por mar los españoles desde fines del siglo XV* (Madrid: La Imprenta Real, 1829), they included this introductory note: "Dos fueron las probanzas que hizo el fiscal.... De la primera probanza remitió el Sr. D. Josef de la Higuera y Lara, archivero del general de Indias, una certificación incompleta, su fecha 23 de Agosto de 1826, que hemos completado, intercalando en sus respectivos lugares las declaraciones de los testigos que faltan en ella, y

se hallan en el extracto que hizo D. Juan Bautista Muñoz de ambas probanzas. De la segunda remitió el mismo archivero otra certificación completa en 7 de Noviembre de 1827, y por consiguiente se han podido colocar en su respectivo lugar las declaraciones que contiene" (538).

138 AHN Estado 5575 exp. 11 docs. 5, 6, 7; and Eric Beerman, "Washington Irving en el Archivo General de Indias (1828–1829)," *Archivo Hispalense,* 2nd ser., 67, no. 207–8 (1985): 159.

139 Irving, *Journals,* 4:197, 202; and AHN Estado 5575 exp. 11 doc. 8.

140 Ezequiel Gómez Murga, "Washington Irving en Sevilla: Los Wetherell y la Casa de la Cera," in *De Colón a la Alhambra: Washington Irving en España,* ed. Antonio Garnica Silva, María Losada Friend, and Eloy Navarro Domínguez (Seville: Universidad Internacional de Andalucía, 2015), 39–58.

141 AGI IG 1858J; AHN Estado 5575 exp. 11 doc. 8; and Irving, *Journals,* 4:214.

142 Washington Irving, *Voyages and Discoveries of the Companions of Columbus* [1831], ed. James W. Tuttleton (Boston: Twayne, 1986), 353; and Washington Irving, *Journals and Notebooks,* vol. 2, *1807–1822,* ed. Walter A. Reichart and Lillian Schlissel (Boston: Twayne, 1981), 215–22; see also Antonio Garnica, *Washington Irving y los lugares colombinos* (Huelva, Spain: Diputación de Huelva, 2001).

143 Irving, *Journals,* 4:223; and Irving, *Letters,* 2:328–30.

144 Irving, *Journals,* 4:224; Beerman, "Washington Irving en el Archivo," 160; and AHN Estado leg. 5575 exp. 11 docs. 9, 10.

145 Irving, *Journals,* 4:227–28.

146 Irving began a first period of working on *Voyages and Discoveries of the Companions of Columbus* from 28 September through 11 October 1828, writing sections on Nuñez de Balboa, Ponce de León, Alonso de Ojeda, and Diego de Nicuesa (Irving, *Journals,* 4:231–33). The project seems to have been inspired by his visit to the Pinzón family and the revisions that it produced in the "Alonso Martin Pinzon" appendix of *A History of the Life and Voyages of Christopher Columbus.* The first appendix of *Voyages and Discoveries,* "A Visit to Palos," appears to have been drafted on 24 and 25 September (Irving, *Journals,* 4:231), just before the start of his two-week writing spree on what would become the main, biographical chapters of

Voyages and Discoveries. See also James W. Tuttleton, "Introduction," in Washington Irving, *Voyages and Discoveries of the Companions of Columbus* [1831], ed. James W. Tuttleton (Boston: Twayne, 1986), xxiii–xxiv.

147 Irving, *Journals,* 4:247.

148 Irving, *Letters,* 2:382.

149 Now NYPL Rich 10-B (folio), copy dated to ca. 1780; thanks to Meredith Mann for her help with dating. See also Brownrigg, *Colonial Latin American Manuscripts and Transcripts,* 24. Note that the original Las Casas Columbus manuscript had been located by Navarrete himself in the early 1790s: Julio F. Guillén y Tato, "Cómo y por qué se formó la colección de manuscritos de Fernández de Navarrete," in *Índice de la colección de documentos de Fernández de Navarrete que posee el Museo Naval,* ed. V. Vicente Vela (Madrid: Instituto Histórico de Marina, 1946), xv.

150 Washington Irving, *Voyages and Discoveries of the Companions of Columbus* (Philadelphia: Carey and Lea, 1931), 7.

151 Navarrete includes these *Probanzas* in document 69 of volume 3 of his *Colección* (538–91); he, too, was working from both a Muñoz copy and a Higuera y Lara copy (see note 137 above).

152 Irving, *History of the Life and Voyages,* 1:159, 172, 175; 4:177–78, 234.

153 Washington Irving, *History of the Life and Voyages of Christopher Columbus,* rev. ed., 2 vols. (New York: G. and C. and H. Carvill, 1831), 2:263; see also https://www.youtube.com/watch?v=__eKB7IdWfE.

154 MS2e, Barrett Collection, UVL. Thanks to librarian David Whitesell for answering questions on this manuscript and its collection history.

155 For a classic biography of Navarrete, see Seco Serrano, "Vida y obra." On the archival project, see Guillén y Tato, "Cómo y por qué se formó la colección de manuscritos"; Higueras Rodríguez, "La colección Fernández de Navarrete"; and María M. Portuondo, "Finding 'Science' in the Archives of the Spanish Monarchy," *Isis* 107, no. 1 (2016): 95–105.

156 "media docena de sillas para los Escribientes de Navarrete" (AGI IG 1858H, "Cuenta con Cargo, y data del Arca de caudales del R[ea]l. Archivo gener[al] de Yndias...1793").

157 This "Academia de Guardias Marias" in the "nueva poblacion de San Cárlos" would replace the older "Colegio de los Guardias Marinas": Antonio Ponz, *Viage de España, en que se da noticia de las cosas mas apreciables, y dignas de saberse, que hay en ella*, vol. 17, *Trata de Andalucia* (Madrid: La Viuda de Joaquín Ibarra, 1792), 307–10; Cesareo Fernández Duro, "Disquisicion décimaséptima: Bibliotecas y museos," in *Los ojos en el cielo, libro cuarto de las Disquisiciones Náuticas* (Madrid: Imprenta, Esterotipa y Galvanoplastia de Aribau y Compañía, 1879), 317–20; Teodoro Falcón Márquez, *La bahía de Cádiz en tiempos de Carlos III* (Cádiz: Consejería de Obras Públicas y Transportes de la Junta de Andalucía, 1988), 27–30; Marcelino González Fernández, "El Museo Naval de Madrid: Su historia y actualidad," *Museos.es* 2 (2006): 140; and Juan Torrejón Chaves, "El cuartel de batallones de marina en la nueva población de San Carlos en la Isla de León (San Fernando)," *Revista General de Marina* 253 (2007): 305–28. On the Isla de León in general (today San Fernando), see Juan Manuel Becerra García, *San Fernando: Informe diagnóstico del Conjunto Histórico* (Seville: Consejería de Obras Públicas y Transportes, 1993). See also this volume, chapter 2, 122n125.

158 Guillén y Tato, "Cómo y por qué se formó la colección de manuscritos," vi–x.

159 Jorge Cañizares-Esguerra, *How to Write the History of the New World: Histories, Epistemologies, and Identities in the Eighteenth-Century Atlantic World* (Stanford, CA: Stanford University Press, 2001), 22–26, 130–32.

160 Martín Fernández de Navarrete, *Colección de los viages y descubrimientos que hicieron por mar los españoles desde fines del siglo XV*, vol. 1 (Madrid: La Imprenta Real, 1825), lix–lx.

161 Guillén y Tato, "Cómo y por qué se formó la colección de manuscritos," xvii, xxi.

162 Guillén y Tato, "Cómo y por qué se formó la colección de manuscritos," xxviii; and Higueras Rodríguez, "La colección Fernández de Navarrete," 40.

163 Guillén y Tato, "Cómo y por qué se formó la colección de manuscritos," xxviii–xxx; and Ana María Vigón, "Los manuscritos del Museo Naval," *Revista de Historia Naval* 5 (1984): 67.

164 Fernández Duro, "Disquisicion décimaséptima," 394–96; and Vigón, "Los manuscritos," 67–68.

165 Fernández Duro, "Disquisicion décimaséptima," 332–43; and Ursula Lamb, "Martin Fernandez de Navarrete Clears the Deck: The

Spanish Hydrographic Office (1809–24)," *Revista da Universidade de Coimbra* 28 (1980): 31.

166 Antonio Prast, "La Marina de Guerra en la Exposición Ibero-Americana de Sevilla," *Cosmópolis* 15 (1929): 30–33; and Amparo Graciani García, "El pabellón de la Marina de Guerra en la Exposición Ibero-Americana," *Aparejadores* 35 (1990): 13–18.

167 See also Susan Boynton, *Silent Music: Medieval Song and the Construction of History in Eighteenth-Century Spain* (Oxford: Oxford University Press, 2011), 55–58, which reconstructs how a team of scribes worked to make archival document copies in the Cathedral of Toledo in the early 1750s.

168 A first step involved coordinating handwriting from the Seville period with handwriting from the Madrid-Escorial phase of the project. Given hiring dates, Hernández Garriga could not have copied documents before 23 May 1791, and Suárez and Finao could not have copied documents before mid-January (Guillén y Tato, "Cómo y por qué se formó la colección de manuscritos," xxi–xxii). Sarmiento also knew Latin, which is why the hand of the Castilian and Latin document verified on 23 April 1793 has been attributed to him (Guillén y Tato, "Cómo y por qué se formó la colección de manuscritos," xxi). Only five scribal hands, and not six, are attested in the AGI copies; since Juaquín Finao is repeatedly praised as a hard worker, and Joséph Miguel Martínez Abad is described as an *auxiliar* (assistant or auxiliary), I have assumed that only Finao was involved in copying documents. Martínez Abad probably assisted Navarrete and Basterrechea with double-checking the copies.

169 "Á veces me sucederá despues de ocupar muchos dias en el reconocimiento de 50 ó 100 legajos el que no hallaré nada" (Guillén y Tato, "Cómo y por qué se formó la colección de manuscritos," xxvii).

170 Guillén y Tato, "Cómo y por qué se formó la colección de manuscritos," xxii, xxvi.

171 Ángel González Palencia, "El Archivo General de Indias," *Revista de Archivos, Bibliotecas, y Museos*, 3rd ser., 33 (1929): 1–3; and Roscoe R. Hill, "Reforms in Shelving and Numbering in the Archivo General de Indias," *Hispanic American Historical Review* 10, no. 4 (1930): 520–24.

172 Now AGI Patronato 258 and 259; Navarrete collection items 1165 and 2252.

173 The main exception is a selection of documents copied from the Justice section in late November and December 1794—about which more starting on page 213.

174 This (key) manuscript is undated and unsigned; the following explains my date-author-place of creation attribution. The main body of the manuscript was written by one person (see below), although there are marginal notations in at least two other hands. The manuscript itself contains several references to the year 1783; one is to a letter from José de Gálvez dated 30 December 1783 (pp. 37–38). The manuscript also contains several reflexive references to "this archive" (*este archivo*), including one naming the (seventeenth-century) Simancas archivist Pedro de Ayala (pp. 11, 37). Part of the hard-to-read inked title on the parchment front cover reads *Colecciones de Simancas*. The writing of the main body of the text matches that of letters signed by Fermín del Río y de la Vega: AGI IG 1852, Francisco Ortiz de Solorzano, Estevan de Larrañaga, Fermín del Río y de la Vega, and Hipólito de la Vega to José de Gálvez, Simancas, 29 January 1785 ("Los oficiales comisionados en el Archivo de Simancas") and 15 February 1785. For a specific comparison, consider the letter forms of del Río y de la Vega's signature with the forms of "del Rio de la Plata" on page 148 of the AGI IG 1858C manuscript index. Other letters in AGI IG 1852 were written and signed by Francisco Ortiz de Solorzano, Estevan de Larrañaga, Hipólito de la Vega, and Simancas archivist Manuel de Ayala y Rosales; none of their handwriting is a match for the AGI IG 1858C manuscript.

175 The documents in AGI IG 1852 also allow for the reconstruction of a bit of Río y de la Vega's employment history. The earliest direct reference to him I have found is a letter he (along with the other three men listed above) signed in Simancas on 20 March 1782 (AGI IG 1852, the addressee is presumably José de Gálvez). However, a year and a half earlier, a letter related to the death of Juan de Echevarría on 23 September 1780 references the recent arrival in Simancas of two scribes to help on the indexing project; one of these was probably del Río y de la Vega (AGI IG 1852: Francisco Ortiz de Solorzano to José de Gálvez, Simancas, 25 October 1780). As discussed in my introduction, in February 1778, Echevarría and Ortiz de Solorzano were nominated to organize and index papers in Simancas (along with Fernando Martínez de Huete, but he would be reassigned to Seville in June). When Echevarría died (on 23 September 1780), Larrañaga was hired as his replacement. Four years later, on 8 December 1784, Ortiz de Solorzano and Larrañaga wrote a letter to Gálvez announcing that they had completed their commission: "hallarese concluidos los Ymbentarios y encajonamiento de los Papeles de Yndias" (referenced in AGI IG 1852, Simancas, 20 January 1785). On 15 February 1785, the four-man team wrote a thank-you note to Gálvez for extra funds—funds they petitioned, and were granted, every year of the project. But the team was about to be broken up: a 2 February 1785 letter from Gálvez ordered Estevan de Larrañaga "con su escribiente" (meaning Fermín) to return to Madrid, with Ortiz de Solorzano and Hipólito de la Vega staying on in Simancas to help with the (eventual) shipment of documents to Seville (AGI IG 1852; see also AGI IG 1854A, "Expediente sobre el establecimiento i progresos del Archivo de Yndias de Sevilla," fol. 18v: "en 1. Febr[er]o se les ordena, que Larrañaga con uno de los Escribientes se venga a Madrid, permaneciendo Ortiz con el otro Escribiente para cuidar de la remision de los Papeles"). In addition, a royal order on 31 March 1785 instructed Ortiz de Solorzano and Hipólito de la Vega to search for documents related to the creation of the Council of the Indies (AGI IG 1852: José de Gálvez to Francisco Ortiz de Solorzano and Hipólito de la Vega, Aranjuez, 31 March 1785; Manuel de Ayala y Rosales to José de Gálvez, Simancas, 15 April 1785; Francisco Ortiz de Solorzano and Hipólito de la Vega to José de Gálvez, Simancas, 15 April 1785). Later that summer, the two men oversaw the packing of the Simancas documents and escorted the crates to Seville; they arrived on 14 October 1785. New jobs awaited: both men were on the (first) list of AGI employees hired on 29 August 1785 (as *Oficial 3* and *Oficial 4*; see this volume, appendix B).

176 A catalog with parallel structure, of documents dated 1600–1640 and sent to Simancas in 1658, is in AGI IG 853.

177 "Colocados en una Arca de Nogal, con las Armas R[eale]s, cantoneras, y Cerradura dorados" (AGI IG 1858C, parchment-bound index on *Colecciones de Simancas,* 1).

178 "Una arquita pequeña con su cerradura dorada, sin llave, donde vinieron las Bulas desde Simancas" (AGI IG 1856). On surviving early modern document chests in the U.K.'s National Archives at Kew, see Heather Wolfe and Peter Stallybrass, "The Material Culture of Record-Keeping in Early Modern England," in *Archives and Information in the Early Modern World,* ed. Liesbeth Corens, Kate Peters, and Alexandra Walsham (Oxford: Oxford University Press, 2018), 200–201.

179 From 3 February 1802 to 30 April 1808, Ceán Bermúdez prepared monthly reports for Antonio Caballero summarizing the work completed by archival officials. (Similar reports from Valbuena exist from 6 October and 9 November 1809.) The report for 31 January 1804 refers to Ceán Bermúdez's own work as the "arreglo del este archivo y separatando los papeles mas interesantes que hai en el"; his "examen y separacion de los papeles mas importantes del Archivo" was reported almost every month thereafter, up until his final report on 30 April ("ordeno y areglo varios documentos preciosos, sacados de los papeles de Simancas"). These reports are scattered throughout AGI IG 1856. Diego Juárez is usually credited/blamed for the expansion of the Royal Patronage holdings ("The section was 'enhanced' during 1818–1820 by the archivist Diego Juárez with documents drawn from different sections but thought to be relevant to its mission as a historical archive"; Portuondo, "Finding 'Science,'" 103), and Juárez suggests as much in a 1 April 1815 report ("Se han coordinado y reducido á Ynventario los papeles llamados de gov[ier]no, y agregado á ellos los de Patronato y Patrimonio Real, como primer titulo de esta Coleccion, los que se han aumentado en lo posible con multitud de documentos que ha ofrecido el reconocimiento de tantos Legajos"; AGI IG 1857B). However, early in the five-year period Juárez spent coordinating and indexing this room, archivist Ventura Collar wrote a letter to Miguel de Lardiabla y Urive (on 26 July 1815) crediting the room's documentary expansion to Ceán Bermúdez ("La coleccion de papeles de que se trata la formo D[o]n Juan Agustin Cean Vermudez oficial que fué de la secretaria de gracia y justicia y comisionado por S[u] M[ajestad] en este archivo, el qual se dedicó á su separacion, coordinacion y extracto"; AGI IG 1857B).

180 AGI IG 1858C, parchment-bound catalog on *Colecciones de Simancas,* 69.

181 AGI IG 1852, Rosales and Francisco Ortiz de Solorzano to José de Gálvez, Simancas, 3 September 1785.

182 Two letters from Ortiz de Solorzano to Gálvez (27 August 1785 and 3 September 1785) ask whether the chest of documents separated out by Muñoz (as well as another chest of documents on Bishop Juan de Palafox) should be sent ahead separately or should travel with the main convoy of Simancas documents (AGI IG 1852). A marginal note on the second letter reads "Que no lo envien por el correo, y si no hay persona de confianza que los traiga, lo haga una de los comisionados q[uan]do

pase á Sevilla," but it is unclear to me exactly how these "dos caxones" traveled to Seville.

183 Scribe 2 (Félix Hernández Garriga) copied documents from 1542, 1549, 1552, and 1555. For a brief summary of the 1542 document, see Paul E. Hoffman, *The Spanish Crown and the Defense of the Caribbean, 1535–1585: Precedent, Patrimonialism, and Royal Parsimony* (Baton Rouge: Louisiana State University Press, 1980), 31 and 293n15. For 1552, see Hoffman, *The Spanish Crown,* 79 and 278n23. For 1555, see Mirjana Polić Bobić, "Un intento de clasificación de la obra 'Tratado del derecho y justicia de guerra que tienen los reyes de España contra las naciones de la India Occidental,'" *Studia Romanica et Anglica Zagrabiensia* 29–30 (1984–85): 259–62. A document from 1581 was also copied (Navarrete document number 2356), which in theory would have come from a separate bundle of royal decrees from 1579 to 1589 (then 41–4–6/16, now AGI Contratación 5014). On reviewing this legajo in July 2017, however, I was unable to find a match for the document copied by scribe 2.

184 Finally, as shown in chart 4.2, in both September and November 1794, Navarrete's scribes copied (respectively) 4 and 83 folios of documents labeled as "Papeles diversos sin fecha" (various undated documents). Since both the "Secretaría de Nueva-España" and "Secretaría del Perú" sections of the *Colecciones de Simancas* manuscript include subsections of "Papeles diversos sin fecha," and since both of those sections were being explored in this third period of copying, I have given those 1794 copies their own category in the chart. Focused research may be able to attribute the sources of those folios more precisely.

185 Guillén y Tato, "Cómo y por qué se formó la colección de manuscritos," xxiv.

186 Marc Morillon, Bertrand Mafart, and Thierry Matton, "Yellow Fever in Europe in 19th Century," in *Ecological Aspects of Past Human Settlements in Europe,* ed. Pia Bennike, Éva B. Bodzsár, and Charles Susanne (Budapest: Eötvös University Press, 2002), 211–22.

187 Portuondo, "Finding 'Science,'" 100.

BARTOLO
Che vuol dir questo dito
Così sporco d'inchiostro?

Why is your finger
so stained with ink?

ROSINA
Sporco? oh nulla!
Io me l'avea scottato,
E coll'inchiostro or or l'ho medicato.

Stained? Oh it's nothing!
I burned myself,
and I used the ink as a medicine.

BARTOLO
(Diavolo!) E questi fogli?
Or son cinque, eran sei.

(The devil!) And these sheets of paper?
Now there are five, there were six.

ROSINA
Que' fogli? . . è vero;
D'uno mi son servita
A mandar de'confetti a Marcellina.

What paper? . . It's true;
I used one
to send candies to Marcellina.

BARTOLO
Bravissima! . . E la penna
Perchè fu temperata?

Well-played! . . And the pen
why was it sharpened?

ROSINA
(Maledetto!) la penna?,.
Per disegnare un fiore sul tamburo.

(Curses!) The pen?
To draw a flower to embroider.

BARTOLO
Un fiore? . . .

A flower? . . .

ROSINA
Un fiore.

A flower.

—Gioachino Rossini (music) and Cesare Sterbini (libretto), *The Barber of Seville*, 1816[1]

CHAPTER 5
THE MONSTERS OF REASON

Juan Bautista Muñoz never used the archive he helped to create. He left Seville for Portugal's Torre do Tombo archive in the spring of 1785, and from that point on directed the AGI's completion mostly by remote, via letters from Madrid and its surroundings. He continued his investigations at other archives, including the Escorial in December 1785, and Madrid's Monastery of Monserrate in November 1786. He briefly returned to Seville for the second half of March 1787, as archival renovations entered their final year.[2] And in 1793, after more than a decade of research, Muñoz published the first—and only—volume of his *Historia del Nuevo-Mundo.*

In many ways, the book was disappointing. It only covered Caribbean history up to 1500. It contained no footnotes or references to sources (Muñoz promised the reader that these would be printed in a forthcoming volume, a volume that never appeared). But the biggest letdown was that the *Historia del Nuevo-Mundo* relied entirely on previously published materials. The years that Muñoz labored in archives, the thousands of documents he and his assistants copied: none were obvious in the *Historia*'s pages.[3]

Another absence is even more surprising. Although writing about Europe's initial exploration and settlement of the Americas, Muñoz never used the words *colonial, colonización,* or *colonialismo.* Such omissions would be unthinkable today. They have long been unthinkable. José Rabasa's *Inventing America* (1993), published two centuries after Muñoz's history, uses the words *colonial, colonization,* and *colonialism* dozens of times. Muñoz, of course, was writing to challenge negative evaluations of the Americas by previous (non-Spanish) authors, so one might be tempted to think he avoided these ideologically charged terms as a matter of strategy.

But these words are also absent (in their French incarnations of *colonial, colonization, colonialisme*) from the Comte de Buffon's Dispute-of-the-New-World-initiating volume 9 of the *Histoire naturelle* (1761). They are also missing from Cornelius de Pauw's two-volume *Recherches philosophiques sur les Américains* (1768–69) and from Abbé Raynal's six-volume *Histoire philosophique et politique, des établissements & du commerce des Europeéns dans les deux Indes* (1772).[4] In English, *colonial* and *colonialism* do not appear in William Robertson's two-volume *History of America* (1777). *Colonization* can be found in the second volume, but only twice and only in the index.[5]

Three years after Robertson, in 1780, the word *coloniale* would at last make its appearance within this polemic corpus, in the revised ten-volume edition of Raynal's

Histoire—but even there, it is used only twice, both times in reference to the *assemblée coloniale* of British Grenada.[6] And these brief cameos are exceptions. The adjectives *coloniale/colonial* would continue to be absent from later eighteenth-century revisions of Pauw and Robertson.[7]

But how was this possible? How could it be that, three centuries into what scholars today unthinkingly refer to as "the colonial period," the term *colonial* was all but absent from a best-selling constellation of polemic books that engaged with the legacies of Iberian invasions and settlements of the New World?

Linguistic history reveals an unexpected answer. The words *colonial* and *colonization* were *new* to European languages in the eighteenth century. *Colonialism* would not emerge until the middle of the nineteenth century. In other words, *coloniality is retrospective.* For most of "the colonial period," words such as *colonial* and *colonization* did not exist. This is not simply an absence in English—it is true for French, Spanish, and Portuguese as well. Authors from the sixteenth century onward certainly wrote about *colonies* or *colonias* in the Americas, and sometimes even *colonists* (*colons* in French, *colonos* in Portuguese). But these were words derived from ancient Roman imperial concepts, and simply referred to satellite settlements and their inhabitants.[8] It was not until the eighteenth century—in the context of newly tense relations between "colonies" and their European capitals—that words such as *colonial* and *colonization* were created.[9]

Colonial and *colonization,* then, are words coined very late in the early modern period, and they emerged—as will be seen in the following pages—from a context of radical Enlightenment debates about governance and sovereignty, debates put into practice during the half century of Atlantic wars and revolutions from 1756 to 1825. The condition of "being colonial" was not inherent to life in the American colonies. It emerged as a polemic, negative foil to an emergent imaginary of political independence. And so the creation of the Archive of the Indies as a space to study the independent history of the Americas took place at the very same time that new words were emerging in various European languages to propose a disjunction between political life in Europe and political life in the New World. The creation of American exceptionalism in the Archive of the Indies needs to be seen as part of a larger discursive separation of the two sides of the Atlantic world in the late eighteenth century, a separation in which imperial formations were replaced by the isolationist dreams of nation-states.

Reconstructing the unexpectedly shallow linguistic history of *colonial, colonization,* and *colonialism* is newly possible thanks to online databases (used, of course, with caution).[10] In English, I consulted *Early English Books Online* (for the years 1473–1700), the *Seventeenth and Eighteenth Century Burney Newspapers Collection* and *Eighteenth Century Collections Online,* as well as the *Oxford English Dictionary.*[11] Resources for French, Spanish, and Portuguese are, alas, not as extensive. I have relied on Google Books and Google Ngram for all three languages—but note that these results always need to be double-checked against the original page scans, due to problems of text recognition. (In Spanish, for example, apparent hits on *colonial* in the sixteenth and seventeenth centuries actually point to a misidentified *celestial.*)[12] French-specific resources include the *Grand Robert,* ARTFL-FRANTEXT, and *Classiques Garnier: Grand Corpus des littératures* databases.[13] For Spanish, I also consulted the *Corpus del Español;* for Portuguese, the *Corpus do Portugês* and the *Dicionário Houaiss.* Here is what these engines revealed.[14]

THE GENEALOGY OF COLONIALITY

The English word *colonial* seems to be the earliest of these politically charged neologisms. But even though British overseas expansion often chartered "colonies" named as such (in contrast to the legal-political status of Spanish "kingdoms" in the Americas), the oldest uses of *colonial* that I have found are from 1729.[15] Tellingly, they appear in an English translation of an Italian work, *The Civil History of the Kingdom of Naples,* in reference to ancient Roman settlements. Curiously, the original Italian does not read *coloniale* but rather *di Colonia* (of the colony) and *le Colonie* (the colony).[16]

This neologism had little impact at the time. *Colonial* disappeared from English usage for forty years, only to explode in popularity after 1765. And if we look at the contexts in which *colonial* then reemerges, its political edge becomes clear. The Stamp Act (a tax on all printed paper used in the Thirteen Colonies) was passed in 1765, followed two years later by the Townshend Acts (a series of taxes on imports to the colonies, including—most famously—tea). *Colonial* was a word used strategically in the polemics these acts triggered. Consider, for example, *The Conduct of the Late Administration Examined* (1767): "If the public see with regret the power of government in the hands of lord C__m, it is from the dread not so much even of his continental, as of his colonial system: It was from the commerce of the American part of our dominions that those resources were to be drawn, which his extravagance have rendered so necessary."[17] Or *A Letter to G. G.* (1767): "Enough has been said to shew how far we are obliged to the stamp author for his colonial system with respect to its advantageousness."[18] Or *An Inquiry into the Nature and Causes of the Present Disputes between the British Colonies in America and Their Mother-Country* (1768): "To convene indeed our colonial representatives at London, would certainly be attended with very great, though I dare not say quite insurmountable, difficulties."[19] Uses of *colonial* then had a slight recess in the early 1770s (the Stamp Act was repealed in March 1766; the Townshend Acts partially so in March 1770), but burst again into popularity after 1775: that is, with the start of the War of the Thirteen Colonies (chart 5.1).

A fascinating microhistory of how *colonial* emerged into English popular use is provided by the writings of Thomas Pownall, governor of the Province of Massachusetts Bay from 1757 to 1760. In 1764, back in London, Pownall published a book on *The Administration of the Colonies,* which was sympathetic to North American perspectives. The word *colonial* is never used in the first edition.[20] Nor does it appear in the second edition of 1765, nor the third edition of 1766. Pownall finally uses the word *colonial,* once, in the fourth edition of 1768 (in "colonial legislature").[21] That single usage is repeated in the first volume of his two-part expanded edition of 1774. But where the first volume of 1774 was basically a reprint of the book Pownall had been reissuing for

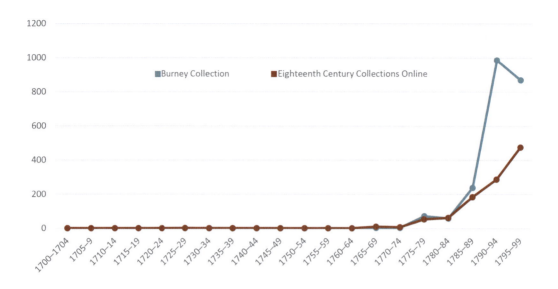

CHART 5.1

Frequency of the English word *colonial* in the *Seventeenth and Eighteenth Century Burney Newspapers Collection* and in *Eighteenth Century Collections Online,* 1700–1799.

CHART 5.2

Frequency of the English word *colonization* in the *Seventeenth and Eighteenth Century Burney Newspapers Collection* and in *Eighteenth Century Collections Online,* 1700–1799.

a decade, the second volume was newly composed. Its pages use the word *colonial* more than two dozen times, for "colonial government" and "colonial jurisdiction." In other words, we can precisely track the "becoming colonial" of Thomas Pownall's ideas, a transformation that took place in the charged years of the mid-1770s.[22]

In French, *colonial* emerges in the mid-1750s—that is, in the early years of the Seven Years' War with Britain over territories in North America (1754–63). This rhetorical connection is direct: *coloniales* is used seven times in the 1756 *Essai sur les intérêts du Commerce National pendant la guerre* (Essay on the interests of national commerce during the war). For example: "by competition from foodstuffs from Europe, and from foreign buyers of foodstuffs from the colonies, the current prices of colonial foodstuffs during peace will be maintained."[23] That same year, questions of war and commerce also frame the word's appearance in *L'Année Littérarie* (The literary year): "the disproportion of National and Colonial foodstuffs, during the war"; the same is true of the 1757 *Roman Politique sur l'état présent des affaires de l'Amerique* (Political account of the present state of America's affairs): "in the very transformations of commerce and of the colonial population."[24] But despite this flurry of midcentury uses, not until the late 1780s and early 1790s was *colonial* really taken up by French writers, in the politically explosive contexts of the French and Haitian Revolutions.[25]

In Spanish, by contrast, most early uses of *colonial* are in works translated from English—that is, *colonial* enters Spanish as a loan word. Spanish translations of English-language news items on Caribbean wars provide uses of *colonial* in 1778 and 1791; the 1794 Spanish edition of Adam Smith's *The Wealth of Nations* provides dozens of additional examples.[26] Once introduced, the new term was quickly taken up in original works. In 1787, Ignacio Gala refers to *generos coloniales, efectos Coloniales, Milicias Coloniales,* and *agricultura Colonial* in his *Memorias de la colonia francesa de Santo Domingo* (Memoranda on the French colony of Santo Domingo).[27]

In Portuguese, the *Dicionário Houaiss* reports *colonial* entering the language in 1776, via a loan from French. Alas, a specific text is not cited.[28] The adjectival variant *coloniaes* appears in the *Gazeta de Lisboa* by the turn of the century,[29] and both *coloniaes* and *colonial* appear together in publications from the first decade of the 1800s.[30]

Turning to the English *colonization,* we find patterns similar to those for *colonial.* The earliest usage of *colonization* that I have found is from 1748—and, tellingly, it appears in the charged political context of a Dublin-published book on the (failed) 1745 Jacobite rising in Scotland: "Something seems yet further wanting to compleat this great Work, which may be the Glory of his Majesty's Reign. This is the Colonization of the new depopulated parts of the *Highlands* by an industrious Set of People, who, by intermixing with the Natives, may teach them the inestimable Advantages arising from Diligence and Commerce."[31] *Colonization* continues to make occasional appearances over the next two decades[32] and then goes viral after 1765, during the polemic context of the Stamp Act.[33] It spikes again after 1775, with the start of the War of the Thirteen Colonies (chart 5.2).

In French, all of the earliest uses of *colonisation* appear in translations of, or commentaries on, English texts. In 1769, the word appears in two commentaries on *The*

THE MONSTERS OF REASON   231

Present State of the Nation: Particularly with respect to its trade, finances, &c., &c. (attributed to George Grenville, actual author William Knox).[34] During the 1770s, *colonisation* is used in a news item on the British in the Falkland Islands (1771);[35] in a review of John Symond's "Remarks on an Essay on the History of Colonisation" (1778); and in a news item from the war-torn Thirteen Colonies (1778).[36] During the 1780s, the word appears in a translation of William Macintosh's 1782 *Travels in Europe, Asia, and Africa* (1786)[37] and in translated quotations from John Andrews's *History of the War with America* (1787).[38]

The same genealogy holds true—at basically the same time—for Spanish. *Colonización* is first attested in translations of books originally published in English. Indeed, the earliest usage I have found of the Spanish *colonización* is in a translation of the English book that also produced my earliest example of the French *colonisation:* William Knox's *The Present State of the Nation* (rendered in Spanish as *Pintura de la Inglaterra: Estado actual de su comercio, y hacienda).*[39] Subsequent uses appear in the aforementioned edition of Adam Smith's *The Wealth of Nations* and in the translated title (*Ensayo sobre la colonizacion*) of C. B. Wadstrom's 1794 *An Essay on Colonization, Particularly Applied to the Western Coast of Africa, with Some Free Thoughts on Cultivation and Commerce.*[40]

And in Portuguese, the *Dicionário Houaiss* reports *colonização* as a loan from French sometime in the middle of the eighteenth century. However, the earliest uses I have found are from 1812 and 1817.[41]

Finally, moving to the third term of the trilogy, *colonialism* and its cognates do not appear until the middle of the nineteenth century. In English, *colonialism* first emerges as a word akin to *provincial,* often referring to "colonialisms" of speech in Australia or the United States.[42] *Colonialism* in the present-day sense ("the colonial system") developed in the late 1880s.[43] In French, *colonialisme* in the present-day sense appears by 1857, in a book on penal colonies.[44] But the term does not really become popular in French until the final years of the century—at the peak of France's imperial expansion—when it shows up in a wide range of journals: *Annuaire de Législation Étrangère* (Annual of foreign legislation),[45] *Journal des Économistes* (Journal of economists),[46] *La Revue Scientifique* (The scientific review),[47] *La Revue Socialiste* (The socialist review),[48] and *Revue Blanche* (White review).[49] In Spanish, *colonialismo* appears in the 1870s in a series of works on the recent history of Argentina by José Manuel Estrada[50]—but (as in English and French) the term would not be used more widely until the 1890s, during the final years of Spain's global empire: in Miguel Blanco Herrero's 1890 *Política de España en ultramar* (Politics of Spain overseas);[51] in the anonymous 1891 *Filipinas: Problema fundamental* (The Philippines: A fundamental problem);[52] and in Martín García Mérou's 1900 *Estudios americanos* (American studies).[53] The same trend holds in Portuguese as well: *colonialismo* became popular at the end of the nineteenth century.[54]

COLONIAL HISTORY, COLONIAL LITERATURE

Given this surprisingly shallow history of three keywords across four languages, when did people begin to imagine that an era of "colonial history" existed? Not surprisingly, this periodization emerged *after* wars of independence. Examples from both history and literary studies in English (for the United States), Spanish (for Mexico), French (for Haiti), and Portuguese (for Brazil) tell surprisingly parallel histories. Although ideas about a colonial period of history and literature emerged at different points in these different languages, all of them link the naming of a colonial period to three-part visions of history (suspiciously Hegelian in their trinities) that culminate in the "national period" of the author's present.[55]

For English, in the United States, the concept of "colonial history" appears as a category already in 1789, in the first pages of David Ramsay's *The History of the American Revolution*.[56] His three-volume sequel, published posthumously in 1816 and 1817, maps out a tripartite vision of U.S. history. Volume 1 covers "Colonial Civil History"; volume 2, the "History of the American Revolution"; and volume 3, "Civil History of the United States." This chronological division would be very influential, both in history and in literature. For example, Jared Sparks begins his 1837 essay "American History" by informing the reader that "we shall speak of this history, as divided into two periods, the Colonial, and the Revolutionary," and throughout his essay the categories of "colonial history," "colonial period," and "Revolutionary period" make frequent appearances.[57] Just over a decade later, Sparks's essay was reprinted in Rufus Wilmot Griswold's *The Prose Writers of America,* thus importing tripartite historical periodizations to literary studies. In that same volume, Sparks's periodization is evoked in the entry on William Gilmore Sims (for his interest in "all that related to the colonial and revolutionary periods in the Carolinas").[58] Seventeen years later, in 1866, the preface of Evert A. Duyckinck and George L. Duyckinck's *Cyclopaedia of American Literature* tells the reader that "as a record of National Literature, the Cyclopaedia may be divided into three general periods; the Colonial Era, the Revolutionary Period, and the Present Century."[59]

A parallel story, in which periodizations first proposed by historians are later taken up by literary scholars, holds true for Mexico.[60] Tadeo Ortiz suggests a three-phase national history ("dividio en tres épocas") in his 1832 *México considerado como nación independiente y libre* (Mexico considered as an independent and free nation). First came the pre-Hispanic (literally "ancient," *anticua*) era, followed by "the modern or middle epoch, which encompasses the whole interval of the colonial regime," and finally "the third epoch, encompassing the period from the war of independence or insurrection up until the constitution of the nation."[61] Four decades later, this schema was applied directly to literary studies in José María Vigil's 1876 "Algunas observaciones sobre la literatura nacional" (Some observations on national literature). "The history of Mexico in its three great divisions, ancient, middle, and modern (that is to say the great epochs of time before the Conquest, during the period of Spanish domination, and that which runs from 1810 to our present days) presents scenes of the greatest interest."[62]

The 1870s also saw the emergence of three-part historical and literary models for Haiti. Before then, Thomas Madiou's three-volume *Histoire d'Haiti* (History of Haiti, published in Port-au-Prince in 1847 and 1848) presented Haiti's history from 1492

THE MONSTERS OF REASON   233

to 1630 in the first chapter (pp. 1–12), and from 1630 to 1789 in the second chapter (pp. 13–31)—but then the rest of volume 1, as well as volumes 2 and 3, focused on Haiti's War of Independence from 1789 up to 1807.[63] Beaubrun Ardouin's eleven-volume *Études sur l'histoire d'Haïti* (Studies on the history of Haiti, published in Paris from 1855 to 1860) divides Haitian history into two parts: the *Période Française* (volumes 1–5, from 1789 to 1802) and then the *Période Haïtienne* (volumes 6–11, from 1802 to 1738).[64] Although both works reference the *régime coloniale* and the *système colonial,* neither names a period of *histoire colonial.*[65]

A tripartite historical model finally appears in Énélus Robin's two-volume *Abrégé de l'histoire d'Haïti* (Summary of the history of Haiti), written for use in Haiti's schools:

> The first part encompasses the period during which this Island was under foreign domination. It begins in 1492, age of discovery, and ends in 1803, at the end of which year the Haitians won their political independence and took the decision to govern themselves.
>
> The second part begins in 1803 and ends in 1838, when Haiti was officially recognized by France as a free and independent nation.
>
> As for the contemporary age, that is to say of our history which extends from 1838 to our own days, I have not written it.[66]

The baptism of a colonial period in Haitian history doesn't take place until 1875, in a work of literary history: Edgar La Selve (who cites Robin as well as Madiou and Ardouin) divides his *Histoire de la littérature haïtienne* (History of Haitian literature) into three *epoques* or *périodes:* "Indian epoch, Colonial epoch, Modern epoch."[67]

As for Brazil, surveys of its history had long been arranged by century, or irregular spans of specific years. Perhaps the first attempt at sweeping periodizations was in 1854, when Francisco Adolpho de Varnhagen divided his *História geral do Brasil* (General history of Brazil) into two volumes, the first covering the history of "Brazil-Colonial," the second the "history of the Principality and the Kingdom, with the declaration of independence and of Empire" (that is, events up until 1822).[68] Brazilian literary history adopted colonial periodization a decade later—a fascinating case study that, as with the Englishman Thomas Pownall in the 1770s, reveals a writer "becoming colonial."

In 1836, Domingos José Gonçalves de Magalhães published his groundbreaking "Ensaio sobre a História da Literatura do Brasil" (Essay on the literary history of Brazil). Like his U.S. contemporary Jared Sparks, Gonçalves de Magalhães divides national literary history into two periods and implies a third: a future when Brazilian writing would come into its own. But unlike Sparks, Gonçalves de Magalhães does not call the earliest period "colonial." Instead, following the century-structured writings of Brazilian historians, he simply labels the first era with numbered centuries: "The history of Brazil consists of two distinct parts: the first comprises the sixteenth, seventeenth, and eighteenth centuries; the second the short period that runs from 1808 to the present day."[69]

Thirty years later, in 1865, Gonçalves de Magalhães included a revised version of this essay in his collected *Opusculos historicos e litterarios* (Historical and literary sketches). There, he presents a newly colonial vision of past periodization. His previously quoted

234 CHAPTER 5

FIGURE 5.1
Francisco de Goya y Lucientes (Spanish, 1746–1828).
El sueño de la razon produce monstruos (The sleep of reason produces monsters / The dream of reason produces monsters), 1799, etching, aquatint, drypoint, and burin, 21.5 × 15 cm.
New York, Metropolitan Museum of Art, acc. no. 18.64(43). Gift of M. Knoedler & Co., 1918.

sentence is revised as follows: "The history of Brazil consists of two distinct parts: the first comprises the three colonial centuries [*os tres seculos coloniaes*]; the second the short period that runs from 1808 to the present day."[70]

Thus, in 1865, Brazil's literary history became colonial.

On Ash Wednesday 1799, two years after Juan Agustín Ceán Bermúdez completed the third *Inventario* for House of Trade documents in the AGI, his friend Francisco de Goya placed an advertisement in the *Diario de Madrid*. It announced the sale of an eighty-print set of etchings known today as the *Caprichos*.[71] This famous series savagely critiqued the hypocrisy of fin-de-siècle Spanish life: obsessions with genealogy (*Asta su Abuelo, Capricho* 39), corruptions of the Church (*Devota profesion, Capricho* 70), superstitions of the people (*Donde vá mamà?, Capricho* 65). Perhaps the most famous of these images is *Capricho* 43: *El sueño de la razon produce monstruos* (fig. 5.1). In the foreground, brightly lit, a man slouches at a desk piled with papers, his head buried in his arms. Behind him is grainy shadow, agitated and alive with wide-eyed beasts.

The image's title has two possible interpretations, given the ambiguity of the word *sueño*, which can mean either "sleep" or "dream." Goya presents the viewer with an irresolvable choice: does "the sleep of reason" produce monsters, or are they engendered by "the *dream* of reason"?

But perhaps the most curious thing about *Capricho* 43 is not the *sueño* of its title, but the *monstruos*. The supposed monsters gathered around the image's dreaming artist are not, in fact, the strange boundary-blurring beasts seen in other prints of the *Caprichos*: the chicken-men of *Caprichos* 19 and 20, the lion-men of *Capricho* 21, the donkey-bear of *Capricho* 63. Instead, the monsters are real-world creatures: a cat, owls, bats, a tufted-eared lynx.[72] Their assembly is significant. All of these animals were famed for their ability to see in the dark. So what does it mean that, for Goya, reason's dreaming in the Enlightenment is of the ability, not to banish darkness with illumination, but to see within darkness itself?[73]

Documents neatly stacked, a table illuminated with light. This is the vision of the AGI championed by Juan Bautista Muñoz, in contrast to his descriptions of chaotic attics and entry floors in Cádiz and Simancas where documents of the Indies had once been stored—places of "darkness," "confusion," and "disorder," uncomfortable and ridiculous. An ordered, brightly lit desk: this was the site from which a new history of

THE MONSTERS OF REASON 235

the New World could be written, overturning the critiques of American inferiority penned by foreigners. The previous chapters have tried to argue that if we look to the archival spaces of Cádiz and Simancas and Madrid with different eyes, their supposed chaos reveals instead a different kind of order, where a different kind of history could be written: one in which the histories of Iberia and the histories of the Americas were connected.

Seeing within darkness itself: this is the perfect image to bring to bear on Muñoz's claims about the *obscuridad i confusion* in which "documents were entombed, scattered and confused in the various Archives of the peninsula"—archives he plundered and recombined to create the Archive of the Indies.[74] What alternative orders, what other ways of thinking about the world, can we see if we turn from the blinding illumination of the windows and shelves and flat desks of the Archive of the Indies and look instead, with the eyes of the lynx, to the older archival spaces from which the AGI was assembled? Despite the name "Enlightenment," darkness was key to late eighteenth-century aesthetics. As Michael Baxandall makes clear in his study *Shadows and Enlightenment,* eighteenth-century observers did not see shadows as absolute voids. Instead, shadows were subtle and colored, with hazy, indistinct edges. Georges-Louis Leclerc, the future Comte de Buffon, described shadows in just this way. Architectural historian Anthony Vidler emphasizes the importance of darkness for Edmund Burke's theory of the architectural sublime, and argues that both Claude-Nicolas Ledoux and Étienne-Louis Boullée experimented with an "architecture of shadows." And Claudia Mattos reveals how, from the 1780s on, the viewing of classical statuary by tourists in Roman museums was ideally conducted at night, in a darkness lit only by the flickering fires of torches.[75]

This visual metaphor of shadow and illumination can be expanded to philology. We are used to looking at the first three centuries of European presence in the Americas through the lens of coloniality. So what does it mean that *colonial* and *colonization* become visible in the lexical record only in the second half of the eighteenth century?

And although Muñoz speaks of the metaphorical light his new archive will bring to history—

> In the present century, with its new light [*luz*] and scholarship, archival documents have been looked upon with greater interest and love.... Government, religion, justice, prudence, the sciences, the arts, commerce, the interests of the nation: all has to receive light [*luz*] from the Archive. And this light [*luz*] will be proportional to the method with which the documents are ordered, and the form of their inventories.[76]

> But these documents were entombed, scattered and confused in various Archives of the peninsula, so much so that an immense effort was needed to uncover them and bring them into full light [*a la clara luz*].[77]

—actual light is dangerous to documents. It bleaches their ink and damages their paper. Sevillian sunlight can also be hot. Very hot: "it is true that the heat of this city is excessive," complained three archival employees in a petition from 1788.[78] This heat

236 CHAPTER 5

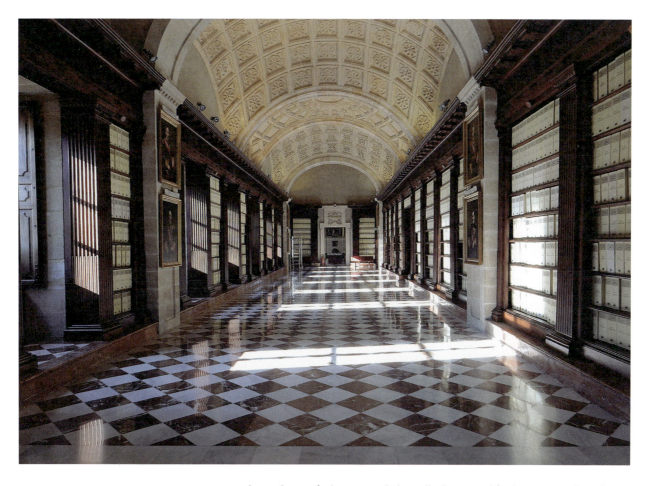

can be unpleasant for humans and physically detrimental for documents—"very harmful to the same shelves, and papers"[79]—which is why in archival and bibliographic practice today, documents are often stored at icy temperatures quite uncomfortable for human archivists and researchers.[80]

And so, as the remodeling of Seville's Lonja into a metaphorically light-filled Archive of the Indies entered its final year, steps were taken to block out actual sunlight (fig. 5.2). Work orders and receipts from 1787 and 1788 include woven mats and cloth curtains for the windows as well as a cloth sunscreen to shade the central patio.[81] A decade later, in May 1799—four months after Goya announced the publication of the *Caprichos*—eight taffeta curtains were purchased and installed in the four windows of the archive's front office: "where work is done, to prevent the glare of sunlight in the eyes."[82]

FIGURE 5.2
Midday sunlight in the southern gallery of the Archive of the Indies, November 2016.

THE MONSTERS OF REASON 237

NOTES

1 Cesare Sterbini Romano, *Almaviva, o sia l'inutile precauzione* (Rome: Crispino Puccinelli, 1816), 30. See also https://www.youtube.com/watch?v =enEVv02f6bo (at 1:06:08): Teatro alla Scala, conductor Riccardo Chailly, Milan, Teatro alla Scala, 1999.

2 Manuel Ballesteros Beretta, "Juan Bautista Muñoz: La creación del Archivo de Indias," *Revista de Indias* 4 (1941): 85; and Nicolás Bas Martín, *El cosmógrafo e historiador Juan Bautista Muñoz (1745–1799)* (Valencia: Universitat de València, 2002), 130–31, 145.

3 Cesáreo Fernández Duro, "D. Juan Bautista Muñoz: Censura por la Academia de su 'Historia del Nuevo Mundo,'" *Boletín de la Real Academia de la Historia* 52, no. 1 (1903): 5–59; Jorge Cañizares-Esguerra, *How to Write the History of the New World: Histories, Epistemologies, and Identities in the Eighteenth-Century Atlantic World* (Stanford, CA: Stanford University Press, 2001), 195–200; Bas Martín, *El cosmógrafo,* 160–61, 171–75; and Richard L. Kagan, *Clio and the Crown: The Politics of History in Medieval and Early Modern Spain* (Baltimore: Johns Hopkins University Press, 2010), 283–89. A manuscript for Muñoz's second volume was drafted, of which only books 7 and 8 survive (in the NYPL and the AHN); see Bas Martín, *El cosmógrafo,* 161–64.

4 Cornelius de Pauw does use the neologism *coloniaires* (referring to *troupes coloniaires*) once in volume 1 of *Recherches philosophiques sur les Américains* (Berlin: George Jacques Decker, 1768), 1. The fact that he does not actually use *colonial* points to the relative rarity of this word in European languages at the time. On the dating of Raynal's *Histoire* ("1770" vs. 1772), see this volume, introduction, 32n60.

5 William Robertson, *History of America,* 2 vols. (Dublin: Whitestone et al., 1777), 2:542, 545. In *History of America,* Robertson also uses *colonizing* (1:xx; 2:360, 387) and *colonized* (2:549).

6 Guillaume-Thomas Raynal, *Histoire philosophique et politique, des établissemens & du commerce des Européens dans les deux Indes,* 10 vols. (Geneva: Jean-Leonard Pellet, 1780), 3:573, 7:471.

7 Editions of Pauw published in London (1771, 1774), Bath (1789), and Paris (1795); editions of Robertson published in London (1780, 1792).

8 Ricardo Levene, *Las Indias no eran colonias* (Madrid: Espasa-Calpe, 1951); Anthony Pagden, "Identity Formation in Spanish America," in *Colonial Identity in the Atlantic World, 1500–1800,* ed. Nicholas Canny and Anthony Pagden (Princeton, NJ: Princeton University Press, 1987), 64–65; François Xavier Guerra, "The Implosion of the Spanish American Empire: Emerging Statehood and Collective Identities," in *The Collective and the Public in Latin America: Cultural Identities and Political Order,* ed. Luis Roniger and Tamar Herzog (Brighton: Sussex Academic Press, 2000), 72–73; and Mark A. Burkholder, "Spain's America: From Kingdoms to Colonies," *Colonial Latin American Review* 25, no. 2 (2016): 125–53.

9 Note that *colonial* isn't one of the ten keywords analyzed in Javier Fernández Sebastián's fascinating *Diccionario político y social del mundo iberoamericano: La era de las revoluciones, 1750–1850* (Madrid: Fundación Carolina, 2009).

10 For the dangers of "culturomics" and the naive use of online databases for the study of linguistic history, see Ben Zimmer, "When Physicists Do Linguistics: Is English 'Cooling'? A Scientific Paper Gets the Cold Shoulder," *Boston Globe,* 10 February 2013. See also the discussion of Google's Ngram in Daniel Rosenberg, "Data before the Fact," in *"Raw Data" Is an Oxymoron,* ed. Lisa Gitelman (Cambridge, MA: MIT Press, 2013), 22–35.

11 All of these resources require subscriptions to access: *Early English Books Online,* https://www .proquest.com/legacyredirect/eebo; *Seventeenth and Eighteenth Century Burney Newspapers Collection,* https://www.gale.com/c/seventeenth-and -eighteenth-century-burney-newspapers-collection; *Eighteenth Century Collections Online,* https://www .gale.com/primary-sources/eighteenth-century -collections-online; and the *Oxford English Dictionary,* https://www.oed.com.

12 On the optical character recognition (OCR) errors corrupting even English-language databases, see Rosenberg, "Data before the Fact," 30–31.

13 All of these resources require subscriptions to access: *Grand Robert,* https://www.lerobert .com/dictionnaires/francais/langue/dictionnaire -le-grand-robert-de-la-langue-francaise-edition -abonnes-3133099010289.html; ARTFL -FRANTEXT, https://artfl-project.uchicago.edu /content/artfl-frantext; and *Classiques Garnier: Grand Corpus des littératures,* https://classiques -garnier.com/grand-corpus-des-litteratures-moyen -age-xxe-s.html.

14 *Corpus del Español,* https://www .corpusdelespanol.org, and *Corpus do Português,* https://www.corpusdoportugues.org (both open access); and *Dicionário Houaiss,* https://houaiss .uol.com.br (requires subscription).

15 Burkholder, "Spain's America."

16 Pietro Giannone, *The Civil History of the Kingdom of Naples, in Two Volumes,* trans. James Ogilvie (London: W. Innys, 1729), 1:5, 46; compare with Pietro Gianonne, *Dell' Istoria Civile del Regno di Napoli,* vol. 1 (Naples: Niccolò Naso, 1723), 7, 60.

17 Charles Lloyd, *The Conduct of the Late Administration Examined: With an Appendix, Containing Original and Authentic Documents* (Boston: Edes and Gill, 1767), 82.

18 L., *A Letter to G. G.* (London: J. Williams, 1767), 84.

19 *An Inquiry into the Nature and Causes of the Present Disputes between the British Colonies in America and Their Mother-Country* (London: Printed for J. Wilkie, 1769 [1768]), 42–43.

20 Thomas Pownall, *The Administration of the Colonies,* 1st ed. (London: J. Wilkie, 1764).

21 Thomas Pownall, *The Administration of the Colonies,* 4th ed. (London: J. Walter, 1768), 165.

22 For example, Thomas Pownall does not use *colonial* at all in *The Right, Interest, and Duty of the State, as Concerned in the Affairs of the East Indies* (London: Printed for S. Bladon, 1773).

23 *Essai sur les intérêts du Commerce National pendant la guerre; ou, Lettres d'un cityoen, sur la Permission de commercer dans les colonies, annoncée* *pour les Puissances Neutres* (1756), 62; see also 67, 134, 223, 245, 257.

24 "Lettres d'un Citoyen," *L'Année Littérarie* 4 (1756): 10; and Pierre-Louis de Saintard, *Roman Politique sur l'état présent des affaires de l'Amerique* (Amsterdam: 1757), 52.

25 *Observations presentées au Roi par les bureaux de l'Assemblée de notables, sur les mémoires remis à l'Assemblée ouverte par le Roi, à Versailles, le 23 février 1787* (Lyon: De l'imprimerie du Roi, 1787), 169; Louis-Marthe de Gouy d'Arsy, *Lettre du Comité colonial de France au Comité colonial de Saint-Domingue, contenant le Journal historique de toutes les assemblées, délibérations, démarches et opérations de la Commission nommée par les colons résidans à Paris, d'après les pouvoirs de ceux residans dans la colonie, depuis le 15 Juillet 1788; époque de la nomination de la Commission jusqu'à ce jour. Le tout rédigé et mis en ordre par M. le marquis de Gouy d'Arsy, commissaire rapporteur. Approuvé et signé par MM. les Commissaires. Première partie. Du 15 Juillet au 16 septembre 1788* (1788), 1; *Extrait du registre des délibérations du comité colonial de St-Domingue, séant à Paris, du 27 janvier 1789* (1789), 1; Charles de Casaux, *Argumens pour et contre le commerce des Colonies* (Paris: Imprimerie de Demonville, 1791), 3; Claude Milscent, *Du Régime colonial* (Paris: Imprimerie du Cercle Social, 1792), 1; and Jean-Adrien Queslin, *Rapport et projet de décret présentés au nom du comité colonial: Sur l'organisation des établissements français aux Côtes d'Afrique* (Paris: Imprimerie Nationale, 1792), 1.

26 "Relación de la Toma de la Isla de la Dominica," *Mercurio histórico y político,* November 1778, 225; "Noticias de Francia," *Mercurio histórico y político,* November 1791, 220; "Noticias de Gran Bretaña," *Mercurio histórico y politico,* November 1791, 248; Adam Smith, *Investigación de la naturaleza y causas de la riqueza de las naciones,* trans. Joséf Alonso Ortiz, 4 vols. (Valladolid: Oficina de la Viuda e Hijos de Santander, 1793); and see also Robert Sidney Smith, "The *Wealth of Nations* in Spain and Hispanic America, 1780–1830," *Journal of Political Economy* 65, no. 2 (1957): 105–17.

27 Ignacio Gala, *Memorias de la colonia francesa de Santo Domingo, con algunas reflexiones relativas a la isla de Cuba* (Madrid: Hilario Santos Alonso, 1787), 14, 42, 66, 89.

28 Instituto Antônio Houaiss, *Dicionário Houaiss da língua portuguesa* (Rio de Janeiro: Editora Objectiva, 2001), 762.

29 "Londres: Continuação das noticias de 18 de Maio," *Gazeta de Lisboa* 24, 14 June 1796;

"Hespanha: Madrid 12 de Agosto," *Supplemento a' Gazeta de Lisboa* 34, 23 August 1805; and "Italia: Veneza 11 de Fevereiro," *Gazeta de Lisboa* 11, 17 March 1807.

30 "Commercio e artes," *Correio Brazilense,* October 1808, 380; "Templo da immortalidades dia 5 de Setembro de 1808," in *Correio do outro mundo* (Lisbon: Na. Offici. de João Evangelista Garcez, 1808), 19; and José Da Silva Lisboa, *Observações sobre a prosperidad do estado* (Rio de Janeiro: Impressão Regia, 1810), iii, 41, 54.

31 Samuel Boyse, *An Impartial History of the Late Rebellion in 1745* (Dublin: Edward and John Exshaw, 1748), 170–71.

32 Ben Sedgly and Timothy Beck, *Observations on Mr. Fielding's Enquiry into the Causes of the Late Increase of Robbers, &c.* (London: Printed for J. Newbery and W. Owen, 1751), 66; William Burke, *An Account of the European Settlements in America: In Six Parts,* 2 vols. (London: R. and J. Dodsley, 1757), 1:46, 2:133; and An Englishman, *A New History of England, from the Time of Its First Invasion by the Romans, Fifty-Four Years before the Birth of Christ, to the Present Time,* vol. 4 (London: Printed for J. Newbery and W. Owen, 1757), 95.

33 Daniel Dulany, *Considerations on the Propriety of Imposing Taxes in the British Colonies, for the Purpose of Raising a Revenue, by Act of Parliament* (New York: John Holt, 1765), 27; John Fothergill, *Considerations Relative to the North American Colonies* (London: Henry Kent, 1765), 30; and Thomas Whately, *The Regulations Lately Made Concerning the Colonies, and the Taxes Imposed upon Them, Considered* (London: Printed for J. Wilkie, 1765), 58.

34 Aubert Abbé, "Article IV: Tableau de l'Angleterre," *Journal des Beaux-Arts et des Sciences* 4 (Paris: P. Fr. Didot Le Jeune, 1769), 54; and "Observations de M. Burke sur les Assertions de M. Grenville, au sujet des Colonies," *Journal de l'Agriculture, du Commerce, des Arts, et des Finances* (October 1769): 74.

35 *Courier du Bas-Rhin,* no. 12, 9 February 1771, 91.

36 "Remarks upon an Essay, &c.," *L'Esprit des Journaux, François et Étrangers* 12 (December 1778): 393; and "États-Unis de l'Amérique-Septent.[rionale]," *Mercure de France,* 25 September 1778, 348.

37 William Macintosh, *Voyages en Europe, en Asie et en Afrique,* 2 vols., trans. J. P. Brissot de Warville (Paris: Regnaut, Libraire, 1786), 1:274. Translated from William Macintosh, *Travels in Europe, Asia, and Africa,* 2 vols. (London: John Murray, 1782), 1:284.

38 "History of the War with America, &c.," *Journal Encyclopédique ou Universel* 3, no. 3 (May 1787): 427. This article is a book review of John Andrews, *History of the War with America, France, Spain, and Holland: Commencing in 1775 and Ending in 1783,* 4 vols. (London: J. Fielding, 1785–86), 1:14.

39 William Knox, *Pintura de la Inglaterra: Estado actual de su comercio, y hacienda,* trans. Domingo de Marco (Madrid: Blas Román, 1770), 128.

40 Smith, *Investigación,* 3:181; and "Población," *Miscelánea Instructiva, Curiosa y Agradable ó Anales de Literatura, Ciencias y Artes: Sacados de los Mejores Escritos que se Publican en Europa en Diversas Idiomas* 7, no. 19 (Madrid: Antonio Cruzado, 1794), 3–4.

41 "Literatura," *O Investigador Portugues em Inglaterra* 5, no. 17 (November 1812): 30; and Manoel Ayres de Cazal, *Corografia brazilica, ou relação historico-geografica do reino do Brazil,* vol. 2 (Rio de Janeiro: Impressão Regia, 1817), 53, 56, 87, 140, 195, 219, 252, 253.

42 Ellen Clacy, *A Lady's Visit to the Gold Diggings of Australia in 1852–53* (London: Hurst & Blackett, 1853), 48; Henry Kingsley, *The Hillyars and the Burtons: A Story of Two Families* (Boston: Ticknor and Fields, 1865), 148; "Long Odds, Chapters 1 and 2," *The Colonial Monthly: An Australian Magazine* 2 (Melbourne: Clarson, Massina, & Co., March 1868): 50; "Long Odds, Chapters 11 and 12," *The Colonial Monthly: An Australian Magazine* 2 (Melbourne: Clarson, Massina, & Co., July 1868): 333; George Carrington, *Behind the Scenes in Russia* (London: George Bell and Sons, 1874), 215; and Richard Grant White, "Americanisms, Part V," *Atlantic Monthly* 42, no. 253 (November 1878): 622.

43 Albert V. Dicey, *England's Case against Home Rule* (London: John Murray, 1886), 273; Joshua Tyler, *Forty Years among the Zulus* (Boston: Congregational Sunday-School and Publishing Society, 1891), 284; and "Cape Colony and South Africa," in *Appleton's Annual Cyclopaedia and Register of Important Events of the Year 1889* (New York: D. Appleton, 1889), 103, 104.

44 Charles Ogé Barbaroux, *De la transportation: Aperçus législatifs, philosophiques et politiques sur la colonisation pénitentiaire* (Paris: Firmin Didot Freres, Fils et Compagnie, 1857), 179, 182.

45 Paul Hamel, "Empire d'Allemagne: Notice générale sur les travaux du parlement allemand pendant l'année 1895," *Annuaire de Législation Étrangère* 25 (Paris: Librairie Cotillon, 1896), 86.

46 G. de Molinari, "1895," *Journal des Économistes: Revue Mensuelle de la Science Économique et de la Statistique,* 5th ser., 25 (Paris: Libraire Guillaumin et Compagnie, 1896), 10; and M. F. Rouxel, "Revue des principales publications economiques en langue française," *Journal des Économistes,* 5th ser., 39 (1889): 224.

47 G. de Molinari, "Esquisse de l'organisation politique et économique de la société future," *La Revue Scientifique,* 4th ser., 12 (1899): 340.

48 Paul Louis, "La grandeur des États-Unis," *La Revue Socialiste* 30 (1899): 198; and Paul Louis, "L'évolution économique du globe," *La Revue Socialiste* 30 (1899): 707, 708.

49 Paul Louis, "La guerre économique," *Revue Blanche* 18 (1899): 241, 250; and Paul Louis, "Notre décadence commerciale," *Revue Blanche* 18 (1899): 589.

50 José Manuel Estrada, "La iglesia y el estado," *Revista Arjentina* 10 (1871): 217; José Manuel Estrada, *Política liberal bajo la tirania de Rosas* (Buenos Aires: Imprenta Americana, 1873), 168, 181, 186, 187; and José Manuel Estrada, *Nociones de derecho federal: Notas in-extenso de las conferencias del catedratico* (Buenos Aires: Imprenta Americana, 1878), 90.

51 Miguel Blanco Herrero, *Política de España en ultramar* (Madrid: Imprenta F. G. Pérez, 1890), 15, 395, 409, 570, 659, 660.

52 Un español de larga residencia en aquellas islas, *Filipinas: Problema fundamental* (Madrid: Imprenta don Luis Aguado, 1891), 59.

53 Martín García Mérou, *Estudios americanos* (Buenos Aires: F. Lajouane, 1900), 201.

54 *Annaes do parlamento braziliero,* vol. 4 (Rio de Janeiro: Imprensa Nacional, 1888), 96; and Ruy Barbosa, *O estado de sitio: Sua natureza, seus effeitos, seus limites* (Rio de Janeiro: Companhia Impressora, 1892), 78.

55 This historiographic analysis of disciplinary periodizations could also be extended to histories of art: Ray Hernández-Duran, *The Academy of San Carlos and Mexican Art History: Politics, History, and Art in Nineteenth-Century Mexico* (London: Routledge, 2017); and Carmen Fernández-Salvador, "La invención del arte colonial en la era del progreso: Crítica, exposiciones y esfera pública en Quito durante la segunda mitad del siglo XIX," *Procesos: Revista Ecuatoriana de Historia* 48 (2018): 49–76.

56 David Ramsay, *The History of the American Revolution,* vol. 1 (Philadelphia: R. Aitken & Son, 1789), 16, 17; and Jill Lepore, *The Whites of Their Eyes: The Tea Party's Revolution and the Battle over American History* (Princeton, NJ: Princeton University Press, 2010), 21–22, 146.

57 Jared Sparks, "American History," in *The Boston Book: Being Specimens of Metropolitan Literature,* ed. B. B. Thatcher (Boston: Light & Stearns, 1837), 121, 122, 125, 127, 129, 130, 131. Also, on page 126, Sparks writes: "The colonial wars form another combining principle in the unity of that period."

58 Rufus Wilmot Griswold, *The Prose Writers of America* (Philadelphia: Carey and Hart, 1849), 308, 503.

59 Evert Augustus Duyckinck and George Long Duyckinck, *Cyclopaedia of American Literature,* vol. 1 (New York: Charles Scribner, 1866), vi.

60 Burkholder, "Spain's America," 148n131, points out that a Spanish-language three-stage American history was first published by Cartagena author Juan García del Río in his introduction to the 1823 *Biblioteca Americana.* García del Río wrote, "su historia, que dividirémos en *antigua, media i moderna….* Designarémos con el nombre de edad media la época colonial." Juan García del Río, "Prospecto," *Biblioteca Americana, o miscelánea de literatura, artes i ciencias, por una sociedad de Americanos: Tomo I* (London: G. Marchant, 1823), vi–vii.

61 Tadeo Ortiz, *México considerado como nación independiente y libre* (Burdeos: Carlos Lawalle Sobrino, 1832), 148–49.

62 José María Vigil, "Algunas observaciones sobre la literatura nacional" [1876], in *La misión del escritor: Ensayos mexicanos del siglo XIX,* ed. Jorge Ruedas de la Serna (Mexico City: UNAM, 1996), 274. See also Beatriz Garza Cuarón, "Historia de la literatura mexicana: Hacia la elaboración de historias nacionales en lengua español," in *Actas del IX Congreso de la Asociación Internacional de Hispanistas, 18–23 agosto 1986* (Frankfurt: Vervuert, 1986), 551–58; and Mónica Quijano Velasco, "José María Vigil y la recuperación del pasado colonial en la primera historia de la literatura mexicana," *Literatura Mexicana* 26, no. 1 (2015): 65–82. A few years before Vigil, Joaquín Baranda gestured to a parallel model: "un distinguido literato mexicano ha dicho otra vez que no hubo poesía mexicana en la época del gobierno colonial….Desde donde debemos empezar á estudiar la poesía mexicana es desde el momento glorioso en que la colonia salió de una lucha desesperada y sangrienta para

recobrar su independencia y soberanía." Joaquín Baranda, "Discurso sobre la poesía mexicana" [1866], in *Joaquín Baranda: Obras; Discuros, articulos literarios* (Mexico City: Imprenta de V. Agüeros, 1900). On the complicated relations of these three eras in the 1890s (specifically, a desire to leap from the pre-Hispanic to the national by underemphasizing three centuries of viceregal rule), see Barbara Mundy and Dana Leibsohn, "Of Copies, Casts, and Codices: Mexico on Display in 1892," *Res: Anthropology and Aesthetics* 29/30 (1996): 326–43.

63 Thomas Madiou, *Histoire d'Haiti,* 3 vols. (Port-au-Prince: Imprimerie de Jh. Coutois, 1847–48).

64 Beaubrun Ardouin, *Études sur l'histoire d'Haïti,* 11 vols. (Paris: Dezobry et E. Magdeleine, 1855–60).

65 See also Michel-Rolph Trouillot, *Silencing the Past: Power and the Production of History* (Boston: Beacon, 1995), 105.

66 Énélus Robin, *Abrégé de l'histoire d'Haïti,* vol. 1 (Port-au-Prince: Imprimerie de l'Auteur, 1880), vi; and Énélus Robin, *Abrégé de l'histoire d'Haïti,* vol. 1 (Port-au-Prince: J. Chenet, 1894), v–vi. Although Edgar La Selve references an 1874 *Résumé de l'histoire d'Haïti* by Robin, I have not tracked down a copy. The text of the 1880 and 1894 *Abrégé* printings, at least, is identical.

67 Edgar La Selve, *Histoire de la littérature haïtienne* (Versailles: Cerf et Fils, 1875), 7.

68 Francisco Adolpho de Varnhagen, *História geral do Brasil,* 2 vols. (Rio de Janeiro: E. e H. Laemmert, 1854). For an overview of earlier nineteenth-century histories of Brazil, see A. Curtis Wilgus, *Histories and Historians of Hispanic America* (New York: H. W. Wilson, 1942), 55–57.

69 Domingos José Gonçalves de Magalhães, "Ensaio sobre a História da Literatura do Brasil," *Nitheroy, Revista Brasilense: Sciencias, Lettras, e Artes* 1 (1836): 151, 153.

70 Domingos José Gonçalves de Magalhães, *Opusculos historicos e litterarios,* 2nd ed. (Rio de Janeiro: Livraria de E. L. Garnier, 1865), 262.

71 Victor I. Stoichita and Anna Maria Coderch, *Goya: The Last Carnival* (London: Reaktion, 2000).

72 See Alfonso E. Pérez Sánchez and Eleanor A. Sayre, *Goya and the Spirit of Enlightenment* (Boston: Bulfinch, 1989), 110–17; and Stoichita and Coderch, *Goya,* 165–74.

73 Agamben's remarks in "What Is the Contemporary?" are resonant here: "The contemporary is he who firmly holds his gaze on his own time so as to perceive not its light, but rather its darkness. The contemporary is precisely the person who knows how to see this obscurity, who is able to write by dipping his pen in the obscurity of the present." Giorgio Agamben, *What Is an Apparatus? And Other Essays* (Stanford, CA: Stanford University Press, 2009), 44–47. See also Piero Camporesi on the Enlightenment "revenge of the night": Piero Camporesi, *Exotic Brew: The Art of Living in the Age of Enlightenment,* trans. Christopher Woodall (London: Polity, 1994), 12–26, 40, 100.

74 "obscuridad i confusion" (AHN Diversos-Colecciones 29 N16, Juan Bautista Muñoz to José de Gálvez, "Idea de la Historia general de America, i del estado de ella," fols. 3v–4r, Madrid, 28 November 1783; for full quotation, see this volume, chapter 2, 118n62). "Pero estos documentos estavan sepultados, derramados i confundidos en varios Archivos de la peninsula, tanto que era menester un trabajo inmenso para descubrirlos i sacarlos a clara luz" (AHN Diversos-Colecciones 29 N17, Juan Bautista Muñoz to José de Gálvez, "Razon de la obra cometida a D.[on] Juan B[autis]ta Muñoz," Madrid). Another copy, dated 16 November 1785, can be found in AJB Div. XIII leg. 5 carp. 8 doc. 10. Thanks to AJB archivist Esther García Guillén for helping me track down these various copies.

75 Michael Baxandall, *Shadows and Enlightenment* (New Haven, CT: Yale University Press, 1995); Jesusa Vega, *Ciencia, arte e ilusión en la España ilustrada* (Madrid: CSIC, 2010), 279–90, 465–70; Jacques Roger, *Buffon: A Life in Natural History,* ed. L. Pearce Williams, trans. Sarah Lucille Bonnefoi (Ithaca, NY: Cornell University Press, 1997), 78; Anthony Vidler, "Transparency and Utopia: Constructing the Void from Pascal to Foucault," in *Regimes of Description: In the Archive of the Eighteenth Century,* ed. John Bender and Michael Marrinan (Stanford, CA: Stanford University Press, 2005), 183–97; and Claudia Mattos, "The Torchlight Visit: Guiding the Eye through Late Eighteenth- and Early Nineteenth-Century Antique Sculpture Galleries," *Res: Anthropology and Aesthetics* 49/50 (2006): 139–50. Scholarly images of sources, light, and darkness had a long history; see Fernando Jesús Bouza Álvarez, "La biblioteca de El Escorial y el orden de los saberes en el siglo XVI," in *El Escorial: Arte, poder, y cultura en la Corte de Felipe II* (Madrid: Universidad Complutense de Madrid, 1988), 98–99.

76 AGI IG 1853; for full quotation, see this volume, chapter 2, 120n104.

77 AHN Diversos-Colecciones 29 N17, Juan Bautista Muñoz to José de Gálvez, "Razon de la obra cometida a D.[on] Juan B[autis]ta Muñoz," Madrid; for full quotation, see note 74 above.

78 "es verdad que son excesivos los calores de esta ciudad" (AGI IG 1854A, letter signed by Juan Manuel de Uricutua y Villanueva, Manuel José Guillén, and Pedro de Mucla, Seville, 21 May 1788).

79 "Procurarè se limite esta obra material al mandato de V[uestra] E[xcelencia] pero creo no comprenderà las cortinas, y Bela del Patio, y ventanas del Archivo; porq[u]e sin ellas serà intolerable el calor, y muy prejudicial à las mismas Estantes, y Papeles" (AGI IG 1854A, Antonio de Lara y Zúñiga to Antonio Porlier, Seville, 13 February 1788).

80 Carolyn Steedman, "'Something She Called a Fever': Michelet, Derrida, and Dust (Or, in the Archives with Michelet and Derrida)," in *Archives, Documentation, and Institutions of Social Memory: Essays from the Sawyer Seminar,* ed. Francis X. Blouin Jr. and William G. Rosenberg (Ann Arbor: University of Michigan Press, 2006), 13.

81 "Veinte, y dos Esteras con Lona p[ar]a cortinas de las Ventanas q[u]e caen al mediodia, y Poniente, q[u]e las resguarden del sol, y temporales recios; regulada cada vna con ierros, palos, y cuerdas.... Y[bi]dem. la Vela p[ar]a el Patio, ò cortinas de crudo p[ar]a cubrir los Corredores en Verano" (AGI IG 1854A, Antonio de Lara y Zúñiga to Antonio Porlier, Seville, 24 November 1787); see also Antonio de Lara y Zúñiga's letter from 13 February 1788 (quoted in note 79 above). Royal approval for the cost of these coverings was granted: "Conformandose el Rey con la propuesta de V[uestra] S[eñoría] en su representacion de 13. del presente, ha venido S[u] M[ajestad] en que se continuen los estantes en la tercera cruxia de ese Archivo, se hagan las cortinas i vela del patio i de las ventanas" (AGI IG 1854A, Antonio Porlier to Antonio de Lara y Zúñiga, El Pardo, 26 February 1788). Item-by-item accounts for the dozens of curtains (and their hanging accessories) are listed in AGI IG 1854B, expenditures for October 1788, receipt 1 ("Razon de lo q[ue] han costado las cortinas de crudo del Archivo, Arambrados, y demas"). But these were apparently not enough to ward off the damaging effects of hot Sevillian summers. In July 1793, a carpenter was paid to repair the archive's heat-cracked wooden infrastructure: "Por la compostura, y reparo de Carpinteria, que se ha hecho à la Estanteria, puertas del Archivo de las Ventanas, y de vidrieras que se hallaba todo con infinidad de aberturas, y hendiduras bastante considerables por causa de los calores segun consta de recibo del M[aest]ro Carpintero n[umer]o 10" (AGI IG 1858H, "Cuenta con Cargo, y data del Arca de caudales del R[ea]l Archivo gener[al] de Yndias 1793").

82 "Por ocho cortinas de tafetan que se han puesto en las quatro ventanas de la pieza donde se trabaja, p[ar]a evitar el reflexo del sol á la vista" (AGI IG 1858H, parchment-bound "Libro en que se sientan las Cuentas mensuales desde el mes de Marzo de 1789," list of expenditures for 1799). Heat had been an issue at the Lonja since its construction: Alfonso Pleguezuelo Hernández, "La Lonja de Mercaderes de Sevilla: De los proyectos a la ejecución," *Archivo Español de Arte* 249 (1990): 26–27. Note that French eighteenth-century archival theory was especially concerned with *humidity:* Pierre Camille Le Moine, *Diplomatique-Pratique, ou traité de l'arrangement des archives et trésors des chartes* (Metz: Joseph Antoine, 1765): 5, 19; and M. Mariée, *Traité des archives* (Paris: L'auteur and Cailleau, 1779), 4, 82, 102.

BEAUMARCHAIS
Fireworks at Versaille. Oh, how the people loved you.

MARIE ANTOINETTE
I was such a homesick little girl.... Poor Florestine, don't let him marry her!

BEAUMARCHAIS
Don't be afraid, Your Majesty. I won't let that happen.
And Almaviva and Figaro will foil Bégearss and bring you to the New World.
(She makes a disdainful face.)
And I'll be there to amuse you. Just the two of us.

LOUIS
The two of you? This time you go too far!
(His hand goes to his sword.)
I warned you. Defend yourself.

MARIE ANTOINETTE
(Putting her hand over her husband's)
Don't be absurd.

LOUIS
How dare he?

MARQUIS
Beaumarchais, do something!

(Marie Antoinette looks at Beaumarchais expectantly.)

BEAUMARCHAIS
(Leaping onto apron of little stage)
New Scene: Rosina's boudoir.
(To Marie Antoinette as he opens the curtains)
They say New York is a lovely town.

— John Corigliano (music) and William M. Hoffman (libretto), *The Ghosts of Versailles,* 1991[1]

EPILOGUE
ARCHIVAL MEMORY

During the first half century of its existence, staffing at the AGI was marked by a high degree of continuity. From 1785 to 1832, the eight main archival positions (archivist, officials 1–4, scribe, doorman, and assistant) were filled by only seventeen individuals (table E.1; see appendix B). Employees often worked their way up the ranks. José de la Higuera y Lara (nephew of Antonio de Lara y Zúñiga, archival superintendent director from 1785 to 1791) was originally hired as fourth official in 1788. He was promoted to third official in 1797, second official in 1800, first official in 1819, and finally head archivist in 1825. He remained in that position until his retirement on 3 January 1844. Long-term staffing continuity applies even to the doorman and assistant. Antonio Lorenzo was hired as assistant in 1805, and in 1820 was promoted to doorman, a position he filled until his death in 1828. His replacement as assistant in 1820 was Francisco García, who in turn replaced Lorenzo as doorman in 1828, and was still working at the AGI in 1841. These long-term staffing continuities probably explain some of the more difficult document searches described in chapter 4—searches not easily conducted with available finding aids. Such searches were possible thanks to the embodied knowledge of long-term employees who worked in the AGI's spaces for decades.[2]

But this long-term continuity was also marked, starting in 1819, by attrition. As older employees died and younger employees were promoted, the positions those younger employees left behind were no longer filled. After 1818, the post of fifth official was left empty. The same fate awaited the post of fourth official in 1820, third official in 1825, and second official in 1833. Employee deaths also resulted in a waning of institutional memory. When the Napoleonic Wars ended in 1814, four archival employees had been working at the AGI since the eighteenth century, two of them starting in the 1780s. A decade later, in 1824, only two employees (Ventura Collar and Higuera y Lara) still remembered the archive from the first years of its existence. Ventura Collar died the next year. And so, as the AGI's human experts dwindled, its paper finding aids (the seventeen volumes of indexes and inventories created from 1791 to 1819) became more and more important.

Jeffrey Garrett would see this shift as symptomatic of broader changes taking place in theories of information storage circa 1800.[3] During the seventeenth and eighteenth

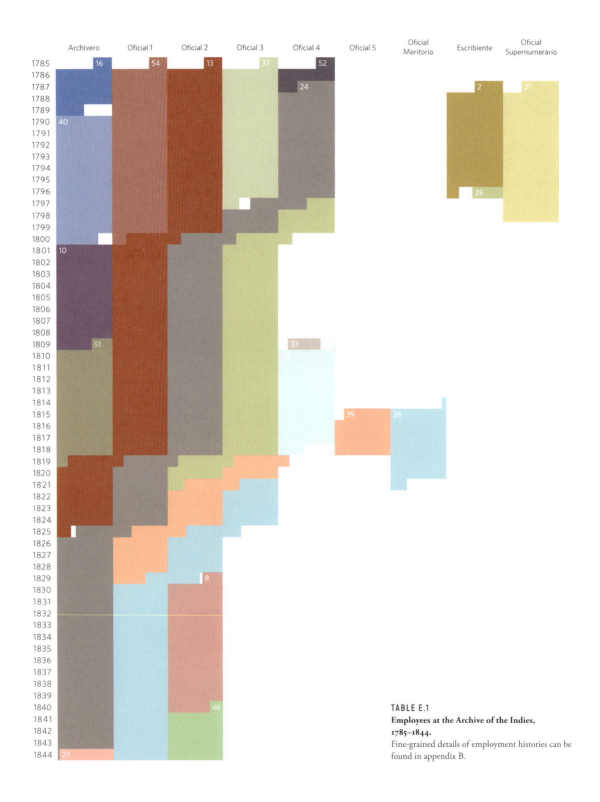

TABLE E.1
Employees at the Archive of the Indies, 1785–1844.
Fine-grained details of employment histories can be found in appendix B.

244 EPILOGUE

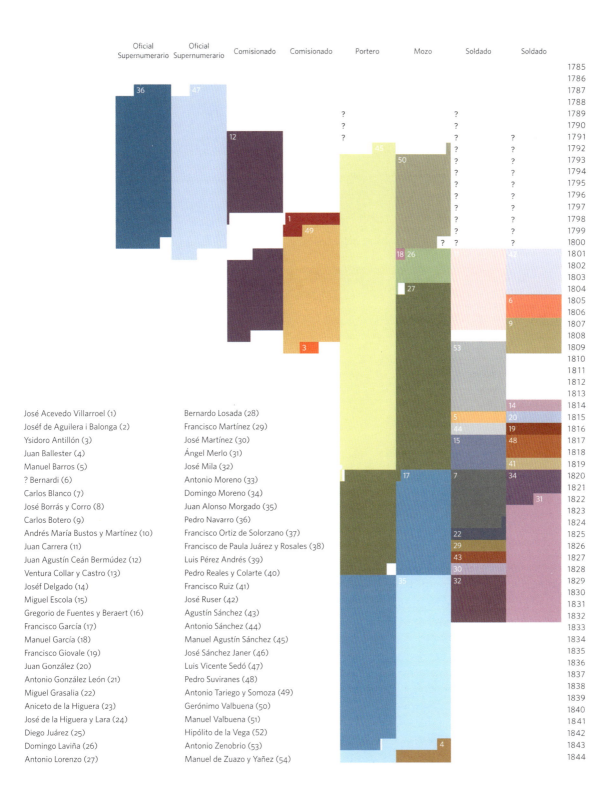

ARCHIVAL MEMORY 245

centuries, libraries were ideally overseen, and organized, by a single genius intimately familiar not only with each item in the collection but also with how every item connected to every other item in a microcosmic whole. Wall-system installations were often accompanied by very poor finding aids (such as lists of book titles that simply followed the same order in which those books were found on the shelves). Garrett argues that the real finding aid in this period was the very mind of the librarian, who had organized the collection in the first place.

Juan Bautista Muñoz briefly dreamed of applying this bibliographic model to Seville. Early modern archives (in Spain and elsewhere) were often run by family "dynasties" of archivists. In theory, this enabled knowledge of an archive's holdings (as well as skills such as paleography) to be passed down across generations. Such was certainly the case for two of the AGI's donor institutions: the Archive of Simancas, overseen for centuries by the Ayalas; and the archive of Seville's House of Trade, overseen for much of the eighteenth century by the Zuazos.[4] But although Manuel de Zuazo y Yañez eventually went to work for the Archive of the Indies, his inherited knowledge only applied to a part of its collections. The great challenge (and opportunity) presented by the AGI was that its document collections had been severed from previous institutional frameworks. Could these archival fragments be (re)assembled into something unprecedented?

Muñoz thought so. In an early letter about how the AGI's new holdings should be installed, he imagined an informational polymath who could, in his mind, integrate the scattered document collections into a microcosmic whole, a whole that would then be materially translated onto shelf space:

> I only see but one difficulty, but it is extremely grave: proper judgment in the selection of a person under whose direction such lofty ideas can be realized. What is needed is a man who would be able to devise a complete plan, with full knowledge of each one of the parts that have to make up the whole, and all of their functions. This whole, and these parts, are nothing less than all the branches of a great Monarchy. What talent! What sweeping ideas will not be necessary for understanding so many relations, in whose union enters all that there are in the physical and moral universe! Government, religion, justice, prudence, the sciences, the arts, commerce, the interests of the nation: all have to receive light from the Archive. And this light will be proportionate to the method with which the documents are ordered, and to the form of their inventories: operations so complicated, so varied, so prolix, that the only person capable of executing them with judgment is one who would have the talent and training sufficient to design the plan, and an extremely unusual dedication to the work. Thus must be the Director who plans the Archive. Once established, there will be many who can competently serve in the office of Archivist.[5]

That was on 8 June 1784. But by August, Muñoz had simplified his archival theory and embraced the more manageable "principle of provenance"—that is, keeping document collections in the order in which they arrived from their source archives.[6] And

FIGURE E.1
The northern gallery of the Archive of the Indies before the shelving reforms of the late 1920s.
New York, The Hispanic Society of America, GRF 849 ("Presented to the Hispanic Society of America by Arthur Byne and Mildred Stapley," 1915).

so when the creation of finding aids began under Juan Agustín Ceán Bermúdez in the spring of 1791, he (mostly) inventoried and indexed subcollections according to orders inherited from their source archives.

In the early nineteenth century, similar developments would follow in French and German bibliographic practice. Faced with massive libraries created by the national confiscations and compilations of formerly separate monastic collections, data specialists who tried to assimilate this vastness in their minds before starting on catalogs were (on more than one occasion) literally driven insane.[7] It often took several decades for an institution's librarians to give up dreams of personally embodying organizational microcosms and to focus instead on organizing their collections with paper finding aids, cross-referenced by author, title, and subject matter.

Seville's precocious finding aids—the indexes and inventories started in 1791—would have a long future. Their handwritten entries form the basis of data entries in PARES, Spain's online catalog of government archives. Although now encompassing some eleven locations, the PARES project began at the Archive of the Indies, during the quincentennial commemorations of 1992.[8] But a century and a half earlier, when just-retired head archivist José de la Higuera y Lara died on 11 April 1844, a very different kind of finding aid, with its roots in the 1780s, died with him.

And so it is poignantly appropriate that nine days later, on 20 April 1844, Queen Isabel II decreed that all of Spain's government archives would be opened to scholarly investigation.[9] One era of institutional memory ended at the Archive of the Indies, and a new one began (fig. E.1).[10]

NOTES

1 John Corigliano and William M. Hoffman, *The Ghosts of Versailles: A Grand Opera Buffa in Two Acts* (New York: G. Schirmer, 1991), 24. See also https://www.youtube.com/watch?v=-yB1IDdP_O8 (at 44:26): Wolf Trap Opera, conductor Eric Melear, Fairfax County, Virginia, The Barns at Wolf Trap, 2015.

2 Inherited-embodied archival knowledge was quite common in the early modern period; see Francisco Tomás y Valiente, "El gobierno de la monarquía y la administración de los reinos en la España del siglo XVII," in *La España de Felipe IV: El gobierno de la monarquía, la crisis de 1640, y el fracaso de la hegemonía europea* (Madrid: Espasa-Calpe, 1982), 123–24; Tamar Herzog, *Mediación, archivos y ejercicio: Los escribanos de Quito (siglo XVII)* (Frankfurt: V. Klostermann, 1996), 22–23, 71–73; and Markus Friedrich, *The Birth of the Archive: A History of Knowledge,* trans. John Noël Dillon (Ann Arbor: University of Michigan Press, 2019), 88–89. On the Ayala archivistic dynasty at Simancas, see Ángel de la Plaza Bores, *Archivo General de Simancas: Guía del investigador,* 4th ed. (Madrid: Ministerio de Cultura, 1992), 31–69; and Patrick Williams, "The Ayala Family and the Development of the Archivo General de Simancas, 1546–1676," in *Hacer historia desde Simancas: Homenaje a José Luis Rodríguez de Diego,* ed. Alberto Marcos Martín (Valladolid: Junta de Castilla y León, 2011), 847–58. See also note 10, as well as the entries for José de la Higuera y Lara, Francisco de Paula Juárez y Rosales, and Manuel de Zuazo y Yañez in this volume, appendix B.

3 Jeffrey Garrett, "Redefining Order in the German Library, 1775–1825," *Eighteenth-Century Studies* 33 (1999): 103–23.

4 On the Ayalas, see Plaza Bores, *Archivo General de Simancas,* 31–69; and Williams, "The Ayala Family." On the Zuazos, see this volume, chapter 2 and appendix B.

5 "No veo sino una sola dificultad, pero sea gravísima; conviene a saber el acierto en el elección del sugeto por cuya dirección se ponga en obra tan alto pensamiento. Se pide un hombre que medite un plan cumplido con pleno conocimiento de cada una de las partes que han de componer el todo, i de todos los usos de ellas. Este todo y

esas partes son nada menos que todos los ramos de una gran Monarquía. Qué talento! Qué ideas tan generales no son menester para comprender tantas relaciones, en cuyo complexo entra quanto hay en el universo físico y moral! El gobierno, la Religión, la justicia, la prudencia, las ciencias, las artes, el comercio, los intereses de la nación, i los de todas las mas naciones del globo con las quales tiene conexión la nuestra: todo ha de recibir luz del Archivo. Y esa luz será proporcional al método con que se ordenen los documentos, i a la forma de sus inventarios: operaciones tan complicadas, tan varias, tan prolijas, que solo es capaz de egecutarlas con acierto, quien tenga el talento y la instrucción suficiente para disponer el plan, y un rarísima constancia en el trabajo. Tal debe ser el Director que plantifique el Archivo: ya establecido, habrá muchos que puedan servir el oficio de Archivero con utilidad" (AGI IG 1853, Juan Bautista Muñoz to José de Gálvez, Seville, 8 June 1784). Not incidentally, elsewhere in the same letter (when talking about the House of Trade documents that remained in Seville), Muñoz imagines an archivist with the "ability to revolutionize the papers and give them a new order and organization."

6 "Con la misma se pueden traer los papeles de Simancas, de Cadiz, i de Madrid para exonerar las oficinas: i desde luego, como se vayan vistiendo Salas, ir colocando los legajos segun el orden que tenian en su lugar originario" (AGI IG 1853, Juan Bautista Muñoz and Francisco Miguel Maestre to José de Gálvez, Seville, 4 August 1784); and "Al paso que se trabaja en la obra material, debe irse adelantando lo posible en el arreglo de los Papeles. Bien entendido que en aquellos ramos que ahora están ordenados con regularidad, no se haga más operación sino colocar los legajos con la misma disposición que tenían anteriormente en sus respectivas oficinas. Así podrán servirse de ellos los Tribunales y particulares, gobernándose por los inventarios que hay de cada clase" (AGI IG 1854A, Juan Bautista Muñoz, "Razón del origen, progreso, i actual estado del Archivo general de Indias," 3 August 1787, fols. 8v–9r).

7 Garrett, "Redefining Order," 113, 122n36. See also Zeynep Çelik Alexander, "Stacks, Shelves, and the Law: Restructuring the Library of Congress," *Grey Room* 82 (2021): 6–29.

8 Ministerio de Cultura (Dirección General de Bellas Artes y Archivos), Fundación Ramón Areces, and IBM España, *Proyecto de informatización del Archivo General de Indias* (Torrejón de Ardoz, Madrid: Julio Soto Impresor, 1990); Pedro González García, "El Archivo General de Indias y su proyecto de informatización: Nuevas posibilidades para la investigación," *Cuadernos de Historia Moderna* 15 (1994): 231–49; Pedro González García, "Introduction," in *Discovering the Americas: The Archive of the Indies,* ed. Pedro González García (New York: Vendome, 1997), 28; Pedro González García, *Informatización del Archivo General de Indias: Estrategias y resultados* (Madrid: ANABAD, 1999), 83–92; María García-González and Celia Chaín Navarro, "Pares: Portal de archivos españoles; Generando puentes entre el investigador y los fondos archivísticos," *Investigación Bibliotecológica* 24, no. 51 (2010): 43–68; and María Jesús Álvarez-Coca González, "La investigación histórica y los archivos en Internet: La presencia del Archivo Histórico Nacional en el Portal de Archivos Españoles (*PARES*)," *Cuadernos de Historia Moderna* 35 (2010): 183–85.

9 Magdalena Canellas Anoz, "El Archivo General de Indias: La recreación de un espacio para la cultura," in *La Casa Lonja de Sevilla: Una casa de ricos tesoros,* ed. María Antonio Colomar Albajar (Madrid: Ministerio de Cultura, 2005), 27; José Luis Rodríguez de Diego, "La apertura de Simancas a la investigación histórica en el año 1844," in *Archivi e storia nell'Europa del XIX secolo: Alle radici dell'identità culturale europea,* ed. Irene Cotta and Rosalia Manno Tolu, vol. 2 (Rome: Direzione generale per gli archivi, 2006), 601–26; and Eduardo Pedruelo Martín, "El Archivo General de Simancas: De archivo real a archivo público," in *Valladolid, ciudad de archivos,* ed. Soledad Carnicer Arribas and Alberto Marcos Martín (Valladolid: Universidad de Valladolid, 2011), 37–97. On the photographers of this epilogue's closing image (the controversial art dealers Arthur Byne and Mildred Stapley Byne), see Richard L. Kagan, *The Spanish Craze: America's Fascination with the Hispanic World, 1779–1939* (Lincoln: University of Nebraska Press, 2019), 225–26, 290–302. The ghostly figure looks like archivist José González Verger, AGI employee from 1894 and vice director at the time of his death on 4 February 1914. The

ARCHIVAL MEMORY 249

photo, however, is dated to 1915. See the (labeled) photograph of "The officials of the Archives of the Indies" in the University of California at Berkeley's Bancroft Library (Roscoe R. Hill Photograph Collection, BANC PIC 1962.024 Box 1); thanks to archivist James A. Eason for helping me track down the trove of Hill photographs. For González Verger's employment history, see "Ministerio de Fomento: Escalafón del Cuerpo facultativo de Archiveros, Bibliotecarios y Anticuarios en 27 de Octubre de 1894," *Gaceta de Instrucción Pública: Periódico Decenal* 6, no. 202 (5 December 1894): 1528; and "Sección oficial y de noticias," *Revista de Archivos, Bibliotecas y Museos 18,* no. 1–2 (1914): 164.

10 Of course, no rupture is ever absolute—Bruno Latour, *We Have Never Been Modern,* trans. Catherine Porter (Cambridge, MA: Harvard University Press, 1993), 48, 69—and although a monograph on the AGI after 1844 still needs to be written, at least three 1860s employees were connected to its earlier history. From 1844 to 1868, the archivist was Aniceto de la Higuera López del Prado, the nephew of former archivist José de la Higuera y Lara (and hired one day after his uncle's retirement). Aniceto's inherited employment was not (merely) a case of (literal) nepotism: he had already been helping at the archive "for many years": AHN Ultramar 2430 exp. 2; see also Manuel Gómez Zarzuela, *Guia de Sevilla, su provincia, arzobispado, capitanía general, audiencia territorial y distrito universitario, para 1868* (Seville: Establecimento Tipográfico de Andalucía, 1868), 275. In turn, Aniceto's *Oficial 1* (and eventual successor as archivist, starting 30 November 1868) was Francisco de Paula Juárez y Rosales, who had started working at the AGI as *Oficial Meritorio* in 1814. He, in turn, was the son of Diego Juárez, an archival employee from 13 June 1796 until his death on 1 April 1821 (AHN Ultramar 2431 exp. 51). The doorman in 1844 was Juan Alonso Morgado, who was hired to work at the AGI as an assistant (*mozo*) in December 1828. See Manuel Gómez Zarzuela, *Guía de Sevilla* (Sevilla: La Andalucía, 1865), 206–7. For genealogies and employment histories, see this volume, appendix B, as well as the personnel files of Aniceto (AHN Ultramar 2430 exp. 2) and Francisco (AHN Ultramar 2431 exp. 51). On the opening of Spain's archives to researchers in 1844, see Centro de Información Documental de Archivos (CIDA), "175 aniversario de la Real Orden de 1844 de Acceso a los Archivos Históricos," https://www.culturaydeporte.gob.es/cultura/areas/archivos/mc/centros/cida/4-difusion-cooperacion/4-2-guias-de-lectura/real-orden-1844-acceso-archivos.html.

APPENDIX A
THE FINANCES OF THE ARCHIVE OF THE INDIES: ACCOUNT BOOKS AND RECEIPTS, 1785–1832

Nearly fifty years of economic information on the archive's costs, spanning 1785 to 1832, can be found in the papers of Indiferente General (legajos 1853, 1854B, 1856, 1857A, 1857B, 1858J, and 1858H). These accounts, which range from construction-worker payments to archivist salaries to "food for the archive's cats" (*comida para los gatos del Archivo,* from September 1786 to November 1787) are mainly preserved in two types of documents. The first are account books (often titled "Cuenta…"), which provide a running day-by-day, month-by-month record of expenses over the course of a year. The second are bundles of individual receipts (*recibos*), usually grouped by month. Finally, accounts of funds entering and leaving the archive's money chest (*arca de caudales*) from March 1789 to January 1810 (deposits) and January 1801 to January 1810 (withdrawals) can be found in AGI IG 1858H; however, in contrast to account books and receipts, these records generally provide only quantities and dates, not explanatory information.

The following is a guide for locating account books and receipts from specific years:

1785	AGI IG 1853 (accounts, receipts), 1858H (accounts)
1786	AGI IG 1853 (accounts, receipts), 1858H (accounts)
1787	AGI IG 1854B (accounts, receipts), 1858H (accounts)
1788	AGI IG 1854B (accounts, receipts), 1858H (accounts)
1789	AGI IG 1858H (accounts)
1790	AGI IG 1854B (accounts, receipts), 1858H (accounts)
1791	AGI IG 1858H (accounts)
1792	AGI IG 1858H (accounts)
1793	AGI IG 1858H (accounts)
1794	AGI IG 1858H (accounts)
1795	AGI IG 1858H (accounts)
1796	AGI IG 1858H (accounts)
1797	AGI IG 1858H (accounts)
1798	AGI IG 1858H (accounts)
1799	AGI IG 1858H (accounts)
1800	AGI IG 1858H (accounts)
1801	AGI IG 1856 (accounts, receipts), 1858H (accounts)
1802	AGI IG 1856 (accounts, receipts), 1858H (accounts)
1803	AGI IG 1856 (accounts, receipts), 1858H (accounts)
1804	AGI IG 1856 (accounts, receipts), 1858H (accounts)
1805	AGI IG 1856 (accounts, receipts), 1858H (accounts)
1806	AGI IG 1856 (accounts, receipts), 1858H (accounts)
1807	AGI IG 1856 (accounts, receipts), 1858H (accounts)
1808	AGI IG 1856 (accounts, receipts), 1858H (accounts)
1809	AGI IG 1858H (accounts)
1810	AGI IG 1858H (accounts: January only)
	[Joseph Bonaparte captures Seville 1 February]
1811	[Napoleonic occupation of Seville, no records]
1812	[Napoleonic occupation of Seville until 27 August, no records]
1813	AGI IG 1857A (accounts, receipts)
1814	AGI IG 1857A (accounts, receipts)
1815	AGI IG 1857A (accounts, receipts)
1816	AGI IG 1857B (accounts, receipts)
1817	AGI IG 1857B (accounts, receipts)
1818	AGI IG 1857B (accounts, receipts)
1819	AGI IG 1857B (accounts, receipts)
1820	AGI IG 1858J (accounts, receipts)
1821	AGI IG 1858J (accounts, receipts)
1822	AGI IG 1858J (accounts, receipts: January–June), 1857B (accounts, receipts: July–December)
1823	AGI IG 1857B (accounts, receipts)
1824	AGI IG 1857B (accounts, receipts: January–November), 1858J (accounts, receipts: December)
1825	AGI IG 1858J (accounts, receipts)
1826	AGI IG 1858J (accounts, receipts)
1827	AGI IG 1858J (accounts, receipts)
1828	AGI IG 1858J (accounts, receipts)
1829	AGI IG 1858J (accounts, receipts)
1830	AGI IG 1858J (accounts, receipts)
1831	AGI IG 1858J (accounts, receipts)
1832	AGI IG 1858J (receipts)

APPENDIX B

FROM ARCHIVISTS TO SOLDIERS: THE EMPLOYEES OF THE ARCHIVE OF THE INDIES, 1785–1844

This appendix tracks the careers of fifty-four employees during the first six decades of the AGI's existence. Most of this information has been compiled from the archive's economic records (see appendix A), which list salaries and promotions as well as mentioning transfers and deaths. Appointment information is sometimes found in written correspondence as well. In several cases, there is a gap between the date of official appointment and the date when an employee actually started to work in the archive; the former is favored below, since appointment dates can reveal the hiring of a whole cohort of employees (as with the first five official hires in August 1785, or the three supernumerary hires in June 1787).

Support staff—*porteros* (doormen), *mozos* (assistants), and *soldados* (soldiers)—were not always named in the available records during the first years of the archive's existence. Main construction work on the archive was completed by mid-November 1788. Support staff begin to be mentioned in monthly expense tallies starting in January 1789, with a *peon* (helper) serving as *portero* (in weekly segments beginning on 7 January, the day after Epiphany), and also a *soldado q[u]e custodia el Zaguan* (soldier who watches the front room), starting on 26 January. By mid-February, the doorkeeper's usual title becomes *portero de arriva* (upstairs doorman), in contrast to the soldier posted on the building's ground floor (generally referred to as *portero de abajo* or *soldado de la puerta*). Starting in March 1791, two soldiers were employed to guard the archive, and a *mozo* began to be paid for several weeks of work every month (twenty-two days in March, eighteen days in April, twenty-four days in May). In these entries, *mozo* seems to be a change in title for the *peon* employed for cleaning starting in March 1789: only two days that month, but up to twenty-two days in February 1791). A *portero interino* (interim doorkeeper) starts being listed in February 1791, and in August 1792 a note explains that Manuel Agustín Sánchez, formerly the interim doorkeeper, would now receive an annual salary as *portero*. That November, Gerónimo Valbuena is named as *mozo propietario* (salaried assistant). Valbuena may have been working (by the day) as *mozo* in the archive since March 1791 (or as *peon* going back to March 1789), and Sánchez may have been (interim) *portero* since January 1792—but even if so, these two men are not named in the archive's financial records until 1792.

For an overview of the core employee categories described in the AGI's 1790 *Ordenanzas*, see this volume, chapter 1, 68n17. For a graphic representation of all of these employee histories, see table E.1 in the epilogue. The numbers in that table are keyed to the numbers that follow each employee's name in this appendix.

José Acevedo Villarroel (1)
Comisionado starting 18 January 1798 to April 1799
(AGI IG 1858H)

Joséf de Aguilera i Balonga (2)
Escribiente starting 25 June 1787 (AGI IG 1858H)
Dies 21 March 1796 (AGI IG 1858H)

Ysidoro Antillón (3)
Comisionado starting 19 April 1809 to 13 August 1809 (AGI IG 1858H)

Juan Ballester (4)
Mozo starting 3 October 1843 (AGI Caja 1 Expedientes Personales
1787–1861, Francisco García)

Manuel Barros (5)
Soldado from January 1815 to December 1815 (AGI IG 1857A)

? Bernardi (6)
Soldado from January 1805 to December 1806 (AGI IG 1856)

Carlos Blanco (7)
Soldado from January 1820 to November 1824
(AGI IG 1858J, 1857B)

José Borrás y Corro (8)
Oficial 2 starting 14 August 1829 (AGI Caja 1 Expedientes Personales
1787–1861, José Borrás y Corro; AGI IG 1858J)
Still employed 1834 (*Guía general de forasteros de Sevilla para el año de
1834* [Seville: Imprenta García, 1834], 133)
Transfers elsewhere 5 October 1840 (AGI Caja 1 Expedientes Personales
1787–1861, José Borrás y Corro; AHN Ultramar 2430 exp. 35; AHN
Ultramar 2430 exp. 2)

Carlos Botero (9)
Soldado from January 1807 to December 1809 (?) (AGI IG 1857A)

Andrés María Bustos y Martínez (10)
Archivero starting 30 December 1800 (AGI IG 1858J)
Dies 13 August 1809 (AGI IG 1858H)

Juan Carrera (11)
Soldado from January 1801 to December 1807 (AGI IG 1856)

Juan Agustín Ceán Bermúdez (12)
Comisionado for first time from 30 December 1790 (AGI IG 1854A)
to 16 January 1798 (AGI IG 1858H), when he returns to Madrid (see
chapter 2)
Comisionado for second time from 18 June 1801 to May 1808 (AGI IG
1858H), when he returns to Madrid (see chapter 2)

Ventura Collar y Castro (13)
Oficial 2 starting 29 August 1785 (AGI IG 1853, 1854A)
Oficial 1 starting 4 April 1800 (AGI IG 1858H)
Archivero starting 10 March 1819 (AGI IG 1857B)
Dies March 1825 (AGI IG 1858J)

Joséf Delgado (14)
Soldado from January 1814 to December 1814 (AGI IG 1857A)

Miguel Escola (15)
Soldado from January 1817 to December 1819 (AGI IG 1857B)

Gregorio de Fuentes y Beraert (16)
Archivero starting 29 August 1785 (AGI IG 1853, 1854A)
Dies July 1789 (AGI IG 1858H)

Francisco García (17)
Mozo starting 1 February 1820 (AGI Caja 1 Expedientes Personales
1787–1861, Francisco García; AGI IG 1858J)
Portero starting 30 December 1828 (AGI IG 1858J)
Still employed as *portero* 10 August 1841 (testament of José de la
Higuera y Lara, AHPS Protocolos 870, fol. 597r)
Dies 19 August 1843 (AGI Caja 1 Expedientes Personales 1787–1861,
Francisco García; see also AHN Ultramar 2430 exp. 2)

Manuel García (18)
Mozo interino starting 1 January to 24 February 1801 (AGI IG 1856)
After the previous *mozo* (Gerónimo Valbuena) died on 8 October
1800, an unnamed *mozo interino* (perhaps referring to Manuel García)
appears in accounts for October, November, and December 1800
(AGI IG 1858H)

Francisco Giovale (19)
Soldado from January 1816 to December 1816 (AGI IG 1857B)

Juan González (20)
Soldado from January 1815 to December 1815 (AGI IG 1857A)

Antonio González León (21)
Oficial Supernumerario from 26 April 1787 (AGI IG 1854A)
Transferred to become *Contador de Tabacos de las Reales Fabricas,*
10 December 1798 (AGI IG 1858H)

Miguel Grasalia (22)
Soldado from December 1824 to December 1825 (AGI IG 1858J)

Aniceto de la Higuera (23)
Nephew of José de la Higuera y Lara, archival employee from 26 April
1787 (*Oficial 4*) to 10 January 1844 (*Archivero*)
Archivero from 11 January 1844 to 1868 (AHN Ultramar 1637 exp. 25;
AHN Ultramar 2430 exp. 2; AHN Ultramar 2431 exp. 51; Manuel
Gómez Zarzuela, *Guia de Sevilla, su provincia, arzobispado, capitanía
general, audiencia territorial y distrito universitario, para 1868* [Seville:
Establecimento Tipográfico de Andalucía, 1868], 275)

FROM ARCHIVISTS TO SOLDIERS 253

José de la Higuera y Lara (24)

Nephew of Antonio de Lara y Zúñiga, the *Superintendente Director del Archivo* (29 August 1785 to 1 February 1791; relation described in letter from Lara to Antonio Porlier, 17 October 1787; and letter from Manuel Zuazo, Pedro Navarro, Ventura Collar y Castro, and Francisco Ortiz de Solorzano to Antonio Porlier, 11 October 1788 (both in AGI IG 1854A)

Oficial 4 starting 26 April 1787 (AGI IG 1853, AGI IG 1854A)

Oficial 3 starting July 1797 (AGI IG 1858H) [account book does not specify day but mentions royal order of promotion]

Oficial 2 starting 4 April 1800 (AGI IG 1858H)

Oficial 1 starting 10 March 1819 (AGI IG 1857B)

Archivero starting 1 May 1825 (AGI IG 1857B, AGI IG 1858J)

Still working as archivist 1834 (José María Montero de Espinosa, *Guía general de forasteros de Sevilla para el año de 1834,* 133)

Retires 10 January 1844 (AHN Ultramar 2430 exp. 2)

Dies 11 April 1844 (AMS Registro Civil Defunciones 1844 Lib. 12, fol. 142r)

Diego Juárez (25)

Before being hired by the archive, Juárez had worked with Juan Bautista Muñoz for fifteen years, starting in 1781 (AGI IG 1857A)

Escribiente starting 13 June 1796 (AGI IG 1858H)

Oficial 4 starting July 1797 (AGI IG 1858H)

Oficial 3 starting 4 April 1800 (AGI IG 1858H)

Oficial 2 starting 10 March 1819 (AGI IG 1857B)

Dies 1 April 1821 (AGI IG 1857B, 1858J)

Domingo Laviña (26)

Mozo starting 25 February 1801 (AGI IG 1858H)

Dies 17 January 1804 (AGI IG 1858H)

Antonio Lorenzo (27)

Mozo starting 6 March 1804 (AGI IG 1858H)

Portero from 1 February 1820 (AGI IG 1858J)

Dies 24 October 1828 (AGI IG 1858J)

Bernardo Losada (28)

Oficial 4 starting 14 December 1809 (AGI IG 1858H)

Transferred to Contaduría de Crédito Público, 17 June 1818 (AGI IG 1857B)

Francisco Martínez (29)

Soldado from January 1826 to December 1826 (AGI IG 1858J)

José Martínez (30)

Soldado from January 1828 to December 1828 (AGI IG 1858J)

Ángel Merlo (31)

Soldado from July 1822 to December 1832 (AGI IG 1858J, 1857B)

José Mila (32)

Soldado from January 1829 to December 1832 (AGI IG 1858J)

Antonio Moreno (33)

Oficial 4 starting 7 March 1809 (AGI IG 1858H)

No longer employed (?) after 30 September 1809 (AGI IG 1858H)

Domingo Moreno (34)

Soldado from January 1820 to June 1822 (AGI IG 1858J, 1857B)

Juan Alonso Morgado (35)

Mozo starting 30 December 1828 (AGI Caja 1 Expedientes Personales 1787–1861, Francisco García; AGI IG 1858J)

Still employed as *mozo* 10 August 1841 (testament of José de la Higuera y Lara, AHPS Protocolos 870, fol. 597r)

Portero starting 3 October 1843 (AGI Caja 1 Expedientes Personales 1787–1861, Francisco García)

Still employed as *portero* 1866 (Manuel Gómez Zarzuela, *Guía de Sevilla: Su provincia, arzobispado, capitanía general, Tercio Naval, audiencia territorial, y distrito Universitario; Para 1866* [Seville: La Andalucía, 1866], 183)

Pedro Navarro (36)

Oficial Supernumerario starting 26 April 1787 (AGI IG 1854A)

Dies 13 October 1800, plague year (AGI IG 1858H)

Francisco Ortiz de Solorzano (37)

Commissioned on 11 October 1778, along with Juan de Echevarría, to order and index New World documents in the Archive of Simancas; he worked in Simancas until late September 1785, when he escorted one convoy of those documents from Simancas to Seville, arriving 14 October (AGI IG 1852)

Oficial 3 starting 29 August 1785 (AGI IG 1853, 1854A)

Dies 15 April 1797 (AGI IG 1858H)

Francisco de Paula Juárez y Rosales (38)

Son of Diego Juárez, archival employee from 13 June 1796 (*escribiente*) to 1 April 1821 (*Oficial 2*) (AGI IG 1857B, letter from Juárez 21 Sept 1814)

Oficial Meritorio starting 1 December 1814 (AGI IG 1857B)

Oficial 3 starting 20 April 1821 (AGI IG 1858J; see also AGI IG 1857B)

Oficial 2 starting May 1825 (AGI IG 1858J)

Oficial 1 starting 1 August 1829 (AGI IG 1858J)

Still employed 1834 (*Guía general de forasteros de Sevilla para el año de 1834,* 133)

Still employed 10 August 1841 (testament of José de la Higuera y Lara, AHPS Protocolos 870, fols. 595r, 597r)

Still employed 1866 (Manuel Gómez Zarzuela, *Guía de Sevilla…para 1866,* 183)

Archivero starting 30 November 1868 through 1884 (AHN Ultramar 2431 exp. 51; Manuel Gómez Zarzuela, *Guía de Sevilla, su provincia, &c para 1884* [Seville: Imprenta y Litografía de José María Ariza, 1884], 303)

Dies 18 July 1884 (AHN Ultramar 2431 exp. 51)

Luis Pérez Andrés (39)

Oficial 5 starting 1 March 1815 (AGI IG 1857A)

Oficial 4 starting 1 January 1819 (AGI IG 1857B)
Oficial 3 starting 10 March 1819 (AGI IG 1857B)
Oficial 2 starting 20 April 1821 (AGI IG 1858J; see also AGI IG 1857B)
Oficial 1 starting 1 May 1825 (AGI IG 1858J)
Dies 31 July 1829 (AGI IG 1857B)

Pedro Reales y Colarte (40)
Archivero starting January 1790 (AGI IG 1858H)
Dies 22 September 1800, plague year (AGI IG 1858J)

Francisco Ruiz (41)
Soldado from January 1819 to December 1819 (AGI IG 1857B)

José Ruser (42)
Soldado from January 1801 to December 1804 (AGI IG 1856)

Agustín Sánchez (43)
Soldado from January 1827 to December 1827 (AGI IG 1858J)

Antonio Sánchez (44)
Soldado from January 1816 to December 1816 (AGI IG 1857B)

Manuel Agustín Sánchez (45)
Portero starting 9 August 1792 (AGI IG 1858H)
Dies 13 January 1820 (AGI IG 1857B, 1858J)

José Sánchez Janer (46)
Oficial 2 starting 20 October 1840 (AGI Caja 1 Expedientes Personales 1787–1861, José Sánchez Janer; AHN Ultramar 2430 exp. 35)
Transfers elsewhere 31 January 1866 (AHN Ultramar 2430 exp. 35)

Luis Vicente Sedó (47)
Oficial Supernumerario starting 26 April 1787 (AGI IG 1854A)
Dies 13 July 1801 (AGI IG 1858H)

Pedro Suviranes (48)
Soldado from January 1817 to December 1818 (AGI IG 1857B)

Antonio Tariego y Somoza (49)
Comisionado starting 29 April 1799 to 18 April 1809 (AGI IG 1858H)

Gerónimo Valbuena (50)
Mozo starting 28 November 1792 (AGI IG 1858H)
Dies 8 October 1800 (AGI IG 1858H)

Manuel Valbuena (51)
Archivero starting 14 August 1809 (AGI IG 1858H, 1857B)
Retires 9 March 1819 (AGI IG 1857B)

Hipólito de la Vega (52)
Commissioned in the fall of 1780 to work as a scribal assistant to Francisco Ortiz de Solorzano in the Archive of Simancas sorting-and-indexing project; he also worked in Simancas until late September 1785, when he escorted one convoy of New World documents from Simancas to Seville, arriving 14 October (AGI IG 1852)
Oficial 4 starting 29 August 1785 (AGI IG 1853, 1854A)
Transferred to Secretaría del Despacho Universal, 2 May 1787 (AGI IG 1853)

Antonio Zenobrio (53)
Soldado from January 1809 to December 1814 (AGI IG 1857A)

Manuel de Zuazo y Yañez (54)
Previously archivist of the House of Trade, Seville; his father, Joséph de Zuazo y Castillo, was also a House of Trade employee (AHPC caja 10796 no. 16)
Oficial 1 starting 29 August 1785 (AGI IG 1853, 1854A)
Dies 3 April 1800, plague year (AGI IG 1858H)

APPENDIX C
PARASOLS, SHIELDS, BUTTERFLY: THE DOCUMENT CASE METOPES OF THE ARCHIVE OF THE INDIES, 1786-88

The carved mahogany metopes that crown the document cases of the Archive of the Indies have never been systematically documented in either words or images. The following descriptions are organized by gallery and then by case number. Metope designs are listed from the viewer's left to right. See also figs. 1.9–1.22.

THE MAIN GALLERIES

Eastern gallery, interior wall, cases 1–13

Corner panel: Crossed spears and crescent shield (facing left).

[Stone pilaster]

1: Feather headdress (profile, facing right). Crossed spears and round shield. Torso. Cuirass with feather skirt. Round shield with hanging feathers.

2: Crossed axes and helmet (facing left). Crossed quivers. Crossed spears and crescent shield (facing right). Parasol (tilted right). Round shield with hanging feathers.

[Stone pilaster]

3: Crossed axe and quiver. Ship. Crossed arrows and round shield. Drum.

4: Crossed quivers. Parasol (upright). Feather headdress (profile, facing left). Two worlds.

5: Crossed swords and octagonal shield. Crossed arrow and quiver. Two worlds. Parasol (upright).

6: Crossed spears and crescent shield (facing right). Crossed arrows and irregular shield. Feather headdress (frontal). Crossed arrows and round shield.

7 [Door]: Cuirass with feather skirt. Crossed arrows and oval shield. Hat (tilted right). Crossed arrow and bow. Crossed arrow and fasces.

8: Hunting horn. Crossed arrows and petal shield. Crossed arrows and crescent shield (facing down). Crossed spears and octagonal shield.

9: Ship. Crossed arrows and helmet (facing left). Ship. Helmet (facing right).

10: Crown on pillow. Crossed arrows and octagonal shield with helmet (facing left). Ship. Crossed arrow and quiver.

11: Feather headdress (frontal). Crossed arrows and round shield. Pillars of Hercules. Round shield with hanging feathers (upside down).

[Stone pilaster]

12: Crossed spear and fasces. Cuirass with feather skirt. Feather headdress (frontal). Crossed spears. Crossed quivers and round shield.

13: Crossed arrows and round shield. Parasol (upright). Round shield with hanging feathers. Cuirass with feather skirt. Crossed fasces and spear.

[Stone pilaster]

Corner panel: Crossed spears and round shield.

[Interior corner, pointing to northeast]

Northern gallery, interior wall, cases 14–26

Corner panel: Crossed spear and quiver.

[Stone pilaster]

14: Feather headdress (frontal). Crossed arrows and round shield. Crossed arrow and fasces. Crossed quiver and spear. Drum.

15: Cuirass with feather skirt. Crossed bow and arrow. Feather headdress (profile, facing left). Crossed arrows and oval shield. Round shield with hanging feathers.

[Stone pilaster]

16: Crossed spears and round shield. Crossed arrows and crescent shield (facing left). Crossed arrows and helmet (facing left). Crossed bow and arrow.

256

17: Crossed arrows and octagonal shield. Crossed arrow and fasces. Parasol (tilted left). Crossed axes.

18: Feather headdress (frontal). Crossed bow and arrow. Crossed arrows and oval shield. Crossed arrow and quiver.

19: Torso. Feather headdress (frontal). Crossed arrow and quiver. Crossed arrows and crescent shield (facing left).

20 [Door]: Crossed quivers. Crossed spear and fasces. Crossed arrows and crescent shield (facing down). Crossed spear and quiver. Crossed spears and cuirass with feather skirt.

21: Crossed bow and arrow. Crossed spears and crescent shield (facing left). Feather headdress (profile, facing left). Crossed spear and quiver.

22: Crossed arrows and round shield. Cuirass with feather skirt. Crossed swords and oval shield. Crossed spears and round shield.

23: Crossed arrow and bow. Ship. Crossed arrows and octagonal shield. Crossed spears and oval shield (facing left).

24: Crossed arrow and quiver. Crossed spears and octagonal shield. Crossed arrow and fasces. Crossed quivers.

[Stone pilaster]

25: Hat (tilted left). Crossed spear and quiver. Helmet (facing right). Crossed arrow and quiver.

26: Two worlds with crown. Crossed quiver and spear. Crossed swords and oval shield. Ship.

[Interior corner, pointing to southwest]

Northern gallery, western wall, cases 27–28

27: Crossed quiver and spear. Parasol (upright). Crossed axe and quiver. Side panel: Parasol (tilted left).

[Door]

28: Crossed spears and round shield. Torso. Round shield with hanging feathers. Side panel: Crossed spears and oval shield.

[Exterior corner, pointing to northwest]

Northern gallery, exterior wall, cases 29–40

29: Crossed spears and crescent shield (facing left).

Window: Ship. Crossed arrows and octagonal shield. Feather headdress (frontal). Torso.

30: Ship. Crossed spears and octagonal shield. Crossed arrows and crescent shield (facing left).

[Stone pilaster]

31: Hat (tilted left). Crossed arrow and quiver.

Window: Crossed arrows. Cuirass with feather skirt. Crossed spears and round shield. Feather headdress (frontal).

32: Crossed spears and oval shield (facing left). Feather headdress (frontal). Crossed spears and oval shield. Crossed arrows and octagonal shield.

Window: Crossed arrows and round shield. Feather headdress (frontal). Ship. Crossed arrows and feather headdress (profile, facing left).

33: Crossed spears and round shield. Feather headdress (frontal). Round shield with hanging feathers. Crossed spears with crescent shield (facing up).

Window: Helmet (facing right). Feather headdress (frontal). Hat (upright). Cuirass with feather skirt.

34: Ship. Hat (tilted left). Parasol (upright). Round shield with hanging feathers.

Window: Cuirass. Crossed spears and octagonal shield. Round shield with hanging feathers. Two worlds with crown.

35: Crossed arrow and fasces. Crossed axes. Helmet (facing right). Feather headdress (frontal).

Window: Crossed bow and arrow. Crossed spears and octagonal shield. Two worlds with crown. Torso.

36: Drum. Parasol (upright).

[Stone pilaster]

37: Crossed arrows and octagonal shield. Crossed arrows and octagonal shield. Feather headdress (frontal).

Window: Crossed arrows and round shield. Torso. Crossed arrows and round shield. Crossed arrows and octagonal shield.

38: Crossed spear and fasces. Feather headdress (frontal). Crossed arrows.

[Stone pilaster]

39: Cuirass with feather skirt. Crossed arrows with crescent shield (facing left).

Window: Crossed bow and arrow. Round shield with hanging feathers. Crossed arrows and oval shield. Arrow and bow (upright).

40: Feather headdress (profile, facing left). Cuirass with feather skirt. Helmet (facing left). Feather headdress (frontal).

Window: Crossed quiver and spear. Crossed arrow and fasces. Crossed bow and arrow. Crossed arrows and oval shield.

[Exterior corner, pointing to northeast]

Eastern gallery, exterior wall, cases 41–54

Window: Crossed arrows and octagonal shield. Ship. Crossed swords and round shield. Crossed arrows and cuirass with feather skirt.

41: Crossed bow and quiver. Crossed bow and arrow. Crossed arrows and oval shield. Feather headdress (frontal).

Window: Crossed bow and arrow. Crossed spears and octagonal shield. Crossed arrows and crescent shield (facing up). Parasol (upright).

42: Crossed spears. Crossed arrows and octagonal shield.

[Stone pilaster]

43: Torso. Crossed arrow and fasces. Feather headdress (frontal).

Window: Crossed bow and arrow. Crossed arrows and oval shield. Crossed arrows and oval shield. Crossed quivers.

44: Feather headdress (frontal). Crossed spears and round shield. Crossed spears and crescent shield (facing left).

[Stone pilaster]

45: Cuirass with feather skirt. Ship.

Window: Crossed arrow and quiver. Hat (tilted left and upside down). Crossed arrows and oval shield. Pillars of Hercules.

46: Feather headdress (profile, facing left). Arrow and bow (upright). Parasol (upright). Crossed quiver and arrow.

Window: Crossed spears and octagonal shield. Crossed arrows and round shield. Feather headdress (frontal). Crossed arrows and octagonal shield.

47: Crossed arrow and bow. Crossed arrow and fasces. Crossed bow and arrow. Pillars of Hercules.

Window: Crossed spears and octagonal shield. Feather headdress (frontal). Crossed arrow and quiver. Two worlds.

48: Round shield with hanging feathers (upside down). Crossed arrows and round shield. Crossed arrow and quiver. Crossed axe and quiver.

Window: Feather headdress (frontal). Crossed spears and crescent shield (facing left). Drum. Parasol (upright).

49: Crossed swords and octagonal shield. Crossed arrows and irregular shield. Parasol (upright). Crossed arrows and round shield.

Window: Crossed quivers. Ship. Two worlds with crown. Crossed arrows and round shield.

50: Feather headdress (profile, facing left). Feather headdress (frontal).

[Stone pilaster]

51: Torso. Crossed arrow and quiver. Crossed swords and octagonal shield.

Window: Hat (tilted left). Crossed spears and octagonal shield. Round shield with hanging feathers. Parasol (upright).

52: Crossed arrows and round shield. Crossed swords and round shield. Feather headdress (profile, facing left).

[Stone pilaster]

53: Feather headdress (frontal). Crossed arrows.

Window: Crossed spears and octagonal shield. Crossed arrow and quiver. Spear and cuirass. Ship.

54: Torso. Crossed spears and octagonal shield. Cuirass. Two worlds.

Window: Ship. Crossed arrow and quiver. Crossed bow and arrow. Round shield with hanging feathers.

[Exterior corner, pointing to southeast]

Southern gallery, exterior wall, cases 55–66

Window: Cuirass with feather skirt. Feather headdress (profile, facing left). Parasol (upright). Round shield with hanging feathers.

55: Crossed arrows and octagonal shield. Crossed spear and fasces. Crossed arrows and round shield. Helmet (frontal).

Window: Ship. Round shield with hanging feathers. Helmet (facing left). Pillars of Hercules.

56: Crossed arrows. Crossed spears and crescent shield (facing left).

[Stone pilaster]

57: Feather headdress (frontal). Arrow and bow (upright). Crossed quivers.

Window: Parasol (tilted right). Feather headdress (frontal). Crossed arrows and oval shield. Crossed swords and heart-shaped shield.

58: Crossed spears and crescent shield (facing left). Cuirass with feather skirt. Crossed quiver and axe.

[Stone pilaster]

59: Feather headdress (frontal). Drum.

Window: Crossed spears and oval shield (facing right). Crossed spears. Crossed arrow and quiver. Crossed arrows and octagonal shield.

60: Crossed bow and quiver. Crossed swords and octagonal shield. Feather headdress (frontal). Crossed swords.

Window: Arrow and bow (upright). Pillars of Hercules. Two worlds. Parasol (upright).

61: Crossed spears and cuirass. Crossed bow and spear. Cuirass with feather skirt. Crossed spear and fasces.

Window: Crossed arrows with crescent shield (facing left). Crossed arrows and helmet (facing left). Crossed quivers. Crossed arrows and round shield with hanging feathers.

62: Cuirass with feather skirt. Ship. Crossed arrows and round shield. Crossed spears and crescent shield (facing left).

Window: Feather headdress (profile, facing right). Crossed spears and octagonal shield. Crossed spears and irregular shield. Crossed arrow and bow.

63: Torso. Crossed spears and round shield. Crossed quivers. Cuirass with feather skirt.

Window: Torso. Crossed arrows. Crossed arrows and oval shield. Crossed spears and round shield.

64: Round shield with hanging feathers. Feather headdress (frontal).

[Stone pilaster]

65: Crossed quivers and feather headdress (profile, facing left). Ship. Crossed swords and octagonal shield.

Window: Feather headdress (frontal). Crossed quivers and round shield. Crossed arrows and crescent shield (facing down). Crossed sword and arrow and drum.

66: Ship.

[Exterior corner, pointing to southwest]

Southern gallery, western wall, cases 67–68

67: Crossed bow and arrow. Crossed bow and axe with cuirass. Crossed bow and quiver. Side panel: Crossed arrow and quiver.

[Door]

68: Crossed arrow and quiver. Crossed swords and octagonal shield. Crossed bow and arrow. Side panel: Arrow and feather headdress (profile, facing left).

[Interior corner, pointing to northwest]

Southern gallery, interior wall, cases 69–81

69: Ship. Drum. Crossed arrows and crescent shield (facing down). Crossed arrows and cuirass.

70: Feather headdress (profile, facing left). Crossed quivers. Crossed arrows and helmet (facing left). Crossed quivers and round shield.

[Stone pilaster]

71: Crossed arrows and irregular shield. Parasol (upright). Ship. Cuirass with feather skirt.

72: Crossed bow and arrow. Spear and crescent shield (facing right). Crossed swords and octagonal shield. Parasol (tilted left).

73: Butterfly. Torso. Feather headdress (profile, facing left). Cuirass with feather skirt.

74: Crossed arrows and crescent shield (facing up). Crossed quivers. Feather headdress (profile, facing left). Round shield with hanging feathers.

75 [Door]: Mask. Crossed arrows and round shield. Crossed arrows and crescent shield (facing down). Crossed arrows and helmet (facing left). Crossed arrows and cuirass.

76: Crossed swords and octagonal shield. Crossed arrows and round shield. Crossed arrow and bow. Crossed bow and quiver.

77: Feather headdress (frontal). Hunting horn. Crossed arrows and round shield. Ship.

78: Octagonal shield and fasces. Crossed spears and round shield. Round shield with hanging feathers. Torso.

79: Crossed sword and fasces. Round shield with hanging feathers. Crossed bow and arrow. Crossed bow and quiver.

[Stone pilaster]

80: Crossed arrow and quiver. Crossed spear and fasces. Parasol (tilted left). Ship. Helmet (frontal).

81: Two worlds. Cuirass with feather skirt. Parasol (tilted right). Feather headdress (frontal). Parasol (upright).

[Stone pilaster]

Corner panel: Crossed swords and round shield.

[Interior corner, pointing to southeast]

ROYAL PATRONAGE ROOM

Western case: Crossed arrow and quiver. Ship. Crossed spear and fasces. Crossed arrows and oval shield.

Eastern case: Feather headdress (frontal). Crossed arrows and crescent shield (facing up). Crossed arrows and feather headdress (facing left). Crossed bow and arrow.

ILLUSTRATION CREDITS

The following sources have granted permission to reproduce illustrations in this volume.

Figure P.1. Archivo ABC, Reference Number 5708678.

Figure P.2. © ICAS-SAHP Fototeca Municipal de Sevilla, Fondo Sánchez del Pando, Signatura sp4_pu-vi_sf_047.

Figures P.3, 1.5. Photo by the author, May 2016.

Figure P.4. Erich Lessing / Art Resource, NY.

Figure P.5. Museo de la Real Academia de Bellas Artes de San Fernando, Madrid.

Figures I.1–I.13, 1.8, 1.25, 1.29, 1.30, 2.3–2.6, 2.12, 3.2–3.5, 3.8–3.10, 4.1–4.4, 4.20–4.23. Spain – Ministerio de Educación, Cultura y Deporte.

Figure I.14. © The Board of Trustees of the Science Museum, London.

Figure 1.1. © ICAS-SAHP Fototeca Municipal de Sevilla, Fondo Sánchez del Pando, Signatura sp4_pu-vi_sf_049.

Figure 1.2. Photo by the author, July 2017.

Figure 1.3. © ICAS-SAHP Fototeca Municipal de Sevilla, Fondo Serrano, Signatura se16_e-c2_sf_008.

Figures 1.4, 1.23, 3.6. Getty Research Institute.

Figures 1.6, 1.7. Photo by the author, June 2017.

Figures 1.9–1.22, 1.24, 2.26, 5.2. Photo by the author, November 2016.

Figure 1.26. © ICAS-SAHP Fototeca Municipal de Sevilla, Fondo Serrano, Signatura se16_e-c2_sf_009.

Figure 1.27. Plan by the author.

Figures 1.28, 2.7, 2.8, 2.13–2.15, 2.17–2.20. Biblioteca Nacional de España, Madrid.

Figures 1.31–1.33. University of California, Berkeley, Bancroft Library.

Figure 2.1. Photo by the author, July 2017.

Figure 2.2. Museo de Historia de Madrid.

Figure 2.9. Reconstruction by the author.

Figures 2.10, 2.11. Photo by the author, July 2019.

Figure 2.16. Archivo ABC, Reference Number 4482994.

Figure 2.21. Archivo General del Palacio Real, Madid.

Figures 2.22, 2.23. © Real Academia de la Historia. España.

Figure 2.24. Biblioteca Nacional de España, Madrid.

Figure 2.25. Photo by the author, December 2015.

Figures 3.1, 3.7, 4.5, 4.11. Collection of the author.

Figure 3.11. University of Connecticut, Dodd Research Library.

Figure 3.12. Diagram by the author.

Figure 4.6. © Bilboko Arte Ederren Museoa – Museo de Bellas Artes de Bilbao.

Figure 4.7. Map from Archivo General de la Villa de Madrid, Signatura 10-204-17.

Figure 4.8. London, The John Murray Collection.

Figures 4.9, 4.10, 4.12–4.19. Ministry of Defense. Madrid, Naval Museum.

Figure 5.1. © The Metropolitan Museum of Art.

Figure E.1. Courtesy of The Hispanic Society of America, New York.

Tables 3.1, 4.1, E.1. Created by the author.

ABOUT THE AUTHOR

Byron Ellsworth Hamann's research is focused on the art and writing of pre-Hispanic Mesoamerica, as well as on the connections linking the Americas and Europe in the early modern Mediterratlantic world. His work explores the histories of globalizations, archaeologies, commodity circulation, landscape interpretation, the nature of writing, methods of archival research, processes of religious conflict and toleration in sixteenth-century Christian-Muslim and Christian-Native American contexts, and the legacies of the antique Mediterranean in early modern Latin America. Hamann is an editor of *Grey Room* (www.greyroom.org); codirector (with Liza Bakewell) of Mesolore (www.mesolore.org); and author of *Bad Christians, New Spains: Muslims, Catholics, and Native Americans in a Mediterratlantic World* (2020) and *The Translations of Nebrija: Language, Culture, and Circulation in the Early Modern World* (2015).

INDEX

Note: page numbers in italics refer to figures or tables. Those followed by n refer to notes, with note number.

account books and receipts for AGI, location of, 251

Accounting (Contaduría) department of Council of the Indies (Madrid)
documents in AGI from (cases #1–11), 52–57, *53;* as first shelved and first indexed, 52, 125; number of chests of documents, 52, 63
types of documents in, 55–57

Acevedo Villaroel, José, 58, *244–45,* 253

aesthetic of simplicity
association with masculine virtue and economy, 138–40
and design of AGI document cases, 143
in Muñoz and Maestre plan for Lonja building, 135–38
and revival of interest in Herrera, 140

AGI. *See* General Archive of the Indies

Alva, Duke of, stipend request, 167, 218n15

America, invention of, vii, xivn3

American War of the Thirteen Colonies
and emergence of "colonial" as term, 229
impact on AGI creation, x, 21, 207
impact on Spain, 21, xvn13

Americas as separate land
creation of Archive of the Indies as indication of, x, 228, 236
imagining of, in late 18th century, viii
and Spanish government councils, 102

architecture, mechanics of function, 6–9

architectures of place and knowledge, vii

archives
archival turn refocusing on, 3
metaphoric overextension in scholarship, 2–3
scholarship on, 3–4, 29–30n21, 29n19

Archivo General de Indias. *See* General Archive of the Indies

Basterrechea, Joséph de, 198, 200, 204, 205, *205,* 212, 214

bears, 138

Beaumarchais, Pierre-Augustin Caron de, x

Benjamin, Walter, 152–53

Bentham, Jeremy, 7–9

Betis. See Real Fernandino [Betis] (steamboat)

Black Legend critiques of Spain, x, 12

Bonaparte, Joseph, as king of Spain, 60, 61, 182, 221n75, 251

Borcht, Sebastian van der, *104,* 105

Bourbons
move of council offices from royal palace, 77
move of House of Trade to Cádiz, 57, 103, 108
transfer of Habsburg archives to Simancas, 78, 90–91

Briarly, Alexandro, 179, 180

Brosses, Charles de, 11–12, 15

Brunel, Antoine de, 76–78

Buffon, Georges-Louis Leclerc, Comte de, 11–12, 15, 25–26, 227, 236

Burke, Edmund, 10, 236

Bustos y Martínez, Andrés María, 171–73, *244–45,* 253

Cabarrús, Francisco de, 55, 63

Cádiz, *54*
distinctive architecture of, 112
evacuation of AGI documents to, during French occupation of Seville, 60, 182, 221n75
map of (1811), 108, *109*
wooden model of, 109, *110, 111*
See also House of Trade, Cádiz offices and archives

cafés, 109, 122n122

Carazas, Félix, 125–28, 130, 139

Carlos III (King of Spain)
and AGI, approval of plan for, viii, 21, 22, 34n105, 74
and gate added to AGI, 39
and Library of Naval Science (Isla de León), 198
and Muñoz's *Historia del Nuevo-Mundo,* 21, 73
and remodeling of Lonja building, 125, 130, 139
removal of Royal Academy of History's authority to write chronicles of Americas, 15–16, 21
and Robertson's *History of America,* 15–16
and widow of Francisco Manjón, 123n131

Carlos IV (king of Spain), 182, 222n107

Carlos V (Holy Roman Emperor), and Simancas archive, 88–89, 99–100, 101, 102

cases. *See* document cases (AGI)

cats, archival, 251

Ceán Bermúdez, Juan Agustín
as AGI archival commissioner, 128, *244–45,* 253
and AGI document requests, 221n74
at AGI during Ticknor's visit, 37, 43, 44, 67n5
biography of Herrera by, 37, 67n5

career of, 55, 58, 63

cataloging of AGI collection, 55, 128

and Cervantes documents in AGI, 181–82

and *Colecciones de Simancas* documents, distribution within AGI collection, 211, 214, 215–16

departure from AGI, 58

Diccionario histórico by, 58

Goya's visit to, 58

indexing of AGI documents, 44, 52, 54–55, 58, 63, 212, 248

monthly reports on indexing progress, 218n18, 225n179

order of original collections and, 248

period of residence in Seville, 55

reports on AGI research requests, 168–69

and Royal Patronage room, addition of documents to, 211, 214, 215–16, 225n179

schematic of cases #1–11 (Contaduría), 54, *56*

cedar, 132–33, 139–40, 144, 147

Cervantes Saavedra, Miguel, 61–62, 181–82

Cintora, Lucas, and trade exchange (Lonja) building
controversy over renovation of, 149–50, *150*
decision to create three galleries, *148,* 149
evaluation as site for AGI, 128
renovation of, 39, 67n10, 125–28, 130, 139, 147

Coelho, Francisco Manuel, 105, *106, 107*

Colecciones de Simancas
attribution of, 224n174
documents recorded in: arrival at AGI, 210; distribution within AGI collection, 211, 214, 215–17; Muñoz subcollection in, 212, 225n182
location in AGI, 207
and Navarrete project: copying of, by collection and month, *211,* 211–13; document numbers *vs. Colecciones',* 207–10, *208–9*
organization of, 207–10

Collar y Castro, Ventura, 63, *64,* 170, 243, *244–45,* 253

Colón, Cristóbal. *See* Columbus, Christopher

Colón, Diego, 177–78, 194

Colón, Fernando, 194

Colón, José, 177–78

colonial Americas
vs. colonies in Americas, 1–2
comparative study of practices, 2, 27–28n9
invention of, viii, 1–2, 24–26, 227–28

colonial/colonialism/colonization, as terms
databases on, 228–29

262

introduction of, 2, 24, 227–32, *230*
colonial period, as retrospective term, 228, 232–35, 236
Columbus, Christopher, 23, 51, 61, 62
Company for Navigation of the Guadalquivir, 179–80
Council of the Indies (Consejo de Indias, Madrid)
  and AGI, establishment of, 16
  building housing, 74, *75*
  documents sent to AGI, 73, 125
  and indexing of archives, 16, 33n99
  Muñoz's research in, 73, 74, 86–87
  offices at Palace of the Councils, 81, *83,* 84–87, 116n34
  other councils sharing building with, 74
  requests for AGI documents, 167
  and Spanish councils as institutional complex, 74–75
  See also Justice (Justicia), legal proceedings from Council of the Indies
councils of Spain
  council system, history of, 75, 77
  decreased number of, by early 18th century, 77
  founding dates of, 76, 114–15n18
  general and territorial types, in early 17th century, 76
  as indivisible whole, 74–75
  move from royal palace under Bourbons, 77–78
  office locations, early 18th century, 77–78
  offices in Madrid's royal palace, in 16th century, 76–77
  reorganization of 1718, 75
  typical functions of, 75

data
  and data fetishism, 163n89
  first appearances of term, 5
  metadata records, 5, *5*
data of the AGI, 4–9
  bundles of documents: labels on, 5–6, *7,* 43–44, 68n22, 153, *214, 215;* metadata indicating archive of origin, 163n89; paper used to wrap, 71n63
  cover sheets summarizing document contents, 5, *5*
  document folders summarizing contents, 5, *6*
  Documentos de Data receipt packet, *4,* 5
  explicit identification as data, *4,* 5, 30n27
  as metadata-tagged database, 5, 153
  similarities to architecture of digital data storage, 4–5
  system structuring, 4–6, *4–8*
  three-part number of each document, 52, 154, 173–74; broader thematic information given by, 156; grid created by, 154–56, *155*
  See also index (*Índice*) volumes; inventory (*Inventario*) volumes; wall-system shelving
data retrieval in AGI first decades
  available evidence on, 165

embodied knowledge of staff and, 167, 243–47; replacement with paper finding aids, 243–48
  for government agencies, 167–71
  for individuals, 171–78; general requests about family information, 177–78; royal permission required for, 166, 172, 173, 174, 177, 178, 182, 219nn33–34
  Ordenanzas on, 165–67
  for scholarship, 178–82
Díaz y Herrero, Francisco Antonio, 171–72
Digueri, Vicente Ignacio Imperial, *196, 197*
Dispute of the New World, 9–15
  Buffon's *Histoire naturelle* and, 10–12
  common references used by works on, 15
  creation of Archive of the Indies and, x, 10, 15
  critiques of, 15
  Muñoz's *Historia del Nuevo-Mundo* as response to, 73
  and new longitude model of Earth, 25–26
  notable contemporaneous events, 24
  Pauw's *Recherches philosophiques* and, 12–13
  Raynal's *Histoire philosophique et politique* and, 13–14
  Robertson's *History of America* and, 14–15, 73
document cases (AGI), *44*
  building and installation of, *126–27,* 151, 157n4
  decorative frieze above, 44–47, *45–47,* 146–47; metopes on, 256–59
  design of, *126,* 131–32, *132,* 135–37, 139–40; and aesthetic of simplicity, 143; influence of Herrera's Escorial monastery-palace library on, 140–46, *142, 143,* 152; three phases of, 125, *126,* 140–44, *143–45*
  number of, 47
  numbers on, *47,* 47–51
  and wall-system shelving, 152
  wood used for, 43, 139–40, 144, 161n54
document cases #1–11 (Contaduría), 52–57, *53*
  as documents from Accounting department of Council of the Indies (Madrid), 52
  as first shelved and first indexed, 52
  indexing of cases #1–11, 54–55
  schematic of cases #1–11 (1791–92), 54, *56*
  types of documents in, 55–57
document cases #12–46 (Contratación), *53,* 57–59
  as documents from House of Trade, 57
  indexing of, 57–58
  types of documents, 58–59
document cases #47–52 (Justicia), *53,* 59–61
  indexing of, 60
  as legal proceedings from Council of the Indies, 59
  sorting and shelving of documents, 60
  types of documents in, 60–61
document cases #53–81 (Gobierno), 62–64
  arrival of additional documents over decades, 63, 64
  as documents from Spain's ultramarine territories, 63

  indexing of, 63
  new shelving required to accommodate, 63, 64
  organization of, 63–64
  plan for (1819), 63, *64*
  poor organization of arriving documents, 63
  types of documents, 63
Du culte des dieux fétisches (Brosses), 11–12, 15

Echevarria, Juan de, 16, 33n90, 224n175
Enlightenment
  and colonial/colonialism as term, 228
  darkness and shadow in aesthetic of, 236
  reforms, Spanish suppression of, 55
Escorial monastery-palace of Felipe II, 128, *129*
  Herrera's design of, 128, *129;* influence on AGI design, 140–41, 152
  Irving at, 190
  library of: bookcases, and AGI cases, 140–46, *142, 143,* 152; bookcase woods, 143–44; Muñoz's research at, 227; Navarrete's research in, 198; and wall-system shelving, 151–52
Everett, Alexander, 184, 187, 189, 191
Exposición Ibero-Americana, Naval Pavilion at, 199, *199*

Felipe II (king of Spain), 89, 91, 128, *129*
Felipe III (king of Spain), 24
Felipe V (king of Spain), 91, 108
Fernando VII (king of Spain), 51, 61, 182, 210
Figaro operas (Beaumarchais et al.), x–xiii, xvn14, xvn17, 193, 222n105
finding aids
  of early libraries, poor quality of, 247
  replacement of staff's embodied knowledge, 243–48
  in Simancas archive, 95
finding aids for AGI
  first four sets of, 65
  Muñoz's early ideas for, 247–48
  in PARES (Portal de Archivos Españoles), 248
  reconstruction of original order of volumes using, 52, *53*
  three-part number assigned to each document, 52, 154, 173–74; broader thematic information given by, 156; grid created by, 154–56, *155*
  See also index (*Índice*) volumes; inventory (*Inventario*) volumes
Foucault, Michel, 3, 8–9
French Revolution, Spanish effort to contain, 55
Fuentes, Gregorio de, 125–28

Gabriel, Joséf de, 167–69, *169*
Gálvez, José de
  and AGI, establishment of, 9–10, 16–22, 74, 128, 130, 139, 147
  and Cintora's *Justa Repulsa,* 150
  and Spanish translation of Robertson's *History,* 15, 16

INDEX 263

García, Francisco, 243, *244–45,* 253
General Archive of the Indies (Archivo General de Indias, AGI), *40–43*
  arrival of documents at, 57, 63, 64, 125, 210
  Carlos III's approval of plan for, viii, 21, 22, 34n105, 74
  central patio, 39, *40,* 43; door leading to, 49; walled-in areas used for storage, 49, 60, 63, 64, 71n67
  closure of, in 1810–11, 182
  creation, reasons for, x, 10, 16
  dedication stone above northern entrance, 37, *38*
  design, Muñoz's early thoughts on, 128–29, 130–34
  dimensions of galleries, 43
  documents concerning archive's history, 167
  donor archives, *54,* 73
  eastern gallery, 49, *49, 65, 66*
  entrance(s), 39, *40*
  first decades, uses of basement and first floor, 39
  first documents to arrive at, 52–54
  floating spiral staircase to roof, *42,* 43
  floors in galleries, 43, *43*
  gate added in late 1780s, 39, 67n10
  generation of new, synthetic knowledge by, 1, 5
  genesis of idea for, 16–22
  and idea of Americas as separate space, x, 228, 236
  indexing of documents in: by Acevedo Villaroel, 58; by Ceán Bermúdez, 44, 52, 54–55, 58, 63, 212, 248; by Juárez, xiii, 37, 61, 62, 67n14, 207; by Tariego y Somoza, 58; at time of Spain's loss of territories in Americas, 37; by Valbuena, 63; by Zuazo y Yañez, 216–17
  loaning of documents from: example of, 169–70; *Ordenanzas* on, 165
  location of, 39
  main office, 43
  main stairs to upper floor, 39–43, *41,* 67n10
  as monumental U-shaped space, 37, 43
  northern gallery, *43,* 49, *237, 246*
  number of document pages stored in, 64
  papers on Irving's visit in, 191
  presentation as unified system of knowledge, 153
  projecting cornices in galleries, 47
  reception room/doorman's office, 43
  roof, *42,* 43
  southern gallery, *viii, 50,* 51, 125
  storage of uncatalogued documents, 49, 64, *65, 66*
  and sunlight damage to documents, 237, *237*
  Ticknor's journal on (1818), 37–52
  as tourist destination in early 19th century, 37
  visual unity of, and wall-system theory, 152
  western facade entrance, *ix,* 39, *40*
  See also data of the AGI; data retrieval in AGI first decades; document cases (AGI); *entries under* document cases; renovation of trade exchange (Lonja) building; Royal Patronage (Patronato Real) room of AGI; staff of AGI
González, Luis, 174–77

González Azaola, Gregorio, 178–80
González Dávila, Gil, 76–77
González Salmón, Manuel, 170–71, 191, 192
Goya y Lucientes, Francisco de
  in Bordeaux, 183
  Caprichos by, 235, *235*
  death of, 191
  designs for Royal Tapestry Factory, *xi,* xvn13
  as friend of Ceán Bermúdez, 55, 58
  portrait of Moratín, *183*
  El sueño de la razon produce monstruos, 235, 235–36
  The Tobacco Guards, x, *xi*
grid, wall-system shelving as type of, 153–56

hairdressing satires (mid-18th century), 138
Harrison, John, 24, *25*
Harwood, John, 6–7, 134, 152–53
Herrera, Juan de
  Ceán Bermúdez's biography of, 37
  design of Escorial, 128, *129,* 140–41, 152
  design of trade exchange (Lonja), 125, 128
  and plan for AGI, 90
  revival of interest in, in late 18th century, 140, 149
Higuera, Aniceto de la, 63, 71n63
Higuera y Lara, José de la
  career at AGI, 243, *244–45,* 253
  and embodied knowledge of AGI collection, 243, 248
  Irving and, 188, 191, 194
  retirement of, 71n63
Hill, Roscoe R., 64, *65, 66,* 250n9
Histoire naturelle (Buffon), 10–12, 15, 25–26, 227
Historia del Nuevo-Mundo (Muñoz)
  AGI not used in research for, 178
  approval for writing of, 21, 33n85, 73
  as disappointment, 227
  no indication of archival research in, 227
  research for, 21, 60, 73–74, 78, 128, 198, 227
  as response to Dispute of the New World, 73
Historia del Reino de Quito (Velasco), 15
Historia de Nueva-España (Lorenzana y Buitron), 47, *48*
Histoire philosophique et politique . . . dans les deux Indes (Raynal), 13–15, 26, 227–28
History of America (Robertson), 14–16, 26, 73, 227
History of the Life and Voyages of Christopher Columbus (Irving)
  abridged version of, 193
  appendices, writing of, 190
  documents from AGI used in, 188
  first edition, writing of, 181, 187, 188, 189
  second edition, 178, 181, 191–93, 195
  on sources in Madrid, 188–89
  submission of completed manuscript, 189–90
History of the Reign of Charles V (Robertson), 14
House of Trade (Casa de la Contratación)
  areas of responsibility, 102–3

  on Coelho map of Seville (1771), 105, *106, 107*
  documents from, at AGI, *53,* 57–59, 63, 73, 125
  history of, 57, 102–3
House of Trade, Cádiz offices and archives, 108–13
  buildings used for, 108–9, *109, 110, 111*
  documents sent to AGI, 57, 73, 125
  establishment of, 57
  mix of American and European documents in, 236
  Muñoz's criticisms of, 109–11
  Muñoz's research in, 73, 74, 122n125
  opening of, 57, 103, 106, 108
  planned permanent building for, 111–12
  president's residence in, 109, 111, 112, 123n131
  rooms used for document storage in, 111, 112–13
House of Trade, Seville offices and archives
  apartments in, 105, 106
  archivist at, 103–5
  in Borcht's plan of Seville palace, *104,* 105
  documents transferred to AGI, 54, 125
  fires in, 103, 105, 106, 107
  Muñoz on state of documents in, 103–5
  Muñoz's reluctance to criticize, 103
  Muñoz's research in, 73, 74, 102
  as original location, 57
  poor conditions for document storage, 107–8
  rooms used for document storage in, 105–8
  separation of Cádiz offices from, 73
  uses after opening of Cádiz offices, 106–7
  volume of documents stored in, 108
Humboldt, Alexander von, 37, 170–71
Hydrographic Office, 198–99

index (*Índice*) volumes, 5, *9*
  for cases #1–11 (Contaduría), 54–55
  for cases #12–46 (Contratación), 57–58
  for cases #47–52 (Justicia), 60
  number of volumes, 52
  ordering of documents in, 55
  in PARES, 248
  of Royal Patronage room, 51–52, 62
  suspension of work on, during French occupation, 61
  See also finding aids for AGI
The Interface (Harwood), 6–7
Inventing America (Rabasa), 227, xivn3
The Invention of America (O'Gorman), vii
inventory (*Inventario*) volumes, 5, *8*
  for cases #1–11 (Contaduría), 55
  for cases #12–46 (Contratación), 57–58
  for cases #47–52 (Justicia), 60
  documents ordered by shelf location in, 55
  number of volumes, 52
  in PARES, 248
  of Royal Patronage room, 51–52, 62
  system used in, 52
  See also finding aids for AGI
Irving, Peter, 183–84, 187, 189, 190

Irving, Washington
  in Andalusia, 190
  and *The Barber of Seville,* 193
  books about Spain by, 184
  in Bordeaux (1825–26), 183–84
  in Cádiz, 193, 195
  Chronicle of the Conquest of Granada, 186, 192, 193
  at Escorial monastery-palace, 190
  in Madrid, 184–90; libraries and archives visited by, 186, 188–89, 190; Navarrete's Columbus sources and, 184, 191, 194, 199; notable sites related to, 184, *185;* other projects researched in, 190; period of writer's block, 186; research on Columbus in, 186; residences, 184–86, 187, 190, 221n90; use of Rich's library, 184–85, 186, 194; visit from Longfellow, 189; visits with Navarrete, 186, 187–88, 189, 194, 198–99; visits with Uguina, 187–89, 190, 194, 198–99; work on *Chronicle of the Conquest of Granada,* 186
  in Palos and Rábida, 193, 195
  research at AGI: and difficult script of documents, 194; limited impact on his work, 194–95; permission for, 181, 191–92, 193–94; as well-documented, 181–82
  in Seville, 191–95; libraries and archives visited by, 191; residences, 191, 192–93; work accomplished, 191, 192
  on Spanish houses, size of, 187
  travel to Seville, 181, 190
  Voyages and Discoveries of the Companions of Columbus, 193–94, 223n146
  Wetherell and, 181
  Wilkie portrait of, 191, *192*
  See also History of the Life and Voyages of Christopher Columbus (Irving)
Isabel II (queen of Spain), 116n29, 218n3, 248

Jovellanos, Gaspar Melchor de, 55, 63, 101
Juárez, Diego
  career of, 67n4, *244–45,* 253
  and data retrieval from archives, 167–68, 178
  and return of evacuated documents from Cádiz, 182
  and Royal Patronage section: expansion of, 225n179; indexing of, xiii, 37, 62, 67n4, 207; Ticknor's visit to, 37, 43
Justa Repulsa de Ignorantes (Cintora), 149–50, *150*
Justice (Justicia), legal proceedings from Council of the Indies
  AGI location, 59
  sorting and shelving of, 60
  types of documents in, 60–61
  Zuazo y Yáñez indexes of, 216–17

Laraviedra, Manuel de, 173–74
Lara y Zúñiga, Antonio de
  as AGI director, 128, 147, 243
  on Council of Indies documents, 52
  on document case installation, 157n4

installation of documents at AGI, 125, 128
and Lonja remodeling, 125, 144, 147–49, *148*
replacement by Ceán Bermúdez, 128
on Simancas archive documents, 60
Larrañaga, Estevan de, 33n90, 207, 224–25n175
latitude, and zonal theory of Earth's climates, 24
Ledoux, Claude-Nicolas, 9, 236
libraries, early
  poor quality of finding aids, 247
  turn to paper finding aids, 243–48
Library of Naval Science (Isla de León), 196, 198
Library of Naval Science, Navarrete group copying books for, 196–200
  copies of works at AGI, 198, 200; file number of, *vs.* AGI filing system, 206–7; file number of, *vs. Colecciones de Simancas* numbers, 207–10, *208–9;* file number of, *vs.* Zuazo y Yáñez indexes, 216–17; location of works then *vs.* now, 211, 215–17; vision of early AGI provided by, 215
  copies of works at Escorial monastery-palace, 198
  copies of works in Madrid libraries, 198
  dates on copies, as date of review, 200
  document's origin recorded on copy, 206
  number of documents copied, 200
  parts of work now missing, 200, 215
  procedures used by, 200–205
  scribes for, 200; identification of work through handwriting style, 200–206, *201–4,* 224n168; individual scribe's production, *205,* 213–15; Navarrete's and Basterrechea's views on, 214; productivity, by month, 205, *205;* sources of documents copied, by month, *211,* 211–13; work across multiple subjects, 213–14
  sources on, 196
  storage of copied documents, 198–200
  and travel narrative compilations as genre, 198
licenses, AGI retrieval requests for, 172–73
Longfellow, Henry Wadsworth, 189
longitude, determining at sea
  Harrison's clock and, 24
  search for accurate measure of, 23, 24
Longitude Act of 1714 (Great Britain), 23
longitude model of Earth, replacement of latitude-based zonal theory, 24–26
Lonja building. *See* trade exchange building (Lonja de Mercaderes, Seville)
Lorenzana y Buitrón, Francisco Antonio, 47, *48*
Lorenzo, Antonio, 243, *244–45,* 254
Louisiana Purchase, AGI search for documents on, 167–69, *168, 169*

Madrid, archives in, *54*
  documents transferred to AGI, 52, 59, 63
  Irving's research in, 186, 188–89, 190
  mix of American and European documents in, 236
  Muñoz's research in, 21
  See also Council of the Indies (Consejo de Indias, Madrid)

Maestre, Francisco Miguel
  proposal for creation of Archive, 9–10
  and renovation of trade exchange (Lonja) building, 125–28, 130–34, *133*
  See also renovation of trade exchange (Lonja) building, Muñoz and Maestre plan for
mahogany, 132–133, 135, 139–140, 144, 147, 160n53
Maison de Plaisir (Ledoux), 9
Marcos, José, 92, 94
Martin, Reinhold, 152–53
Martínez de Huete, Fernando, 16, 21, 34n98
Mason & Dixon (Pynchon), 23
Mattos, Claudia, xvn18, 236
Méndez, Ramón, 172–73
mining regulations, request for AGI documents on, 170–71
Molner y Zamora, Blas, *44–47, 133, 145,* 147
Moratín, Leandro Fernández de, *183,* 183–84
Muñoz, Juan Bautista
  and AGI, call for creation of, 9–10, 21, 73, 74, 105; as motive for denigrating existing archives, 73–74; thoughts on design of, 128–29, 130–34
  archive work with Juárez, 167
  Colecciones de Simancas subcollection by, 212, 225n182
  Columbus document copies used by Navarrete, 194, 195
  familiarity with Dispute of the New World, 15
  on finding aids for AGI, 247–48
  in House of Trade archives, 102
  on order of AGI *vs.* disorder of source archives, 235–36
  at Palace of the Councils archives, 86–87
  papers willed to Carlos IV, 222n107
  and renovation of trade exchange (Lonja) building: aesthetic of simplicity and, 135–40; detailed proposal for, 130–34, *132, 133,* 135–37, *136;* evaluation of site, 74, 128–30; influence of Herrera's style on, 140–46; oversight of, 125–28, 227; progress report (July 1787), 146; proposal *vs.* final plan, 134
  on Simancas archive, disorder in, 21, 60, 91–92; *vs.* evidence from other sources, 100–102; reasons for perception of, 91, 101–2
  on Spanish archives' condition, *vs.* evidence from other sources, 92, 100–102, 113
  Uguina and, 187–88, 189
  visit to Naval Archive, 92, 100–102, 113, 122n125
  See also Historia del Nuevo-Mundo (Muñoz); renovation of trade exchange (Lonja) building, Muñoz and Maestre plan for
Murray, John, 190, 193

Nangle, Francisco, 92, 93–94, 99, 101, 102
Napoleonic Wars
  evacuation of AGI documents during, 60, 182, 221n76

Napoleonic Wars, *continued*
  evacuation of Library of Naval Science documents during, 198–99
  suspension of work at AGI, 61
Naval Academy of San Carlos, 196, *196, 197*
  See also Library of Naval Science (Isla de León)
Naval Museum (Madrid), Library of Naval Science documents at, 196, 199–200
Navarrete, Martín Fernández de
  Colección de los viajes y descubrimientos que hicieron por mar los españoles, 186, 191, 199, 223n137
  Irving and, 182, 184, 186–89, 191, 194, 198–99
  Vida de Miguel de Cervantes Saavedra, 182
  See also Library of Naval Science (Isla de León)
New World House of Trade. *See* House of Trade (Casa de la Contratación)
Nouveau voyage dans les états-unis de l'Amérique septentrionale (Brissot), 15

***Ordenanzas para el Archivo General de Indias* (1790)**
  on annual roof inspection, 101
  on charges for document copies, 166
  document use regulations, 165–67, 218nn3–4
  on labels, 43–44
  private use of documents, restrictions on, 166, 219nn33
  on staff, 68n17
  on tourist access to Archive, 167
Ortiz de Solorzano, Francisco, 16, 33n90, 207, 224–25n175, *244–45,* 254

Páez de la Cadena, Juan Miguel, 170–71
Palace of the Councils (Madrid), 74–87, *75*
  Council of the Indies offices, 81, *83,* 84–87, 116n34
  councils currently located in, 79
  councils sharing building, 74–75
  Crown purchase of, 112
  damage in Spanish Civil War, 79, 116n30
  floor plans and sections of, *178,* 79, 79–81, *80, 81*
  floor plan with office locations, 81–85, *83,* 117nn36–37
  front and rear facades (1770s–80s), 81, *82*
  ground-floor room layouts (1786), 81, *83,* 116nn31–32
  hierarchy of councils in, 87
  lack of Europe *vs.* Americas binary in, 87, 101–2
  move of council offices to, 77–78, 91, 114n9, 115n22
  Muñoz's research at, offices visited during, 86–87
  remodeling for councils' use, 78, *78*
  as rented building, 111–12
  space limitations: and jumbled mix of office space, 84–85; and transfer of archives to Simancas, 78–79, 91

structural problems caused by archives' weight, 85–86
Panopticon prison, 7–9
parageography, 26
PARES (Portal de Archivos Españoles), 206–7, 248
Pauw, Cornelius de, 12–13, 227
Pérez, Joséph, *78,* 116n30
Pérez de Laserna, Joséf Antonio, 171–72
Perovani, Joseph, x, *xii*
Pinzón, Martín Alonzo, 193, 195
Plano de los Reales Alcázares de Sevilla (Borcht), *104, 105*
polecats, 91, 118n60
Portrait of George Washington (Perovani), x, *xii*
Portrait of John Harrison (Tassaert, after King), *25*
Pownall, Thomas, 229–31

Quesada, Vincente G., 64, 71n63

Rabasa, José, xivn3, 227
Raynal, Guillaume, 13–15, 26, 227–28
Real Fernandino [Betis] (steamboat), *180, 181,* 190, 193
Recherches philosophiques sur les Américains (Pauw), 12–13, 26, 227
renovation of trade exchange (Lonja) building
  and architectural imagism, 134
  arrival of documents prior to completion of, 125
  chronology of, *126–27*
  completion of, 125
  designers of, 125–28
  doors and windows, design of, 133, *136, 137,* 147
  evaluation of site, 74, 128–30
  eviction of tenants for, 22, 34n107, 130, 134
  flooring choice, 140, *141,* 146
  furniture design, 133, 147
  gallery design and construction, *126–27*
  influence of Herrera's style on, 140–41
  Muñoz and Maestre plan for: aesthetic of simplicity and, 135–40; detailed proposal, 130–34, *132, 133,* 135–37, *136;* differences from final plan, 134; and unifying effect of color, 135; upper floor plan proposal, *133,* 133–34, *136*
  Muñoz's progress report (July 1787) on, 146
  staircase design and installation, *126–27*
  and three galleries, removal of walls to create, 146, 147–49, *148;* controversy caused by, 149–51, *150;* and wall-system shelving, 151–53
  time required for, 125
  See also document cases (AGI); trade exchange building (Lonja de Mercaderes, Seville)
Rich, Obadiah, 184–86, 187, 190, 194
Riol, Santiago Agustín, 92, 93–94, 137–38, 153
Río y de la Vega, Fermín del, 207, 224–25n175
Robertson, William. *See History of America* (Robertson)
rodents, 108
Rodríguez, Ventura
  Palace of Councils section and floor plan, *80–81*

Simancas archive sections, floor plans, and elevations, 92, *92, 93, 95, 97–100,* 101, *102*
Royal Academy of History (Real Academia de la Historia), 15–16, 21
Royal Academy of Spain dictionary, viii, 5
royal palace in Madrid
  burning of (1734), 78–79
  council offices in, in 16th century, 76–77
  Courtyard of the Queen in, 76, *76*
  described, 76–77
  move of council offices from, 77–78, 91, 114n9, 115n22
Royal Patronage (Patronato Real) room of AGI, 50, *51*
  addition of documents to, 211, 214, 215–16, 225n179
  artworks and "precious things" in, 51, 61–62, 69n26, 69n30
  filing system used in, 51–52
  indexing of, after restoration of Fernando VII, 61
  indexing of, by Juárez, xiii, 37, 62, 67n4, 207
  location of, *53,* 62
  as most famous part of AGI, 61
  overview of documents in, 62
  theft from, 69n30
  Ticknor on, 61–62
  time required for completion of, 125
Royal Tapestry Factory, x, *xi,* xvn13

Sabatini, Francisco, *79,* 85, 112
Seven Years' War, 11, 24
Seville, *54*
  aerial views of, *ix, 38*
  archives, Muñoz's research in, 74
  Coelho map of (1771), *106, 107*
  plague of 1649, 128
Shadows and Enlightenment (Baxandall), 236
shipping records, AGI retrieval requests for, 173–77, *175–76*
Siegert, Bernhard, 2, 153, 156
Sigüenza, José de, 141, 143–44
Simancas archive, *54,* 88–102
  and aesthetics of simplicity, 137–38
  AGI locations of documents from, 54
  archivist's residence, 89–90, 93, 97–98
  attic windows, maintenance issues with, 101
  brick addition to tower, 88, *88, 89,* 99
  castle housing, 88, *88, 89;* remodeling as archive, 88, 89–90, *90*
  and *Colecciones de Simancas,* 207
  data retrieval requests, record of, 165
  document chest from, at AGI, *210*
  documents transferred to AGI, 52–54, 59–60, 210–11; number of chests of documents, 54, 60, 63, 125; preparation of, 207; royal patronage documents, 51; sorting and cataloging of, 168–69
  as donor archive for AGI, 73
  elevation drawing of, *92*

entrance to, 93
filing system in, 21, 60
finding aids in, 95
indexing of documents at, 16
Instrucción for running, 90
mix of American and European documents in, 63, 236; separation of, for AGI, 102
Muñoz's criticism of disorder in, 21, 60, 91–92; *vs.* evidence from other sources, 92, 100–102; reasons for seeming disorder noted by, 91, 101–2
Muñoz's research in, 21, 60, 73, 74, 79, 91–92
original transfers of documents to, 88–89
planned expansion (1774), 16–17, *17–20,* 92, 100, 133
records on upkeep of, 92
rooms, and document storage, 92–100; attic, *98,* 98–101; Carlos V's original archive atop north tower, 88–89, 95, 99–100, 101, 102; first floor, 94–97, *95;* ground floor, *93,* 93–94; Royal Patronage (Patronazgo Real) room, 94, 95–97, *96,* 102; second floor, *97,* 97–98; section drawings of, *99, 100;* sources on, 92; stability of, in 18th century and earlier, 100; winter office, 95, 97
Royal Patronage archive in, 89, 90, *90,* 137–38
transfer of documents to, over three centuries, 90
transfer of records from Madrid's Palace of the Councils to, 78–79, 91
transfer of records to, under Queen Isabel II, 116n29
turn from royal to general archive, 89
windows, doors, and roof, maintenance, 101
Sisto, Tomás de, 108, *109*
Spanish America, first uses of *colonia* to describe, 1–2
Spanish American wars of independence, 37
staff of AGI
from 1785 to 1844, 243–47, *244–45,* 252–55
attrition of, 243
continuity in first half-century, 243
embodied knowledge of, and data retrieval, 167, 243–47
Ordenanzas on, 68n17
original positions, and additions, 68n17

Tariego y Somoza, Antonio, 58, 245, 255
tax payments, AGI retrieval requests for, 173–74, *175–76*
Tercera parte de la historia de la orden de San Geronimo (Sigüenza), 141, 144
Ticknor, George
on Ceán Bermúdez, 54–55
description of AGI, 37–52
on House of Trade archive papers, 57
on Royal Patronage room, 51–52, 61–62
on Spanish wars of independence, 37
visit to AGI, 63
on visual unity of AGI collection, 153
trade exchange building (Lonja de Mercaderes, Seville)
construction of, 128

history of, Ticknor on, 38
history of occupancy, 128–29
location of, ix
original architect of, 125, 128
original purpose of, 128
pre-renovation condition of (1784), 130–31
selection as site for AGI, 21, 128–30
study of, as site for AGI, 16, 21–22, 74
See also renovation of trade exchange (Lonja) building
travel licenses, AGI retrieval requests for, 172–73
"Treaty of Friendship, Limits, and Navigation Between Spain and The United States; October 27, 1795," x, *xii,* xvn16
Treaty of Paris (1783), x, 21
Tropics of Empire (Wey-Gómez), 23

Uguina, Antonio de, 187–89, 190, 194, 198–99

Val, Miguel Esteban de, 172–73
Valbuena, Manuel de, indexing of cases #53–81, 63
Veragua, Duke of, 188–89, 222–23n119
Vidler, Anthony, 8–9, 236
Villanueva, Juan de
and AGI document case design, *145*
plans for Simancas addition, 16–17, *17–20,* 92, 133

wall-system shelving
AGI donor archives' lack of, 153
and design of AGI galleries, 152–53
and erasure of previous document contexts, 153, 156, 163n89
history of, 151, 163n82
as information structuring system, 151
as type of information grid, 153–56
War of the Spanish Succession, 77
Washington, George, x, *xii*
Wetherell, John, 181–82, 193
Wetherell, Nathan, 181–82
Wey-Gómez, Nicolás, 23
Wilkie, David, 191, *192*
wills, AGI retrieval requests for, 171–72

Ximénez, Andrés, 144

zonal theory of Earth's climates, 23
on climate effects on human development, 23–24
replacement by longitude model, implications of, 24–26
Zuazo y Yañez, Joséph de, 103
Zuazo y Yañez, Manuel de
career of, *244–45,* 255
and House of Trade archives, 107–8
index of Justice documents at AGI, 216–17
Muñoz on, 103–5
residence of, 106
and transfer of documents to AGI, 103

Getty Research Institute Publications Program
Mary E. Miller, *Director, Getty Research Institute*

© 2022 J. Paul Getty Trust

Published by the Getty Research Institute, Los Angeles
Getty Publications
1200 Getty Center Drive, Suite 500
Los Angeles, California 90049-1682
getty.edu/publications

Laura Santiago, *Editor*
Kurt Hauser, *Designer*
Michelle Woo Deemer, *Production*
Karen Ehrmann, *Image and Rights Acquisition*

Type composed in Adobe Garamond Pro

Distributed in the United States and Canada by the University of Chicago Press
Distributed outside the United States and Canada by Yale University Press, London

Printed in China

Library of Congress Cataloging-in-Publication Data
Names: Hamann, Byron Ellsworth, 1972- author. | Getty Research Institute, issuing body.
Title: The invention of the colonial Americas : data, architecture, and the Archive of the Indies, 1781–1844 / Byron Ellsworth Hamann.
Description: Los Angeles : Getty Research Institute, [2022] | Includes bibliographical references and index. | Summary: "The Invention of the Colonial Americas is an architectural history and media-archaeological study of changing theories and practices of government archives in Enlightenment Spain"— Provided by publisher.
Identifiers: LCCN 2021053740 (print) | LCCN 2021053741 (ebook) | ISBN 9781606067734 (hardback) | ISBN 9781606067758 (pdf)
Subjects: LCSH: Archivo General de Indias—History. | Lonja de mercaderes (Seville, Spain) — History. | Archives—Spain—Administration—History—18th century. | Archives— Spain—Administration—History—19th century. | Archive buildings—Spain—History. | Spain—Colonies—America—Archival resources.
Classification: LCC CD1864 .A546 2022 (print) | LCC CD1864 (ebook) | DDC 946/.054—dc23 /eng/20211209
LC record available at https://lccn.loc.gov/2021053740
LC ebook record available at https://lccn.loc.gov/2021053741

Cover: The northern gallery of the Archive of the Indies before the shelving reforms of the late 1920s (detail). See fig. E.1.

p. i: Joseph Perovani (U.S. American, 1765–1835). *Portrait of George Washington* (detail), 1796. See fig. P.5.

Frontispiece: The floating spiral staircase of the Lonja, leading up to the roof (detail), June 2017. See fig. 1.6.

pp. iv–v: Blas Molner y Zamora (Spanish, 1737–1812). First document case design for the Archive of the Indies (detail), 4 August 1784. See fig. 3.2.

p. xix: Tomás López (Spanish, 1730–1802). *Mapa General de España* (detail), 1795. See fig. 1.28.

Every effort has been made to contact the owners and photographers of illustrations reproduced here whose names do not appear in the captions or in the illustration credits at the back of this book. Anyone having further information concerning copyright holders is asked to contact Getty Publications so this information can be included in future printings.